CLEP®
The College-Level Examination Program®
Third Edition

RELATED TITLES

Grammar Source

Math Source

Word Source

Writing Source

Shortcut Series
Shortcut Algebra I
Shortcut Algebra II
Shortcut Calculus I
Shortcut Calculus II

CLEP®
The College-Level Examination Program®
Third Edition

By Anaxos, Inc.

PUBLISHING

New York

CLEP® is a registered trademark of the College Entrance Examination Board, which neither sponsors nor endorses this product.

This publication is designed to provide accurate and authoritative information in regard to the subject matter covered. It is sold with the understanding that the publisher is not engaged in rendering legal, accounting, or other professional service. If legal advice or other expert assistance is required, the services of a competent professional should be sought.

Vice President and Publisher: Maureen McMahon
Editorial Director: Jennifer Farthing
Development Editor: Janell Lantana
Production Editor: Julio Espin
Cover Designer: Carly Schnur

© 2008 by Anaxos, Inc.

Published by Kaplan Publishing, a division of Kaplan, Inc.
1 Liberty Plaza, 24th Floor
New York, NY 10006

All rights reserved. No part of this book may be reproduced or transmitted in any form or by any means, electronic or mechanical, including photocopying, recording, or by any information storage and retrieval system, without the written permission of Kaplan, Inc.

Notre Dame Cathedral, Steve Vidler. Digital image courtesy of SuperStock, Inc.
The Birth of Venus, Sandro Botticelli; Galleria degli Uffizi, Florence, Italy. Digital image courtesy of SuperStock, Inc.
The Holy Family with Saints Elizabeth and John the Baptist, Peter Paul Rubens; Wallace Collection, London. Digital image courtesy of SuperStock, Inc.
David, Michelangelo Buonarroti; Galleria Dell Academia, Florence, Italy. Digital image courtesy of SuperStock, Inc.
Guernica, Pablo Picasso; copyright 2007 Estate of Pablo Picasso/Artists Rights Society (ARS), New York. Digital image courtesy of SuperStock, Inc.
Casa Mila, copyright 2007 Howard Davis. Digital image courtesy of Artifice, Inc.
Starry Night, Vincent van Gogh; The Museum of Modern Art, New York. Digital image courtesy of SuperStock, Inc.
Bathers at Asniers, Georges Pierre Seurat; The National Gallery, London. Digital image courtesy of SuperStock, Inc.
Eiffel Tower, Dean Fox. Digital image courtesy of SuperStock, Inc.
Christina's World, Andrew Wyeth Digital image, copyright 2007, The Museum of Modern Art, 1948, tempera on panel copyright licensed by SCALA/ Art Resource, New York.
Girl with a Pearl Earring, Jan Vermeer; Mauritshuis, The Hague, the Netherlands. Digital image courtesy of SuperStock, Inc.
Self-Portait with Grey Felt Hat, Vincent van Gogh; Van Gogh Museum, Amsterdam, the Netherlands. Digital image courtesy of SuperStock, Inc.
Nighthawks, Edward Hopper; copyright 2007 Art Institute of Chicago. Digital image courtesy of SuperStock, Inc.
Lavendar Mist, Jackson Pollock; copyright 2007 The Pollock-Krasner Foundation/Artists Rights Society (ARS), New York. Digital image courtesy of the National Gallery of Art; Washington, DC.

Printed in the United States of America

March 2008
10 9 8 7 6 5 4 3 2 1

ISBN-13: 978-1-4195-5277-9

Kaplan Publishing books are available at special quantity discounts to use for sales promotions, employee premiums, or educational purposes. Please email our Special Sales Department to order or for more information at kaplanpublishing@kaplan.com, or write to Kaplan Publishing, 1 Liberty Plaza, 24th Floor, New York, NY 10006.

Table of Contents

Contributors xi
How to Use This Book xiii

Section One: Introduction to the CLEP
Chapter One: Introduction 3
    Which CLEP Exam Should I Take? 3
    Registering for the Exams 4
    Your CLEP Score 4
    CLEP and the Military 6
    How This Book Can Help You 7

Chapter Two: The CLEP Computer Interface 9
    Call It the CCLEP 9
    Should You Take the Computer-Based Test? 9
    The Basics of the Computer CLEP Exam Format 10
    Final Thoughts 17

Chapter Three: Specific CLEP Exam Strategies 19
    Specific Strategies for Specific Tests 19
    General Test-Taking Strategies 20
    CLEP English Composition Strategies 21
    CLEP College Mathematics Strategies 27
    CLEP Humanities Strategies 32
    CLEP Social Sciences and History Strategies 36
    CLEP Natural Sciences Strategies 40
    Final Thoughts 43

Section Two: The CLEP English Composition Exam

Chapter Four: Practice Test 1: Diagnostic 47

    Practice Test 1: Diagnostic Answers and Explanations 71

Chapter Five: CLEP English Composition Review 79

    The Big Picture: CLEP English Composition 79

    Two Versions of the Test 79

    Nuts and Bolts 80

    Skills at the Sentence Level 80

    Skills in Context 90

    The Essay 94

    Final Thoughts 98

Chapter Six: Practice Test 2 99

    Practice Test 2 Answers and Explanations 127

Chapter Seven: Practice Test 3 137

    Practice Test 3 Answers and Explanations 155

Section Three: The CLEP College Mathematics Exam

Chapter Eight: Practice Test 1: Diagnostic 163

    Practice Test 1: Diagnostic Answers and Explanations 175

Chapter Nine: CLEP College Mathematics Review 181

    The Big Picture: CLEP College Mathematics 181

    Nuts and Bolts 182

    CLEP College Mathematics Strategy Checklist 183

    Set Theory 184

    Logic 186

    Real Number System 189

    Functions and Graphs 191

    Probability and Statistics 193

    Additional Topics from Algebra and Geometry 196

    College Mathematics Resources 199

    Final Thoughts 200

Chapter Ten: Practice Test 2 201
    Practice Test 2 Answers and Explanations 211

Chapter Eleven: Practice Test 3 219
    Practice Test 3 Answers and Explanations 229

Section Four: The CLEP Humanities Exam
Chapter Twelve: Practice Test 1: Diagnostic 237
    Practice Test 1: Diagnostic Answers and Explanations 259

Chapter Thirteen: CLEP Humanities Review 271
    The Big Picture: CLEP Humanities 271
    Nuts and Bolts 272
    How to Score at Scoring 272
    Visual Arts and Architecture 273
    Performing Arts: Music, Dance, and Film 277
    Drama 282
    Poetry 284
    Fiction, Nonfiction, and Philosophy 287
    Final Thoughts 289

Chapter Fourteen: Practice Test 2 291
    Practice Test 2 Answers and Explanations 311

Chapter Fifteen: Practice Test 3 323
    Practice Test 3 Answers and Explanations 341

Section Five: The CLEP Social Sciences and History Exam
Chapter Sixteen: Practice Test 1: Diagnostic 353
    Practice Test 1: Diagnostic Answers and Explanations 375

Chapter Seventeen: CLEP Social Sciences and History Review 385
    The Big Picture: CLEP Social Sciences and History 386
    Nuts and Bolts 386
    History 387
        What You Need to Know 387
        United States History 387
        Western Civilization 387
        World History 387
        Master Timeline 388
        History Resources 390
    The Social Sciences 391
        What You Need to Know 391
        Government/Political Science 391
        Sociology 392
        Economics 393
        Psychology 394
        Geography 395
        Anthropology 396
    Final Thoughts 397

Chapter Eighteen: Practice Test 2 399
    Practice Test 2 Answers and Explanations 419

Chapter Nineteen: Practice Test 3 429
    Practice Test 3 Answers and Explanations 451

Section Six: The CLEP Natural Sciences Exam
Chapter Twenty: Practice Test 1: Diagnostic 463
    Practice Test 1: Diagnostic Answers and Explanations 485

Chapter Twenty-One: CLEP Natural Sciences Review 495
    The Big Picture: CLEP Natural Sciences 495
    Nuts and Bolts 496
    Biological Sciences 496
        Evolution and Diversity of Life 496
        Diversity of Life Chart 499
        Cell Biology and Biochemistry 500
        Organisms and Heredity 503
        Ecology and Population Biology 508
    Physical Sciences 510
        The Metric System 510
        Atoms and Subatomic Structures 511
        Elements, Molecules, and Compounds 513
        Energy, Matter, and Mechanics 516
        Electricity, Magnetism, and Waves 519
        The Universe 520
        Earth Science 522
    Natural Sciences Resources 524
    Final Thoughts 525

Chapter Twenty-Two: Practice Test 2 527
    Practice Test 2 Answers and Explanations 549

Chapter Twenty-Three: Practice Test 3 559
    Practice Test 3 Answers and Explanations 579

Section Seven: Computing Your Practice Test Score

Chapter Twenty-Four: Scoring Your Test 591

Section Eight: CLEP Resources
    A Special Note for International Students 595
    Word Roots 599
    Vocabulary Word List 607
    Math in a Nutshell 673
    Math Glossary 691

FOR ANY TEST CHANGES OR LATE-BREAKING DEVELOPMENTS

kaptest.com/publishing

The material in this book is up-to-date at the time of publication. However, the College Board may have instituted changes in the tests after this book was published. Be sure to carefully read the materials you receive when you register for your test. If there are any important late-breaking developments—or any changes or corrections to the Kaplan test preparation materials in this book—we will post that information online at **kaptest.com/publishing**.

FEEDBACK AND COMMENTS

kaplansurveys.com/books

We'd love to hear your comments and suggestions about this book. We invite you to fill out our online survey form at **kaplansurveys.com/books**. Your feedback is extremely helpful as we continue to develop high-quality resources to meet your needs.

Contributors

Bay Anapol

Ron Davis

Jeremiah A. Gilbert

Elizabeth Haserick Jackson

Drew Johnson

Mark Metz

Stephanie Reents

Amy Shoultz

Linda Brooke Stabler

How to Use This Book

The following chapters contain strategies, review information, and practice tests covering the topics on the CLEP exams in English Composition, College Mathematics, Humanities, Social Sciences and History, and Natural Sciences.

Step 1

First, read Section One: Introduction to the CLEP, for basic information. Chapter One gives a general introduction to the exams, while Chapters Two and Three offer vital strategies for the computer interface and each of the five subject tests.

Step 2

Once you've gotten familiar with the tests and strategies, turn to the section that addresses the test you plan to take. To ensure that you get the most out of your review time, take a moment for the appropriate full-length diagnostic test. After you take it, you can use the results to give yourself a broad idea of what topics you are strong in and what topics you need to review more.

Step 3

You can use your diagnostic test results to tailor your approach to the following review chapter. Hopefully you'll have time to read the entire chapter, but if pressed, you can start with the subjects you know you need to work on.

Step 4

You can then take the two practice tests, giving yourself practice at taking a test similar to the actual CLEP exam. By the time the real test comes around, you will be highly familiar with this CLEP test and its format. If you're short on time, take the diagnostic test and review the subjects that need the most work. When taking practice tests, time yourself and take the entire test without interruption—you can always call your friend back after you finish. And remember, you won't get to watch television while taking the real CLEP exam.

Step 5

Be sure to read the answer explanations for all questions, even those you answered correctly. Even if you got the problem right, reading another person's answer can give you insights that will prove helpful on the real exam.

Step 6

Finally, to see how your practice test score stacks up, turn to Section Seven: Computing Your Score. You'll be able to see if you're ready to take the actual CLEP exam.

Be sure to take some time to relax before test day, and best of luck!

| SECTION ONE |

Introduction to the CLEP

Chapter One: **Introduction**

- Which CLEP Exam Should I Take?
- Registering for the Exams
- Your CLEP Score
- CLEP and the Military
- How This Book Can Help You

Many students go to college to learn, while others seem to go simply to party. A select few valiantly attempt to do as much of both as humanly possible. Yet regardless of your intentions, college is expensive and some parts aren't worth your time or money. For instance, taking introductory classes with two hundred other students isn't very educational or interesting, especially if you're already familiar with the material.

This is where the CLEP® comes in. Taking an exam through the College Level Examination Program (CLEP) can help you leapfrog over some basic college coursework—provided, of course, that you score well enough. Overall, it's a good exchange: 90 minutes of testing can get you credit that allows you to bypass entire semesters of college courses.

The decision to take a CLEP test and get college credit doesn't rest entirely in your hands, however. Every university in the United States has its own ideas about whether or not to accept CLEP scores for credit. Some colleges don't accept them at all. Others schools give you college credit, but only if you exceed a certain score on the scale of 20–80. Every school has its own take on the test, so make sure you do some homework on the schools you are thinking about applying to before forking over the $65 CLEP registration fee.

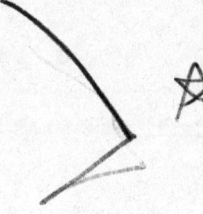

WHICH CLEP EXAM SHOULD I TAKE?

There are over thirty different CLEP exams. You can find a complete list of the test titles, as well as other basic information, at collegeboard.com/student/testing/clep/about.html. This is the official CLEP website, and it contains all of the general facts about the CLEP program.

Some exams are more popular than others. The exams covered in this book are the ones in the popular crowd. Think of them as the Homecoming Court of CLEP exams.

- English Composition
- College Mathematics
- Humanities
- Social Sciences and History
- Natural Sciences

If you're thinking about taking any of these exams, this book can help. If you have your heart set on acing the German Level 2 CLEP exam, then all we can say is, *"Viel glück!"*

As for which CLEP test (or tests) you should take, try to balance the advantage gained by earning a good score with the extra studying you will have to do for each exam. Perhaps you think you won't need any additional studying, since you're already an expert in a particular subject. That may be true (and you can take one of the practice tests in this book to find out if you're right or wrong). Most students however, expert or not, will need to put in some preparation for any new exam.

REGISTERING FOR THE EXAMS

You can register for any of the CLEP exams by contacting a CLEP test center. To find a center in your area, visit collegeboard.com/student/testing/clep/reg.html. After you learn about the center's procedures and schedule your test, you'll fill out a registration-admission form that you can download from the CLEP website. Mail it along with your payment to the test center. The fee for each test is $65 plus an extra $10 for tests with an optional essay, and the average test center registration fee is around $15—be sure to ask your center of choice about its policy. If you want to take the CLEP exam the old-fashioned way, on paper instead of on the computer, be prepared to pay $120. Members of the U.S. Armed Forces should refer to the section in this chapter called "CLEP and the Military" for registration information.

YOUR CLEP SCORE

Scores on the CLEP exams range from 20–80. The number of questions you get correct is called your *raw score*. Each *correct* multiple-choice answer receives one point, while each *wrong* or *skipped* answer does not receive any points. There are no points subtracted for incorrect answers, so it is in your best interest to answer all questions on the exam. The raw score is not reported; it is adjusted according to a formula specified by the College Board to compensate for differences in question difficulty on various forms of the test. The final score that is reported, called the scaled score, is computed based on this formula.

While most of the CLEP exams are scored by computer, the English Composition essay is graded by at least two College English professors who are specially trained in the scoring guidelines set forth by the College Board.

Receiving Your Score

With the exception of the English Composition exam with essay, you will receive your score on the computer screen right after you have completed the test. Since the CLEP exam is completed through Computer-Based Testing (CBT), it is possible to designate through test software the schools, certifying agency, or employer that you would like to receive your CLEP test score right away. You cannot recall your score once you have viewed it, however. Only after you designate institutions to have your score sent to can you view your scores.

If you have any questions about the test or your score report that cannot be answered at the testing center, write to:

CLEP

P.O. Box 6600

Princeton, NJ 08541-6600

clep@info.collegeboard.org

Canceling Your Score

You can only cancel your score before you view it. Once you have viewed your CLEP test score, the score has been recorded and you cannot recall it. If you feel that you have done very poorly on the exam and you wish to cancel your score, do so, but realize that no record will be kept of how you did on the test. If you cancel your score, the computer will prompt you to confirm that you really want to cancel your score before the score is nullified.

Obtaining Additional Score Reports

To send a CLEP score report/transcript to additional schools or institutions after you have viewed your score, fill out a transcript request form on the College Board's website: collegeboard.com/student/testing/clep/scores.html, or call (800) 257-9558 to order one. Your CLEP transcript will include scores on any CLEP exam that you have taken in the last 20 years. Each transcript request costs $20.

A Passing Score

For the CLEP exams, a passing score is a score that you can either get college credit for or use to skip a course. The following table shows the minimum scores recommended by the American Council on Education (ACE) to receive college credit for each exam. The minimum exam scores that are recommended are equivalent to an average class grade of a C. Each college and/or institution can have its own credit-granting policies, so check with the school or institution about what scores are acceptable to it before taking the exam.

Minimum Credit-Granting Scores The American Council on Education (ACE)		
Subject	*Minimum Recommended Score*	*Semester Hours*
College Mathematics	50	6
English Compostion	50	6
Humanities	50	6
Natural Sciences	50	6
Social Sciences and History	50	6

Tests in This Book

While your estimated score on any of the sample full-length tests in this book cannot determine the exact score you will receive on the actual CLEP test, they can help you determine what areas to work on before taking the test, as well as whether or not you are ready to take the test in general.

The College Board has not released the exact scoring guidelines for each test, but you can estimate whether or not you have achieved a passing grade on the sample tests in this book. In general, if you score over 70 percent (a grade of C) on a given test, you probably are well prepared for that CLEP exam. See Chapter Twenty-Four, Scoring Your Test, for more information.

CLEP AND THE MILITARY

The CLEP exams offer an especially good opportunity for American servicemen and women. Most members of the United States Armed Services (and some civilian employees) can take the CLEP exams for free. Go to collegeboard.com/students/testing/clep/military.html to find a list of eligible personnel. In addition, CLEP exams are offered at College Test Centers on many military bases, on college campuses, and at DANTES Education centers. DANTES stands for Defense Activity for Non-Traditional Education Support, and this organization offers a variety of opportunities including distance learning and tuition assistance. In addition to the CLEP, it administers a number of other standardized tests. See dantes.doded.mil for information. The difference between taking a CLEP exam on a military base or college campus and at a DANTES Education center is that DANTES only offers the paper-and-pencil tests, while most bases and campuses only offer the computer-based test. To register for a CLEP exam in either location or for information, contact your Educational Services Officer or Navy College Specialist, or visit DANTES online at www.dantes.doded.mil.

HOW THIS BOOK CAN HELP YOU

If you are taking any of the five CLEP exams discussed in this chapter, Kaplan's *Guide to the CLEP* can help you focus your studying and maximize your results. Our book covers the following key points.

1. **Test strategies geared specifically to the computer-based CLEP exam in general, and additional strategies for each subject test.** Many books give the same talk about strategies like Pacing and the Process of Elimination that have been used for every standardized test given in the past twenty years. By now, most of this stuff is common knowledge (although we'll review it again for you, just in case you haven't had enough of it). Since most CLEP exams are given only on the computer, knowledge of specific techniques to improve your skills at navigating this computer interface is something every student should have. These strategies are covered in the next chapter, and they are very useful regardless of what specific subject test you are taking. Before you read anything else in this book, thoroughly review the contents of the next chapter.

   In addition to the strategies designed to help you attack the computer-based CLEP exams, we have also developed techniques geared specifically for each of the five tests covered in this book. These subject-specific strategies—combined with the computer-specific CLEP strategies—are powerful tools to have at your disposal.

2. **A well-crafted review of all the relevant subjects**. The best test-taking strategies alone won't help you take the CLEP College Mathematics test if you don't know a square from a triangle. Every CLEP exam covers a broad range of topics, and a basic familiarity with these topics is necessary if you want to score well. Obviously, you wouldn't even be trying to take a CLEP test in a particular subject if you didn't feel pretty confident about your mastery of that subject. That's why we won't waste your time with an exhaustive subject review. Instead, we've tailored our review section to focus on how the CLEP tests present information, and what you need to know in order to answer the questions correctly.

3. **Three full-length practice tests for each subject**. There's no substitute for experience when it comes to standardized testing. Taking a practice CLEP exam gives you an idea of what it's like to answer multiple-choice questions on a particular topic for 90 minutes. That's not a fun experience, granted, but it is helpful. Practice exams give you the opportunity to find out what areas are your strongest, and what topics you should spend some additional time studying. And the best part is . . . it doesn't count! Mistakes you make on our practice exams are mistakes you won't make on the real test.

   In the section devoted to each CLEP exam covered in this book, we've placed one diagnostic test at the very beginning of the section. Think of this exam as a "Here's what you would score if you took that CLEP exam without much studying" test. You can use the results of this exam to tailor your approach to the review section, which follows the diagnostic. Note the topics or categories where you missed the most questions, and then concentrate on the section of the review that covers the categories. You may also want to create an additional study plan to shore up these weaker areas. For this, use the relevant sections of the review as your starting point.

Once you've had a chance to work on your weak areas, you have two more full-length tests to take as practice. Also, each test has detailed explanations for each question, so you can learn from all your mistakes. You may even learn from some problems you got right in the first place, so don't neglect to read through the explanations section thoroughly.

Those three points describe the general outline of this book: Strategies, Review, and Practice Exams. Check out the next chapter to learn some specific skills you can use on the five CLEP subject tests covered in this book.

Section One: Introduction to the CLEP

Chapter Two: The CLEP Computer Interface

- Call it the CCLEP
- Should You Take the Computer-Based Test?
- The Basics of the Computer CLEP Exam Format
- Final Thoughts

CALL IT THE CCLEP

That first "C" stands for "Computer-based," since most of you reading this book will take your CLEP exam or exams on a computer. There are pencil-and-paper versions of the five CLEP tests covered in this book, but they cost twice as much as the computer-based version. For reasons of cost and availability, many of you won't be able to choose between a computer version and a pencil-and-paper version. If you do have a choice, though, consider the pros and cons of the computer test before making your decision.

SHOULD YOU TAKE THE COMPUTER-BASED TEST?

Pro: No Waiting for Results

Once you finish answering all the questions on a computer-based CLEP exam, you get to see your score. (The only time this isn't true is when you take a CLEP test that has an essay portion to it.) Waiting for results from a pencil-and-paper test can take anywhere between two to six weeks. With the computer version, you get your results back after two to six *seconds*. It's quite a difference, and one that will save you weeks of anxiety about your scores.

Con: No Experience with the Format

You probably know or remember from your high-school days so-called "good test-takers," people with average grades who always seem to do very well on exams. What makes them "good" test-takers? There are many factors, but having confidence and a positive attitude are two attributes

most good test-takers have. This mindset allows them to avoid anxiety, take educated guesses, and not get bogged down on one or two questions. In general, a positive attitude leads to positive results.

Now here's the question to consider: How confident can you be taking a test in a format you've never experienced before? Most people haven't taken 90-minute multiple-choice tests on a computer, so the experience is something new. This acclimation process adds another layer of difficulty to the test. Not only do you have to take a CLEP exam, but you have to take time and learn the format needed to take a CLEP exam. For some people, this is a nuisance, and for others it's a bigger problem. Either way, though, having to learn the computer format doesn't make your life any easier.

Pro: The Computer Commands Are Easy to Learn

Although you do have to take the time to learn the computer format, the instructions are fairly simple. There are 8–10 buttons on the screen that have self-explanatory labels: If you see a button called "time," you can make a fairly confident guess about what it's for. How to use buttons like "review" and "mark" may be less apparent initially, but they're still easy to learn about. However, you'll want to get familiar ahead of time with all of the buttons, because some of them can really help you in your test-taking strategy.

Con: The Best Strategies Are Not Always Obvious

When you get to the end of your exam, should you review from the back to the front? When you finish a section, should you immediately exit and go on to the next one? The computer format gives you a lot of options, but not all of them will help you. Going back through your exam question by question using the "previous" button may seem like a good idea, but it would be a very inefficient (not to mention potentially confusing) approach to reviewing your exam. Hitting the "quit" button as soon as you're done with a section may make you feel like you're getting ahead, but it doesn't buy you any time for the next section of the exam.

The best way to use the commands is not always clear, and without some preparation, you can waste precious time and brain power on the day of the exam. This chapter will help you learn how to use the test format to your advantage.

THE BASICS OF THE COMPUTER CLEP EXAM FORMAT

Now that we've convinced you that you need to prepare not only for the subject matter of the CLEP exam you're taking, but also for taking it on the computer, where do you begin? This section will take you through everything you'll need to know to navigate the screens you'll actually see in front of you when you take the CLEP exam. After you get familiar with the commands and strategies, we'll tell you how to get some hands-on practice before you take the exam.

Basic Computer Skills for the CLEP Exams

While some computer experience is important if you're taking a CLEP exam, the test won't require any computer skills more advanced than you would use for browsing the Internet or using a word-processing program. You should be sure that you know how to do the following.

1. Type on a computer keyboard
2. Identify a computer icon
3. Use a mouse to navigate a computer screen
4. Scroll through a document

Basically, you need to be able to get around on a computer and be comfortable doing it. If any of the above concepts make you nervous, find some help learning the basics of computer usage. If they are familiar, you'll be fine using the exam software.

A Quick Review of the Question Screen

The question screen has three basic parts: the title bar at the top, the test question in the center, and the icons at the bottom of the screen. Before we look at each part in depth, take a moment to familiarize yourself with what the CLEP will look like.

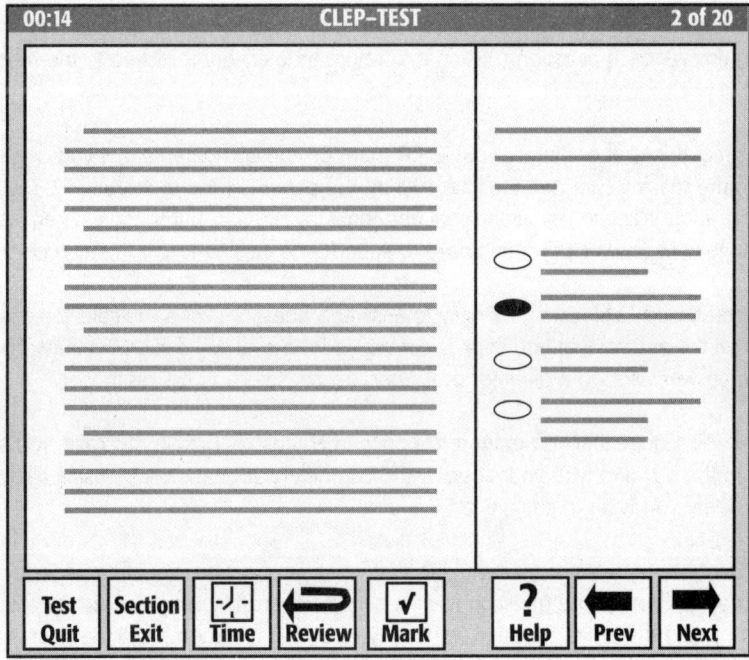

It looks pretty simple, doesn't it? Let's look more closely.

The Title Bar

Across the top of the question screen is the title bar. It's the simplest part of the question screen and is fairly self-explanatory.

1. On the left of the title bar is the time remaining for the section of the exam that you are taking. It is not the time remaining in the exam as a whole (unless you're taking the final section). Checking your time remaining is a good way of keeping track of your progress on the exam. However, if always having the time in front of you makes you nervous, you can hide it. We'll explain how when we go over the icons.

2. In the center of the title bar is the test or section title. It may be useful to be reminded of what section of the exam you are taking, but if the title at the top isn't for the test you planned on taking, you'll want to see a test administrator immediately.

3. On the right of the title bar is the number of the question you are on and the total number of questions in the section. This is helpful for keeping track of where you are. If you're on question 10 out of 20, you know you're halfway through. But remember that some types of questions will take longer than others, so don't use question number alone to gauge your progress.

The Test Questions

You'll always find the test questions in the center of the screen. They will appear one at a time and you can answer each question (or skip it to return to later) and proceed to the next at your own pace.

One of the great things about taking your CLEP exam on the computer is that you don't need to spend your time making sure that the little oval on the paper is filled in thoroughly. You don't have to worry about filling in the wrong oval and throwing off your numbering system. And if you want to change your answer, you don't have to spend time erasing to get the lead off the paper.

On a computer-based CLEP exam, it's easy to answer a question. For a multiple-choice question, simply click on the answer that you think is correct and the oval will darken. If you want to change your answer, click on a different oval. Your original selection will disappear.

Some exams will require that you enter a response in an answer box. In this case, you simply put your cursor in the box and type your answer. You can delete your answer by using backspace and type a new one if you want to change it.

Recording your answer is easier on the CLEP than when you're working with a paper exam, but sometimes getting through the question itself is harder. The test question section is sometimes too small to contain the entire question, especially when the question has a long passage associated with it. When this happens, a scroll bar will appear and you will have to use it to navigate through the question. This may be frustrating. You won't have all of the information for the question in front of you at one time. It's a limitation of the computer format, and there's not much to do about it but be prepared for it.

The Icons

The icons are the tools that will enable you to take the test. Using them correctly and effectively can make or break your score, so take time to get to know them well.

The icons you see may vary depending on what test you're taking, though the basic ones will stay consistent. However, if you are taking a math exam, you may find a calculator icon available. Sometimes an icon may appear gray. That means it's disabled and not needed (or allowed) on this exam.

Moving from the right to the left, here are the icons you'll encounter on the CLEP exam along with some strategies to help you use them most effectively.

1. **Next**. To move through the test, you will use the "next" icon. When you answer a question, you will not proceed to the next question until you hit "next." You can also skip a question by hitting "next." This one is pretty obvious.

2. **Previous**. The "prev" icon is also designed to help you move through the test, but in this case it takes you backward through the questions. You're most likely to use the "prev" icon if you suddenly change your mind about a question you just answered or for a multipart question where you might want to move back and forth between questions.

    It is not a good use of your time to scan through earlier parts of the exam using the "prev" button. The "review" button is a much better option, as we'll explain later on.

3. **Help**. Help? Didn't you think that you couldn't get additional help on this exam?

    Clicking on the "help" icon opens the help window. There you will find directions for the section of the test that you are taking, which can be very useful if you don't remember some specifics when you get to a new question.

    The "help" icon can also give you other useful information, such as how to answer a question in general or a review of the tools available for the question. You'll find the available help categories as icons along the right side of the help screen. At the bottom you'll find the "return to where I was" icon, which will take you back to the question you were working on.

    You may never use the "help" icon, especially if you take time to prepare for the computer functions up front. The exam will be set up so that it isn't essential that you turn to the help window. However, know that it's there if you need it.

4. **Mark**. Pay attention here: The "mark" icon can be one of the most important tools for taking the exam if you use it effectively. Paired with the "review" icon, it can give you a terrific strategy for dealing with questions whose answers you're not absolutely sure about.

    The "mark" icon allows you to mark a question so that you can return to it easily. It's kind of like adding something to your "favorites" list on your Web browser, except often the questions you will choose to mark won't be your favorites. They'll be the ones you aren't sure you answered correctly.

    To mark a question, just hit the "mark" icon while you're still on that question. A check mark will appear in the "mark" box. If you click on "mark" again, the check mark will be erased. "Mark" is meant to be used in conjunction with the next icon on the list.

5. **Review**. Clicking on the "review" icon opens the review window. In this window you will find a list of all of the questions in the current section of the exam. For each question, you can see its status:
   - answered
   - not answered
   - not seen

Any question you have marked will have a check mark next to it.

You can choose between two ways of sorting the list in the review window. You can sort it by question, which keeps it in the numerical order from the beginning of the section. You can also choose to sort it by status, which will group together all the questions that have been answered, not answered, or not seen. To sort the list, simply click on the "question" or "status" headings at the top of the questions list.

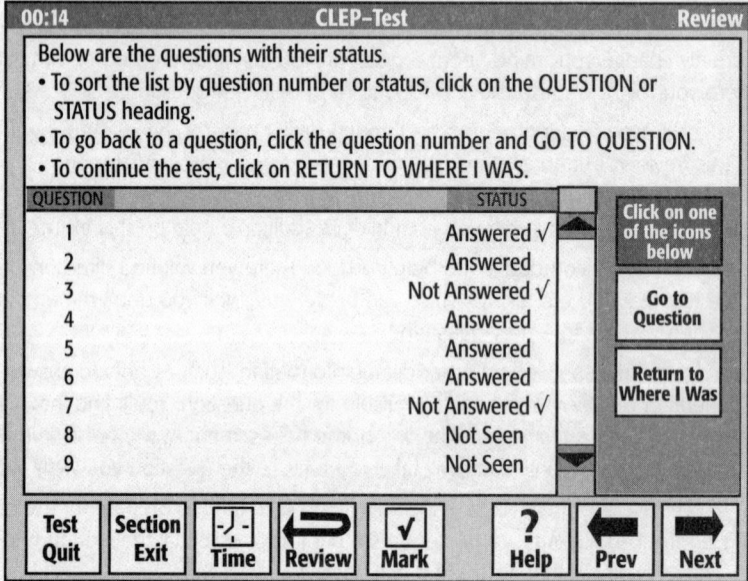

The review window also allows you to return to any question in the section or to go back to where you were in the section. Therefore, if you know that you want to return to question 15, you can sort by question number and simply click on number 15. Then click on the Go to Question icon on the right of the screen. You'll return directly to that question.

You may also want to go back to all of the questions that you didn't answer or, alternately, all of the questions that you marked. To do this, sort the questions by status. Now you can click on any question that says "not answered" or that has a check mark next to it.

Using the review window can give you a quick snapshot of where you are on the section. You can click on "review," glance at how many questions you've answered, not answered, and not seen, then click on the "Return to Where I Was" icon and go directly back to the question you were working on. It can also be used more comprehensively, however. Here's how.

Strategies for Using Mark and Review

You always want to make at least two passes through any section of the CLEP exam. Mark and Review will make your second pass much more efficient by giving you a simple way to find the questions you want to return to. On your first pass through the exam, move through the questions, answering them if you are sure about the answer. If you don't know the answer to a question, don't waste time trying to decipher it. Move on and return to it later. But what about when you have an idea about a question but just aren't sure?

One strategy is to make your best guess about an answer, but then mark the question to return to later. You will have to choose for yourself under what parameters you answer and mark versus leaving a question blank. Perhaps for a multiple-choice question you answer and then mark the question when you can eliminate one choice. Perhaps when you can eliminate two. Remember, there is no penalty for guessing on the CLEP exams. You're better off answering a question than leaving it blank. Before you leave a section, you'll want to have answered all of the questions.

When you make your second pass through an exam, begin at the review window. How much time you spend on the remaining questions will depend on your approach and how much time you have left. Ideally, when you are done with the section, you'll have reviewed all the questions you either didn't answer or you marked, and each question will have an answer.

Using mark and review will save you time on your exam. It will save you the stress of trying to figure out which questions to go back to.

6. **Time.** Clicking on the "time" icon will hide or show the time remaining for the section you are working on. You can use this button to get rid of the potentially stressful countdown happening on the far left of the title bar. You cannot, unfortunately, use it to buy more time on your exam.

    — DO NOT USE

7. **Section Exit.** The "section exit" icon allows you to leave a section and move on to the next. You won't be able to return to a section once you exit it. We don't recommend that you use the "section exit" icon. Here's why.

    Each section of the exam is allotted a specific amount of time. Leaving a section early will not afford you any more time on subsequent sections of the exam. You will simply lose the time you didn't use. So leaving a section early may get you out of the exam earlier, but what are you in such a rush for anyway? Instead of clicking on "section exit," click on "review." Go through the questions again. Check your answers.

8. **Test Quit.** We're even more adamant about this button than the "section exit" button. "Test quit" will exit the exam for you. There will be no going back, no reconsidering your answers. We don't recommend it. We really don't recommend it.

    — DO NOT USE

"Test quit" is there for an emergency, and you should only use it in the case of a bona fide emergency. Don't use it if you just need to get up and use the bathroom. Don't use it if you're frustrated and wish you'd studied harder. What's a bona fide emergency? We heard about a guy who was taking a computerized exam and yawned so widely that his jaw locked. This poor guy had to get up and go to the emergency room in the middle of his exam. We think it was all right for him to hit "test quit." This is unlikely to happen to you. Stay for your entire testing session.

9. **Calculator**. On some exams, a "calculator" icon will appear. If it is shaded gray, it is not available for use, but if it is dark, you can use it on the exam questions. You'll find there's not much that's surprising about the calculator. It has the same basic functions as your typical handheld scientific calculator; you'll just be using it on the computer instead of in your palm.

There are just a few things to know about the calculator function. You can use either your mouse or the numbers of your keyboard to enter figures into the calculator. You can choose to display your calculations using either a floating decimal or by scientific notation by clicking your mouse on either "flo" or "sci," respectively. There is also one available memory location. You can access it by using the ">>M" or "M>>" buttons.

The coolest thing about the calculator is that for some questions you can transfer your answer directly from the calculator to the answer box without having to retype it. There's no chance of entering misplaced decimals or inadvertent typos. To use this feature, hit "transfer display" on the bottom left of the calculator. You'll see your figure appear in the answer box of the question.

Don't Take Our Word For It

This is a lot of information to take in, we realize, and learning computer commands by reading about them is kind of like learning to play tennis by poring through a tennis manual. You need to try it out yourself on the court, in the sun, with a little yellow ball coming straight at you. Or, in this case, you'll want to do so with a mouse and a computer screen before your eyes.

Fortunately, you have the opportunity to do just that before taking the CLEP exam. The College Board offers a free demo to allow you to practice taking a CLEP exam on the computer. It won't help you with the material you'll be tested on, but it will help you get used to what the material will look like when you actually sit down for the exam.

So try it yourself. You'll need to go to the College Board's CLEP website and download the CLEP Sampler. You can do so at collegeboard.com/student/testing/clep/prep.html. The program requires a PC running Microsoft Windows; at this time a Macintosh version is not available.

Once you have it, the sampler will take you step by step through all of the windows and all of the commands you'll see when taking the exam. We strongly recommend you take the time to run through the sampler a few times before you ever set foot in the testing center. Get familiar with seeing the questions on the computer. Picture yourself answering them like an expert.

FINAL THOUGHTS

Mastering a subject is hard work. Before you even decided to take a CLEP exam, you probably put in a significant amount of time and effort learning the materials you'll be tested on. This was a good investment, and part of the return on it will be being able to go on to more interesting and challenging subjects and not having to learn it again. You can also save a lot of money by finishing college earlier. It would be a shame to blow that opportunity because you weren't prepared for the format of the exam.

Taking a computer-based CLEP exam can have many benefits over the pencil-and-paper version, but only if you are prepared for it. Get familiar with the screens. Learn the commands. Go through the demos. Then turn your attention to proving just how well you know your stuff. We're ready to share more strategies for helping you do just that.

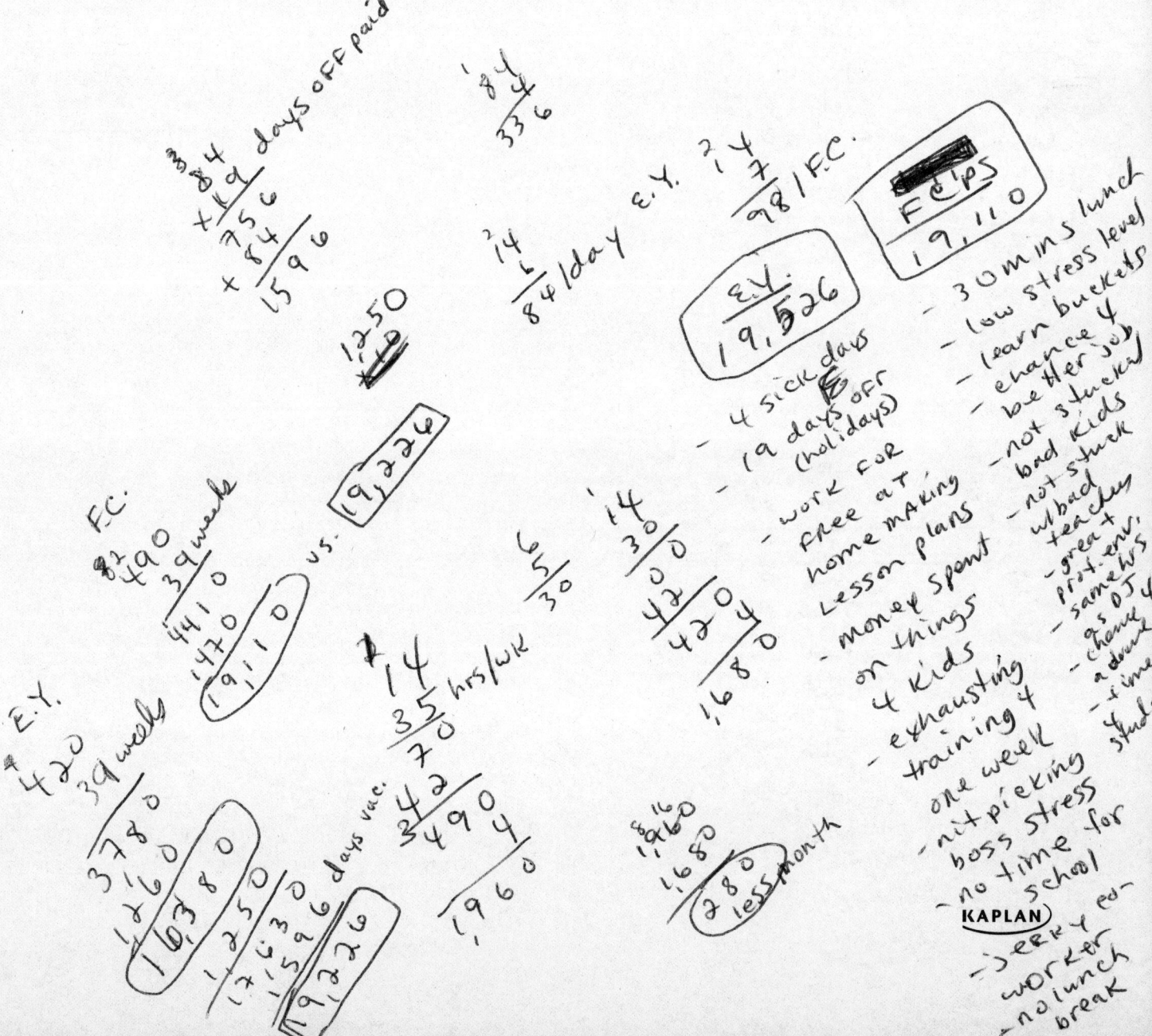

Wed 10	Sat 13
Th 11	Sun 14
Fri 12	Mon 15
Sat 13	Tu 16
Su 14	Wed 17
Mon 15	Th 18
Ty 16	Fri 19
Wed 17	Sat 20
Th 18	Sun 21
Fri 19	Mon 22
Sat 20	Tues 23
Sun 21	Wed 24
Mon 22	Thurs 25
Tues 23	Fri 26
Wed 24	Sat 27
Th 25	Sun 28
Fri 26	Mon 29
Sat 27	Tues 30
Sun 28	Wed 31
Mon 1	Thurs 1
Tues 2	Fri 2
Wed 3	Sat 3
Th 4	Sun 4
Fri 5	Mon 5
Sat 6	Tues 6
Sun 7	Wed 7
Mon 8	
Tues 9	
Wed 10	
Th 11	
Fri 12	

//Section One: Introduction to the CLEP | 19//

Chapter Three: Specific CLEP Exam Strategies

- Specific Strategies for Specific Tests
- General Test-Taking Strategies
- CLEP English Composition Strategies
- CLEP College Mathematics Strategies
- CLEP Humanities Strategies
- CLEP Social Sciences and History Strategies
- CLEP Natural Sciences Strategies
- Final Thoughts

SPECIFIC STRATEGIES FOR SPECIFIC TESTS

Now that you have an idea of how to navigate through the CLEP computer wonderland, it's time to talk about formulating the right approach to each of the five CLEP tests covered in this book. Every standardized test requires a combination of skills (facts) and strategy in order to get a good score. Think about it: If you've read over a thousand books but are a lousy test-taker, your CLEP Humanities exam score will suffer. If you have no problem working fast and guessing aggressively, that will help, but it won't help much if you think Beethoven is a large dog you saw in a movie once.

Before we talk about specific strategies, a quick review of general strategies is in order. Most of these ideas will not be new to you, although one or two might be. Either way, review them, because you need to do more than just be aware of these ideas. You need to understand and feel comfortable using them. Most students know what the process of elimination is, but sadly, too few actually use the process of elimination when taking a test. Don't let this happen to you.

GENERAL TEST-TAKING STRATEGIES

1. **Pacing**. Since many tests are timed, proper pacing allows someone to attempt every question in the time allotted. Poor pacing causes students to spend too much time on some questions to the point where they run out of time before getting a chance at every problem.

2. **Two-Pass System**. Using the two-pass system is one way to help your pacing on a test. The key idea is that you don't simply start with question 1 and trudge onward from there. Instead, you start at the beginning, but take a first pass through the test answering all the questions that are easy for you. If you encounter a tough problem, you spend only a small amount of time on it and then move on in search of easier questions that might exist after that problem. This way, you don't get bogged down on a tough problem when you could be earning points answering later problems that you do know. On your second pass, you go back through the section and attempt all the tougher problems that you passed over the first time. You should be able to spend a little more time on them, and this extra time might help you answer the problem. Even if you don't reach an answer, you might be able to employ techniques like the process of elimination to cross out some answer choices and then take a guess.

3. **Process of Elimination**. On every multiple-choice test you ever take, the answer is given to you. The only difficulty resides in the fact that the correct answer is hidden among incorrect choices. Even so, the multiple-choice format means you don't have to pluck the answer out of the air. Instead, if you can eliminate answer choices you know are incorrect, and only one choice remains, then that must be the correct answer.

4. **Patterns and Trends**. The key word here is the *standardized* in "standardized testing." Being standardized means that tests don't change greatly from year to year. Sure, each question won't be the same, and different topics will be covered from one administration to the next, but there will also be a lot of overlap from one year to the next. That's the nature of *standardized* testing: if the test changed wildly each time it came out, it would be useless as a tool for comparison. Because of this, certain patterns can be uncovered about any standardized test. Learning about these trends and patterns can help students taking the test for the first time.

5. **The Right Approach**. Having the right mindset plays a large part in how well people do on a test. Those who are nervous about the exam and hesitant to make guesses often fare much worse than students with an aggressive, confident attitude. Students who start with question 1 and go on from there don't score as well as students who pick and choose the easy question first before tackling the harder ones. People who take a test cold have more problems than those who take the time to learn about the test beforehand. In the end, factors like these create people who are good test-takers and those who struggle even when they know the material.

Those are the basics. On to the next level.

CLEP ENGLISH COMPOSITION STRATEGIES

There are two versions of this exam: one that's all multiple-choice (MC) and one that's half multiple-choice, half essay. In this section we will cover all the different multiple-choice question types and the strategies that you need to use for each one. For the essay, check out the English Composition review in Chapter Five of this book.

The all-MC version of the CLEP English Composition exam features 90 questions in 90 minutes, making it very easy for you to figure out the average amount of time you should spend on every question. The half-and-half test presents you with 50 MC questions in a 45-minute Section I. Section II gives you 45 minutes to write an essay. The all-MC test has five different multiple-choice question types, while the exam-with-essay has only three of these five question types.

The three multiple-choice question types that appear on both tests may look familiar to you, since they appear on other standardized tests. In addition, the new Writing section of the SAT features the exact same types of questions, so if you've taken the SAT after February 2005 this will be like a reunion exam. Perhaps not a happy reunion, but it's better to face a question format you've already seen than a problem type you've never encountered before.

Identifying Sentence Errors
(Appears on both versions of the test)

First up on the CLEP English Composition exam are Identifying Sentence Error (ISE) problems, which look like:

> 16. When the pilgrims first came <u>to</u> America, they had <u>few</u>
>   A   B
> supplies and <u>were almost</u> <u>kill off</u> by the harsh winter
>   C   D
> weather and disease. <u>No error</u>
>   E

Four sections of a sentence are underlined, and if there's a mistake under one of the underlined portions, you are supposed to pick that answer choice. If there is no error under (A), (B), (C), or (D), then you are supposed to pick answer (E). On average, 20 percent of the problems will fall under choice (E). This fact causes problems for people determined to find something wrong (they never pick (E)) as well as people too quick to decide that nothing is wrong (they pick (E) half the time). To avoid either extreme, try to keep track of how many times you pick choice (E) on the ISE section. You could write the letter "E" down on a scratch sheet of paper, and every time you pick it, make a small mark. When you leave the ISE section, do some quick division and figure out how many times you picked answer (E) in that section. As long as you're somewhere around 20 percent, don't sweat it. But if you picked (E) too often or too rarely, try to take some time at the end of the exam to go back and look over your answers for these questions.

The English Composition Review in Chapter Five covers the common grammar errors that crop up in the ISE problems and elsewhere. This section is about strategy, and to understand the best strategy for ISE problems, remember the following statement.

The regular (non-underlined) portions of the sentence are just as important as the underlined ones. Since they can't be changed, they often have the clue that shows which underlined portion needs to be changed.

The pilgrim question is a straightforward example of parallelism. With parallelism, each item in a series appears in the same grammatical form. Parallelism is a common grammatical error that crops up on the CLEP English Composition test. For the pilgrim question, the underlined portion (D) has to agree with "were almost." "Were almost" is in the past tense, so (D) has to be in the past tense, not the present. Each underlined answer choice has to be grammatically accurate and agree with the rest of the sentence, so (D) has to be "killed" rather than "kill." Since the first two underlined items are correct and the third underlined item has to agree with (D), choice (D) is the correct answer for this question. The regular portion of the sentence led you to the underlined portion that was the correct answer.

The regular sentence portions won't always provide the clue. Sometime you just have to listen to your inner ear and trust your grammar instincts. Everyone knows more grammar than they think they do, so if you feel that something is wrong but don't know the exact terminology to explain why it is wrong, trust your instincts. They will lead you in the right direction more often than not.

Improving Sentences
(Appears on both versions of the test)

Next up on our tour of the CLEP English Composition test are Improving Sentences problems. These questions begin with a single sentence, and a portion of that sentence—sometimes only a single word, other times every word— is underlined. You are then given four different ways to rewrite the underlined portion of the sentence.

20. During the 1920s, legislators were <u>convinced that prohibition would make</u> people stop drinking and would cut down on crime.

    (A) convinced that prohibition would make
    (B) convincing that prohibition could make
    (C) and it was convinced that prohibition could make
    (D) convinced of prohibition's making
    (E) as they convinced themselves that prohibition would make

The first choice, (A), always repeats the underlined portion exactly as it appears in the question stem. In this sense choice (A) on Improving Sentences is like choice (E), "No Error," on an ISE problem. Again, look to have about one-fifth of your answer choices in this section come up as choice (A).

Improving Sentences problems are very similar to ISE problems, and your approach will reflect this similarity. Again, the non-underlined portion of the sentence plays an important role. If the subject is not underlined but the verb is, you had better start looking at subject/verb agreement. If there are two items in a list in the regular portion of the sentence, take a very close look at the third parallel item that is underlined.

If you're not quite sure what the right answer is, a good fallback strategy is to remind yourself that:

More words ≠ better grammar

Most people have this idea that grammar is horribly complex and difficult to understand. Well, they may be on to something, but just because grammar is hard, that doesn't mean it takes up a lot of space and requires a lot of words. Test-takers often get psyched out on Improving Sentences problems and pick choices with long strings of words like *will might could have been searching* when a simple *will search* is correct. If you're ever in doubt, avoid the longer convoluted choices and try to keep things simple.

Look at the prohibition question above. Choices (C) and (E) contain a bunch of extra phrases and seem to go on forever. Neither one of them is correct, however, since all those extra words are unnecessary. Choices (C) and (E) are there to trap students who think more words equal better grammar. You, however, know better, so you should be quite leery of picking (C) and (E). They might be right, but probably not.

Look over the underlined portion and compare the text there with the regular portion. Use your mental voice and "speak" the sentence out loud in your head. Does it seem right? Is *convinced* (past tense) the right verb form, or is something more involved needed?

In fact, the simple past tense is all that's needed for the verb *convince*, and everything else is fine with the sentence as it stands. Choice (A) is the answer. You shouldn't be worried or afraid to pick (A) since some of the Improving Sentences questions will actually need no improvement.

Revising Work in Progress
(Appears on both versions of the test)

Hey, are you the kind of person who enjoys reading badly-written essays? If you answered "yes," today is your lucky day! Revising Work in Progress (RWP) questions present you with a "draft" of an essay, and then ask you roughly five questions about it. All sentences in the draft are numbered so that they can easily be referred to in a problem. Let's look at a small version of a RWP essay and problem.

(1) My friend and I attended camp together last summer. (2) We decided a play would be fun. (3) We didn't know what the play would be about, but we wanted it to be fun. (4) Everyone is always saying that my friend is creative. (5) She wrote the play for us.

40. Which of the following is the best way to revise and combine sentences 4 and 5 (reproduced below)?

    Everyone is always saying that my friend is creative. She wrote the play for us.

    (A) My friend is creative, so she wrote the play for us.
    (B) My friend is creative, and everyone is always saying that she is creative, so she wrote the play.
    (C) Everyone is always talking about how creative my friend is, and she wrote the play.
    (D) The play was written by my friend who is so creative that everyone always talks about her.
    (E) Talking about the creativeness of my friend, she decided to write.

Use the following points to help you handle RWP Problems.

Techniques to Use on RWP Questions

1. **Read the passage quickly for the general idea and nothing else.** Look, the passage has problems—that's the whole point. Spending time trying to understand what those problems are is a waste of your time. You don't get points for reading the passage: you get points for answering questions, so make that your goal. You need to know what each sentence says and have a general idea of what the passage is about, but any deeper understanding is pointless. Get to the questions as soon as you can. Then you can work on fixing some of the problems in the passage . . . if that's what the question asks you to do.

2. **Problems are more structural/organizational than grammatical.** The last two question types focused on proper grammar. That's not stressed as much in the RWP section, although there will be some grammatical errors occasionally. Instead, the focus here is on sentence structure and organization, with questions like, "Where could sentence 7 best be placed?" or "Which of the following sentences would work best after sentence 5?" To answer the latter question, you have to read sentence 5 and gain an idea of where the paragraph is heading in terms of content. What is being discussed in sentence 5? A good sentence 6 will continue that train of thought or move on to a related point.

3. **Other repeating problems deal with the problem of redundant, repeating sentences that repeat sentences redundantly and say same thing over and over again, repeatedly.** You get the feeling the above sentence could be restated with fewer words? You'll get that feeling again and again on this section of the CLEP English Composition test. Two related sentences will need to be stitched together, or a long sentence like the one above will have

to be pruned. When you do this, keep in mind that "more words ≠ better grammar" and that keeping it simple and clear is often the hallmark of good writing. The initial sentence could read, "Other problems deal with redundant sentences" or "Other problems deal with sentences that repeat themselves." Both of these are clear, simple alternatives to the initial mess.

4. **Other question types may drop by for a visit.** Suppose you have a RWP problem that looks like:

> 54. Which is the best version of the underlined portion of sentence 1 (reproduced below)?
>
> Sometimes people like to go out for dinner, and sometimes <u>they like to cook at home</u>.
>
> (A) No change
> (B) they all cook in the house
> (C) a house is a place to eat in
> (D) they thus like to cook food at a house
> (E) eating dinner at home can be a sometimes cooking experience

Look familiar? This is exactly like an Improving Sentences problem, even down to the fact that choice (A) states that things are correct the way they are. Why the test includes the same type of problem in two different sections is a mystery, but since it does, you can use it to your advantage. You know how to approach Improving Sentences problems, so use the correct technique regardless of where the problems appear.

The three question types that appear on both versions of the test are fairly standard question types that you may have encountered before. The next two question types appear only on the all-MC version of the CLEP English Composition exam, and they are somewhat unusual. After looking at them, you might decide that writing an essay isn't such a bad idea after all.

Restructuring Sentences
(Appears only on all-MC version of exam)

These are strange questions, so understand their format before test day.

Anatomy of a Restructuring Sentences Question
1. You are given a fine, upstanding correct sentence.

> The Metropolitan Museum of Art is a famous museum located in New York.

2. You are then given directions on how to change it in some way.

   Begin with <u>New York is home to</u>

3. You must now rewrite (or restructure) the sentence yourself in line with the directions. **It is highly advisable to write your revised sentence down.**

   New York is home to the famous Metropolitan Museum of Art.

4. Snippets of sentences reside in the answer choices. If you rewrote the sentence correctly, you'll find a single snippet that matches a piece of your own revised sentence.

   (A) the famous Metropolitan
   (B) the home of the museum
   (C) the Museum of Art, and is inspired by
   (D) ten museums in its own vicinity
   (E) many places that can be considered museums

Choice (A) repeats a snippet of your revised sentence, so it is the answer.

The answer choices are disjointed snippets of text, so don't look at them before you craft your own restructured sentence. Doing so might influence you in the wrong direction, as you take an incorrect snippet and attempt to create some sentence around it.

The key technique was stated already, but it bears repeating: write out your own sentence. Don't try to craft it in your head. Place it on paper. Once you have done so, *then* you can look at the answer choices.

If you write a sentence and don't find a snippet, them mark that question and come back to it later. You can spend a lot of time on a single Restructuring Sentences problem, churning out sentence after sentence in the hopes that one of them will connect. Instead, avoid a black-hole question like that and move on in search of potentially easier problems.

Analyzing Writing
(Appears only on all-MC version of exam)

Most of you have taken a reading comprehension test—you know, you read a passage and then answer questions about it. Analyzing Writing (AW) looks like regular reading comprehension, but the questions are different. Instead of testing your understanding of what a sentence says, AW problems want to see whether you understand how the sentence is used. You will see questions that ask:

> Which of the following best describes the relationship of sentence 2 to the rest of the paragraph?
>
> Which of the following best describes the function of sentence 3?
>
> In sentence 4, the effect of using "whereas" is to

It doesn't matter what sentence 2 says; what's important is how it fits in with the other sentences in that paragraph. AW problems want you to view a piece of writing as an interwoven fabric of ideas. They then ask you questions about the individual strings and how they fit into the overall weave.

To gain this level of understanding, you have to read the initial passage fairly carefully. What is being discussed is not as critical as *how* it is being discussed. Reading a passage this way takes time, but you really can't cut corners too much or you won't really understand how the sentences thread together.

When you do get a chance to answer questions, keep in mind that standardized tests do all they can to be as uncontroversial as possible. *Bland is Good!* is the motto for most answers. Correct answers are often statements that are positive in a general way, while wrong answer choices are often filled with extreme wording or controversial statements. So if you have a choice between "Creativity is often a matter of luck or chance" and "Artists feel more intensely than other people," ask yourself which answer is more friendly and digestible. The second sentence makes a point that can't really be proven and could be dead wrong, while the first statement contains the qualifying word "often" to lessen any controversy the statement might create. The first statement is definitely the better guess.

Those are the five MC question types. If you still haven't decided which version of the CLEP English Composition exam you would prefer to take, try the sample tests in this book and see how well you fare on both versions.

CLEP COLLEGE MATHEMATICS STRATEGIES

The CLEP College Mathematics exam consists of 60 questions that you have 90 minutes to answer. Most of the questions are multiple-choice questions with four answer choices, but scattered throughout are 5–10 problems that are more like open-ended short answer problems.

For these problems, you will usually be asked to type in the correct numerical value—like 5.3 or −2, for example—but there might also be a couple of problems with graphics that ask you to use the mouse and click on the correct area of a figure. This sounds more difficult than it actually is. Look at the next example.

46. Which of the following figures has the largest area?

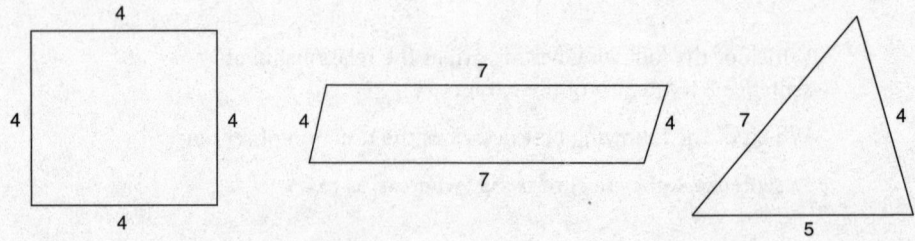

Click inside the figure that has the largest area.

You don't get answer choices. You get a command to move the mouse to the figure with the largest area and then click once. It's a change from just picking an answer, but there's nothing actually difficult about it. It's a regular math question with a strange format, that's all. If you don't let the odd format bother you, you won't have any trouble with this problem.

Speaking of odd...

The Odds and the Straightforwards

Imagine two groups of opposing math teachers seated in a room. Someone asks, "What defines a good math student?" One group—call them the Straightforwards—believes that a deep understanding of all the basic principles of math is the defining characteristic of a good math student. They argue that a student must be able to understand a fundamental concept like algebra so well that he (or she) can use algebra in a variety of situations and in many different ways.

The other group disagrees. This group—let's call them the Odds— feels that knowing the basic concepts is not enough, and that what separates a good math student from everyone else is his or her knowledge of a great range of math subjects, including those that are not as common. The Odds believe that everyone knows a bit about geometry, algebra, and number sense, but that only a good math student can discuss and use topics like set theory and irrational numbers.

If these two groups got together and wrote a math exam, the result would look a lot like the CLEP College Mathematics exam. Half of the questions cover basic topics in a variety of situations, while the other half covers "non-routine problems" including topics that are not standard. The CLEP College Mathematics exam ends up looking like two different tests jammed together: one test covers the basics, and the other hits on all sorts of math topics.

Understanding the dual nature to the test is important, because each kind of question requires a different approach. If you see a problem that has variables in it, you can say, "Ah! A problem written by the Straightforwards. I need to apply a basic idea to solve this problem." If you encounter a problem that starts talking about *truth tables*, you can say, "Here's one by the Odds. What do I remember about this topic from my review? If I can remember the topic, chances are good that I can get this problem correct."

These are two different approaches, and neither one works on the other kind of question. If you have the idea of the Odds versus the Straightforwards in your head, you can navigate through the CLEP College Mathematics exam much more easily.

Vectoring Through the Test

For a simple paper-and-pencil test, using a two-pass system is a matter of using your eyes to scan and your hands to turn the page. Since the CLEP exam is computerized and you see only one question at a time, this version of the two-pass system doesn't quite work, does it?

Here's how to modify the two-pass concept to fit the CLEP College Mathematics exam. When you encounter a problem, realize that you can do one of three things:

1) you can answer it
2) you can "mark" it by hitting the "mark" key on the screen
3) you can leave it alone entirely.

Those are your three options. Even if you could answer every question that shows up, that doesn't mean you want to. For instance, if you encounter a problem that has Roman numerals in it, like

3. Which of the following is NOT true of a rational number?

    I. A rational number can be equal to 0.
    II. A rational number can be the ratio of two nonzero whole numbers.
    III. A rational number cannot be expressed as a fraction.

    (A) I and II
    (B) III only
    (C) II and III
    (D) II only

To answer Roman numeral problems, you often have to address each Roman numeral. This means you have to work three problems to get credit for one. It's not a good use of your time, so you should leave this question blank for now. Move past it and search for problems that are solvable with less time and effort.

In general, Straightforward problems are going to require more time. If you feel you could answer a problem, but that it would take some time, "mark" it on your first pass through a section. There might be easier, simpler problems after it, and you want to try to find all of those on your first pass. On this first run-through, you should "mark" questions that you feel you can answer with a bit of time.

In general, Odd problems are going to require you to have the right facts. Spending a lot of time on these problems might not make a big difference if you don't know the concepts being tested. Leave these problems unanswered during your first pass. You will answer them eventually, even if you don't even attempt them.

After your first pass, you should now have answered all the easy questions that you encountered. You can now go click the Review button and sort the remaining problems by Status. Marked problems will be all those problems you thought you could answer with some more work. Well, you've answered all the easier problems, so the time is now to start in on the marked questions. Many of these marked problems will probably be Straightforwards.

When the marked problems are completed, it's time to tackle the unanswered problems. Give these the best shot that you can, but remember the following fact: **If time is running out, make sure you answer every problem**. If the timer shows 1 minute remaining and there are four problems left, pick (D) (or one of the letters) for every answer and don't worry about it. There's no guessing penalty on the CLEP exam, and the law of averages states that you should get one of those problems right. It's all about getting points wherever, and however, you can.

Here's a recap of an optimal plan of attack.

Problems to Answer on the First Pass:
   Straightforward problems that don't take much time
   Odd problems you know the concept for

Problems to Mark on the First Pass:
   Straightforward problems that might take two minutes
   Odd problems on concepts you remember, but not perfectly
   Open-ended questions (because of the open-ended format, it's best to save these for the second pass to avoid getting bogged down)

Problems to Leave Unanswered (until Time Is Running Out):
   Odd problems on topics you don't know much about
   Roman numeral questions

Make it Real

Many problems on the exam will include variables, either in the answer choices or as part of the question stem. Although variables are an important abstract math concept, working in abstractions on a test is not the best way to get a problem right. **If possible, always replace the variables in a question with actual numbers**. The goal when taking the CLEP College Mathematics exam is to get the highest score possible, not to show off your knowledge of variables. Consider a question like the next example.

13. The width of a farmer's rectangular cornfield is y feet. If he needs 1000 feet of fencing to enclose the field, which of the following represents the length of the field, in feet?

   (A) $1000 - y$
   (B) $1000 - 2y$
   (C) $500 - y$
   (D) $500 - 2y$

For the love of Pythagoras, give the variable y a value and then solve the problem. Look at the answer choices: there's one right algebra answer and four traps designed to catch people who do the algebra incorrectly. If you just decide that $y = 20$ ft, though, then the problem leaves the abstract realm of algebra and becomes an easily workable problem with real-world numbers. Take the formula for the perimeter of a rectangle and place in the values that you know (or just made up).

$$P = 2(l + w)$$
$$1000 = 2(l + 20)$$
$$1000 = 2l + 40$$
$$960 = 2l$$
$$480 = l$$

The length is 480, and that works out to be choice (C), $500 - y$.

Whenever there are variables, remember to try to take the variables out of the equation by making it real.

Work It Out on Paper, Not in Your Head

Since you're staring at a computer screen with a mouse in one hand, there is a great tendency to try to answer questions in your head. It's faster (supposedly), and you've already got one hand tied up using the mouse. The only problem with doing CLEP College Mathematics work in your head is that you almost guarantee yourself a lower score than you need to get.

People—when rushed and under pressure—make mental mistakes. Taking an important exam like this timed CLEP test is almost a textbook definition of a rushed and pressure-filled situation. To avoid the careless errors, make sure to write something down on every problem. Every one. If you make it an automatic habit, you'll find that it doesn't take too long to jot down your thoughts. Writing something down also has a bonus effect on multi-step problems. Quite often, students trying to figure out a knotty problem in their head get lost somewhere along the way, or are unable to visualize how to take the initial facts and reach the required information that the question wants. If you write your work down, you often find yourself staring down at the intermediate steps needed to determine the right answer. You might be able to get there in your head, but what's the point? You want to answer CLEP questions accurately in the fairly brief amount of time, and writing your work down is the best way to accomplish that.

CLEP HUMANITIES STRATEGIES

This test has 140 questions, and even if you're speedy, answering 140 questions in 90 minutes is going to be a rushed affair. When you combine this with the fact that these questions come from a diverse range of topics, the end result is that you are not going to have time to reflect on every question and come up with an answer. Instead, questions will fall into one of three categories:

Category 1: you know the answer right away

Category 2: you can answer the question with a bit of work

Category 3: you have little or no chance of answering these questions correctly

Your goal is to expand Categories 1 and 2, and not spend too much time on problems in that last category. You expand Category 1 by reviewing, while Category 2 questions can be overcome with a mixture of review, strategy, and (a pinch of) luck. Everyone has some Category 3 problems; the key is to accept this fact and not let it bother you. Missing one question won't kill your CLEP Humanities exam score, but spending too much time on a problem you have little chance of even answering correctly can harm your overall performance.

Word Lover or Art Lover?

Half of the CLEP Humanities test covers literature, and the other 50 percent covers fine arts. Ask yourself honestly, which topic do you know more about? You might have an idea by now. If you don't, take the first test in this book and see what problems you find easier to answer.

It doesn't matter if you're a Word Lover (better at literature) or an Art Lover. All that matters is that you have a clear idea which topic you are better at. Once you know, you can take this knowledge and use the computer format of the CLEP exam to craft a killer plan of attack.

Let's say you are a Word Lover. You're not ignorant of art, but you definitely have a better chance on literature questions than art questions. If this is the case, then refine your two-pass approach in the following way.

Word Lover Plan of Attack

1. **On the first pass, look for all Word Lover questions**. Your goal on the first run-through is to find all the Category 1 (you get them right away) questions you can. Since you're better at literature, look for these problems. If you see italics in a question, that's an immediate indicator that it's probably about a book or play. (Art Lover problems can be spotted very easily too; many have ART—like a painting or sculpture—in them. We doubt you'll be confused.)

Give yourself a moment to answer every World Lover question. Even if you are strong in this subject, there will be some questions that you don't know the answer to immediately. That's fine. If you feel you know something about the subject of the question, hit the "mark" button and move on.

2. **If you encounter an Art Lover question that you immediately know the answer to, answer it.** You should be able to hit some art questions out of the park right away. If that's the case, do it and move on. However, don't spend time figuring out an Art Lover question when there are potentially easier literature problems waiting.

3. **If you hit a question you think you know something about but can't answer immediately, "mark" it and move on.** Here is where you can take advantage of the computer format. On your first pass through the CLEP Humanities exam, you can answer all Category 1 questions, "mark" all Category 2 questions, and leave unanswered (for now) all problems that you don't have a strong chance at.

4. **Once you finish your first pass through the test, hit the Review button and sort by status.** You should have three groups, which just so happen to correspond with the three question types we discussed earlier.

   "Answered"—these will be the Category 1 questions.

   "Marked"—these are your Category 2 questions. Start going back through these problems, taking some additional time to work out the right answer (or at least give yourself a good guess). Note that the marked problems won't be sorted into a bunch together, but they will clearly have a check mark next to them.

   "Not answered"—here are the Category 3 problems. As time is running out, leave about three minutes to go through and answer every one of these problems. That doesn't mean you have to look at them. If there's no time, just put an answer and move on. There's no guessing penalty on the CLEP exam, so you should pick up some points even by answering blindly.

Now that is a plan of attack. (If you're an Art Lover, simply switch the two terms and proceed the same way.) While others test-takers are floundering through the section, you will be using your knowledge of the computer format and your understanding of the test structure to maximize your ability to see all questions. This gives you the best possible chance of answering them correctly.

Cluster Questions

Cluster Questions are like the game show *Jeopardy!* because the answers come *before* the question. Cluster Questions start off with A–E, and each answer choice has an initial piece of information next to it. One to three questions follow, and each question describes one of the choices (A–E) in the initial information. You pick the right letter choice for each problem.

Here's an example of a Cluster Question.

> **Questions 6–8** refer to the following texts.
>
> (A) *The Great Gatsby*
> (B) *Sons and Lovers*
> (C) *Beloved*
> (D) *The Grapes of Wrath*
> (E) *The Cider House Rules*

6. Which novel was written by Toni Morrison?

7. Which novel discusses, in part, the immorality and organized crime of the 1920s?

8. Which novel involves love and loss as experienced through the eyes of an orphan named Homer?

Cluster Questions can be answered quickly, so that's good. But a common mistake is to spend time reading over all the answer choices first. Don't. The whole point is to answer questions, not read answer choices. **Once you encounter a Cluster Question set, read the question and then go back and look at the answer choices.** In the example above, you should drop down to question 6, read the question, and then look for an answer. Once you have it, move on to questions 7 and 8.

Sometimes the Cluster Question answer choices are very short, so this approach doesn't save you a lot of time. Other times the Cluster Questions answer choices are lengthier. They might even use a format popular on the CLEP Humanities exam that we call The Lineup.

Unusual Suspects: Lineups on the CLEP Humanities Exam

Sometimes one name just isn't good enough for this test. The CLEP Humanities exam likes to place three names together and then ask you how they are related. Consider the following Cluster Question with Lineup format.

> **Question 10** refers to the following people.
>
> (A) Andy Warhol, Maya Angelou, Jack Kerouac
> (B) Michelangelo, Da Vinci, Rousseau
> (C) Socrates, Aristotle, Plato
> (D) Claude Monet, Auguste Rodin, Edouard Manet
> (E) Charlotte Perkins Gilman, Emily Bronte, Charlotte Bronte

10. Which group is from the twentieth century?

The point to remember about Lineup problems is that because all three names are related in the same way, **you only need to know one of the names**. Sure, there are fifteen names listed, but it's really more like five groups of three. If you know Michelangelo is not from the twentieth century, then it no longer matters who da Vinci and Rousseau are. Similarly, if the Art Lover in you knows that Andy Warhol was a modern artist, the identities of author Maya Angelou and poet Jack Kerouac are irrelevant. The answer has to be (A), because all members of the Lineup are related. You needed to know only one name (Andy Warhol) out of fifteen to get this question right.

Lineup problems can look intimidating at first, since there are a lot of proper names. Students often get worried because they don't recognize all the names. That's the wrong mindset to have, so don't fall prey to it. Instead, when you encounter a Lineup problem in some form or another, tell yourself, "I only need to know one of the names to get the answer right." This can be demonstrated in the following question, which won't be on the CLEP Humanities exam but does show how to attack Lineup questions.

56. Fennis Dembo, Yinka Dare, and Michael Jordan were all

    (A) composers of opera.
    (B) professional basketball players.
    (C) math professors.
    (D) poets.
    (E) playwrights.

You don't really need to know the first two names to get this problem right, do you? All you need is one name.

Uh, I'm Guessing . . .

Whenever you can't find the right answer to a problem, switch gears and start looking for wrong answers to eliminate. The CLEP Humanities exam usually does not have one right answer and four very close wrong answers, which is good news for you. Look back at the sample problems we've gone over so far and you can see that there are one or two choices that are unlikely. Even if you're not a big fan of art, you probably have heard of Michelangelo as a famous *historic* painter. He wasn't painting the Sistine Chapel between World War I and World War II, even if you're not quite sure when he was alive. Using just a smidgeon of factual knowledge can often help you cross out a choice here and there.

Common sense and gut instinct also work well. Look at the following problem.

   (A) Salman Rushdie's *The Satanic Verses*
   (B) Homer's *The Iliad*
   (C) Oscar Wilde's *The Importance of Being Earnest*
   (D) William Carlos Williams' *Paterson*
   (E) Emily Dickinson's *Nature, the gentlest mother*

6. Which takes place in and around London?

Does it seem likely that a book called *The Satanic Verses* takes place in London? If it does, you have a low opinion of London. For that matter, does Salman Rushdie sound like an English name to you? There's always a chance that answer (A) is correct, but if you're guessing, it's not a good guess. Since the work takes place in London, pick one of the British-sounding names like answer (C) or (D). You might be wrong, because there's no law that states that people's names automatically show where they are from. That's not the point. The point is that if you have to guess, don't overthink things too much. Use common sense, since it will give you a good shot at eliminating some unlikely choices and picking the right one.

When you take the practice tests in this book, go back through after the test is over and look at all the answer choices. On the questions you answered immediately, look at the other answer choices and spot the one or two choices that you would have known were wrong, even if you didn't know the right answer. If you get accustomed to looking at answer choices and crossing out the ones that are highly unlikely to be the answer, you should be in good practice when you come to a question and actually have to use this technique.

CLEP SOCIAL SCIENCES AND HISTORY STRATEGIES

When the College Board states that the CLEP Social Sciences and History (SS&H) exam "covers a wide range of topics," they are not kidding. This 120-question test, which you have 90 minutes to complete, throws everything but the kitchen sink at you. A complete breakdown of the topics covered on the CLEP SS&H exam can be found in Chapter Seventeen, but a brief rundown follows.

U.S. History

World History

History of Western Civilization

Government

Political Science

Sociology

Economics

Psychology

Geography

Anthropology

The College Board could have said, "Everything but math, English, and science is on this test," and they wouldn't have been far off.

When you combine a large number of questions (120) with a massive array of topics, you get a situation where getting every question right is almost an impossibility. The truth is that at least one out of every ten CLEP SS&H questions you face will seem completely alien to you. You might not even know what the question is asking for, much less what the answer is. If this happens only 10 percent of the time, consider yourself one of the lucky ones.

A perfect score is impossible, but so what? The goal is to get a good score, one that gets you college credit. This goal is still easily within range. However, you have to make good use of your 90 minutes of testing, and to do that you must accept the fact that there will be some questions that you just won't stand much of a chance on. That doesn't mean you won't answer them—there's no guessing penalty, so every question is going to get answered. It just means that you shouldn't let it bother you when you encounter a problem that you don't have an idea about. That's simply the nature of this many-question, widely ranging exam.

Eating at the Question Smorgasbord

You have less than a minute per question for the CLEP SS&H exam, so managing your time is important. You'll want to use a two-pass system to give yourself a chance to answer every question that you know the answer to. Since the test is on a computer, though, you need to modify the two-pass concept to fit this electronic format. When you encounter a problem, realize that you can do one of three things:

1) You can answer it right away
2) You can "mark" it by hitting the "mark" key on the screen
3) You can leave it alone entirely

Those are your three options. Unlike a math test—where computations often have to be done to find an answer—you are going to know the answer to many of the questions on the CLEP SS&H exam immediately. For example, let's say you know what the Fifth Amendment of the U.S. Constitution is. You get a question that asks, "The Fifth Amendment of the U.S. Constitution declares which of the following?" There's one question you can hit out of the ballpark quickly.

Other questions will be solvable, but not as rapidly. For instance, you might encounter an economics problem that you feel you could answer if you spent just a bit of time thinking about the answer choices. You could spend the time then, but you would be better off using the "mark" function on the computer and marking that question for later. This would allow you to seek out easier, faster questions that might come after that problem.

Still other questions will fall into the third category of, "Whhaaaat? I have little or no idea." Leave these questions unanswered and look for easier prey in the rest of the exam.

After your first pass, you should now have answered all the easy questions that you encountered. **You can now go click the Review button and sort the remaining problems by Status.** It's a great way to make the computer format work to your advantage.

Marked problems will be all those problems you thought you could answer with some more work. Well, you've answered all the easier problems, so the time is now to start in on the marked questions. When the marked problems are completed, it's time to tackle the unanswered problems. Give these the best shot that you can, but remember the following tip: **If time is running out, make sure you answer every problem.** If the timer shows two minutes remaining and there are ten unanswered problems left, pick (B) (or one of the letters) for every answer and don't worry about it. There's no guessing penalty on the CLEP exam, and the law of averages states that you should get two of those problems right (since you have a one-in-five chance

when guessing randomly). Two out of ten might not seem like a lot, but it's good when you consider you didn't stand a chance on any of those questions, and you didn't waste any precious time trying to work them futilely. Shoot for a good score, not a perfect score.

You Can Be Bland

Standardized testing might be a controversial subject to some, but actual standardized tests are *not* controversial. Every standardized test goes to enormous lengths not to offend anyone, and the CLEP tests—not just the Social Sciences and History exam, but all CLEP exams—are no exception.

You can use this fact about the CLEP exams to your advantage when answering a SS&H question you don't anything about. If you have to guess, steer clear of answer choices that are extreme and controversial and pick one of the blander, safer answer choices. Here's a sample question. To illustrate our point, we've crossed out the name of the person.

> XXXXXXX XXXX was a military leader during the American Revolution and
>
> (A) he often was disciplined for fighting with fellow soldiers
>
> (B) was known for defecting to Britain
>
> (C) lived in Maryland
>
> (D) gained power through unscrupulous business dealings in Massachusetts
>
> (E) founded a movement in the Methodist Church

Since we don't even have the name, this question should be very difficult. However, look at the answer choices, and cull out those answers that are negative or controversial. Choice (A) gets the axe, and choice (D) should also go. Choice (E) might seem OK, but it refers to religion, and standardized tests do their utmost to steer clear of religious topics if possible.

That leaves only two choices, (B) and (C). Since the word "Britain" is associated with the American Revolution, you might lean toward (B) as the correct answer. It makes sense that a question on the Social Sciences and History test would refer to a specific place in history. Pick (B) and move on. As it turns out, it is the correct answer for this question.

Looking for the bland is a very effective guessing technique, but it doesn't work all the time. On some questions, the answer will be one of the choices that seem a little more unlikely or extreme. The Mystery Person in the question above might have "gained power through unscrupulous business dealings," for example. Even so, slicing away the extreme while looking for the bland will work more often than not, and on questions that you don't know the answer to, it's one of your best chances to get the problem correct.

Buy a World Map

This technique pretty much explains itself. Ten percent of the CLEP SS&H exam covers geography, and there may even be a map visual or two on your test.

In addition to actively studying geography, gazing at a nice world map is a great way to learn geography almost without trying to. If you have a place where you regularly do your homework or studying, the ideal scenario is to place the world map near there where it is easily visible. If you're studying and need a break, look up and stare at a continent for a moment or two. You don't have to strain yourself to memorize every capital: just let your mind relax and soak in the pretty colors. Stare at a different part of the map every time, and you'll find that as weeks go by you actually will be able to recall the location of countries, cities, and other geographic landmarks better than you used to.

There aren't too many geography questions on the CLEP SS&H exam, but since this is such an easy way to increase your knowledge of geography, you should do it if possible. It will also aid you after the CLEP SS&H exam, since needing to know where countries are is something that tends to crop up from time to time in college and in the rest of the world.

The Test is All Over the Place. So Are the Answer Choices.

Question: What does famous nineteenth-century Dutch painter Vincent van Gogh have to do with contemporary political cartoons?

If you answered "Nothing," you would be correct. However, that wouldn't stop Vincent from appearing as an answer choice on a CLEP SS&H exam question about contemporary political cartoons. You see, the test doesn't have one correct answer and four really close incorrect choices. Instead, there are often one or two answer choices that just cannot be the answer. The catch is that you have to know who Vincent van Gogh is before you can cross him out as a political cartoonist. If you don't know who he is at all, you can't eliminate him as an answer choice.

33. Which of the following was the first major land battle of the Union and Confederate armies in Virginia?

    (A) the Battle of Little Big Horn
    (B) the Battle of Bull Run
    (C) the Battle of Gettysburg
    (D) the Battle of Pearl Harbor
    (E) the Battle of Hastings

Even if you don't know the exact answer, you might know one or two of the answer choices are definitely wrong. If you've ever seen the movie *Pearl Harbor* or paid close attention in history class, you'd know that battle was between the U.S. and Japanese in World War II. That's all you need to cross out choice (D): a vague memory of a movie you saw once or a recollection of class. Similarly, if you know that Little Big Horn involved Native Americans, you can cross out choice (A) as well. That gives you a one-in-three chance on this problem.

Sometimes just a minuscule amount of knowledge is all you need to eliminate an answer choice and give yourself a better chance of determining the right answer.

CLEP NATURAL SCIENCES STRATEGIES

The CLEP Natural Sciences exam shares some basic similarities with the CLEP Humanities exam. Both tests contain a large number of questions and both are split into two major categories. Similar tests require similar strategies, so if you are taking the CLEP Humanities and Natural Sciences tests, you will find that the basic approach to both tests is the same. The strategies that follow have been modified to reflect the CLEP Natural Sciences exam, but they are identical in essence with those to use on the CLEP Humanities exam. You might think it's strange that two tests covering greatly different subjects (humanities and natural sciences) would have identical strategies, but it's not the subject matter that's important, only the design of the tests.

The CLEP Natural Sciences exam has 120 questions. Since you only have 90 minutes, you can see that there's not much time on average for each question. These questions come from a wide spectrum of biological science and physical science subjects, so you are probably not going to have time to reflect on every question and come up with an answer. Instead, questions will fall into one of three categories:

Category 1: you know the answer right away,

Category 2: you can answer the question with a bit of work

Category 3: you have little or no chance of answering these questions correctly

Your goal is to expand Categories 1 and 2, and not spend too much time on problems in that last category. You expand Category 1 by reviewing, while Category 2 questions can be overcome with a mixture of review, strategy, and some luck. Everyone has some Category 3 problems; the key is to accept this fact and not let it bother you. Missing one question won't kill your CLEP Natural Sciences exam score, but spending too much time on a problem you have little chance of even answering correctly can harm your overall performance.

Are you Bio or Phys?

Half of the CLEP Natural Sciences test covers biology, and the other 50 percent covers the physical sciences. Ask yourself honestly, which topic do you know more about? You might have an idea by now. If you don't, take the first test in this book and see what problems you find easier to answer.

It doesn't matter if you're better at Bio or excel at Phys. All that matters is that you have a clear idea of which topic you are better at. Once you know, you can take this knowledge and use the computer format of the CLEP to craft an excellent plan of attack.

Let's say you are better at biology. You're not ignorant of physics, but you definitely have a better chance at cell questions than atom questions. If this is the case, then refine your two-pass approach in the following way.

Bio Plan of Attack

1. **On the first pass, look for all biology questions.** Your goal on the first run-through is to find all the Category 1 (you get them right away) questions you can. Since you're better at biology, look for these problems. There's very little overlap between the biology and physical sciences topics, so you probably won't be confused about what question is which. Questions about organisms and heredity fall pretty obviously under the biology umbrella. If you see chemical symbols in the answer choices, you can guess what kind of problem that is.

    Give yourself a moment to answer every Bio question. Even if you are strong in this subject, there will be some questions that you won't know the answer to immediately. That's fine. If you feel you know something about the subject, hit the "mark" button and move on.

2. **If you encounter a Phys question that you immediately know the answer to, answer it.** You should be able to hit some of these questions out of the park right away. If that's the case, do it and move on. However, don't spend time figuring out a physical science question when there are potentially easier biology problems waiting.

3. **If you hit a question you think you know something about but can't answer immediately, "mark" it and move on.** Here is where you can take advantage of the computer format. On your first pass through the CLEP Natural Sciences exam, you can answer all Category 1 questions, "mark" all Category 2 questions, and leave unanswered (for now) all problems that you don't have a strong chance at.

4. **Once you finish your first pass through the test, hit the Review button and sort by status.** You should have three groups, which just so happen to correspond with the three question types we discussed earlier.

    "Answered"—these will be the Category 1 questions.

    "Marked"—these are your Category 2 questions. Start going back through these problems, taking some additional time to work out the right answer (or at least give yourself a good guess).

    "Not answered"—here are the Category 3 problems. As time is running out, leave about three minutes to go through and answer every one of these problems. That doesn't mean you have to look at them. If there's no time, just put an answer and move on. There's no guessing penalty on the CLEP eaxm, so you should pick up some points even by answering blindly.

Now that is a plan of attack. (If you're better at physical sciences, simply switch the two terms and proceed the same way.) While others students are floundering through the section, you will be using your knowledge of the computer format and your understanding of the test structure to maximize your ability to see all questions. This gives you the best possible chance of answering them correctly.

Cluster Questions

Cluster Questions are like the game show *Jeopardy!* because the answers come *before* the question. Cluster Questions start off with A–E, and each answer choice has an initial piece of information next to it. One to three questions follow, and each question describes one of the choices (A–E) in the initial information. You pick the right letter choice for each problem. Here's an example.

(A) Golgi apparatus
(B) Nucleus
(C) Cell wall
(D) Chloroplast
(E) mRNA

1. Site of protein synthesis.
2. Not found in a plant cell.
3. Site of photosynthesis.

Cluster Questions can be answered quickly, so that's good. But a common mistake is to spend time reading over all the answer choices first. Don't. The whole point is to answer questions, not read answer choices. **Once you encounter a Cluster Question set, read the question and then go back and look at the answer choices**. In the example above, you should drop down to question 1, read the question, and then look for an answer. Once you have it, move on to questions 2 and 3.

The CLEP Natural Sciences exam often starts out with Cluster Questions. This lets you answer a bunch of questions in a short period of time. This helps you in terms of overall time, but there aren't enough Cluster Questions to make a huge impact on the overall pacing picture.

The Long and the Short of It

You can further refine your two-pass approach by skipping long or involved questions on the first pass. For example, some questions will contain Roman numerals (usually I, II, and III). To answer these questions, you often have to address each Roman numeral. This means you have to work three questions to get credit for one. It's not a good use of your time, so you should leave these questions blank during the first pass. Move past it and search for questions that are solvable with less time and effort.

Other questions begin with a 60-word passage describing an experiment. This might interest you, but why spend all this time reading an experiment when you only get credit for one question? You can "mark" it if you like, and come back to it if there's time, but since there are so many short, simple problems, don't spend too much time on a long problem that is worth the same.

A Little Bit of Knowledge Can Go a Long Way

The CLEP Natural Science test rewards students who know biology and physical science. What the test doesn't reward is bad science. It doesn't want answers that are factually incorrect, too extreme to be true, or irrelevant to the topic at hand.

Yet these bad science answers invariably appear, because hey! It's a multiple-choice test and you have to have four incorrect answer choices around the one right answer. So if you don't know how to answer a problem, look at the answer choices and think "Good Science." This may lead you to find some poor answer choices that can be eliminated.

30. Which gland(s) in the human body secrete(s) steroid hormones and is located above the kidneys?

    (A) Pituitary
    (B) Kidney
    (C) Pancreas
    (D) Adrenal
    (E) Heart

Let's say you know about the production of steroid hormones, but during the test your mind draws a blank as to exactly which gland produces them. Even though you don't know the right answer, you still know enough good science to eliminate some incorrect answers. This leads you to whack choices (B), (C), and (E), since they are all organs, not glands. That leaves only two answers. At this point, trust your instincts and take a guess. You have a one-in-two chance of getting the right answer, and over the course of the test these chances will add up and help your final score.

FINAL THOUGHTS

You now have three levels of strategies to approach every CLEP exam: computer strategies, general strategies, and specific strategies. Be sure to employ all relevant techniques when you take the practice tests in this book and the real tests as well.

| SECTION TWO |

The CLEP English Composition Exam

Section Two: The CLEP English Composition Exam | 47

Chapter Four: **Practice Test 1: Diagnostic**

Time—90 minutes
90 Questions

Directions: Each sentence below tests your knowledge of diction (choice of words), idiom, grammar, and usage. Some sentences are correct, and each sentence can contain no more than one error.

Elements of the sentence that are underlined and lettered may be incorrect. Parts of the sentence that are not underlined can be assumed to be correct. When choosing an answer, follow the rules of written English.

If a sentence contains an error, select the <u>one underlined portion</u> that must be changed in order to form a correct sentence. For sentences with no error, choose answer (E).

1. The button, <u>which is</u> commonly used to fasten
              A
   two pieces of cloth together, <u>and was</u> <u>originally</u>
                                   B   C
   <u>viewed</u> as an ornament and <u>worn</u> like jewelry.
     C   D
   <u>No error</u>
     E

2. If <u>you are</u> preparing to take the SAT, <u>it's important</u>
       A   B
   that the person familiarize him- or herself with
   the test, <u>work</u> on areas of weakness, and <u>get</u> a
           C   D
   good night's sleep the night before. <u>No error</u>
                                                E

3. <u>According</u> to some experts, playing video games is
     A
   no better than <u>television</u> because it is a passive
                     B
   activity that <u>draws children</u> away from reading or
                 C
   <u>participating in</u> physical activities. <u>No error</u>
       D   E

4. The author of nine detective <u>mysteries, Linda</u>
                                           A
   <u>Kong</u>, <u>frequented</u> the police headquarters because
     A   B
   <u>they</u> provided her with inspiration for her <u>work</u>,
     C   D
   <u>especially</u> when she was beginning a new novel.
     D
   <u>No error</u>
     E

GO ON TO THE NEXT PAGE

KAPLAN

5. Mrs. Gwen has been teaching third grade for
            A
   twenty years, and though she has found the work
                        B   C
   rewarding, she has decided to apply for a job as a
                    D
   school administrator this year. No error
                                    E

6. In the eyes of some social critics, the quality of life
   A
   in the United States is poorer than that in England
                         B   C
   and other European countries because many
                                         D
   Americans do not have access to adequate health
   D
   care. No error
         E

7. The pioneering spirit of the men and women
   A
   who settled the frontier have all but disappeared,
   B   C
   except in the state of Alaska where adventure and
   D
   hardship still characterize everyday life. No error
                                              E

8. Diving, which began in the latter half of the
           A
   nineteenth century when gymnasts performed
                       B
   in swimming areas, is now an Olympic sport,
                      C
   and it takes finely tuned coordination and
   D
   strength. No error
             E

9. Explaining the causes of drought is not easy since
   A   B   C
   lack of precipitation is one of many factors,
   C
   including high temperatures, low humidity, and
   strong wind, that lead to a deficiency of water.
                D
   No error
   E

10. Opened in 1809, Luther Goddard built hundreds
                    A
    of watches, manufacturing some parts in the
                B
    United States and importing others from England.
    C   D
    No error
    E

11. Eudora Welty's novels almost always address the
                         A
    complexities of family life, while in her short
                                B   C
    stories she focus on the isolation of individuals.
    C   D
    No error
    E

12. No single characteristic or behavior separate
                             A   B
    moths from butterflies because for every rule
                          C
    that seems to apply to either moths or butterflies,
    D
    there is an exception. No error
                           E

13. Excepting 30 percent more students than there are
    A   B
    spots is common practice among colleges and
         C
    universities since not all students will decide to
                                D
    attend. No error
    D   E

14. London was the first large city to use sewers for
    A
    the disposal of waste water, following its lead were
                          B   C   D
    Paris, New York, and Boston. No error
                                 E

15. Meteorologists predict changes in the weather,
                                          A
    both immediate and long term, through careful
    A   B   C
    scrutiny of atmospheric conditions. No error
             D   E

16. In the eighteenth century when the philosopher
              A   B
    Voltaire lived and wrote, there was no press, no
    B   C
    equality of individuals before the law, and
    freedom of thought was forbidden. No error
    D   E

17. The other cyclists and her narrowly missed
    A   B   C
    crashing into the small, wily dog that had
    wiggled free of its leash and trotted onto the race
                   D
    course. No error
            E

Directions: The sentences below test your knowledge of effective and correct expression. Use the conventions of written English to choose your answer: pay attention to choice of words (diction), punctuation, sentence structure, and grammar.

In each of the following sentences, either the entire sentence or part of the sentence is underlined. There are five versions of the underlined portion below the sentence. Choice (A) is the same as the original sentence, and choices (B)–(E) are different.

Choose the answer that produces the best sentence with the same meaning as the original sentence. If none of the alternatives are as effective as the original sentence, choose (A). The final sentence should be precise and unambiguous.

18. Candy grew more popular during World War II when the Army began buying sweets in great quantities, <u>convinced that candy could increase</u> men's combat effectiveness and sustain them when there was nothing else to eat.

    (A) convinced that candy could increase
    (B) convincing that candy could increase
    (C) and it was convinced that candy could increase
    (D) convinced of candy's increasing of
    (E) as they convinced themselves that candy could increase

19. Some people claim the hamburger was invented in New Haven, Connecticut in 1903 where the owner of a local lunch counter <u>ground lean beef, broils it, and presented it</u> between two slices of bread.

    (A) ground lean beef, broils it, and presented it
    (B) grinds lean beef, broils it, and presents it
    (C) ground lean beef, broiled it, and presented it
    (D) ground lean beef, broiled it, presenting it
    (E) grinds and broils lean beef, presenting it

20. The stories told about the role of Sacagawea in the Lewis and Clark expedition are most certainly exaggerated, though it is true that <u>her presence as a woman and a mother signals that the group was on a peaceful mission</u>.

    (A) her presence as a woman and a mother signals that the group was on a peaceful mission
    (B) her presence as a woman and a mother signals that the group is on a peaceful mission
    (C) her presence as a woman and a mother signaled that the group was on a peaceful mission
    (D) her presence as a woman and a mother, signaling that the group was on a peaceful mission
    (E) her presence as a woman and a mother was the signal that the group is on a peaceful mission

21. The movie examines the antislavery movement and the fight for women's suffrage, <u>and it shows how the</u> first gave rise to the second and eventually helped the United States live up to the promises of the Constitution.

    (A) and it shows how the
    (B) and it showed how the
    (C) thus by showing how the
    (D) nevertheless showing how the
    (E) showing how the

22. "Art for art's sake" was the slogan of the late nineteenth-century Aesthetic Movement that grew out of their emphasis on beauty and art's potential to please.

    (A) that grew out of their emphasis
    (B) that grew out of its emphasis
    (C) growing out of their emphasis
    (D) and it grew out of its emphasis
    (E) the growth of their emphasis

23. The pilot announced to them that he would be collecting them, and it would help the flight attendant if the passengers passed the headphones towards the aisle.

    (A) The pilot announced to them that he would be collecting them, and it would help the flight attendant if the passengers passed the headphones towards the aisle.
    (B) The pilot announced to the passengers that the flight attendant would be collecting the headphones, and it would help the flight attendant if they passed them towards the aisle.
    (C) The pilot announced to headphones that he would be collecting the passengers, and it would help the flight attendant if the passengers passed the headphones towards the aisle.
    (D) The pilot announced to the flight attendant that he would be collecting the headphones, and it would help the passengers if they passed the headphones towards the aisle.
    (E) Announcing to them that he would be collecting the headphones, the pilot said it would help the flight attendant if they passed them towards the aisle.

24. According to the poll that was conducted by the principal, two-thirds of the tenth-grade class plan to participate in a competitive sport.

    (A) two-thirds of the tenth-grade class plan to participate
    (B) two-thirds of the tenth graders plans to participate
    (C) two-thirds of the tenth-grade class are planning to participate
    (D) two-thirds of the tenth-grade class plans to participate
    (E) two-thirds of the tenth-grade class have plans to participate

25. A pacemaker is an electronic device; it produces steady electrical impulses that help regulate the heartbeat in people who have certain heart diseases.

    (A) A pacemaker is an electronic device; it produces
    (B) A pacemaker is an electronic device, it produces
    (C) A pacemaker is an electronic device in the production of
    (D) A pacemaker, is an electronic device, produces
    (E) A pacemaker is an electronic device that produces;

26. A contradictory statement is known as a paradox. A paradox is designed to capture a reader's attention and make her think.

   (A) A contradictory statement is known as a paradox. A paradox is designed to capture a reader's attention and make her think.
   (B) A contradictory statement is known as a paradox, and a paradox is designed to capture a reader's attention and make her think.
   (C) A paradox and a contradictory statement are designed to capture a reader's attention and make her think.
   (D) A contradictory statement, known as a paradox, is designed to capture a reader's attention and make her think.
   (E) A contradictory statement is known as a paradox, and that is designed to capture a reader's attention and make her think.

27. The parachute, initially proposed by Leonardo da Vinci to aid in evacuations from burning buildings, slows the speed of a body falling through the air, it works by increasing the surface area of the body, and thus increasing air resistance.

   (A) slows the speed of a body falling through the air, it works
   (B) slows the speed of a body falling through the air, but works
   (C) slows the speed of a body falling through the air? It works
   (D) slows the speed of a body falling through the air. It works
   (E) slows the speed of a body falling through the air, works

28. The chess club archives that were stored in the basement with their delightful descriptions of the club's colorful history were damaged, and most likely destroyed, by the flood last week.

   (A) The chess club archives that were stored in the basement with their delightful descriptions of the club's colorful history were damaged, and most likely destroyed, by the flood last week.
   (B) The chess club archives, stored in the basement and delightfully describing the club's colorful history, were damaged and most likely destroyed in the flood last week.
   (C) Stored in the basement and damaged, and most likely destroyed, by the flood last week, the chess club archives have delightful descriptions of the club's colorful history.
   (D) Stored in the basement with their delightful descriptions of the club's colorful history, the chess club archives were damaged, and most likely destroyed, by the flood last week.
   (E) The chess club archives with their delightful descriptions of the club's colorful history that were stored in the basement were damaged, and most likely destroyed, by the flood last week.

29. The circulation of the New York Times is greater than that of any other newspaper in the United States while, at the same time, the readership of local newspapers is shrinking.

   (A) greater than that of
   (B) greater than the circulation of
   (C) greater than
   (D) greater than of
   (E) a greater circulation than of

GO ON TO THE NEXT PAGE

30. <u>Of all the dishes on the menu, spaghetti and meatballs are</u> still the most popular, especially among patrons who remember what Italian food was like before it became fancy.

    (A) Of all the dishes on the menu, spaghetti and meatballs are
    (B) Of all the dishes on the menu, spaghetti and meatballs is
    (C) Spaghetti and meatballs, of all the dishes on the menu, are
    (D) Of all the dishes on the menu, spaghetti and meatballs being
    (E) Of all the dishes on the menu, spaghetti and meatballs have been

31. After losing her brother to suicide and her infant son to cholera, <u>Harriet Beecher Stowe's faith and empathy deepened</u>, and she began writing her most famous book, *Uncle Tom's Cabin*.

    (A) Harriet Beecher Stowe's faith and empathy deepened
    (B) Harriet Beecher Stowe experienced a deepening of her faith and empathy
    (C) which deepened the faith of Harriet Beecher Stowe's faith and empathy
    (D) deepening Harriet Beecher Stowe's faith and empathy
    (E) and Harriet Beecher Stowe's faith and empathy deepened

32. May Sarton, the American writer and feminist, corresponded with Virginia Woolf, and <u>her and the poet Louise Bogan exchanged letters about their art</u>.

    (A) her and the poet Louise Bogan exchanged letters about their art
    (B) exchanged between she and the poet Louise Bogan letters about their art
    (C) the poet Louise Bogan and her exchanged letters about their art
    (D) exchanging letters about art with the poet Louise Bogan
    (E) she and the poet Louise Bogan exchanged letters about their art

33. <u>Coca-Cola first appeared in a pharmacy in Atlanta in 1886, and it</u> was advertised as an "esteemed Brain Tonic and Intellectual Beverage."

    (A) Coca-Cola first appeared in a pharmacy in Atlanta in 1886, and it
    (B) In 1886, when Coca-Cola first appeared in a pharmacy, and it
    (C) Appearing in a pharmacy in Atlanta in 1886, Coca-Cola
    (D) Appearing in a pharmacy in Atlanta in 1886, however Coca-Cola
    (E) It was 1886 when Coca-Cola appeared in a pharmacy in Atlanta, and it was

34. <u>The Picasso Museum in Barcelona, along with the Prado Museum in Madrid, offers</u> an extensive collection of Picasso's work, showing the master's evolution over time.

    (A) The Picasso Museum in Barcelona, along with the Prado Museum in Madrid, offers
    (B) It is the Picasso Museum in Barcelona and the Prado Museum in Madrid offering
    (C) Offering the Picasso Museum in Barcelona, along with the Prado Museum in Madrid, are
    (D) The Picasso Museum in Barcelona and the Prado Museum in Madrid offers
    (E) The Picasso Museum in Barcelona, along with the Prado Museum in Madrid, offer

GO ON TO THE NEXT PAGE

Directions: The passages below are first drafts of student essays. The sentences in each passage have been numbered. Parts of the essays require revision.

After reading each passage, answer the questions that follow. Some questions require you to improve sentences by changing word choice (diction) and sentence structure. Other questions ask you to review the entire essay or part of the essay and evaluate its organization, development, and the suitability of its language for the intended audience and purpose. Follow the rules of standard written English in your answer choices.

Questions 35–39 are based on the following draft of a letter that a student plans to send to the school principal.

Dear Mr. Simms,

(1) *Because I feel so strongly about this issue, I decided to write you a letter.* (2) *The food in the cafeteria stinks!* (3) *The cafeteria features three food groups: starch, fat, and meat.* (4) *If you are a vegetarian, you might as well give up your beliefs.* (5) *If you want to be healthy, you better plan to skip a meal.* (6) *If you dislike fried food and fatty sauces, you better look elsewhere.* (7) *Shredded iceberg lettuce and bits of carrot don't really make a salad.* (8) *Ketchup is not a vegetable.* (9) *Hot dogs can barely be included in the category of meat.* (10) *Rather than face another soggy sloppy joe or glob of starchy spaghetti, students avoid the cafeteria.* (11) *Students bring brown-bag lunches from home, or they go out to lunch.*

(12) *Who is forced to eat in the cafeteria?* (13) *Students who qualify for free or reduced-price lunches; students who can't, for whatever reason, bring a lunch from home; students who don't have the cash for a $3 lunch at the local drive-in.* (14) *Is this fair?* (15) *No!* (16) *Why should the poor kids in our school be forced to eat disgusting food?* (17) *They shouldn't be.*

(18) *Obviously, it would be terrific if all students could eat where they pleased, and since this is impossible, I have a simple suggestion: improve the food in the cafeteria.* (19) *Get a salad bar.* (20) *Plan vegetarian options.* (21) *Stop frying everything.* (22) *If this happened, more kids would choose the cafeteria, and that will have ultimately built more community in our school.*

35. Which of the following is the best way to revise the underlined portions of sentences 10 and 11 (reproduced below) so that the two sentences are combined into one?

    Rather than face another soggy sloppy joe or glob of starchy spaghetti, <u>students avoid the cafeteria. Students</u> bring brown-bag lunches from home, or they go out to lunch.

    (A) students avoid the cafeteria, but
    (B) students avoid the cafeteria and
    (C) avoiding the cafeteria, students
    (D) students avoid the cafeteria, so they
    (E) students avoided the cafeteria and

36. Which of the following sentences, if added after sentence 11, would best link the first paragraph with the rest of the letter?

    (A) This is what students face in the cafeteria.
    (B) The mediocre quality of the food drives students away and penalizes students who have no other lunch alternatives.
    (C) The quality of the food has declined since my sophomore year.
    (D) Surely, you've noticed that hot dogs aren't as popular as they used to be.
    (E) Every time I eat in the cafeteria I feel sick and wish I hadn't.

GO ON TO THE NEXT PAGE

37. In light of the fact that this letter is being written to a school principal, what would be the best way for the writer of the letter to improve sentence 2?

   (A) The quality of the food in the cafeteria is mediocre.
   (B) The food in the cafeteria should be tossed.
   (C) The food in the cafeteria is absolutely disgusting!
   (D) The cafeteria food is gross beyond belief.
   (E) The food in the cafeteria is pure garbage.

38. Which is the best version of the underlined version of sentence 15 (reproduced below)?

   Obviously, it would be terrific if all students could eat where they pleased, and since this is impossible, I have a simple suggestion: improve the food in the cafeteria.

   (A) however in light of the possibility
   (B) but barring the impossibility of this
   (C) and because of the impossibility of this
   (D) but because this is impossible
   (E) and yet this is impossible

39. In the context of the third paragraph, which of the following is the best version of the underlined portion of sentence 22 (reproduced below)?

   If this happened, more kids would choose the cafeteria, and that will have ultimately built more community in our school.

   (A) No change
   (B) that will ultimately build more community
   (C) ultimately building more community
   (D) that would be ultimately building more community
   (E) that would ultimately build more community

Questions 40–44 are based on the following draft of a student essay.

(1) Last summer, I had a very unique experience. (2) My brother and I decided that we wanted to do something positive in our community. (3) We didn't know exactly what, but we knew we wanted to do something to make a difference. (4) Everyone is always talking about how our generation is selfish. (5) Everyone focuses on the bad things that happen instead of the good things that happen.

(6) We decided to start basketball camp for kids in our neighborhood. (7) It wasn't anything fancy. (8) My brother and I both are good basketball players. (9) We divided the kids into two groups: beginning and experienced. (10) The beginning kids came in the morning for two hours of drills. (11) They were mainly younger so we didn't want to work them too hard. (12) We mainly wanted to teach them the fundamentals: ball handling, shooting, and the rules of the game. (13) The experienced kids were a blast. (14) We could play real games with them and run real plays. (15) Some of them really improved. (16) Nevertheless, we're going to tell the high school coach to look out for them.

(17) The kids who came to our camp really enjoyed it. (18) Now everyone in the neighborhoods knows each other. (19) They've kept playing basketball on their own. (20) I think the key to making a difference is doing something you enjoy. (21) At least that's what my brother and I learned.

40. Which of the following is the best way to revise and combine sentences 4 and 5 (reproduced below)?

    Everyone is always talking about how our generation is selfish. Everyone focuses on the bad things that happen instead of the good things that happen.

    (A) Everyone is always talking about how our generation is selfish, and everyone focuses on the bad things that happen instead of the good things that happen.
    (B) Focusing on the bad, instead of the good, things that happen, everyone is always talking about how our generation is selfish.
    (C) Everyone is always talking about the selfishness of our generation, focusing on the bad instead of the good.
    (D) Everyone is always talking about how our generation is selfish and focuses on the bad things that happen instead of the good things that happen.
    (E) Talking about the selfishness of our generation, the focus is on the bad things instead of the good things.

41. Which of the following is the best description of how the essay is organized?

    (A) It relates an anecdote.
    (B) It identifies a problem and offers a solution.
    (C) It explains the chronology of an experience.
    (D) It refutes an argument.
    (E) It provides step-by-step instructions.

42. The writer of the essay could best improve sentence 3 by

    (A) illustrating the idea with an example.
    (B) explaining what "making a difference" means to him.
    (C) including the conversation he had with his brother.
    (D) discussing the drawbacks of trying to do something positive.
    (E) describing what other young people have done to make a difference.

43. Which of the following would best replace "nevertheless" at the beginning of sentence 16?

    (A) And so,
    (B) Instead,
    (C) As a result,
    (D) However,
    (E) Perhaps

44. To improve the development of paragraph 2, which would be the best way to reorder the first four sentences?

    (A) Sentence 9, 8, 7, 6
    (B) Sentence 7, 8, 6, 9
    (C) Sentence 6, 7, 9, 8
    (D) Sentence 8, 6, 7, 9
    (E) Sentence 6, 9, 7, 8

Questions 45–50 are based on the following draft of an announcement that a student plans to make to recruit students for the history club.

(1) *Did President Washington really chop down the cherry tree?* (2) *Did President Jackson carry around two bullets in his body while he was president?* (3) *Can President Carter read two thousand words per minute with 95 percent comprehension?*
(4) *If you're dying to know the answer to these and other questions, then you're the perfect person to join the history club.* (5) *History club, you may think, is only for nerds.* (6) *And that's completely wrong.* (7) *History club is for students with inquiring minds.* (8) *It's for students who think understanding the past will make it easier to understand the present.* (9) *Weekly trivia competitions give you an opportunity to flex your mind (and to study for the Advanced Placement American and European history tests).* (10) *Researching the history of our school will let you see whether you have what it takes to be a historian.* (11) *Finally, there's an annual banquet honoring a local historian at the end of the school year that gives students responsibility.*
(12) *Convinced?* (13) *If you still have doubts, at least come by our meeting in Room 201 next Wednesday at lunch.* (14) *We'll have pizza, and while we can't promise that it will be gourmet, at least it won't be old.* (15) *Do you need another reason?* (16) *Lots of history club members have been accepted at their first-choice colleges.*

45. The writer of the passage could best improve sentence 16 by

    (A) providing the names of the colleges to which students were accepted.
    (B) including the names of some students.
    (C) acknowledging that this is an advertising gimmick to lure students into joining history club.
    (D) explaining what happened to students who weren't accepted to their first-choice colleges.
    (E) citing the percentage of students who have been accepted at their first-choice colleges.

46. Which of the following would best replace "And" at the beginning of sentence 6?

    (A) Excepting this
    (B) Still
    (C) Therefore
    (D) But
    (E) As a result

47. Which of the following is the best way to revise and combine sentences 7 and 8 (reproduced below)?

    History club is for students with inquiring minds. It's for students who think understanding the past will make it easier to understand the present.

    (A) Inquiring mind students who think understanding the past will make it easier to understand the present are for history club.
    (B) History club is for students who, with inquiring minds, want to understand the past to understand the present.
    (C) History club is for students with inquiring minds who think understanding the past will make it easier to understand the present.
    (D) For students with inquiring minds, history club will make understanding the past easier to understand the present.
    (E) Understanding the past to understand the present, this is the inquiring that students of history club will do.

48. In context, the best phrase to replace "gives students responsibility" in sentence 11 is

    (A) allows students to understand the work and explore the contributions of contemporary historians.
    (B) allows students to have a lot of fun.
    (C) introduces students to different historians working in the community.
    (D) helps students explore different historical theories about contemporary life.
    (E) makes it possible for students to share a meal with a real historian.

49. Which of the following is the best way to revise and combine sentences 12 and 13 (reproduced below)?

    Convinced? If you still have doubts, at least come by our meeting in Room 201 next Wednesday at lunch.

    (A) Convinced but still have doubts, at least come by our meeting in Room 201 next Wednesday at lunch.
    (B) Even if you are convinced, at least come by our meeting in Room 201 next Wednesday at lunch.
    (C) Even if you still have doubts about your convictions, at least come by our meeting in Room 201 next Wednesday at lunch.
    (D) Even if you still aren't convinced, at least come by our meeting in Room 201 next Wednesday at lunch.
    (E) Convinced and doubting, at least come by our meeting in Room 201 next Wednesday at lunch.

50. Which of the following BEST describes the strategy used by the writer of the first paragraph?

    (A) piquing the listener's curiosity
    (B) using a formal tone
    (C) dispelling myths about presidents
    (D) building suspense by not providing the answers
    (E) describing public figures to make a point

GO ON TO THE NEXT PAGE

Questions 51–56 are based on the following early draft of a letter to the editor of a local newspaper.

(1) I am writing to protest the zoo's decision to build Maggie, the elephant, a treadmill so that she will still be able to exercise during the long winter in Alaska. (2) This is a good plot for a surreal short story, but it is emphatically not a good plan of action for an elephant. (3) Elephants are native to regions with warm temperatures. (4) They do not thrive in cold places. (5) Many zoos are beginning to recognize this fact. (6) The Baltimore Zoo, for example, is moving its elephants to a place where the temperature does not dip below 50 degrees. (7) Zookeepers recognize that elephants have particular needs. (8) Just as it would be unkind to expect polar bears to be happy spending summers in Florida, it's cruel to expect Asian elephants to weather cold winters. (9) Furthermore, experts note that female elephants are social animals, and they need the company of other elephants. (10) Officials are not keeping Maggie's needs in mind by keeping her in a cage all by herself. (11) Maggie should be moved to a warm place where she can roam vast tracts of land with other elephants like her. (12) If you truly love animals, you should put their needs first. (13) I hope the zoo will take this into consideration.

51. Which is the best version of the underlined portion of sentence 2 (reproduced below)?

    This is a good plot for a surreal short story, <u>but it is emphatically not a good plan</u> of action for an elephant.

    (A) No change
    (B) emphatically not a good plan
    (C) and it is emphatically not a good plan
    (D) and thus is emphatically not a good plan
    (E) being emphatically not a good plan

52. Which of the following is the best way to revise and combine sentences 3 and 4 (reproduced below)?

    Elephants are native to regions with warm temperatures. They do not thrive in cold places.

    (A) Elephants are native to regions with warm temperatures, but they do not thrive in cold places.
    (B) Though they are native to regions with warm temperatures, elephants do not thrive in cold places.
    (C) Native to regions with warm temperatures, elephants do not thrive in cold places.
    (D) Elephants are native to regions with warm temperatures, not thriving in cold places.
    (E) Cold places do not thrive elephants because they are native to regions with warm temperatures.

53. Which of the following sentences in the second paragraph could be eliminated without affecting its clarity?

    (A) Elephants are native to regions with warm temperatures.
    (B) They do not thrive in cold places.
    (C) The Baltimore Zoo, for example, is moving its elephants to a place where the temperature does not dip below 50 degrees.
    (D) Zookeepers recognize that elephants have particular needs.
    (E) Just as it would be unkind to expect polar bears to be happy spending summers in Florida, it's cruel to expect Asian elephants to weather cold winters.

54. Why does the author of this letter refer to the Baltimore Zoo?

    (A) to back up her argument with an expert opinion
    (B) to bring in her personal experience
    (C) to illustrate her point about elephants' need for company
    (D) to provide evidence for her argument
    (E) to broaden the scope of her criticism

55. How could the transition between the second and third paragraph be improved?

    (A) by discussing why elephants are social creatures
    (B) by providing a physical description of Maggie
    (C) by explaining what happened to the other elephants in the zoo
    (D) by specifying the size of Maggie's cage
    (E) by clarifying the impact of the zoo's plans on Maggie

56. The purpose of this letter is to

    (A) explain the habits of elephants.
    (B) put pressure on the Alaska Zoo to give up its elephant.
    (C) specify which kinds of animals would be happiest at the Alaska Zoo.
    (D) increase community support for animals.
    (E) help the zoo raise money to move Maggie to a warmer place.

Questions 57–62 are based on the following draft of a student essay about education.

(1) The American educator Horace Mann once said, "As an apple is not in any proper sense an apple until it is ripe, so a human being is not in any proper sense a human being until he is educated." (2) This may be true, but what does it really mean to be educated?

(3) In prehistoric times, education revolved around learning practical skills. (4) Children are taught to farm, hunt, fish, and make tools by following the examples set for them by their elders. (5) They didn't have formal schooling, except before undergoing puberty rites when they needed to learn about tribal customs.

(6) In colonial America, education was both practical and morally rectifying. (7) If you were wealthy enough to attend elementary school, you could. (8) In school, you would learn reading, writing, and arithmetic alongside religion. (9) Although most poor children didn't attend school, the New England colonies tried to change this by passing a law in 1642 that said all children had to be taught to read, though the underlying reason for the decision was not purely altruistic. (10) Public officials wanted to ensure that citizens developed good morals by reading the Scriptures.

(11) Afterwards, the emphasis of education changed again. (12) Science and commerce made learning more practical skills important. (13) People started academies that offered classes in history, geography, math, languages, and navigation. (14) This trend continued into the nineteenth century with growing public support for free education for students.

57. Which of the following sentences, if added after sentence 2, would best link the first paragraph with the rest of the essay?

    (A) No one can agree upon what it means to be educated.
    (B) How has education been viewed at different times in history?
    (C) What is the connection between apples and human minds?
    (D) Horace Mann was very influential in establishing public schools in the United States.
    (E) Education plays an important role in helping people develop their potential.

58. In the context of the second paragraph, which of the following is the best version of the underlined portion of sentence 4?

   Children are taught to farm, hunt, fish, and make tools by following the examples set for them by their elders.

   (A) No change.
   (B) Taught to farm, hunt, fish, and make tools, children
   (C) Farming, hunting, fishing, and making tools are taught to children
   (D) Children are taught farming, hunting, fishing, and making tools
   (E) Children were taught to farm, hunt, fish, and make tools

59. Which is the best version of the underlined portion of sentence 9 (reproduced below)?

   Although most poor children didn't attend school, the New England colonies tried to change this by passing a law in 1642 that said all children had to be taught to read, *though the underlying reason for the decision was not purely altruistic.*

   (A) No change.
   (B) the underlying reason for the decision not being purely altruistic
   (C) and the underlying reason for the decision was not purely altruistic
   (D) based upon not purely altruistic, underlying reasons for the decision
   (E) though the underlying reason and the decision were not purely altruistic

60. Which of the following is the best way to revise the underlined portions of sentences 7 and 8 (reproduced below) so that the two sentences are combined into one?

   If you were wealthy enough to attend elementary school, you *could. In school, you would learn* reading, writing, and arithmetic alongside religion.

   (A) could, but in school you would learn
   (B) could, and in school you would learn
   (C) would learn
   (D) learn
   (E) learning

61. In context, which is the best phrase to replace "afterward" in sentence 11?

   (A) Thereafter
   (B) Shortly later
   (C) By the middle of the next century
   (D) Sometime in the future
   (E) When the time was right

62. All of the following strategies are used by the writer of the passage EXCEPT

   (A) drawing examples from history.
   (B) opening with the words of an expert to frame the issue discussed in the rest of the essay.
   (C) comparing and contrasting education in the past with education in the present.
   (D) using an informational tone to convey what she has learned.
   (E) answering the question that is posed in the first paragraph.

Directions: The questions below test your ability to revise sentences.

Each sentence below is followed by directions on how to revise it. Some directions require you to change the entire sentence, while others only require you to change part of the sentence. Words may be added or omitted so that the final version of the sentence is grammatically correct. The meaning of the revised sentence should be as close to the meaning of the original sentence as possible. The final sentence should follow the rules of standard written English.

Answer choices (A)–(E) contain words or phrases that could be used to revise the sentence. If you had a different revision to the sentence in mind, try to revise the sentence in a new way so that it includes the wording listed in the correct answer choice.

63. You can determine whether your tabby is of show quality by checking to see whether it has stripes and whorls on its face and cheeks, a butterfly wing pattern on its back, rings on its chest, tail, and legs, and bands on its back and sides.

    Begin with The show quality.

    (A) has the determination by
    (B) is determined by
    (C) is determining by
    (D) could have been determined by
    (E) determining is

64. Could it be possible for the union to be mollified if management raised the workers' wages and provided a more comprehensive health insurance package?

    Change so that the sentence ends with a period instead of a question mark.

    (A) not it be possible
    (B) could be more of a possibility
    (C) could not be possible
    (D) could be possible
    (E) will have to be possible

65. American and European playwrights were inspired to address political subjects by the Theater of Fact, a German theatrical movement.

    Begin with A German theatrical movement.

    (A) the Theater of Fact inspired
    (B) the Theater of Fact was inspired
    (C) the Theater of Fact and inspired
    (D) the Theater of Fact inspiring
    (E) the Theater of Fact had been inspired by

66. Describing nature in objective terms and evoking a distinct emotional feeling in readers were the original purposes of the haiku, a Japanese form of poetry.

    Begin The haiku's original purposes.

    (A) was describing
    (B) is describing
    (C) were to describe
    (D) in the description
    (E) described

GO ON TO THE NEXT PAGE

67. When we consider how conflict between Africans and Muslims in the Sudan has escalated in recent months, we can understand why the international community is becoming more alarmed.

    Change we can understand to explains.

    (A) Conflict recently escalating
    (B) In light of recently escalating conflict
    (C) As a result of the recently escalating conflict
    (D) Due to the recent escalation of conflict
    (E) Recently escalating conflict

68. Most people who vote in elections have little expectation of having an impact on the overall results.

    Begin with Few people.

    (A) except their being
    (B) lack expectation
    (C) expect to have
    (D) have no expectation
    (E) have much to expect

69. The Supreme Court's 1948 ruling against censorship of crime literature was based on its rejecting the difference between "the informing and the entertaining."

    Begin with The Supreme Court.

    (A) basing its rejection on
    (B) by rejecting the basis of
    (C) by having the difference rejected
    (D) by rejecting
    (E) differing in its rejection

70. The purpose of the outdoor experience is to teach leadership skills to young people and to make them more self-reliant.

    Begin with Teaching leadership skills.

    (A) and self-reliance to young people
    (B) and making them more self-reliant
    (C) for the purpose of self-reliance
    (D) and teaching self-reliance
    (E) with self-reliance

71. When you think about how frequently you check your e-mail, it makes you wonder how you spent your time before the proliferation of this technology.

    Change it makes you wonder to begs the question of.

    (A) Due to the frequency of checking email
    (B) Based upon the frequency of checking email
    (C) The frequency with which you check email
    (D) How frequently checking email
    (E) Checking frequently email

72. The elaborate wedding plans that were designed to guarantee that everything went smoothly backfired and caused havoc the week before the ceremony.

    Change backfired to but they backfired.

    (A) wedding plans with the design
    (B) wedding plans, designed
    (C) wedding plans, which were
    (D) wedding plans, ostensibly designed
    (E) wedding plans were designed

73. The inexperienced beachcomber will be pleased with the abundance of pink conch shells littering the seashores of the West Indies.

    Begin with The abundance of pink conch shells.

    (A) will please the inexperienced beachcomber
    (B) pleasing the inexperienced beachcomber
    (C) the inexperienced beachcomber will be pleased
    (D) having pleased the inexperienced beachcomber
    (E) are pleasing to the inexperienced beachcomber

74. In the most popular comics of the 1930s, adventure themes and domestic problems were explored in *Terry and the Pirates* and *Mary Worth*.

    Begin with *Terry and the Pirates* and *Mary Worth*.

    (A) had adventure and domestic problems as their themes to be explored
    (B) explored adventure themes and domestic problems
    (C) exploring adventure themes and domestic problems
    (D) was explored by adventure themes and domestic problems
    (E) were explorations of adventure themes and domestic problems

75. The proximity of Colombia to the "Ring of Fire," an area in the Pacific Basin that is characterized by seismic instability, is the cause of many earthquakes and volcanic eruptions in the country.

    Change is the cause of to causes.

    (A) In the proximity of the "Ring of Fire"
    (B) Approximating Colombia, the "Ring of Fire"
    (C) The proximity of the "Ring of Fire" to Colombia
    (D) Colombia's proximity to the "Ring of Fire"
    (E) Because of the proximity of the "Ring of Fire" to Colombia

76. Might it not be wiser for politicians to be driven by their convictions instead of public opinion polls?

    Change so that the sentence ends with a period instead of a question mark.

    (A) might be wiser
    (B) not it be wiser
    (C) will have to be wiser
    (D) would not be wiser
    (E) might not be wiser

77. Some education reformers argue that, because of the rise of dual earner families, public schools need to offer longer school days and extended school years.

    Change that, because of to that the.

    (A) families is making
    (B) families, making
    (C) families had made
    (D) families, and it has made
    (E) families will have made

78. Should the stock market rebound from the recent slump, nervous investors would cautiously begin putting money into stocks again.

    Begin with If the stock market rebounds from the recent slump.

    (A) should cautiously begin
    (B) will cautiously begin
    (C) will cautiously have begun
    (D) will cause the cautious beginning of
    (E) have cautiously begun

GO ON TO THE NEXT PAGE

Directions: The passages below consist of numbered sentences. These passages are taken from longer writing samples, so a complete discussion of all issues in the longer writing samples may not appear.

Read each passage and answer the questions below it. The questions for each passage test your understanding of the writer's purpose and the characteristics of good writing.

Questions 79–83 refer to the following paragraph.

(1) *These passages raise the issue of "travel class consciousness," a phrase coined by Mark Cocker.* (2) *Travel class consciousness, according to Cocker, refers to travel writers' concern with differentiating themselves from other travelers and tourists whose presence threatens their sense of originality and pluckiness; this consciousness is expressed both intratextually and intertextually for travel writers are equally concerned with their position to other authors.* (3) *The reason is quite simple: the genre of the travel narrative can't appear too formulaic.* (4) *Whereas tourists can relax and follow the routes plotted for them in their guidebooks, travelers, especially travel writers, eschew guides and are driven, instead, by a need to discover wonders and exotica in places far off the well-trodden path.* (5) *Women travelers are no exception.* (6) *In her tale of bicycling from Kenya to Zimbabwe,* The Ukimwi Road, *Dervla Murphy cites and dismisses all other female-authored accounts of life in East Africa.* (7) *In her account of visiting China, Julia Kristeva wonders, at one point, whether tourists know the schedule of the train passing by and who is riding on it.* (8) *Finally, Robyn Davidson, author of* Tracks, *constantly worries about whether the Aborigines who she meets on her journey by camel through the desert heart of Australia consider her a traveler or a tourist.*

79. This paragraph is most likely written for

    (A) women who are interested in exploring East Africa, China, and Australia.
    (B) the authors of travel narratives who want to make their stories more engaging.
    (C) experts on world politics who are gathering information on the economies of foreign countries.
    (D) literary critics who study and explore issues of representation in different types of writing.
    (E) tourists who want to explore areas off the well-trodden path.

80. Which of the following best describes the relationship of sentence 2 to the rest of the paragraph?

    (A) It describes the author's personal experience, which the paragraph will further explore.
    (B) It offers an idea that will be refuted in the rest of the paragraph.
    (C) It establishes the organization for the paragraph as a whole.
    (D) It presents an idea that the rest of the paragraph will explore.
    (E) It describes how all travel writers feel.

81. Which of the following best describes the function of sentence 3?

    (A) It explains why travel writers are concerned with "travel class consciousness."
    (B) It suggests the difference between travelers and tourists.
    (C) It alludes to the difficulty of writing a travel narrative.
    (D) It asks readers to evaluate the travel narratives they have read.
    (E) It provides an example of "travel class consciousness" in a travel narrative.

82. In sentence 4, the effect of using "whereas" is to

    (A) further explain the idea of travel class consciousness by referring back to it.
    (B) differentiate between the goals and expectations of tourists and travel writers.
    (C) prepare the reader for examples of how travel writers express their individuality.
    (D) reveal the author's disdain for tourists who depend on guidebooks.
    (E) emphasize the differences between guidebooks, which point people toward known sites, and travel narratives, which describe unfamiliar places.

83. The function of sentence 6 is primarily to

    (A) introduce the evidence of "travel class consciousness" that follows in sentences 7 and 8.
    (B) present a specific example of travel writers' attempts to distinguish themselves from other tourists.
    (C) provide an example of the travel writer's concern for her originality vis-à-vis other travel writers.
    (D) show why Dervla Murphy's account of her travels in East Africa is superior to other written accounts.
    (E) illustrate the concept of "travel class consciousness" by interviewing a travel writer.

84. The purpose of this paragraph is primarily to

    (A) expose the reader to a genre of literature that is gaining popularity.
    (B) demonstrate the futility of trying to write a book that is not formulaic.
    (C) dismiss the value of traveling as a tourist to see another country's treasures.
    (D) describe a particular idea, the reasons for it and explore how it is realized in specific examples.
    (E) analyze how female-authored travel narratives are more interesting than male-authored travel narratives.

Questions 85–90 refer to the following passage.

(1) *In the beginning of Desert Solitaire*, *Edward Abbey writes, "This is the most beautiful place on earth.* (2) *There are many such places.* (3) *Every man, every woman, carries in heart and mind the image of the ideal place, the right place, the one true home, known or unknown, actual or visionary."* (4) *To others it may look overgrown, but outside my window is my ideal place.*

(5) *The garden is an oasis in this city, a quiet hidden paradise that seems miles away from the concert of car horns and the clip clop of passing pedestrians and the hungry yips of dogs returning from their romps.* (6) *There is no order here.* (7) *The aristocratic roses mingle with the common sunflowers, native grasses surround a clump of delicate African violets, the hardy apple tree is weighted down with hanging pots of delicate things.* (8) *What the garden lacks in rhyme or reason, it wholly compensates for with surprise.* (9) *Tucked into the corner is jar of orange guppies, but you must look carefully to see them through the green seaweed.* (10) *The jay has a twig holder of beautiful blue eggs and fiercely protects them from the prowling cat.* (11) *The humming birds torpedo forth from who-knows-where, and then defy physics by standing still in the air.* (12) *The squirrels tuck their peanuts into flowerpots, chirping madly when the whereabouts of their next meal slips their small minds.* (13) *This garden.* (14) *I could spend many afternoons there, and I would still discover something new, a tender green shoot, a flower in its last throes of splendor, a strawberry or a tomato patiently ripening in the sun.*

85. Which of the following most accurately describes what happens in the second paragraph?

    (A) The author tries to escape the stress of city life by retreating to the chaos of her garden.
    (B) The author depicts the idiosyncrasies of her garden to show how beauty is relative.
    (C) The author describes her garden in an attempt to convince everyone that it should be their ideal place.
    (D) The author conjures up an imaginary garden that she wishes were real.
    (E) The author explains why we must accept chaos and disorder as a necessary part of life.

86. The descriptive details in sentence 5 provide a(n)

    (A) evocation of different senses.
    (B) description of the neighborhood.
    (C) sense of the city's noisiness.
    (D) depiction of urban decay.
    (E) view from the window of the house.

87. The purpose of sentence 7 is to

    (A) catalogue all of the different plants in the garden.
    (B) substantiate the claim made in sentence 6.
    (C) refute the generalization made in sentence 6.
    (D) engage the readers' senses.
    (E) describe the author's one true home.

88. Which of the following best characterizes the author's reaction to her garden?

    (A) tranquility and interest
    (B) delight and confusion
    (C) complacency and wonder
    (D) wonder and curiosity
    (E) interest and fatigue

89. The main implication of this passage is that

    (A) imaginary places are often more real than real places.
    (B) the author finds the natural world more inviting than the urban environment.
    (C) in order to be surprised, you must look carefully at the small things.
    (D) the most beautiful places usually appear ugly to others.
    (E) the author finds beauty in surprises, both small and large.

90. Which of the following is the best description of the overall organization of this passage?

    (A) The second paragraph offers a personal example to support the idea described in the first.
    (B) The second paragraph actively refutes the idea offered in the first.
    (C) The second paragraph continues generalizing about the idea described in the first.
    (D) The second paragraph offers an analysis of the idea put forth in the first.
    (E) The second paragraph goes off on a tangent, offering little that is related to the first.

END OF TEST. STOP

ANSWER KEY

1. B	16. D	31. B	46. D	61. C	76. A
2. A	17. B	32. E	47. C	62. C	77. A
3. B	18. A	33. C	48. A	63. B	78. B
4. C	19. C	34. A	49. D	64. D	79. D
5. D	20. C	35. B	50. A	65. A	80. D
6. E	21. E	36. B	51. A	66. C	81. A
7. C	22. B	37. A	52. C	67. E	82. B
8. D	23. B	38. D	53. D	68. C	83. C
9. E	24. D	39. E	54. D	69. D	84. D
10. A	25. A	40. C	55. E	70. A	85. B
11. C	26. D	41. B	56. B	71. C	86. C
12. B	27. D	42. B	57. B	72. E	87. B
13. A	28. E	43. C	58. E	73. A	88. D
14. B	29. A	44. D	59. A	74. B	89. E
15. E	30. B	45. E	60. C	75. D	90. A

DIAGNOSTIC TEST QUICK REFERENCE TABLES

Use the following tables to determine which topics you need to review most.

Topic	Test Question
Complete Sentences	14, 25, 27
Economy and Clarity	8, 21, 33, 63, 64, 67, 68, 71, 72, 76, 77, 78
Agreement	2, 4, 5, 7, 9, 12, 17, 19, 20, 22, 23, 24, 30, 32, 34
Active versus Passive Voice	65, 66, 69, 73, 74, 75
Diction and Idiom	13, 16
Syntax and Structure	1, 3, 6, 10, 11, 15, 18, 28, 29, 31, 59, 70
Sentence Variation	26
Central Idea	84, 85, 89
Organization	41, 44, 53, 57, 80, 82, 90
Evidence (Relevance, Detail, Specificity)	42, 45, 48, 62
Audience and Purpose	37, 56, 79
Logic	38, 54, 83, 87
Paragraph Structure and Function	36, 43, 46, 55, 61, 81
Rhetorical Emphasis	50, 86, 88
Consistency of Tense and Viewpoint	39, 58
Combination and Variation of Sentences	35, 40, 47, 49, 51, 52, 60

Topic	Number of Questions on Test	Number Correct
Complete Sentences	3	
Economy and Clarity	12	
Agreement	15	
Active versus Passive Voice	6	
Diction and Idiom	2	
Syntax and Structure	12	
Sentence Variation	1	
Central Idea	3	
Organization	7	
Evidence (Relevance, Detail, Specificity)	4	
Audience and Purpose	3	
Logic	4	
Paragraph Structure and Function	6	
Rhetorical Emphasis	3	
Consistency of Tense and Viewpoint	2	
Combination and Variation of Sentences	7	

Answers and Explanations

1. (B)
The sentence, as it appears, is incomplete because the verb "is" is part of a subordinate clause modifying "the button": "which is commonly used to fasten two pieces of cloth together." To correct the mistake, the "and" should be eliminated. "Was originally viewed" will then serve as the verb.

2. (A)
All the pronouns in a sentence must agree. Here the pronoun shifts from the second person ("you") to the third person ("the person").

3. (B)
Comparisons must be written in similar grammatical form. In this sentence, which compares video games to television, the first comparison is written as a phrase ("playing video games") while the second is written as a noun ("television"). To make the comparison parallel, they both should be grammatically alike. Therefore, you would write: "playing video games is no better than <u>watching</u> television . . . ."

4. (C)
Pronouns must agree with their antecedents (the nouns that they are replacing). In this sentence, "they" is replacing the noun, "police headquarters." Although "police headquarters" appears to be plural, it is actually singular because it refers to a single place. "They" should be "it."

5. (D)
This sentence refers to two different times: Mrs. Gwen's teaching over the last twenty years and her current decision to apply for a job as school administrator. Because Mrs. Gwen's decision is not ongoing, the verb phrase ("has decided") should be written in the simple past tense (decided).

6. (E)
"That" refers to "quality of life" (in England and Europe). Therefore the sentence is parallel and there is no error. You may be tempted to choose (B), "is poorer" because you may want to substitute "more poor," but the term "is poorer" is correct.

7. (C)
Verbs always agree with subjects. Intervening words—such as the prepositional phrase "of the men and women who settled the frontier"—should not be confused with the subject. In this case, since the subject is singular ("the pioneering spirit"), the verb should be singular as well ("has" instead of "have").

8. (D)
A compound sentence can often be simplified, especially if the second independent clause in the compound sentence describes some part of the first. In this question, the clause "and it takes finely tuned coordination and strength" describes diving. Therefore, "that" could be used instead of "and" to make it a dependent clause. The comma after "sport" must be removed if "that" is added.

9. (E)
Nouns and verbs must always agree. "Explaining the causes" and "is" are both in the singular form. "Factors" and "lead" are both in the plural form.

10. (A)
Modifiers are words, phrases, or clauses that further describe a word. In this sentence, the modifier is "opened in 1809." Obviously, this describes Goddard's watch factory. However, because of where the modifier has been placed, it sounds like Luther Goddard was opened in 1809. To fix this sentence, change "Luther Goddard" to "Luther Goddard's factory." Modifiers must always be placed as close as possible to whatever they are describing.

11. (C)
Answer (D) is a tempting choice, as the plural verb "focus" does not match the singular subject "she." However, remember that each part of a comparison has to be grammatically similar. The first half of the comparison describes what Welty's writing says while the second half describes

what Welty herself says. To make this sentence parallel, the second half should be modified so that it reads, *"her short stories* focus on the isolation of individuals."

12. (B)
Singular nouns joined by "nor" or "or" are modified by singular verbs. "Separate" must agree with the singular noun, "behavior."

13. (A)
Don't confuse "except" and "accept." "Except" means "not including" while "accept" means "to admit." The wrong word choice can express a totally different meaning in a sentence.

14. (B)
This sentence is a run-on. The comma that follows "water" should be replaced with a semicolon.

15. (E)
There are no errors in this sentence. The modifier ("both immediate and long term") is close to the noun it is modifying ("changes").

16. (D)
In a series of items, such as the one that occurs at the end of the sentence, each item has to be grammatically similar. In this case, the first two items ("no press" and "no equality of individuals before the law") are nouns. The third item, however, is a phrase because it contains a verb ("freedom of thought *was* forbidden). For consistency, it should be rewritten as a noun: "no freedom of thought."

17. (B)
When pronouns are used as the subjects of sentences, you need to use the nominative case: I, he, she, they, we, and you. Instead of "her," "she" would be grammatically correct in the sentence. ("She and the other cyclists" is a more familiar way of phrasing this.)

18. (A)
Answer (A) is the correct form of the modifier. It clarifies why the Army began buying greater quantities of sweets, an issue answer (C) does not adequately address. "Convincing that candy" in answer (B) is not parallel with the rest of the sentence. Answer (D), "convinced of candy's increasing of" contains too many prepositions within one phrase.

19. (C)
Answer (C) is correct because all of the verbs should agree. They should also be in the simple past tense (unlike answers (B) and (E)) since the sentence makes it clear that the action happened in the past. Answers (A) and (D) are wrong because the verbs do not agree.

20. (C)
Answer (C) is the best choice because the two verbs ("signaled" and "was") are both in the past tense. The reference to the Lewis and Clark expedition makes it clear that the action happened in the past. Answer (D) is ungrammatical because the form of the verb ("signaling") makes the independent clause incomplete.

21. (E)
Answer (E) is the best way to revise this sentence since the second half of the sentence modifies the first by further describing the movie. While there's nothing grammatically incorrect about writing the sentence as two independent clauses (answer choice (A)), since "it" refers to the "movie" the most efficient revision makes the second clause a modifying phrase.

22. (B)
Answer (B) is correct because "Aesthetics Movement" and "its emphasis" are both singular. The possessive pronoun must always agree with the noun it is replacing. In answer (D), the possessive pronoun agrees with the noun, but this is not the most efficient way to write the sentence.

23. (B)
In this question, the pronoun references are unclear. The best answer choice is (B) because it clarifies the role of each person and makes reference to the object. The pilot makes an announcement to the passengers; the flight attendant will collect the headphones.

24. (D)
When the noun is a fraction, the verb should agree with the object of the preposition that follows it. In this question, "class" is singular and should be modified by a

singular verb, "plans." None of the verbs agree in number with the nouns in the other answer choices.

25. (A)
Semicolons are used to connect two closely related sentences. Using a comma instead of a semicolon makes the sentence a run-on (answer B) and placing the semicolon after "produces" (answer (E)) makes the second phrase incomplete. Answers (C) and (D) are also incorrect.

26. (D)
Answer (D) is the best choice because it combines the two sentences in the most efficient way while staying close to the spirit of the original sentence. The word "that" makes answer (E) incorrect—it is superfluous and misplaced wording that can be taken out of the sentence.

27. (D)
This original sentence is a run-on, thus the best choice is answer (D) because it breaks the run-on into two sentences. Answer (B) is incorrect because the two sentences do not contradict each other, as "but" implies. Answer (C) is incorrect because the first sentence is not a question. Finally, answer (E) is incorrect because it lacks a subject.

28. (E)
The problem with the original sentence is that it sounds as though the basement had "delightful descriptions," which clearly doesn't make sense. The best answer choice is the one in which the descriptive phrase ("with their delightful descriptions . . .") is placed next to the noun it modifies ("the chess club archives"). This is accomplished by answer choice (E).

29. (A)
Answer (A) correctly compares the circulation of the *Times* with the circulation of other newspapers. Answer (B) is repetitive. Answer (C) compares the *Times'* circulation with other newspapers, which doesn't make sense. Answer (D) is missing a noun, and answer (E) is simply ungrammatical.

30. (B)
Spaghetti and meatballs refers to a single dish, which makes it a singular noun. Answer (B) is correct because the noun and verb agree in number. In answers (A), (C), and (E), the noun and verb do not agree. In answer (D), the use of the verb form "being" leads to an incomplete sentence.

31. (B)
The first part of the sentence is a modifier. It describes something that happened to Harriet Beecher Stowe. The original sentence is written, however, so that the phrase describes Stowe's faith and empathy instead of Stowe herself. Answer (B) is the correct answer because it makes Stowe the subject of the sentence, so that the modifier clearly refers to her.

32. (E)
The answer is (E). "She" is the correct pronoun to use instead of "her." Answer (D) contains the wrong verb tense, and answer (C) merely switches the order of "the poet Louise Bogan" and "her."

33. (C)
Since the subject of both dependent clauses is "Coca-Cola," it is best to combine the sentence as has been done in answer (C). "And" is superfluous wording in answer (B) and "however" is unnecessary wording in answer (D).

34. (A)
Remember that intervening phrases that begin with "in addition to," "along with," and "as well as" do not change the subject of the sentence. For this question, answer (A) is correct because the subject ("The Picasso Museum") is singular and the verb ("offers") agrees with it. In answer (D), because the two museums have been joined by "and," the subject is now a compound subject that requires a plural verb.

35. (B)
Since these two sentences share the same subject, "students," it's easy to combine them by eliminating the subject in the second sentence and adding an "and." Answer (A) is incorrect because the two sentences do not contradict each other, and therefore "but" is unnecessary. Answer (C) doesn't make sense. Answer (D) is wordy, and answer (E) is the wrong tense.

36. (B)
The final sentence in a paragraph has two purposes: to summarize and serve as a bridge to the next paragraph.

Since the second paragraph deals with students who have no other choice but to eat in the cafeteria, answer (B) is best. Answer (A) isn't a good choice because its scope is too limited. Answers (C), (D), and (E) offer random bits of information that don't add anything to the letter.

37. (A)

Since the audience for this letter is the principal, the writer probably wants to use fairly formal language that will appeal to a person in a position of authority. That means answers (B), (C), (D), and (E) aren't great since they're emotional, inflammatory, and not objective. In contrast, answer (A) sounds more objective.

38. (D)

Answer (D) is correct because the author is making a suggestion that is not possible (and contradicts the first part of the sentence). Answer (E) "and yet this is impossible" is the ending to a sentence, not the middle, where it is stuck in this sentence.

39. (E)

The first part of the sentence is written using the conditional verb tense. For the sake of consistency, the rest of the sentence should use the same tense, which makes answer (E) the correct choice. Although answer (D) uses the conditional, it is too wordy.

40. (C)

Since the subject ("everyone") of sentences 4 and 5 is the same, the two sentences can be combined, and answer (C) is the most effective way to do it. Answer (A) is unnecessarily repetitive (with "everyone" appearing twice), answer (B) is choppy, answer (D) is ungrammatical since the two verbs are not in the same form, and answer (E) is weakened by a dangling modifier since the sentence never says who is doing the talking.

41. (B)

This is structured as a problem-solution essay. The problem is that teenagers have a poor reputation, and the solution is that the essay writer and his brother try to disprove this idea by starting a basketball camp.

42. (B)

"Make a difference" is vague. The sentence would be stronger if the author discussed what making a difference means to him. The other ideas for improvement, while good, are not as necessary or relevant to the sentence.

43. (C)

"Nevertheless" suggests that the brothers recommended the basketball players even though they weren't good. However, according to the passage, some of the kids were good and improved dramatically. Thus, recommending them is a "result" of the progress they made over the summer, which makes answer (C) correct.

44. (D)

Beginning with sentence 8 would be the best way to restructure paragraph 2 because it provides a context for why the two boys decided to start a basketball camp. Sentence 6 could even be moved to the end of sentence 8: "My brother and I are both good basketball players, so we started a basketball camp for kids in our neighborhood." The sentence is made into a cause-effect relationship: the brothers are good at basketball, so they started a camp to teach kids how to play the game.

45. (E)

Citing the percentage of students who were accepted to their first-choice college is the most effective way for the speaker to sell students on the value of history club. While the other answer choices do provide more specifics, the information is not necessarily persuasive.

46. (D)

Answer (D) ("But") is the correct choice since the speaker is trying to disprove that history club is for nerds. Answer (A) doesn't make sense grammatically, and answers (B), (C), and (E) suggest that the speaker agrees that history club is for nerds.

47. (C)

The two sentences simply say that history club is for students with inquiring minds who believe in the value of understanding the past. The answer choice that shares this meaning is (C). The other answers are wordy, grammatically incorrect, or incoherent.

Section Two: The CLEP English Composition Exam
Practice Test 1: Diagnostic Answers and Explanations

48. (A)

What responsibility would students assume in choosing an honoree for the history club banquet? Answer (A) is the best choice because students would have to evaluate the work and contributions of an historian to decide who to honor.

49. (D)

The key to answering this question is finding the answer choice that doesn't significantly change the meaning of the original sentences and is grammatically correct.

50. (A)

Questions are designed to arouse people's curiosity, which is the purpose of the first paragraph.

51. (A)

Since the author is contrasting two ideas, the sentence is correctly written using "but" to suggest a difference. Answer (C) contains "and," which connects two phrases rather than contributing to the meaning of this sentence. Answer (B) creates an incomplete sentence.

52. (C)

The most efficient way to combine these sentences is to refer to the subject just once, as in answer (C). Answers (A), (B), and (E) are incorrect because they have strayed too far from the meaning of the original sentence.

53. (D)

Answer (D) ("Zookeepers recognize that elephants have particular needs") could be eliminated because sentence 5 ("Many zoos are beginning to recognize this fact") expresses the same idea.

54. (D)

The reference to the Baltimore Zoo does not represent an expert opinion (A). However, it does provide evidence for her argument by showing that other zoos are taking into account the elephant's climate preferences.

55. (E)

The first two paragraphs of the letter don't make it clear that Maggie is leading a solitary life at the Alaska Zoo. Therefore, the transition to the third paragraph would be stronger if the writer explained how the zoo's plans would impact Maggie's need for company.

56. (B)

While the letter does describe some habits of elephants (A), and while it may indirectly make people more supportive of animals (D) or help the zoo raise money (E), its main purpose is to make the Alaska Zoo reconsider its decision to keep an elephant.

57. (B)

Since the essay goes on to discuss different methods of education during different periods, it would be nice to have a transition preparing the reader for this.

58. (E)

Since the author is discussing the past ("prehistoric times") the underlined portion of sentence 4 should be revised so that it is in the past tense. While answer (B) is in the past, it doesn't make grammatical sense with the rest of the sentence. Therefore, the best answer is (E).

59. (A)

Although this sentence is long, it is free of grammatical errors. "Though" sets up the relationship between the two clauses more clearly than "and" (C).

60. (C)

The best way to approach this question is to replace the underlined portion with each answer choice. By doing this, it's clear that answer (C) is the only one that makes sense.

61. (C)

"Afterwards" is vague. Far more specific is "by the middle of the next century" (C), and by looking at the dates referenced in the passage you can determine that this answer is accurate. "Shortly later" (B) should just be "later" or "in a little while"—"shortly" is an unnecessary adjective in the sentence. "Sometime in the future" (D) and "When the time was right" (E) are vague as well.

62. (C)

Although the author does discuss education in the past, she never explores contemporary education. Therefore, she does not compare and contrast past and present education.

63. (B)

If you begin with "the show quality," the sentence must be written using the passive voice. Therefore, answer (B) is correct. The restructured sentence would be:

"The show quality of a tabby is determined by stripes and whorls on its face and cheeks, a butterfly wing pattern on its back, rings on its chest, tail, and legs, and bands on its back and sides."

64. (D)

To change the sentence to a statement, it must begin with "it," and the verb must remain in the conditional tense. That means answers (A) and (E) are not correct because they do not use the correct form of the verb. Answers (B) and (C) are also wrong because they have changed the spirit of the sentence. Answer (B) is wordy and diffident, and answer (C) makes the sentence negative. The restructured sentence would be:

"It could be possible for the union to be mollified if management raised the workers' wages and provided a more comprehensive health insurance package."

65. (A)

The best approach to this question is to think about the relationship between the Theater of Fact and American and European playwrights along with who influenced whom. Since the Theater of Fact influenced Americans and Europeans, the newly constructed sentence needs to reflect this idea. Since the sentence begins with the Theater of Fact as the subject, the verb needs to be active (A). The restructured sentence would be:

"A German theatrical movement called the Theater of Fact inspired American and European playwrights to address political subjects."

66. (C)

Answer (C) is correct because the verb agrees with the noun and refers to an action that took place in the past. The restructured sentence would be:

"The haiku's original purposes were to describe nature in objective terms and to evoke a distinct emotional feeling in readers."

67. (E)

Answer (E) is the most efficient way to convey the cause and effect relationship between violence in the Sudan and the reaction of the international community. The restructured sentence would be:

Recently escalating conflict between Africans and Muslims in the Sudan explains why the international community is becoming more alarmed."

68. (C)

The key to answering this question is to try out each of the answer choices. If most people don't expect much, then it stands to reason that few people expect much. Answer (C) comes closest to expressing this idea in a grammatical way. The restructured sentence would be:

"Few people who vote in elections expect to have an impact on the overall results."

69. (D)

By beginning with "The Supreme Court," the sentence is being expressed actively instead of passively: "The Supreme Court ruled against censorship of crime literature . . . ." The rest of the sentence should modify how it achieved this ruling. While answer (A) may sound correct, the Supreme Court didn't base its rejection on the difference between "the informing and the entertaining." Instead, it simply rejected the idea that such a difference existed. This means that answer (D) is the best choice. The restructured sentence would be:

"The Supreme Court ruled against censorship of crime literature by rejecting the difference between 'the informing and the entertaining.'"

70. (A)

This sentence is being revised so that the two skills mentioned are grammatically parallel. Since leadership skills is a noun, self-reliance is also expressed as a noun in answer choice (A). The restructured sentence would be:

"Teaching leadership skills and self-reliance to young people is the purpose of the outdoor experience."

71. (C)

In this revision, the beginning of the sentence is now a noun instead of a descriptive modifier. What question could the choices be answering? Something related to how

often you check your e-mail. The best approach for this question is to try each of the answer choices and see which one makes grammatical sense with the revision. The restructured sentence would be:

"The frequency with which you check e-mail begs the question of how you spent your time before the proliferation of this technology."

72. (E)

If you revise the sentence using "but" you know you must end up with the two independent clauses that must stand in opposition to each other. Answers (A), (B), (C), and (D) are incorrect because they do not express complete thoughts. However, answer (E) does: The elaborate wedding plans were designed to guarantee that everything went smoothly . . . ." The restructured sentence would be:

"The elaborate wedding plans were designed to guarantee that everything went smoothly, but they backfired and caused havoc the week before the ceremony."

73. (A)

This sentence has simply been flipped. The correct answer choice (A) explains the effect the shells will have on the beachcomber. The restructured sentence would be:

"The abundance of pink conch shells littering the seashores of the West Indies will please the inexperienced beachcomber."

74. (B)

"*Terry and the Pirates* and *Mary Worth*" is the compound subject of the sentence. Therefore, the correct answer (B) contains a verb that agrees with the compound subject. The restructured sentence would be:

"*Terry and the Pirates* and *Mary Worth*, the most popular comics of the 1930s, explored adventure themes and domestic problems."

75. (D)

Answer (D) is correct because the change requires the beginning of the sentence to be written as a noun. Although answer (C) isn't bad, it's much wordier than (D). The other choices are not grammatical. The restructured sentence would be:

"Colombia's proximity to the 'Ring of Fire' causes many earthquakes and volcanic eruptions in the country."

76. (A)

In changing the question to a statement, you still want to express the tentativeness of the claim that it would be wiser for politicians to be driven by their convictions. That means the correct answer will likely include "might." Answer choices (A) and (E) both have "might" in them, but answer (E) is incorrect because it expresses a view at odds with the opinion expressed in the original sentence: "It might not be wiser for politicians to be driven by their convictions . . . ." That means answer (A) is the best choice. The restructured sentence would be:

"It might be wiser for politicians to be driven by their convictions instead of public opinion polls."

77. (A)

Due to the revision, the phrase "because of the rise of dual earner families" must become a noun. The best way to answer this question is to take the revision: "the rise of dual earner families" and try each of the answer choices. The best answer is (A) because the noun ("the rise") agrees with the verb ("is making"). The restructured sentence would be:

"Some education reformers argue that the rise of dual earner families is making public schools need to offer longer school days and extended school years."

78. (B)

Since the sentence has been revised using a dependent "if" clause, the future tense of the verb must be used in the main sentence. The restructured sentence would be:

"If the stock market rebounds from the recent slump, nervous investors will cautiously begin putting money into stocks again."

79. (D)

Although all of the answer choices related to travel or international relations may seem correct, it's important to keep in mind that the essay focuses on how travel writers express themselves, rather than on travel itself. Therefore, the paragraph would be most interesting to a literary critic—someone who studies literature.

80. (D)

Answer (D) is the best choice because sentence 2 defines the essay's central idea more than it sets up an idea that will be refuted (B), establishes an organizational strategy (C), or asserts a universal truth (E).

81. (A)

Sentence 2 asserts that travel writers are concerned with their position vis-à-vis other travel writers, and sentence 3 tries to explain why this is the case. Thus, answer (A) is the best choice.

82. (B)

"Whereas" signals to the reader that the writer is differentiating between two things. In this case, the purpose of "whereas" in sentence 4 is to show how tourists are different from travelers.

83. (C)

Answer (C) is the best choice. The reference to Dervla Murphy serves as an example of how she strives to prove that her book is more original than others. While answer (D) may seem correct, it's important to keep in mind that the author of the essay is *not* showing that Dervla Murphy's account is superior. Instead, she is pointing out that Dervla Murphy tries to establish her book as superior.

84. (D)

Use process of elimination to answer this question. You can eliminate (A) because the author doesn't mention whether travel literature is becoming more popular. While she does mention that travel writers are concerned with not being formulaic, she doesn't evaluate whether it's difficult to be original (B). Answer (C) is also not mentioned in the essay. Finally, the author doesn't compare female and male travel writers, so you can also eliminate (E). That means answer (D) is the best choice.

85. (B)

In light the of the Edward Abbey quote, it's clear that the author is striving to show how her garden is beautiful, even though it may appear overgrown to others. This means that answer (B) is correct.

86. (C)

All the details that the author focuses on in sentence 5 describe different noises in the city. Therefore, she is trying to convey a sense of the city's noisiness (B) to the reader.

87. (B)

Although the author is describing the different plants that grow in her garden (A) she does not provide a complete catalogue. Answer (B) is better because she is focusing on how everything in the garden is mixed together without regard for category or type.

88. (D)

The best way to answer this question is to consider each answer choice in light of the passage. Make sure that you look at both adjectives because while one may be true, the other may not. While the author is clearly interested in her garden, there is nothing in the passage to indicate that she is tranquil (A). Similarly, while she seems delighted, she doesn't appear confused (B). Likewise, while it's true she conveys a sense of wonder, she isn't complacent or self-satisfied (C). Finally, answer (E) is incorrect because she is interested, but she isn't fatigued. The best choice is answer (D).

89. (E)

The author focuses on the disorderliness of her garden and the pleasure this brings her. She may find the natural world more inviting than the urban environment (B), but the author's joy in surprises both large and small is what is implied most succinctly by the passage.

90. (A)

The first paragraph in this passage states an idea about the perfect place in the form of a quote from nature writer Edward Abbey. In the second paragraph, the author uses a personal example (her disorderly garden) to explore the idea of what perfect is, thereby supporting the idea described in the first paragraph.

Section Two: The CLEP English Composition Exam | 79

Chapter Five: **CLEP English Composition Review**

- The Big Picture: CLEP English Composition
- Two Versions of the Test
- Nuts and Bolts
- Skills at the Sentence Level
- Skills in Context
- The Essay
- Final Thoughts

Congratulations! You've decided to get a head start on your college education by taking the CLEP English Composition exam. While preparing for the exam takes work, a good score can get you credit or advanced placement at many schools. (Check with the schools of your choice to find out their policies.) This review chapter will help you get there.

THE BIG PICTURE: CLEP ENGLISH COMPOSITION

The CLEP English Composition exam evaluates the writing ability that is expected of students in freshman-level composition courses. Test-takers must demonstrate the ability to write grammatically, to analyze how arguments are made, and to write coherent essays (in one version of the exam).

TWO VERSIONS OF THE TEST

As mentioned in the Strategies chapter, there are two versions of the test, one of which features an essay. The first option comprises approximately 90 multiple-choice questions to be answered in 90 minutes. Fifty-five percent of the questions test your knowledge of grammar at the sentence level, while 45 percent test your understanding of how arguments are made. The second version of the exam tests your knowledge of grammar and the structure of arguments via multiple-choice questions, but it also contains a section featuring one essay question. The test with an

essay includes approximately 50 multiple-choice questions to be answered in 45 minutes plus an essay to be typed in 45 minutes (using the CLEP computer interface). Colleges differ in their policies on granting credit for the English Composition exam. Some schools require the exam with essay, so be sure to check with the schools you are considering. In this book, Tests 1 and 2 are all-multiple-choice exams, while Test 3 is an exam with essay.

NUTS AND BOLTS

The following information summarizes the two tests.

	Multiple-Choice Exam	Exam with Essay
Skills at the Sentence Level	55%	30%
Identifying Sentence Errors		
Improving Sentences		
*Restructuring Sentences		N/A
Skills in Context	45%	20%
Revising Work in Progress		
*Analyzing Writing		N/A
Essay	N/A	50%

*Restructuring Sentences and Analyzing Writing appear *only* on the all-multiple choice exam.

In the following review, we'll discuss what you need to know to do your best on each part of the CLEP English Composition exam.

SKILLS AT THE SENTENCE LEVEL

The first multiple-choice section of the CLEP English Composition exam is called "Skills at the Sentence Level" and contains two or three parts: Identifying Sentence Errors and Improving Sentences appear on both versions of the test, but Restructuring Sentences is reserved for the version without the essay. (When it occurs, it follows Revising Work in Progress.) Questions in "Skills at the Sentence Level" cover many specific topics, which we'll explore in depth in this section.

- Complete Sentences
- Economy and Clarity
- Agreement
- Active versus Passive Voice
- Diction and Idiom
- Syntax and Structure
- Sentence Variation

Most people who have grown up speaking English have an intuitive sense of topics such as subject-verb agreement; however, there are other grammatical rules that may surprise even native speakers. For a thorough review of uncommon or confusing grammatical constructions, you should consult a book on writing and grammar.

Complete Sentences

A complete sentence contains a noun and a verb and expresses a complete thought. An incomplete sentence may begin with a capital letter and end with a punctuation mark, but often it will be missing either a subject or a verb or both. In other cases the sentence will contain a subject and verb, but express an incomplete thought, as in this example:

> Because she had an appointment early in the morning.

In a run-on sentence, two complete thoughts, or *independent clauses*, are ungrammatically joined by a comma.

> The school board chair called the meeting into session, the high school principal presented the athletic calendar.

To correct this sentence, a period or semicolon must be added between the two independent clauses. If a period is added, the first word of the second clause must be capitalized—creating two separate sentences.

> The school board chair called the meeting into session. The high school principal presented the athletic calendar.

Generally, the best way to handle run-on sentences is to split them into more than one sentence. However, if the two complete thoughts are closely related, a semicolon may be used to separate them. In addition, if the second sentence amplifies an idea expressed in the first sentence, a colon may be used.

Alternatively, you can use a conjunction (i.e. "and," "but," "for," "so") to join two sentences into one. In this instance the conjunction indicates the end of one complete thought and the beginning of another. A comma should precede it.

> The school board chair called the meeting into session, and the high school principal presented the athletic calendar.

Economy and Clarity

Good writing is clear to the reader and not monotonous or repetitive. This means finding the most efficient and straightforward way to express ideas through words. On the CLEP English Composition exam, some of the questions will ask you to find better ways to write sentences that are grammatically correct but wordy or awkwardly phrased. For example:

> The writer James Baldwin, who was raised in Harlem, moved to France in the middle of his writing career, and this gave him the necessary distance to explore the social problems in the United States.

Although this example is grammatically correct, it can be written more economically by combining the two independent clauses (or complete thoughts) as follows.

> The writer James Baldwin, who was raised in Harlem, moved to France in the middle of his writing career, gaining the necessary distance to explore the social problems in the United States.

Issues of economy also arise in sentences that only contain one complete thought. These sentences can be redundant or verbose.

> I am capable of speaking the language of France.

The main idea can be stated more simply.

> I speak French.

Agreement

Subject-Verb Agreement

The subject and verb of a sentence must agree with each other. That means a singular subject is modified by a singular verb, and a plural subject is modified by a plural verb. Sometimes identifying the subject of a sentence can be difficult, especially when a clause or phrase comes between the subject and the verb.

> His understanding of the math concepts always increase after the teacher reviews the homework.

The subject of the above sentence, "understanding," is singular. The phrase that follows, "of the math concepts," is a prepositional phrase that further describes "understanding," but "the math concepts" is not the subject of the sentence. Since the subject ("understanding") is singular, the plural verb "increase" must be changed to the singular form, "increases."

> His <u>understanding</u> of the math concepts always <u>increases</u> after the teacher reviews the homework.

In other sentences, the verb will come before the subject. In these sentences, the verb must agree with the subject that follows it.

> There <u>are</u> many <u>allusions</u> in Eliot's poem, *The Waste Land*, which make it extremely difficult to understand without seriously studying it.

In this sentence, the noun ("allusions") is plural, and so is the verb ("are"). The sentence is correct as written.

Let's look at what happens when the subject of a sentence includes more than one person, place or thing ("Billy and I," "chocolate or vanilla"). In sentences with compound subjects (two nouns joined by a conjunction), the verb may be singular or plural. When the conjunction "and" creates the compound subject, the subject is plural.

> A dry winter and hot summer increase the likelihood of forest fires.

Since the compound subject ("dry winter and hot summer") is plural, the verb ("increase") is also plural. The sentence is correct as written.

When "or" or "nor" is used to join the subjects, whether the compound subject is plural depends on the subjects themselves. If both are singular, the compound subject is singular and calls for a singular verb.

> A dry winter or hot summer increases the likelihood of forest fires.

Since the compound subject ("dry winter or hot summer") is singular, the verb ("increases") is also singular. The sentence is correct as written.

If both subjects are plural, the compound subject is plural and calls for a plural verb. If one is singular and one is plural, the verb should agree with the subject closest to it.

> Park rangers believe that either campers or lightning is most likely to cause the next wildfire here.

Since the compound subject ("campers or lightning") contains both a plural and a singular subject, the verb ("is") agrees with the subject closest to it (the singular "lightning"). The sentence is correct as written.

Verb Tense Agreement

Verbs are used to express action ("walk," "jump," "dive," "grin") or states of being ("are," "is"). They appear in six different grammatical tenses in the English language.

Present:	I study for three hours every evening.
Past:	I studied for three hours last night.
Future:	I will study for three hours tomorrow afternoon.
Present Perfect:	I have studied for three hours for three weeks.
Past Perfect:	I had studied for three hours every evening for a week.
Future Perfect:	I will have studied for three hours every evening for a month by the time I take the exam.

The present tense, as you know, means that the action is currently taking place. The present perfect refers to an action that started in the past and may or may not still be continuing ("I have studied").

The past tense describes an action that has already been completed. The past prefect refers to an action that ended at a particular point in the past: "I had studied for three hours every evening for a week when I passed the test."

The future tense, as the name suggests, means that the action has not yet happened. The future perfect tense signals that the action will take place in the future after something else happens ("I will have driven fifty miles by the time I get to the mountains.").

On the CLEP English Composition exam, you will need to watch for inconsistencies in verb tense. In some instances, the sentences will contain simple shifts in verb tense.

> *Poets and Writers* contains reviews of recently published books and offered a list of contests and publishing opportunities for writers.

For the sake of consistency, both verbs should be in the present tense ("contains" and "offers") or in the past tense ("contained" and "offered").

Other questions on the exam will be more complicated because all the verbs in a sentence do not always have to be in the same tense. In fact, different verb tenses are used to show when one event happened in relationship to another. For example, the following sentence must be revised.

> Julie will look for a job as a lifeguard after she finished her CPR training.

In the example above, the future tense ("will look") is being used. Since the future takes place after the present, the present tense (use of the verb "finishes") is necessary to show when Julie will begin looking for a job.

Here's another sample sentence that needs revision.

> When he has finished his first full-length work, the novelist Caryl Phillips had already graduated from Oxford University.

In the example above, the subject is Caryl Phillips, and the verb ("had graduated") is in the past perfect tense. As we've seen, the past perfect indicates that the action of the verb ("graduating") was completed before another action in the *past*. The first verb ("has finished") should appear in the simple *past* tense and not the present perfect, which doesn't necessarily mean that the action is over. Therefore, the sentence should be revised.

> When he <u>finished</u> his first full-length work, the novelist Caryl Phillips <u>had already graduated</u> from Oxford University.

Incomplete Verbs

Finally, watch out for incomplete verbs used in sentences. Some verb forms must be used in conjunction with helping verbs (such as "are," "is," and "have"). If the helping verb is missing, the sentence will be incomplete or ungrammatical.

> Jose writing the final paragraph of his essay when the electricity failed and the computer shut down without saving his final changes.

The subject of the sentence is Jose. The verb ("writing") is missing the helping verb ("was"), making the sentence incomplete. Again, this should sound incorrect.

Pronoun Reference

Pronouns (he, she, they, we, it) must agree with the nouns or *antecedents* that they replace. The *antecedent* is the word, clause, or phrase that a pronoun repaces. If the noun is singular, then the pronoun must be singular. Similarly, if the noun is plural, then the pronoun must be plural.

> <u>Professors Judith Meyers and Tony Abel</u> asked the English department chair for sabbaticals so that <u>they</u> could finish their collaborative project.

"They" agrees with the plural subject, "Professors Judith Meyers and Tony Abel," making this sentence grammatically correct.

Shifts in the number of subjects (or pronouns) in a sentence can occur when you aren't sure whether the antecedent is singular or plural. Keep in mind that indefinite subjects, such as *everyone*, *anybody*, and *everything*, are singular even though they sound plural.

For example, the following sentence is correct as written.

> Everyone who takes my creative writing class must write thirty pages in her journal each week.

Besides watching for agreement in number, you must also make sure that pronouns appear in the same voice as the nouns they replace. As you probably know, pronouns can be categorized by point of view or voice in a sentence. When you read a sentence, note whether the subject is the speaker (I/me/we), someone the speaker is addressing (you), or someone/something not being directly addressed (he/she/they).

<u>First-person pronouns</u>:   I, we, me, us, my, mine, our, ours

<u>Second-person pronouns</u>:   you, your, yours

<u>Third-person pronouns</u>:   she, he, it, one, they, him, her, them, his, her, hers, its, their, theirs, ours

Shifts in point of view and voice can occur when you aren't paying attention to whether the sentence is written in the first, second, or third person. Remember that point of view must stay consistent throughout a sentence. The point of view changes within the next sentence.

> Training for the marathon is tricky: if he logs too many miles, you risk getting an injury, but if you run too few, you may not finish.

The error in the example above is that it shifts from the third person ("he") to the second person ("you"). The sentence must be written using either second- or third-person pronouns, but not both.

Active versus Passive Voice

The test makers and most teachers usually prefer the active voice to the passive voice. Sentences that use the active voice more clearly express *who* is performing an action and *what* action is being performed. In active sentences, the person or thing that performs the action comes at the beginning of the sentence.

> Mrs. Solomon traveled to South America over her vacation and returned with lots of colorful photographs to show the students.

Mrs. Solomon is the one who traveled to South America, returned with photographs, and shared them with her students. It's clear who completed the actions. In contrast, in passive sentences, the person or thing performing the actions doesn't appear until the end of the sentence. In some cases, the agent of the action is not mentioned at all. Here is the same sentence written in the passive voice.

> The students were shown many colorful photographs by Mrs. Solomon who traveled to South America over her vacation.

The passive voice can be even more vague. The same sentence would be grammatically correct if it simply stated, "The students were shown many colorful photographs." Here there is no agent at all.

Remember: on the English Composition test, you always should pick the answer choice that has the sentence written in the active voice.

Diction and Idiom

Diction refers to word choice, and idiom refers to phrases that have a meaning different from their literal meaning. On the CLEP English Composition exam, you need to watch for misused words, language that is not appropriate given the context, and idiomatic phrases that are incorrectly used. Often, language is misused when the writer is faced with two words that sound alike or seem to share the same meaning. For example:

> *Torturous* means terrible or painful
>
> *Tortuous* means winding or twisting

Therefore, the following use of "tortuous" would be incorrect:

> Running a mile around the track is tortuous for me because I'm out of shape.

On the English Composition test, you will need to identify errors in appropriate word choice. A word or phrase may not necessarily be used incorrectly, but its style or tone may be at odds with the rest of the sentence or paragraph.

> Sarah Burnhardt was one of the most famous actresses ever to grace the stage. The people of her day thought she was hot stuff.

Clearly the informal slang expression "hot stuff" doesn't fit the formal style of the rest of the example. In formal writing, the words are formal, and in informal writing, the words are informal. You need to be able to recognize the tone of different words and the purpose of each section of writing.

Syntax and Structure

Syntax refers to the order of words in a sentence. In some sentences, the order of words clouds the overall meaning of the sentence. In others, faulty syntax can make the sentence ungrammatical. On the CLEP exam, you will want to pay close attention to parallel structure, subordination, and misplaced or "dangling" modifiers.

Parallel Structure

Parallel structure means that each item in a series or a comparison appears in the same grammatical form. The next example presents a list that is parallel.

> Next summer, I plan to take piano lessons, attend basketball camp, baby-sit on the weekends, and help my mother with her vegetable garden.

Each of the items in this list is grammatically similar. Each part of the sentence is a simple verbal phrase that begins with a verb in the present tense: *take, baby-sit, help*. This sentence would be unparallel if it was written as follows.

> Next summer, I plan to take piano lessons, attend basketball camp, baby-sit on the weekends, and gardening with my mother.

The last item ("gardening with my mother") is grammatically different from the other items in the series. It should sound wrong or different to you. The other items are verbs while the final item is a noun ("gardening," the thing the speaker will be doing).

Parallel structure also applies to items in a comparison. Look at the next example. How would you make it parallel?

> My father believes that eating a home-cooked meal is healthier than what you can get in a restaurant.

Which two things are being compared in the sentence? "Eating a home-cooked meal" and "what you can get in a restaurant" are being compared, but the two phrases are in different grammatical forms. To correct the sentence, put them in the same form.

> My father believes that eating a home-cooked meal is healthier than dining at a restaurant.

You should be able to hear that "eating a home-cooked meal" is in the same form as "dining at a restaurant."

Subordination

Subordination refers to how writers show relationships between ideas or emphasize the relative importance of different ideas. Generally, the most important ideas appear in the independent clauses, while less important ideas take their place in dependent clauses or phrases. An independent clause is part of a sentence that expresses a complete idea and could be a grammatically correct sentence on its own.

The CLEP English Composition exam will ask you to correct sentences in which the relationship between ideas is unclear or misstated. Here's a sentence that has an error in subordination.

> Transferring to a large university, Leo was disappointed with his small college's lack of an astronomy department.

The sentence doesn't make sense. It sounds as though Leo transferred before he realized that his college didn't have an astronomy department. There are better ways to write the sentence.

> Disappointed with his small college's lack of an astronomy department, Leo transferred to a large university.

In the revision, the relationship between the two ideas is more clearly expressed. Leo transferred because he was disappointed by his college's course offerings. The most important idea—Leo's decision to transfer—appears in the independent clause. The cause of it—his disappointment—appears in the dependent clause. "Leo transferred to a large university" forms a complete sentence, but "Disappointed with his small college's lack of an astronomy department" does not.

Misplaced Modifiers

Modifiers provide more information about a word or phrase in a sentence. When they are misplaced, it means they aren't positioned close enough to the part of the sentence they are describing. As a result, the modifier seems to be modifying something else, making the meaning of the sentence unclear or ridiculous.

> I brought my parrot to the school assembly who only speaks when it rains.

In this sentence, the modifier ("who only speaks when it rains") is too far from the word that it modifies ("parrot"). As a result, the sentence seems nonsensical—does the school assembly only speak when it rains? However, this error is easy to correct.

> I brought my parrot who only speaks when it rains to the school assembly.

When a modifier is dangling, it means the word it is supposed to describe is missing from the sentence as in the next example.

> Sprinting around the track, Lindsey's shoes came untied, and she tripped and lost the race.

"Sprinting around the track" describes what Lindsey is doing. However, because of how the sentence is constructed, it appears that Lindsey's shoes are sprinting around the track without her. To correct the sentence, either add Lindsey as the subject or rewrite the modifier to include a reference to Lindsey. The second sentence here does this by making the modifier into an adverbial phrase.

> Sprinting around the track, Lindsey tripped and lost the race when her shoes came untied.

OR

> While she was sprinting around the track, Lindsey's shoes came untied, and she tripped and lost the race.

Sentence Variation

It's important to vary sentence length when you write. Some sentences should be long; others short. Mixing up sentence length keeps the reader engaged in what she or he is reading. It's also important to vary the structure of your sentences. Think about how bored you would be if you read an essay of simple subject-verb-object sentences.

> David went to the store. His mother sent him. She gave him a list. He realized he had lost the list at the store. He couldn't remember the items on the list. He decided to buy his favorite food. He hoped his mother wouldn't be angry.

For some questions on the exam, the sentences may be perfectly grammatical, but there may be a better way to write them so that text is more interesting for the reader.

SKILLS IN CONTEXT

The second multiple-choice portion of the CLEP English Composition exam is called "Skills in Context." Of this portion's two question types, Revising Work in Progress appears on both versions of the test while Analyzing Writing only appears on the version without the essay. In the Revising Work in Progress section, you will be asked to read early drafts of student essays and improve the way they are written on the sentence and paragraph level. The Analyzing Writing section asks you to examine the organization of written passages and identify the writing strategies used by the authors. Questions in the "Skills in Context" portion cover several topics.

- Central Idea
- Organization
- Evidence (Relevance, Degree of Detail, and Specificity)
- Audience and Purpose
- Logic
- Paragraph Structure and Function
- Rhetorical Emphasis
- Consistency of Tense and Viewpoint
- Combination and Variation of Sentences

Central Idea

The central idea is the main point that any piece of writing, whether an essay, letter to the editor, or literary analysis, is attempting to make. The main idea is usually introduced in the first paragraph of a piece of writing in the form of a thesis statement. Don't confuse the thesis statement with the subject of the essay. For example, while an essay may be about Emily Dickinson, the thesis will express an opinion about her poetry: "Emily Dickinson's poetry reveals how nineteenth-century women escaped the narrow confines of their domestic responsibilities." In other words, the thesis statement takes a stand on a topic.

Each paragraph in an essay may contain a separate central idea that supports the thesis of the essay. Usually, the writer will state the central idea at the beginning of each paragraph in the form of a topic sentence. On the CLEP exam, you will be asked to identify the central idea of essays and individual paragraphs.

Organization

There are countless ways to organize essays. Your job on the CLEP English Composition exam will be to recognize patterns that indicate how the author has ordered the essay. Some common ways to structure essays include the following.

- Cause and effect
- Chronological
- Problem and solution
- Question and answer
- Compare and contrast
- Narrative

For each passage, ask yourself how every paragraph relates to the thesis. This will help you determine the passage's structure. Keep in mind that some of the essays on the exam will be deliberately disorganized, especially in the Revising Work in Progress section. You may discover that one paragraph is totally unrelated to the thesis. If this is the case, you may be asked to identify ways to improve the organization of the essay—perhaps by removing that paragraph!

In addition, you should be able to identify how ideas are ordered within a paragraph. Generally, a topic sentence will indicate the main point of the paragraph, and the rest of the paragraph will be devoted to providing evidence or making an argument to support the main point. Keep in mind that just as some of the essays will seem disorganized, some of the paragraphs within essays will also seem jumbled or confused. Your job will be to determine which evidence is unnecessary, which evidence is necessary but missing, and how a paragraph can be restructured so that it makes its main point more effectively.

Evidence (Relevance, Degree of Detail, and Specificity)

The best way to make a point is to provide evidence that is specific and concrete. Evidence can take many forms: it can be based upon experience, analysis, expert opinions, or observation. On the CLEP English Composition exam, you will be asked to do two things: identify the evidence that an author presents to support his or her points, and judge the value of the evidence presented.

Some of the writing that appears on the exam will seem vague to you. The author may make a strong claim, such as, "A mandatory community service program for students would be easy to start," but may not provide examples of how she or he would go about launching it. Your job will be to identify the answer choice that offers evidence that is both specific and relevant to the point being made in the passage.

Audience and Purpose

For whom is the essay or letter in the passage being written? This is known as the audience. Why is the passage being written? This is known as the purpose. The audience affects the style, tone, and rhetorical strategies of each piece of writing. If you wrote the editor of your local newspaper, it would sound very different from a letter that you might write to a close friend or relative. You would probably use more formal language in the letter to the editor, whereas in the letter to your friend you would be more casual and perhaps use slang.

The purpose of a piece of writing dictates its tone and structure. There are many different reasons for writing. Writers may write to inform, to relate a personal experience, to persuade the reader of something, or to explain how something is done. Let's look at the last reason for writing: to explain. If your purpose is to explain how to play soccer, you will probably use clear language and relate the rules in a straightforward, methodical way. You may address your readers in the second person (as "you"), since you are telling them what they need to do to play soccer. Your tone and structure would be different if you wanted to write a scary story. In the story, you would use emotional language. You also would present characters and use dialogue to build suspense.

On the English Composition test, you will be asked to consider how the writer could more effectively address his or her audience by choosing more appropriate language for a written passage. If you are taking the all-multiple-choice exam, you will also be asked to analyze written passages to determine their purpose and ideal audience.

Logic

There are two basic types of logical reasoning: inductive and deductive. An inductive argument usually moves from a specific observation to a generalization while a deductive argument starts with a general statement and ends with specific points.

- **Inductive**: I've noticed that whenever it snows more than six inches, the school district closes the schools for the day. I think that means that the next time it snows six inches, we'll have a snow day.
- **Deductive**: The school district policy states that school must be cancelled if more than six inches of snow fall in twenty-four hours. That means if it snows six inches tonight, we'll have a snow day.

On the CLEP English Composition exam, you won't be asked to determine whether an inductive or deductive argument is being made in a passage; however, you may be asked to explain the role that specific sentences play in how the argument is being made. For example, does the first sentence offer a generalization or a specific detail? How does a sentence in the middle of a passage function? Does it provide a counterexample? Does it serve as a transition to a new idea? Does it provide evidence to support the argument?

Paragraph Structure and Function

A paragraph is like a very short essay. The topic sentence (which is usually the first or second sentence) should announce the main point, and the rest of the paragraph should provide logical support for this point. You should be able to understand how each sentence supports the main idea of the paragraph. Alternatively, you may identify sentences that don't seem related to the main idea and that should be revised or omitted. A paragraph may end with a concluding sentence that returns the reader's attention to the main idea. A concluding sentence also may serve as a transition to the next paragraph.

You should be able to see the connection between all of the different paragraphs in an essay. Sometimes paragraphs will contain transitional sentences that help connect each paragraph to the previous or subsequent one. At other times, it will be up to you to determine the relationship between paragraphs. The best way to evaluate the excerpt's coherence between paragraphs is to try to summarize the purpose of each paragraph and then explore how they are interrelated. Consider the following main points of a hypothetical essay:

Paragraph 1:	Our town should have a recycling program.
Paragraph 2:	Recycling is important because it reduces waste and helps preserve the environment.
Paragraph 3:	Because new items can be made from recycled materials, recycling programs are not expensive.
Paragraph 4:	By starting a recycling program, we can reduce waste and preserve the environment without spending too much money.

You could say that the essay follows a problem-solution organizational pattern. The first paragraph states the need or problem. The second paragraph explains why this need should be addressed. The third paragraph offers a solution, with the final paragraph serving as a conclusion that sums everything up. Having identified the essay's organization, you can answer almost any question about how the paragraphs relate to one another. If the paragraphs are presented in the wrong order, you can unscramble them once you discover their internal logic.

Rhetorical Emphasis

Rhetorical emphasis simply refers to the way writers use language to create a feeling or effect. Consider the rhetorical device known as personification—giving human qualities to animals or inanimate objects. Read the next example, which makes use of personification, and consider the effect it has on you.

> The house looked blankly at the fields. It seemed to say, "Even though you are in front of me, I refuse to see you." On windy days when the trees shook their branches at the sky, the house held itself very still. Whatever had happened long ago lingered. The house was frozen with grief—or shock.

Personification makes the house seem capable of feeling emotions like grief and shock. Overall, it gives the passage an eerie feeling. Especially in the Analyzing Writing section but in other parts of

the exam as well, you will be asked to examine specific details in the passages and determine their effect on the passage. Read carefully, ask yourself what the author is trying to accomplish, and think about how the description makes you feel.

Consistency of Tense and Viewpoint

In each sentence or passage on the exam, you have to be on the lookout for shifts in verb tense. If a passage is mostly written in the past tense, it would be inconsistent if one sentence appeared in the present tense for no particular reason. Likewise, be aware of shifts in point of view (first person, second person, etc.). Most essays are written without reference to a point of view (in other words, they don't refer to "you" or "I" or "she"). Other writing, especially memoir, does have a point of view. If the point of view shifts from the first person to third person, then you know that the point of view has not been sustained throughout the written piece.

Combination and Variation of Sentences

The Revising Work in Progress section puts a heavy emphasis on combining and varying sentences. A paragraph that is composed of many short sentences, all of which contain a single idea, is boring to read. It may also be potentially confusing since you don't know how the ideas in the paragraph are related to each other. The CLEP English Composition exam will evaluate your ability to combine sentences by asking you to revise and combine certain sentences from a passage. Look at the next example.

> Derek completed the project two weeks before the deadline. Derek got a raise at work.

To combine these two sentences, you must ask yourself how they are related. Did Derek complete the project before the deadline because he got a raise at work? Or vice versa? Once you understand the connection between the two events, you can revise the sentence accordingly to covey the "missing link."

> After Derek completed the project two weeks before the deadline, he got a raise at work.

THE ESSAY

Nuts and Bolts

In this section of the CLEP English Composition exam, you will be given an essay topic and 45 minutes to respond. The essay counts for 50 percent of your grade on the exam. Usually the prompt will ask you to take a stand on a general statement, such as, "We are living in the best of all possible worlds." Your essay should reflect the extent to which you agree or disagree. Practice Test 3 has an essay question, and a sample essay appears in the Answers and Explanations section of that test.

On the computer-based CLEP exam, you will type your essay in the box on the screen. The interface resembles a typical word-processing program. Commands that will be available to you include Cut, Paste, and Undo. You will navigate using the arrow keys, Page Up, and Page Down. The Help icon will take you to a screen explaining the different commands in the typing program. Download the CLEP Sampler from collegeboard.com/clep to practice using the essay-writing program.

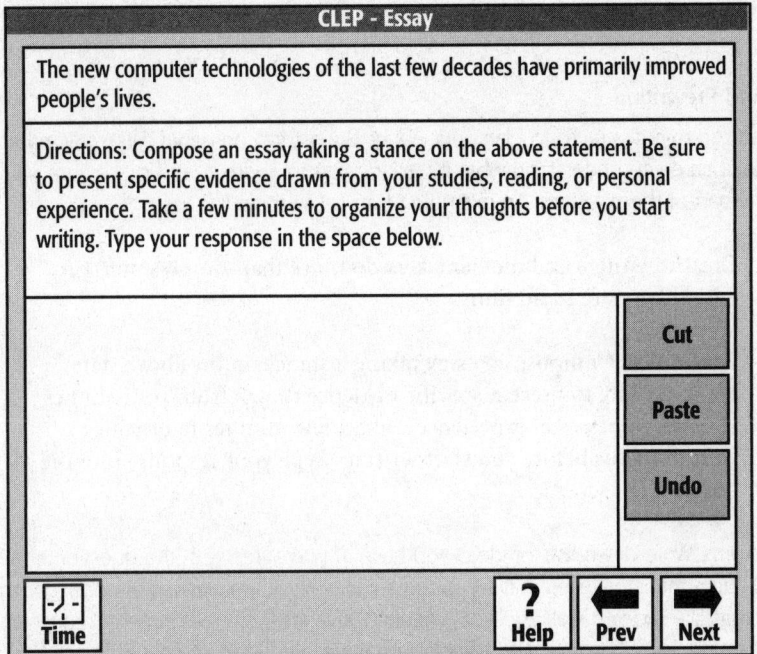

How the Essay Is Scored

Unlike the rest of the exam, which is scored by computer, the essay is read by two college English teachers. Each reader assigns it a grade on a scale of 1 to 6, and the sum of their grades is your final score. If the essay is blank or completely off the topic, you will receive a zero from the grading supervisor. Grading is holistic and graders look for the following: well-developed ideas, good use of evidence, a focused and organized essay, facility with vocabulary, sentence variation, and grammatical writing. The scoring criteria are discussed more thoroughly in the Answers and Explanations section of Practice Test 3, which features an essay question and a sample answer.

Preparing for the Essay

Since the essay is worth half of the points on the exam, it definitely pays to prepare. Practice planning and writing essays using the method given below. Respond to the sample essay question in Practice Test 3. It's better to type your practice essays into a computer to simulate the testing experience. You should practice writing on a variety of topics, and if at all possible, have someone else read and grade your essays. You also can practice by reading the work of different authors and trying to identify the rhetorical strategies and logical structures they use.

Writing the Essay

Everything that you have learned about writing good essays applies here! That means you need to make sure you address the topic completely and effectively, organize your ideas, make a clear argument, provide support for each of your points, and demonstrate your mastery of English by not only writing grammatically but also with sophistication and flair. However, you must do all of this in only 45 minutes. How should you approach this daunting task? Break it down into the following steps.

Planning and Prewriting

Give yourself ten minutes or so to plan your essay. Brainstorm on paper. First, study the question carefully. Make sure you understand what it's asking you to address, and make sure you don't overlook any part of the question. An example of an essay topic follows.

> Creative writers and moviemakers do more than simply entertain with their stories and films.
>
> **Directions:** Compose an essay taking a stance on the above statement. Be sure to present specific evidence drawn from your studies, reading, or personal experience. Take a few minutes to organize your thoughts before you start writing. Type your response into the box on your screen.

Next, brainstorm. Write down lists of ideas you have. If you agree with the question above, perhaps you thought that storytellers have inspired technological innovations or social progress. You might list things like space travel, abolition, medical advances, or environmental conservation that emerged after a novel or film sparked people's imaginations. After you have taken a few minutes to generate ideas, look carefully at what you have written down. How can you narrow down the topic? Are some of your ideas or examples related to each other? Circle the ideas that seem connected. Jot down how they are related.

Since the topic is so broad, you need to choose a specific focus for your answer. Perhaps, if you were responding to the question above, you might focus on science fiction. You might think of submarines, cloning, microsurgery, robots, and pacemakers as innovations first described in fiction. You might start by describing the origins of inventions in the writer's imagination. In your next paragraph you could discuss how these imagined advances became part of our reality. You could finish by looking forward to technology we hope to soon possess because fiction has helped us imagine it. Alternatively, if you disagree with the statement you might argue that imaginative stories do nothing more than entertain us, providing an escape from daily chores and troubles.

There are no right or wrong answers on the essay portion of the exam. You only need to make sure that you have a narrow focus, a clear position, and examples to support your argument.

Writing and Organization

Given the time limit for the essay, it's best to write a traditionally structured essay that includes an introduction, two or three body paragraphs depending upon the topic, and a conclusion.

In your introduction, you should pique the reader's curiosity and clearly state your thesis. Remember that your thesis explains your point of view. You need to take a stand on the question in order to create an effective essay. Simply restating the question or theme will inevitably lead to a vague essay.

Each of the body paragraphs in your essay should address a single idea that reinforces your thesis statement. Body paragraphs should begin with a topic sentence that tells the reader what you will address in each paragraph. The remainder of each paragraph should support the main idea with examples and specific evidence. By the end of each paragraph, the reader should firmly grasp the main idea of that paragraph.

The conclusion gives you a chance to summarize your main points, reiterate your solution to the topic, or leave your reader with a question. Given the limited time you have to write the CLEP English Composition essay, don't agonize over the conclusion. It's far more important to have a strong introduction and well-developed body paragraphs. However, try to allow time to wrap up your essay with a concluding paragraph.

Sophistication of Expression

You may have the best ideas in the world, but if you don't express them grammatically, readers won't be able to understand the points you are trying to make. Grammatical mistakes can be eliminated or reduced by proofreading your essay after you complete it.

In your essay, you must also demonstrate your mastery of English. This goes beyond writing an essay that is free of grammatical errors. As you complete the essay, focus on writing clearly, which means choosing words that are interesting, appropriate, and precise. Use a mix of simple and advanced vocabulary words. Write using the active voice. Include strong verbs in your essay. Vary the length of your sentences to energize the rhythm of the essay and demonstrate that you understand the relationships between different ideas. Use transitional words to help the reader follow the progress of your argument.

Even though you are writing an essay, you are also telling a story. That means you should use all the writing techniques that you have learned so far to keep the reader engaged and interested in your essay.

Proofreading

Be sure to pace yourself and allow three minutes to proofread your work. When writing under time pressure, most people make a few mistakes. Common errors include confused sentences, omitted words, and misspellings. The extra time will allow you to reread the essay as a whole for sense, and to look for grammatical errors and typos. That way, you'll finish knowing that you produced a solid, polished piece of writing.

FINAL THOUGHTS

After completing this review and the practice tests in this book, you will be on your way to an excellent score on the CLEP English Composition exam. For further preparation, consult college textbooks or other books on grammar and writing. Keep reading works by many different authors in a range of subjects, and hone your essay-writing skills by taking a stand on a variety of issues.

Good luck!

Chapter Six: Practice Test 2

Time—90 minutes
90 Questions

Directions: Each sentence below tests your knowledge of diction (choice of words), idiom, grammar, and usage. Some sentences are correct, and each sentence can contain no more than one error.

Elements of the sentence that are underlined and lettered may be incorrect. Parts of the sentence that are not underlined can be assumed to be correct. When choosing an answer, follow the rules of written English.

If a sentence contains an error, select the <u>one underlined portion</u> that must be changed in order to form a correct sentence. For sentences with no error, choose answer (E).

1. Dr. Levars found <u>his searching</u> for good problem
                   A
   sets <u>for his chemistry class</u> to be more
         B
   <u>efficient</u> online <u>than in the library</u>. <u>No error</u>
      C   D   E

2. Dates, which <u>were originally grown</u> in the Middle
                 A
   East, <u>and are now</u> cultivated in regions <u>around</u> the
        B   C
   world <u>with desert climates</u>. <u>No error</u>
         D   E

3. After <u>Sarah Clark resigned</u>, word spread quickly
         A
   among politicians <u>who speculated</u> about the real
               B
   reason behind <u>their decision</u> to step down from
           C
   office <u>so abruptly</u>. <u>No error</u>
       D   E

4. <u>The members</u> of the Electoral College <u>meets</u> after
     A   B
   the general election and <u>cast</u> their votes <u>to choose</u>
                          C   D
   the next President of the United States. <u>No error</u>
                                     E

5. During the Middle Ages, monasteries <u>were centers</u>
                                     A
   of learning with <u>their own libraries</u> and copying
                   B
   <u>chambers, here</u> monks <u>copied in</u> beautiful
       C   D
   calligraphy the great works of their age. <u>No error</u>
                                     E

6. The <u>gray storm clouds</u> <u>that darkened</u> the after-
         A   B
   noon <u>and caused</u> the temperature to plummet
          C
   gave <u>the allusion</u> of the arrival of autumn
          D
   although it was only the middle of July. <u>No error</u>
                                     E

GO ON TO THE NEXT PAGE →

7. Although it was debated for many years and even
        A
   became the subject of a legal case, the difference
              B
   between fruits and vegetables is simple: fruits are
                                      C
   usually eaten after a meal, and vegetables are
                         D
   served with a meal. No error
                       E

8. After the heat wave sent temperatures into the
              A
   hundreds and overburdened the city's
   power system, causing an extended blackout, Lee
          B
   and her friends congratulated each other on
                   C
   having had enough good sense to have gone
                D
   camping for the weekend. No error
                             E

9. Nutritional fads that promised to help Americans
                   A
   lose weight and lead healthier lives were
   B   C
   ubiquitous in the nineteenth century and in the
   C   D
   twentieth century. No error
                      E

10. The young scholar had been working at the
                      A   B
    American Antiquarian Society for three
    months before she locates the nineteenth-century
                      C
    captivity narrative that changed her perspective.
                                     D
    No error
    E

11. The American architect, Frank Lloyd Wright,
                   A
    insisted that he did not have a personal style, and
                                                    B
    he was guided by a vision, termed "organic
    B
    architecture," that emphasized harmony between
                  C
    the building and its natural surroundings.
                       D
    No error
    E

12. The new student, who our teacher introduced to
                     A   B
    us today in calculus class, has evidently skipped
    B   C
    three grades and is a math and science prodigy.
          D
    No error
    E

13. Although many people assume that President George W. Bush and his father are cut in the same
    _____A
    cloth, sharing the same convictions and moral
         ___B___   _C_
    fiber, history will show that each had a different
                                  ____D___
    leadership style. No error
                      ___E____

14. To choose the best camera, a photographer should
    _____A_____ _____B_____
    consider what kind of pictures she wants to take,
    her needs in terms of mobility, and how much
    _____C_____
    control she desires over composition and
            ____D_____
    exposure. No error
              ___E____

15. Neither high winds nor rain are expected on the
    ___A___   _B_ ____C_____
    Fourth of July, which means the fireworks show
              _____D____
    will likely take place. No error
                            ___E____

16. As an insect, the praying mantis is better known
                                       ____A_____
    for its cannibalistic eating habits than for how it
                                                __B__
    can disappear into foliage by camouflaging itself
    _____B_____   __C__
    to look like a leaf or twig. No error
                   ____D_____ ___E____

17. The cause of the South African War was disagree-
    ____A____   _B_
    ments between Boers and the British about
    whether British citizens that had settled around
                     ____C_____
    Johannesburg should be given the right to vote.
                  _____D_____
    No error
    ___E____

Directions: The sentences below test your knowledge of effective and correct expression. Use the conventions of written English to choose your answer: pay attention to choice of words (diction), punctuation, sentence structure, and grammar.

In each of the following sentences, either the entire sentence or part of the sentence is underlined. There are five versions of the underlined portion below the sentence. Choice (A) is the same as the original sentence, and choices (B)–(E) are different.

Choose the answer that produces the best sentence with the same meaning as the original sentence. If none of the alternatives are as effective as the original sentence, choose (A). The final sentence should be precise and unambiguous.

18. <u>While San Francisco is known for its architectural sights, many people visit Los Angeles for the beaches.</u>

    (A) While San Francisco is known for its architectural sights, many people visit Los Angeles for its beaches.
    (B) San Francisco is known for its architectural sights, but visiting Los Angeles is for its beaches.
    (C) The reason people visit San Francisco is for its architectural sights, Los Angeles beaches.
    (D) San Francisco is known for its architectural sights, Los Angeles for its beaches.
    (E) A city with beaches is Los Angeles, but San Francisco is known for its architectural sights.

19. <u>Poor planning made the meeting run three hours, which upset board members, and the facilitator of the meetings streamlined the agenda.</u>

    (A) Poor planning made the meeting run three hours, which upset board members, and the facilitator of the meetings streamlined the agenda.
    (B) After poor planning made the meeting run for three hours, upsetting board members, the facilitator of the meetings streamlined the agenda.
    (C) Poor planning, which made the meeting run three hours and upset board members, resulting in the facilitator of the meetings writing a more efficient agenda.
    (D) After poor planning makes the meeting run three hours and upsets board members, the facilitator of the meetings streamlined the agenda.
    (E) The agenda was streamlined by the facilitator of the meetings for the reason a three-hour meeting caused by poor planning upset board members.

GO ON TO THE NEXT PAGE

20. Theodore Dreiser, an American naturalist novelist who distanced himself from Victorian propriety and realistic fiction, best known for his critiques of the American dream and industrialization.

    (A) best known for his critiques of
    (B) best known for critiquing
    (C) is best known for his critique of
    (D) being best known for his critiques of
    (E) knew his critiques of

21. Microeconomics, a branch of economics that focuses on the interaction of individual economic units, concerning the behavior of consumers, producers, and the markets that bring the two together.

    (A) Microeconomics, a branch of economics that focuses on the interaction of individual economic units, concerning
    (B) It is microeconomics, a branch of economics that focuses on the interaction of individual economic units, concerning
    (C) Concerning microeconomics, a branch of economics that focuses on the interaction of individual economic units, was
    (D) Microeconomics, a branch of economics that focuses on the interaction of individual economic units, is concerned with
    (E) Concerned with microeconomics, a branch of economics that focuses on the interaction of individual economic units, is

22. After fuel and power shortages caused by World War I, a daylight saving time plan was adopted in England.

    (A) a daylight saving time plan was adopted in England
    (B) England adopted a daylight saving time plan
    (C) a daylight saving time was the plan of England
    (D) England's adoption of daylight saving became a plan
    (E) plans for daylight saving became increasingly adopted in England

23. In the early twentieth century, Picasso and others invented a new movement in modern art that immediately has distorted the individual figure and nature and eventually leads to the advent of nonobjective art.

    (A) that immediately has distorted the individual figure and nature and eventually leads to the advent of nonobjective art
    (B) with distorting the individual and nature and eventually leading to the advent of nonobjective art
    (C) that immediately distorts the individual figure and nature and leads to the advent of nonobjective art
    (D) that immediately distorted the individual figure and nature and led to the advent of nonobjective art
    (E) that immediately has distorted the individual figure and nature and has led to the advent of nonobjective art

24. In Cyprus, we toured many ancient archaeological sites, including ruins on the eastern coast, and these feature a theater, forum, and aqueduct that date back to the classical era.

    (A) including ruins on the eastern coast, and these feature a theater, forum, and aqueduct that date back to the classical era.
    (B) including ruins on the eastern coast by featuring a theater, forum, and aqueduct that date back to the classical era.
    (C) including ruins on the eastern coast and with a theater, forum, and aqueduct and dates back to the classical era.
    (D) including ruins on the eastern coast that feature a theater, forum, and aqueduct dating back to the classical era.
    (E) including ruins on the eastern coast that feature a theater, forum, and aqueduct while dating back to the classical era.

25. The first academy was founded by Plato in 387 B.C.E., and it was ostensibly committed to the study of the Muses, though in practice, Plato taught philosophy.

    (A) The first academy was founded by Plato in 387 B.C.E., and it
    (B) In 387 B.C.E., Plato founded the first academy and it
    (C) Founded by Plato in 387 B.C.E., the first academy
    (D) Founding the first academy in 387 B.C.E., Plato was
    (E) The year was only 387 B.C.E. when Plato founded the first academy, and it

26. In people with allergies, the body's defense system goes haywire, the antibodies that are produced to combat foreign substances end up attacking the body instead of protecting it.

    (A) system goes haywire, the antibodies
    (B) system goes haywire; the antibodies
    (C) system goes haywire being the antibodies
    (D) system goes haywire with the antibodies
    (E) system goes haywire so the antibodies

27. In J.M. Coetzee's novel, *Disgrace*, he explores ideas about humans' responsibility toward one another.

    (A) In J.M. Coetzee's novel, *Disgrace*, he explores ideas about humans' responsibility toward one another.
    (B) In *Disgrace*, J.M. Coetzee explores ideas about humans' responsibility toward one another.
    (C) In J.M. Coetzee's novel, *Disgrace*, ideas about humans' responsibility toward one another are explored.
    (D) *Disgrace* explores ideas about humans' responsibility toward one another in the novel by J.M. Coetzee.
    (E) J.M. Coetzee's novel, *Disgrace*, is a novel in which he explores ideas about humans' responsibility toward one another.

GO ON TO THE NEXT PAGE

28. The last lecture dealt with two classifications of deafness—congenitally deaf and adventitiously deaf—and explained why the distinction is important: it helps predict how easily a child will acquire language skills.

    (A) distinction is important: it helps predict how easily a child will acquire language skills
    (B) distinction is important: predicting how easily a child with acquire language skills
    (C) distinction is important: they help predict how easily a child will acquire language skills
    (D) distinction is important in the acquisition of language skills predicted in a child
    (E) distinction is important helping to predict how easily a child will acquire language skills

29. Mia's father often espoused to his children and any other young people who happened to be listening that success was a result of hard work, a few lucky breaks along the way, and graduating from a top-notch college.

    (A) a few lucky breaks along the way, and graduating from a top-notch college
    (B) getting a few lucky breaks along the way and graduating with good grades from a top-notch college
    (C) have a few lucky break along the way and graduate from a top-notch college
    (D) a few lucky breaks along the way, and graduation from a top-notch college
    (E) obtaining a few lucky breaks along the way and graduation from a top-notch college

30. When an odorous substance stimulates the olfactory cells, it has reached the inside of the nose and dissolved in the mucous lining.

    (A) When an odorous substance stimulates the olfactory cells, it has reached the inside of the nose and dissolved in the mucous lining.
    (B) An odorous substance reaches the inside of the nose, dissolves in the mucous lining, and stimulates the olfactory cells.
    (C) When an odorous substance reaches the inside of the nose and dissolves in the mucous lining, it stimulates the olfactory cells.
    (D) Stimulating the olfactory cells, an odorous substance reaches the inside of the nose and dissolves in the mucous lining.
    (E) Dissolving in the mucous lining, an odorous substance stimulates the olfactory cells by reaching the inside of the nose.

31. Anyone who lives in the United States, regardless of whether you studied history, should know that Thomas Paine is the author of *Common Sense*, which called for the American colonies to declare independence from Britain.

    (A) regardless of whether you studied history
    (B) regardless of education
    (C) regardless of whether they studied history
    (D) regardless of the study of history
    (E) irregardless of education

GO ON TO THE NEXT PAGE

32. While stilts are generally used by clowns and other performers for entertainment purposes, fruit pickers may wear them to avoid having to climb up and down ladders.

    (A) fruit pickers may wear them to avoid having to climb up and down ladders
    (B) they may also be worn by fruit pickers to avoid having to climb up and down ladders
    (C) fruit pickers avoid having to climb up and down ladders by wearing them
    (D) fruit pickers, who want to avoid climbing up and down ladders, may wear them
    (E) avoidance of climbing up and down ladders may lead fruit pickers to wear them

33. Because paper was invented in China in 105 C.E., the Chinese are the first to realize that paper could be used to make shades for lamps and lanterns as well as coverings for windows.

    (A) the Chinese are the first to realize
    (B) the Chinese first realize
    (C) the realization of the Chinese was
    (D) the Chinese were the first to realize
    (E) first realizing are the Chinese

34. Flattened by the recent tornado, the school district is meeting to discuss whether they must pass an emergency bond to raise funds to repair the middle school.

    (A) Flattened by the recent tornado, the school district is meeting to discuss whether they must pass an emergency bond to raise funds to repair the middle school.
    (B) Flattened by the recent tornado, the middle school is meeting to discuss whether they must pass an emergency bond to raise funds to repair the school district.
    (C) Flattened by the recent tornado was the middle school, and the school district is meeting to discuss whether they must pass an emergency bond to repair it.
    (D) The middle school was flattened by the recent tornado, which is why the school district is meeting to discuss whether they must pass an emergency bond to repair it.
    (E) The school district is meeting to discuss whether it must pass an emergency bond to raise funds to repair the middle school that was flattened by the tornado.

Directions: The passages below are first drafts of student essays. The sentences in each passage have been numbered. Parts of the essays require revision.

After reading each passage, answer the questions that follow. Some questions require you to improve sentences by changing word choice (diction) and sentence structure. Other questions ask you to review the entire essay or part of the essay and evaluate its organization, development, and the suitability of its language for the intended audience and purpose. Follow the rules of standard written English in your answer choices.

Questions 35–39 are based on the following draft of a student essay.

(1) I used to hate traveling. (2) I didn't see the point of visiting different places when everything and everyone I loved, except for my grandparents, were nearby. (3) Last year, however, my mother announced that we were going to spend the next year in Uganda in East Africa.

(4) I almost choked. (5) My mother, who is a professor, had an opportunity to work at the medical school in Kampala. (6) "In light of the growing disparities between industrialized and developing countries, volunteering is an obligation I must fulfill," she said. (7) "But what about my friends?" I wailed. "What about school?" (8) "It's just for nine months," she told me, "and I think it will be very educational."

(9) Even though adjusting to a new culture was difficult, my mother has the right instincts about what I would get out of the experience. (10) I attended an international school in Kampala with students hailing from countries located in Africa, Europe, and Asia. (11) My new friends introduced me to foreign food (like ugali, a starch that is a staple in Uganda), new traditions, and even new languages. (12) Even though we all looked different, dressed differently, and disagreed about whether American football is more exciting than soccer, we shared many things.

(13) When we left the United States, I was certain I would be miserable in Uganda. (14) When we left Uganda, I vowed to return as soon as I could. (15) Traveling truly expands your horizons.

35. Which of the following is the best way to revise the underlined portions of sentences 1 and 2 (reproduced below) so that the two sentences are combined into one?

    I used <u>to hate traveling. I didn't see</u> the point of visiting different places when everything and everyone I loved, except for my grandparents, were nearby.

    (A) to hate traveling because I didn't see
    (B) to hate traveling, and I didn't see
    (C) to hate traveling, though I didn't see
    (D) to hate traveling because not seeing
    (E) to hate traveling, not seeing the

36. Which of the following sentences, if added after sentence 3, would best link the first paragraph with the rest of the essay?

    (A) I was excited by the opportunity to have an adventure.
    (B) This made me change my opinions completely.
    (C) You can imagine my surprised reaction to the news.
    (D) I have lived in the same town for my whole life.
    (E) My mother had spent several years in East Africa when she was in the Peace Corps.

37. In the context of the third paragraph, which of the following is the best version of the underlined portion of sentence 9 (reproduced below)?

    Even though adjusting to a new culture was difficult, my mother has the right instincts about the experience.

    (A) No change
    (B) my mother having the right instincts
    (C) my mother had the right instincts
    (D) my mother is having the right instincts
    (E) my mother has had the right instincts

38. What is the main idea of the passage?

    (A) People have an obligation to do service in less wealthy countries.
    (B) Living abroad is the best way to understand a different culture.
    (C) Traveling increases your appreciation for the things you left behind at home.
    (D) Traveling is a good way to learn more about the world.
    (E) Traveling is stressful but brings you closer to your travel companions.

39. All of the following strategies are used by the writer of the passage EXCEPT

    (A) using an informal tone.
    (B) using personal experience to make a point.
    (C) using narrative strategies to explain the experience.
    (D) citing specific facts to back an argument.
    (E) showing a different point of view in the end.

Questions 40–45 are based on the following early draft of a letter to the editor of a local newspaper.

(1) Volunteering should be a mandatory part of every student's high-school education. (2) Doing service for others is a good way to teach teenagers empathy, the value of hard work, respect for diversity, and the meaning of community. (3) In contrast, a mandatory service program would help meet nonprofits' needs for more volunteers.

(4) A mandatory volunteer program would be easy to run. (5) Local service organizations, ranging from food cupboards to soup kitchens to tutoring programs, could put together a menu of volunteer needs. (6) Students could choose from the offerings, and schools could support the volunteering by giving students high-school credit for their work. (7) Teachers could act as liaisons between the students and volunteer organizations, supervising the students' service work.

(8) A mandatory volunteer program would address this issue by getting students into "real-world" situations. (9) We need this country's best and brightest young minds to begin thinking about problems like poverty and educational inequity. (10) The program I'm proposing will do this. (11) And it will go a long way toward instilling tolerance in young people by making them see that the less fortunate have names, faces, and stories. (12) Once they realize this, our young people won't be able to look past those in need.

(13) We have an opportunity to meet our community's desperate need for more volunteers and to shape our youth into civic-minded individuals; this is a win-win situation. (14) In closing, I hope you will urge the city council to support the mandatory volunteer program and to get our young people out of the classroom, where abstract ideas reign, and into the world, where they can make a difference.

40. Which of the following would best replace "In contrast" at the beginning of sentence 3?

    (A) At the same time
    (B) And
    (C) Therefore
    (D) Nevertheless
    (E) In short

41. The writer could best improve the first paragraph by

    (A) explaining why her letter on volunteering is relevant.
    (B) detailing her own volunteer experience.
    (C) revealing whether she teaches in the public schools.
    (D) citing statistics on the number of teenagers who currently volunteer.
    (E) anticipating what critics will say about her idea.

42. Which of the following sentences, if added before sentence 9, would provide the best transition to the third paragraph?

    (A) The real world is very complicated.
    (B) A mandatory volunteer program would be easy to implement with little cost to the schools.
    (C) Our current education system is inadequate and old-fashioned.
    (D) One oft-repeated criticism of our educational system is students don't learn skills relevant in today's world.
    (E) The gap between the rich and poor is increasing by an alarming rate in this country.

43. Which of the following would best replace "And" at the beginning of sentence 11?

    (A) Nevertheless
    (B) Furthermore
    (C) Instead
    (D) But
    (E) In general

44. In context, the best phrase to replace "do this" in sentence 10 is

    (A) cause this to happen.
    (B) get young people into their communities.
    (C) help social service agencies have greater success.
    (D) solve these problems immediately.
    (E) plant the seeds for a new generation of problem solvers.

45. Which is the best version of the underlined portion of sentence 13 (reproduced below)?

    We have an opportunity to meet our community's desperate need for more volunteers and to shape our youth into civic-minded individuals; this is a win-win situation.

    (A) No change
    (B) individuals, and this will be a win-win situation
    (C) individuals, this being a win-win situation
    (D) individuals, a win-win situation
    (E) individuals, this is a win-win situation

Questions 46–51 are based on the following early draft of a student essay about the Great Pyramid of Egypt.

(1) *The construction of the Great Pyramid in Egypt has been portrayed in many pictures and books.* (2) *These pictures showing Egyptian workers carrying bricks up the side of the pyramid are only legends.* (3) The difficulty of carrying the rocks up the side has been debated by top experts, who have proven that these pictures are false. (4) *The idea that one long ramp extending up the side of the large rectangular box would have been sufficient for moving materials is dubious.* (5) The ramp would have been a struggle to build itself and would have been too steep for workers to move up and down.

(6) Even if it had been possible for the workers to carry the stones up the tall ramp, which most experts doubt, building the ramp would have still remained an insurmountable challenge for Egyptian engineers. (7) Historians have calculated the amount of materials needed for a single ramp. (8) They found that it would have required more materials than were needed to build the entire pyramid.

(9) Many myths have surrounded the building of the Great Pyramid. (10) Some illustrations picture "teams of laborers hauling stones on sleds up a single giant earth ramp." (11) This theory has been rejected by many experts, including Peter Hodges. (12) He argued that "a single straight ramp connecting the quarry and the pyramid" would have been insufficient. (13) If hauling the stones "up a mile-long ramp had been practical," it would have been prohibitively expensive. (14) *Not only a "monumental engineering challenge," the ramp would have "required at least three times as much building material as the pyramid."*

46. Which of the following is the best way to revise the underlined portions of sentence 1 and 2 (reproduced below) so that the two sentences are combined into one?

    The construction of the Great Pyramid in Egypt has been portrayed in many pictures and <u>books. These pictures showing</u> Egyptian workers carrying bricks up the side of the pyramid are only legends.

    (A) books, however the pictures showing
    (B) books, showing these pictures
    (C) books, and the pictures showing
    (D) books, but having shown
    (E) while these picture have shown

47. Which of the following describes the weakness of the third paragraph in terms of the overall development of the essay?

    (A) It should follow the first paragraph instead of the third paragraph.
    (B) It is completely unrelated to the ideas developed in the first and second paragraphs.
    (C) It restates the theories described in the first and second paragraphs.
    (D) It contradicts the theories offered in the first and second paragraphs.
    (E) It should serve as the opening paragraph of the essay instead of the final one.

48. If the third paragraph were eliminated, where could you BEST use the quotes from the experts in sentence 14?

    (A) sentence 1
    (B) sentence 2
    (C) sentence 3
    (D) sentence 4
    (E) sentence 7

49. Which of the following is the best way to revise and combine sentences 11 and 12 (reproduced below)?

   This theory has been rejected by many experts, including Peter Hodges. He argued that "a single straight ramp connecting the quarry and the pyramid" would have been insufficient.

   (A) This theory has been rejected by many experts, including Peter Hodges, and he argued that "a single straight ramp connecting the quarry and the pyramid" would have been insufficient.

   (B) Rejected by many experts, including Peter Hodges, because it would have been insufficient is the theory of a "single straight ramp connecting the quarry and the pyramid."

   (C) The theory of a "single straight ramp connecting the quarry and the pyramid" has been rejected by experts and Peter Hodges because it would have been insufficient.

   (D) Arguing that "a single straight ramp connecting the quarry and the pyramid," experts, including Peter Hodges, reject the theory as insufficient.

   (E) Peter Hodges, along with other experts, rejects this theory, arguing that "a single straight ramp connecting the quarry and the pyramid" would have been insufficient.

50. Which of the following is the best way to revise the underlined portion of sentence 6 (reproduced below)?

   <u>Even if it had been possible for the workers to carry the stones up the tall ramp, which most experts doubt</u>, building the ramp would have still remained an insurmountable challenge for Egyptian engineers.

   (A) No change
   (B) Although it had been possible for the workers to carry the stones up the tall ramp, which most experts doubt
   (C) Most experts doubt it had been possible for the workers to carry the stones up the tall ramp
   (D) Given the possibility for the workers to carry the stones up the tall ramp, which most doubt
   (E) Even if it had been possible for the workers to carry the stones up the tall ramp, that most experts doubt

51. Which of the following is the best way to revise and combine sentences 7 and 8 (reproduced below)?

    Historians have calculated the amount of materials needed for a single ramp. They found that it would have required more materials than were needed to build the entire pyramid.

    (A) Historians have calculated the amount of materials needed for a single ramp and found that it would have required more materials than were needed to built the entire pyramid.

    (B) Building a single ramp would have required more materials than building the entire pyramid according to historians' calculations.

    (C) Calculating the amount of materials needed for a single ramp, it has been found by historians that it would have required more materials than building the entire pyramid.

    (D) Historians, in calculating the amount of materials for a single ramp, have found that it would have required more materials than building the entire pyramid.

    (E) In terms of the amount of materials needed for a single ramp, the calculations of historians show that it would have required more materials than were needed to build the entire pyramid.

Questions 52–56 are based on the following draft of a student essay.

(1) Although advertisements are designed to be deceptive, advertisers love the audience that doesn't question the message, the viewer who swallows the whole claim. (2) What's the claim? (3) It is the verbal or print part of the advertisement that makes the assertion that its product is superior. (4) You can either believe that the magician can make the elephant disappear—or learn to see through it.

(5) Claims run the gamut: a few are patently false, a few undeniably true, but most are worded so that it's hard to distinguish between the true and false. (6) Advertisers do this in an attempt to distinguish between products that are almost identical. (7) These are called parity products.

(8) The first rule in advertisement goes against common sense: "better" actually means "best," and "best" means "equal to." (9) That means that if the advertisement says, "Great Grape Soda is the best there is," it actually means "Great Grape Soda is as good as other sodas." (10) In contrast, "better" is still used as a comparative. (11) If an ad claims, "Great Grape Soda is better than other sodas," then Great Grape Soda is indeed superior to other sodas. (12) However, since it's impossible to prove that it is better than other sodas, the comparative is only used to compare products with things other than competing brands. (13) As an example, it would perfectly legal to say that "Great Grape Soda is better than fruit."

(14) Being bombarded by advertisements with messages aiming to deceive you, it is important that you learn to be a discriminating viewer who can see through the rhetoric.

52. The writer of the passage could best improve sentence 4 by

 (A) shortening the length of the sentence.
 (B) explaining the connection between elephants and claims.
 (C) switching from second person to third person.
 (D) being more descriptive.
 (E) using straightforward, concrete language.

53. Sentence 6 would improve if the writer

 (A) explained how it is possible for products to be similar.
 (B) added examples of some products that are almost identical.
 (C) offered a definition of parity products.
 (D) discussed what tactics advertisers use when products are different.
 (E) described some current advertisements.

54. Which of the following sentences, if added after sentence 7, would best complete the main idea explored in the second paragraph?

 (A) Disparity products are products that have nothing in common.
 (B) Because the products are so similar, advertisers resort to using misleading language to convince you that one product is better than another.
 (C) Companies spend tens of millions of dollars on advertising.
 (D) The next time you buy something, you should think about what influenced you to buy a particular product.
 (E) Another advertising strategy is to create a catchy jingle that you remember when you walk into a store.

55. Which of the following best describes the strategy used by the writer in the third paragraph?

    (A) using the story to illustrate an idea
    (B) explaining a concept by providing examples
    (C) providing the pros and cons of an argument to allow the reader to draw his or her own conclusion
    (D) offering information about the history of something to make sense of it
    (E) analyzing two products to explore different approaches to advertising

56. Which of the following is the best way to revise the underlined portion of sentence 14?

    Being bombarded by advertisements with messages aiming to deceive you, it is important that you learn to be a discriminating viewer who can see through the rhetoric.

    (A) Bombarding advertisements with messages aiming to deceive you, you must
    (B) Aiming to deceive you, the messages that bombard you, you need to
    (C) You are bombarded by advertisements with messages aimed to deceive you, it is important that you
    (D) Being bombarded by advertisements with messages aiming to deceive you, the important thing is to
    (E) Bombarded by advertisements with deceptive messages, you need to

Questions 57–62 are based on the following draft of an editorial in a school newspaper.

(1) Having attended public schools for last twelve years, I've earned the right to call myself an expert on school. (2) While it's true that there are many aspects of running schools and teaching that I don't understand, I've observed firsthand the effects of class size, especially the negative consequences of being in large classes. (3) For the past year, I was part of a pilot program in which students were broken into pods and taught in small, interdisciplinary classes with no more than fifteen students. (4) Now that I have returned to "regular school" and large classes, the advantages of small classes are shockingly clear to me.

(5) The learning environment in small classes leads to higher academic achievement. (6) Last year, it was the norm, rather than the exception, for all students to participate in class discussions. (7) Our teacher got to know each of us individually. (8) We developed mutual respect for each other and our teacher. (9) Moreover, because we were such a small class, our teacher had time to work with us one-on-one, and as everyone knows, this kind of individual instruction is invaluable. (10) Finally, the students in the class dug each other in a really cool way. (11) We organized a weekly study group, and the discussions we had in class often continued into the lunch hour.

(12) In my regularly sized classes, my passion for learning has disappeared, and I think many of my classmates share my sentiment. (13) Only a handful of students contribute their ideas in class discussions; it's impossible to meet one-on-one with our teachers; and it takes ages to get our graded papers returned to us. (14) Although I understand that the current budget squeeze has led to larger classes, if the school board really wants to improve education it should invest in small classes.

57. The writer of the editorial could strengthen sentence 4 by

(A) specifying the size of the large classes.
(B) clarifying the definition of "regular school."
(C) discussing the advantages of small classes.
(D) explaining why the pilot program ended.
(E) specifying the size of the small classes.

58. The writer could best improve the second paragraph by

(A) supporting the claims about the educational benefits of small classes with research.
(B) including the opinions of other students.
(C) discussing some of the disadvantages of small classes.
(D) specifying the subject and grade level of the class being discussed.
(E) exploring other changes that can have a positive effect on student achievement.

59. Which of the following is the best way to revise sentence 9 (reproduced below)?

    Moreover, because we were such a small class, our teacher had time to work with us one-on-one, and as everyone knows, this kind of individual instruction is invaluable.

    (A) Moreover, our teacher had time to work with us one-on-one because we were such a small class, and everyone knows this kind of individual instruction is invaluable.
    (B) Moreover, because we were such a small class, our teacher had time to give us invaluable one-on-one teaching instruction.
    (C) Moreover, being such a small class, our teacher gave us what everyone knows is the invaluable time to work one-on-one in this kind of individual instruction.
    (D) With time to work with us one-on-one, moreover, our teacher gave us individual instruction that is invaluable.
    (E) Moreover, our teacher had time to work with us one-on-one and give us invaluable instruction because we were such a small class.

60. In context, the best phrase to replace "dug each other in a realy cool way" in sentence 10 is

    (A) "became fast and furious friends."
    (B) "hung out all the time."
    (C) "bonded in a positive way."
    (D) "liked each other a lot."
    (E) "had a lot of fun."

61. The writer's strategy for organizing this passage is to

    (A) present one side of an argument and then refute it with the other side.
    (B) offer theories from many different experts.
    (C) ask a question in the beginning of the essay and then answer it.
    (D) compare and contrast two experiences to make a point.
    (E) identify a problem, explore different aspects of it, and present a solution.

62. Which of the following could be added after sentence 14 to help the writer strengthen her argument?

    (A) an anecdote from the writer's experience in small classes
    (B) evidence proving the value of small classes
    (C) an acknowledgment of the limitations of small classes
    (D) a quote from a school board member in support of small classes
    (E) a proposed solution for funding smaller classes

Directions: The questions below test your ability to revise sentences.

Each sentence below is followed by directions on how to revise it. Some directions require you to change the entire sentence, while others only require you to change part of the sentence. Words may be added or omitted so that the final version of the sentence is grammatically correct. The meaning of the revised sentence should be as close to the meaning of the original sentence as possible. The final sentence should follow the rules of standard written English.

Answer choices (A)–(E) contain words or phrases that could be used to revise the sentence. If you had a different revision to the sentence in mind, try to revise the sentence in a new way so that it includes the wording listed in the correct answer choice.

63. The elaborate sculptures and reliefs carved by the Mayans is one of the reasons anthropologists believe they had developed into a highly sophisticated culture.

    Begin with <u>Anthropologists believe</u>.

    (A) because of their elaborate sculptures and reliefs
    (B) in contrast to their elaborate sculptures and reliefs
    (C) and their elaborate sculptures and reliefs
    (D) resulting from their elaborate sculptures and reliefs
    (E) while their elaborate sculptures and reliefs

64. Owing to the lack of precipitation, the high temperatures, and the number of dead trees, the forest fire in the eastern part of the state was not contained by firefighters for three weeks.

    Begin with <u>Firefighters did not contain</u>.

    (A) so
    (B) because
    (C) although
    (D) while
    (E) and

65. The art historian noted that because of the political unrest during World Wars I and II, abstract art was rejected and surrealism and socially critical realism rose in its place.

    Change <u>abstract art was rejected</u> to <u>led to the rejection of abstract art</u>.

    (A) therefore the rise of
    (B) but the rise of
    (C) and the rise of
    (D) in rising
    (E) which rose

66. It is not impossible that campaign finance reform will keep big business from unduly influencing politicians.

    Change so that the sentence ends with a question mark instead of a period.

    (A) possibly
    (B) it not impossible
    (C) it not possible
    (D) the possibility
    (E) it impossible

GO ON TO THE NEXT PAGE

67. Because of the its reputation for exclusivity rather than inclusiveness, the pep club was put on probation by the principal for the rest of the school year.

    Begin with <u>Having concluded the pep club</u>.

    (A) are to be put on probation
    (B) its probation
    (C) had the pep club put on probation
    (D) they are put on probation
    (E) put it on probation

68. Palestine and Israel have been locked in an intractable stalemate, and American presidents and other world leaders have tried to end it without any success.

    Begin with <u>American presidents</u>.

    (A) have tried unsuccessfully to end
    (B) trying unsuccessfully to end
    (C) and tried unsuccessfully to end
    (D) unsuccessfully ending
    (E) with no success at ending

69. Most people who live in large apartment buildings in cities have little communication with their neighbors.

    Change <u>most people</u> to <u>few people</u>.

    (A) communicating
    (B) having communication
    (C) have communication
    (D) have little communication
    (E) have much communication

70. Arabesque designs that featured intertwining leaves and branches were drawn by artists in the Renaissance period who embellished everything from manuscripts to furniture to pottery.

    Begin with <u>Artists in the Renaissance period</u>.

    (A) and Arabesque designs that features
    (B) with the features of Arabesque designs
    (C) in featuring Arabesque designs
    (D) with Arabesque designs that featured
    (E) featuring Arabesque designs

71. Betsey's expected news about her promotion to district attorney filled her family with considerable pride.

    Change <u>filled</u> to <u>but it still filled</u>.

    (A) district attorney was expected
    (B) district attorney which was expected
    (C) district attorney, expecting
    (D) district attorney, despite being expected
    (E) district attorney wasn't expected

72. The work of Jane Austen and other female novelists has been dismissed by many male critics who don't recognize the significance of family and marriage in society.

    Begin with <u>Dismissing the work</u>.

    (A) many male critics not recognizing
    (B) many male critics that don't recognize
    (C) many male critics don't recognize
    (D) many male critics recognizing
    (E) many male critics recognize

GO ON TO THE NEXT PAGE

73. Our holiday feast was created by many people contributing the dishes that they remembered as their favorites from childhood.

    Begin with Many people contributed.

    (A) and our holiday feast was created
    (B) thus our holiday feast was created
    (C) and the creation of our holiday feast
    (D) to create our holiday feast
    (E) to creating our holiday feast

74. Strong organizational abilities, good writing skills, and a cheerful demeanor were the characteristics that the president was seeking in his new assistant.

    Change was seeking to sought.

    (A) cheerful demeanor being
    (B) cheerful demeanor in
    (C) cheerful demeanor having
    (D) cheerful demeanor that
    (E) cheerful demeanor of

75. The CEO said that, in light of increases in the cost of electricity, the company would shut down for a week over Christmas to save money.

    Change that, in light of to that increases.

    (A) electricity would cause
    (B) electricity would be the cause
    (C) electricity, causing
    (D) electricity would have the cause
    (E) electricity, and they have caused

76. When you consider how much levels of carbon dioxide and methane in the atmosphere have increased since the preindustrial age, you can understand why some scientists are concerned about global warming.

    Change you can understand to explain.

    (A) The fact of increasing level of carbon dioxide
    (B) In light of increasing levels of carbon dioxide
    (C) Due to increases in the level of carbon dioxide
    (D) On account of increasing levels of carbon dioxide
    (E) Increasing levels of carbon dioxide

77. The audience was presented with alarming statistics about the pace of temperature rise during the last century by the co-directors of the National Climatic Data Center.

    Begin with the Co-directors of the National Climatic Data Center.

    (A) were presented the audience
    (B) had presented the audience
    (C) caused the audience to be presented with
    (D) were prepared to present
    (E) presented the audience

78. If the hurricane reaches the eastern coast before diminishing in force, flash floods will occur and hundred of thousands of households will lose their electricity.

    Begin with Should the hurricane reach the eastern coast.

    (A) will be occurring
    (B) would have occurred
    (C) will have occurred
    (D) could occur
    (E) the occurrence would be

GO ON TO THE NEXT PAGE

Directions: The passages below consist of numbered sentences. These passages are taken from longer writing samples, so a complete discussion of all issues in the longer writing samples may not appear.

Read each passage and answer the questions below it. The questions for each passage test your understanding of the writer's purpose and the characteristics of good writing.

Questions 79–90 refer to the following passage.

(1) *American criticism of captivity narratives traditionally begins with Mary Rowlandson who was captured February 10, 1675, at Lancaster.* (2) *She returned to white civilization in May of the same year, and shortly thereafter wrote and published* The Sovereignty and the Goodness of God. (3) *Her text offered a seventeenth-century reader a complicated number of possibilities.* (4) *Reminiscent of a Puritan sermon, the text surely drew people for religious reasons.* (5) *The detailed descriptions of her Indian captor's life must have interested people concerned about Native Americans.* (6) *Still others may have read it purely for adventure's sake.* (7) *As a "novel" it offered a thrilling tale about a woman's survival among strangers in the howling wilderness.*

(8) *It's impossible to "extract" from the text what Rowlandson might have wanted her contemporaries to think.* (9) *Instead, her text offers contradictory images of a woman, trying to save herself and sanity in an unprecedented situation, among another culture and people.* (10) *Rowlandson shifts between recognizing her own strengths and becoming overwhelmed by her vulnerability.* (11) *Although her faith eases the hardships, sometimes Rowlandson expresses dissatisfaction, her restlessness and pain unassuaged by the Holy Word.* (12) *Rowlandson's relationship to her Indian captors is not straightforward either.* (13) *She vacillates between berating the Indians for their cruelty and admiring their ability to survive in an environment that has appeared to her only a desolate wilderness, grateful for the kindnesses they offer her.*

79. Which of the following best describes the relationship between the two paragraphs in this passage?

   (A) The first paragraph offers a generally held opinion and the second refutes it.
   (B) The first paragraph introduces Mary Rowlandson while the second describes her book.
   (C) The second paragraph provides evidence to support the first paragraph's assertion that there are many ways to read Rowlandson's book.
   (D) The first paragraph provides the historical context for understanding the description of Rowlandson's book in the second.
   (E) The first paragraph describes how others viewed Rowlandson's book while the second explores how she complicates a straightforward reading.

80. Which of the following could be added to the first paragraph to make the passage more clear?

   (A) a biography of Mary Rowlandson's life
   (B) a short explanation of the genre of the captivity narrative
   (C) a reference to when the book was published
   (D) an explanation of how others viewed the book
   (E) a description of Puritan sermons

81. Why is "novel" placed in quotations marks in sentence 7?

    (A) to call into question the traditional definition of the novel
    (B) to emphasize that Rowlandson's text has many novelistic qualities
    (C) to remind readers that Rowlandson's text was not truly a novel, even though it could be read for recreational reasons
    (D) to indicate that the author of the passage does not approve of calling Rowlandson's text a novel
    (E) to underscore the originality and creativity of Rowlandson's captivity narrative

82. Which treatment of sentence 9 is most needed?

    (A) No change
    (B) It should be omitted.
    (C) It should be placed after sentence 10.
    (D) "Instead" should be changed to "Therefore."
    (E) "Instead, her text offers contradictory images" should be changed to "Instead, a contradictory image is offered by her text."

83. The purpose of sentence 13 is primarily to

    (A) reinforce the idea of the complexity of representation expressed in sentence 9.
    (B) provide a counterexample to the assertion made at the beginning of the second paragraph.
    (C) present a specific example of the text's novelistic qualities.
    (D) refute the generalization presented in sentence 12.
    (E) indicate the reason for the shifts in Rowlandson's self-awareness described in sentence 10.

84. The author of this passage is attempting to illustrate the point that

    (A) Mary Rowlandson's text has been misinterpreted by readers for centuries.
    (B) Mary Rowlandson lacked the resources to overcome her captivity.
    (C) Mary Rowlandson was not very sympathetic to her captors.
    (D) Mary Rowlandson was a poor writer who wasn't in control of her meaning.
    (E) Mary Rowlandson's text defies easy interpretation.

Questions 85–90 refer to the following passage.

(1) *Suppression is the act of keeping back, restraining, checking.* (2) *Omission means to leave out or fail to include.* (3) *Remembering is the process of bringing an event, person, or thing to the mind again.* (4) *Both remembering and suppressing or omitting, though working in opposite directions, produce accounts that are half true at best.* (5) *When I moved back to Idaho in my early twenties to work as a reporter, I often told people that I was born and raised there, which was only a small part of the story.*

(6) *In fact, I had just graduated from Oxford University.* (7) *I had just flown across the Atlantic and traveled by train across Canada, reading the plays of England's greatest playwright, Shakespeare; the autobiography of a medieval mystic named Margery Kempe who lived in England, and the British magazine* Granta's *issue about journeys to far-flung, exotic places.* (8) *During the train trip, I read through the night, not glancing out the window, until the train climbed through the Rockies and started its slow, rhythmic slide to the Pacific Ocean.* (9) *Then, I started to panic.* (10) *Moving back to Idaho and taking up work as a reporter was a romantic idea to me.* (11) *It represented an idea that I possessed about myself as a westerner, what I remembered about my childhood in Idaho.* (12) *Whenever the talk at Oxford turned to subjects I didn't understand or didn't care to understand, like the fall of communism or tax cuts or New York private schools or Flemish painting, I withdrew, telling myself that I was a westerner, and we westerners were a different breed.* (13) *"I'm a cross between a barbed-wire fence and a wild coyote," my grandpa was fond of saying.* (14) *I thought I was, too, but the fact was my time outside of the state had changed me.*

85. Which of the following best describes the relationship between the two paragraphs in the passage?

    (A) The first paragraph introduces several ideas that the second paragraph explores.
    (B) The first paragraph introduces a thesis that the second paragraph contradicts.
    (C) The first paragraph offers a concrete experience that the second paragraph generalizes upon.
    (D) The first paragraph explains the meaning of remembering while the second paragraph explores the significance of forgetting.
    (E) The first paragraph is completely abstract while the second paragraph is personal.

86. Which of the following is the best summary of the second paragraph?

    (A) The author emphasizes how adrift she felt during her time at Oxford.
    (B) The author shows that she is relieved to be returning to Idaho.
    (C) The author admits that she is uncertain about her identity.
    (D) The author revels in her feelings about being an outsider.
    (E) The author indicates that reading is her favorite pastime.

87. Which of the following best describes the function of sentence 4?

 (A) It indicates how the process of remembering is always imperfect.
 (B) It draws a clear distinction between the acts of suppression or omission and remembering.
 (C) It alerts the reader to be suspicious of the truthfulness of the writer.
 (D) It alludes to the similarities between trying to forget something and trying to remember something.
 (E) It proves the author is telling the whole story when she says she is an Idaho native.

88. The books and magazines that the author reads on the train suggest that she

 (A) will not stop reading British literature even though she has left the country.
 (B) is trying to fill the hours of the long train ride across Canada.
 (C) enjoys British literature more than American literature.
 (D) is beginning to prepare for her work in Idaho as a reporter.
 (E) is very connected to England and the world she is leaving behind.

89. Which word best describes the writer's reaction to her homecoming?

 (A) confusion
 (B) excitement
 (C) comfort
 (D) fear
 (E) happiness

90. The main idea of this passage is that

 (A) moving back home is not complicated for the author.
 (B) it's difficult for the author to know who she is and where she belongs.
 (C) people's personalities are defined by where they grow up.
 (D) traveling by train allows time for important reflections.
 (E) memories are always wholly accurate.

END OF TEST. STOP

THE ANSWER KEY APPEARS ON THE FOLLOWING PAGE.

ANSWER KEY

1.	A	14.	C	27.	B	40.	A	53.	B	66.	C	79.	E
2.	B	15.	C	28.	A	41.	A	54.	B	67.	E	80.	B
3.	C	16.	B	29.	D	42.	D	55.	B	68.	A	81.	C
4.	B	17.	C	30.	C	43.	B	56.	E	69.	E	82.	A
5.	C	18.	D	31.	B	44.	E	57.	A	70.	D	83.	A
6.	D	19.	B	32.	B	45.	A	58.	A	71.	A	84.	E
7.	E	20.	C	33.	D	46.	A	59.	B	72.	C	85.	A
8.	C	21.	D	34.	E	47.	C	60.	C	73.	D	86.	C
9.	D	22.	B	35.	A	48.	E	61.	D	74.	B	87.	D
10.	C	23.	D	36.	C	49.	E	62.	E	75.	A	88.	E
11.	B	24.	D	37.	C	50.	A	63.	A	76.	E	89.	A
12.	A	25.	C	38.	D	51.	B	64.	B	77.	E	90.	B
13.	A	26.	B	39.	D	52.	E	65.	C	78.	D		

Answers and Explanations

1. (A)

The object in a sentence must be able to be substituted by the word "it." In this sentence, "his searching" and the prepositional phrases that follow it comprise the object of the sentence. The correct form of "it" would be "his search."

2. (B)

The sentence, as it appears, is incomplete because the verb "were" is part of the dependent clause: "which were originally grown in the Middle East." To correct the mistake, the "and" should be eliminated. "*Are* now cultivated" will serve as the verb.

3. (C)

Pronouns must agree in number and person with their antecedents (the words they replace). Since the antecedent is "Sarah Clark", the pronoun should be "her." The way the sentence currently is written, the pronoun "their" refers back to "politicians." The politicians were speculating about Sarah Clark's decision, not their own decision.

4. (B)

Verbs always agree with subjects. Here, the subject is "the members." Intervening words such as the prepositional phrase "of the Electoral College," should not be confused with the subject. In this case, since the subject is plural, the verb must take the plural form as well ("meet" instead of "meets").

5. (C)

This sentence is a run-on. "During the Middle Ages, monasteries were centers of learning with their own libraries and copying chambers" is one complete thought, and "here monks copied in beautiful calligraphy the great works of their age" is another. The two independent clauses can be connected (with "where") or separated with a semicolon or a period.

6. (D)

"Allusion" is defined as a reference to something such as a piece of literature, which doesn't make sense in the context of the sentence. The correct answer is "illusion," which means an unreal or misleading image. These two words are homonyms, or words that sound the same but are spelled differently and have different meanings.

7. (E)

This sentence is correctly written. Colons can be used as punctuation between two independent clauses when the second clause clarifies or adds meaning to the first. In this example, the first independent clause establishes a broad concept (the difference between fruits and vegetables), and the second independent clause clarifies the first and makes it more specific. Answer (C) looks attractive because it appears that the first letter after the colon should be capitalized. However, the only time that letter should be capitalized is if it is the beginning of a direct quote or if it is a proper noun.

8. (C)

"Each other" is used with two people. "One another" refers to more than two people. The sentence refers to "Lee and her friends," which adds up to at least three people. The comma after "system" in answer (B) is correct, because it sets off a clause that further defines the effects of the heat wave.

9. (D)

It's unnecessary to use the preposition "in" twice. The sentence could be simplified by revising it so it read, "Nutritional fads . . . were ubiquitous in the nineteenth century and twentieth century." Answer (A) looks attractive because the reader may think that "which" should replace "that." Either would technically be fine although "which" would require a comma preceding it.

10. (C)

The verb tense shifts in this sentence. Because the first verb ("had been working") is in the past perfect tense, the second verb ("locates") should be in the past tense. This indicates the order of events happening in the sentence. The scholar was working, and *then* she located the captivity narrative.

11. (B)

The "he" that comes after "and" is unnecessary, since the sentence has already established that the subject is "Frank Lloyd Wright." The sentence is perfectly grammatical and more economical if the second "he" is eliminated.

12. (A)

"Whom" is the correct form of the pronoun when referring to something being done to a person. Since the new student is being introduced by the teacher, the sentence should read, "whom our teacher introduced to us today in calculus class."

13. (A)

The correct form of the idiomatic phrase is "cut from the same cloth," not "cut in the same cloth." Remember that products are made from their materials, not in them. Answer (D) looks like it could be correct because the reader is thinking that each man has (currently) a different leadership style. But the sentence is saying that in the future, both men's terms will be over, at which time it will be apparent that they "had" different leadership styles.

14. (C)

Each item in a series needs to be grammatically alike, conforming to the pattern established by the first item, "what kind of pictures she wants to take." Since the first item is a phrase, the second item should also be written as a phrase: "what she needs in terms of mobility."

15. (C)

When the subject of a sentence consists of a plural noun ("high winds") and a singular noun ("rain") that are linked by "nor," the verb agrees with the noun closest to it. Therefore, the sentence should read, "Neither high winds nor rain is expected . . . ."

16. (B)

When two items are being compared, they must be written in a similar grammatical form. Since the first part of the comparison is written as a noun ("cannibalistic eating habits"), the second should also be written as a noun ("its ability to disappear"). One might think that answer (A) is the correct choice, because "better known" should be changed to "best known." However, only two traits are being compared and one is the better of the two, so "better known" is appropriate.

17. (C)

Whenever there is a phrase that modifies a person or people, the word "who" should be used. Inanimate objects and animals are referred to as "that." Therefore, the corrected phrase would read, "British citizens who had settled."

18. (D)

Items in a comparison must be grammatically alike. Since the name of a city (San Francisco) is the subject of the first clause, then "Los Angeles" should be the subject of the second clause. Once the two phrases are grammatically similar, the second one can also be simplified by eliminating the verb.

19. (B)

Answer (B) is correct because it shows the correct relationship between actions in the sentence. The long meeting caused the facilitator to streamline the agenda. The original sentence implies that the two things happened simultaneously.

20. (C)

The original sentence lacks a verb and is therefore incomplete. Correct the error by adding "is" before "best known" (C). Answers (A) and (B) both lack verbs, answer (D) uses the wrong verb form, and answer (E) makes little sense.

21. (D)

This original sentence is incomplete because "concerning" is not a complete verb. In this sentence, the correct form of the verb is "is concerned with," which makes answer (D) correct. Neither answers (A) nor (B) correct the problem, and answer (C) implies that microeconomics is an obsolete field of study, which it isn't. Answer (E) is unnecessarily convoluted.

22. (B)

It's usually better to write sentences in the active voice. This means stating early in the sentence who or what completed the action. In answers (A), (C), and (E), the subject ("England") does not appear until the end of the sentence. Answer (D) is very wordy. Therefore, the best answer is (B) which shows succinctly the relationship between the subject ("England") and the action ("adopted").

23. (D)
The sentence refers to something that happened in the past (as indicated by the verb, "invented"). All of the verbs, even those in the dependent clause, must agree. Answer (D) is the only option with all the verbs in the past tense.

24. (D)
The key to revising this sentence is to find the answer that most clearly shows the relationship between the descriptive clauses. The list of architectural sites (a theater, forum, and aqueduct") describes the ruins; therefore, the sights can be joined to "ruins on the eastern coast" by the subordinating conjunction, "that."

25. (C)
The original sentence is inefficiently written. Two independent clauses sharing the same subject ("the first academy" and "it") can usually be combined. Answer (B) also simplifies the original sentence, but answer (C) is less wordy.

26. (B)
The original sentence is a run-on. The two independent clauses ("In people with allergies, the body's defense system goes haywire" and "The antibodies that are produced to combat foreign substances end up attacking the body instead of protecting it") need to be separated by a period or semicolon or joined by a conjunction. Only answer (B) accomplishes this.

27. (B)
This question is tricky. Remember that pronouns have to refer back to their antecedents, or the nouns that they are replacing. Although "he" seems to refer to "J.M. Coetzee's novel," this doesn't make sense because the subject clearly is Coetzee himself. While answer (C) is not ungrammatical, it is wordy. Answer (B) conveys the same meaning efficiently written and eliminates the problem with the pronoun reference.

28. (A)
The way the sentence is written is correct. Colons can be used to separate independent clauses when the second clause clarifies something in the first. In answer (B), the clause following the colon is a fragment.

29. (D)
Remember that items in a series must be in the same grammatical form. The first and second items in the series ("hard work" and "a few lucky breaks") are nouns. That means the third item must also be a noun ("graduation from a top-notch college").

30. (C)
The original sentence is incorrect because the relationships between the actions are misstated. It implies that the odorous substance stimulates the olfactory cells before it reaches the inside of the nose. However, the odorous substance must reach the inside of the nose and dissolve in the mucous lining to stimulate the olfactory cells. The sentence that expresses this idea is answer (C).

31. (B)
The best way to answer this question is to use process of elimination. First, keep in mind that the pronoun and its antecedent must agree, or the pronoun must be eliminated so that there is no shift between them. Answers (A) and (C) are incorrect because the pronouns "you" and "they" do not agree with the subject "anyone." Answer (D) veers too much from the meaning of the original sentence, and answer (E) uses the nonstandard word, "irregardless." That means that answer (B) is the best choice. "Regardless of education" is nearly synonymous with "regardless of whether you studied history."

32. (B)
When you are comparing or contrasting two ideas, they should be written as grammatical equivalents. In the first item, the noun is "stilts." Therefore, to make the second half of the sentence parallel, the noun should remain "stilts," which makes answer (B) correct.

33. (D)
The verb tense has shifted in this sentence. Since the action happened in the past, all of the verbs in the sentence should be in the past tense. Answers (A), (B), and (E) all contain present-tense verbs, and answer (C) is clumsy and verbose.

34. (E)
The original sentence has a misplaced modifier so that it sounds like the school district was flattened by a recent

tornado. However, if you read the sentence carefully you should be able to determine that the middle school was flattened by the tornado, which is why the school district is meeting. Answer (E) best expresses this meaning. Answer (D) is overly wordy while answer (C) is ungrammatical.

35. (A)
The second sentence explains the first sentence, which means that there is a causal relationship between them. "Because" is the best word to express this relationship. Answers (B) and (C) do not express the correct relationship between the two ideas. Answer (D) is not grammatical.

36. (C)
The last sentence of a paragraph provides a summary and serves as a transition to the next paragraph. In this case, the best choice is answer (C) because it suggests how the author reacted to his mother's news, preparing the reader for the description in the next paragraph.

37. (C)
Because the author is describing an experience that happened in the past, the past tense (C) should be used throughout the sentence. Answer (B) is incomplete. Answer (D) suggests that the action is ongoing, and answer (E) implies the action is happening in the present.

38. (D)
The best way to answer this question is to use process of elimination. Answer (A) is a detail from the essay, but not the main idea. Answer (B) is tricky because the author does learn about different cultures, but he doesn't try to persuade that living abroad is the best way to do this. The essay never mentions anything about answers (C) or (E). Therefore, the best answer is (D). As the author writes at the end of the essay, "Traveling truly expands your horizons."

39. (D)
This is mostly a personal essay. The author uses an informal tone, describes his experiences to show he learned the value of traveling, offers pieces of the dialogue he had with his mother, and shows how his attitudes toward traveling changed by the end of the essay. The only strategy he does not use is citing facts (D).

40. (A)
Because the author is trying to describe how a mandatory volunteer program would meet two different needs simultaneously, the best choice is answer (A). While "And" (B) isn't ungrammatical, it's more precise to say that the two things can happen at the same time.

41. (A)
By the final paragraph, the reasons for the author to write this letter are clear: the city council is considering some kind of plan for a mandatory volunteer program. Knowing this information in the first paragraph would make the occasion for the letter clearer and the letter more persuasive.

42. (D)
Sentence 8 refers to an issue and says it would be solved by getting students involved in "real-world" situations. Since you know the correct answer is related to the real world, the best choice is answer (D) since it refers to students' need to learn skills that are "relevant in today's world."

43. (B)
The author is discussing the positive benefits of the program in sentences 8, 9, 10, and 11. That means the ideas are related, and you need a transitional word that shows this. Answers (A), (C), and (D) suggest that the final idea is different from the previous ones, which isn't true. Answer (E) prepares the reader for a generalization that doesn't occur. The best choice, therefore, is answer (B) because it signals that another positive benefit will be noted.

44. (E)
In sentence 9, the author suggests that a mandatory volunteer program will give young people the opportunity to begin exploring social problems. With this in mind, look at each of the answer choices. Answer (A) is just as vague as the original sentence. Answer (B) is not specific enough. Answer (C) is not related to the young volunteers. Answer (D) is focused on the present while sentence 9 is focused on the future. Therefore, the best answer is (E). If the country's best and brightest young minds begin thinking about social problems, the seeds will be planted for a new generation of problem solvers.

45. (A)

The sentence, as it is currently written, is correct. A semicolon is correct punctuation for separating two independent but closely related clauses. Answer (A) is a run-on, and answer (B) is unnecessarily set in the future tense. Answer (C) is verbose and in answer (D), the phrase "a win-win situation" mistakenly describes the last noun, "individuals," which is inaccurate.

46. (A)

The use of the word "legends" in the second sentence tells you that the second sentence qualifies the first. Whatever pictures you may have seen depicting the construction of the Great Pyramid are only "legends." Answers (A) and (E) both begin with words that signal contrasting ideas ("however" and "while"), but answer (E) is not grammatically correct.

47. (C)

The third paragraph's weakness is that it is repetitive (C). It simply restates the myths about the construction of the Great Pyramid and describes why they are false. The only difference is that it includes quotes from experts.

48. (E)

Since sentence 7 discusses the amount of materials that would have been needed to build a ramp, and Peter Hodges' quote refers to the same issue, the material in sentence 14 could be used to support the assertion in sentence 7.

49. (E)

To answer this question, read each answer choice, paying attention to which one expresses the same ideas as the original efficiently and grammatically. The relationship between the two independent clauses is unclear in answer (A). Answers (B) and (C) are awkwardly worded. Answer (D) is incorrect because the ramp is insufficient, not the theory.

50. (A)

The sentence is correctly written. The clause "which most experts doubt" is correctly placed to qualify the idea of the workers carrying the stones up the ramp. Answer (B) contradicts itself, first saying that it was possible for workers to carry the stones up the ramp, and then saying that experts doubt it was possible.

51. (B)

The key to answering this question is to look for the answer that is grammatical, economical, AND faithful to the meaning of the original two sentences. Eliminate answer (C) because it contains a dangling modifier. Answers (D) and (E) are wordy. Finally, although there is nothing ungrammatical about answer (A), it is not as economical as answer (B).

52. (E)

The image used by the writer in sentence 4 is unclear. Since the essay is mostly informational, and not creative, the writer would be better off using more straightforward language that matches the style of the rest of the essay.

53. (B)

The reader would have a better understanding of parity (or nearly identical) products if the writer illustrated the concept with a few examples. Using examples is always a good way to explain abstract concepts.

54. (B)

The best way to answer this question is to use process of elimination. Eliminate answer (A) because "disparity products" is not related to the article. Eliminate answer (C) because the article is not about the size of different companies' advertising budgets. Eliminate answers (D) and (E) because they would be more relevant if they appeared in paragraph 1. That leaves you with answer (B), which is the best choice because it explains why advertisers use language that goes against common sense.

55. (B)

The writer uses the example of "Great Grape Soda" to show how advertisers manipulate common comparisons so that they can say things about their products that are not necessarily true.

56. (E)

Answer (E) simplifies the descriptive phrases without compromising the meaning of the original sentence. Answers (A), (C), and (D) are grammatically incorrect, and answer (B) is awkwardly worded.

57. (A)

Since the writer is discussing class size, and she has specified the size of the small classes she attended in her pilot program, it would be helpful to know the size of the large classes to which she is drawing her comparison. Expanding on the other topics would not help clarify the points she is making in that part of her essay.

58. (A)

The writer does an excellent job of presenting her experience in a small class, but she could strengthen her argument by including support from educational researchers. Objective facts would validate what she has observed.

59. (B)

The original sentence can be simplified by combining "one-on-one" with "individualized instruction." Since these two phrases refer to the same thing, it's possible to compress the two independent clauses as long you don't lose any meaning. That means you need to make sure you keep the idea that individualized instruction is "invaluable." Answer (B) accomplishes this: it is economical, clear, and grammatically correct.

60. (C)

The tone of this essay is mostly formal and informational. "Dug each other in a really cool way," however, is much more informal. Answers (B), (D), and (E) are also informal ways of describing relationships, and answer (A) makes no sense, as a friendship cannot be "fast and furious." Answer (C) most closely matches the tone of the essay.

61. (D)

The author discusses her experiences in a small class and a large class, drawing implicit comparisons between the two. The author does not examine two sides of an argument (A), offer anybody's theories but her own (B), ask a question and answer it (C), or identify a problem and then present its solution (E).

62. (E)

The best way to make a persuasive argument is to anticipate all of the arguments the other side might make. If the school board can't offer small classes because of budget constraints, it would be very good for the author to address funding issues in the essay.

63. (A)

What is the relationship between anthropologists' belief in the Mayans' sophisticated culture and the Mayans' elaborate sculptures and reliefs? It's a causal relationship to which the sculptures and reliefs provide evidence. "Because" is the only subordinating conjunction that shows causality, and therefore answer (A) is correct. The restructured sentence would be:

"Anthropologists believe that the Mayans had developed a highly sophisticated culture because of their elaborate sculptures and reliefs."

64. (B)

In this revision, you must choose the word that establishes the correct relationship between firefighters' inability to contain the fire and the causes of the fire. Answer (A) is incorrect because "so" suggests that the second half of the sentence happened as a consequence of the first. Answers (C) and (D) are incorrect because "although" and "while" imply the two parts of the sentence contrast with one another. Answer (E) does not establish the relationship between the independent and dependent clause. That means (B) is the correct answer because one thing happened as a result of another thing. The restructured sentence would be:

"Firefighters did not contain the forest fire in the eastern part of the state for three weeks because of lack of precipitation, high temperatures, and the number of dead trees."

65. (C)

In the revision, the verb "was rejected" has been changed into a noun, "rejection." To keep the construction parallel, the second verb, "rose", should also appear in the noun form. Answer (C) is correct because "rose" appears as a noun ("the rise"), and the sentence expresses that the rejection of abstract art and the rise of surrealism and socially critical realism occurred at the same time. The restructured sentence would be:

"The art historian noted that the political unrest during World Wars I and II led to the rejection of abstract art and the rise of surrealism and socially critical realism."

66. (C)

The original sentence suggests the possibility that campaign finance reform will work. To turn the statement into a question, it needs to begin with "is." If you try each of the answer choices with "is," it's clear that (C) is correct because it expresses the idea (in the form of a question) that campaign finance reform is possible. The restructured sentence would be:

"Is it not possible that campaign finance reform will keep big business from unduly influencing politicians?"

67. (E)

The revision means that the principal becomes the subject of the sentence, and the verb must agree with it. The restructured sentence would be:

"Having concluded the pep club was exclusive rather than inclusive, the principal put it on probation for the rest of the year."

68. (A)

Beginning with "American presidents" simplifies the sentence, combining two independent clauses into one. In the correct answer, the verb agrees with the new subject and expresses what American presidents have been trying to accomplish with respect to Palestine and Israel. The restructured sentence would be:

"American presidents and other world leaders have tried unsuccessfully to end the intractable stalemate between Palestine and Israel."

69. (E)

If most people have little communication, then few people have much communication. The correct answer reflects this relationship, even though the subject has been changed. The restructured sentence would be:

"Few people who live in large apartment buildings in cities have much communication with their neighbors."

70. (D)

The revision calls for beginning with the subject and putting the sentence into the active voice. The restructured sentence would be:

"Artists in the Renaissance period embellished everything from manuscripts to furniture to pottery with Arabesque designs that featured intertwining leaves and branches."

71. (A)

If you revise the sentence using "but" you know you must end up with two independent clauses that oppose each other. Answer (A) is the only option that turns the first part of the sentence into a clause that can stand on its own. The restructured sentence would be:

"Betsey's news about her promotion to district attorney was expected, but it still filled her family with considerable pride."

72. (C)

Who is dismissing the work of Jane Austen? Male critics. To make the sentence grammatical, "male critics" must follow the modifier. It must serve as the beginning of an independent clause. Answers (C) and (E) are the only two choices with verbs that make the sentence complete. Answer (E) expresses the opposite meaning of the original sentence. The restructured sentence would be:

"Dismissing the work of Jane Austen and other female novelists, male critics don't recognize the significance of family and marriage in society."

73. (D)

The revision forces you to rewrite the sentence in the active voice. Answers (A) and (B) are both written in the passive voice, and answers (C) and (E) are not grammatically correct. The restructured sentence would be:

"Many people contributed their favorite childhood dishes to create our holiday feast."

74. (B)

The revision means that the sentence must begin with "the president" and list the qualities that he was seeking. The restructured sentence would be:

"The president sought strong organizational abilities, good writing skills, and a cheerful demeanor in his new assistant."

75. (A)

Because of the changes, the new sentence must show the effect of the increases in electricity costs on the company. In other words, the increased costs "would cause" the shutdown. The restructured sentence would be:

"The CEO said that increases in the cost of electricity would cause the company to shut down for a week over Christmas to save money."

76. (E)

By changing the verb, you need to change the phrase "how much levels of carbon dioxide and methane in the atmosphere have increased" to a noun, "increasing levels of carbon dioxide . . . ." The restructured sentence would be:

Increasing levels of carbon dioxide and methane in the atmosphere since the preindustrial age explains why some scientists are concerned about global warming.

77. (E)

By beginning with the subject, the sentence must be written in the active voice. The restructured sentence would be:

"Co-directors of the National Climatic Data Center presented the audience with alarming statistics about the pace of temperature rise during the last century."

78. (D)

Since the sentence begins with "should" the rest of the sentence must be written using the conditional tense, "could." The restructured sentence would be:

"Should the hurricane reach the eastern coast before diminishing in force, flash floods could occur and hundreds of thousands of households could lose their electricity."

79. (E)

Answer choices (C) and (E) both might seem correct at first glance; however, answer (C) is not entirely accurate. The first paragraph doesn't merely assert that Mary Rowlandson's book offers different readings. Instead, it actually presents some of the ways that early readers might have viewed it. That means that both paragraphs discuss ways of understanding the book, the first from readers' perspectives, and the second from Rowlandson's own contradictory descriptions of herself.

80. (B)

The first paragraph implies but never actually offers a definition of captivity narratives. Since this essay deals with a captivity narrative, having a clear explanation of what they are would be helpful. While the other answers may provide some insight, the genre the piece belongs to would tell the most about its age and the environment in which it was written.

81. (C)

Quotation marks are often used to call something into question. Here, as answer (C) states, the question marks emphasize that Rowlandson's narrative was not a fictional piece of work. There is no questioning of the traditional definition of the novel (A). The quotation marks do not emphasize the work's novelistic qualities (B) or its originality and creativity (E). The quotes do not reflect the author's personal feelings of approval or disapproval (D).

82. (A)

Although sentence 9 is quite long, it is in the correct place in the essay and does not need to be changed. Since the sentence introduces the idea of Rowlandson's instability, it wouldn't make sense to place it after sentence 10.

83. (A)

Sentence 13 is an example of the complex way that Rowlandson characterizes herself, and therefore it provides evidence for the assertion made in sentence 9. It does not provide a counterexample to the previously made statement (B) or refer to the text's novelistic qualities (C). Neither does it refute the statement made in sentence 12 (D) nor provide a reason for her change in self-awareness (E).

84. (E)

The best way to answer this question is through process of elimination. Although the author says that Rowlandson's book has been interpreted many different ways, she doesn't say it has been misinterpreted (A). It's also clear from the examples that Rowlandson vacillates between different emotions during her captivity, so neither answer (B) nor answer (C) is a good choice. Finally, the author never comments on Rowlandson's writing abilities (D). That means answer (E) is correct.

85. (A)

In the first paragraph, the author explores the idea of how we remember and forget the past, and how this shapes who we are. In the second paragraph, she explores how these ideas are relevant to her life.

86. (C)

In the second paragraph, the author discusses feeling out of place in Oxford, but also confesses her anxiety about returning to her home. As a result, she is uncertain about her identify.

87. (D)

Sentence 4 indicates that suppressing information and remembering things are similar because neither presents an entirely accurate picture of the situation. It does not refer only to the process of remembering (A) and does not differentiate among suppression, omission, and remembering (B). It certainly doesn't warn the reader to beware of the writer's truthfulness (C) and, contrary to answer (E), states clearly that the author is not telling the whole story.

88. (E)

Since the author is reading books that are all by British authors or related to travel, it suggests that she is still connected to England. Answer (A) simplifies the emotions the writer is feeling toward England and her time spent there. The author does not mention boredom or a need to fill hours (B) and does not downplay the value of American literature (C). There is also no indication that the books she is reading will contribute to her work as a journalist (D).

89. (A)

The author returns several times to her feeling of not knowing who she is or where she belongs. This suggests that returning home has caused her to feel confused. She was once familiar with her home state, but hasn't lived there in a long time and fears that she may have lost touch with it. This mixture of feelings—both gratitude to be home and fear that she will not fit in—is best described as confusion.

90. (B)

When the author feels out of place in Oxford, she attributes this to being a westerner. But as she is returning to Idaho, she is uncertain about whether she will feel at home there. You can conclude from this that the author is having trouble determining who she is and where she belongs.

Section Two: The CLEP English Composition Exam | 137

Chapter Seven: Practice Test 3

PART I
Time—45 minutes
50 Questions

Directions: Each sentence below tests your knowledge of diction (choice of words), idiom, grammar, and usage. Some sentences are correct, and each sentence can contain no more than one error.

Elements of the sentence that are underlined and lettered may be incorrect. Parts of the sentence that are not underlined can be assumed to be correct. When choosing an answer, follow the rules of written English.

If a sentence contains an error, select the <u>one underlined portion</u> that must be changed in order to form a correct sentence. For sentences with no error, choose answer (E).

1. <u>Neither</u> the attorney <u>nor</u> the client <u>were</u> <u>pleased</u>
     A   B   C   D
   <u>with</u> the outcome of the trial. <u>No error</u>
    D   E

2. <u>There was</u> a brief silence <u>in the room</u> after the
       A   B
   windows <u>was broken by</u> a <u>falling</u> branch. <u>No error</u>
            C   D   E

3. Margaret <u>told</u> Leticia that <u>she</u> could not <u>continue</u>
            A   B   C
   in <u>her present</u> job. <u>No error</u>
      C   D   E

4. The group <u>marveled at</u> the <u>tour guide's</u> fluency in
               A   B
   Chinese, <u>her</u> knowledge of history, and <u>how well</u>
          C   D
   <u>she managed</u> to keep them on a tight schedule.
       D
   <u>No error</u>
     E

5. <u>It was discovered</u> <u>the following day</u> that the fire
        A   B
   alarm <u>had not been</u> a drill <u>but resulted from</u> some
            C   D
   burned toast in the staff lounge. <u>No error</u>
                                     E

6. For <u>hour after hour</u>, <u>jolting along</u> the bumpy road,
         A   B
   leaving <u>both passenger and driver</u> <u>exhausted and</u>
               C   D
   <u>nauseous</u>. <u>No error</u>
     D   E

7. <u>Between</u> you and <u>I</u>, Julia's novel <u>is</u> the <u>worst</u> thing
      A   B   C   D
   I've ever read! <u>No error</u>
                   E

8. Though the attorney requested a summary <u>of</u> ten
                                                     A

   pages or <u>less</u>, her assistant <u>found that</u> he needed
           B   C

   twelve pages to convey the complexities <u>in</u> the
                                                D

   case. <u>No error</u>
             E

9. Nora was frustrated <u>to discover</u>, <u>upon arriving</u> at
                       A   B

   the theater box office, that <u>tickets</u> <u>sold</u> out earlier
                               C   D

   that day. <u>No error</u>
                 E

10. <u>Since</u> many <u>remain committed to</u> the city funding
        A   B

    proposal <u>as it stands</u>, others are convinced that it
              C

    will not <u>succeed in improving</u> the deficit. <u>No error</u>
                  D   E

11. The student radio station recently <u>aired</u> <u>a news</u>
                                       A   B

    story <u>where</u> the reporter exposed the <u>infighting</u>
      B   C   D

    <u>among</u> the board members. <u>No error</u>
       D   E

12. The number of vehicles <u>on the road</u> <u>that</u> <u>are</u>
                              A   B   C

    <u>considered</u> trucks <u>have</u> increased dramatically in
        C   D

    the last ten years. <u>No error</u>
                        E

13. The young man missed <u>his</u> bus <u>and</u> <u>had been</u>
                       A   B   C

    <u>slowed</u> down <u>by</u> his sprained ankle. <u>No error</u>
      C   D   E

14. The safety measures <u>imposed by school adminis-</u>
                                  A

    <u>trators</u> <u>have improved</u> the learning <u>environment,</u>
      A   B   C

    however, students' grades have declined since they
       C

    took effect. <u>No error</u>
      D   E

15. Terrycloth, which <u>consists of</u> looped cotton fiber,
                       A

    <u>and becomes</u> <u>more absorbent</u> <u>as the loops get</u>
        B   C   D

    longer. <u>No error</u>
      D   E

GO ON TO THE NEXT PAGE →

Directions: The sentences below test your knowledge of effective and correct expression. Use the conventions of written English to choose your answer: pay attention to choice of words (diction), punctuation, sentence structure, and grammar.

In each of the following sentences, either the entire sentence or part of the sentence is underlined. There are five versions of the underlined portion below the sentence. Choice (A) is the same as the original sentence, and choices (B)–(E) are different.

Choose the answer that produces the best sentence with the same meaning as the original sentence. If none of the alternatives are as effective as the original sentence, choose (A). The final sentence should be precise and unambiguous.

16. After spending so much time with her new puppy, <u>going back to work was an abrupt change for Candace</u>.

    (A) going back to work was an abrupt change for Candace
    (B) Candace found going back to work to be an abrupt change
    (C) for Candace, going back to work was an abrupt change
    (D) to go back to work was an abrupt change for Candace
    (E) Candace's going back to work was an abrupt change

17. Both Tina and Mario have exhibited their artwork in galleries, but <u>only one of the two have had commercial success</u>.

    (A) only one of the two have had commercial success
    (B) only one of the two artworks are commercially successful
    (C) only one of the two artworks has had commercial success
    (D) only one of the two has had commercial success
    (E) one only had been successfully

18. Although Mr. Stern supervises the research project, <u>he has no training in the social sciences and has never designed a project of his own</u>.

    (A) he has no training in the social sciences and has never designed a project of his own
    (B) he has no training in the social sciences and has never designed one
    (C) he has no training in the social sciences nor has designed a project of his own
    (D) it is without training in the social sciences or designing a project of his own
    (E) it is without the benefit of training or designing projects

19. As a young man, Robert dreamed of working with the heart transplant team at the university hospital, <u>because they have earned a reputation for providing cutting-edge care</u>.

    (A) because they have earned a reputation for providing cutting-edge care
    (B) because they have earned a reputation for providing cutting edge care
    (C) because it has earned a reputation for providing cutting-edge care
    (D) having earned a reputation for providing cutting-edge care
    (E) because they had earned a reputation and provide cutting-edge care

GO ON TO THE NEXT PAGE

20. The National Oceanic Atmospheric Administration predicted that 2004 will be a particularly busy hurricane season.

    (A) 2004 will be a particularly busy hurricane season
    (B) the year of 2004 will be a particularly busy hurricane season
    (C) 2004's will be a particularly busy hurricane season
    (D) 2004 being a particularly busy hurricane season
    (E) 2004 would be a particularly busy hurricane season

21. The many varieties of coffee from around the world offering Coffee Emporium's customers an endless, diverse selection.

    (A) offering Coffee Emporium's customers an endless, diverse selection
    (B) offering Coffee Emporium's customers and endlessly diverse selection
    (C) offer Coffee Emporium's customers an endless, diverse selection
    (D) offer the customers of Coffee Emporium and endless, diverse selection of coffee
    (E) offers Coffee Emporium's customers an endless, diverse selection

22. In the first half of the twentieth century, Albert Einstein presented scientific theories, which radically changed the way scientists think of the world and continues to provide new problems for them to explore.

    (A) which radically changed the way scientists think of the world and continues to provide new problems for them to explore
    (B) which radically changed the way scientists think of the world and continue to provide new problems for them to explore
    (C) which radically changed the way scientists think of the world and which continues to provide new problems for them to explore
    (D) which radically changed the way scientists think of the world having provided new problems for them to explore
    (E) which, by radically changing the way scientist think of the world, continued to provide new problems for them to explore.

23. *Don Quixote*, by Miguel Cervantes, is the quintessential example of a picaresque novel, consisting of a series of adventures undertaken by the main character.

    (A) consisting of a series of adventures undertaken by the main character
    (B) and a series of adventures undertaken by the main character is narrated
    (C) and with this was the serialization of adventures undertaken by the main character
    (D) it consists of a series of adventures undertaken by the main character
    (E) consisting a series of adventures undertaken by the main character

GO ON TO THE NEXT PAGE

24. The new manager's ability <u>for resolving conflicts was put to the test when two employees quarreled over who would close that night</u>.

    (A) for resolving conflicts was put to the test when two employees quarreled over who would close that night
    (B) for resolving conflicts was put to the test when two employees quarreled regarding who would close that night
    (C) for resolving conflicts was put to the test when two employees quarreled over who will be closing that night
    (D) for resolving conflicts was put to the test when two employees were quarreling over who would close that night
    (E) to resolve conflicts was put to the test when two employees quarreled over who would close that night

25. Scientists have used the Hubble telescope to photograph star clusters, <u>and they reveal a great deal about star development because all their stars are the same age</u>.

    (A) and they reveal a great deal about star development because all their stars are the same age
    (B) and they reveal a great deal about star development, all their stars being the same age
    (C) and the star clusters reveal a great deal about star development because all their stars are the same age
    (D) which reveal a great deal about star development because all their stars are the same age
    (E) revealing a great deal about star development because all their stars are the same age

26. <u>Among the most ferocious animals is the polar bear</u>, a mammal that can reach the height of an elephant when standing on its hind legs.

    (A) Among the most ferocious animals is the polar bear
    (B) Among the most ferocious animals are the polar bear
    (C) Among the most ferocious animals is polar bears
    (D) Between the most ferocious animals is the polar bear
    (E) Included in the most ferocious animals is the polar bear

27. Not only did the peoples of the Arab empire adopt the Indian concept of zero, <u>they also made great advances in philosophy and medicine</u>.

    (A) they also made great advances in philosophy and medicine
    (B) these peoples also made great advances in philosophy and medicine
    (C) but they also made great advances in philosophy and medicine
    (D) additionally making great advances in philosophy and medicine
    (E) they also accomplished great advances in philosophy and medicine

28. The most innovative quality of modern poetry is not so much the urban themes the poems explore, but the nontraditional forms being used.

   (A) but the nontraditional forms being used
   (B) but the nontraditional forms they use
   (C) but the nontraditional forms being used by the poems
   (D) but that the poems use nontraditional forms
   (E) but rather the nontraditional forms being used

29. The Los Angeles Dodgers were originally from Brooklyn, New York, where they were first known as the Trolley Dodgers.

   (A) where they were first known as the Trolley Dodgers
   (B) having been known there as the Trolley Dodgers
   (C) where people first knew them as the Trolley Dodgers
   (D) being known as the Trolley Dodgers
   (E) and it was then that they were first known as the Trolley Dodgers

30. Whether the woman actually committed the crime or did not remains a mystery, but she has been convicted and sentenced.

   (A) Whether the woman actually committed the crime or did not
   (B) Whether in reality the woman committed the crime or did not commit it
   (C) The truth of whether the woman committed the crime or not
   (D) Whether or not the woman actually committed the crime
   (E) That the woman really might have committed the crime

Directions: The passages below are first drafts of student essays. The sentences in each passage have been numbered. Parts of the essays require revision.

After reading each passage, answer the questions that follow. Some questions require you to improve sentences by changing word choice (diction) and sentence structure. Other questions ask you to review the entire essay or part of the essay and evaluate its organization, development, and the suitability of its language for the intended audience and purpose. Follow the rules of standard written English in your answer choices.

Questions 31–35 are based on the following early draft of a student essay.

(1) *I used to hate exercise.* (2) *I was the one in gym class who played sick to avoid running the mile.*

(3) *Two years ago, my Aunt Sarah got breast cancer.* (4) *It was a real scare for all of us.* (5) *She had surgery then went through chemotherapy.* (6) *Now, she is a survivor.* (7) *To celebrate, last year she decided to participate in a triathlon that benefits breast cancer survivors.* (8) *She asked my cousin Leah, my mother, and I to participate too.*

(9) *I couldn't possibly say no.* (10) *I knew I'd hate it and would probably finish last.* (11) *My mother suggested that we start swimming together—at least it isn't as bad as running.* (12) *We made it a habit to go to the pool every other day to swim half a mile.* (13) *Then, my mother suggested all four of us go on a bike ride together.* (14) *It was actually a lot of fun.* (15) *We started going every week.* (16) *My Aunt Sarah had to force me to go running with her.* (17) *We started with a half a mile.* (18) *I huffed and puffed and was sweating, but I did it.*

(19) *By the time the triathlon came around, we were ready for it.* (20) *We all stuck together.* (21) *We took our time and drank lots of water.* (22) *But we finished, and we didn't finish last, either.* (23) *My Aunt Sarah was so thankful, she cried and hugged us all for a long time.*

31. Which of the following sentences, if added after sentence 2, would best connect the first paragraph to the rest of the essay?

    (A) This year, to my surprise, I began to enjoy exercise.
    (B) But, changing all that, a strange thing happened.
    (C) It seems I hated exercise for as long as I can remember.
    (D) Then a terrible thing happened.
    (E) For many, exercise is a pleasant experience.

32. Which of the following is the best revision of sentence 8?

    (A) She asked my cousin, Leah, my mother and I to participate, too.
    (B) My Aunt Sarah asked my cousin Leah, my mother and I to participate, too.
    (C) She asked my cousin Leah, my mother, and me to participate too.
    (D) Asking, my cousin Leah, my mother and I participated too.
    (E) She had asked my cousin Leah, my mother, and me to participate too.

33. Which of the following is the best way to combine sentences 9 and 10 (reproduced below)?

    I couldn't possibly say no. I knew I'd hate it and would probably finish last.

    (A) I couldn't possibly say no, but I knew I'd hate it and would probably finish last.
    (B) Being impossible to say no, I knew I'd hate it and would probably finish last.
    (C) Despite not being able to say no, I knew I'd hate it and would probably finish last.
    (D) Since I couldn't possibly say no, it was then I knew I'd hate it and would probably finish last.
    (E) Knowing I'd hate it and would probably finish last, it was impossible to say no.

34. In keeping with the tone and meaning of the essay, which of the following would be the best transition at the beginning of sentence 15 (reproduced below)?

    We started going every week.

    (A) However
    (B) Therefore
    (C) For example
    (D) Rather
    (E) So

35. Which of the following represents the best revision of sentence 18 (reproduced below)?

    I huffed and puffed and was sweating, but I did it.

    (A) I was huffing and puffing and getting sweaty, but I did it.
    (B) I was huffing and puffing, sweaty, but I did it.
    (C) I huffed and puffed and sweated, but I did it.
    (D) I huffed and I puffed and I was sweating, but I did it.
    (E) I would huff and puff and get sweaty, but I did it.

GO ON TO THE NEXT PAGE

Questions 36–40 are based on the following early draft of a student essay.

(1) The subways of all major cities ought to run all night. (2) Subways prevent a lot of traffic and provide transportation to people who don't have cars or cannot drive.

(3) It is important to alleviate traffic as much as possible. (4) In most major cities, cars are the biggest factor in air pollution. (5) They contribute to smog, greenhouse gases, and acid rain. (6) Traffic also lessens the quality of life for people who live in a city. (7) Subways that run only during limited hours discourage people from riding them. (8) You never know when you might decide to change your plans and come home later.

(9) The other major function of subway systems is to provide transportation for people who cannot drive cars. (10) Some people cannot afford a car and some are not able to drive one. (11) Many people who cannot afford a car may also have to work night shifts, so they really need one that runs all night. (12) People who cannot drive cars also have the right, like all of us, to go out at night and they can't do that unless the subway runs all night. (13) So all subway systems should run twenty-four hours a day, even if they don't run often during the late-night hours.

36. Which sentence, if added to the end of paragraph 1, would best connect it to the rest of the essay?

    (A) Also, the cities people like the most in the world have all-night subways.
    (B) Subways that run all night offer significantly more of both of these important benefits.
    (C) But it seems cities are reluctant to operate subway systems all night.
    (D) Traffic is one of the most important problems we face.
    (E) Reliable subways also encourage tourism.

37. Which of the following is the best way to revise and combine sentences 9 and 10 (reproduced below)?

    The other major function of subway systems is to provide transportation for people who cannot drive cars. Some people cannot afford a car and some are not able to drive one.

    (A) The other major function of subway systems is to provide transportation for people who cannot drive cars, being either that some people cannot afford a car and some are not able to drive one.
    (B) The other major function of subway systems is to provide transportation for people who cannot drive cars because some people cannot afford a car and some are not able to drive one.
    (C) Some people not affording a car and some not being able to drive one, the other major function of subway systems is to provide transportation for people who cannot drive cars.
    (D) The other major function of subway systems is to provide transportation for people who cannot drive cars, either because they cannot afford one or because they are not able to drive one.
    (E) The other major function of subway systems is to provide transportation for people who cannot drive cars; some people cannot afford cars and some are not able to drive them.

38. Which of the following offers the best revision of sentence 11 (reproduced below)?

    Many people who cannot afford a car may also have to work night shifts, so they really need one that runs all night.

    (A) No change.
    (B) Really needing one that runs all night, many people who cannot afford a car may also have to work night shifts.
    (C) Needing a subway system that runs all night, many people cannot afford a car and have to work night shifts.
    (D) Because many people who cannot afford a car may also have to work night shifts, they really need one that runs all night.
    (E) Many people who cannot afford a car may also have to work the night shift, so they really need a subway system that runs all night.

39. In the context of the essay as a whole, which of the following is the best revision of sentence 13 (reproduced below)?

    So all subway systems should run twenty-four hours a day, even if they don't run often during the late-night hours.

    (A) No change.
    (B) For these reasons, all subway systems in major cities should run twenty-four hours a day.
    (C) So, even if they don't run often during the late-night hours, all subway systems should run twenty-four hours a day.
    (D) Even when not running often during the late-night hours, all subway systems should run twenty-four hours a day.
    (E) So all subway systems should not run often during the late-night hours.

40. The writer uses all of the following strategies in the passage EXCEPT

    (A) making a personal appeal.
    (B) using scientific information.
    (C) suggesting solutions to a problem.
    (D) making an appeal to morality.
    (E) employing a historical reference.

Questions 41–45 are based on the following early draft of a student essay.

(1) *There are three basic functions physical education serves in our education.* (2) *First, it gives students a break from schoolwork during the day, allowing them to return refreshed.* (3) *Second, it teaches students an active, healthy lifestyle.* (4) *Third, ideally, it can teach students self-confidence.*

(5) *For these reasons, it is very important that school districts should continue to fund physical education programs.* (6) *Students should have physical education every day.* (7) *The activities should be well planned.* (8) *If the teacher just leaves students on their own to play, the students who need physical education the most will be the ones who don't join in.* (9) *They may even be teased by the other students.* (10) *Students cannot teach themselves about the importance of nutrition or stretching in an active lifestyle.* (11) *They need a qualified teacher for their physical education classes.*

41. Which of the following represents the best way to revise sentence 1?

    (A) No change.
    (B) There is physical education in our education, serving three basic functions.
    (C) Physical education serves three basic functions.
    (D) Physical education has served three basic functions in our education.
    (E) Physical education serves three basic functions in our education.

42. Which of the following is the best way to revise sentence 2?

    (A) No change.
    (B) First, it gives students a break from schoolwork during the day, and it allows them to return refreshed.
    (C) First, allowing them to return refreshed, it gives students a break from schoolwork during the day.
    (D) The first reason is that it gives students a break from schoolwork during the day, allowing them to return refreshed.
    (E) First, because it gives students a break from schoolwork during the day, it has allowed them to return refreshed.

43. In the context of the essay as a whole, which of the following is the best way to revise sentence 5 (reproduced below)?

    For these reasons, it is very important that school districts should continue to fund physical education programs.

    (A) No change.
    (B) Continuing to fund physical education programs for these reasons, it is very important.
    (C) For these reasons being very important, school districts should continue to fund physical education programs.
    (D) For these reasons, it is very important that school districts continue to fund physical education programs.
    (E) That schools are continuing to fund physical education programs being very important for these reasons.

44. Which of the following represents the best way to combine sentences 6 and 7 (reproduced below)?

    Students should have physical education every day. The activities should be well planned.

    (A) Students should have physical education every day, and should participate in well-planned activities.
    (B) Students should have physical education every day, being well-planned activities.
    (C) Students should have physical education every day; the activities should be well planned.
    (D) Students should have physical education every day, having the right to participate in well-planned activities.
    (E) Having physical education every day means participating in well-planned activities.

45. The author could improve sentence 8 by
    (A) defining his/her terms.
    (B) using a concrete example.
    (C) suggesting ways to increase student participation.
    (D) suggesting reasons why teachers leave children alone.
    (E) providing personal opinions.

Questions 46–50 are based on the following early draft of an editorial for the school newspaper.

(1) *We should all take a moment to think about how much we will miss Ms. Garcia.* (2) *Ms. Garcia just retired.* (3) *A dedicated, passionate teacher, our school counts on teachers like Ms. Garcia.* (4) *Principal Natto's idea to establish a scholarship in her name is a great one.*

(5) *It would be impossible to mention everything that Ms. Garcia has meant to us.* (6) *She began the Student Action Club before any of us were born.* (7) *It became a very popular extracurricular activity.* (8) *The Student Action Club has made many important contributions to our school over the years.* (9) *They got the school district to stop using toxic pesticides at the schools.* (10) *We also got the school district to commit to green areas at all of the schools.* (11) *The Student Action Club also raised a lot of money for the Teen Runaway Hotline.* (12) *Ms. Garcia taught us that we could talk right to school officials and companies.* (13) *Even though they didn't always listen, we always felt we had tried.*

(14) *Ms. Garcia always believed in her students.* (15) *Ms. Garcia was also nationally known as an excellent teacher.* (16) *We learned from her both in class, in our after-school activities and out of them.* (17) *She continues to be an inspiration for all of us.* (18) *We should remember her inspiration and pass it on to others by developing a scholarship fund in her name.* (19) *It might be a lot of work, but Ms. Garcia would tell us not to let that stop us.*

46. Which of the following is the best way to revise and combine sentences 1 and 2 (reproduced below)?

    We should all take a moment to think about how much we will miss Ms. Garcia. Ms. Garcia just retired.

    (A) We should all take a moment to think about how much we will miss Ms. Garcia, having just retired.
    (B) We should all take a moment to think about how much we will miss Ms. Garcia, and Ms. Garcia just retired.
    (C) We should all take a moment to think about how much we will miss Ms. Garcia, who just retired.
    (D) Having just retired, we should all take a moment to think about how much we will miss Ms. Garcia.
    (E) We should all take a moment to think about how much we will miss Ms. Garcia—Ms. Garcia just retired.

47. Which of the following is the best, most concise revision of sentence 3 (reproduced below)?

    A dedicated, passionate teacher, our school counts on teachers like Ms. Garcia.

    (A) Our school counts on dedicated, passionate teachers like Ms. Garcia.
    (B) Our school counts on teachers like Ms. Garcia, a dedicated, passionate teacher.
    (C) Like Ms. Garcia, our school counts on dedicated, passionate teachers.
    (D) Like Ms. Garcia, a dedicated, passionate teacher, our school counts on teachers.
    (E) Our school counts on teachers like Ms. Garcia, being a dedicated, passionate teacher.

48. In the context of the second paragraph, which of the following is the clearest way to revise sentences 9 and 10 (reproduced below) so that the two sentences are combined?

   They got the school district to stop using toxic pesticides at the schools. We also got the school district to commit to green areas at all of the schools.

   (A) They got the school district to stop using toxic pesticides at the schools, and we also got the school district to commit to green areas at all of the schools.
   (B) They got the school district to stop using toxic pesticides at the schools, and got them to commit to green areas.
   (C) We got the school district to stop using toxic pesticides and commit to green areas at all of the schools.
   (D) We got the school district to stop using toxic pesticides at the schools, committing to green areas at all of them.
   (E) Getting the school district to commit to green areas at all of the schools, we got them to stop using toxic pesticides.

49. The author could improve sentence 15 by

   (A) including an additional sentence with more personal information about Ms. Garcia.
   (B) expressing more enthusiasm.
   (C) defining the word "excellent" more specifically.
   (D) citing examples of national recognition.
   (E) giving counterexamples.

50. Which of the following versions of sentence 16 (reproduced below) is the clearest?

   We learned from her both in class, in our after-school activities and out of them.

   (A) We learned from her both during school hours and outside of them, whether in class or in our after-school activities.
   (B) We learned both in our after-school activities and in class and outside of our after-school activities and classes.
   (C) Whether in class or after-school activities or out of them, we learned from her.
   (D) Whether we were in our out of them, class or after-school activities or both, we learned from her.
   (E) Whether in school hours, in after-school activities or out of, we learned from Ms. Garcia.

END OF PART I. **STOP**

PART II
Time—45 minutes

ESSAY

Directions: Read the following essay topic and plan out how you want to structure your essay. You will have 45 minutes to complete your response.

It is often said that "the more things change, the more they stay the same." Explore this idea in relation to the effects technology has had on people's lives in the last several years.

THE ANSWER KEY APPEARS ON THE FOLLOWING PAGE.

ANSWER KEY

1. C
2. C
3. B
4. D
5. E
6. B
7. B
8. D
9. D
10. A

11. C
12. D
13. B
14. C
15. B
16. B
17. D
18. A
19. C
20. E

21. C
22. B
23. A
24. E
25. D
26. A
27. C
28. B
29. A
30. D

31. A
32. C
33. A
34. E
35. C
36. B
37. D
38. E
39. B
40. E

41. C
42. A
43. D
44. A
45. B
46. C
47. A
48. C
49. D
50. A

Answers and Explanations

PART I

1. (C)
With neither/nor, you must use a singular verb, but "were" is plural.

2. (C)
In a passive voice construction like this one, the object of the action is the subject of the verb—"windows," which is plural, is the subject of "was broken," so "was" should be "were."

3. (B)
"She" does not have a clear reference, because it could mean either Margaret or Leticia could not continue at her job. For this sentence to be correct, the person's name should appear again.

4. (D)
This sentence exhibits a parallel structure problem. The first two clauses refer to nouns ("fluency in Chinese," "knowledge of history.") The final clause does not match because it is in the form of a phrase ("how well she . . ."). It needs to be changed to match the first two clauses. One might say, "her success in keeping the group on schedule."

5. (E)
The verb tenses here are a little tricky, but they are all correct. "It was discovered the following day," indicates that the discovery is a past event that preceded something else in the more distant past (the fire alarm). "Had not been" indicates that more distant past when the fire alarm occurred. "Resulted" takes the simple past tense because it does not refer to something that had definitively ended at the time when it was "discovered."

6. (B)
This is an incomplete sentence as it stands. One of the verbs needs to have a subject attached and to be conjugated in some tense other than the vague "–ing." Since only one of the verbs, "jolting" (B) is underlined, it must be the problem. One possible replacement is, "the car jolted." If "leaving" were also underlined, you would have a choice as to which to make the primary verb of the sentence.

7. (B)
"I" (B) is a subject pronoun, not the object of a preposition. "Between" is a preposition, so "I" should be "me."

8. (D)
Everything is used correctly here until the relatively simple diction problem "complexities in," which should be "complexities *of.*"

9. (D)
Something that has happened prior to an event which is, itself, past, needs to be in the pluperfect tense—which is to say, the tickets "*had* sold out" before the past event of Nora arriving at the ticket office.

10. (A)
The problem here is a logical one. One group is not unconvinced because (or "since") the other group is convinced. "Although" is a much more logical choice.

11. (C)
A "news story" is not a place and should not be followed by "where." This is marginally acceptable in spoken speech, but not acceptable in the "standard written English" the CLEP English Composition exam calls for.

12. (D)
It is the number (singular) that increases, so "have" should be "has." To change the meaning of the sentence slightly, the entire middle of the sentence could be taken out to state, "The number of trucks on the road has increased dramatically in the last ten years."

13. (B)

If the man "had been slowed down" before missing the bus, "and" is the wrong conjunction. "Because" would be more logical ("because he had been slowed down").

14. (C)

The conjunction "however" should occur at the beginning of a new sentence, and you cannot connect two complete sentences with a comma. The comma ought to be a semi-colon.

15. (B)

"And becomes" implies that there has already been a main verb, but there is no main verb prior to it, only the verb in the adjectival phrase "which consists of. . . ". The "and" should be removed to correct the mistake.

16. (B)

"After spending so much time with her new puppy" is a modifier that describes Candace, not "going back to work." This is a classic case of a dangling modifier. These clauses serve as adjectives: they describe something. They must be placed next to what they describe.

17. (D)

The subject of the verb here is "one," which, it goes without saying, takes a singular verb. "Have" should be "has."

18. (A)

This is a complex sentence, but it has no errors so the answer is (A). In the main clause, it is perfectly acceptable to link two verbs with "and" when they refer to the same subject and do not repeat that subject.

19. (C)

"Team" is the subject of the verb, so the pronoun should be "it" instead of "they."

20. (E)

Because "predicted" is in the past tense, the future tense "will be" is incorrect. It should be "would be." "Would be" is the correct way to suggest actions which, although they are in the past, are in the future relative to another past action in the sentence.

21. (C)

There is no main verb here, only the "–ing" form. Everything else is fine, so simply change "offering" to "offer."

22. (B)

This may look similar to question 15 at first, but it does have a main verb: "presented." All that needs to be done is to make "continues" agree with "theories," the subject of the verb.

23. (A)

This is a little tricky because it is one of just a few correct usages of the "–ing" form. Here the clause beginning with "consisting" serves as an adjective to describe the book. Notice that the phrase "consisting of a series of adventures undertaken by the main character" modifies "novel," and that it must appear next to what it modifies.

24. (E)

After "ability," you need the infinitive, "to resolve." Only answer (E) contains this form of the verb. In addition, the night already happened, so "will be" in answer (C) cannot be correct. "Were quarreling" also makes choice (D) incorrect.

25. (D)

There are two problems here: first, "they" has an unclear referent (scientists or star clusters). The meaning of the sentence makes it clear that "star clusters" is what is being described in the second half of the sentence. Second, when the object of the verb of the first clause gets described in another clause, the easiest way to structure the sentence is with a simple "which . . . ". (D) does that.

26. (A)

There is no mistake here. "The polar bear" is used singularly as one of many "animals." Answer (B), "are the polar bear," suggests the bear is more than one animal, which makes no sense. Answer (C) uses the singular verb "is" with the plural subject "bears." The verb and subject must agree in number.

27. (C)
Remember that "not only" goes with "but also." That's answer (C). Answer (D), "additionally making great advances in philosophy and medicine," makes the sentence into a phrase. In answer (A), "they" and "zero" need to have a connecting word.

28. (B)
This is a question of parallel structure. The first clause has the structure "the [noun] the poems [verb]." Only answer (B) uses this same structure for the second clause ("the nontraditional forms they [the poems] use").

29. (A)
There is no error here. The sentence uses the passive voice correctly.

30. (D)
Just simplify the underlined part to "whether the woman committed the crime or not" and you have answer (D). The other choices are wordy or ungrammatical.

31. (A)
Only answers (A) and (D) make any sense at all, but answer (A) covers the whole passage rather than just the second paragraph, so it is the better choice. In answer (C) the verb tenses "seems," "hated," and "can remember" do not fit together.

32. (C)
The problem here is that you can't say "she asked . . . I." "I" refers to the subject of a sentence, not its object. Simply change "I" to "me" and you have answer (C). Answer (D) makes it sound as though the author, the author's mother, and the author's cousin were "asking."

33. (A)
The two sentences express opposing sentiments, so they are best united by "but," which only appears in answer (A). Answer (E) is not logical: you would not refuse to say no *because* you know you'd hate the race.

34. (E)
"Therefore" and "so" both make sense logically. The question also asks you to maintain the *tone* of the passage, which is informal. "So" is the more informal, and better, choice.

35. (C)
This question asks about parallel structure. Just think, "I huffed and puffed and blew the house down." Change "blew the house down" to "sweated" and you have answer (C). In answer (B), "puffing" and "sweaty" are not parallel.

36. (B)
Answers (A), (C), and (E) introduce ideas that don't appear anywhere else in the passage. While answer (D) only connects the first paragraph to the second, answer (B) summarizes the central idea of the whole essay.

37. (D)
Answers (A), (B), and (C) add to the complexity of the sentences and are therefore easy to eliminate. While not ungrammatical, the use of a semicolon to join the two sentences in answer (E) does not specify the relationship between them. Answer (D) does this while simplifying the structure of the statement.

38. (E)
"One" does not have a clear reference and needs to be replaced by "a subway system." Only answers (C) and (E) do that. Answer (C) loses the simple logic of the original, replacing it with an "–ing" verb and vague "and's."

39. (B)
The real problem with this sentence, which is the concluding sentence of the essay, is that it introduces a new idea. The conclusion of an essay should never introduce a new concept. If you eliminate the new idea altogether you have answer (B).

40. (E)
Use the process of elimination. Does the author make a personal appeal (A)? Yes. He or she says, "you never know when you might change your plans" and also "like all of us." The third paragraph, in reference to the rights of people who cannot drive, is an appeal to morality, (D). Does the author use scientific information (B)? More or less, yes, by mentioning that cars contribute to three factors of pollution. Does the author suggest a solution to a problem (C)? Most definitely; that is what the entire passage is about.

41. (C)

"There are" is unnecessary. Get rid of it and make the sentence active and you have "Physical education serves three basic functions in our education." There is no real need to say "education" twice.

42. (A)

All of the revisions complicate this perfectly acceptable sentence. Always avoid the complicated, messy answer choices.

43. (D)

"It is important that they should continue" is awkward. "It is important that they continue" is the standard usage. "It is very important" in answer (B) is a phrase by itself at the end of the sentence.

44. (A)

It is easy to make both sentences have the same subject ("students"), making the connection clearer and the sentences more active. Only answers (A) and (D) do that, but answer (D) has the weird, complicating "–ing" verb form that is almost always incorrect.

45. (B)

It's not entirely clear how this lack of participation occurs. A concrete example of a game that students would select and how certain students would be excluded would help the author's argument.

46. (C)

When the object of the first clause is also described in the second clause, use "which." However, when the object happens to be a person, use "who" (or "whom"). The correct answer is also the most straightforward.

47. (A)

This sentence includes a misplaced modifier. "Our school" is not the "dedicated, passionate teacher." "Ms. Garcia" needs to be right next to this description of her. Answers (A) and (B) make this adjustment, but answer (A) is simpler.

48. (C)

The task here is to get rid of the we/they problem. Both of these pronouns refer to the same group, so only one is necessary. Then there is no need to repeat "got the school district." Answer (A) does not address these issues. Answer (D) has a dangling modifier ("committing . . .") that grammatically describes "we." Answer (E) produces an unnecessarily complicated sentence. Between answers (B) and (C), answer (C) is best because it is the simpler choice.

49. (D)

The original sentence lacks specific information on the type of national recognition Ms. Garcia has received. Giving an example (D) would be the clearest way to fix this. Answer (A) is incorrect because it's not Ms. Garcia's personal life we need to know more about; it's her professional life. Answer (C) is on the right track, but it is not as specific as answer (D). There is no need for the author to undermine his or her own argument by presenting counterexamples.

50. (A)

This is a tough question, because none of the answer choices is great. Answer (B) is clearly wrong because it uses "both" then has three options. Answer (C) could be right but it just sounds really clunky. Both answers (D) and (E) have grammatical mistakes. Opting between answers (A) and (C), the better-sounding answer is (A).

PART II

Essay Section

Scoring Guidelines

The essay is read by two college English teachers who each assign it a grade of 1–6, based on the following holistic criteria. Their scores are added to form the essay's raw score, which comprises 50 percent of the exam. Read the scoring guidelines and the sample essay that follows, and try to decide what score you would give it.

Level 6 essays:
- cover all aspects of the assignment in an insightful manner
- contain thoroughly developed ideas supported with specific, relevant evidence
- are organized and focused
- exhibit superior skill with vocabulary and sentence variation
- display grammar mastery only with minor errors if any

Level 5 essays:
- cover the assignment effectively
- contain well-developed ideas supported with appropriate evidence
- are organized and focused for the most part
- exhibit skill with vocabulary and some sentence variation
- display a good grasp of grammar with only minor errors

Level 4 essays:
- cover the assignment competently
- contain adequately developed ideas supported with evidence
- are adequately organized and focused
- exhibit competence with vocabulary but little sentence variation
- display a grasp of grammar for the most part, some errors possible

Note that for categories below Level 4, an essay only has to contain one of the specified problems.

Level 3 essays:
- cover only part of the assignment
- contain uneven development and unsupported assertions
- are poorly organized and focused
- exhibit multiple problems in communicating
- display mediocre or inconsistent grammar

Level 2 essays:
- cover a small part of the assignment
- lack development and contain little evidence
- are unfocused and disorganized
- display grammar and usage errors that obscure meaning

Level 1 essays:
- fail to cover the assignment
- are undeveloped
- display persistent errors in grammar and usage that significantly obscure meaning

If your essay is on a different topic than the one given, if it merely restates the topic, or if it can't be understood by the graders, it will receive a score of 0.

Pay close attention to the differences between categories. For example, to make a Level 4 essay into a Level 5, you need to add sentence variation, make sure your evidence is appropriate, eliminate grammatical errors, and make your essay more focused.

Sample Essay

Look at the following sample essay and think about how you would grade it. What are its strengths, and how might it be improved?

    The expression "the more things change, the more they stay the same" is often used to express frustration when things don't change as someone hoped they would. But, with technology, life often changes in ways people could not have expected. Life usually changes in a million little ways. It is fair to say that the average person's life since the widespread use of computers has changed more in little ways than it has in big ways. In this sense, the expression rings true. But there is at least one dramatic change that computers have brought to an average person's life, which is that an individual can be a more active, informed consumer.

    Life may seem to be more of the same with the use of computers. E-mail means we don't hear our friends' and family's voices as often, but on the other hand, we see more pictures of them because they are so easily sent. Computers have reduced paperwork in offices, but there is always busywork to fill the time. Some people can work from home, but it wasn't impossible for people to work from home using regular mail before computers.

    Shopping online may also seem, in many cases, very similar to shopping at an outlet mall or buying airline tickets over the phone. But we can compare so many more prices so much more quickly that we definitely save money over time. We can also bookmark a particular Web site and check every day to see if an item we want is on sale. This would have been impossible when people had to check prices by car or even by phone. Finally, we can buy the shoes or books we want from a faraway place, so we have a much better chance of getting the best price.

    Perhaps the most concrete examples of how we have become better consumers are Web sites like Amazon.com and eBay. Amazon.com (and other book-searching Web sites like Bookfinder) allow us to locate a used copy of a book that may be out of print. Some of these used copies are like new. Before computers, we would have had to pay very high prices for them. Or we may not have been able to find the book at all. The Web site eBay also helps us find things that we may not have been able to find before. Anything you can think of is on sale right now on eBay. In addition, eBay lets us sell things we have. A garage sale is not a good place to sell an unusual item. You can't assume that a collector of 1940s jewelry will show up and be willing to pay what your heirlooms are worth. So eBay has really put people in touch in new ways.

    Sometimes, then, it may seem like "the more things change, the more they stay the same." After all, we've always been buying and selling things. But technology really has changed the way that happens and to the benefit of the consumer.

| SECTION THREE |

The CLEP College Mathematics Exam

Section Three: The CLEP College Mathematics Exam

Chapter Eight: Practice Test 1: Diagnostic

Time—90 minutes
60 Questions

Directions: For the following questions, either select the BEST answer of the choices given, or input your answer into the box provided.

You can use the computer-based scientific calculator during this exam.

Notes:

(1) Unless otherwise stated, the domain of any function f consists of the set of all real numbers x for which $f(x)$ is a real number.

(2) i represents $\sqrt{-1}$

(3) Unless otherwise indicated, all geometric figures lie in a plane. The appearance of all figures is accurate UNLESS the question states that the figure is not drawn to scale.

1. If A = $\{x \mid x$ is a whole number$\}$ and B = $\{x \mid x$ is an odd integer less than 10$\}$, which of the following is a subset of A $\cap$ B?

    (A) $\{3, 5, 7, 9\}$
    (B) $\{-3, 7, 9\}$
    (C) $\{2, 3, 5, 7\}$
    (D) $\{1, 7, 9, 11\}$

2. If $f(x) = x^2 - 3x$, then $f(x - 1) - 1 =$

    (A) $x^2 - 5x - 2$
    (B) $x^2 - 5x + 2$
    (C) $x^2 - 5x + 4$
    (D) $x^2 - x + 4$

3. Which of the following is NOT true of a prime number?

    I. A prime number is always divisible by itself.
    II. A prime number is always divisible by 1.
    III. A prime number is always odd.

    (A) I and II only
    (B) III only
    (C) II and III only
    (D) II only

GO ON TO THE NEXT PAGE

KAPLAN

4. Below is a Truth Table:

p	q	r
T	T	T
T	F	T
F	T	T
F	F	F

According to this table, which of the following statements describes r?

(A) $p \wedge q$
(B) $p \rightarrow q$
(C) $p \leftrightarrow q$
(D) $p \vee q$

5. Sue is on vacation and wants to dine at 3 different restaurants while in town. In how many ways could she choose 3 restaurants if there are 10 restaurants in all to choose from and order doesn't matter?

6. Which of the following numbers is NOT divisible by 3?

(A) 48
(B) 51
(C) 87
(D) 92

7. What is the domain of the function $f(x) = \dfrac{x}{x^2 - 4}$?

(A) All real numbers except for 2 and –2
(B) All real numbers except for 4 and –4
(C) All real numbers except for 0
(D) All real numbers

8. Which of the following is a factor of $2x^3 - x^2 + 3x - 4$?

(A) $x + 1$
(B) $x + 2$
(C) $x - 1$
(D) $x - 2$

9. Suppose the mean for a set of numbers is 6. If all the numbers in the set are doubled, what would the mean then be?

(A) 12
(B) 6
(C) 3
(D) 24

10. Which is the converse of "If P, then Q"?

(A) If Q, then P
(B) If not P, then not Q
(C) If not Q, then not P
(D) If P, then not Q

11. Suppose R = {u, v} and S = {x, y}. Which of the following ordered pairs is NOT in the Cartesian product R × S?

(A) (u, x)
(B) (v, x)
(C) (v, y)
(D) (u, v)

12. Values for the functions f and g are given in the following tables:

x	2	3	4
f(x)	5	6	7

x	4	5	6
g(x)	2	3	4

What is the value of $f(g(4))$?

(A) 7
(B) 5
(C) 4
(D) 2

GO ON TO THE NEXT PAGE

13. The width of a rectangular yard is *x* feet. If 200 feet of fencing is needed to enclose the yard, which of the following represents the length of the yard, in feet?

    (A) $200 - x$
    (B) $200 - 2x$
    (C) $100 - x$
    (D) $100 - 2x$

14. Find the smallest positive integer which is divisible by both 15 and 18.

    (A) 3
    (B) 30
    (C) 60
    (D) 90

15. One digit from the number 5,473,343 is written on each of seven cards. What is the probability of drawing a card that shows 4?

    (A) $\frac{4}{7}$
    (B) $\frac{2}{7}$
    (C) $\frac{5}{7}$
    (D) $\frac{1}{7}$

16. In a right triangle, what is the sum in degrees of the measures of the two acute angles?

    [   ]

17. Which of the following could be the graph of a function of *x*?

    (A)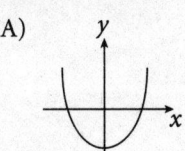

    (B)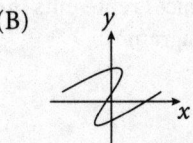

    (C)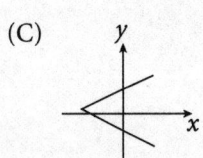

    (D)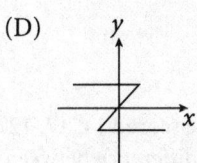

18. If $\frac{a}{b}$ and $\frac{c}{d}$ are rational numbers, then $\frac{a}{b} \div \frac{c}{d} =$

    (A) $\frac{(a-c)}{(b-d)}$
    (B) $\frac{ac}{bd}$
    (C) $\frac{ad}{bc}$
    (D) $\frac{a \div d}{b \div c}$

19. A family has three children. What is the likelihood all three are boys, given that the first child is a boy?

    (A) $\frac{1}{8}$
    (B) $\frac{1}{4}$
    (C) $\frac{3}{4}$
    (D) $\frac{3}{8}$

20. If $\log_4 x = 3$, then $\log_8 x =$

    (A) 6
    (B) 8
    (C) 4
    (D) 2

21. Which of the following choices represents the shaded area of the Venn diagram?

    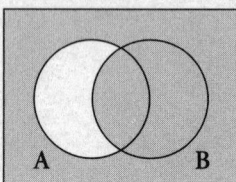

    (A) $(A \cup B) \cap A'$
    (B) $(A \cup B)'$
    (C) $(A \cup B)' \cup B$
    (D) $(A \cup B)' \cup A$

22. In five basketball games, Joe scored 14, 17, 12, 18, and 24 points. What is the difference between his mean and median score?

    [   ]

23. What is the range of the function $f(x) = (x-2)^2$?

    (A) All real numbers greater than or equal to 0
    (B) All real numbers except for 2
    (C) All real numbers greater than or equal to 2
    (D) All real numbers

24. The statement "A is a necessary condition for B" is equivalent to which of the following?

    (A) If not A, then B
    (B) If not B, then A
    (C) If A, then B
    (D) If B, then A

25. What is the slope of a line perpendicular to a line with slope $\frac{4}{5}$?

    (A) $-\frac{5}{4}$
    (B) $-\frac{4}{5}$
    (C) $\frac{4}{5}$
    (D) $\frac{5}{4}$

26. What is the prime factorization of 60?

    (A) 6×10
    (B) $2 \times 2 \times 3 \times 5$
    (C) $3 \times 4 \times 5$
    (D) $2 \times 3 \times 3 \times 5$

27. The low temperatures for the past seven days at a mountain resort are given in the table below:

Day	Low Temp.
Sunday	11°
Monday	15°
Tuesday	7°
Wednesday	−3°
Thursday	13°
Friday	9°
Saturday	2°

    If the low temperature for one day was chosen at random, what is the probability that the temperature would be a prime number?

    (A) $\frac{2}{7}$
    (B) $\frac{3}{7}$
    (C) $\frac{4}{7}$
    (D) $\frac{5}{7}$

28. What is the median low temperature for the days listed in problem 27?

    (A) 9°
    (B) −3°
    (C) 7°
    (D) 5°

29. Which of the following is the inverse of the function $f(x) = \dfrac{x-4}{3}$?

    (A) $f^{-1}(x) = 3x + 4$
    (B) $f^{-1}(x) = \dfrac{x+4}{3}$
    (C) $f^{-1}(x) = \dfrac{x-3}{4}$
    (D) $f^{-1}(x) = 3x - 4$

30. Which of the following numbers is irrational?

    (A) $\sqrt{9}$
    (B) $\sqrt{25}$
    (C) $\sqrt{49}$
    (D) $\sqrt{50}$

31. The volume of a rectangular box is found by multiplying its length, width, and height. If each dimension of a particular box is doubled, then the volume of the new box is how many times the volume of the original box?

    (A) 2
    (B) 8
    (C) 6
    (D) 4

32. In a barrel of 25 apples, 5 are green. If you select two apples, without replacement, what is the probability they are both green?

    (A) $\dfrac{2}{25}$
    (B) $\dfrac{1}{5}$
    (C) $\dfrac{1}{30}$
    (D) $\dfrac{11}{30}$

33. If X = {$x \mid x$ is a prime number} and Y = {$x \mid x$ is an even integer less than 15}, how many elements are in X ∩ Y?

    (A) 1
    (B) 0
    (C) 5
    (D) 6

34. If a and b are both odd integers, what can be said about $a^2 + 2ab + b^2$?

    (A) It is always odd.
    (B) It is sometimes odd.
    (C) It is always divisible by 3.
    (D) It is always even.

35. A friend tells you that if n is any number, then $2n + 1$ is always odd. Which of the following provides a counterexample to this?

    (A) 2
    (B) $\dfrac{1}{2}$
    (C) 3
    (D) −1

36. Suppose $f(x) = 3x + 4$ and $g(x) = x − 2$. For what value of x does $f(x) = g(x)$?

    (A) 3
    (B) 1
    (C) −2
    (D) −3

37. Which of the following sets contains all of the other sets?

    (A) real numbers
    (B) rational numbers
    (C) irrational numbers
    (D) integers

38. If you roll three standard dice, how many outcomes are possible?

   _____

39. If $\log_n x = 4$ and $\log_n y = 6$, then $\log_n\left(\dfrac{x^2}{y}\right) =$

    (A) 10
    (B) 2
    (C) 14
    (D) $\dfrac{8}{3}$

40. If $x - 2$ is a factor of $x^4 - 2x^3 + kx - 4$, what is the value of k?

   _____

41. A train has gone 120 miles from its point of origin (O) when Sally gets on. Five hours later, the train has traveled 420 miles total. If its speed is constant, which of the following represents the total distance (D) the train has traveled from its origin in miles, t hours after Sally has embarked?

    (A) $D = 120 + 300t$
    (B) $D = 120 + 300(t - 5)$
    (C) $D = 120 + 60t$
    (D) $D = 120 + 60(t + 3)$

42. If $A \subset B$ and $C \subset B$, then which of the following is NEVER true?

    (A) $A \subset C$
    (B) $B \subset C$
    (C) $C \subset A$
    (D) $A = \varnothing$

43. The graph of $y = f(x)$ is given below:

    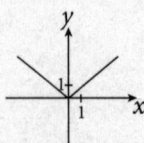

    Which of the following could be the graph of $y = -3f(x)$?

    (A)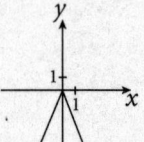

    (B)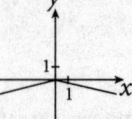

    (C)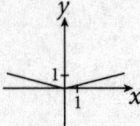

    (D)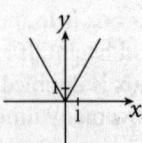

44. A jar contains 6 red, 5 yellow, and 4 blue jellybeans. If two jellybeans are selected one after the other without replacing the first, what is the probability that the first one is red and the second one is yellow?

    (A) $\dfrac{2}{15}$
    (B) $\dfrac{8}{75}$
    (C) $\dfrac{11}{15}$
    (D) $\dfrac{1}{7}$

GO ON TO THE NEXT PAGE

45. If A → B and B → C, what does ~C imply?

    (A) A
    (B) B
    (C) ~A
    (D) It implies a contradiction.

46. If $x^2 + 9 = 0$, then which of the following are the two roots of the equation?

    (A) $3i, -3i$
    (B) $3i, -3$
    (C) $3, -3i$
    (D) $3, -3$

47. Which of the following is a composite number?

    (A) 11
    (B) 27
    (C) 43
    (D) 61

48. In base two (binary), a six-digit number looks like 110101. How many six-digit numbers are possible in base two?

    (A) 12
    (B) 6
    (C) 64
    (D) 32

49. If $f(g(x)) = \dfrac{1}{x-4}$ and $g(x) = x + 4$, what is $f(x)$?

    (A) $\dfrac{1}{x+4}$
    (B) $\dfrac{x}{x-4}$
    (C) $\dfrac{1}{x-4}$
    (D) $\dfrac{1}{x-8}$

50. The number 1011 is written in binary notation. How would it be written in decimal notation?

    (A) 13
    (B) 11
    (C) 9
    (D) 7

51. You are dealt 5 cards in a game of draw poker. If 3 of the cards are aces, what is the probability you will get another ace if you draw two cards?

    (A) $\dfrac{2}{47}$
    (B) $\dfrac{1}{26}$
    (C) $\dfrac{1}{13}$
    (D) $\dfrac{4}{47}$

52. If $g(x) = 2x^3 - 3x^2 + 5x - 4$, then $g(-2) =$

    (A) -10
    (B) 10
    (C) -42
    (D) 12

53. Josh is five years older than Sam. Three years ago, Josh was twice as old as Sam. How old is Sam now?

54. Which of the following are finite sets?

    I. The set of hours in the day
    II. The set of days in the week
    III. The set of weeks in the year

    (A) I and II only
    (B) II and III only
    (C) I and III only
    (D) I, II, and III

GO ON TO THE NEXT PAGE

KAPLAN

55. Suppose $f(x) = (x-2)^3$. What is the y-intercept of this function?

    (A) 2
    (B) −8
    (C) 8
    (D) −6

56. The probability it will snow on Monday is 0.6, while the probability it will snow on Tuesday is 0.3. What is the probability it will snow on Monday but not on Tuesday?

    (A) 0.18
    (B) 0.12
    (C) 0.42
    (D) 0.9

57. All doctors are men. My sister is a doctor. What can you logically conclude?

    (A) Some doctors are women.
    (B) My sister is not a man.
    (C) My sister is not a doctor.
    (D) My sister is a man.

58. Suppose you toss a coin three times. What is the probability of getting three heads given you have at least two heads?

    (A) $\frac{1}{4}$
    (B) $\frac{1}{8}$
    (C) $\frac{3}{4}$
    (D) $\frac{3}{8}$

59. What is the inverse of the function $f(x) = \{(1, 3), (2, 5), (3, 7)\}$?

    (A) $f^{-1}(x) = \{3, 5, 7\}$
    (B) $f^{-1}(x) = \{1, 2, 3\}$
    (C) $f^{-1}(x) = \{(3, 1), (5, 2), (7, 3)\}$
    (D) The function has no inverse.

60. Consider the set consisting of the first seven prime numbers {2, 3, 5, 7, 11, 13, 17}. What is the difference between the mean and the median?

    (A) $\frac{5}{7}$
    (B) $1\frac{2}{7}$
    (C) $7\frac{2}{7}$
    (D) $1\frac{5}{7}$

END OF TEST. STOP

THE ANSWER KEY APPEARS ON THE FOLLOWING PAGE.

ANSWER KEY

1. A	11. D	21. C	31. B	41. C	51. A
2. C	12. B	22. 0	32. C	42. B	52. C
3. B	13. C	23. A	33. A	43. A	53. 8
4. D	14. D	24. D	34. D	44. D	54. D
5. 120	15. B	25. A	35. B	45. C	55. B
6. D	16. 90	26. B	36. D	46. A	56. C
7. A	17. A	27. C	37. A	47. B	57. D
8. C	18. C	28. A	38. 216	48. C	58. A
9. A	19. B	29. A	39. B	49. D	59. C
10. A	20. D	30. D	40. 2	50. B	60. B

DIAGNOSTIC TEST QUICK REFERENCE TABLES

Use the following tables to determine which topics you need to review most.

Topic	Test Question
Sets	1, 11, 21, 33, 42, 54
Logic	4, 10, 24, 35, 45, 57
Real Number System	3, 6, 8, 14, 18, 26, 30, 34, 37, 40, 47, 50
Functions and Graphs	2, 7, 12, 17, 23, 29, 36, 43, 49, 52, 55, 59
Probability and Statistics	5, 9, 15, 19, 22, 27, 28, 32, 38, 44, 48, 51, 56, 58, 60
Additional Topics	13, 16, 20, 25, 31, 39, 41, 46, 53

Topic	Number of Questions on Test	Number Correct
Sets	6	
Logic	6	
Real Number System	12	
Functions and Graphs	12	
Probability and Statistics	15	
Additional Topics	9	

Answers and Explanations

1. (A)

$A \cap B$ would be the set of odd whole numbers less than 10. So a subset of this set must also include odd whole numbers that are less than 10. (B) includes a negative number (the whole numbers are positive), (C) includes an even number, and (D) includes a number greater than 10, so none of these are the right answer. (A) is the only set listed that includes only odd whole numbers less than 10.

2. (C)

The quickest way to solve this problem is to replace x with $(x - 1)$ in the function and simplify:

$$f(x - 1) = (x - 1)^2 - 3(x - 1)$$
$$= x^2 - 2x + 1 - 3x + 3$$
$$= x^2 - 5x + 4$$

3. (B)

A prime number is only divisible by itself and 1, so I and II are true. Since 2 is a prime number, it can be presumed that a prime number is not always odd. (B) is the correct answer.

4. (D)

Notice that r is only false when both p and q are false. Of the choices given, r, p, and q are only false in the statement $p \vee q$.

5. (120)

A subset of restaurants is selected in this problem, with no sense of order. That means this is a combination problem. The problem can be solved using the combination formula, $C(n, r) = \dfrac{n!}{r!(n - r)!}$. Here $n = 10$ and $r = 3$, so:

$$C(10, 3) = \frac{10!}{3!(10 - 3)!} = \frac{10!}{3!7!} =$$

$$\frac{(10 \times 9 \times 8 \times 7 \times 6 \times 5 \times 4 \times 3 \times 2 \times 1)}{(3 \times 2 \times 1) \times (7 \times 6 \times 5 \times 4 \times 3 \times 2 \times 1)}$$

Canceling and reducing will leave you with 120.

6. (D)

A number is divisible by 3 if its digits add up to a number that is divisible by 3. If the digits of each number given are added together, you will be able to see that only (D) doesn't add up to a number that is divisible by 3:

(A) $4 + 8 = 12$

(B) $5 + 1 = 6$

(C) $8 + 7 = 15$

(D) $9 + 2 = 11$

7. (A)

The domain of a function includes all the values of x for which the function is defined. The given function is defined for all real numbers except for those that make the denominator 0. This happen when $x^2 - 4 = 0$. Solving this equation gives us $x = 2$ or $x = -2$. The domain is therefore all real numbers except for 2 or -2.

8. (C)

If any number c is plugged into a polynomial to get 0, then $x - c$ is a factor of the polynomial. Looking at the possible answers, there are four choices for c: 1, -1, 2, and -2. Plugging 1 into the polynomial gives us:

$$2(1)^3 - (1)^2 + 3(1) - 4 = 2 - 1 + 3 - 4 = 0$$

Thus, $x - 1$ is a factor of the polynomial.

9. (A)

The mean (or average) of a set of numbers is found by adding all the numbers then dividing by how many numbers were added. If these numbers are doubled, then the mean should also be doubled. For instance, the mean of the set of numbers 2, 4, 6, 8, 10 is 6 because $\dfrac{2 + 4 + 6 + 8 + 10}{5} = \dfrac{30}{5} = 6$. If you double each number, you get the set 4, 8, 12, 16, 20, whose mean is 12 because $\dfrac{4 + 8 + 12 + 16 + 20}{5} = \dfrac{60}{5} = 12$.

10. (A)

To find the converse of a conditional statement, we switch the two statements that make up the conditional. That is, "If P, then Q" becomes "If Q, then P."

11. (D)

Since R and S are small sets, the Cartesian product can quickly be determined: $R \times S = \{(u, x), (u, y), (v, x), (v, y)\}$. The only answer choice that is not in this set is (u, v).

12. (B)

First you need to find $g(4)$. According to the second table, if $x = 4$, then $g(x) = 2$; therefore $g(4) = 2$. Now find $f(2)$. According to the first table, when $x = 2$, $f(x) = 5$, so $f(2) = 5$. Thus $f(g(4)) = f(2) = 5$.

13. (C)

If you add the length and width of a rectangle, you've gone half the distance around the rectangle, in this case 100 feet. So length + width = 100. Since width is x, the equation becomes length + x = 100 or length = 100 − x.

14. (D)

A quick way to do this problem is to start listing the multiples of 15 and 18 and see which number appears on both lists first:

Multiples of 15: 15, 30, 45, 60, 75, 90, 105, …

Multiples of 18: 18, 36, 54, 72, 90, 108, 126, …

Since 90 is the first number to appear in both lists, the answer is (D). You also can solve this problem quickly by looking at the answer choices and determining whether each is a multiple of 15 and 18.

15. (B)

Out of seven cards, two will have 4 written on them, since 4 appears twice in the number 5,473,343. The probability of getting a 4 would therefore be $\frac{2}{7}$.

16. (90)

The sum of the three angles of any triangle is 180°. Since we are talking about a right triangle, we know one of the angles must measure 90°. This leaves 90° for the sum of the other two angles.

17. (A)

The graph of a function of x must pass the *vertical line test*, which says that any vertical line drawn on the Cartesian plane should intersect the graph of a function no more than once. (B), (C), and (D) all fail this test.

18. (C)

To divide two fractions, multiply the first by the reciprocal of the second. The reciprocal of $\frac{c}{d}$ is $\frac{d}{c}$, so $\frac{a}{b} \div \frac{c}{d} = \frac{a}{b} \times \frac{d}{c} = \frac{ad}{bc}$.

19. (B)

The probability of a given child being a boy is $\frac{1}{2}$. If the first child is a boy, the chance of both subsequent children also being boys is $\frac{1}{2} \times \frac{1}{2}$ or $\frac{1}{4}$.

20. (D)

$\log_4 x = 3$ means that $4^3 = x$, so $x = 64$. Substituting 64 for x gives us $\log_8 64 = ?$ The equation can be phrased as: 8 to what power equals 64? The answer is 2, because $8^2 = 64$.

21. (C)

Notice that the area outside of the two circles is shaded. The shaded area is what is not in A or B, which is $(A \cup B)'$. Also, all of circle B is shaded. So the Venn diagram here represents $(A \cup B)' \cup B$.

22. (0)

Joe's mean score is $\frac{14 + 17 + 12 + 18 + 24}{5} = \frac{85}{5} = 17$.

To find his median score, list the numbers from smallest to largest and identify the number in the middle. The middle number of 12, 14, 17, 18, 24 is 17, so his median score is 17. Since the mean and median scores are the same, the difference in scores is 0.

23. (A)

No matter what value we substitute for x, x^2 will always be greater than or equal to 0. Likewise, $(x − 2)^2$ will always be greater than or equal to 0, so the range of the function is all real numbers greater than or equal to 0.

24. (D)

"A is a necessary condition for B" means that whenever B happens, A happens. In other words, if B, then A.

25. (A)

Two lines are perpendicular if their slopes are negative reciprocals of each other. The negative reciprocal of $\frac{4}{5}$ is $-\frac{5}{4}$, so the answer is (A).

26. (B)

We are looking for 60 written as a product of prime numbers. Answer choices (A) and (C) can be discounted because they both include numbers that are not prime. If answer choice (D) is multiplied we get 90, so this answer can also be discarded. This leaves us with (B).

27. (C)

Of the seven temperatures listed, four of them are prime: 2, 7, 11, and 13. While 3 is a prime number, −3 is not because prime numbers do not include negative numbers. The probability of choosing a prime number is therefore $\frac{4}{7}$.

28. (A)

By listing the temperatures from smallest to largest we get: −3, 2, 7, 9, 11, 13, 15. Since 9 is the number in the middle, 9° is the median low temperature.

29. (A)

The inverse of a function "undoes" the function. In this problem, the function takes x, subtracts 4, then divides by 3. To undo this, we would need to multiply by 3, then add 4. Answer choice (A) completes this calculation.

30. (D)

If you simplify the first three choices, you get rational numbers: $\sqrt{9} = 3$, $\sqrt{25} = 5$, and $\sqrt{49} = 7$. Answer choice (D), therefore, is the correct choice.

31. (B)

Suppose the original box had a length of 2, width of 3, and height of 4. The volume of the box would be $2 \times 3 \times 4 = 24$. If each of these dimensions were doubled, the new volume would be $4 \times 6 \times 8 = 192$, which is 8 times the original volume.

32. (C)

When choosing the first apple, 5 out of 25 apples are green, so the probability of getting a green apple would be $\frac{5}{25} = \frac{1}{5}$. Once this apple has been chosen, there are 4 out of 24 remaining apples that are green, so the probability of the second apple being green would be $\frac{4}{24} = \frac{1}{6}$. Thus, the probability of them both being green is $\frac{1}{5} \times \frac{1}{6} = \frac{1}{30}$.

33. (A)

$X \cap Y$ denotes the set of elements that are both prime and even integers less than 15. There is only one even prime number, and that is the number 2. This is the only number that would be in the set $X \cap Y$, so the number of elements in the set is 1.

34. (D)

$a^2 + 2ab + b^2 = (a + b)^2$, so for any odd numbers a and b, $(a + b)$ and $(a + b)^2$ will always be even.

35. (B)

$2n + 1$ is always odd if n is an integer, but plugging $\frac{1}{2}$ into the equation produces $2\left(\frac{1}{2}\right) + 1 = 1 + 1 = 2$, which is not odd.

36. (D)

Set $f(x)$ equal to $g(x)$ and solve:
$$3x + 4 = x - 2$$
$$2x + 4 = -2$$
$$2x = -6$$
$$x = -3$$

37. (A)

Integers are rational numbers, so the set of integers is contained in the set of rational numbers. Both rational and irrational numbers are real numbers, so the set of real numbers contains the other three sets.

38. (216)

Each time you roll a die there are 6 possible outcomes, so if you roll three dice, there are $6 \times 6 \times 6 = 216$ possible outcomes.

39. (B)

This problem requires using some properties of logarithms:
$\log_n\left(\frac{x^2}{y}\right) = \log_n x^2 - \log_n y = 2\log_n x - \log_n y = 2(4) - 6 = 2$.

40. (2)

If $x - 2$ is a factor of $x^4 - 2x^3 + kx - 4$, then plugging 2 into the polynomial would make the polynomial 0. Solving the equation:

$(2)^4 - 2(2)^3 k(2) - 4 = 0$
$16 - 16 + 2k - 4 = 0$
$2k - 4 = 0$
$2k = 4$
$k = 2$

41. (C)

In five hours, the train has traveled 300 additional miles, which is 60 miles per hour (mph). As the speed of the train remains constant, it is represented by $60t$, where t is the number of hours since Sally embarked. The distance of $60t$ will be added to the original distance traveled by the train before Sally came aboard, so the formula for the total distance traveled by the train is $D = 120 + 60t$.

42. (B)

The symbol $\subset$ in the problem states that both A and C are proper subsets of B. While it could be true that $A \subset C$, $C \subset A$, or $A = \emptyset$, it is never true that if $C \subset B$ then $B \subset C$. This is because C must have fewer elements than B, since it is a proper subset of B.

43. (A)

Having −3 before the function will make the graph open down instead of up and will make the graph more narrow.

44. (D)

When you choose the first jellybean, there are 6 red out of 15 total, so the probability of selecting a red jellybean would be $\frac{6}{15} = \frac{2}{5}$. The first jellybean is not replaced, so there are 14 jellybeans left. Five of the 14 remaining jellybeans are yellow, so the probability of choosing a yellow jellybean second would be $\frac{5}{14}$. The probability of choosing a red then a yellow jellybean would be $\frac{2}{5} \times \frac{5}{14} = \frac{1}{7}$.

45. (C)

Since $A \to B$ and $B \to C$, it can be concluded that $A \to C$. This is logically equivalent to $\sim C \to \sim A$, so $\sim C$ implies $\sim A$.

46. (A)

Solving the equation produces:
$x^2 + 9 = 0$
$x^2 = -9$
$x^2 = \pm\sqrt{-9}$
$x^2 = \pm 3i$

47. (B)

A composite number is divisible by at least one number other than itself and 1. 27 is divisible by 3 and 9, so it is composite.

48. (C)

In base two, there are two choices for each digit (0 or 1). However, the first digit must be 1 because if it were 0, the number would only have five digits. The other five digits can be either 0 or 1, so there would be $2 \times 2 \times 2 \times 2 \times 2 = 64$ possibilities.

49. (D)

Since $f(g(x)) = \frac{1}{x - 4}$, $x + 4$ needs to be plugged into each choice to see which gives us the desired result. Plugging $x + 4$ into (D) we get: $\frac{1}{(x + 4) - 8} = \frac{1}{x - 4}$

50. (B)

The answer needs to be computed in base two:
$1011_2 = (1 \times 8) + (0 \times 4) + (1 \times 2) + (1 \times 1)$
$= 8 + 0 + 2 + 1$
$= 11$

51. (A)

5 cards have been dealt, with 47 cards left, only one of which is an ace. The chance that you will draw an ace if you draw two of the cards is $\frac{2}{47}$.

52. (C)

Replacing x with -2 produces:
$$g(-2) = 2(-2)^3 - 3(-2)^2 + 5(-2) - 4$$
$$= -16 - 12 - 10 - 4$$
$$= -42$$

53. (8)

If we let x represent Sam's current age, Josh's age is $x + 5$. Three years ago, Josh's age was $(x + 5) - 3$ and Sam's was $(x - 3)$. Josh's age was also twice Sam's, or $2(x - 3)$. We now have two equivalent expressions for Josh's age three years ago, allowing us to solve the problem:
$$(x + 5) - 3 = 2(x - 3)$$
$$x + 2 = 2x - 6$$
$$2 = x - 6$$
$$8 = x$$

54. (D)

A set is finite if all elements in the set can be listed. The answer is (D), since a list can be made of the elements of all three sets described.

55. (B)

The y-intercept of a function is found by setting $x = 0$. In this case: $f(0) = (0 - 2)^3 = -2^3 = -8$.

56. (C)

The probability it will snow on Tuesday is 0.3, so the probability it will not snow on Tuesday is 0.7. The probability it will snow on Monday but not on Tuesday would be $0.6 \times 0.7 = 0.42$.

57. (D)

"All doctors are men" means that if you are a doctor, then you are a man. So, if my sister is a doctor, she must be a man. Even though this may not make sense to you, it is true according to the logic of the question.

58. (A)

If you flip a coin three times, there are eight possible outcomes: HHH, HHT, HTH, HTT, THH, THT, TTH, TTT. Of these outcomes, only four have at least two heads: HHH, HHT, HTH, THH. The probability of getting three heads given that you have at least two heads would be $\frac{1}{4}$.

59. (C)

To find the inverse of a function listed as a series of ordered pairs, simply reverse the numbers in each ordered pair.

60. (B)

The mean is $\frac{2 + 3 + 5 + 7 + 11 + 13 + 17}{7} = \frac{58}{7} = 8\frac{2}{7}$. The median is 7. So the difference between the mean and median is $8\frac{2}{7} - 7 = 1\frac{2}{7}$.

Section Three: The CLEP College Mathematics Exam | 181

Chapter Nine: CLEP College Mathematics Review

- The Big Picture: CLEP College Mathematics
- Nuts and Bolts
- CLEP College Mathematics Strategy Checklist
- Set Theory
- Logic
- Real Number System
- Functions and Graphs
- Probability and Statistics
- Additional Topics from Algebra and Geometry
- College Mathematics Resources
- Final Thoughts

You've decided to get a head start on higher education by taking the CLEP College Mathematics exam. Many institutions of higher learning will grant six semester hours of credit to high-scoring candidates. (You should check with the schools you are considering to find out their policies.) This guide will help you achieve your goal of a great score.

THE BIG PICTURE: CLEP COLLEGE MATHEMATICS

Let's start with some good news. Since the College Mathematics exam consists of material generally taught in a college course for non-mathematics majors, the material on the test can easily be learned by most students (that includes you). None of the material covered on the exam requires advanced mathematical knowledge. In fact, most of the material on the exam has been taught to students by the tenth grade.

Before you delve into any subject, it is important to know what you are getting into. Understanding the structure of the CLEP College Mathematics exam will help you maximize your score, so let's start talking facts.

This particular exam consists of 60 questions to be completed in 90 minutes. Do some basic math, and you can see that means that you can spend one and a half minutes on each question.

Approximately half of the questions on the exam require you to understand and solve simple, routine problems, which should be as easy to solve as going through your day-to-day activities.

KAPLAN

The other half of the exam involves non-routine problems that require test-takers to understand concepts and the application of these concepts. The non-routine problems require you to call upon your bank of mathematical concepts, your "troops," to carry out your plan. Most of the exam questions are multiple choice, with four possible answers to choose from. Some problems may require a numerical answer to be tallied and entered into the box provided.

The different areas or topics covered on the exam include sets, logic, the real number system, functions and their graphs, and probability and statistics. There are also additional topics from algebra and geometry, including complex numbers, logarithms, properties of triangles and circles, and application problems. Just as it is important to keep up with current events, you should be familiar with currently taught mathematical notation, symbols, and vocabulary.

The exam does not focus on arithmetic, and a calculator will not be required for any problems. However, a scientific (non-graphing) calculator will be provided for you on the computer, as a test-taking tool during the exam.

NUTS AND BOLTS

The key mathematical topics to study, along with how much of the CLEP College Mathematics exam each of these mathematical topics covers, can be found in the following list.

10% Sets
- Intersection and union
- Subsets
- Venn diagrams
- Cartesian product

10% Logic
- Truth tables
- Conjunctions, disjunctions, implications, and negations
- Conditionals and biconditionals
- Necessary and sufficient
- Converse, inverse, and contrapositive
- Hypotheses, conclusions, and counterexamples

20% Real Number System
- Prime versus composite numbers
- Odd versus even numbers
- Factors and divisibility
- Rational versus irrational numbers
- Absolute value
- Binary (base two) system

20% Functions and Graphs
- Properties of functions and graphs
- Domain and range
- Structure of functions and inverse functions

25% Probability and Statistics
- Counting problems (includes permutations and combinations)
- Probabilities of single and compound events
- Conditional probability
- Calculating mean and median

15% Additional Topics from Algebra and Geometry
- Imaginary and complex numbers
- Exponents and logarithms
- Perimeter and area
- Triangles and circles (with Pythagorean Theorem)
- Finding parallel and perpendicular lines
- Word problems

Percentage of the exam and the number of problems that are from each topic are approximate. There may be more or fewer problems from a particular topic on the actual exam.

While this list may seem intimidating, keep in mind that some of the subtopics listed above will only appear once on the exam, while some may not appear at all. It is best to study all of them, however, just in case you are tested on every topic. It is important to have a solid knowledge base so that few questions are complete surprises to you during the CLEP College Mathematics exam.

CLEP COLLEGE MATHEMATICS STRATEGY CHECKLIST

Preparing for any exam takes time. In order to maximize your study time and be prepared for the fast-paced format of the actual exam, consult the following list:

Be familiar with all the symbols and terms that may appear on the exam. While you may be familiar with symbols such as ≠, ≤, and ≈, more specific symbols may not be as familiar, such as ∪, ⊆, and ∈ from set theory, or ~, ∧, and ∨ from logic. Similarly, terms such as *contrapositive* or *permutation* may not immediately be familiar.

Be on the lookout for general keywords such as "all," "never," or "always." While it may sometimes be true that n^2 is greater than n, for example, it is not *always* true. Likewise, adding two odd numbers will *never* produce an odd number.

Be on the lookout for specific keywords such as "positive," "negative," "odd," "even," or specific types of numbers such as "integers" or "whole numbers." Knowing that you are dealing with integers in a problem, for instance, indicates that you can have negative numbers, but not fractions, which may be important.

Know probability. Approximately a fourth of the exam covers probability and statistics, so be sure to be familiar with the types of problems that may appear here. Also keep in mind that probability is often written as a fraction and this fraction will need to be reduced in your answer.

Backsolve. If you're asked which number solves a particular equation, there's no need to solve the equation if you're provided possible answers. Plug the answer choices into the equation until the right answer is found.

Many test-takers stay up late and try to cram a lot of information in the night before, which makes them too tired to answer exam questions in the most efficient way possible. When your mind is dragging due to lack of sleep, it is difficult to answer 60 questions in 90 minutes. If you skip breakfast the day of the exam, your mind may be focused on how hungry you are, rather than how to solve the next problem on the test.

SET THEORY

The CLEP College Mathematics exam will cover the general topic of *sets*, which are collections of objects. Sets can be represented by words, letters, or numbers. A CD collection, for instance, would be a set. The objects that make up a set are called *elements*. For example, if you have 50 CDs in a collection, the set of 50 CDs would be composed of 50 individual elements, each CD in the collection.

Sets are typically represented by capital letters. Braces, { and }, are often used to enclose the elements of a set. For instance, sets can be written as:

A = {a, b, c, d, e} or B = {1, 3, 5}.

The order in which the elements are listed is not important. The number of elements in a set is called the *cardinal number* of the set. If a set has 5 elements, then its cardinal number is 5. A set is considered *well defined* when its component elements are objectively clear. For example, "all the CDs in my collection" is a well-defined set but "the best television shows on Monday night" is not because that category is definitely subjective!

The symbol $\in$ can be used to indicate that an element belongs to a particular set and the symbol $\notin$ —which contains the "not" slash you've seen on so many signs—can indicate that an element does not belong to a set. So, if A = {1, 3, 5, 7}, it can be said that $3 \in A$ and $6 \notin A$. The set that contains no elements is called the *empty set*, or *null set*, and is denoted as either $\emptyset$ or { }. A set can contain elements and later become a null set, provided that all elements of the set are no longer available. For example, as a species becomes extinct, the set of individuals of that species gradually dwindles until there are no individuals left in the set. When there are no individuals left to fill the set, the set becomes null. (The dodo set is a null set.)

Listing the elements of a set between braces is called *roster notation*. Another way to write a set is called *set-builder notation*. In this notation a variable such as x is used to represent an element of the set, and a vertical bar, | , stands for the phrase "such that," followed by a brief description of the variable. For example, the set of all integers less than 10 could be written as:

{x | x is an integer less than 10}.

A set can be broken down into smaller units. A is a *subset* of B, denoted $A \subseteq B$, if every element in A is also in B. For instance, if A = {a, b, c} and B = {a, b, c, d, e}, then $A \subseteq B$. Sets A and B are *equal*, denoted A = B, if they contain the exact same elements. If $A \subseteq B$ but $A \neq B$, then we say A is a *proper subset* of B, denoted $A \subset B$. If, for example, A= {peanut butter, jelly, milk, bananas} and B={peanut butter, jelly, milk, bananas, butter, raisins, and lettuce}, A is a proper subset of B, since A contains some, but not all, of the elements of B.

Now let's look at the big picture. The *universal set*, U, is the set that contains all the possible elements needed for a particular problem. The *complement* of set A, denoted A′, is the set of elements that are in U but not in A. For example, suppose U is the set of all integers for a particular problem. If A represents the set of all negative integers, A′ represents the set of all non-negative integers.

The *union* of sets A and B, denoted A ∪ B, is the set of elements in A or in B. The *intersection* of two sets A and B, denoted A ∩ B, is the set of elements in A and B. For example, if A = {1, 2, 3} and B = {2, 3, 4, 5}, then A ∪ B = {1, 2, 3, 4, 5} and A ∩ B = {2, 3}. If A ∩ B = ∅, then A and B are called *disjoint* and do not have any values in common.

A way to visualize sets is to use a *Venn diagram*. Each Venn diagram uses a rectangle to represent the universal set and circles within the rectangle to represent all other sets. Anything that belongs to set A is inside circle A:

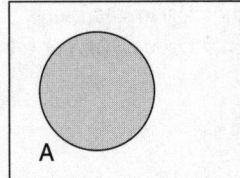

Anything not in A is outside of circle A:

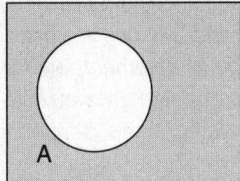

The operations of union and intersection are represented in the following Venn diagrams:

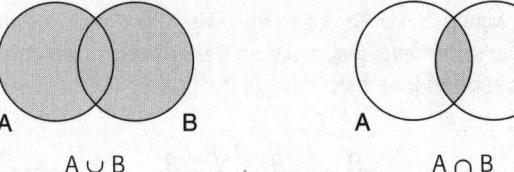

There is another way to combine two sets beyond union and intersection. Let A = {2, 3} and B = {5, 6, 7}. The set of all possible ordered pairs (a, b), with a ∈ A and b ∈ B, is called the Cartesian Product of A and B, denoted A × B. In this case, A × B = {(2, 5), (2, 6), (2, 7), (3, 5), (3, 6), (3, 7)}.

Set Theory Review Questions

1. If A = {1, 3, 5, 7} and B = {2, 3, 4, 5}, find A ∪ B and A ∩ B.

    Solution: A ∪ B is the set of elements that are in A or in B, so A ∪ B = {1, 2, 3, 4, 5, 7}. A ∩ B is the set of elements that are in A and in B, so A ∩ B = {3, 5}.

2. If U = {2, 4, 6, 8, 10, 12} and A = {2, 8, 10}, find A'.

    Solution: A' represents the set of elements in U that are not in A, so A' = {4, 6, 12}.

3. What is the notation for the following Venn diagram?

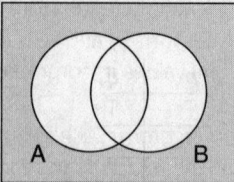

Solution: The shaded area of the diagram represents the set of elements that are not in A or in B. Since there are no elements inside circle A or circle B, the notation would be (A ∪ B)′.

LOGIC

In logic, algebraic techniques are used to determine when statements are true and when they are false. A *statement* conveys one idea and can be labeled either true or false. Examples of statements are "She has green eyes" and "My dog is a beagle." Letters such as p, q, r, and s are used to represent statements. *Compound statements* are formed by connecting two or more statements. An example of a compound statement would be "She has green eyes and my dog is a beagle." Two separate ideas are conveyed in this compound statement.

If two statements are connected using the word "and," the resulting compound statement is called a *conjunction*. This math term means pretty much the same thing that it does when talking about conjunctions in grammar; it combines two statements. If p and q are statements, then the conjunction "p and q" is written $p \wedge q$. To determine when a compound statement is true, we have to consider when the statements that make up the compound statement are true and when they are false. This can be done by creating a *truth table*. The truth table for the conjunction above is:

p	q	$p \wedge q$
T	T	T
T	F	F
F	T	F
F	F	F

Conjunction

The first row of this table tells us that when p is true and q is true, $p \wedge q$ is true. The second row says that when p is true and q is false, $p \wedge q$ is false. The third and fourth rows also give us results of "false," telling us that the conjunction is only true when both p and q are true.

If two statements are connected using the word "or," the resulting compound statement is called a *disjunction*. If p and q are statements, then the conjunction "p or q" is written $p \vee q$. The truth table for the disjunction p or q is:

p	q	$p \vee q$
T	T	T
T	F	T
F	T	T
F	F	F

Disjunction

The table shows that a disjunction is only false when both p and q are false. Note that in logic, the word "or" is used to mean "either or both."

If p is a statement, its *negation* can be found by inserting the word "not" into it. For instance, the negation of "It is raining" is "It is not raining." The negation of statement p is symbolized $\sim p$ and read "not p." The truth table for the negation is:

p	$\sim p$
T	F
F	T

Negation

So when p is true, $\sim p$ is false and when p is false, $\sim p$ is true. For example, it cannot be raining (p) and not raining ($\sim p$ or not p) at the same time and place.

If p and q are statements, then $p \rightarrow q$ represents the compound statement "if p, then q." A compound statement of this form is called an *implication* or *conditional statement*. Its truth table is:

p	q	$p \rightarrow q$
T	T	T
T	F	F
F	T	T
F	F	T

Implication/Conditional

The compound statement $p \rightarrow q$ is also read "p implies q" and is only false when p is true and q is false. Another compound statement is the *biconditional*, which is symbolized $p \leftrightarrow q$ and is read "p if and only if q." The biconditional is true only when p and q are both true or both false. The truth table for the biconditional is:

p	q	$p \leftrightarrow q$
T	T	T
T	F	F
F	T	F
F	F	T

Biconditional

If we start with the conditional statement $p \to q$, then its *converse* is $q \to p$. For example, the converse of "If it is sunny, then it is warm" is "If it is warm, then it is sunny." Similarly, $\sim p \to \sim q$ is the *inverse* of $p \to q$, while $\sim q \to \sim p$ is called the *contrapositive* of $p \to q$.

In logic, necessary and sufficient conditions are discussed. A is *necessary* for B if and only if B cannot occur without A. That is, whenever you have B, you have A. For instance, being female is necessary for being pregnant. On the other hand, A is *sufficient* for B if and only if A guarantees B. That is, whenever you have A, you have B. For example, getting an 83 on a test is sufficient for passing.

An *argument* is a claim that a series of statements, called *hypotheses* or *premises*, imply a final statement, called the *conclusion*. An argument is called *valid* if its conclusion is true whenever all of its hypotheses are true. An argument that is not valid is called a *fallacy*.

One way to show that an argument or assertion is not valid is to provide a *counterexample*. This is an example that satisfies the hypotheses of the argument but does not agree with the conclusion. For instance, suppose it is asserted that "If m and n are odd numbers, then $m + n$ is an odd number." For a counterexample, choose two odd numbers, say $m = 3$ and $n = 5$. According to the assertion, $m + n$ should also be odd, but $m + n = 3 + 5 = 8$, which is even.

Logic Review Questions

1. Write the converse, inverse, and contrapositive of "If it is milk, then it contains calcium."

    Solution: If we think of this statement as $p \to q$, then the converse is $q \to p$ or "If it contains calcium, then it is milk"; the inverse is $\sim p \to \sim q$ or "If it is not milk, then it does not contain calcium"; and the contrapositive is $\sim q \to \sim p$ or "If it does not contain calcium, then it is not milk."

2. If p represents a true statement and q represents a false statement, determine the truth values of the compound statements $p \wedge \sim q$, $\sim p \vee q$, and $\sim(p \vee q)$.

    Solution: As q is a false statement, $\sim q$ is true, so $p \wedge \sim q$ is the conjunction of two true statements, which is true. Similarly, as p is true, $\sim p$ is false, so $\sim p \vee q$ is the disjunction of two false statements, which is false. Finally, as p is true and q is false, $p \vee q$ is true, so $\sim(p \vee q)$ must be false.

3. Provide a counterexample to the assertion "If n is an integer, then $2n > n$."

    Solution: You need to find an integer that doesn't satisfy $2n > n$. One choice would be $n = -3$, for $2n = -6$ and -6 is not greater than -3.

REAL NUMBER SYSTEM

The real number system is divided into many different types of numbers. The numbers that are used for counting {1, 2, 3, 4, 5 . . .} are called *natural* or *counting numbers*. If we add zero to this set, we get *whole numbers*. If we also include negative versions of the counting numbers we get *integers*.

A real number is rational if it can be written as the ratio of two integers, where the denominator is not 0. For instance, $\frac{2}{3}$, $-\frac{5}{8}$, and $\frac{11}{3}$ are all rational numbers. This set also includes mixed numbers and decimals that stop or repeat, such as 0.25 and 7.6888. Think of a rational number as a bag of apples. Regardless of how many apples are in the bag, you cannot start out with zero apples in the bag and expect five apples to magically appear, when there are none to begin with. If you started out with three apples in the bag, and removed one, you would still have a rational number to deal with, since $\frac{2}{3}$ of the apples are left.

Any real number that cannot be written as the ratio of two integers is called *irrational*. These numbers include decimals that do not stop and do not repeat. Examples of irrational numbers are $\sqrt{2}$, $-\sqrt{7}$, and π.

Whole number *m* is divisible by whole number *n* if, when *m* is divided by *n*, there is no remainder. For example, if you divide 35 by 7, there is no remainder, so we say 35 is divisible by 7. Furthermore, 7 is said to be a factor of 35.

Any integer that is divisible by 2 is called an *even* integer. Any integer that is not divisible by 2 is called an *odd* integer. These definitions include negative integers, so that −4 is even and −5 is odd.

A whole number greater than 1 that is only divisible by itself and 1 is called a *prime number*. Examples of prime numbers are 2, 3, 5, 7, 11, 13, and 17. Note that 2 is the only even prime number. A whole number greater than 1 that is divisible by some number other than itself and 1 is called *composite*. Composite numbers include 4, 6, 8, 9, 10, 12, 14, 15, etc.

Every composite number can be written as a product of prime numbers. For instance, the composite number 20 can be written as $2 \times 2 \times 5$, while the composite number 30 can be written as $2 \times 3 \times 5$. This is known as *prime factorization*.

The *absolute value* of a number is its distance from zero on the number line. If *n* is a number, its absolute value is indicated by |*n*|. As distance is always positive, absolute value is always positive. The absolute value of a positive number is just the number, while the absolute value of a negative number is that number without the negative sign. For example, |5| = 5 and |−3| = 3.

Number A is *greater than* number B, written A > B, if A is to the right of B on the number line. Number A is *less than* B, written A < B, if A is to the left of B on the number line. These definitions can help when ordering negative numbers, for while it may be easy to see that 7 > 5 without using a number line, it is not always so easy to see that −7 < −5.

The number system that is used to represent numbers is called a *decimal* system because it represents numbers in terms of powers of 10. Think of the place values of whole numbers: ones ($10^0 = 1$), tens ($10^1 = 10$), hundreds ($10^2 = 100$), thousands ($10^3 = 1000$), and so on. Any number in the decimal system can be broken down using these powers of ten. For example:

$$1862 = 1000 + 800 + 60 + 2$$
$$= 1(1000) + 8(100) + 6(10) + 2(1)$$
$$= 1(10^3) + 8(10^2) + 6(10^1) + 2(10^0)$$

A different number system is called the *binary system*. In this system, numbers are expressed in terms of powers of 2 and only two digits, usually 0 and 1, are required. So numbers in the binary system look like 1011_2 or 1100101_2. The small, low two ($_2$) at the far right is there to denote that this is a binary number. The rightmost digit indicates how many "ones" you have ($2^0 = 1$), the next digit how many "twos" you have ($2^1 = 2$), the next digit how many "fours" ($2^2 = 4$), the next how many "eights" ($2^3 = 8$), and so on. The binary system is used in computer coding, but you won't see it on many wristwatches.

A number written in binary can be translated into a decimal number. For example, say we want to translate 10111_2 into its decimal equivalent. The rightmost digit tells you that you have 1 "one," the next digit tells you that you have one "two," then one "four," no "eights," and one "sixteen." So:

$$10111_2 = 1(2^4) + 0(2^3) + 1(2^2) + 1(2^1) + 1(2^0)$$
$$= 1(16) + 0(8) + 1(4) + 1(2) + 1(1)$$
$$= 23$$

To turn a decimal number into binary, start by finding the largest power of 2 less than the number. Subtract this power of 2 from the number, then look for the largest power of 2 less than this number. Repeat this process until you end up with 0 or 1.

For example, say you want to convert 47 into binary. The largest power of 2 less than 47 is 32, which is 2^5, and $47 - 32 = 15$. The largest power of 2 less than 15 is 8, which is 2^3, and $15 - 8 = 7$. The largest power of 2 less than 7 is 4, which is 2^2, and $7 - 4 = 3$. The largest power of 2 less than 3 is 2, which is 2^1, and $3 - 2 = 1$. We can stop as 1 is a power of 2. This tells us that:

$$47 = 1(2^5) + 0(2^4) + 1(2^3) + 1(2^2) + 1(2^1) + 1(2^0)$$
$$= 101111_2$$

Real Number System Review Questions

1. Determine the rational and irrational numbers in the set of numbers $\{\frac{5}{4}, 3.7, \sqrt{8}, 9.525, \sqrt{9}, \sqrt[3]{4}, \frac{2}{3}\}$.

    Solution: Rational numbers are fractions and decimals that either stop or repeat, so the rational numbers in the set are $\frac{5}{4}$, 3.7, 9.525, $\sqrt{9}$ ($= 3$), and $\frac{2}{3}$.

This leaves $\sqrt{8}$ and $\sqrt[3]{4}$ as the irrational numbers (decimals that don't stop and don't repeat).

2. Which one of the numbers 42, 45, 49, 51, and 53 is prime?

   Solution: The only even prime number is 2, so it's not 42. 45 is divisible by 5, 49 is divisible by 7, and 51 is divisible by 3. This leaves only 53.

FUNCTIONS AND GRAPHS

Let X and Y be any two sets. A *function* is a rule that assigns to each element $x \in X$ one and only one $y \in Y$. A function is usually notated $f(x)$, which is read "f of x." For example, $f(x) = 2x + 5$ is the function that takes a number x, doubles it, then adds 5. By replacing x with different numbers, we can see each function has a different outcome. For instance, $f(2) = 2(2) + 5 = 9$ while $f(-1) = 2(-1) + 5 = 3$.

The *domain* of a function is the set of numbers that can be plugged into a function so that the function is defined. If $f(x) = x^2$, then the domain is the set of all real numbers, since any real number can be squared. On the other hand, if $f(x) = \sqrt{x}$, the domain is the set of real numbers such that $x \geq 0$, because the square root of a negative number cannot be taken.

The *range* of a function is the set of numbers that the function produces. For example, the range of the function $f(x) = x^2$ is all real numbers such that $y \geq 0$ because if you square a number, you always get a nonnegative result. Similarly, the range of $f(x) = |x|$ is the set of real numbers such that $y \geq 0$ because the absolute value of any number is always nonnegative.

Functions can be added, subtracted, multiplied, and divided. Let $f(x)$ and $g(x)$ be two functions. The following four functions can then be defined:

The *sum* of $f(x)$ and $g(x)$ is given by $(f + g)(x) = f(x) + g(x)$.

The *difference* of $f(x)$ and $g(x)$ is given by $(f - g)(x) = f(x) - g(x)$.

The *product* of $f(x)$ and $g(x)$ is given by $(f \times g)(x) = f(x) g(x)$.

The *quotient* of $f(x)$ and $g(x)$ is given by $\left(\dfrac{f}{g}\right)(x) = \dfrac{f(x)}{g(x)}$, where $g(x) \neq 0$.

For example, suppose $f(x) = 3x - 2$ and $g(x) = x + 5$. Then:

$(f + g)(x) = (3x - 2) + (x + 5) = 4x + 3$

$(f - g)(x) = (3x - 2) - (x + 5) = 2x - 7$

$(f \times g)(x) = (3x - 2)(x + 5) = 3x^2 + 13x - 10$

$\left(\dfrac{f}{g}\right)(x) = \dfrac{(3x - 2)}{(x + 5)}$

Note that this last function is not defined when $x = -5$, so its domain is all real numbers except -5.

There is a fifth way of combining two functions f and g, known as a *composition function*. This is written $f \circ g$ and is defined as $(f \circ g)(x) = f(g(x))$. The idea is to substitute whatever the g function is into f and then simplify the result. If $f(x) = 3x - 2$ and $g(x) = x + 5$, then $(f \circ g)(x) = f(g(x)) = 3(x + 5) - 2 = 3x + 13$. Note that $(g \circ f)(x) = g(f(x))$, which is not the same as $(f \circ g)(x)$. In the above example, $(g \circ f)(x) = g(f(x)) = (3x - 2) + 5 = 3x + 3$.

The *inverse* of a function, which is written $f^{-1}(x)$, "undoes" the action of a function. That is to say that if the function assigns the domain value of 2 to 5, then the inverse assigns 5 back to 2. An inverse can be obtained by replacing $f(x)$ with y, then interchanging x and y in the resulting equation. Solving this equation for y will result in the inverse of the original function.

For example, to find the inverse of $f(x) = 3x - 2$, we first write $y = 3x - 2$. Now interchange x and y, resulting in $x = 3y - 2$. Solving this equation for y we get $y = \frac{x + 2}{3}$. So $f^{-1}(x) = \frac{x + 2}{3}$.

Functions can be graphed on a coordinate system by plotting domain values on the x-axis and their corresponding y values on the y-axis. A function of the form $f(x) = c$, where c is a constant, is called a *constant function*. Its graph is a horizontal line passing through the y-axis at c. A function of the form $f(x) = mx + b$, where m and b are constants, is called a *linear function*. Its graph is a straight line that crosses the y-axis at b and has a slope of m (that is, for every unit the graph moves horizontally, it rises m units vertically). For example, the graph of $f(x) = 3x + 2$ is linear, so we only need to find two values to draw the graph. As $f(0) = 2$ and $f(1) = 5$, we have:

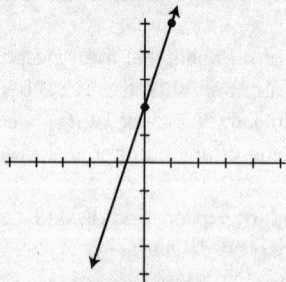

A function of the form $f(x) = ax^2 + bx = c$ is called a *quadratic function* and its graph is always a parabola. For instance, $f(x) = x^2 + 2x - 3$ is a quadratic function. To draw its graph, we need to find several points to plot:

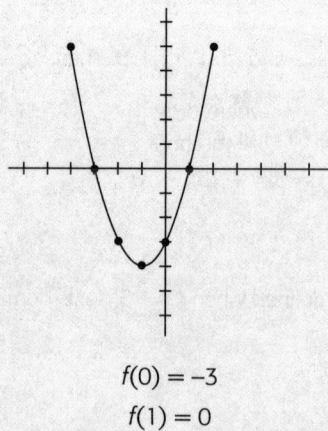

$f(0) = -3$
$f(1) = 0$

$$f(2) = 5$$
$$f(-1) = -4$$
$$f(-2) = -3$$
$$f(-3) = 0$$
$$f(-4) = 5$$

To determine whether or not a graph is the graph of a function, apply the *Vertical Line Test*, which says that a vertical line will cross the graph of a function at no more than one point. Applying this rule to the graphs above will show you that they are indeed graphs of functions.

Functions and Graphs Review Questions

1. If $f(x) = 2x^2 - 3x + 1$, find $f(2)$, $f(3)$ and $f(-1)$.

    Solution: $f(2) = 2(2)^2 - 3(2) + 1 = 8 - 6 + 1 = 3$
    $f(3) = 2(3)^2 - 3(3) + 1 = 18 - 9 + 1 = 10$
    $f(-1) = 2(-1)^2 - 3(-1) + 1 = 2 + 3 + 1 = 6$

2. State the domain and range of the function $f(x) = \frac{1}{x^2}$.

    Solution: This function is defined for all values of x except for $x = 0$ (which would give us division by 0), so the domain is the set of all real numbers except for 0. As for the range, any number we plug into the function will turn out to be positive because of x^2. So the range is the set of all positive real numbers.

PROBABILITY AND STATISTICS

Suppose you have a series of choices to make. You go out to dinner and want to have an appetizer, entree, and dessert. If the restaurant has 5 choices of appetizer, 12 choices of entree, and 3 choices of dessert, how many possible meals could you order? In a problem like this, take the number of ways each choice can be made and multiply:

5 appetizers × 12 entrees × 3 desserts = 5 × 12 × 3 = 180 possible meals.

This principle can be extended to however many choices you have.

A *permutation* is a selection of items where order matters. For instance, suppose you want to arrange three books on a shelf. If we call the books A, B, and C, then there are six possible ways to do this:

ABC, ACB, BAC, BCA, CAB, CBA

To compute the permutation without listing every possible outcome, simply note that for the first book (book A) there are 3 choices. Once the first book has been selected, there are 2 books left to choose from. Once the second book has been selected, there is only 1 left. By multiplying these together, we get the result 3 × 2 × 1 = 6.

The product 3 × 2 × 1 can be written in what is known as *factorial notation* as 3!, which is read "three factorial." Similarly, 5! = 5 × 4 × 3 × 2 × 1. In general, $n! = n \times (n-1) \times (n-2) \times \cdots \times 3 \times 2 \times 1$. As can be seen with the above example, the number of permutations of a set with n items is $n!$.

Things get more involved when we select a subset of items. For example, suppose you want to arrange 3 books on a shelf, but you have 12 books to choose from. In this case you have 12 ways to make your first choice, then 11, then 10, so that there are 12 × 11 × 10 = 1,320 ways to do this. The number of ways the books can be arranged can be computed using the *permutation formula*: The number of permutations of n items taken r at a time is given by $_nP_r = \frac{n!}{(n-r)!}$. In this example, $n = 12$ and $r = 3$, so that $_{12}P_3 = \frac{12!}{(12-3)!} = \frac{12!}{9!} = 12 \times 11 \times 10 = 1320$.

A *combination* is a selection of items where order does not matter. For example, suppose a department of 10 wants to select 3 members for a selection committee. We can compute how many ways these 3 members can be selected by using the *combination formula*: The number of combinations of n items taken r at a time is given by $_nC_r = \frac{n!}{r!(n-r)!}$. For the above example, $n = 10$ and $r = 3$, so $_{10}C_3 = \frac{10!}{3!(10-3)!} = \frac{10!}{3!7!} = \frac{10 \times 9 \times 8}{3 \times 2 \times 1} = 120$.

Probability is a measure of the likelihood that some event will occur. The value of probability is always between 0 and 1. The closer the value is to 0, the less likely it is that the event will occur; the closer it is to 1, the more likely the event is to occur. The probability of an event occurring = $\frac{\text{The number of favorable outcomes}}{\text{The total number of possible outcomes}}$

Suppose you roll a die. The total number of possible outcomes is 6 (you could roll 1, 2, 3, 4, 5, or 6). Now say you are interested in rolling an even number. This is what we consider a favorable outcome. In this case there are 3 favorable outcomes: 2, 4, or 6. So the probability of rolling an even number is $\frac{3}{6} = \frac{1}{2}$.

Two events are *independent* if the occurrence of one does not affect the probability of the occurrence of the other. For instance, if you toss a die then roll a coin, getting a 2 on the die has no affect on getting tails on the coin. When two events are independent, the probability of both happening is the product of their individual probabilities. In the example above, the probability of getting a 2 when rolling a die is $\frac{1}{6}$, while the probability of getting tails when tossing a coin is $\frac{1}{2}$, so the probability of both happening is $\left(\frac{1}{6}\right)\left(\frac{1}{2}\right) = \frac{1}{12}$.

If there are two events and the first event affects the second, be careful when computing the probability of the events occurring. While the probability of both events happening is still the product of their individual probabilities, it is necessary to see how the first event affects the second one.

For instance, suppose you choose two cards from a deck of cards by selecting the first card, leaving it out of the deck, then selecting the second card; and you want to find the probability of selecting two aces. The probability of selecting the first ace would be $\frac{4}{52} = \frac{1}{13}$ as there are 4 aces in a deck of 52 cards. Once the first ace has been selected, there are only 3 aces left in a deck of 51 cards, so the probability of getting a second ace is $\frac{3}{51} = \frac{1}{17}$. The probability of getting two aces in this instance would be $\left(\frac{1}{13}\right)\left(\frac{1}{17}\right) = \frac{1}{221}$.

This last example brings up what is known as *conditional probability*. Remember that when you roll a die, there are 6 possible outcomes, so the probability of rolling a 5 is $\frac{1}{6}$. Suppose the number you rolled was odd. There are only three possible odd outcomes (1, 3, and 5), so the probability of rolling a 5 would now be $\frac{1}{3}$. When new information is presented about the experiment you are interested in, the probability of certain events can be affected.

Given a set of numbers, the *mean* (or *average*) can be found by first adding the numbers, then dividing by how many numbers were added. For example, suppose you want to find the mean of the numbers 22, 25, 14, 26, and 18. This can be found by adding the numbers and dividing by 5:
$\frac{22 + 25 + 14 + 26 + 18}{5} = \frac{105}{5} = 21$.

Given a set of numbers, the number in the middle if you arrange the values from smallest to largest is called the *median*. In the example above, if we arrange the numbers in order from smallest to largest (14, 18, 22, 25, 26), the median is 22. If there is no middle number, the median is the mean of the middle two numbers. For instance, to find the median of 11, 13, 14, 16, 18, and 20, the middle two numbers, 14 and 16, are used to find the mean. The middle two numbers are added and divided by 2: $\frac{14 + 16}{2} = \frac{30}{2} = 15$.

Probability and Statistics Review Questions

1. A student code requires you to enter a four-digit number. If you can repeat digits, how many codes are possible?

    Solution: For each digit, there are 10 possible choices (0, 1, 2, 3, 4, 5, 6, 7, 8, or 9) and there are four digits, so there are 10 × 10 × 10 × 10 = 10,000 possible codes.

2. If a jar contains 3 red, 4 yellow, and 5 blue jellybeans, what is the probability of selecting a red or yellow jellybean if you select one jellybean at random?

    Solution: There are 12 jellybeans in all. Three of the jellybeans are red, so the probability of selecting a red jellybean is $\frac{3}{12}$. Four jellybeans are yellow, so the probability of selecting a yellow jellybean is $\frac{4}{12}$. The probability of selecting a red or yellow jellybean is then $\frac{3}{12} + \frac{4}{12} = \frac{7}{12}$.

ADDITIONAL TOPICS FROM ALGEBRA AND GEOMETRY

What follows are many concepts that may crop up on the CLEP College Mathematics exam in some form or another. The test is not going to be full of these ideas, but some of them will definitely make an appearance, so it always helps to be ready.

Imaginary and Complex Numbers

In the real number system, the square root of a negative number cannot be taken. We can get around this in the complex number system by defining $i = \sqrt{-1}$. Then, for any real number n, $\sqrt{-n} = \sqrt{(-1)n} = \sqrt{(-1)}\sqrt{n} = i\sqrt{n}$. For example, $\sqrt{-36} = 6i$.

A number of the form bi, where b is any real number, is called an *imaginary number*. Any number of the form $a + bi$, where a and b are real numbers, is called a *complex number*. For example, $7i$ is an imaginary number, while $2 + 3i$ is a complex number. For any complex number $a + bi$, $a - bi$ is called its *complex conjugate*. The complex conjugate of $2 + 3i$ is $2 - 3i$.

Exponents and Logarithms

An *exponent* indicates repeated multiplication. For instance, $5^3 = 5 \times 5 \times 5 = 125$ and $2^5 = 2 \times 2 \times 2 \times 2 \times 2 = 32$. In the first example, 5 is called the *base* while the exponent is 3. In the second example, 2 is the base while the exponent is 5. Exponents are not just positive integers. Negative exponents are defined by $a^{-n} = \frac{1}{a^n}$, so that $4^{-3} = \frac{1}{4^3}$. Also, by definition, $a^0 = 1$.

There are five basic rules to keep in mind when dealing with exponents. In general, if m and n are integers, and a and b are any numbers:

Rule 1: $\quad a^m \times a^n = a^{m+n}$

Rule 2: $\quad (a^m)^n = a^{mn}$

Rule 3: $\quad (ab)^m = a^m \times b^m$

Rule 4: $\quad \left(\frac{a}{b}\right)^m = \frac{a^m}{b^m}$

Rule 5: $\quad \frac{a^m}{a^n} = a^{m-n}$

An *exponential equation* is an equation whose variable appears as an exponent. An equation of this type can be solved algebraically if both sides of the equation can be expressed as powers of the same base. For example, to solve the equation $2^{x+4} = 64$, 64 would be rewritten as 2^6, giving the equation $2^{x+4} = 2^6$. This means that $x + 4 = 6$, so that $x = 2$.

If the bases cannot both be changed to the same number, then the equation can be solved using a logarithm. The logarithm of a number is the power to which a given base is raised to in order to produce the number. For example, $\log_3 81 = 4$ because $3^4 = 81$. While logarithms can be written to any base, logarithms to base 10 are used so often that they are referred to as common logarithms and "log" is often used to stand for "$\log_{10}$." A "log" button can be found on scientific calculators and can be a great shortcut to finding the "log" of a number, provided you know what you're doing and input correct numbers. The calculator available to you as part of the CLEP testing software will have the "log" function.

Note that the logarithm of 0 or of a negative number cannot be found. As with exponents, there are several rules for logarithms. The three most common rules are:

Rule 1: $\log_b xy = \log_b x + \log_b y$

Rule 2: $\log_b \left(\dfrac{x}{y}\right) = \log_b x - \log_b y$

Rule 3: $\log_b x^n = n\log_b x$

Perimeter and Area

To find the *perimeter* of a plane figure, simply add the lengths of the sides of the figure. For instance, if a triangle has sides measuring 4 ft, 6 ft, and 10 ft, its perimeter would be 4 + 6 + 10 = 20 ft.

Area is a measure of the surface covered by a plane figure. There is a formula for finding area depending upon the figure in question. The three most common formulas for different figures are:

The area A of a rectangle with length l and width w is given by $A = lw$

The area A of a square with sides measuring s is given by $A = s^2$

The area A of a triangle with base b and height h is given by $A = \dfrac{1}{2}bh$

So if a rectangle has width 5 ft and length 12 ft, its area is (5 ft)(12 ft) = 60 ft^2.

Triangles and Circles

A *triangle* is a plane figure with three sides and three angles. If all three sides of a triangle have different lengths, the triangle is called *scalene*. If two of the sides have the same length, the triangle is called *isosceles*. If all three sides have the same length, the triangle is called *equilateral*.

The sum of the three interior angles of a triangle is always 180°. If all three angles of a triangle are less than 90°, the triangle is called *acute*. If one of the angles measures 90°, the triangle is called a *right triangle*. If one of the angles is more than 90°, the triangle is called *obtuse*. If all three angles have the same measure, then the triangle is called *equiangular*.

A *circle* is the set of all points a fixed distance from a given point, called the *center*. The distance from the center to the circle is called *radius*, while the distance between two points on the circle described by a line that passes through the center is called *diameter*. The distance around a circle is called *circumference* and is given by the formula $C = 2\pi r$, where r is the radius and $\pi \approx 3.14$. Circumference is also given by the formula $C = \pi d$, where d is the diameter of the circle.

The area of a circle is given by the formula $A = \pi r^2$. So if a circle has a radius of 5 in, then its area would be $(3.14)(5 \text{ in})^2 = (3.14)(25 \text{ in}^2) = 78.5 \text{ in}^2$.

The Pythagorean Theorem

The side opposite the right angle in a right triangle is called the *hypotenuse* while the other two sides are called *legs*. There is a special relationship between the hypotenuse and legs of a right triangle, which is given by the Pythagorean Theorem: If the hypotenuse of a right triangle has length c and the legs have lengths a and b, then $c = \sqrt{a^2 + b^2}$.

For example, if the legs of a right triangle measure 3 cm and 4 cm, then the hypotenuse c would be given by $c = \sqrt{3^2 + 4^2} = \sqrt{25} = 5$ cm.

Finding Parallel and Perpendicular Lines

Two lines are *parallel* if they never intersect. This means that they have the same slope. Train tracks are like parallel lines. If the equation of a line is written in the form $y = mx + b$, m indicates the slope of the line. For instance, the line $y = 3x + 5$ has slope 3. To see if two lines are parallel, just check to see if they have the same slope.

For example, to see if $y = 2x - 4$ and $2y - 4x = 6$ are parallel, first write the second equation in the form $y = mx + b$ to solve for y. In doing this we obtain $y = 2x + 3$. The slope of both lines is 2, so they are parallel.

Two lines are *perpendicular* if their intersection forms right angles. If two lines are perpendicular, their slopes are negative reciprocals of each other. For example, if the slope of a line is $\frac{2}{3}$, then the slope of a line perpendicular to it would be $-\frac{3}{2}$. As with parallel lines, putting the equation of both lines in the form $y = mx + b$ and comparing the slopes will quickly tell us if the lines are perpendicular.

Word Problems

Word problems provide real-world examples of mathematics. Most problems involve representing something in the problem by the variable x then finding an equation to solve.

Example 1:

The sum of a number and three times the number is 60. Find the number.

> *Solution:* Let x represent the number we are looking for. According to the problem, $x + 3x = 60$. Solving this equation we get $4x = 60$, so $x = 15$.

Example 2:

If Joe can carpet a house alone in 5 hours, and Susan can carpet a house alone in 7 hours, how long will it take them to carpet a house if they both work together?

Solution: Let x represent the number of hours it will take if they work together. In an hour, Joe can carpet $\frac{1}{5}$ of a house and Susan can carpet $\frac{1}{7}$, and together they can carpet $\frac{1}{x}$. This gives us the equation $\frac{1}{5} + \frac{1}{7} = \frac{1}{x}$. Multiplying each term by $35x$ will clear the fractions, leaving us with:

$$7x + 5x = 35$$
$$12x = 35$$
$$x = 2\frac{11}{12} \text{ hours}$$

Additional Topics from Algebra and Geometry Review Questions

1. Add $3 + 2i$ and $4 - 5i$.

   Solution: We add complex numbers like we do polynomials, by combining like terms. So $(3 + 2i) + (4 - 5i) = (3 + 4) + (2i - 5i) = 7 - 3i$.

2. Write $5^3 = 125$ as a logarithm.

   Solution: Any exponential expression can be written as a logarithm. Remember that a logarithm is the power to which the base is raised in order to produce a specific number. In this case, base 5 is raised to the power 3 to produce 125, which can be written as $\log_5 125 = 3$.

3. Suppose a triangle has sides of length 3 ft, 5 ft, and 3 ft. What type of triangle is this?

   Solution: Notice that two of the three sides have the same length. When this is the case, the triangle is called *isosceles*.

COLLEGE MATHEMATICS RESOURCES

For an in-depth, detailed review—we've covered the basic points—of the material found on the CLEP College Mathematics exam, consult textbooks that contain explanations and practice problems. Almost any textbook used in college-level mathematics classes covers at least some of the topics you need to study. As textbooks may have differing approaches to solving problems, it's always good to look at two or more different texts to find the approach that makes the most sense to you.

Algebra and geometry topics covered on the exam can usually be found in an Elementary Algebra text. This text should also include information on the real number system and functions. Sets, logic, and probability can often be found in texts for courses with names like "Finite Mathematics" or "Ideas of Mathematics." These texts typically also have chapters on algebra and geometry. It is, of course, best to obtain the textbooks for free at the library, through teachers at your school if you are a student, or through the local college.

When selecting a text to study from, be sure to compare its table of contents against the outline of topics on the exam, so that during your study time you are able to cover every topic that you need to know.

FINAL THOUGHTS

While there are many rules to learn in mathematics, a lot of math is the use of common sense and logic. Even if you are not a "logic" person, math can be learned based on the principles reviewed in this chapter. The review section, the diagnostic test, and the two practice tests should prepare you well for the CLEP College Mathematics exam, but there is always more information that can be studied prior to the test. Many of the concepts on the exam are covered in Elementary Algebra and Geometry. If you don't remember much from your algebra and geometry classes, have no fear—with a bit of outside study and the use of this book, you are on your way to a solid base of knowledge to apply to the CLEP College Mathematics exam.

Good luck!

Section Three: The CLEP College Mathematics Exam | 201

Chapter Ten: Practice Test 2

Time—90 minutes
60 Questions

Directions: For the following questions, either select the BEST answer of the choices given, or input your answer into the box provided.

You can use the computer-based scientific calculator during this exam.

Notes:

(1) Unless otherwise stated, the domain of any function f consists of the set of all real numbers x for which $f(x)$ is a real number.

(2) i represents $\sqrt{-1}$

(3) Unless otherwise indicated, all geometric figures lie in a plane. The appearance of all figures is accurate UNLESS the question states that the figure is not drawn to scale.

1. Which of the following is NOT an integer?

    (A) $\sqrt{49}$

    (B) $\dfrac{4}{\sqrt{9}}$

    (C) $\sqrt[3]{-27}$

    (D) $\dfrac{\sqrt{36}}{3}$

2. If set A contains 25 elements and set B contains 35 elements, and the two sets are disjoint, how many elements are in A or B?

    ☐

3. Suppose A is any event. Which of the following statements about event A are true?

    I. The probability that event A will occur can be greater than 1.
    II. The probability that event A will occur can be equal to 0.
    III. The probability that event A will occur plus the probability that event A will not occur is less than 1.

    (A) I and II only

    (B) II and III only

    (C) II only

    (D) III only

GO ON TO THE NEXT PAGE ⇒

KAPLAN

4. Which of the following is the inverse of "If R, then S"?

    (A) If S, then R.
    (B) If not R, then not S.
    (C) If not S, then not R.
    (D) R and not S.

5. If m is an odd integer, which of the following is also odd?

    (A) $m + 1$
    (B) $m - 1$
    (C) $m^2 - m$
    (D) $m^2 + m + 1$

6. If $f(x) = x^3 - 3x + 1$, then $f(-1) =$

    (A) 3
    (B) -3
    (C) -1
    (D) 5

7. If $i = \sqrt{-1}$, then $i + i^2 + i^3 =$

    (A) i
    (B) $-i$
    (C) -1
    (D) 1

8. How many odd prime numbers are there between 1 and 30?

    (A) 9
    (B) 10
    (C) 14
    (D) 28

9. If $f(x) = \{(4, 2), (5, 3), (6, 4)\}$ and $g(x) = \{(3, 4), (4, 6), (5, 8)\}$, what is the value of $f(g(4))$?

    (A) 6
    (B) 4
    (C) 2
    (D) 3

10. Which of the following are infinite sets?

    I. The set of all integers between 0 and 10
    II. The set of all rational numbers between 0 and 10
    III. The set of all real numbers between 0 and 10

    (A) I and II only
    (B) II and III only
    (C) I and III only
    (D) I, II, and III

11. When Ted goes to lunch, he can choose from 3 kinds of soup, 5 kinds of sandwiches, and 4 kinds of drinks. If he chooses one soup, one sandwich, and one drink, how many different lunches could he choose from?

    (A) 12
    (B) 19
    (C) 32
    (D) 60

12. If x is an odd integer and y is an even integer, which of the following must be even?

    (A) $x + y$
    (B) $x - y$
    (C) xy
    (D) $\dfrac{x}{y}$

13. Given the functions $f(x) = 4x + 3$ and $g(x) = x - 5$, what is the value of $(f+g)(x)$ when $x = 2$?

    (A) $\{8\}$
    (B) $\{11\}$
    (C) $\{-3\}$
    (D) $\{5\}$

14. Which of the following is logically equivalent to: "If it rains, then the park will be closed"?

    (A) If the park is closed, then it rains.
    (B) If it rains, then the park is not closed.
    (C) If it does not rain, then the park is not closed.
    (D) If the park is not closed, then it does not rain.

15. The sum of five times a number n and the reciprocal of n is equal to 11. Which of the following is an algebraic representation of the statement above?

    (A) $5\left(n + \dfrac{1}{n}\right) = 11$

    (B) $(5n)\left(\dfrac{1}{n}\right) = 11$

    (C) $5n + \dfrac{1}{n} = 11$

    (D) $(5 + n)\left(\dfrac{1}{n}\right) = 11$

16. Thirty employees took a training course. Afterwards, each took a 5-question multiple choice test. The results are summarized in the table below:

Number Correct:	0	1	2	3	4	5
Frequency:	7	8	6	3	5	1

    If an employee who answered at least 2 questions correctly is selected at random, what is the probability that the employee who answered all 5 questions correctly will be selected?

    (A) $\dfrac{1}{30}$

    (B) $\dfrac{1}{15}$

    (C) $\dfrac{6}{30}$

    (D) $\dfrac{6}{15}$

17. What is the smallest positive integer that is divisible by both 12 and 15?

18. If $f(x)$ is a linear function such that $f(5) = 7$ and $f(1) = -1$, then $f(x)$ equals

    (A) $x + 2$
    (B) $x^2 - 1$
    (C) $2x - 3$
    (D) $x - 2$

19. If $A = \{x \mid x > 2\}$ and $B = \{x \mid x \leq 6\}$, what is the number of integers in $A \cap B$?

    (A) 4
    (B) 3
    (C) 6
    (D) 0

20. The difference between the mean and median of the numbers 16, 18, 17, 27, and 22 is

    (A) 7
    (B) 4
    (C) 3
    (D) 2

21. A fair coin is tossed three times. What is the probability that it will come up tails three times in a row?

    (A) $\dfrac{3}{8}$

    (B) $\dfrac{1}{3}$

    (C) $\dfrac{1}{8}$

    (D) $\dfrac{1}{2}$

22. The product of all distinct positive factors of which number below is the smallest?

    (A) 7
    (B) 6
    (C) 4
    (D) 8

23. If $f(x) = x^2 - x$, then $f(x + 2) =$

    (A) $x^2 + 3x + 6$
    (B) $x^2 + 3x + 2$
    (C) $x^2 - x + 2$
    (D) $x^2 - x + 6$

24. If $\log_2 x = 6$, then $\log_4 x =$

    (A) 3
    (B) 2
    (C) 1
    (D) 4

25. If $f(x) = 2x$ and the domain of $f(x)$ is all positive integers less than 50, what is the range of $f(x)$?

    (A) positive integers less than 100
    (B) even positive integers less than 50
    (C) even positive integers less than 100
    (D) even positive integers less than 200

26. In a group of 51 students, 27 have brown eyes, 13 have blue eyes, 8 have green eyes, and 3 have hazel eyes. The likelihood that a person chosen at random from this group will have either blue or green eyes is

    (A) $\dfrac{7}{17}$
    (B) $\dfrac{9}{17}$
    (C) $\dfrac{13}{51}$
    (D) $\dfrac{8}{51}$

27. A student claims that n^3 is greater than or equal to n for all real numbers n. Of the following, which is a value of n that provides a counterexample to the student's claim?

    (A) 2
    (B) -1
    (C) $\dfrac{1}{2}$
    (D) 1

28. What is the measure of angle M?

    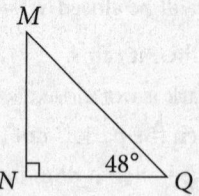

    (A) 48°
    (B) 42°
    (C) 52°
    (D) 132°

29. If $0 \le x \le 150$, how many values of x are both the square of an integer and the cube of an integer?

    ☐

30. A collector of vases wants to arrange five different pieces from her collection on a shelf in her home. In how many different ways could she arrange the five vases?

    (A) 120
    (B) 625
    (C) 15
    (D) 1

31. Suppose $A = \{1, 2\}$ and $B = \{2, 3\}$. Which of the following ordered pairs is NOT in the Cartesian product $A \times B$?

    (A) (1, 2)
    (B) (1, 3)
    (C) (2, 2)
    (D) (3, 2)

32. If the probability it will rain on Friday is 0.6 and the probability it will rain on Saturday is 0.7, what is the likelihood it will rain on neither Friday nor Saturday?

    ☐

GO ON TO THE NEXT PAGE

33. Which of the following is NOT a prime number?

    (A) 17
    (B) 11
    (C) 23
    (D) 51

34. Your favorite band is coming to town, but you're not sure if you should go to the concert. You reason, "If I go to the concert, I will have to call in sick. If I call in sick, then my boss will get angry. If my boss gets angry, then I'll lose my job." What conclusion can you draw from this?

    (A) If I go to the concert, then I'll lose my job.
    (B) If my boss gets angry, then I called in sick.
    (C) If I lose my job, then I went to the concert.
    (D) If I don't go to the concert, then I won't lose my job.

35. Let $f(x) = \dfrac{x+1}{x(x+2)}$. Which of the following is the domain of $f(x)$?

    (A) All real numbers
    (B) All real numbers except for –1
    (C) All real numbers except for –2
    (D) All real numbers except for 0 and –2

36. The sum of three consecutive even numbers is 42. What is the smallest of the even numbers?

    (A) 10
    (B) 14
    (C) 12
    (D) 16

37. If $x = -3$, then $|x - 5| =$

    (A) 2
    (B) –2
    (C) 8
    (D) –8

38. Let $M = \{4, 7, 9, 13, 17\}$. What is the sum of the mean and median of M?

    (A) 10
    (B) 19
    (C) 59
    (D) 90

39. What are the x-intercepts of the curve defined by $x^2 - 3xy + y^2 = 6y + 9$?

    (A) $x = \pm 3$
    (B) $y = \pm 3$
    (C) $x = \pm 2$
    (D) $y = \pm 2$

40. Which of the following is equal to $(2a^3 b^{\frac{3}{4}})^4$?

    (A) $8a^7 b^3$
    (B) $8a^{12} b^3$
    (C) $16a^7 b^3$
    (D) $16a^{12} b^3$

41. If $A \subset C$ and $B \subset C$, which of the following statements is always true?

    (A) A is a subset of B
    (B) B is a subset of A
    (C) $A \cup B$ is a subset of C
    (D) $A \cap C = C$

42. If you roll a pair of fair dice, the sum of the numbers on the two dice can be any number from 2 to 12. Which is more likely, getting an odd sum or an even sum?

    (A) An odd sum
    (B) An even sum
    (C) They are equally likely
    (D) None of the above

GO ON TO THE NEXT PAGE

43. If $x > y > 0$, which of the following is NOT true?

    (A) $|x| > |y|$
    (B) $\frac{1}{x} > \frac{1}{y}$
    (C) $x^2 > y^2$
    (D) $\frac{1}{y} > \frac{1}{x}$

44. Below is a Truth Table:

p	q	r
T	T	T
T	F	F
F	T	F
F	F	F

    According to this table, which of the following statements describes r?

    (A) p or q
    (B) if p then q
    (C) p or not q
    (D) p and q

45. If $-3 < x < 4$, which of the following expresses the range of possible values of x^2?

    (A) $0 \leq x \leq 16$
    (B) $-9 < x < 16$
    (C) $9 < x < 16$
    (D) $-6 < x < 8$

46. A deck of 52 cards contains 13 cards of each of four suits—clubs, spades, diamonds, and hearts. If you select three cards from a deck without replacement, what is the probability the third card is a spade given that the first two cards were spades?

    (A) $\frac{13}{52}$
    (B) $\frac{11}{52}$
    (C) $\frac{11}{50}$
    (D) $\frac{12}{51}$

47. What type of figure is the figure below?

    (A) rectangle
    (B) trapezoid
    (C) rhombus
    (D) quadrilateral

48. The number 10110 is written in binary notation. How would it be written in decimal notation?

    (A) 13
    (B) 22
    (C) 31
    (D) 3

49. What is the slope of the line defined by $3y + 6x = 15$?

    [ ]

50. The number of absences and their probabilities for any given day in a math class are given in the table below:

Absences:	0	1	2	3	4
Probability:	0.10	0.25	0.30	0.15	0.20

    What is the expected number of absences for any given day of the class?

    (A) 1
    (B) 2.1
    (C) 1.9
    (D) 3.2

GO ON TO THE NEXT PAGE

51. Let A represent the statement "x is an even integer" and B represent the statement "x is an integer divisible by 2." What can be said about statements A and B?

    (A) A is necessary but not a sufficient condition for B.
    (B) A is not necessary but is a sufficient condition for B.
    (C) A is a necessary and sufficient condition for B.
    (D) A is neither necessary nor sufficient for B.

52. Alan can paint a house in 5 hours, while Tim can paint a house in 3 hours. How long would it take both of them to paint a house together?

    (A) $1\frac{7}{8}$ hours
    (B) 2 hours
    (C) 8 hours
    (D) $\frac{1}{8}$ hour

53. Which of the following choices represents the Venn diagram?

    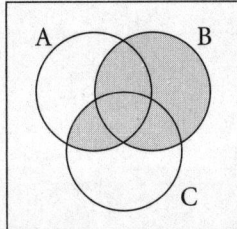

    (A) $A \cup B \cup C$
    (B) $(A \cup B) \cap C$
    (C) $(A \cap C) \cup B$
    (D) $(A \cap B) \cup (A \cap C)$

54. Which is the inverse of the function $f(x) = \frac{1}{x}$?

    (A) $f^{-1}(x) = x$
    (B) $f^{-1}(x) = \frac{1}{x}$
    (C) $f^{-1}(x) = \sqrt{x}$
    (D) $f^{-1}(x) = \frac{1}{\sqrt{x}}$

55. Joe, Michael, Ralph, Terry, and Steve have formed a band. Larry, Joe, Terry, William, and Ralph have formed another band. How many musicians are in both bands?

    (A) 3
    (B) 2
    (C) 1
    (D) 0

56. Given an equation of the form $ax^2 + bx + c = 0$, with $b^2 - 4ac > 0$, how many real values of x satisfy the equation?

    (A) 0
    (B) 1
    (C) 4
    (D) 2

57. How many different ways can you make up a committee of 3 people from a group of 8 people?

58. If a fair die is tossed, what is the probability of tossing a number less than 3 or greater than 4?

    (A) $\frac{1}{3}$
    (B) $\frac{5}{6}$
    (C) $\frac{2}{3}$
    (D) $\frac{1}{2}$

59. Which of the following could be the graph of a function of x?

(A)

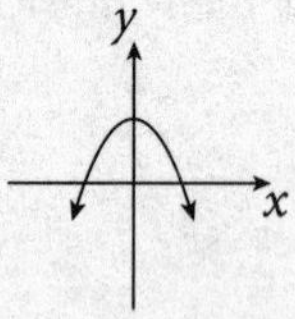

(B)

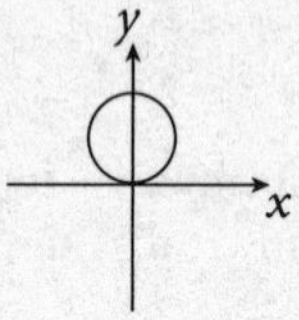

(C)

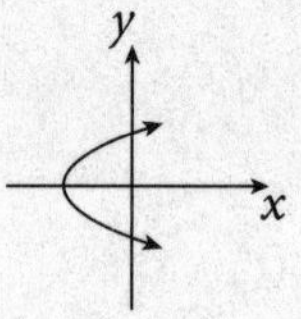

(D)

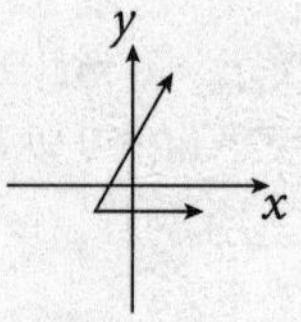

60. A rectangle has a width of 5 cm and a length of 12 cm. What is the measure of a diagonal of the rectangle?

(A) 17 cm

(B) 13 cm

(C) 16.9 cm

(D) 34 cm

END OF TEST. STOP

THE ANSWER KEY APPEARS ON THE FOLLOWING PAGE.

ANSWER KEY

1. B	11. D	21. C	31. D	41. C	51. C
2. 60	12. C	22. A	32. 0.12	42. C	52. A
3. C	13. A	23. B	33. D	43. B	53. C
4. B	14. D	24. A	34. A	44. D	54. B
5. D	15. C	25. C	35. D	45. A	55. A
6. A	16. B	26. A	36. C	46. C	56. D
7. C	17. 60	27. C	37. C	47. D	57. 56
8. A	18. C	28. B	38. B	48. B	58. C
9. B	19. A	29. 3	39. A	49. −2	59. A
10. B	20. D	30. A	40. D	50. B	60. B

Section Three: The CLEP College Mathematics Exam
Practice Test 2 Answers and Explanations

Answers and Explanations

1. (B)
Simplifying the possible answers produces:

(A) $\sqrt{49} = 7$

(B) $\dfrac{4}{\sqrt{9}} = \dfrac{4}{3}$

(C) $\sqrt[3]{-27} = -\sqrt[3]{27} = -3$

(D) $\dfrac{\sqrt{36}}{3} = \dfrac{6}{3} = 2$

All of these are integers except for (B).

2. (60)
Two sets are *disjoint* if they have no elements in common. If set A has 25 elements and set B has 35 elements, and they have none of these elements in common, then there are $25 + 35 = 60$ elements in A or B.

3. (C)
This problem requires being familiar with two basic properties of probability:

1) The probability that event A will occur is always between 0 and 1, including 0 and 1.

2) The probability that event A will occur plus the probability that event A will not occur is always equal to 1.

With these properties in mind, you can quickly see that II is the only choice that is true, which means the solution is (C).

4. (B)
To find the *inverse* of a conditional statement, negate both statements in the conditional. That is, the inverse of "If P, then Q" is "If not P, then not Q." In this case, the inverse of "If R, then S" is "If not R, then not S." Choice (A) represents the converse, while (C) represents the contrapositive.

5. (D)
The easiest way to solve a problem like this is to pick a number for m and plug it into the possible solutions. Since m is an odd integer, 3 would be a good choice for m. Substitute 3 for m in each possible solution:

(A) $m + 1 = 3 + 1 = 4$
(B) $m - 1 = 3 - 1 = 2$
(C) $m^2 - m = 3^2 - 3 = 9 - 3 = 6$
(D) $m^2 + m + 1 = 3^2 + 3 + 1 = 9 + 3 + 1 = 13$

(D) is the only answer that ends up being odd, so it is the solution to the problem.

6. (A)
Substitute -1 for x in the function and simplify: $f(x) = x^3 - 3x + 1$, so $f(-1) = (-1)^3 - 3(-1) + 1 = -1 + 3 + 1 = 3$. A common mistake here is to not change the sign of the second term, which would give you choice (B). Also, remember that $(-1)^3 = -1$, otherwise you could end up with answer choice (C) or (D).

7. (C)
Quickly compute i^2 and i^3, then add these two values to i:
$i^2 = (\sqrt{-1})^2 = -1$
$i^3 = i^2 \times i = -1 \times i = -i$
So $i + i^2 + i^3 = i + (-1) + (-i) = -1$

8. (A)
There are two easy mistakes that could be made in this problem. The first mistake would be to only read "odd" numbers; there are 14 odd numbers between 1 and 30. The second mistake would be to only read "prime" numbers; there are 10 prime numbers between 1 and 30. Notice that the problem is asking for "odd prime" numbers. Make a quick list of odd prime numbers between 1 and 30: {3, 5, 7, 11, 13, 17, 19, 23, 29}. The list shows that there are 9 odd prime numbers between 1 and 30.

9. (B)
The functions here are given as ordered pairs; the first number tells you what number is going into the function and the second part of the pair tells you what number is coming out of the function. With this in mind, to compute $f(g(4))$, you first need to see what the function $g(x)$ does to 4. If you look at the ordered pairs in this function you'll

find (4, 6), which says the function $g(x)$ takes 4 and turns it into 6. Now we need to see what $f(x)$ does to 6. Looking at the ordered pairs listed for $f(x)$ you'll find (6, 4), which means $f(x)$ takes 6 and turns it into 4. Thus, $f(g(4)) = 4$.

10. (B)

An infinite set is a set with an infinite number of elements. In other words, if you were to try to list all of the elements in an infinite set, you could never list them all. You could easily list all of the elements in the set described in I, so this set is not infinite. The sets in II and III are infinite, since you could never list all of the numbers described by either set. This eliminates all the answer choices except (B).

11. (D)

This is a simple counting problem. For a problem like this, you just need to see how many ways you can make a series of choices, then multiply. In this case, a lunch is made up of soup, a sandwich, and a drink. There are 3 soups, 5 sandwiches, and 4 drinks to choose from, so there are $3 \times 5 \times 4 = 60$ different possible lunches. A common mistake is to add the parts of the lunches together, which would give you the incorrect solution (A).

12. (C)

Choose values for x and y, say $x = 5$ and $y = 2$. Then
(A) $x + y = 5 + 2 = 7$
(B) $x - y = 5 - 2 = 3$
(C) $xy = (5)(2) = 10$
(D) $\frac{x}{y} = \frac{5}{2}$

Since only (C) yields an even number, it is the correct answer.

13. (A)

The problem states that $f(x) = 4x + 3$ and $g(x) = x - 5$. The value of $(f + g)(x) = (4x + 3) + (x - 5) = 5x - 2$. So when $x = 2$, $(f + g)(x) = 5(2) - 2 = 8$.

14. (D)

If you are given a conditional statement and asked to find a logically equivalent statement, keep in mind that the contrapositive is always equivalent. To find the contrapositive, switch and negate the statements that make up the original conditional. That is, the conditional "If P, then Q" is equivalent to its contrapositive, "If not Q, then not P." In this case, "If it rains, then the park will be closed" is equivalent to "If the park is not closed, then it does not rain." Be sure to switch *and* negate the statements.

15. (C)

In a problem like this, keep your eyes open for key words. *Sum* means addition, so expect to see addition in the answer. What is being added? According to the problem, five times (multiplication) a number n and the reciprocal of n, which are $5n$ and $\frac{1}{n}$, are being added. When these two values are added you get 11, so the answer is $5n + \frac{1}{n} = 11$. Misreading the question could lead you to choose (A), which is 5 times the sum of a number and its reciprocal.

16. (B)

This is a conditional probability problem, meaning that instead of using all of the employees to chose from we only use those the employees that the problem specifies. In this case, instead of using all 30 employees to choose from, we only want those that got at least two problems correct on the test, which means answers (A) and (C) can be eliminated. There was only one person who got all 5 correct answers, so the answer is (B), $\frac{1}{15}$.

17. (60)

If you start to list the multiples of 12 and the multiples of 15, the first number to appear in both lists will be the number we want:

Multiples of 12: 12, 24, 36, 48, 60, 72, …

Multiples of 15: 15, 30, 45, 60, 75, 90, …

Since 60 is the first number to appear in both lists, the answer is 60.

18. (C)

First, we can discount (B) because $x^2 - 1$ is not linear. For the other choices, substitute in 5 and 1 to see which one gives you the desired results. (A) isn't the answer because $f(1) = 1 + 2 = 3$, not −1. (D) is not the answer because $f(5) = 5 - 2 = 3$, not 7. But (C) works because

$f(5) = 2(5) - 3 = 10 - 3 = 7$ and $f(1) = 2(1) - 3 = 2 - 3 = -1$.

19. (A)

We are looking for integers greater than 2 and less than or equal to 6, which is the set {3, 4, 5, 6}. There are 4 elements in this set.

20. (D)

To find the mean, add the numbers and divide by 5 (how many numbers you've added), which gives you $(16 + 18 + 17 + 27 + 22) \div 5 = 100 \div 5 = 20$. The median is the middle number if you list the numbers from smallest to largest: 16, 17, 18, 22, 27. The median is thus 18, so the difference between the mean and median is $20 - 18 = 2$. A common mistake is to find the median without listing the numbers from smallest to largest, which would give you 17 as the median and a difference of 3 instead of 2.

21. (C)

There are two ways to solve this problem. The first is to realize that the probability of a coin coming up tails in one toss is $\frac{1}{2}$, so the probability of it being tails in three tosses is $\frac{1}{2} \times \frac{1}{2} \times \frac{1}{2} = \frac{1}{8}$. The other way to solve the problem is to list all the possible outcomes of tossing a coin three times: HHH, HHT, HTH, HTT, THH, THT, TTH, TTT. Of these 8 outcomes, only one has three tails.

22. (A)

It's easy to think that one of the smallest numbers listed will be the right choice, but this is not the case. The positive factors of 4 are 1, 2, 4 and $1 \times 2 \times 4 = 8$. The positive factors of 6 are 1, 2, 3, 6 and $1 \times 2 \times 3 \times 6 = 36$. 7 is prime, so its only factors are 1 and 7, which have a product of 7.

23. (B)

Plug $x + 2$ into the function:
$f(x + 2) = (x + 2)^2 - (x + 2)$
$= (x^2 + 4x + 4) - (x + 2)$
$= x^2 + 4x + 4 - x - 2$
$= x^2 + 3x + 2$

There are two common mistakes that you could make in solving the problem, which have been anticipated in the possible solutions. The first mistake is to not distribute the negative to the 2 at the end of the equation, which would end up giving you answer (A). The second is to multiply $(x + 2)^2$ incorrectly, ending up with $x^2 + 4$ instead of $x^2 + 4x + 4$. This mistake is represented by answers (C) and (D).

24. (A)

First we need to find x: $\log_2 x = 6$. means that $2^6 = x$, so $x = 64$. Next, find $\log_4 x$. Substituting 64 for x gives us $\log_4 64 = ?$ The equation can be verbalized as 4 to what power equals 64? The answer is 3.

25. (C)

The range of $f(x)$ is all possible values of $2x$, where x is a positive integer less than 50. This means that whatever value we plug in for x, it will be doubled. Not only would 50 become 100, but all the numbers in the range would be even. Thus, the answer is (C).

26. (A)

The problem is asking for the probability of one event *or* another event, so we need to find each probability and then add them. The probability of a student with blue eyes being chosen is $\frac{13}{51}$, while the probability of a student with green eyes being chosen is $\frac{8}{51}$. Their sum is $\frac{21}{51}$, which can be reduced to $\frac{7}{17}$.

27. (C)

The student in the problem claims that $n^3 \geq n$ for all real numbers n, which may not sound too unreasonable at first. To see which number works as a counterexample, plug each in to see which one is not correct:

$2^3 \geq 2$ is true because $8 \geq 2$

$(-1)^3 \geq -1$ is true because $-1 \geq -1$

$\left(\frac{1}{2}\right)^3 \geq \frac{1}{2}$ is not true because $\left(\frac{1}{2}\right)^3 = \frac{1}{8}$ and $\frac{1}{8}$ is less than $\frac{1}{2}$, not greater than it. So the answer is (C).

28. (B)

The sum of the angles of a triangle is always 180°. Here we are given a right triangle, so we know one of the angles is 90°. We're given a second angle that measures 48°, so that leaves $180° - 90° - 48° = 42°$ for the third angle.

29. (3)

It's easiest to list the cubes from 0 to 150 and see which, if any, are also squares. The cubes are 0, 1, 8, 27, 64, and 125. Only three of these are also squares: 0, 1, and 64. The answer is 3. Be sure to notice that the range given for x includes 0, which is both a square and a cube.

30. (A)

If you want to arrange five items, then you have 5 choices for the first item, 4 for the second, 3 for the third, and so on. This is 5!, where $5! = 5 \times 4 \times 3 \times 2 \times 1 = 120$. Keep in mind that you are counting the number of ways to arrange the items, which always involves multiplication.

31. (D)

The *Cartesian product* of two sets is the set of all ordered pairs whose first entry comes from the first set and whose second entry comes from the second set. Since A and B are small sets, we can easily list the Cartesian product: $A \times B = \{(1, 2), (1, 3), (2, 2), (2, 3)\}$. We can see that $(3, 2)$ is not in this set, so the correct answer is (D). If you don't want to list the elements in $A \times B$, you could also keep in mind that the first number in the ordered pairs comes from A, meaning it has to be 1 or 2. Since (D) begins with 3, it can't be one of the elements.

32. (0.12)

If the probability of rain on Friday is 0.6, then the probability it will not rain on Friday is 0.4 (probability has to add up to 1). Likewise, the probability it will not rain on Saturday is 0.3. So the probability it will not rain on both days is $0.4 \times 0.3 = 0.12$.

33. (D)

At first glance the choices may all appear to be prime numbers, but keep in mind that a prime number is only divisible by itself and 1. This is certainly true for the first three choices, but 51 is divisible by 3, so it is not prime.

34. (A)

Following the logic of the problem, you start by going to the concert, which means calling in sick. But if you call in sick, you know your boss will get angry. If your boss gets angry, you know you'll lose your job. Going to the concert ultimately means you will lose your job.

35. (D)

When a function is written as a fraction, you have to be concerned when its denominator is equal to zero, since the function will not be defined there. In this case, the denominator is zero when $x(x + 2) = 0$, which happens when either $x = 0$ or $x = -2$.

36. (C)

Since there are three numbers that add up to 42, the quickest way to do this problem is to divide 42 by 3, which produces 14. 14 is the middle number that is added to get 42. The even number before 14 is 12 and after 14 is 16. You can check to see that $12 + 14 + 16 = 42$ and can see that the smallest of these even numbers is 12.

37. (C)

If $x = -3$, then $x - 5 = -3 - 5 = -8$. Therefore, $|x - 5| = |-8| = 8$. Remember that the absolute value of a negative number is its opposite. Be sure to do the subtraction carefully. At a quick glance you may just notice the difference between 3 and 5 and mistakenly end up with an answer of 2 or -2.

38. (B)

To find the mean of the numbers, first add them (4 + 7 + 9 + 13 + 17 = 50), then divide by 5 (how many numbers you added). The mean is 50 ÷ 5 = 10. To find the median, list the numbers from smallest to largest and find the number in the middle. The middle number, or median, is 9. The sum of the mean and median is 10 + 9 = 19. Notice that answer choice (A) is just the mean, while choice (D) is the product of the mean and median. You get answer (C) if you forget to divide by 5 to get the mean.

39. (A)

To find the x-intercepts, simply replace y with 0 and solve for x:

$$x^2 - 3xy + y^2 = 6y + 9$$
$$x^2 - 3x(0) + (0)^2 = 6(0) + 9$$
$$x^2 = 9$$
$$x = \pm 3$$

Note that since you are looking for the x-intercepts, you could quickly eliminate answers (B) and (D) because they give you values for y, not x.

40. (D)

This problem requires using some rules of exponents:

$$(2a^3 b^{\frac{3}{4}})^4 = (2)^4 (a^3)^4 (b^{\frac{3}{4}})^4$$
$$= 16 a^{12} b^3$$

First we distribute the exponent to every term inside the parentheses and then we multiply the exponents. A common mistake here is to either compute 2^4 as 8, which is done in choices (A) and (B), or to add instead of multiply the exponents, which is done in (A) and (C).

41. (C)

We are told that A is a subset of C and that B is a subset of C. While it may be true that either $A \subset B$ or $B \subset A$, we don't know this for sure (it could be true but is not *always* true), so answer choices (A) and (B) can be discarded. What is true is that $A \subset C$, so if both A and B are subsets of C, then $A \cup B$ is also a subset of C.

42. (C)

Each die has six sides: 1, 2, 3, 4, 5, 6. Notice that half of the numbers are odd and half of them are even. It should make sense that when you roll two dice, the likelihood of them adding up to an odd number and the likelihood of them adding up to an even number should be the same (half of the sums will be odd and half of the sums will be even).

43. (B)

Choose values for x and y, such as x = 5 and y = 2. These values satisfy the conditions of the problem because 5 > 2 > 0. Plug the values into each possible solution:

(A) $|5| > |2|$ True
(B) $\frac{1}{5} > \frac{1}{2}$ False
(C) $5^2 > 2^2$ True
(D) $\frac{1}{2} > \frac{1}{5}$ True

You can always stop plugging in values when you reach the solution that does not work, in this case (B).

44. (D)

Notice that r is only true when both p and q are true. This is true of the statement "p and q." Process of elimination can also be used to find the solution: The answer is not (A) because "p or q" is only false once, but r is false three times. Answer choices (B) and (C) can be discounted for the same reason.

45. (A)

If you remember that x^2 is always greater than or equal to zero, you can eliminate (B) and (D) from the choices. Also note that 0 is between −3 and 4, and since $0^2 = 0$, it must be included in the range. Answer choice (C) does not include 0, so the answer must be (A).

46. (C)

When you select the first card, there are 13 spades in a deck of 52 cards, so the probability of getting a spade is $\frac{13}{52}$. If you know the first card was a spade, then when you select the second card, not only is there one less card in the deck, but there is also one less spade. The probability of getting a spade is now $\frac{12}{51}$. For the third card, there are two less cards in the deck and two less spades, leaving 11 spades and 50 cards, so the probability of getting a spade the third time is $\frac{11}{50}$.

47. (D)

Since no further information is given about this figure, all we can conclude is that it is a quadrilateral, meaning it has four sides. For it to be a rectangle, we'd need to know that the opposite sides were parallel and that the angles measured 90°. To be a rhombus, we'd need to know that the opposite sides were parallel and that all four sides had the same length. A trapezoid could never look like this, so (B) can easily be discarded.

48. (B)

The answer needs to be computed in base two:

$10110_2 = (1 \times 16) + (0 \times 8) + (1 \times 4) + (1 \times 2) + (0 \times 1)$

$ = 16 + 4 + 2$

$ = 22$

Remember that binary starts from the right and goes to the left. Reversing this would give you an answer of 13.

49. (−2)

If you solve the equation of a line for y, then the coefficient of x is the slope of the line. In this case:

$3y + 6x = 15$

$ 3y = -6x + 15$

$ y = -2x + 5$

The slope is therefore −2.

50. (B)

This is an *expected value* problem. For a problem like this, we need to find the product of each outcome and its probability, then add the two together. In this case:

$(0 \times 0.10) + (1 \times 0.25) + (2 \times 0.30) + (3 \times 0.15) + (4 \times 0.20)$

$= 0.25 + 0.60 + 0.45 + 0.80$

$= 2.1$

Notice that the number of absences with the largest probability is 2, so we should expect the result to be around 2. With this in mind, answer choices (A) and (D) can be discounted.

51. (C)

In order for an integer to be even, it must be divisible by 2. Likewise, if an integer is divisible by 2, then we know that it is even. A number must be an even integer for it to be divisible by 2. Therefore, A is both necessary and sufficient for B.

52. (A)

Alan paints $\frac{1}{5}$ of the house each hour, while Tim paints $\frac{1}{3}$ of the house each hour. Solving the equation $\frac{x}{5} + \frac{x}{3} = 1$ for x will tell us how many hours it will take to paint the house:

$\frac{x}{5} + \frac{x}{3} = 1$

$3x + 5x = 15$

$8x = 15$

$x = \frac{15}{8}$

$x = 1\frac{7}{8}$

53. (C)

Notice in the diagram that all of B is shaded, so we will be looking for a B union with another area or areas. The other shaded piece comes from where A and C intersect. This means the diagram represents $(A \cap C) \cup B$.

54. (B)

To find the inverse of a function, replace $f(x)$ with y, interchange x and y, then solve the equation for y. The result will be $f^{-1}(x)$, the inverse of the function. In this case:

$f(x) = \frac{1}{x}$

$y = \frac{1}{x}$ Replace $f(x)$ with y

$x = \frac{1}{y}$ Interchange x and y

$xy = 1$ Solve for y

$f^{-1}(x) = \frac{1}{x}$ Replace y with $f^{-1}(x)$

This is sort of a trick question because the function and inverse are the same. A common mistake here is to think that since $f(x)$ is a fraction, the reciprocal is the inverse, which would give you the incorrect answer (A).

55. (A)

Since this is a counting problem, all you need to do is see which names appear in both lists. Looking at the lists, you will find that Joe, Terry, and Ralph are in both bands, answer (A).

56. (D)

First, this equation has at most two solutions, so answer (C) can be discarded. Since $b^2 - 4ac > 0$, we will get two real solutions to the equation. $b^2 - 4ac$ is what's under the radical in the quadratic formula and is called the *discriminant*. If the discriminant is greater than zero, there are two real solutions. If it's less than zero, then there are two complex solutions. If $b^2 - 4ac = 0$, then there is one real, repeated solution.

57. (56)

Note that we are selecting a subset of people and that there is no sense of order. That means this is a *combination* problem. The problem can be solved using the combination formula, $C(n, r) = \dfrac{n!}{r!(n-r)!}$. Here $n = 8$ and $r = 3$, so:

$$C(8, 3) = \dfrac{8!}{3!(8-3)!} = \dfrac{8!}{3!5!} = \dfrac{(8 \times 7 \times 6 \times 5 \times 4 \times 3 \times 2 \times 1)}{(3 \times 2 \times 1)(5 \times 4 \times 3 \times 2 \times 1)}$$

Reducing the fraction will leave you with 56. If you had used the permutation formula (which is used when there is a sense of order) instead of the combination formula, your answer would be 336.

58. (C)

When you toss a fair die, there are six possibilities: 1, 2, 3, 4, 5, or 6. Of these possibilities, two are less than 3 and two are greater than 4. Four out of the six possible outcomes are less than 3 or greater than 4, so the probability of this happening is $\dfrac{4}{6}$, which can be reduced to $\dfrac{2}{3}$.

59. (A)

The graph of a function of x must pass the *vertical line test*, which says that any vertical line drawn on the Cartesian plane should intersect the graph of a function no more than once. (B), (C), and (D) all fail this test.

60. (B)

The diagonal of a rectangle forms the hypotenuse of a right triangle, with the width and length of the rectangle forming the legs of the triangle. With this in mind, this problem can be solved using the *Pythagorean theorem*, which says that the square of the hypotenuse of a right triangle equals the sum of the squares of the legs. In symbols, if c is the measure of the hypotenuse with a and b as the measures of the legs, then $c^2 = a^2 + b^2$. In this case $a = 5$, $b = 12$, and we want to find c, so

$$c^2 = 5^2 + 12^2$$
$$c^2 = 25 + 144$$
$$c^2 = 169$$
$$c = \sqrt{169}$$
$$c = 13$$

Section Three: The CLEP College Mathematics Exam | 219

Chapter Eleven: Practice Test 3

Time—90 minutes
60 Questions

Directions: For the following questions, either select the BEST answer of the choices given, or input your answer into the box provided.

You can use the computer-based scientific calculator during this exam.

Notes:

(1) Unless otherwise stated, the domain of any function f consists of the set of all real numbers x for which $f(x)$ is a real number.

(2) i represents $\sqrt{-1}$

(3) Unless otherwise indicated, all geometric figures lie in a plane. The appearance of all figures is accurate UNLESS the question states that the figure is not drawn to scale.

1. Which of the following is logically equivalent to "If you are not young, then you are old"?

   (A) If you are young, then you are not old.
   (B) If you are old, then you are not young.
   (C) You are not young or you are old.
   (D) If you are not old, then you are young.

2. If $x = -3$, then $|x| - 3 =$

   (A) 6
   (B) 0
   (C) 9
   (D) –6

3. An athlete wants to arrange four different trophies on a shelf. In how many ways could he arrange the four trophies?

   [   ]

4. Which of the following statements includes a cardinal number?

   (A) Today is my 25th birthday.
   (B) Our class meets in room 409.
   (C) There are 30 volumes in that set of encyclopedias.
   (D) My ID number is 555345.

5. How many prime numbers are there between 1 and 20?

   (A) 19
   (B) 10
   (C) 7
   (D) 8

GO ON TO THE NEXT PAGE

KAPLAN

6. What is the range of the function graphed below?

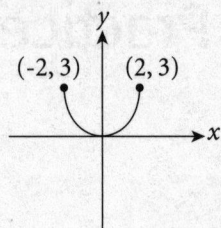

(A) $-2 \leq x \leq 2$
(B) $0 \leq y \leq 3$
(C) $y \geq 0$
(D) $-2 \leq y \leq 2$

7. The sum of the mean and median of the numbers 22, 41, 13, 17, and 32 is

(A) 147
(B) 47
(C) 550
(D) 38

8. Which of the following is an irrational number?

(A) $\sqrt{49}$
(B) $\sqrt{36}$
(C) $\sqrt{27}$
(D) $\sqrt{9}$

9. Which is the inverse of the function $f(x) = 3x + 4$?

(A) $f^{-1}(x) = 3x - 4$
(B) $f^{-1}(x) = 4x + 3$
(C) $f^{-1}(x) = \dfrac{x}{3} - 4$
(D) $f^{-1}(x) = \dfrac{x - 4}{3}$

10. Below is a Truth Table:

p	q	r
T	T	T
T	F	F
F	T	F
F	F	T

According to this table, which of the following statements describes r?

(A) $p \leftrightarrow q$
(B) $p \rightarrow q$
(C) $p \vee q$
(D) $p \wedge q$

11. Which of the following lines is perpendicular to the line $2y - 3x = 8$?

(A) $y = 3x - 4$
(B) $y = \dfrac{2}{3}x + 6$
(C) $y = -\dfrac{2}{3}x - 4$
(D) $y = \dfrac{3}{2}x + 4$

12. The probability an event will occur is 0.4. What is the probability the event will not occur?

(A) 0.6
(B) 0.4
(C) 0
(D) 1

13. Which of the following is a factor of $x^4 + 5x^3 - x^2 - 3x - 2$?

(A) $x^2 + 3x + 2$
(B) $x - 1$
(C) $x + 1$
(D) $x - 2$

14. If A = {$x \mid x$ is a positive integer} and B = {$x \mid x$ is an even integer less than 50}, which of the following is a subset of A ∩ B?

    (A) {12, 15, 16, 18}
    (B) {−4, 6, 8, 10}
    (C) {22, 34, 56}
    (D) {12, 20, 36, 48}

15. Simplify $\sqrt{-49} + \sqrt{-36} - \sqrt{-25}$

    (A) 8
    (B) 15
    (C) $8i$
    (D) $15i$

16. If $f(x) = 2x - 3$ and $g(x) = x^2 + 1$, then $f(g(-3)) =$ ☐

17. If a and b are prime numbers, which of the following is NEVER true?

    I. $a + b$ is a prime number
    II. $a - b$ is a prime number
    III. ab is a prime number

    (A) I only
    (B) II only
    (C) I and II only
    (D) III only

18. At a music store, there are 10 types of guitars, 3 types of cases, and 5 types of amplifiers. If Leo wants to purchase one of each, how many different combinations of guitars, cases, and amplifiers are possible?

    (A) 18
    (B) 150
    (C) 35
    (D) 80

19. What is the domain of the function $f(x) = \{(1, 4), (2, 5), (3, 6)\}$?

    (A) {1, 2, 3}
    (B) {4, 5, 6}
    (C) {1, 4, 2}
    (D) {5, 3, 6}

20. A friend claims that $2n$ is always greater than or equal to n for all integers n. Of the following, which is a value of n that provides a counterexample to your friend's claim?

    (A) 2
    (B) $\frac{1}{2}$
    (C) 0
    (D) −1

21. What type of triangle is given below?

    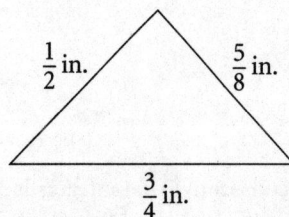

    (A) isosceles
    (B) scalene
    (C) equilateral
    (D) obtuse

22. A family adopts a second cat. What is the probability of both cats being males, given the first cat is a male?

    (A) $\frac{1}{4}$
    (B) $\frac{3}{4}$
    (C) $\frac{1}{2}$
    (D) $\frac{2}{3}$

GO ON TO THE NEXT PAGE

23. Suppose $A = \{a, b\}$ and $B = \{c, d\}$. Which of the following ordered pairs is in the Cartesian product $A \times B$?

    (A) (a, b)
    (B) (a, c)
    (C) (c, d)
    (D) (d, a)

24. How would the number 69 be written in binary notation?

    (A) 1101101
    (B) 1001100
    (C) 1000101
    (D) 1000100

25. If $f(x) = 3x^2 - 2x + 5$ and $g(x) = 4x - 5$, then $(f - g)(x) =$

    (A) $3x^2 - 6x + 10$
    (B) $3x^2 - 6x$
    (C) $3x^2 - 2x + 10$
    (D) $3x^2 - 6x - 10$

26. The sum of three consecutive odd integers is 39. What is the value of the largest odd integer?

27. Given an equation of the form $ax^2 + bx + c = 0$, with $b^2 - 4ac < 0$, how many real values of x satisfy the equation?

    (A) 2
    (B) 0
    (C) 1
    (D) 3

28. Consider the set of numbers $\{4, 9, 11, 17, 23, 27\}$. If one number is chosen at random from this set, what is the probability the number would be prime?

    (A) $\dfrac{1}{2}$
    (B) $\dfrac{2}{3}$
    (C) $\dfrac{1}{3}$
    (D) $\dfrac{3}{4}$

29. Consider the set of numbers $\{3, 6, 7, 9, 10\}$. What is the relation between the mean and the median of this set?

    (A) The median is greater than the mean
    (B) The mean is greater then the median
    (C) The median and the mean are exactly the same
    (D) More information is required

30. Let A represent the statement "You are 18 years old" and B represent the statement "You can register to vote." What can be said about statements A and B?

    (A) A is a sufficient but not a necessary condition for B.
    (B) A is a necessary but not a sufficient condition for B.
    (C) A is a necessary and sufficient condition for B.
    (D) A is neither necessary nor sufficient for B.

GO ON TO THE NEXT PAGE

31. Which of the following choices represents the Venn diagram?

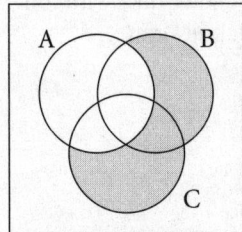

(A) $(A \cup B) \cap C'$
(B) $(B \cup C) \cap A'$
(C) $(B \cap C) \cup A'$
(D) $A' \cap B \cap C$

32. What is $2^4 = 64$ written as a logarithm?

(A) $\log_2 64 = 4$
(B) $\log_2 4 = 64$
(C) $\log_4 2 = 64$
(D) $\log_{64} 2 = 4$

33. If $f(x) = x^3 - 2x^2 + 5$, then $f(-2) =$

(A) 5
(B) 21
(C) -2
(D) -11

34. Which of the following is NOT a factor of 924?

(A) 2
(B) 3
(C) 5
(D) 6

35. In a race with 8 runners, in how many ways could there be prizes given for first, second, and third place, assuming there are no ties?

36. What is the area of the rectangle given below?

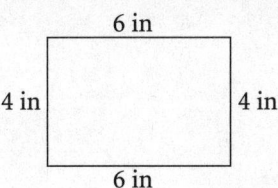

(A) 24 in^2
(B) 20 in^2
(C) 576 in^2
(D) 36 in^2

37. Let $f(x) = \sqrt{x - 3}$. Which of the following is the domain of $f(x)$?

(A) All real numbers
(B) All real numbers greater than or equal to 0
(C) All real numbers greater than or equal to 3
(D) All real number greater than or equal to -3

38. Which is the prime factorization of 45?

(A) 9×5
(B) 1×45
(C) $3 \times 3 \times 5$
(D) $2 \times 3 \times 5$

39. The number of absences and their probabilities for any given day in an English class are given in the table below:

Absences:	0	1	2	3	4
Probability:	0.15	0.15	0.30	0.30	0.10

What is the probability that there will be an odd number of absences for any given day of the class?

(A) 0.45
(B) 0.55
(C) 0.50
(D) 0.30

40. Which of the following is the converse of "If not R, then not S"?

    (A) If R, then S.
    (B) If S, then R.
    (C) If not S, then not R.
    (D) If R, then not S.

41. If $2^{2x-3} = 32$, then $x =$

    [_____]

42. Which of the following is NOT the graph of a function of x?

    (A)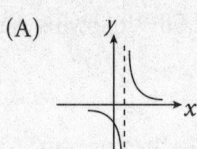

    (B)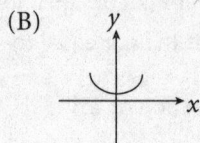

    (C)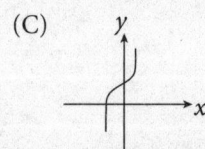

    (D)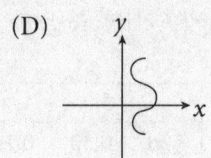

43. Suppose A and B are distinct sets such that $A \cap B = \emptyset$. What do we know about sets A and B?

    (A) A is a subset of B
    (B) B is a subset of A
    (C) A and B are disjoint
    (D) A and B are both empty

44. In how many ways could you mark your answer sheet (with an answer for each question) for a five-question multiple-choice quiz with four answer choices for each question?

    (A) 1024
    (B) 625
    (C) 20
    (D) 5

45. Suppose a is a positive integer and b is a negative integer. Which of the following is always true?

    (A) $a + b$ is negative
    (B) $a \div b$ is positive
    (C) ab^2 is negative
    (D) $a - b$ is positive

46. Suppose A is any event. Which of the following statements about event A are NEVER true?

    I. The probability that event A will occur can be greater than 1.
    II. The probability that event A will occur can be less than 0.
    III. The probability that event A will not occur is less than the probability event A will occur.

    (A) I only
    (B) I and II only
    (C) II and III only
    (D) III only

47. If $f(x) = 5^x$ and $f(y) = 1$, then $y =$

    (A) 1
    (B) −1
    (C) −2
    (D) 0

GO ON TO THE NEXT PAGE

48. What is the length of the side marked ? in the figure below?

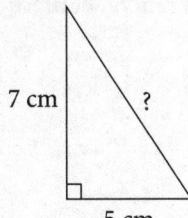

(A) 12 cm
(B) $\sqrt{35}$ cm
(C) $\sqrt{74}$ cm
(D) 9 cm

49. A number that is the sum of its proper factors is called "perfect." Which of the following numbers is perfect?

(A) 28
(B) 8
(C) 12
(D) 4

50. A jar contains 3 blue, 4 red, and 7 yellow marbles. If you select two marbles without looking from the jar, one after the other without replacement, what is the probability that they will both be red?

(A) $\frac{1}{7}$
(B) $\frac{2}{7}$
(C) $\frac{3}{13}$
(D) $\frac{6}{91}$

51. All dogs bark. Sparky barks. What can you conclude about Sparky?

(A) Sparky is a dog.
(B) Sparky is not a dog.
(C) Sparky doesn't bark.
(D) None of the above conclusions is warranted.

52. What is the range of the function $f(x) = |x - 3|$?

(A) All real numbers
(B) All real numbers except for 3
(C) All real numbers greater than or equal to 0
(D) All real numbers greater than or equal to 3

53. To win a certain state lottery, you need to select three distinct numbers from the set 1 through 25, where order makes no difference. How many different ways can you make your selection?

54. The product of all distinct positive factors of which number below is the largest?

(A) 5
(B) 6
(C) 8
(D) 11

55. Which of the following sets are well defined?

I. $\{x \mid x \text{ is an even number}\}$
II. $\{x \mid x \text{ is a good movie}\}$
III. $\{x \mid x \text{ is a difficult instructor}\}$

(A) I only
(B) II only
(C) III only
(D) II and III only

56. A deck of 52 cards contains 13 cards of each of four suits—clubs, spades, diamonds, and hearts. If you select three cards from a deck without replacement, what is the probability the third card is a spade given that the first two cards were diamonds?

    (A) $\dfrac{13}{52}$

    (B) $\dfrac{11}{52}$

    (C) $\dfrac{11}{50}$

    (D) $\dfrac{13}{50}$

57. What are the x-intercepts of the function $f(x) = x^2 - x - 12$?

    (A) 1 and 12
    (B) −3 and 4
    (C) 3 and −4
    (D) −3 and −4

58. Which of the following is equal to $(2a^{\frac{2}{5}} b^{\frac{3}{5}})^5$?

    (A) $2a^2 b^3$
    (B) $10a^{10} b^{15}$
    (C) $32a^2 b^3$
    (D) $32a^{10} b^{15}$

59. If the probability it will rain on Saturday is 0.7 and the probability it will rain on Sunday is 0.5, what is the likelihood it will rain on both Saturday and Sunday?

    (A) 1.2
    (B) 0.35
    (C) 0.2
    (D) 0.12

60. Which of the following functions does NOT have two distinct zeros?

    (A) $f(x) = (x-1)^2$
    (B) $f(x) = x^2 - 1$
    (C) $f(x) = -x^2 - 1$
    (D) $f(x) = x^2 + 1$

END OF TEST. **STOP**

THE ANSWER KEY APPEARS ON THE FOLLOWING PAGE.

ANSWER KEY

1. D	11. C	21. B	31. B	41. 4	51. D
2. B	12. A	22. C	32. A	42. D	52. C
3. 24	13. B	23. B	33. D	43. C	53. 2,300
4. C	14. D	24. C	34. C	44. A	54. C
5. D	15. C	25. A	35. 336	45. D	55. A
6. B	16. 17	26. 15	36. A	46. B	56. D
7. B	17. D	27. B	37. C	47. D	57. B
8. C	18. B	28. A	38. C	48. C	58. C
9. D	19. A	29. C	39. A	49. A	59. B
10. A	20. D	30. A	40. C	50. D	60. A

Answers and Explanations

1. (D)
Given a conditional statement, the contrapositive is always equivalent. To find the contrapositive, switch and negate the statements that make up the original conditional. In this case, "If you are not young, then you are old" is equivalent to "If you are not old, then you are young."

2. (B)
If $x = -3$, then $|x| = 3$. Therefore, $|x| - 3 = |-3| - 3 = 3 - 3 = 0$.

3. (24)
If you want to arrange four items, then you have 4 choices for the first item, 3 for the second, 2 for the third, and 1 for the fourth. There are $4 \times 3 \times 2 \times 1 = 24$ total ways to arrange the four items.

4. (C)
A cardinal number indicates the number of elements in a set. Of all the possible answers, only (C) could be thought of as a set (the set of books that make up the encyclopedia).

5. (D)
If you can make a quick list of the prime numbers between 1 and 20 you get the set {2, 3, 5, 7, 11, 13, 17, 19}. This gives you 8 numbers.

6. (B)
The range of a function is always in terms of y or $f(x)$, so we can eliminate (A) as a possible answer. Notice the graph is always above the x-axis, meaning it is always positive, so choice (D) can also be eliminated. In terms of the y-axis, the function never goes above 3 or below 0, so the range is $0 \leq y \leq 3$.

7. (B)
To find the mean, add the numbers and divide by 5. This gives you: $\frac{22 + 41 + 13 + 17 + 32}{5} = \frac{125}{5} = 25$. The median is the middle number if you list the numbers from smallest to largest: 13, 17, 22, 32, 41. The median is 22, so the sum of the mean and median is $25 + 22 = 47$.

8. (C)
Square roots often give us irrational numbers, but three of the square roots here simplify to whole numbers: $\sqrt{49} = 7$, $\sqrt{36} = 6$, and $\sqrt{9} = 3$. This leaves only $\sqrt{27}$, which is irrational.

9. (D)
The inverse of a function "undoes" the function. The function in this problem multiplies x by 3 then adds 4. To undo this, we would need to subtract 4 then divide by 3. Answer (D) completes this process.

10. (A)
Notice that r is true when p and q are both true or both false. Of the four choices, r is only true in the statement $p \leftrightarrow q$.

11. (C)
Two lines are perpendicular if their slopes are negative reciprocals of each other. If we solve the given line for y, we can find its slope:
$2y - 3x = 8$
$2y = 3x + 8$
$y = \frac{3}{2}x + 4$

The slope of this line is $\frac{3}{2}$ (the number in front of x), so the slope of a line perpendicular to it would be $-\frac{2}{3}$. Choice (C) is the only line with this slope.

12. (A)
The probability that an event will occur plus the probability that it will not occur always equals 1. In this case, the probability the event will occur is 0.4, so we need to add 0.6 to get 1. Therefore, the probability that the event will not occur must be 0.6.

13. (B)

If we plug any number c into a polynomial and get 0, then $x - c$ is a factor of the polynomial. Looking at answers (B), (C), and (D), there are three choices for c: 1, −1, and 2. Plugging 1 into the polynomial produces $(1)^4 + 5(1)^3 - (1)^2 - 3(1) - 2 = 1 + 5 - 1 - 3 - 2 = 0$. Thus, $x - 1$ is a factor of the polynomial.

14. (D)

$A \cap B$ denotes the set of positive even integers less than 50. A subset of this set must also include positive integers that are less than 50. (A) includes an odd number, (B) includes a negative number, and (C) includes a number greater than 50, so none of these are the right answer. (D) is the only set listed that includes only positive even integers less than 50.

15. (C)

Keeping in mind that $i = \sqrt{-1}$, we can simplify each square root in the problem as follows: $\sqrt{-49} = \sqrt{49(-1)} = \sqrt{49}\sqrt{-1} = 7i$. Similarly, $\sqrt{-36} = 6i$ and $\sqrt{-25} = 5i$, so $\sqrt{-49} + \sqrt{-36} - \sqrt{-25} = 7i + 6i - 5i = 8i$.

16. (17)

First we need to find $g(-3)$. Since $g(x) = x^2 + 1$, $g(-3) = (-3)^2 + 1 = 9 + 1 = 10$. Therefore, $f(g(-3)) = f(10) = 2(10) - 3 = 20 - 3 = 17$.

17. (D)

If a and b are prime numbers, $a + b$ will also be prime sometimes (for instance, 2 + 3 = 5). Likewise, $a - b$ will also be prime sometimes (for example, 7 − 5 = 2). If you multiply two prime numbers, the result will always be a composite number and never a prime number.

18. (B)

For a problem like this you need to see how many ways you can make each choice, then multiply. In this case, there are 10 guitars, 3 cases, and 5 amplifiers, so there are $10 \times 3 \times 5 = 150$ different combinations.

19. (A)

When a function is written as a series of ordered pairs, the first number in each ordered pair comes from the domain. With this in mind, the domain of this function would be the first number in each ordered pair, which is the set {1, 2, 3}.

20. (D)

First, we can exclude (B) because $\frac{1}{2}$ is not an integer. To see which of the remaining numbers works as a counterexample, plug each number in to see which one is not correct:

$2(2) \geq 2$ is true because $4 \geq 2$;

$2(0) \geq 0$ is true because $0 \geq 0$;

$2(-1) \geq -1$ is not true because $-2 < -1$.

The answer is (D).

21. (B)

Notice that all three sides of the triangle have different lengths. When this is the case, the triangle is called scalene.

22. (C)

If we let M represent a male and F represent a female, there are four possible gender combinations if a family has two cats: MM, MF, FM, and FF. The problem states that the first cat is a male, which narrows the possibilities down to two: MM and MF. Of these two options, only one represents two males, so the probability of having two males given the first cat is a male is $\frac{1}{2}$.

23. (B)

Since A and B are small sets, we can quickly list the Cartesian product: $A \times B = \{(a, c), (a, d), (b, c), (b, d)\}$. Ordered pair (a, c) is only choice listed that is in this set.

24. (C)

Since 69 is odd, the binary can be expected to end in 1, which is displayed in choices (A) and (C). If we expand (C), we can see that it is the correct choice:

$1000101_2 = (1 \times 64) + (0 \times 32) + (0 \times 16) + (0 \times 8) + (1 \times 4) + (0 \times 2) + (1 \times 1) = 64 + 4 + 1 = 69$.

25. (A)

To find the answer, use the fact that $(f - g)(x) = f(x) - g(x)$:

$(f - g)(x) = f(x) - g(x)$
$= (3x^2 - 2x + 5) - (4x - 5)$
$= 3x^2 - 2x + 5 - 4x + 5$
$= 3x^2 - 6x + 10$

26. (15)

Since there are three numbers that add up to 39, the quickest way to do this problem is to divide 39 by 3, which produces 13. This is the middle number we are adding to get 39. The odd number before 13 is 11 and after 13 is 15. You can check to see that $11 + 13 + 15 = 39$ and can see that the largest of these odd numbers is 15.

27. (B)

An equation of this form has at most two solutions, so you can discard choice (D). Since $b^2 - 4ac < 0$, there will be no real solutions to this equation.

28. (A)

Of the six numbers listed, three are prime: 11, 17, and 23. The probability of selecting a prime number would therefore be $\frac{3}{6} = \frac{1}{2}$.

29. (C)

The mean of this set is $\frac{3 + 6 + 7 + 9 + 10}{5} = \frac{35}{5} = 7$.

The median is the middle number when the numbers are put in order from smallest to largest, which they are above, so the median is also 7. The answer is therefore (C).

30. (A)

It is true that if you are 18 years old, you can register to vote. This means that A is sufficient for B. On the other hand, it is not necessarily true that if you can register to vote, then you are 18 years old. You could be older than 18. So A is a sufficient but not necessary condition for B.

31. (B)

None of A is shaded, so we are looking for something with A′, which eliminates choice (A). Most of B and C are shaded, except where A is. A′ can be found in the regions where B ∪ C. This Venn diagram therefore represents (B ∪ C) ∩ A′.

32. (A)

The base of the exponential expression is 2, so the base of the logarithm also needs to be 2. This narrows our choices down to (A) or (B). The logarithm of a number is the power to which a given base is raised to in order to produce that number. Here the power is 4, so the logarithm must equal 4. The only answer with base 2 that equals 4 is (A).

33. (D)

Substitute −2 for x into the function and simplify: $f(x) = x^3 - 2x^2 + 5$, so $f(-2) = (-2)^3 - 2(-2)^2 + 5 = -8 - 8 + 5 = -11$.

34. (C)

5 is a factor of a number if the number ends in 0 or 5. 924 does not end in 0 or 5, so 5 is not a factor of it.

35. (336)

There are 8 possible runners for first place. Once first place has been taken, there are 7 runners left for second place. After that, there are only 6 runners left for third place. In total, there are $8 \times 7 \times 6 = 336$ ways prizes could be given for first, second, and third place.

36. (A)

The area of a rectangle is given by length × width. In this case, the area of the rectangle is 6 in × 4 in = 24 in^2.

37. (C)

The domain of a function includes all the values of x for which the function is defined. The function $f(x) = \sqrt{x}$ is only defined for $x \geq 0$, so the function $f(x) = \sqrt{x - 3}$ is only defined for $x - 3 \geq 0$, which means $x \geq 3$.

38. (C)

The prime factorization of a number is the number written as a product of prime numbers. 9 is not prime, so choice (A) is out. Likewise, 45 is not prime, so choice (B) is out. Choice (D) multiplies to 30, not 45, so it's also out. This leaves only choice (C).

39. (A)

The possible number of absences listed are 0, 1, 2, 3, and 4. The only odd numbers here are 1 and 3. The probability of 1 person being absent is 0.15, while the probability of 3 people being absent is 0.30. The total probability of 1 or 3 people being absent is therefore 0.15 + 0.30 = 0.45.

40. (C)

The converse of a conditional statement $p \to q$ is $q \to p$. In this case, the converse of "If not R, then not S" would be "If not S, then not R."

41. (4)

To solve a problem where the variable is given in the exponent, we first need to make the bases the same. In this case, $32 = 2^5$, so $2^{2x-3} = 2^5$. Once the bases are the same, then the exponents must be equal, so we can solve the resulting equation:

$2^{2x-3} = 2^5$
$2x - 3 = 5$
$2x = 8$
$x = 4$

42. (D)

The graph of a function of x must pass the *vertical line test*, which says that any vertical line drawn on the Cartesian plane should intersect the graph of a function no more than once. (A), (B), and (C) all pass this test, but (D) fails it.

43. (C)

Since A and B are distinct sets, they cannot both be empty, so choice (D) can be eliminated. By definition, two sets are disjoint if $A \cap B = \varnothing$, so the answer is (C).

44. (A)

Each question has 4 possible answer choices and there are 5 questions, so the number of ways to mark your answer sheet would be $4 \times 4 \times 4 \times 4 \times 4 = 1024$.

45. (D)

Choice (A) is sometimes true, but not always. A positive number divided by a negative number is always negative, so (B) is not the answer. If a negative number is squared the result is a positive number, so (C) will always be positive. But if a negative number is subtracted, it will always become positive, producing a positive answer (D).

46. (B)

For any event A, the probability that event A will occur is always between 0 and 1, so I and II are never true. While the probability that event A will not occur can be greater than the probability that event A will occur, it can also be less. Choice (B) is the right answer.

47. (D)

If $f(y) = 1$ then $5^y = 1$. This is only true when $y = 0$ because $5^0 = 1$.

48. (C)

The figure shown is a right triangle and the side marked ? is the hypotenuse. The length of the hypotenuse of a right triangle can be found by using the Pythagorean Theorem, which says that if the length of the hypotenuse of a right triangle is given by c and the length of the legs are a and b, then $c = \sqrt{a^2 + b^2}$. In this problem, $a = 5$, $b = 7$, and c is what we want to find, so:

$c = \sqrt{a^2 + b^2}$
$c = \sqrt{5^2 + 7^2}$
$c = \sqrt{25 + 49}$
$c = \sqrt{74}$

49. (A)

The proper factors of a number are factors of the number that are less than the number. The proper factors of 28 are 1, 2, 4, 7, and 14. Adding these factors produces $1 + 2 + 4 + 7 + 14 = 28$. The number 28 is therefore "perfect." A quick check will show you the other choices are not "perfect."

50. (D)

Altogether there are 14 marbles, 4 of which are red. The probability that the first marble you select is red would be $\frac{4}{14} = \frac{2}{7}$. Once the first selection has been made, there are only 13 marbles left, 3 of which are red. The probability that the second marble is red would be $\frac{3}{13}$. Thus, the probability of them both being red would be $\frac{2}{7} \times \frac{3}{13} = \frac{6}{91}$.

51. (D)

Being told that "All dogs bark" means that "If it is a dog, then it barks." All we know about Sparky is that he barks. This does not guarantee that he's a dog. For instance, he could be a parrot that's been trained to bark, or a child that is imitating the bark of a dog. Consequently, there is no conclusion that can be drawn, so the answer must be (D).

52. (C)

The range of a function is all the values that come out of the function. Since absolute value is always greater than or equal to 0, all numbers that come out of the function are greater than or equal to zero.

53. (2,300)

A subset of items is being selected where order does not matter. This is a combination problem. The problem can be solved using the combination formula, $C(n, r) = \frac{n!}{r!(n-r)!}$. Here $n = 25$ and $r = 3$, so:

$C(25, 3) = \frac{25!}{3!(25-3)!} = \frac{25!}{3!22!} = \frac{(25 \times 24 \times 23)}{(3 \times 2 \times 1)}$

Reducing this last fraction produces 2,300.

54. (C)

The distinct positive factors of 11 are only 1 and 11, and $1 \times 11 = 11$. Similarly, the only distinct positive factors of 5 are 1 and 5, whose product is 5. On the other hand, the distinct positive factors of 6 are 1, 2, 3, and 6, and $1 \times 2 \times 3 \times 6 = 36$, which is considerably larger than 5 or 11. The distinct positive factors of 8 are 1, 2, 4, and 8, and $1 \times 2 \times 4 \times 8 = 64$. Hence, (C) is the right answer.

55. (A)

A set is well defined if it is clear what elements make up the set. This is true of the set {$x \mid x$ is an even number} because an even number can easily be defined and elements from the set can easily be listed. The choices for II and III are not well defined because they are too subjective.

56. (D)

Knowing the first two cards are diamonds affects the number of cards left (50 instead of 52) but does not affect the number of spades. For the third card there are 13 spades out of a total of 50 remaining cards, so the probability of the third card being a spade is $\frac{13}{50}$.

57. (B)

The x-intercepts of a function are where the function equals zero, so set the function equal to zero and factor to find the answer:

$f(x) = x^2 - x - 12$
$0 = x^2 - x - 12$
$0 = (x + 3)(x - 4)$

This tells us that the function equals zero when either $x + 3 = 0$ or $x - 4 = 0$. Solving these equations produces the values $x = -3$ or $x = 4$.

58. (C)

This problem requires using some rules of exponents:
$$(2a^{\frac{2}{5}}b^{\frac{3}{5}})^5 = (2)^5 (a^{\frac{2}{5}})^5 (b^{\frac{3}{5}})^5$$
$$= 32a^2b^3$$

59. (B)

Probability is always between 0 and 1, so we can discount (A) because it is greater than 1. Since the probability of rain on Saturday is 0.7 and the probability of rain on Sunday is 0.5, the probability it will rain both days is $0.7 \times 0.5 = 0.35$.

60. (A)

The values of x that make a function equal to zero can be found by setting the function equal to 0 and solving for x. In the case of (A), $f(x) = (x-1)^2$ only equals zero when $x = 1$, so it is the correct answer. Every other function listed has two x values that make the function equal to zero: $x^2 - 1 = 0$ when $x = \pm 1$, and both (C) and (D) equal zero when $x = \pm i$.

| SECTION FOUR |

The CLEP Humanities Exam

Chapter Twelve: Practice Test 1: Diagnostic

Time—90 minutes
140 Questions

Directions: For each of the following questions or incomplete statements, select the best answer or completion from the five options given.

1. Elizabeth Barrett Browning, Matthew Arnold, and Charles Algernon Swinburne are all poets of

   (A) the Byzantine period.
   (B) the Age of Reason.
   (C) the medieval period.
   (D) the postmodern period.
   (E) the Victorian period.

2. Which of the following is a group of "Beat" poets?

   (A) Goethe, Dante, Petrarch
   (B) Pablo Neruda, Federico Garcia Lorca, Gabriel Garcia Marquez
   (C) Allen Ginsberg, Lawrence Ferlinghetti, Gregory Corso
   (D) Virginia Woolf, Stevie Smith, Naomi Shahib Nye
   (E) Bertrand Russell, Henri Bergson, A.J. Ayer

3. Sigmund Freud had a profound impact on which literary movement?

   (A) modern
   (B) Victorian
   (C) Restoration
   (D) Romantic
   (E) Renaissance

Questions 4–6 refer to the following people.

   (A) Immanuel Kant, David Hume, Voltaire
   (B) Ted Hughes, Robert Browning, Edmund Spenser
   (C) Auguste Rodin, Henri Matisse, Jean-Auguste Dominique Ingres
   (D) Frank Lloyd Wright, Buckminster Fuller, Louis Sullivan
   (E) Paul Verlaine, Paul Valery, Simone de Beauvoir

4. Which group consists of American architects?

5. Which is the only group that does NOT consist of three people from the same country?

6. Which group consists of figures from the eighteenth century?

7. The Romantic movement in poetry could best be characterized as

    (A) a movement away from all things vigorous and naturalistic.
    (B) the triumph of emotion and nature over logic and systematic thinking.
    (C) a combination of geometry and Aristotelian philosophy.
    (D) a movement that gave way to the Renaissance.
    (E) a sacrifice of the individual imagination to objectivism.

8. Which type of music contains the descriptive word "Bel Canto"?

    (A) chamber music
    (B) orchestral music
    (C) opera
    (D) jazz
    (E) church music

9. Which of the following are poets of the Harlem Renaissance?

    (A) Rita Dove and Jimmy Santiago Baca
    (B) Ovid and Terence
    (C) T.S. Eliot and Ezra Pound
    (D) Jacob Lawrence and Jean-Michel Basquiat
    (E) Gwendolyn Brooks and Langston Hughes

10. Which of the following poets is famous for his/her poetic "Essays"?

    (A) Sappho
    (B) Alexander Pope
    (C) Pindar
    (D) Marina Tsvetayeva
    (E) Octavio Paz

11. In musical terminology, a movement means

    (A) a section.
    (B) a tone.
    (C) parallel motion.
    (D) tempo.
    (E) faster motion.

12. Which of the following works was written in Old English?

    (A) *The Winter's Tale*
    (B) "A Valediction Forbidding Mourning"
    (C) *Beowulf*
    (D) *To the Lighthouse*
    (E) *White Teeth*

13. "When the evening is spread out against the sky Like a patient etherised upon a table;" This is an example of which of the following?

    (A) metaphor
    (B) synecdoche
    (C) synesthesia
    (D) simile
    (E) couplet

Photograph by Steve Vidler. Courtesy of SuperStock, Inc.

14. Based on the picture above, which of the following structures was the chief preoccupation of Gothic architecture?

    (A) bridge
    (B) cathedral
    (C) triumphal arch
    (D) lighthouse
    (E) aqueduct

15. Which of the following would best describe the Rococo period?

    (A) expressionistic, esoteric
    (B) devotional, sacred
    (C) somber, stark
    (D) political, agenda driven
    (E) voluptuous, lighthearted

16. Illusionism came into prominence in which period?

    (A) Hellenic
    (B) Baroque
    (C) Romantic
    (D) postmodern
    (E) modern

17. What do Max Ernst, El Greco, Mary Cassatt, and Marc Chagall all have in common?

    (A) They all started out as architects.
    (B) They all worked in the Impressionist period.
    (C) Their primary medium was watercolor.
    (D) They all made their reputations as expatriates.
    (E) They all based their works on the relationship between mother and child.

18. Which bold experimental film did Alfred Hitchcock create to appear as if it had been shot as a single continuous take?

    (A) *Rope*
    (B) *Rear Window*
    (C) *Vertigo*
    (D) *Shadow of a Doubt*
    (E) *Sabotage*

Questions 19–21 refer to the following people.

   (A) D.H. Lawrence, Thomas Hardy, Rudyard Kipling, H.D.
   (B) Ezra Pound, Marianne Moore, Emily Dickinson, Rumi
   (C) Henrik Ibsen, Anton Chekhov, August Strindberg, Luigi Pirandello
   (D) Jacques Derrida, Paul de Man, Helen Cixous, Julia Kristeva
   (E) Edward Gibbon, Suetonius, Herodotus, Thomas Macaulay

19. Which of these is a group of historians?

20. Which of these is a group of authors who were both poets and novelists?

21. Which of these is a group of dramatists?

GO ON TO THE NEXT PAGE

22. Which of the following philosophers influenced the French Revolutionaries?

    (A) Jean-Paul Sartre and Claude Levi-Strauss
    (B) Henri Bergson and Jan Husserl
    (C) Voltaire and Henri Rousseau
    (D) Marcus Aurelius and Thomas Hobbes
    (E) The Buddha and Bertrand Russell

23. Which of the following adjectives best describes Cubism?

    (A) geometrical
    (B) uniform
    (C) political
    (D) bulbous
    (E) realistic

24. Which of the following writers' life and work is associated with the painter Pablo Picasso?

    (A) Robert Browning
    (B) Emily Bronte
    (C) Gertrude Stein
    (D) Jane Austen
    (E) Eudora Welty

25. A term used to denote "background" music is

    (A) a gala.
    (B) furniture music.
    (C) skating music.
    (D) gamelan.
    (E) fusion.

26. Of the following, which story has not been made into a ballet?

    (A) *Carmen*
    (B) *Don Quixote*
    (C) "Sleeping Beauty"
    (D) "Scheherazade"
    (E) "Goldilocks and the Three Bears"

27. *Troy*, Wolfgang Petersen's 2004 film starring Brad Pitt and Orlando Bloom, is based on which work of classical Greek literature?

    (A) *History of the Peloponnesian War*, by Thucydides
    (B) *Iliad*, by Homer
    (C) *The Art of War*, by Sun Tzu
    (D) *Oedipus Rex*, by Sophocles
    (E) *Odyssey*, by Homer

28. Which of the following might be a synonym for "hubris"?

    (A) intelligence
    (B) empathy
    (C) regret
    (D) pride
    (E) reticence

29. Which of the following artists was known simply as "M," short for Michelangelo Merisi?

    (A) Dubuffet
    (B) Rivera
    (C) Caravaggio
    (D) Gentileschi
    (E) Picasso

Questions 30–32 refer to the following playwrights.

    (A) August Wilson
    (B) Lope de Vega
    (C) George Bernard Shaw
    (D) Friedrich von Schiller
    (E) John Osborne

30. Which of these playwrights is NOT a European?

31. Which of these playwrights was a contemporary of Johann von Goethe?

GO ON TO THE NEXT PAGE

32. The musical and film *My Fair Lady* are based on a work by which of these playwrights?

33. Blanche DuBois is the protagonist of which of the following plays?

    (A) *The Caucasian Chalk Circle*
    (B) *Outward Bound*
    (C) *Six Characters in Search of an Author*
    (D) *Our Town*
    (E) *A Streetcar Named Desire*

34. Kate Chopin's *The Awakening*, Sylvia Plath's *The Bell Jar*, and Edith Wharton's *The House of Mirth* all have this in common.

    (A) They were self-published novels.
    (B) They won the Pulitzer Prize.
    (C) They are considered feminist novels.
    (D) They were written in the nineteenth century.
    (E) They were banned books.

35. "Call me Ishmael." This is the famous opening line in what novel?

    (A) *Death Comes to the Archbishop*
    (B) *The Handmaid's Tale*
    (C) *For Whom the Bell Tolls*
    (D) *Of Mice and Men*
    (E) *Moby-Dick*

36. John Updike's *Rabbit, Run*, the story of an ordinary man trying to get ahead in his profession is based upon the similarly themed, classic novel *Babbit*, written by which earlier writer?

    (A) Theodore Dreiser
    (B) Sinclair Lewis
    (C) Preston Sturges
    (D) Margaret Mitchell
    (E) F. Scott Fitzgerald

37. This memoir, written in a series of volumes, contains many experiences from the narrator's childhood and later life, written with bittersweet regret for time's passing.

    (A) Proust's *Remembrance of Things Past*
    (B) Wolfe's *You Can't Go Home Again*
    (C) Austen's *Northanger Abbey*
    (D) Woolf's *Mrs. Dalloway*
    (E) Didion's *Slouching Towards Bethlehem*

38. Siblings from this Victorian family were noted for their stirring, often socially astute romantic novels set in the secluded English countryside.

    (A) Bronte
    (B) James
    (C) Rossetti
    (D) Austen
    (E) Shelley

39. The play and movie *Amadeus* are based on the life of which noted composer?

    (A) Bach
    (B) Mozart
    (C) Beethoven
    (D) Strauss
    (E) Wagner

40. Sherwood Anderson's *Winesburg, Ohio* and Edgar Lee Master's *Spoon River Anthology* both chronicle the lives of what kind of people?

    (A) urban
    (B) impoverished
    (C) small town
    (D) depressed
    (E) wealthy

41. Alexander Pope, Sir Joshua Reynolds, and Johann Sebastian Bach were all considered part of what eighteenth-century movement?

    (A) Restoration
    (B) Enlightenment
    (C) Neoclassical
    (D) Elizabethan
    (E) Renaissance

42. The eighteenth-century philosopher Diderot's *Memoirs of a Nun* famously attacked

    (A) capitalism.
    (B) Martin Luther's 95 Theses.
    (C) atheism.
    (D) religion.
    (E) reason.

43. Which composer was known as the Master of the Symphony?

    (A) Johann Sebastian Bach
    (B) Claude Debussy
    (C) Ludwig van Beethoven
    (D) Bela Bartok
    (E) Antonin Dvorak

44. The poet William Carlos Williams and playwright Anton Chekhov both learned compassion while working at which profession?

    (A) law
    (B) missionary work
    (C) philanthropy
    (D) farming
    (E) medicine

45. Which of the following artists is correctly matched to his/her discipline?

    (A) Berthe Morisot . . . etching
    (B) Phidias . . . oil painting
    (C) Fernand Leger . . . architecture
    (D) Frank Lloyd Wright . . . installation art
    (E) Louise Nevelson . . . sculpture

46. In a novel, "roman a clef" involves characters that are

    (A) based on real historical figures.
    (B) unacquainted with each other.
    (C) Italian.
    (D) of mixed ethnicity.
    (E) predominantly female.

47. *Steppenwolfe* and *Siddhartha* are novels by which of the following authors?

    (A) Thomas Mann
    (B) W.G. Sebald
    (C) Gunther Grass
    (D) Vladimir Nabokov
    (E) Herman Hesse

48. Which of the following artists was famous for his/her murals?

    (A) Auguste Rodin
    (B) Jenny Holzer
    (C) Christo
    (D) Theodore Gericault
    (E) Diego Rivera

GO ON TO THE NEXT PAGE

Questions 49–51 refer to the following portion of a poem.

THE KNIGHT'S TALE

WHILOM*, as olde stories tellen us,   *formerly*
There was a duke that highte* Theseus.   *was called*
Of Athens he was lord and governor,
And in his time such a conqueror
That greater was there none under the sun.
Full many a riche country had he won.
What with his wisdom and his chivalry,
He conquer'd all the regne of Feminie,
That whilom was y-cleped* Scythia;   *called*
And weddede the Queen Hippolyta
And brought her home with him to his country
With muchel* glory and great solemnity, *great*
And eke her younge sister Emily,
And thus with vict'ry and with melody
Let I this worthy Duke to Athens ride,
And all his host, in armes him beside.

49. What type of language is the poem written in?

    (A) Gaelic
    (B) standard English
    (C) Old Earlton
    (D) Middle English
    (E) American

50. Who is the author of this tale?

    (A) Sir Arthur Conan Doyle
    (B) Henrik Ibsen
    (C) Christopher Marlowe
    (D) William Shakespeare
    (E) Geoffrey Chaucer

51. What is the name of another part of *The Canterbury Tales*?

    (A) "The Second Nun's Tale"
    (B) "The Mariner's Tale"
    (C) "The Princess' Tale"
    (D) "The King's Tale"
    (E) "The Midwife's Tale"

52. Which of the following poets did NOT compose his major work in Latin?

    (A) Ovid
    (B) Virgil
    (C) Terence
    (D) Catullus
    (E) Dante

53. Which modern classical composer composed "The Rite of Spring"?

    (A) Ludwig van Beethoven
    (B) Igor Stravinsky
    (C) Franz Schubert
    (D) Leo Delibes
    (E) David Oistrakh

54. A sonata is a

    (A) musical form created by Wolfgang Amadeus Mozart.
    (B) piece that is played prior to the entrance of the principal characters in a play.
    (C) short piece that is played as the melody of an opera.
    (D) composition in three or four different movements, using one or more solo instruments.
    (E) tragic melody sung by the principal actor of a play.

55. The Symbolist or Decadent movement originated in

    (A) Japan.
    (B) Russia.
    (C) Bolivia.
    (D) Saudi Arabia.
    (E) France.

56. Orson Welles made his cinematic masterpiece, *Citizen Kane*, at age 25. For his next film, he adapted Booth Tarkington's 1918 Pulitzer Prize-winning novel. The film and novel are titled

    (A) *The Magnificent Ambersons.*
    (B) *Alice Adams.*
    (C) *Touch of Evil.*
    (D) *The Age of Innocence.*
    (E) *The Hours.*

57. During which holiday does *The Nutcracker* take place?

    (A) Thanksgiving
    (B) Christmas
    (C) Easter
    (D) Bastille Day
    (E) New Year's Eve

58. Which composer, who wrote primarily for the piano, is known for his use of ambiguous chords and unconventional clashes of melody?

    (A) George Gershwin
    (B) Aaron Copland
    (C) Antonio Vivaldi
    (D) Frederic Chopin
    (E) Wolfgang Amadeus Mozart

59. The Blue Rider and The Bridge were both expressionistic movements in

    (A) Ireland.
    (B) Australia.
    (C) Germany.
    (D) the United States.
    (E) India.

60. Which of the following is NOT associated with the painter Vincent van Gogh?

    (A) sunflowers
    (B) Paul Gauguin
    (C) self-portraits
    (D) madness
    (E) elongated faces

61. Which of the following painters was a member of the Pre-Raphaelite brotherhood?

    (A) Claude Monet
    (B) Dante Gabriel Rossetti
    (C) Amedeo Modigliani
    (D) Alberto Giacometti
    (E) Damien Hirst

Questions 62–64 refer to the following people.

    (A) Ludwig van Beethoven, William Wordsworth, Eugene Delacroix
    (B) Arnold Schoenberg, Gertrude Stein, Pablo Picasso
    (C) Wolfgang Amadeus Mozart, Samuel Johnson, Sir Joshua Reynolds
    (D) Phillip Glass, Rita Dove, Chuck Close
    (E) Claudio Monteverdi, William Shakespeare, Caravaggio

62. Which choice above is a group of modernists?

63. Which of the above groups worked in the eighteenth century?

64. Which group consists of Romantics?

GO ON TO THE NEXT PAGE

65. Max Ernst, Mark Rothko, and Willem De Kooning all emigrated from their native countries to live and work in

    (A) the United States.
    (B) Spain.
    (C) Algeria.
    (D) Australia.
    (E) Tahiti.

66. Which of the following matches the writer to his/her discipline?

    (A) Czeslaw Milosz . . . philosopher
    (B) Rabindranath Tagore . . . novelist
    (C) George Santayana . . . dramatist
    (D) W.H. Auden . . . poet
    (E) Flannery O'Connor . . . journalist

67. Contemporary writers Ann Beattie, Raymond Carver and Lori Moore are best known for which kind of fiction?

    (A) essays
    (B) memoirs
    (C) novels
    (D) historical fiction
    (E) short stories

68. A novel written in the second person addresses the reader with which pronoun?

    (A) we
    (B) I
    (C) you
    (D) us
    (E) he or she

Questions 69–71 refer to the following terms.

    (A) aside
    (B) play within the play
    (C) soliloquy
    (D) tableau vivant
    (E) prologue

69. Which of the above choices is spoken before the beginning of a play?

70. Which of the following involves an actor, alone on stage, giving a speech to the audience?

71. The players' performing *The Murder of Gonzago* in Shakespeare's *Hamlet* is an example of what?

72. Which of the following artists is a key figure in the photorealism movement?

    (A) Artimesia Gentileschi
    (B) Phillip Guston
    (C) Max Ernst
    (D) Hans Holbein
    (E) Chuck Close

73. Which of the following is a famous tragicomic figure often painted by Rococo artists like Jean-Antoine Watteau?

    (A) Mephistopheles
    (B) Pierrot
    (C) Aphrodite
    (D) Rasputin
    (E) Bismarck

74. A pas de deux is a dance for how many people?

    (A) two
    (B) three
    (C) four
    (D) five
    (E) one

75. Which of the following people is NOT associated with existentialism?

    (A) Albert Camus
    (B) Jean-Paul Sartre
    (C) Soren Kierkegaard
    (D) Samuel Beckett
    (E) Blaise Pascal

76. Which of the following figures are from the nineteenth century?

    (A) Friedrich Nietzsche, Lord Byron, Richard Wagner
    (B) Plutarch, Marcus Aurelius, Galen
    (C) Rene Descartes, John Milton, Aphra Behn
    (D) Montesquieu, Edward Gibbon, George Handel
    (E) Hannah Arendt, Jhumpa Lahiri, Merce Cunningham

77. Mark Twain's Huckleberry Finn has his adventures on and along which of the following rivers?

    (A) Ohio River
    (B) Snake River
    (C) Mississippi River
    (D) Missouri River
    (E) Po River

Questions 78–80 refer to the following novels.

    (A) *The House of the Seven Gables*
    (B) *Moby-Dick*
    (C) *Beloved*
    (D) *Fathers and Sons*
    (E) *A Connecticut Yankee in King Arthur's Court*

78. Which of these novels was NOT written in the nineteenth century?

79. Which of these novels was NOT written by an American?

80. Which of these novels was written by Nathaniel Hawthorne?

81. The novel *A Day in the Life of Ivan Denisovich* by Aleksandr Solzhenitsyn takes place

    (A) in the Gulag (Russian prison camp).
    (B) in an upscale Moscow neighborhood.
    (C) in a cemetery.
    (D) during the Napoleonic wars.
    (E) in a Cossack village.

82. Thomas Hardy's novels and poems are marked by

    (A) pessimism and resignation.
    (B) joie de vivre and optimism.
    (C) mysticism and imagination.
    (D) technology and futurism.
    (E) indifference and apathy.

In classical music, tempo marks are used to indicate a steady rate of speed, an acceleration, or a slackening in speed. Identify the following in relation to these indications.

83. "Largo" means

    (A) increasing rapidity.
    (B) twice as fast.
    (C) slow, steady tempo.
    (D) a walking tempo.
    (E) a moderate tempo.

84. "Tardando" means to

    (A) speed up quickly.
    (B) gradually grow slower.
    (C) gradually speed up.
    (D) grow slower and softer.
    (E) be slower than the preceding movement.

85. This Indian filmmaker known for his Apu trilogy brought international attention to Indian cinema for the first time in its history.

    (A) Satyajit Ray
    (B) Raj Kapoor
    (C) Bimal Roy
    (D) Guru Dutt
    (E) Mebeeb Khan

86. *The Persistence of Memory* is all of the following EXCEPT

    (A) a Surrealist work.
    (B) a painting by Salvadore Dali.
    (C) a landscape with timepieces.
    (D) a twentieth-century work.
    (E) a mosaic.

87. The word "Dada"

    (A) refers to a city in Switzerland.
    (B) means "ancient" in Old English.
    (C) has no meaning.
    (D) means "liberty" in French.
    (E) refers to a Norse God.

88. Which of the following books was illustrated by the author?

    (A) William Faulkner's *Absalom, Absalom*
    (B) William Blake's *The Marriage of Heaven and Hell*
    (C) Flannery O'Connor's *The Violent Bear it Away*
    (D) Ludovico Ariosto's *Orlando Furioso*
    (E) Sharon Olds' *The Dead and the Living*

Courtesy of SuperStock, Inc.

89. The *Birth of Venus*, shown above, is a painting by which of the following artists?

    (A) Edvard Munch
    (B) Sandro Botticelli
    (C) Christo
    (D) Edward Hopper
    (E) Sonia Delaunay

90. Wole Soyinka's *The Strong Breed* takes place on which continent?

    (A) Asia
    (B) North America
    (C) Africa
    (D) Australia
    (E) Europe

91. The poems and novels of D.H. Lawrence are most concerned with what subject?

    (A) children
    (B) politics
    (C) injustice
    (D) sexuality
    (E) life in the big city

92. *Satyricon* and *La Dolce Vita* are some of the films made by this internationally acclaimed Italian filmmaker.

    (A) Michelangelo Antonioni
    (B) Bernardo Bertolucci
    (C) Sergio Leone
    (D) Roberto Rossellini
    (E) Federico Fellini

93. Which of the following novels begins with a long poem?

    (A) Vladimir Nabokov's *Pale Fire*
    (B) Herman Melville's *Moby-Dick*
    (C) F. Scott Fitzgerald's *The Great Gatsby*
    (D) Aldous Huxley's *Brave New World*
    (E) Emily Bronte's *Wuthering Heights*

94. Lorraine Hansberry's depiction of an African-American family's struggle to survive and flourish in an urban world is entitled

    (A) *for colored girls who have considered suicide/when the rainbow is enuf.*
    (B) *Broken Glass.*
    (C) *West Side Story.*
    (D) *A Raisin in the Sun.*
    (E) *Sonny's Blues.*

95. Jack Kerouac's *On the Road* and Allen Ginsberg's "Howl" are landmark works from

    (A) the Restoration period.
    (B) the Beat generation.
    (C) the Fugitive poets.
    (D) the Imagists.
    (E) the Dadaist Conference in Zurich.

96. Henri Matisse, Vincent van Gogh, and Pablo Picasso are all considered to be

    (A) Cubists.
    (B) Post-Impressionists.
    (C) Impressionists.
    (D) Minimalists.
    (E) Color Field painters.

GO ON TO THE NEXT PAGE

Courtesy of SuperStock, Inc.

97. Which of the following painters is best known for his rotund and rosy nudes, as in his painting above?

    (A) Claude Monet
    (B) Jean-Michel Basquiat
    (C) Jacob Lawrence
    (D) Peter Paul Rubens
    (E) Willem de Kooning

98. Robert Frost's poetry can best be described as a blend of

    (A) Surrealism and fascism.
    (B) free verse and Greek drama.
    (C) Romanticism and Rococo hedonism.
    (D) mysticism and colloquial wisdom.
    (E) cosmopolitanism and elitism.

99. Satan is the protagonist of which of the following works?

    (A) *The Canterbury Tales*
    (B) *Paradise Lost*
    (C) *The Alchemist*
    (D) *1984*
    (E) *Love in the Time of Cholera*

100. Thomas Gray's "Elegy Written in a Country Churchyard" sings the praises of

    (A) technology.
    (B) peasant folk.
    (C) royalty.
    (D) continental philosophy.
    (E) priests.

101. Which of the following would be considered a picaresque novel?

    (A) *Pride and Prejudice*
    (B) *The Color Purple*
    (C) *Tom Jones*
    (D) *Diary of a Superfluous Man*
    (E) *The Recognitions*

102. David Hume famously contested standing theories of

    (A) time and space.
    (B) thermodynamics.
    (C) cause and effect.
    (D) supply and demand.
    (E) heat and energy.

GO ON TO THE NEXT PAGE

103. Which late Romantic-era composer was a contemporary of the philosopher Friedrich Nietzsche?

    (A) Dmitri Shostakovich (1906–1975)
    (B) Wolfgang Amadeus Mozart (1756–1791)
    (C) Niccolo Paganini (1782–1840)
    (D) Johannes Brahms (1833–1897)
    (E) Robert Fayrfax (1464–1521)

104. "A cappella" is a form used in which type of music?

    (A) choral
    (B) orchestral
    (C) jazz
    (D) bebop
    (E) opera

105. Margot Fonteyn, Darci Kissler, and Mikhail Baryshnikov are all best known as

    (A) composers.
    (B) jazz musicians.
    (C) modern dancers.
    (D) ballet dancers.
    (E) novelists.

106. Which of Ludwig van Beethoven's symphonies is often described as "Fate knocking at the door?"

    (A) Ninth
    (B) Fifth
    (C) First
    (D) Eroica
    (E) Pastoral

107. Which of the following is a novel written by Jane Austen?

    (A) Daniel Deronda
    (B) Wuthering Heights
    (C) Frankenstein
    (D) The Yellow Wallpaper
    (E) Sense and Sensibility

108. Which of the following novels is recounted by a recluse from his basement apartment?

    (A) Diary of a Superfluous Man
    (B) Invisible Man
    (C) Man Walks into a Room
    (D) Man's Fate
    (E) The Man Without Qualities

109. Which of the following authors' names is synonymous with clichéd writing?

    (A) Robert Bulwer-Lytton
    (B) T.S. Eliot
    (C) Marcel Proust
    (D) Leo Tolstoy
    (E) Virginia Woolf

110. What is the title of Niccolo Machiavelli's most famous work?

    (A) Being and Time
    (B) The Will as Representation
    (C) Civilization and its Discontents
    (D) The Prince
    (E) The Raw and the Cooked

GO ON TO THE NEXT PAGE

111. Robert Browning's "My Last Duchess" and "Porphyria's Lover" are

    (A) sonnets.
    (B) romances.
    (C) epics.
    (D) sestinas.
    (E) dramatic monologues.

112. Which of the following lines are taken from Matthew Arnold's "Dover Beach"?

    (A) "Where ignorant armies clash by night"
    (B) "To strive, to seek, to find, and not to yield."
    (C) "How can we know the dancer from the dance?"
    (D) "Because I could not stop for Death—"
    (E) "The old lie: Dulce et decorum est / Pro patria mori."

113. Whose famous maxim was, "No ideas but in things"?

    (A) Robert Frost
    (B) Anna Akhmatova
    (C) Gwendolyn Brooks
    (D) William Carlos Williams
    (E) Oscar Wilde

Courtesy of SuperStock, Inc.

Questions 114–116 refer to the sculpture above.

114. The sculptor of the piece is

    (A) Donatello.
    (B) Bernini.
    (C) Michelangelo.
    (D) Ghiberti.
    (E) Verrochio.

115. The piece was produced in which of the following periods?

    (A) Renaissance
    (B) Baroque
    (C) postmodern
    (D) Romantic
    (E) Hellenic

116. The sculptor's attitude toward the human form resembles

    (A) Alberto Giacommetti's.
    (B) Jean Arp's.
    (C) Henri Matisse's.
    (D) Fernand Botero's.
    (E) Phidias'.

117. Which of the following is NOT a poem?

    (A) *The Faerie Queene*
    (B) "Song of Myself"
    (C) *As I Lay Dying*
    (D) "Howl"
    (E) "Skunk Hour"

Questions 118–120 refer to the following poem.

Let me not to the marriage of true minds
Admit impediments; love is not love
Which alters when it alteration finds,
Or bends with the remover to remove:
O, no, it is an ever-fixed mark,
That looks on tempests and is never shaken;
It is the star to every wand'ring bark,
Whose worth's unknown, although his higth be taken.
Love's not Time's fool, though rosy lips and cheeks
Within his bending sickle's compass come;
Love alters not with his brief hours and weeks,
But bears it out even to the edge of doom.
If this be error and upon me proved,
I never writ, nor no man ever loved.

118. Who is the author of this work?

    (A) William Shakespeare
    (B) John Milton
    (C) Djuna Barnes
    (D) Boris Pasternak
    (E) Robert Browning

119. What sort of poem is this?

    (A) villanelle
    (B) sestina
    (C) epic
    (D) sonnet
    (E) rondeau

120. Which might best paraphrase the lines ". . . love is not love / Which alters when it alteration finds,"?

    (A) Love is fickle.
    (B) Infidelity is the inevitable outcome of a romantic relationship.
    (C) Love is constant, come what may.
    (D) Love is like stitching trousers.
    (E) Love changes and changes and changes ad infinitum.

121. Which of the following would be considered an epic poem?

    (A) *The Faerie Queene* by Edmund Spenser
    (B) "In a Station of the Metro" by Ezra Pound
    (C) "The Man-Moth" by Elizabeth Bishop
    (D) "America" by Allen Ginsberg
    (E) "Ulysses" by Alfred Lord Tennyson

122. Samuel Beckett's *Waiting for Godot* is which type of play?

    (A) realist
    (B) romantic
    (C) absurdist
    (D) anarchist
    (E) comedy of manners

GO ON TO THE NEXT PAGE

123. In which of the following ballets does the Sugar Plum Fairy appear?

(A) *Swan Lake*
(B) *Coppelia*
(C) *Peter and the Wolf*
(D) *The Nutcracker*
(E) *Sleeping Beauty*

124. Goya's later paintings can best be described as

(A) optimistic and joyful.
(B) bleak and disturbing.
(C) diffuse and colorless.
(D) natural and authentic.
(E) sane and moralistic.

125. Tony Kushner's *Angels in America* confronts the tragedy of

(A) poverty.
(B) AIDS.
(C) teen pregnancy.
(D) terrorism.
(E) genocide.

126. *La Giocanda* is another name for which of the following paintings?

(A) *The Scream*
(B) *The Blue Boy*
(C) the *Mona Lisa*
(D) *Self-Portrait in a Convex Mirror*
(E) *Impression: Sunrise*

Used by permission. See copyright page (iv) for information.

Questions 127–129 refer to the painting above.

127. Who is the artist?

(A) Emily Carr
(B) Pablo Picasso
(C) Goya
(D) Eugene Delacroix
(E) Paul Klee

128. What is the subject of this painting?

(A) religion
(B) philanthropy
(C) war
(D) sport
(E) democracy

129. In which century was this work produced?

(A) fifteenth
(B) sixteenth
(C) eighteenth
(D) nineteenth
(E) twentieth

Casa Mila © 2006
Howard Davis/Great Buildings.com. Used by permission.

130. The architecture of Antoni Gaudi, as shown in the picture above, could best be described as

   (A) amorphous.
   (B) geometric.
   (C) Cubist.
   (D) minimalist.
   (E) utilitarian.

131. Which of the following novels was NOT written by Henry James?

   (A) *The Ambassadors*
   (B) *Daisy Miller*
   (C) *The Golden Bowl*
   (D) *Portrait of a Lady*
   (E) *This Side of Paradise*

132. Which of the following novelists is/was most prolific?

   (A) Malcolm Lowry
   (B) J.D. Salinger
   (C) Djuna Barnes
   (D) Joyce Carol Oates
   (E) Ralph Ellison

133. Which of the following musicians wrote *The Well-Tempered Clavier* in 1722?

   (A) Johann Sebastian Bach
   (B) Aaron Copland
   (C) Antonio Salieri
   (D) Emmanuel Ax
   (E) Isaac Stern

134. Of the following operas, which were written by Wolfgang Amadeus Mozart?

   (A) *La Boheme, Madame Butterfly*
   (B) *The Tales of Hoffman, Orpheus in the Underworld*
   (C) *Don Giovanni, The Marriage of Figaro*
   (D) *William Tell, The Barber of Seville*
   (E) *Salome, Elektra*

GO ON TO THE NEXT PAGE

135. Which of the following works does NOT deal with the horrors of war?

    (A) "In Parenthesis"
    (B) *The Red Badge of Courage*
    (C) "Dulce et Decorum est"
    (D) *Apocalypse Now*
    (E) *The Jungle*

136. *Poetics* is a philosophical work written by

    (A) Thales of Miletus.
    (B) Pythagoras.
    (C) Aristotle.
    (D) Ptolemy.
    (E) Anaximander.

137. Which of the following adjectives best describes the poetry of William Blake?

    (A) understated
    (B) logical
    (C) prophetic
    (D) prosaic
    (E) inhibited

138. What is the setting of Edgar Lee Masters' *Spoon River Anthology*?

    (A) a graveyard
    (B) the desert
    (C) the sea
    (D) an industrial warehouse
    (E) an anonymous city

139. What do Gerard Manley Hopkins and Emily Dickinson have in common?

    (A) They were both conventional poets.
    (B) They were dramatists of the Romantic period.
    (C) They were both largely unpublished in their lifetimes.
    (D) They both used pen names.
    (E) They were both born in the United States.

140. Which of the following is NOT an aspect of the heroic couplet?

    (A) iambic
    (B) rhyming
    (C) consists of two lines
    (D) common in Elizabethan poetry
    (E) common in short stories

END OF TEST. STOP

ANSWER KEY

1. E	21. C	41. B	61. B	81. A	101. C	121. A
2. C	22. C	42. C	62. B	82. A	102. C	122. C
3. A	23. A	43. C	63. C	83. E	103. D	123. D
4. D	24. C	44. E	64. A	84. B	104. A	124. B
5. A	25. B	45. E	65. A	85. A	105. D	125. B
6. A	26. E	46. A	66. D	86. E	106. B	126. C
7. B	27. B	47. E	67. E	87. C	107. E	127. B
8. C	28. D	48. E	68. C	88. B	108. B	128. C
9. E	29. C	49. D	69. E	89. B	109. A	129. E
10. B	30. A	50. E	70. C	90. C	110. D	130. A
11. A	31. D	51. A	71. B	91. D	111. E	131. E
12. C	32. C	52. E	72. E	92. E	112. A	132. D
13. D	33. E	53. B	73. B	93. A	113. D	133. A
14. B	34. C	54. D	74. A	94. D	114. C	134. C
15. E	35. E	55. E	75. E	95. B	115. A	135. E
16. B	36. B	56. A	76. A	96. B	116. E	136. C
17. D	37. A	57. B	77. C	97. D	117. C	137. C
18. A	38. A	58. D	78. C	98. D	118. A	138. A
19. E	39. B	59. C	79. D	99. B	119. D	139. C
20. A	40. C	60. E	80. A	100. B	120. C	140. E

DIAGNOSTIC TEST QUICK REFERENCE TABLES

Use the following tables to determine which topics you need to review most. Many questions may fall into more than one category.

Topic	Test Question
Fine Arts	
Architecture	4, 14, 130
Dance	26, 57, 74, 105, 123
Drama	21, 28, 30, 31, 32, 33, 39, 44, 69, 70, 71, 94, 122, 125
Film	18, 27, 32, 39, 56, 85, 92
Music	8, 11, 25, 41, 43, 53, 54, 58, 62, 63, 64, 83, 84, 103, 104, 133, 134
Visual Arts	5, 15, 16, 17, 23, 24, 29, 45, 48, 59, 60, 61, 62, 63, 64, 65, 72, 73, 86, 87, 89, 96, 97, 114, 115, 116, 124, 126, 127, 128, 129
Literature	
Fiction	12, 20, 24, 27, 34, 35, 36, 38, 40, 46, 47, 56, 62, 66, 67, 68, 77, 78, 79, 80, 81, 82, 90, 91, 93, 95, 101, 107, 109, 131, 132, 135
Nonfiction/Philosophy	3, 5, 19, 22, 37, 42, 63, 66, 75, 102, 110, 136
Poetry	1, 2, 5, 6, 7, 9, 10, 12, 13, 20, 24, 27, 28, 40, 41, 44, 49, 50, 51, 52, 55, 61, 62, 63, 64, 66, 76, 82, 87, 88, 91, 93, 95, 98, 99, 100, 111, 112, 113, 117, 118, 119, 120, 121, 137, 138, 139, 140

Bear in mind that the number of questions below will not add up to 140, as many questions are listed for multiple topics.

Topic	Number of Questions on Test	Number Correct
Fine Arts		
Architecture	3	
Dance	5	
Drama	14	
Film	7	
Music	17	
Visual Arts	30	
Literature		
Fiction	40	
Nonfiction/Philosophy	12	
Poetry	48	

Answers and Explanations

1. (E)
All three poets are representative of the style and mode of the late nineteenth-century Victorians. Victorians wrote about contemporary social problems. The Byzantine period (A) occurred with the ascension of the Roman emperor Constantine in 8 C.E., and came well before the poets in question. The Age of Reason (B) occurred in the eighteenth century. The medieval period (C) began in approximately 410 C.E. and represented poets such as Geoffrey Chaucer in the fourteenth century. Answer (D), the postmodern period, is a twentieth and twenty-first century phenomenon.

2. (C)
These three poets are part of the first flourishing of experimental Beat poetry. Smith, Ayer, and Garcia Marquez would be near contemporaries, but have nothing to do with the movement. Goethe, Dante, and Petrarch (A) lived well before the generation of Beat poets. Neruda, Lorca, and Marquez (B) are/were Latin poets, whereas the Beat generation comprised American poets. Answer (D) includes twentieth-century philosophers.

3. (A)
Along with Darwin, Nietzsche, and Einstein, Freud (1856–1939) was a key figure in the break with classical ideas. None of the other choices (except for the very late Victorian period) could have been chronologically possible.

4. (D)
Note that Wright, Fuller, and Sullivan are the only Americans listed. Kant, Hume, and Voltaire (A), were philosophers. Hughes, Browning, and Spenser were poets (B). Rodin, Matisse, and Ingres (C), were artists. Verlaine, Valery, and de Beauvoir (E) were writers and poets.

5. (A)
Kant, Hume, and Voltaire were born in Germany, Scotland, and France respectively. All the other choices include people from the same country, namely England (B), the United States (D) and France ((C) and (E)).

6. (A)
Kant, Hume, and Voltaire all lived during the eighteenth century. Hughes and Browning lived during the nineteenth century, while Spenser lived in the sixteenth century (B). Answer (C) is not correct because Ingres was born in the eighteenth century, but did most of his work in the nineteenth. The other figures listed all lived in the nineteenth and twentieth centuries.

7. (B)
The Romantic Movement was a reaction against the sterile scientific view of the universe held by philosophers and poets in the Age of Reason. The Romantic Movement emphasized emotion in poetry much more than earlier writers had.

8. (C)
"Bel Canto" literally means "beautiful song" in Italian, and always refers to operatic singing.

9. (E)
Rita Dove and Jimmy Santiago were poets, but not of the Harlem Renaissance (A). Ovid was an Augustan poet and Terence was an Italian poet (B). T.S. Eliot and Ezra Pound (C) were famous figures in modern poetry, but neither was part of the Harlem Renaissance. While Jacob Lawrence began his career in the late Harlem Renaissance period, he was an artist, not a poet; Basquiat was an artist in the late twentieth century (D).

10. (B)
Pope's "Essay on Man" is the most notable and representative of the somewhat dry, clinical approach of the Restoration poets. The work of the other poets could not be termed essay-like.

11. (A)

A section of a classical piece is called a movement. A tone (B) is a distinct pitch. While parallel motion (C) is a tempting choice, this refers to the movement of intervals in the same direction. Tempo (D) refers to the speed at which a piece is played, while faster motion (E) refers to a descent of pitch and melodic ascent.

12. (C)

While *The Winter's Tale* by Shakespeare (A) and "A Valediction Forbidding Mourning" by Donne (B) were written in an older version of present-day English, they are not considered Old English. *White Teeth* by Zadie Smith (E) is a recent novel, and *To the Lighthouse* by Virginia Woolf (D) is a modernist novel from 1927.

13. (D)

The sky being "like" (rather than simply being) an etherized patient makes the quote a simile rather than a metaphor (A). A synecdoche (B) is a part is used for a whole part of speech, and vice-versa. Synesthesia (C) is the use of words that normally describe one sense impression (such as vision) to describe another (such as hearing). A couplet (E) is a unit of two lines of verse that usually rhyme and express a complete thought.

14. (B)

While Gothic architects did not relegate themselves to the erection of a single edifice, their central concern was the glorification of God with grand and imposing cathedrals. None of the other choices were central to Gothic architecture.

15. (E)

The Rococo period was the first flourishing of art for art's sake, and was sensual and celebratory. The period was far from stark and somber (C), and did not express overtones of religion (B) or politics (D). The Rococo period was not esoteric (A): it was not meant to be understood by only a small group of people.

16. (B)

Illusionism came into prominence during the Baroque period, although all but the Hellenistic period involved elements of Illusionism (especially the postmodern). Illusionist painters use foreshortening and perspective to create images that trick the eye.

17. (D)

All of the people mentioned were painters, but not all of them worked during the Impressionist period (B), primarily used watercolor (C), or based their work on the relationship between mother and child (E). However. they all left the country of their birth, so the correct answer is (D).

18. (A)

The other films listed are also works by Hitchcock but were not created to appear as if they were shot in a single continuous take. *Rope* was Hitchcock's first film as a producer, and was shot in scenes of ten minutes, without cuts in between the scenes.

19. (E)

Some of the literary critics listed in the other answer choices may have done some historical work, and Pound's poetry is steeped in history, but none would be considered historians. Lawrence, Hardy, Kipling, and H.D. were poets and novelists (A). Pound, Moore, Dickinson, and Rumi were poets (B). Answer (C), Ibsen, Chekhov, Strindberg, and Pirandello, consists of dramatists. Answer (D), Derrida, de Man, Cixous, and Kristeva, includes literary critics and theorists.

20. (A)

D.H. Lawrence and Rudyard Kipling were prominent novelists who also made a name for themselves as poets. H.D. was a notable twentieth-century poet who published a few novels. Thomas Hardy was prominent as a novelist and as a poet in the late nineteenth and early twentieth centuries.

21. (C)

Henrik Ibsen, Anton Chekhov, August Strindberg, and Luigi Pirandello were four of the most influential playwrights in the modern theater.

22. (C)

Voltaire and Henri Rousseau are representative of the nineteenth century's demand for equality and rights regardless of class or birth. Jean-Paul Sartre was a twentieth-century philosopher, while Claude Levi-Strauss (A) is a modern anthropologist. Both Henri Bergson and Jan Husserl (B) were philosophers of the late nineteenth and early twentieth centuries. Marcus Aurelius was a Roman emperor, while Thomas Hobbes was a seventeenth-century English philosopher (D). The Buddha created the religion of Buddhism in the sixth century B.C.E., and Bertrand Russell was a twentieth-century logician (E).

23. (A)
Picasso, Gris, and Braque used the sharp lines of geometry to express a kind of psychic rigidity. Picasso's work was neither uniform (B), political (C), bulbous (D), nor realistic (E).

24. (C)
A simple knowledge of life chronologies will help you deduce that there are only two real options. Robert Browning (A), Emily Bronte (B), and Jane Austen (D) did not live at the same time as Picasso. Eudora Welty (E), who was Picasso's contemporary, had no contact or affinity with the artist.

25. (B)
"Furniture music" is a term created by the composer Erik Satie to denote "background" music. A gala (A) is a festive occasion, skating music (C) is played while a person is skating, and a gamelan (D) is an Indonesian orchestra of primarily percussion instruments. Fusion (E) in reference to music describes the blending of two or more styles, especially jazz and rock.

26. (E)
"Goldilocks and the Three Bears" is the only story listed that has not been made into a ballet.

27. (B)
Homer's *Iliad* is an epic poem nearly three thousand years old that tells of the legendary war between the Greeks and the people of Troy. *History of the Peloponnesian War* (B) was written by Thucydides in 431 B.C.E. *The Art of War* (C) was written by the Chinese author Sun Tzu. Sophocles' *Oedipus Rex* (D) is a play about Oedipus, the king of Thebes. Homer's *Odyssey* (E) recounts the adventures of King Odysseus on his return home from the Trojan War.

28. (D)
"Hubris" is pride, particularly in relation to defiance of or negligence of the gods. The other terms have no relation to "hubris."

29. (C)
Caravaggio's given name was Michelangelo, shortened to "M" by his compatriots and many art historians.

30. (A)
August Wilson is an African-American playwright of the late twentieth and early twenty-first centuries. Lope de Vega (B) was from Spain, George Bernard Shaw (C) was a native of Ireland, Friedrich von Schiller (D) hailed from Germany, and John Osborne (E) was from England.

31. (D)
Friedrich von Schiller was a close friend of Goethe, and the two of them were largely responsible for the German Romantic movement. All other playwrights listed were not contemporaries of Goethe.

32. (C)
George Bernard Shaw's *Pygmalion* was the inspiration for the popular musical *My Fair Lady*, which was made into a film in 1964. In *Pygmalion*, Eliza Doolittle is tutored by professor Henry Higgins on the refinement of her speech and manner. Both works comment upon the complexities of human relationships in a social context.

33. (E)
Blanche DuBois, the quintessential faded Southern belle, is the protagonist in *A Streetcar Named Desire* by Tennessee Williams.

34. (C)
While from far-different eras, all three books concern women struggling against their destined roles. The books were not self-published (A), they did not all win the Pulitzer Prize (B), they were not all written in the nineteenth century (D), and they were not banned (E).

35. (E)

Ishmael is an important character in Herman Melville's famous tale, *Moby-Dick*. He is a teacher turned seaman/harpooner who leaves Massachusetts to fulfill his desire to go to sea.

36. (B)

The word "babbit" from the book by Sinclair Lewis came to mean a kind of comic American "go-getter," and was used in the same satiric fashion by John Updike. While Theodore Dreiser (A) also commented on contemporary values and hypocritical notions in books like *Sister Carrie*, it is Lewis who remains a great influence on writers like Updike. Preston Sturges (C) was a playwright and screenwriter, Margaret Mitchell (D) wrote *Gone With the Wind*, and F. Scott Fitzgerald (E) wrote *The Great Gatsby*.

37. (A)

Proust's *Remembrance of Things Past*, a series of volumes, is justifiably famous for its chronicle of one man's life. Of the other choices, only Didion (E) wrote nonfiction; this contemporary writer is not a memoirist like Proust.

38. (A)

Charlotte, Emily, and Anne Bronte wrote novels and poetry, including Emily's classic novel *Wuthering Heights* and Anne's novel *The Tenant of Wildfell Hall*. The James brothers, Henry and William, were American writers not known for the type of novel described (B). Rossetti (C) was a painter and poet, not a novelist. Jane Austen's many siblings (D) did not leave any writings, and Mary Shelley (E), the author of *Frankenstein*, was the sister of a poet, Lord Byron, not a novelist.

39. (B)

The play and film *Amadeus* chronicle the supposed rivalry between Wolfgang "Amadeus" Mozart and the less well-known composer, Salieri. It's a good idea to know the full names of artists.

40. (C)

While one book is prose and the other poetry, both examine the lives of small-town residents at the turn of the century. Some of the books' characters are poor (B), some wealthy (E), some depressed (D), but all are from a small town.

41. (B)

The eighteenth century was the ideal host to this movement (the Enlightenment), which gained strength as the power of the aristocracy declined and revolutions did away with the old order. Note the time period. The Renaissance (E), Elizabethan period (D), and Restoration (A) occurred before the eighteenth century. Although the Neoclassical movement lasted from the seventeenth to the nineteenth centuries, the unemotional, severe overtones of the movement were not adopted by Pope, Reynolds, and Bach.

42. (D)

This French philosopher was a leader of the Enlightenment in the 1700s, before the Age of Reason (E), the advent of the Industrial Age, and capitalism (A) as we know it today. The book did not attack Martin Luther (B); rather, it denigrated the idea of the church deciding how a country should be run. Prior to the Enlightenment, the church was still heavily linked to many European governments, a situation largely unquestioned by most citizens. The book attacked religion, rather than the lack thereof (C).

43. (C)

Beethoven, having composed over nine symphonies, bridged the Classical and Romantic periods in music and was known as the Master of the Symphony. The other composers, while prolific, were not known for their masterful symphonies.

44. (E)

Both writers practiced medicine while finding the time to write distinguished poems, short stories, and plays. The question contains the word "compassion" so you may be tempted to choose answer (B), missionary work, but that answer is incorrect.

45. (E)

Nevelson was an innovative and prominent sculptor of the twentieth century. While she may not be very well known, the correct answer could be arrived at by eliminating the other, better-known options. Berthe Morisot (A) was a French Impressionist who worked with oil on canvas. Phidias (B) was a Greek sculptor, Fernand Leger (C) was a French Cubist painter, and Frank Lloyd Wright (D) was an American architect.

46. (A)

Primary Colors, which satirizes former President Clinton, is a good example of "roman a clef." Only answer (A), based on real historical figures, defines the term "roman a clef."

47. (E)

Both *Steppenwolfe* and *Siddhartha* are indicative of Herman Hesse's preoccupation with spiritual angst and isolation. Thomas Mann (A) wrote *The Magic Mountain* among other novels, W.G. Sebald (B) wrote *After Nature*, Gunther Grass (C) wrote *The Tin Drum*, and Vladimir Nabokov (D) wrote *Lolita*.

48. (E)

Rivera promoted the shift to larger, more socially conscious artwork executed in the public arena. Rodin (A) was a sculptor, Holzer (B) uses media such as LCD screens for her displays, Christo (C) is an environmental artist who uses fabric and other materials in his pieces, and Gericault (D) was an eighteenth-century Romantic painter.

49. (D)

Gaelic is an Irish language (A). The poem is not written in standard English (B), and Old Earlton (C) is a made-up language. While most Americans speak English, the wording used in the poem above is in Middle English. Note how the spelling and usage of many words does not follow conventional English-language standards.

50. (E)

Chaucer wrote this tale in the fourteenth century, as part of *The Canterbury Tales*. Sir Arthur Conan Doyle (A) was a nineteenth-century Scottish author and doctor who wrote the Sherlock Holmes detective novels. Henrik Ibsen (B) was a nineteenth-century Norwegian playwright. Christopher Marlowe (C), was a playwright who may actually have written Shakespeare's plays. He did not write in Middle English. Shakespeare (who may have been Marlowe!) did not write in Middle English either.

51. (A)

"The Second Nun's Tale" is the only choice that represents an actual section from *The Canterbury Tales*. All of the other choices are made up.

52. (E)

Dante's *Commedia* was a landmark work both because of its aesthetic innovations and because it was written in Italian and thus accessible to the average reader. All of the other poets wrote in Latin.

53. (B)

Note the use of the word "modern," which lets you know the time period. Beethoven (A), Schubert (C), and Delibes (D) are earlier composers, while Oistrakh (E) is a violinist.

54. (D)

Mozart (A) did not create the sonata form, but he did create individual sonatas, as did Bach, Beethoven, and various other classical composers. A sonata is not necessarily played for an opera or play ((B), (C), and (E)). A sonata can be shortened into a sonatina, which is less complex.

55. (E)

The Symbolist movement originated in France. The French poet Charles Baudelaire is generally credited as the father of the movement; however, it was heavily influenced by American poets like Poe and Whitman.

56. (A)

The Magnificent Ambersons was made by Welles in 1942. *Alice Adams* (B) was Booth Tarkington's second novel to win the Pulitzer Prize, in 1922. Welles directed *Touch of Evil* (C) in 1958, based on a novel by Whit Masterson. Edith Wharton's *The Age of Innocence* (D) won the Pulitzer Prize in 1921, and was adapted to the screen by Martin Scorcese in 1993. Michael Cunningham's *The Hours* (E) won the Pulitzer Prize in 1999, and was adapted to film by Stephan Daldry in 2002.

57. (B)

The ballet *The Nutcracker* takes place on Christmas Eve, unfolding as a fantasy in the mind of the little girl, Clara.

58. (D)

Frederic Chopin lived and wrote during the 1800s. He is known for composing primarily for the piano and for employing unusual chords and occasionally dissonant melodies. None of the other composers listed have all of these characteristics.

59. (C)

The movements took place in Germany. Both movements were offshoots of German Expressionism.

60. (E)

Elongated faces are associated with Modigliani. Van Gogh was famous for including sunflowers (A) in his work, he knew Paul Gauguin (B), he created many self-portraits (C), and he was known for madness—he chopped off his own ear (D).

61. (B)

Rossetti formed the Pre-Raphaelite brotherhood in response to what he considered to be the contemporary affectation in the arts, which he and his followers traced back to Raphael. None of the other choices were members of the Pre-Raphaelite brotherhood.

62. (B)

In answer (B), each person is exemplary of the modernist movement in their respective disciplines. Schoenberg was a composer, Stein was a writer, and Picasso was a painter. For answer (A), Beethoven was an eighteenth-century Austrian composer, Wordsworth was an English poet, and Delacroix was a French Romantic painter. Answer (C) includes eighteenth-century composer Mozart, eighteenth-century British writer Samuel Johnson, and eighteenth-century English Rococo painter, Sir Joshua Reynolds. Answer (D) is composed of twentieth-century musician Philip Glass, twentieth-century poet Rita Dove, and twentieth-century artist Chuck Close. Answer (E) contains sixteenth/seventeenth-century musician Claudio Monteverdi, sixteenth/seventeenth-century Elizabethan playwright William Shakespeare, and sixteenth-century Italian painter Caravaggio.

63. (C)

Mozart, Johnson, and Reynolds, although from different artistic disciplines, all worked during the eighteenth century.

64. (A)

Beethoven, Wordsworth, and Delacroix were the seminal figures of Romanticism in each of their disciplines. Beethoven was a composer, Wordsworth a poet, and Delacroix a painter. The other choices do not include composers, writers, and artists of the Romantic movement.

65. (A)

The political turmoil of the twentieth century reversed the trend of American artists and writers emigrating to the old country. The United States became the haven of poets, artists, philosophers, and scientists alike.

66. (D)

Although there are philosophical elements in Milosz's work (A) and dramatic elements in Santayana's (C), neither person's vocation matches the one listed. Milosz was a poet born in Poland who emigrated to the United States. Tagore (B) was a poet from India, Santayana was a literary critic, poet, and philosopher, and O'Connor (E) was a Southern writer of stories and novels. Only choice (D), W.H. Auden, matches the discipline given.

67. (E)

While Carver did write essays (A), and Beattie, like Moore, is the author of an accomplished novel (C), the three are best known for their short fiction. The authors are not well known for writing memoirs (B) or historical fiction (D). Memoir is not a form of fiction.

68. (C)

Much less common than third-person or first-person novels, a novel written in second person (like Jay McInerney's *Bright Lights, Big City*) addresses the reader as "you," giving the text a more direct appeal to the reader. First-person voice uses the pronouns "I" (B) and "me." Third-person voice uses "he or she" (E) and "they."

69. (E)

Some plays preface the beginning of the play's dialogue with a brief explanation of the play's point of departure, termed a prologue. An aside (A) is a piece of dialogue intended only for the audience to hear, not the actors on stage. A play within the play (B) is just what it sounds like, for example when *The Murder of Gonzago* is staged in Shakespeare's *Hamlet* (see explanation for question 71). A soliloquy (C) is when a character reveals thoughts without directly addressing a listener, or talks to her/himself. A tableau vivant (D) is a scene on stage where actors, in costume, remain motionless and silent.

70. (C)

Hamlet's "To be or not to be" speech is a prominent example of a soliloquy. An aside (A) is also spoken for the benefit of the audience, but always involves a second character onstage. A play within a play (B) and a tableau vivant (D) involve more than one actor. A prologue is what the audience learns before the play starts, not necessarily from one actor.

71. (B)

Shakespeare fashioned this particular episode from one by Thomas Kyd in *The Spanish Tragedy*. The murder scene is meant to unnerve the king, who is guilty of a similar murder. None of the other answer choices are correct, since the players murdering Gonzago in *Hamlet* do not all have an aside (A), a soliloquy (C), a tableau vivant (D), or a prologue (E). See definitions in explanation for question 69.

72. (E)

Close is one of America's most prominent living artists; he is famous for his blown-up, detailed portraits of average people. Only two of the other artists listed lived during the twentieth century: Max Ernst (C), who worked in abstract art, and Phillip Guston (B), a muralist, Expressive Realist, and Abstract Expressionist. Artimesia Gentileschi (A) was a Baroque painter. Hans Holbein (D) was a late fifteenth- to early sixteenth-century German Northern Renaissance painter.

73. (B)

Watteau's famous painting of Pierrot in his oversized clown's costume is representative of the Rococo period's lighthearted wit tinged with sadness. None of the other choices were subjects often chosen by Rococo artists.

74. (A)

Deux means two, and therefore, a *pas de deux* literally means "step for two" (in French).

75. (E)

Pascal's life's work involved rationalizing the existence of God. Kierkegaard (C) is considered to be the father of existentialism, and the other choices are key figures of the movement in the twentieth century.

76. (A)

Nietzsche, Byron, and Wagner were all working in the spirit of Romanticism. Nietzsche was a philosopher who lived from 1844 to 1900, Byron was a poet who lived from 1788 to 1824, and Wagner was a composer who lived from 1813 to 1883. Answer (B) contains figures from the first and second century C.E., the people in answer (C) lived during the seventeenth century, answer (D) includes individuals from the eighteenth century, and answer (E) contains twentieth-century figures.

77. (C)

The Mississippi River is thought to be allegorical of Odysseus' Aegean in Homer's *Odyssey*. Huckleberry Finn is the main character in Twain's novel *Huckleberry Finn*, but he also appears alongside Tom Sawyer in Twain's *The Adventures of Tom Sawyer*.

78. (C)

Beloved is a novel set in the nineteenth century, but written in the late twentieth century by Toni Morrison. *The House of the Seven Gables* (A) is a Gothic horror novel written by Nathaniel Hawthorne in 1851. *Moby-Dick* (B) was written by Herman Melville in 1851, *Fathers and Sons* (D) was written by Ivan Turgenev in 1861, and *A Connecticut Yankee in King Arthur's Court* (E) was written by Mark Twain in 1889.

79. (D)

Fathers and Sons was written by the Russian novelist, Ivan Turgenev. All the other authors were/are Americans.

80. (A)

The House of the Seven Gables is one of Hawthorne's great novels in which "the sins of the father are visited upon the son." The book is the epitome of the Gothic horror novel. None of the other books listed were written by Hawthorne (see explanation of question 78 for authors and their works).

81. (A)

Solzhenitsyn wrote from firsthand experience, having been imprisoned by Stalin in the Gulag for his subversive writings.

82. (A)
Pessimism and resignation are the cornerstones of almost all of Thomas Hardy's work. Hardy is a sad stoic whose books explore the hardships of being human. Answers (B), (C), and (D) are way off, and answer (E) would be too much of a stretch.

83. (C)
"Largo" means a slow, steady tempo. Largo does not speed up, nor is it a walking or moderate tempo, as suggested by the other answer choices.

84. (B)
"Tardando" means gradually growing slower or to "retard." None of the other answer choices represent "tardando."

85. (A)
The other Indian filmmakers listed were contemporaries of Satyajit Ray's, but none of their works brought as much attention to Indian cinema as Ray's Apu trilogy. Never before had Indian cinema been so widely scrutinized by an international audience.

86. (E)
The Persistence of Memory is Dali's most famous work (B) and perhaps the most prominent painting of the Surrealist period (A). The Surrealist period occurred during the twentieth century (D). *The Persistence of Memory* was a landscape with timepieces (C), but not a mosaic.

87. (C)
The Dadaists chose the term "Dada" because they felt a nonsensical utterance would best represent their subversive aesthetic.

88. (B)
William Blake's *The Marriage of Heaven and Hell* was a landmark book for Romantic poetry, and its author was also a prominent artist of the period. None of the other books were illustrated by the author.

89. (B)
This painting is Sandro Botticelli's most famous and one of the most notable works of the Renaissance. Each of the other artists listed has a style that is radically different from Botticelli's.

90. (C)
Nobel Prize winner Soyinka is the foremost African literary artist of his era. His international fame attests to the postmodern goal of globally known literature. His novel, *The Strong Breed*, takes place in Africa.

91. (D)
Lawrence takes a clinical approach to the sexual instincts and involutions of both man and animal. Most of his work is set in the English countryside. The work of Lawrence is not as concerned with children (A), politics (B), injustice (C), or life in the big city (E).

92. (E)
Antonioni (A), a contemporary of Fellini's, made *L'Avventura* and *Blowup*. Bertolucci (B), from the generation after Fellini, is known for his films *The Conformist* and *The Sheltering Sky*. Leone (C) is known for the films *Ben Hur* and *Helen of Troy*, among others. Rossellini (D) is known for *The Messiah*.

93. (A)
The novel *Pale Fire* is a lengthy extension of a poem. *Moby-Dick* (B) and *The Great Gatsby* (C) open with famous lines, not poetry. The other two choices ((D) and (E)) are full works of prose.

94. (D)
A Raisin in the Sun is a powerful homage to the African-American experience. *for colored girls who have...* (A) and *Sonny's Blues* (E) are also written by African-American authors (Ntozake Shange and James Baldwin, respectively). *for colored girls who have...* is a play, *Broken Glass* (B) is a play by Arthur Miller, and *West Side Story* (C) is a musical by Leonard Bernstein and Stephen Sondheim. *Sonny's Blues* is a short story.

95. (B)
Kerouac and Ginsberg were Beat generation poets, most prominent in the 1950s. Kerouac's novel promotes his maxim "first word, best word" in an organic stream of conference prose-poetry, while Ginsberg's poem recalls Whitman's effusive, unfettered verse. The Restoration period (A) occurred between 1660 and 1800, much earlier than the Beat generation. The Fugitive poets (C) wrote during the twentieth century and were Southern classic poets. The Imagists (D) wrote during the twentieth

century as well. The Dadaist Conference in Zurich (E) occurred between 1916 and 1924, when a group of European artists (the Dadaists) met.

96. (B)

Each painter came into prominence at the end of the Impressionist period. Van Gogh could not be considered a Cubist (A), nor could any of the three be considered Color Field painters (E). The three painters were not Minimalists, which eliminates choice (D).

97. (D)

The term Rubenesque now refers to people (especially women) who are chubby or exaggeratedly curvaceous. The other choices include Claude Monet (A), a French Impressionist; Jean-Michel Basquiat (B), a twentieth-century postcolonialist; Jacob Lawrence (C), a twentieth-century Harlem Renaissance painter; and Willem de Kooning (E), a twentieth-century Abstract Expressionist painter.

98. (D)

Frost presented himself as a kind of homespun rural sage (the opposite of choice (E)), but upon close inspection of his work we find an elusive and somewhat esoteric philosophy. Very little of his work is free verse (B) and while there are Surreal (A) and Romantic elements in his work (C), neither is predominant.

99. (B)

Satan is the protagonist in *Paradise Lost*. Although there may be evil elements in the other works, Satan himself does not actually appear.

100. (B)

Gray's elegy is a touching ode to the soul and character of the common man and woman. "Priests" (E) is a tempting answer, as it references the church. However, it is incorrect.

101. (C)

Fielding's bawdy, episodic masterpiece was a high point in the genre. Turgenev's *Diary* (D) is episodic, but far too sober to be picaresque. A picaresque novel typically is a full-length fictional and usually satirical book, based on the adventures of a social underdog who is the protagonist. The first picaresque novel was Mateo Alemán's *Guzmán de Alfarache*, published in Spain in 1599.

102. (C)

Hume contested theories of cause and effect. He claimed that all we can know (and predict) is that one thing invariably follows another thing; we cannot infer that one thing is the cause of the other.

103. (D)

Johannes Brahms lived from 1833 to 1897. The Romantic era of music spanned from about 1815 to 1910, and Nietzsche lived from 1844 to 1900. Notice the use of dates in this question: none of the other composers lived during a time that was compatible with Nietzsche's.

104. (A)

"A cappella" means "as in chapel" and refers to singing without instrumental accompaniment.

105. (D)

All three people are noted for their principal performances as ballet dancers. They are not known as musicians (answers (A) and (B)), modern dancers (C), or writers (E).

106. (B)

This choice is the correct answer due to the dramatic chords opening the work. None of the other choices are associated with the phrase "Fate knocking at the door."

107. (E)

Jane Austen wrote *Sense and Sensibility*. George Eliot is the author of *Daniel Deronda* (A), Emily Bronte composed *Wuthering Heights* (B), Mary Shelley produced *Frankenstein* (C), and Charlotte Perkins Gilman wrote *The Yellow Wallpaper* (D).

108. (B)

Invisible Man is Ellison's outcry against a restrictive, racist society. *Diary of a Superfluous Man* (A) by Ivan Turgenev is recounted by a wealthy nobleman from his deathbed. *Man Walks into a Room* (C) by Nicole Krauss is the story of Samson Greene, a professor of English at Columbia University, who was found walking in the Nevada desert with a brain tumor. *Man's Fate* (D) by Andre Malraux is a fictional account of the early days of the Chinese Revolution. *The Man Without Qualities* (E), written by Robert Musil, has a main character called Ulrich, the "Man of Qualities."

109. (A)

There is an annual prize for the worst novel opening, awarded in Robert Bulwer-Lytton's name. The other names are synonymous with great writing.

110. (D)

The Prince is Machiavelli's guide to strong-arm government. The other choices are by Heidegger (A), Schopenhauer (B), Freud (C), and Levi-Strauss (E).

111. (E)

Browning was the master of the dramatic monologue. No aspect of either poem could be considered epic (C) or elemental of romance (B). The works are not sonnets (A) or sestinas (D).

112. (A)

"Where ignorant armies clash by night" is taken from "Dover Beach." The other choices are from works by Tennyson (B), Yeats (C), Dickinson (D), and Wilfred Owen (E).

113. (D)

"No ideas but in things" is the famous maxim of William Carlos Williams. Many succeeding poets would try to follow this maxim.

114. (C)

Michelangelo's sculpture *David* may be the most famous sculpture on the planet. Donatello (A) produced a slightly less famous and more diminutive *David*.

115. (A)

The piece is quintessentially high Renaissance style, which bases its principles on the Hellenic period. Michelangelo worked during the Renaissance, not during the other periods listed.

116. (E)

Michelangelo represents the physical form as the Greeks did, glorious and idealized, somewhere between Giacommetti's attenuated figures and Botero's blimpish ones. The other choices are not represented by Michelangelo's work.

117. (C)

As I Lay Dying is a modernist novel by William Faulkner. The other choices are all poems.

118. (A)

This is a Shakespearian sonnet. Of the other choices, only Milton (B) worked significantly with the form, and he is better known for his longer works.

119. (D)

A defining feature of sonnets is that they are fourteen lines long. A villanelle (A) is a nineteen-line poem of fixed form, containing five tercets (three-line groups) and a final quatrain (four-line stanza) with two rhymes. A sestina (B) is a verse form composed of six six-line stanzas and a three-line envoy. The sestina reuses the same line-ending words across stanzas in a specific pattern. An epic (C) is an extended narrative poem written in elevated language. The rondeau (E) originated in France and contains ten or thirteen lines, with an opening phrase repeated two times as a refrain. Be sure to review any unfamiliar poetry terms.

120. (C)

The lines mean "Love is constant, come what may." The other options mean the opposite of "love is constant."

121. (A)

The Faerie Queene is an epic poem. Spenser's long magnum opus is the quintessential epic poem, whereas none of the other poems are longer than a page and a half, nor do they have particularly epic themes.

122. (C)

Beckett's play is the high point of the absurdist movement, which included playwrights like Eugene Ionesco and Jean Genet. While facets of the other choices may be included in the play, overall *Waiting for Godot* is not realist (A), romantic (B), anarchist (D), or a comedy of manners (E).

123. (D)

All of the other choices are ballets, but the Sugar Plum Fairy only appears in Act II of *The Nutcracker* (in the Land of Sweets). *The Nutcracker* is performed on stages throughout the world at Christmastime.

124. (B)

Goya's later works are the products of a burgeoning madness married to the atrocities of his time. They may be authentic, but none of the other adjectives would apply.

125. (B)

Angels in America brought awareness of AIDS to its audience and questioned what Kushner considered to be "the implicit lack of compassion in the Reagan era." It is a perfect example of postmodernism's move toward a more socially conscious art form.

126. (C)

La Giocanda is another name for the *Mona Lisa*, Leonardo da Vinci's most famous painting.

127. (B)

Although the painting displays the violence of Delacroix (D) and the horror of Goya (C), it is in fact Picasso's masterpiece, *Guernica*. Picasso was a famous Cubist painter.

128. (C)

Guernica is Picasso's depiction of the atrocities of war.

129. (E)

Produced in the twentieth century, the work is characteristic of the modern movement away from realistic interpretation.

130. (A)

"Amorphous" refers to a lack of definite form, or shapelessness. Many of Gaudi's buildings seem to be melting like wax, and lack a definite form throughout. While Gaudi's buildings may have some elements of the other answer choices, the best answer is (A), amorphous, since the buildings do not express the clear-cut lines of Cubism (C) or geometric shapes (B), and they are not minimalist (D) or utilitarian (E).

131. (E)

F. Scott Fitzgerald is the author of *This Side of Paradise*. All of the other novels were written by Henry James.

132. (D)

Joyce Carol Oates has written over a hundred novels. Lowry (A), Salinger (B), and Barnes (C) published only a handful of books, and Ellison (E) went through thirty years of writer's block after *Invisible Man*.

133. (A)

Johann Sebastian Bach lived from 1685 to 1750. Aaron Copland (B) is a contemporary composer (1900–1990), Antonio Salieri (1750–1825) was an Italian composer who lived too late to write this music (C), and both Emmanuel Ax (D) and Isaac Stern (E) are musicians but not composers.

134. (C)

Don Giovanni and *The Marriage of Figaro* were written by Mozart. The operas in answer (A) were written by Giacomo Puccini, *The Tales of Hoffman* and *Orpheus in the Underworld* were written by Jacques Offenbach (B), *William Tell* and *The Barber of Seville* were written by Gioacchino Rossini (D), and *Salome* and *Elektra* were written by Richard Strauss (E).

135. (E)

The Jungle is Upton Sinclair's socialist indictment of the meatpacking industry and urban squalor of Chicago. All of the other poems and books deal with the horrors of war.

136. (C)

In this work, Aristotle details the criteria for a work of art or literature to be great and refers often to the playwrights Aeschylus, Sophocles, and Euripides.

137. (C)

Blake's poems are unfettered songs of divine inspiration. All the other adjectives are antonyms of "prophetic."

138. (A)

The *Spoon River Anthology* consists of epitaphs, or poems spoken by deceased individuals. A graveyard is a fit setting for spoken epitaphs.

139. (C)
Gerard Manley Hopkins and Emily Dickinson were both highly unconventional poets, eliminating answer (A). Emily Dickinson was a recluse for most of her life. They did not live during the Romantic period (B), and Hopkins was born in the U.K. so answer (E) is wrong. The authors did not both use pen names (D), but they were both largely unpublished during their lifetimes.

140. (E)
There may be a heroic couplet or two sprinkled in short stories, but they look out of place in most stories. Iambic (A), rhyming (B), consists of two lines (C), and common in Elizabethan poetry (D) are all aspects of the heroic couplet.

Chapter Thirteen: **CLEP Humanities Review**

- The Big Picture: CLEP Humanities
- Nuts and Bolts
- How to Score at Scoring
- Visual Arts and Architecture
- Performing Arts: Music, Dance, and Film
- Drama
- Poetry
- Fiction, Nonfiction, and Philosophy
- Final Thoughts

Congratulations on making the important and exciting decision to challenge yourself by taking the CLEP Humanities exam. The material in this chapter, if studied well, will help you to adequately prepare for the test. While the CLEP Humanities exam may seem daunting at first, don't despair: much of the unfamiliar information on the exam can be acquired with some thought, practice, and study.

THE BIG PICTURE: CLEP HUMANITIES

Before looking at the individual arts sections of the exam, take a look at the big picture. It's important to understand that this test is general in scope and broad in outlook. The CLEP Humanities exam tests for a thorough knowledge of classical to contemporary culture in many different fields: art, architecture, poetry, prose, philosophy, drama, music, dance, and film. You will be asked to demonstrate your understanding of key concepts, to recognize famous works of art and important techniques, and to interpret and recall information from a variety of subject areas. Be prepared to cross-reference categories and interpret dates and eras of work. The reward for studying hard for the exam is definitely worth it: a good score on this exam may get you up to six semester hours of college credit (or fulfillment of a requirement). Some schools may choose to grant credit for a particular course with content that matches the exam.

NUTS AND BOLTS

Brace yourself: it is highly unlikely that you will achieve expert status in every section of the exam. The exam is designed so that you will not know the answer to every question. As mentioned above, the test is exceedingly broad in scope, with 90 minutes allotted to answer 140 multiple-choice questions. Questions on the exam often involve information taught to college students in year-long survey courses. While you will most likely achieve a higher score in some sections than others, it is best to keep in mind the percentage of the exam taken up by each topic.

About half of the exam questions will ask you to identify the names and works of various authors, artists, or composers spanning several centuries. Another 30 percent of the questions will test your ability to recognize the style, rhyme scheme, or characteristics of these writers and artists, or the time period or movement during which their work was created. Finally, you will need to clearly present an interpretation of literary passages and photographs of artwork that may be unfamiliar to you. This level of question (discussion and interpretation) will make up about 20 percent of the test. These question types and the different topics are mixed together on the exam, rather than sorted into separate sections.

Here is the approximate breakdown of subject areas:

- 50%   Fine Arts
  - 20%   Visual arts (painting, sculpture, etc.)
  - 15%   Music
  - 10%   Other performing arts (film, dance, etc.)
  - 5%   Architecture

- 50%   Literature
  - 10%   Drama
  - 15–20%   Poetry
  - 10–15%   Fiction
  - 5–10%   Nonfiction (including Philosophy)

Emphasis is placed on Western culture and art, focusing on the Classical, Medieval, Renaissance, and Romantic periods, as well as the seventeenth, eighteenth, nineteenth, and twentieth centuries. Expect a few questions to touch on Latin American, Russian, African, or Asian studies. Be particularly alert for questions that cross disciplines and/or periods. It's especially important to have a clear understanding of terminology and genre for each topic covered.

HOW TO SCORE AT SCORING

Reading is fundamental to this exam. Read that sentence again! The only way to truly understand the fine arts is by experiencing them, either through books or firsthand. Learning about the fine arts takes effort on your part—you can't learn everything there is to know about the arts through one book. Visit your library on a regular basis. Read college textbooks for survey courses in drama, literature, and fine arts.

Make a conscious effort to attend fine arts events. Go see independent films rather than mainstream movies at the multiplex. Rent classic movies that transformed cinematic history, such as *Citizen Kane*. Go to museums and jazz or classical concerts. Attend a ballet, play, or gallery event. If you must turn on the TV, turn off MTV and turn on PBS. Go online and find websites that discuss the arts. Look up an author you want to know more about, or an art period you would like to study. The broader your range of experience and expertise in the arts, the better you will do on the CLEP Humanities exam.

At the end of each section in this review, there will be suggestions for further reading and study, as well as tips for how to make the most of your prep time. When you're taking the exam, be sure to read each question as quickly and efficiently as you can. If you're familiar with time periods, for example, you'll be able to rule out some multiple-choice answers quickly. Try to remember one important fact about each era. This will help you to remember what occurred during each time period.

Let's examine each category of the arts and discover what you need to know in order to score well—and how to get there.

VISUAL ARTS AND ARCHITECTURE

What You Need to Know
The visual arts portion of the CLEP Humanities exam will contain approximately 28 questions on a variety of artistic genres, including sculpture and painting. There will be another 7 or so questions about architecture. You will be asked to identify familiar and unfamiliar work by creator, discipline, and style. In addition, you'll be asked to recognize terms related to these fields.

Art Terms to Learn
One of the most important things you can do to prepare for each subject on the exam is to create a glossary of significant terms. Take the time to compile, consider, and understand the terminology, along with the types of art the terms are connected with. Here are some of the terms to learn:

Action painting A style of abstract painting that relies on the physical movement of the artist and vigorous brushwork or pouring on the canvas.

Camera obscura A dark room (or box) with a small hole in one side that external images are projected through. An inverted image of what can be seen through the hole is projected onto an opposing surface, where it can be traced. Vermeer was said to have used this instrument to aid his rendering of light and shadow.

Casting The process that involves pouring liquid material like clay, wax, or plaster into a mold.

Chiaroscuro Describes the effect of light and shade in a painting or drawing, especially where strong contrasts are given.

Collage A technique in which an artist uses materials other than paint, such as glass, paper, or wood.

Fresco A technique in which pigments are dispersed in plain water and applied to a damp plaster wall. The wall becomes both the binder and the support.

Mosaic Small pieces of colored glass or tessera embedded into plaster or mortar.

Architecture Terms to Learn

Arcade A series of arches supported by columns or piers, or a passageway between two series of arches.

Arch A curved structure designed to span an opening, usually made of stone or other masonry. Roman arches are semicircular; Islamic and Gothic arches come to a point at the top.

Façade The front exterior of a building.

Gothic An architectural style popular from the twelfth through the fifteenth centuries, characterized by pointed arches, flying buttresses and stone buildings that reached great heights.

Truss A structural framework of wood or metal that reinforces or supports walls, ceilings, piers, or beams.

Since art terms are constantly evolving, look over a recent college art textbook. Put these words on flashcards and practice learning them nightly. Try to find sketches or images to glue to the front of the cards, since you will be asked to identify pictures of various kinds of art. To prepare for the architectural aspect of this exam, find photographs of famous buildings, identifying the trusses, arches, and other components, or look for different styles of architecture as you walk around. Try to remember the time periods associated with each architectural form. Remembering, for example, that pointed arches are connected with Gothic buildings, will be of great help to you.

Different Schools of Art

As you learn the terms above, add the important schools of art to your base of knowledge, along with at least one noted artist in each school. Study the following chart, which lists popular schools of art along with a representative artist for each. Sometimes it is easier to remember a school of art when you are able to connect the works of an artist with a particular school of art.

School of Art	Description	Artist Associated with School of Art
Abstract art	Art that departs significantly from natural appearances.	Willem de Kooning
Art Nouveau	A style of the late 1880s, based on the curves of plants.	Gustav Klimt
Baroque	Popular in the seventeenth century, this style uses dramatic light and shade, strong composition, and exaggerated emotions.	Peter Paul Rubens
Bauhaus	This German school of art existed from 1919 to prewar 1933 and was interested in mass production along with greatly affected design styles.	Paul Klee
Classical	Greek art and architecture during the fifth century B.C.E. or art that emphasizes balance and proportion.	Myron, Polyclitus, Phidias; the Acropolis at Athens, the Parthenon
Conceptual art	This art believes that ideas and process take precedence over a tangible form. Developed in the late 1960s, Conceptual works include performance art.	Judy Chicago
Cubism	Cubism began in 1907. It is based upon the geometric reconstruction of objects into a surface of shifting planes.	Pablo Picasso
Dada	An early twentieth-century anarchic movement, which ridiculed the accepted standards of conventional art.	Marcel Duchamp
Expressionism or Abstract Expressionism	Used to describe emotional art featuring distortion and color. It was popular from the late nineteenth to the early twentieth century.	Vassily Kandinsky
Fauvism	A style of painting from the early twentieth century, with bright color and simple shapes.	Henri Matisse
Futurism	Originating in Italy around 1910, this school aimed to express the violent, energized, ever-changing quality of modern life; it was an outgrowth of Cubism.	Umberto Boccioni
Hellenistic	Style of the last of three phases of ancient Greek art (300–100 B.C.E.), characterized by emotion, drama, and the interaction of sculptural forms with surrounding space.	
Impressionism	A style of painting that originated in France around 1870, with casual outdoor subjects and divided brush strokes to capture the transitory effects of light and color.	Claude Monet
Minimalism	A late 1960s style of sculpture and painting, with simple geometric shapes.	Agnes Martin
Neoclassicism or Romanticism	New Classicism, or the revival of classical Greek and Roman forms in art, music, and literature, particularly during the eighteenth and nineteenth centuries.	Jacques Louis David
Photorealism	A style of painting popular in the 1970s, using photographs as subjects.	Chuck Close

Pointillism	A system of painting using tiny dots or "points" of color, developed in the 1880s.	Georges Seurat
Pop Art	Developed in America and England in the late 1950s and early 1960s, based on the impersonal style of the popular mass media. Think Marilyn Monroe on soup cans.	Andy Warhol
Post-Impressionism	A general term applied to French artists from about 1885 to 1900, concerned with symbols and expressiveness.	Vincent Van Gogh or Paul Cézanne
Postmodernism	A trend of the 1970s, 1980s, and 1990s, characterized by an eclectic acceptance of all periods and styles.	Damian Hirst
Renaissance	The late fourteenth through the sixteenth centuries, with an interest in human subjects and classical art.	Sandro Botticelli
Rococo	Late Baroque style, playful, romantic, pastel, and elaborate.	Jean Antoine Watteau
Surrealism	A term for a type of literature and art from the 1920s to the 1940s concerned with fantastic and dreamlike images.	Salvador Dali

While there are other art movements to keep in mind, the above chart is a good start. Taking out a variety of art books from the library will furnish you with the familiarity that cannot come from memorization alone. If you live in a city or have access to museums, visit them. There is no substitute for seeing actual works: whether via photo, reproduction, or, with luck, the art itself. Remember the identifying characteristics of the artist and time period. For example, Dali's melting clocks should bring to mind Surrealism.

Creating Timelines and Flashcards

A timeline can be an effective way to learn art movements. Create a simple timeline, adding artists and their schools, styles, and periods. Here is an example of a blank timeline for you to copy and fill in:

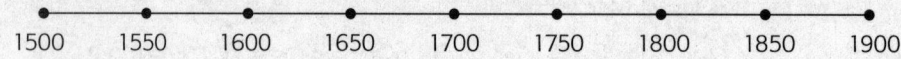

1500   1550   1600   1650   1700   1750   1800   1850   1900

The following is a handy website for creating great looking timelines. Bookmark it for use with your study guide: teach-nology.com/web_tools/materials/timelines.

Flashcards can be created for artwork and art movements as well as for art terms. Search the Internet or magazines for pictures of famous works or examples, and print and paste the pictures on index cards. Focus on remembering what distinguishes one style of art from another.

Art Resources

Besides museums and galleries, there are many fine books to be found on this subject. Some recommendations are: *Architecture: The World's Greatest Buildings Explored and Explained* by Neil Stevenson (Collingdale, PA: DIANE Publishing Company, 2000 (hardcover edition from DK

Publishing, 1997)), *The Annotated Mona Lisa: A Crash Course in Art History* by John Boswell and Carol Strickland (Kansas City, MO: Andrews McMeel, 1992), and *Learning to Look at Paintings* by Mary Acton (New York: Routledge, 1997). Check out great art websites such as the Metropolitan Museum of Art at metmuseum.org (which includes a helpful timeline of art through the ages) or the Art by Period site at teacheroz.com/Art_Periods.htm. For architectural information online, try GreatBuildings.com/gbc.html. This site includes a fine listing of buildings through the ages.

PERFORMING ARTS: MUSIC, DANCE, AND FILM

What You Need to Know

In all these categories, you'll be asked to identify specific works such as symphonies, ballets, operas, or films. You'll also be questioned on important composers, filmmakers, choreographers, and musicians, both classical and jazz. Some questions will ask you to place these artists inside their time period or movement. The largest number of questions will cover music, with a smaller number of questions about dance and film. Plan on being quizzed about the work of such American music greats as Cole Porter, George Gershwin, or Billie Holiday, and dance and film luminaries like Margot Fonteyn, George Balanchine, or Charlie Chaplin.

If you aren't a dancer or musician, these areas will take some study to master. If you do have a background in ballet or if you've ever played an instrument, you're in luck. Many of the questions will focus on musical terms such as the difference between a symphony and a sonata, or how many notes form a scale. If you've been an avid appreciator of music, you may already be familiar with works and composers on the test. Ballet dancers will be relieved to find they are already familiar with the language of dance (French) and are able to recognize notable dancers and ballets. Questions also will be asked about modern dance and notable dancers, such as Isadora Duncan.

The film section will be a breeze if you have a taste for important films older than the *Star Wars* trilogy. You will probably be asked fewer questions about specific terminology in this area, but you should be familiar with the plot and direction of great movies such as those by filmmaker Preston Sturges.

Music

This subject makes up 15 percent of the exam, or approximately 21 questions, so it's not one you can overlook! Let's start with some common terms.

Music Terms to Learn

A cappella Vocal or choral music performed without accompaniment.

Aria A song for solo voice with instrumental accompaniment.

Articulation The way notes are struck, sustained, and released, including legato, staccato, tenuto etc.

Atonality A term for twentieth century music where a "key" is avoided.

Bass The lowest male voice.

Bebop A 1940s term for jazz including improvised solos in dissonant patterns.

Cadence A pause or stopping point.

Contralto The lowest female voice.

Counterpoint Music consisting of two lines or melodic lines played simultaneously.

Crescendo Music getting progressively louder.

Diminuendo Music growing progressively softer.

Harmony The simultaneous occurrence of musical tones, as opposed to melody.

Leitmotiv A short musical passage that brings to mind a character or situation in a musical drama.

Libretto The text of an opera.

Plainsong Gregorian chant of the Middle Ages.

Quartet A composition written for four instruments or voices, or the four performers assembled to play such a work.

Quintet A composition for five instruments or voices.

Scat singing A style of jazz singing with nonsense syllables.

Sonata The most important form of instrumental music from the Baroque era to the present. It usually consists of four independent pieces called movements.

Swing A popular style of jazz that originated about 1935.

While memorizing these and many other music terms may be a good beginning, listening to music is an important aspect of learning as well. Check out the classical section of your local music store or library. Shuffle your CD or MP3 selections and see if you can name the type of music you are listening to. Some online sites have audio samples of various symphonies and compositions. This can be an enjoyable study session, if you use your time to become more familiar with great works. Take the opportunity to attend recitals. In addition to listening to music, it's wise to acquire a book on opera and composers, and to create a series of flashcards for better recognition of terms.

Music Through the Ages

Once again, we'll take a timeline approach to learning this information. We'll start with the Middle Ages, when most music was religious in nature and connected to the Church. As we did before for well-known artists, we will group musicians with their respective centuries and the musical period in which they composed. That done, consult a musical encyclopedia or an online source to connect at least one piece to each musician listed.

Pre-Medieval and Medieval	Renaissance	Seventeenth Century (Baroque)	Eighteenth Century (Classical)	Nineteenth Century (Romantic)	Twentieth Century (Modern)	Postmodern
Giovanni Gabrieli	Landini	Corelli	Handel	Schubert	Schoenberg	John Cage
Jan Pieters Sweelinck	Dunstable	Lully	Mozart	Wagner	Debussy	Phillip Glass
Thomas Morley	Tallis	Bach	Haydn	Mahler	Stravinsky	Miles Davis
Luca Marenzio		Vivaldi	Beethoven	Liszt	George Gershwin	
				Chopin	Cole Porter	
				Berlioz	Duke Ellington	

You also can use another kind of musical timeline, which incorporates other events:

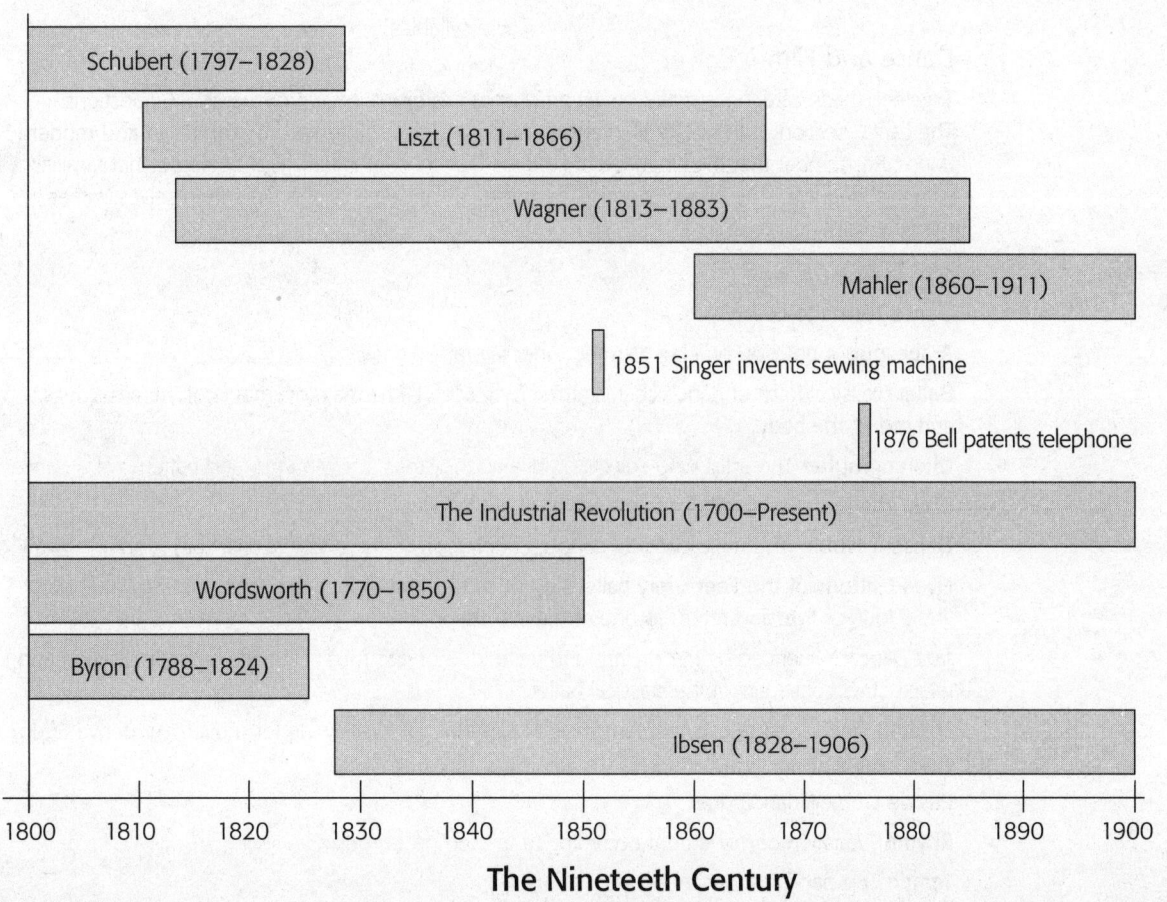

The Nineteenth Century

Music Resources

While music might seem to be a big topic to fully take in, source material in this area is especially diverse. Any text on the history of great composers would not be amiss for studying for the exam. To begin, try *The Lives of the Great Composers* (Third Edition) by Harold Schonberg (New York: Norton, 1997). Other helpful texts include: *The NPR Guide to Building a Classical CD Collection: The 350 Essential Works* (Second Edition) by Theodore Libbey (New York: Workman, 1999), *The Symphony: A Listener's Guide* by Michael Steinberg (New York: Oxford University Press, 1998), and *Guide to Symphonic Music* by Edward Downes (New York: Walker & Company, 1981).

Any guide to the stories behind great opera can be studied, along with a book on jazz roots in American music, such as *The Oxford Companion to Jazz* by Bill Kirshner (New York: Oxford University Press, 2000). If you feel you require more in-depth study in this area, Geoffrey C. Ward and Ken Burns' *Jazz: A History of America's Music* (New York: Knopf, 2002) is highly recommended. There are a plethora of websites containing both valuable information about music and timelines. For classical information, classicalworks.com is a very helpful site that is easy to navigate. One of the best sites, HyperMusic, can be found at hypermusic.ca. The site contains information and quizzes on every category of music.

Dance and Film

Together, these categories make up 10 percent of the exam, or approximately 14 questions. The dance section of the CLEP Humanities exam includes references to both ballet and modern dance. Remember that the language of ballet is French, so it is handy to be somewhat familiar with this language. The film section will be more concerned with the films themselves, rather than the terminology of film.

Dance Terms to Learn

Arabesque A pose on one leg with the other leg raised back.

Ballet Classical form of dance characterized by graceful, precise movements of the arms, legs, and rest of the body.

Choreographer The artist who selects or invents the steps, movements, and patterns of a dance.

Coda The last section of a pas de deux or of a full ballet.

Danseur Noble The male classical dancer, counterpart to the classical ballerina.

Five Positions of the Feet Every ballet step or movement must begin with positions one, two, three, four, or five, and return to one of these positions.

Jazz Dance influenced by the rhythm and technique of jazz music, it relies on improvisation and rejects strict constructs of the classical ballet.

Modern Dance that rejects the constructs of classical ballet, allowing for movement derived from inner feeling.

Pas de Deux A dance duet.

Rhythm Variation of movement according to the tempo of music.

Tempo The pace of a dance.

Film Terms to Learn

Aperture Camera lens with a valve to control the amount of light that comes through.

Dissolve A transition between two shots, where one shot fades away and another shot simultaneously fades in.

Dubbing Recording of dialogue in a sound studio after a film has been shot. Actors match the lip movements on the film to dialogue that they speak.

Edit The arrangement of shots.

Frame A single image on film.

Looping Film is on a loop, to give an actor several tries to get a line correct.

Negative Original film used in the camera, used to make a positive, final print from.

Dance and Film Names to Know

For these subjects, it's more important to remember great works than terminology. Instead of making a timeline, look up information about well-known ballets, dancers, films, and directors. It is important to know the plots of landmark films and ballets. As always, this is not a complete list. It's always important to do your own research.

Ballets	Dancers and Choreographers	Films	Directors
Cinderella	George Balanchine	*8 1/2*	Federico Fellini
Giselle	Mikhail Baryshnikov	*Battleship Potemkin*	Sergei Eisenstein
Manon	Erik Bruhn	*Citizen Kane*	Orson Welles
The Nutcracker	Isadora Duncan	*Metropolis*	Fritz Lang
Romeo and Juliet	Margot Fonteyn	*Modern Times*	Charlie Chaplin
Sleeping Beauty	Martha Graham	*Rashomon*	Akira Kurosawa
Swan Lake	Vaslav Nijinsky	*The Searchers*	John Ford
	Rudolf Nureyev	*Vertigo*	Alfred Hitchcock
	Anna Pavlova		Ingmar Bergman
	Jerome Robbins		Francis Ford Coppola
	Maria Tallchief		Stanley Kubrick
			Jean Renoir
			Billy Wilder

Dance and Film Resources

The most enjoyable way to do research for this section is through your local library or video store. Rent videotapes or DVDs of great ballets and films. Good books on these subjects include *101 Stories of the Great Ballets* by George Balanchine (New York: Anchor Books, 1989), *Technical Manual and Dictionary of Classical Ballet* by Gail Grant (Mineola, NY: Dover Publishing, 1982), *The Classic Ballet: Basic Technique and Terminology* by Lincoln Kirstein (New York: Knopf, 2004), or *Ballet and Modern Dance: A Concise History* by Jack Anderson (Hightstown, NY: Princeton Book Company, 1992). For film, try the book *Film History: An Introduction* by Kristin Thompson (New York: McGraw-Hill, 2002), visit the expansive websites from Sight and Sound and the British Film Institute at bfi.org.uk, or visit the inclusive group of film sites at dmoz.org/Reference/Archives/Arts/Film.

DRAMA

What You Need to Know

The drama section of the exam will ask you to identify the plots, authors, and themes of theater over the course of several centuries. This section comprises 10 percent of the exam, approximately 14 questions. Expect the exam to focus on important playwrights such as Shakespeare. The exam will cover common theatrical terms, such as "soliloquy," "epilogue," or "farce." Finding examples within plays of terms and constructs is a great way to learn this material.

Drama Terms to Learn

Act Major division of an opera or play; composed of scenes.

Allegory Symbolic representation of abstract ideas or principles through characters or events.

Antagonist A character against which another character struggles.

Aside Lines spoken by an actor directly to the audience, which are not "heard" by the other characters.

Catharsis The feelings of pity and fear that, according to Aristotle, occur in the audience of a tragedy.

Climax The turning point in a drama; culmination of a crisis or moment of culminating intensity in a drama.

Denouement The resolution of the plot.

Deus ex machina A god who resolves the entanglements of a play, or the use of artificial means to resolve the plot.

Epilogue Short speech by a character at the conclusion of a play, directed at the audience.

Farce Humorous play with light, dramatic effect and outrageous characters.

Protagonist The main character of a literary work.

Prologue Introduction to a play, a speech providing background information on the scene before the play starts.

Scene Part of an act in a play in which time is continuous and the setting is fixed.

Soliloquy A speech in a play heard by the audience, usually when only one actor is onstage.

Tableau vivant Scene in a play where costumed actors remain motionless and silent.

Tragedy Play that ends in extreme, meaningful sorrow, typically leading to the downfall of the main character due to a moral weakness or tragic flaw.

Drama Through the Centuries

Theater is a good area to study by forming a timeline and timeline study chart. The study chart is ascending, covering great modern playwrights all the way back to playwrights of the Elizabathan era. While the chart in this section is by no means all-inclusive, you may want to begin studying the chart by finding a famous play by each author. For example, Oscar Wilde's *The Importance of Being Earnest* is a classic farce, and remains, even today, a popular work. You might also want to connect such later works as *My Fair Lady* to the work it is based on, *Pygmalion*. Set up your flashcards! Put the name of a play on the front of each card and the name of the playwright on

the back. Do the same with the time period each playwright worked in. Cluster Shakespeare with Marlowe to remember that they are Elizabethan playwrights. Do the same with plots and titles.

Modern		**Early Modern**		**Restoration (Manners)**	
Albee	1928–	Lady Gregory	1852–1932	Dryden	1631–1700
Anouillh	1910–	O'Neill	1888–1953	Marivaux	1688–1763
Beckett	1906–	Pirandello	1867–1936	Sheridan	1751–1816
Brecht	1898–1956	Synge	1871–1909	Wilde	1854–1900
Cocteau	1889–1963				
Genet	1910–1986	**Naturalist**		**Post-Shakespeare**	
Ionesco	1912–	Chekhov	1860–1904	Corneille	1606–1684
Miller	1915–	Ibsen	1828–1906	Moliere	1622–1673
Sartre	1905–1980	Shaw	1856–1950	Racine	1639–1699
Stoppard	1937–	Strindberg	1849–1912		
Wilder	1897–1975			**Elizabethan-Jacobean**	
Williams	1911–1983	**Romantic**		Jonson	1572–1637
		Byron	1788–1824	Marlowe	1564–1593
		Goethe	1749–1832	Shakespeare	1564–1616
		Schiller	1759–1805	Webster	1580–1625

The following is a simple example of a drama timeline. Copy it or create your own version with more dates and authors, along with the movements to which they belonged (i.e. Shakespeare: Elizabethan).

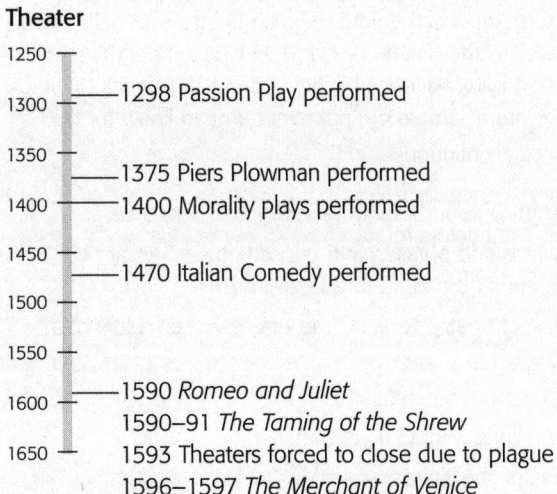

Theater

- 1298 Passion Play performed
- 1375 Piers Plowman performed
- 1400 Morality plays performed
- 1470 Italian Comedy performed
- 1590 *Romeo and Juliet*
- 1590–91 *The Taming of the Shrew*
- 1593 Theaters forced to close due to plague
- 1596–1597 *The Merchant of Venice*

Drama Resources

This is a good time to go to the theater. Important plays are performed fairly often in large cities, and seeing these plays performed live will help you remember important concepts and plotlines. If you cannot attend plays in person, rent DVDs or videos. Keep in mind that movie versions do not always follow the actual text of the play. Try to get a digital recording of the actual play filmed. Books abound on the history of theater as well. A few books to look for include: *Masterpieces of the Drama* (6th Edition) by Alexander W. Allison, et al (New York: Pearson, 1990), *Theories of the Theatre: A Historical and Critical Survey, from the Greeks to the Present* by Marvin Carlson (Ithaca, NY: Cornell University Press, 1994), *The Wadsworth Anthology of Drama* (Fourth Edition) by W. B. Worthen (Boston: Heinle, 2003), and *The Oxford Illustrated History of Theatre* by John Russell Brown (New York: Oxford University Press, 2001). If you'd like to check the Internet for information on particular works, try Open Source Shakespeare at opensourceshakespeare.org. You might also try the Theatre History Online Course at connectedcourseware.com/ccweb/start.htm.

POETRY

What You Need to Know

The poetry section of the CLEP Humanities exam will ask you to identify the name of a poet by his or her genre, identify the work of a particular poet, or correctly note a technique or scheme of a poem. You'll be asked questions about poems and poets from ancient Greece to the twentieth century. This section comprises 15–20 percent of the exam, or approximately 21–28 questions.

Poetry Terms to Learn

If you are unfamiliar with poetry as an art form, now is the time to brush up! It's especially important to know some poetic terminology as well as the difference between types of poems such as free verse and sonnets. You may want to start learning terms by jotting down definitions of words you want to remember. The following terms are a sample of important terms to know for the CLEP Humanities exam.

Alliteration is the repetition of the *s*ame *s*tarting *s*ound in *s*everal words of a *s*entence.

Antithesis is a figure of speech in which words and phrases with opposite meanings are balanced against each other. For example, "To err is human, to forgive, divine."

Caesura is a natural break or pause in a line of poetry. Look for caesura near the middle of a line.

Elegy is typically a poem that laments the death of a person.

Free verse uses either rhymed or unrhymed lines without a set meter.

Haiku Japanese poetic form with three lines of five, seven, and five syllables.

Hyperbole The literary use of exaggeration for effect or emphasis.

Iambic pentameter is a type of meter in poetry, in which there are five iambs to a line. An iamb is an unstressed syllable followed by a stressed syllable or a short syllable followed by a long syllable. For example, "I *know* that *I* will *pass* the *CLEP* ex*am*" is an iambic pentameter line. Say it

out loud to get a sense of the rhythm. Keep in mind that most of Shakespeare's plays were written in iambic pentameter—this is a very common type of meter in English poetry.

Metaphor A figure of speech in which a word or phrase that ordinarily represents one thing is used to denote another, creating a comparison without using *like* or *as*.

Onomatopoeia Use of words to represent the sounds of actions or objects they refer to.

Simile A figure of speech used to compare two unlike things joined by the word *like* or *as*.

Sonnet A verse of fourteen lines with a conventional rhyme scheme.

There are many more poetic terms to learn. It's a good idea to purchase or borrow a poetry textbook from the library and create flashcards. Another good study method is to read poems and write down examples of terms you find within their lines. Reading poetry aloud is helpful as well. It is much easier to hear the differences in meter, rather than simply to see them on a page. Check the Internet for glossaries of poetry terms, if you prefer online sources.

Covering Extensive Time Periods

If knowing every poet from every century seems an impossible task, break the task up into segments. One way to study the names of poets is to create a timeline. Your timeline should include the important poets (or poems) of each period along with the type of verse each poet or poem covers. Before you begin, gather the most important figures of each period according to the time period they lived in. A table of poets by century they lived in might look like this.

Century	Sixteenth Century	Seventeenth Century	Eighteenth Century	Nineteenth Century
Well-Known Poets	Edmund Spenser	John Dryden	Thomas Gray	Samuel Coleridge
	Sir Phillip Sidney	John Milton	Alexander Pope	William Wordsworth
	Christopher Marlowe	Andrew Marvell		John Keats
		John Donne		Lord Byron
				Heinrich Heine

Find a famous example of a poem by each poet (Spenser's classic epic poem *The Fairie Queene* is a good bet for study, as is Andrew Marvell's "To His Coy Mistress") and place it next to the century in which that poet wrote. You may also want to note the time periods for different movements. For example, Romanticism was a product of the late 1700s. Put the different movements on your timeline and memorize them along with poets for each time period.

You can use the following type of timeline to put your thoughts together:

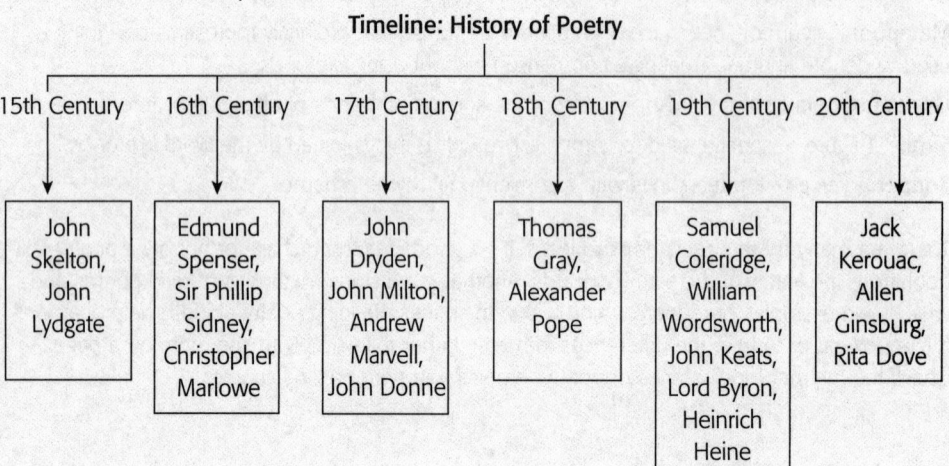

Poetry Resources

There is no shortage of books and websites offering information on poetry. The Norton Anthologies are particularly good for studying poetry. Acquire *The Norton Anthology of Poetry* (Fourth Edition), edited by Margaret Ferguson, Mary Jo Salter, and John Stallworthy (New York: Norton, 1996) and *The Norton Anthology of Modern and Contemporary Poetry* (Third Edition), edited by Jahan Ramazani et al (New York: Norton, 2003). Try reading some poems before bed every night. The Anthologies tie in quite well with a copy of a good college poetry textbook of terms. Consult poets.org for an extensive guide to movements in poetry, including the Beats and Surrealists. The site literatureclassics.com/ancientpaths/timeline.html contains a helpful timeline of literary events. "Voice of the Shuttle" at vos.ucsb.edu is an easy-access look-up for many academic websites.

FICTION, NONFICTION, AND PHILOSOPHY

What You Need to Know
This is a fairly large part of your exam, with 14–21 questions on fiction and 7–14 questions asking about nonfiction and philosophy. Once again, the content tested spans from the days of the ancient Greeks to recent or contemporary work. The fiction and nonfiction section of the CLEP Humanities exam will ask you to identify the names of writers, the particular work of a particular writer, or to correctly note a theme or plot. There will be some questions testing your general knowledge of philosophy, as well as some comparing plot and theme of several works. The philosophy section covers the Western philosophical tradition, with some attention given to principles and thinkers of Eastern traditions such as Hinduism, Buddhism, Taoism, Confucianism, and Islam.

Fiction, Nonfiction, and Philosophy Terms to Learn
Characterization The way writers reveal character, typically through speech, dress, manner, and actions.
Conflict A struggle between opposing forces in a novel or story.
Epistemology The branch of philosophy that investigates the grounds and limits of human knowledge.
Flashback The presentation of an incident that occurred prior to the main timeframe of the work.
Foreshadowing Hints of things to come in a story or a novel.
Metaphor A comparison between unlike things without the use of *like* or *as*.
Metaphysics The branch of philosophy that seeks to understand the nature of reality and existence.
Plot The structure of incidents or events.
Resolution The end of the plot.
Simile A comparison between unlike things using *like* or *as*.
Style Choice of words and actions, aided by description, imagery, and other techniques.
Theme The central idea put forth in a work.
Tone The attitude of a writer toward his/her subject or characters.

Covering Extensive Time Periods
Your fiction, nonfiction, and philosophy timeline should include the important writers (and their works) of each period with the school of literature that they belong to (if applicable). Before you begin, gather the most important writers of each period by dates. Try to remember one great work by each writer.

Authors to Know

Classics/Ancient
Euripides
Herodotus
Homer
Ovid
Sappho
Sophicles
Suetonius
Thucydides
Virgil
*Aristotle
*Confucius
*Lao Tzu
*Plato
*Socrates
*Sun Tzu

Middle Ages
Margery Kempe
Sir Thomas Malory
Julian of Norwich
Geoffrey Chaucer
*Saint Augustine
*Ibn Khaldun
*Ibn Rushd
*Ibn Sina

**Renaissance
(early)**
Dante Alighieri
Francesco Petrarch
*Niccolo Machiavelli
(late)
Giovanni Boccaccio
Miguel de Cervantes
Rene Descartes
Michel de Montaigne
*Francis Bacon
*Thomas Hobbes
*Baruch Spinoza

**Age of
Reason/Restoration
(Eighteenth Century)**
Daniel Defoe
Samuel Richardson
Laurence Sterne
Jonathan Swift
*David Hume
*Immanuel Kant
*Gottfried Wilhelm Leibniz
*John Locke
*Adam Smith

**Romantic
(Eighteenth/Nineteenth
Century)**
Jane Austen
Johann Goethe
Victor Hugo
Sir Walter Scott
Mary Shelley
*G.W.F. Hegel

* indicates philosopher

**Victorian (Nineteenth
Century)**
Charles Dickens
George Eliot
Gustave Flaubert
Henry James
Herman Melville
Leo Tolstoy
Emile Zola
*Soren Kirkegaard
*Karl Marx
*John Stuart Mill
*Friedrich Nietzsche

**Modern (Twentieth
Century)**
F. Scott Fitzgerald
Ernest Hemingway
Zora Neale Hurston
James Joyce
Franz Kafka
Marcel Proust
Virginia Woolf
*Bertrand Russell
*Ludwig Wittgenstein

**Late Modern (Twentieth
Century)**
Ralph Ellison
Andre Gide
Gabriel Garcia Marquez
Flannery O'Connor

**Postmodern (Twentieth
Century)**
Raymond Carver
Phillip Roth
Salman Rushdie
*Jacques Derrida

Fiction, Nonfiction, and Philosophy Resources

As with poetry, there is no shortage of books and websites offering information on fiction, nonfiction, and philosophy. Since it will not be possible to read dozens of novels prior to taking the CLEP Humanities exam, try to write down plot points for yourself. Reading shorter fiction is helpful. The Norton Anthologies are particularly useful. Acquire *The Norton Anthology of English Literature* (Seventh Edition) edited by M.H. Abrams (New York: Norton, 1999) or *The Norton Anthology of American Literature* (Sixth Edition) edited by Judith Tanka and Nina Baym (New York: Norton, 2003) and *The Norton Anthology of World Masterpieces* (Sixth Edition) edited by Maynard Mack (New York: Norton, 1992) and try to read a bit before bed every night. Any Oxford edition is a very good source of information as well.

A good website to consult is literatureclassics.com/ancientpaths/timeline.html, which contains a terrific timeline of literary events. Voice of the Shuttle at vos.ucsb.edu as mentioned in the poetry section, is a great portal to many academic and literary websites. Funtrivia.com has an enjoyable online literary quiz. Check Philosophy by Topic at users.ox.ac.uk/~worc0337/phil_topics.html for a quick review of philosophical terms and works. Philosophypages.com offers an overview of the history of philosophy and a dictionary of philosophical terms and names.

FINAL THOUGHTS

Now that you're armed with enough information to begin studying, it's time to learn the best way to conquer the CLEP Humanities exam. A formula for success includes the following points:

Study Nightly, Don't Cram

Cramming won't help you pass the exam! There is too much to memorize in such a short amount of time, and cramming won't provide you with all the necessary facts you need to learn for the exam. It's best to spend an hour a day studying, without trying to cover everything at once. Break study time down into categories and schedule your time section by section.

Create a Master Timeline

Since a fair number of questions are cross-referential, it would be helpful to take your individual timelines and put them together into a master timeline reference sheet. A master sheet will clearly show various types of art in different eras. For example, Romantic art, poetry, and literature had to do with the emotions. Pinpoint each period or movement on your master list.

Remember One Painting, Book, or Fact

While there is no certainty it will be asked on the exam, it's helpful to know that Cervantes' most famous work is *Don Quixote*. Add to your list of names in each category the most important work by each writer, artist, or playwright.

Relax!

If you take the time to study hard, you can trust that you know the material. On test day, try to relax. Take deep breaths and focus your thoughts on the task at hand. Gentle stretching such as yoga and meditation can relax your mind before the test. Remember, you are prepared!

Good luck!

Chapter Fourteen: Practice Test 2

Time—90 minutes
140 Questions

Directions: For each of the following questions or incomplete statements, select the best answer or completion from the five options given.

1. Which type of ending are the works of O. Henry renowned for featuring?

   (A) tragic
   (B) happy
   (C) twist
   (D) unfinished
   (E) funny

2. Which pair of authors wrote "The Metamorphosis" and *Metamorphoses* respectively?

   (A) Franz Kafka and Ovid
   (B) Edith Wharton and Virgil
   (C) Alice Walker and Geoffrey Chaucer
   (D) William Gaddis and Robert Burns
   (E) Chinua Achebe and Jhumpa Lahiri

3. The Baroque period in music spanned the years 1600–1750. Which composers are associated with this period?

   (A) Frederic Chopin and Richard Strauss
   (B) Ludwig van Beethoven and John Cage
   (C) Wolfgang Amadeus Mozart and Richard Strauss
   (D) George Frideric Handel and Johann Sebastian Bach
   (E) Gustav Mahler and Glenn Miller

4. Rene Descartes' "Cogito ergo sum" translates into

   (A) "do unto others."
   (B) "the set of all subsets."
   (C) "being *qua* being."
   (D) "I think therefore I am."
   (E) "all is vanity."

5. The Russian novel *Anna Karenina* is the story of an adulterous love affair that ends in death. Which famous novel below features a similar story?

   (A) *The House of Mirth*
   (B) *Pride and Prejudice*
   (C) *Death Comes to the Archbishop*
   (D) *Madame Bovary*
   (E) *The Sound and the Fury*

6. *The Bicycle Thief* is a classic example of which movement in cinema history?

   (A) German Expressionism
   (B) French New Wave
   (C) Independent Filmmaking
   (D) Italian Neorealism
   (E) Anticommunist Film

GO ON TO THE NEXT PAGE

7. Which fifth-century B.C.E. Athenian philosopher set the standard for Western philosophy?

    (A) Aristotle
    (B) Henry David Thoreau
    (C) Bertrand Russell
    (D) Plato
    (E) Socrates

8. Zora Neale Hurston, Rita Dove, and Toni Morrison are all acclaimed writers. What else do they have in common?

    (A) Their first novels were creative failures.
    (B) They completed only one book.
    (C) They are all African-American writers.
    (D) They were all educated at Howard University.
    (E) They have all won the Nobel Prize.

9. Thomas Aquinas based his philosophy on the work of which of the following?

    (A) Marcus Aurelius
    (B) Aristotle
    (C) David Hume
    (D) Voltaire
    (E) Erasmus

10. Artist Salvador Dali and this young Spanish filmmaker collaborated on the classic *Un chien andalou*.

    (A) Federico Garcia Lorca
    (B) Diego Rivera
    (C) Luis Buñuel
    (D) Gabriel Garcia Marquez
    (E) Carlos Fuentes

11. Dali's film *Un chien andalou* is a work of

    (A) Super-realism.
    (B) Photorealism.
    (C) Impressionism.
    (D) Surrealism.
    (E) Classical cinema.

12. Which of the following was a contemporary of Franz Schubert?

    (A) Arthur Rubinstein
    (B) Arnold Schoenberg
    (C) Niccolo Paganini
    (D) Igor Stravinsky
    (E) Giuseppi Verdi

13. Which of the following philosophers claimed that all philosophical problems are problems of language and is responsible for the statement, "What we cannot speak of, we must pass over in silence"?

    (A) Adam Smith
    (B) Euclid
    (C) Henri Rousseau
    (D) Ludwig Wittgenstein
    (E) John Dewey

14. Boccaccio's *The Decameron* is what sort of work?

    (A) collection of stories
    (B) epic poem
    (C) essays on government
    (D) opera
    (E) symphony in three movements

15. The film *Battleship Potemkin*, which contains the Odessa massacre sequence—considered to be the greatest and most influential montage sequence in the history of cinema—is the work of this master Soviet filmmaker.

    (A) Dziga Vertov
    (B) Sergei Eisenstein
    (C) Lev Kuleshov
    (D) Vsevolod Pudovkin
    (E) Alexander Dovzhenko

16. In a symphony, the word "modulation" refers to

    (A) descending tones.
    (B) a change of key.
    (C) diapason.
    (D) "built on a second scale step."
    (E) ascending tones.

17. This comic genius of the silent era is known for risking life and limb in his stunts. He wrote, directed, and starred in films that include *The General*.

    (A) Billy Wilder
    (B) Charlie Chaplin
    (C) Howard Hawks
    (D) Buster Keaton
    (E) Frank Capra

18. Renowned choreographer George Balanchine founded this landmark dance company.

    (A) American Ballet Theater
    (B) Ballet Russe
    (C) Ballet Society
    (D) Miami City Ballet
    (E) Ballet New York

"And so we beat on, like boats against the current, bourn back ceaselessly into the past."

19. Which famous novel ends with the lines quoted above?

    (A) *For Whom the Bell Tolls*
    (B) *The Scarlet Letter*
    (C) *Frankenstein*
    (D) *Huckleberry Finn*
    (E) *The Great Gatsby*

20. The phrase "like boats against the current" is an example of which literary device?

    (A) simile
    (B) characterization
    (C) narrative
    (D) structure
    (E) dialogue

21. When the protagonist's voice tells the story of the novel, this is known as

    (A) first-person narration.
    (B) third-person narration.
    (C) second-person narration.
    (D) narrative drive.
    (E) unreliable narrator.

Courtesy of SuperStock, Inc.

22. Who is the painter of this work?

    (A) Jacob Lawrence
    (B) Man Ray
    (C) Kenneth Noland
    (D) Vincent van Gogh
    (E) Mary Cassatt

23. Sinclair Lewis' *Babbit*, Evelyn Waugh's *The Loved One* and Tom Wolfe's *The Bonfire of the Vanities* are all novels that

    (A) proclaim the rights of women.
    (B) call for the end of government.
    (C) politicize world events.
    (D) plead for a return to small-town values.
    (E) satirize American culture.

24. In Hawthorne's *The Scarlet Letter*, the "A" for adultery sewn to the dress of the protagonist is an example of which literary term?

    (A) conceit
    (B) theme
    (C) point of view
    (D) symbolism
    (E) denouement

25. Which of the following is NOT a novel written by Somerset Maugham?

    (A) *Cakes and Ale*
    (B) *The Moon and Sixpence*
    (C) *Tom Jones*
    (D) *The Razor's Edge*
    (E) *Of Human Bondage*

26. N. Scott Momaday, Sherman Alexie, and Louise Erdrich have all written books based on an inside understanding of which culture?

    (A) Eastern European
    (B) Native American
    (C) African American
    (D) Cuban American
    (E) Central Asian

27. *Gigi* tells the story of a young girl groomed to become a courtesan in turn-of-the-century Paris who rebels and marries instead. The film is based on the work of which iconoclastic French writer?

    (A) Colette
    (B) Honore de Balzac
    (C) Jean Cocteau
    (D) Marguerite Duras
    (E) Simone de Beauvoir

28. Aldous Huxley's *Brave New World* and George Orwell's *1984* both envision what sort of future society?

    (A) utopian
    (B) pneumatic
    (C) democratic
    (D) totalitarian
    (E) socialist

29. John Steinbeck's *The Grapes of Wrath* tracks the path of migrant Oklahoma farm workers during

    (A) the Great Depression.
    (B) World War I.
    (C) World War II.
    (D) the turn of the century.
    (E) the Civil War.

30. The unfolding of events within a novel or play is known as

    (A) characterization.
    (B) symbolism.
    (C) plot.
    (D) denouement.
    (E) climax.

31. Which of the following writers is correctly matched with his school of literature?

    (A) Robert Frost . . . play
    (B) Christopher Marlowe . . . essay
    (C) Yukio Mishima . . . poetry
    (D) E.M. Forster . . . novel
    (E) Niccolo Machiavelli . . . prose poem

32. Which of the instruments below is the smallest string instrument found in an orchestra?

    (A) bass
    (B) violin
    (C) cello
    (D) viola
    (E) double bass

33. *Pamela* by Samuel Richardson and *Lady Susan* by Jane Austen are both examples of which early style of novel?

    (A) narrative
    (B) formulaic
    (C) epistolary
    (D) serial
    (E) religious

34. The novel *Grendel* by John Gardner, is based upon this sixth-century Anglo-Saxon poem, but written from the point of view of the monster.

    (A) *Gulliver's Travels*
    (B) *The Inferno*
    (C) *Beowulf*
    (D) *The Seafarer*
    (E) *The Battle of Maldon*

35. In the novel, *Gulliver's Travels*, the Yahoos that Gulliver encounters are meant to be symbolic of

    (A) his English peers.
    (B) early American settlers.
    (C) the Puritans.
    (D) the Shakers.
    (E) mentally ill patients.

GO ON TO THE NEXT PAGE

36. "Bard" is a Middle English word for which type of writer?

   (A) novelist
   (B) poet
   (C) essayist
   (D) short-story writer
   (E) journalist

37. In Isabel Allende's *House of the Spirits* and Toni Morrison's *Beloved*, fantastic and inexplicable events take place amid ordinary lives. This style of novel is often referred to as

   (A) epistolary.
   (B) creative nonfiction.
   (C) magical realism.
   (D) reactionary.
   (E) epic.

38. The opera *Eugene Onegin* is based on a work by which of the following authors?

   (A) William Makepeace Thackeray
   (B) Daniel Defoe
   (C) Anna Akhmatova
   (D) Colette
   (E) Aleksandr Pushkin

39. Li Po and So Shu are famous

   (A) Chinese poets.
   (B) Taiwanese composers.
   (C) Japanese philosophers.
   (D) Indian mystics.
   (E) Korean architects.

40. Which of the instruments below is NOT a woodwind?

   (A) oboe
   (B) flute
   (C) bassoon
   (D) saxophone
   (E) harp

41. The recent Pulitzer Prize-winning novel *The Hours* is based upon *Mrs. Dalloway*, the classic novel by which turn-of-the-century writer?

   (A) Jane Austen
   (B) Charlotte Bronte
   (C) Emily Bronte
   (D) Virginia Woolf
   (E) Harriet Beecher Stowe

42. Langston Hughes, Richard Wright, Jean Toomer, and Zora Neale Hurston were collectively known as part of the

   (A) Brotherhood of the Book.
   (B) Harlem Renaissance.
   (C) Narrative Collective.
   (D) New York Experience.
   (E) Brooklyn Book Circle.

43. Which group of writers is considered to be part of the Romantic movement in British literature?

   (A) Edmund Spenser, John Milton, William Shakespeare
   (B) Mary Shelley, Robert Burns, Jane Austen
   (C) Dante, Thomas More, Mary Herbert
   (D) Thomas Wyatt, John Davies, Philip Sidney
   (E) Charles Dickens, Henry James, Edith Wharton

GO ON TO THE NEXT PAGE

44. Which of the dramatists below was a contemporary of William Shakespeare?

    (A) Christopher Marlowe
    (B) John Dryden
    (C) William Wycherley
    (D) Thornton Wilder
    (E) Harold Pinter

45. *The Four Seasons* is a piece in four movements: "Spring," "Summer," "Autumn," and "Winter." Which of the following composers produced this famous work?

    (A) Richard Strauss
    (B) Johann Sebastian Bach
    (C) Antonio Vivaldi
    (D) Ancangelo Corelli
    (E) Alfredo Casella

46. If a play is called a farce, it might also be called a

    (A) tragedy.
    (B) comedy.
    (C) masterpiece.
    (D) drama.
    (E) romance.

47. In this play and subsequent film, the restless son and isolated daughter of a fading Southern belle invite an old schoolmate to visit, with the forlorn hope that he will be interested in marrying the shy daughter. When this does not happen, the son abandons his mother and sister to their lonely life and inability to accept reality. What is the play's title?

    (A) *Our Town*
    (B) *Sweet Bird of Youth*
    (C) *A Streetcar Named Desire*
    (D) *After the Fall*
    (E) *The Glass Menagerie*

48. When a literary work does not follow or dispenses with traditional patterns of plot, characters, or dialogue, it might be called

    (A) a narrative.
    (B) romantic.
    (C) a genre.
    (D) experimental.
    (E) technical.

49. In musical terminology, what does counterpoint refer to?

    (A) a male singer
    (B) a sequence of single tones
    (C) a composition with two or more simultaneous melodies
    (D) a composition with two or more simultaneous tones
    (E) ascending notes

50. "Lord, what fools these mortals be!" is uttered by Puck in this comedy by Shakespeare.

    (A) *As You Like It*
    (B) *A Midsummer Night's Dream*
    (C) *All's Well that Ends Well*
    (D) *The Tempest*
    (E) *The Comedy of Errors*

51. This country was the birthplace of modern dance.

    (A) Russia
    (B) the United States
    (C) England
    (D) France
    (E) Sweden

GO ON TO THE NEXT PAGE

52. John Webster and Ben Johnson are two playwrights who wrote during the

    (A) Restoration.
    (B) modern era.
    (C) Elizabethan era.
    (D) classical era.
    (E) post-World War II era.

53. The plays of Samuel Beckett, Jean-Paul Sartre, and Harold Pinter are all considered to be

    (A) existential.
    (B) optimistic.
    (C) anticlimactic.
    (D) episodic.
    (E) melodramatic.

54. When a character in a play speaks directly to the audience, this is known as

    (A) "characterization."
    (B) "foreshadowing."
    (C) "peripety."
    (D) "breaking the fourth wall."
    (E) "point of attack."

55. In theater, the Greek term *deus ex machina* refers to

    (A) an implausible ending where everything is resolved.
    (B) a play that ends in death for all the characters.
    (C) a scene leading to another scene.
    (D) a particularly happy ending.
    (E) a character arriving at the last minute.

56. According to Aristotle's *Poetics*, what element is intertwined with plot?

    (A) structure
    (B) character
    (C) setting
    (D) narration
    (E) dialogue

57. *Little Dorrit*, *The Pickwick Papers*, and *Bleak House* were all written by this prolific nineteenth-century English novelist.

    (A) Washington Irving
    (B) Charles Dickens
    (C) Victor Hugo
    (D) Leo Tolstoy
    (E) Edith Wharton

58. This film tells the story of a rich but lonely newspaper magnate, who alienates everyone around him, including his two wives. He dies alone, remembering his forgotten childhood, and uttering the name of his lost sled.

    (A) *The Heart Is a Lonely Hunter*
    (B) *A Clockwork Orange*
    (C) *The Lion in Winter*
    (D) *Citizen Kane*
    (E) *The Last Angry Man*

59. Thornton Wilder won a Pulitzer Prize for the play, *Our Town*. He also had won a Pulitzer Prize ten years earlier for this novel.

    (A) *Breakfast at Tiffany's*
    (B) *The Executioner's Song*
    (C) *Red Sky at Morning*
    (D) *The Bridge of San Luis Rey*
    (E) *Goodbye, Columbus*

GO ON TO THE NEXT PAGE

60. The great composer Ludwig van Beethoven and the poet Lord Byron both died in which century?

    (A) fifteenth
    (B) sixteenth
    (C) seventeenth
    (D) eighteenth
    (E) nineteenth

61. The late composer George Gershwin is renowned for inspiring the symphony form of what type of music?

    (A) ballet
    (B) piano
    (C) violin
    (D) jazz
    (E) chamber

62. The plays *Medea*, *Oedipus Rex*, and *Mourning Becomes Electra* are all considered to be

    (A) romances.
    (B) comedies.
    (C) experimental.
    (D) farces.
    (E) tragedies.

63. The classic operas *The Magic Flute* and *The Marriage of Figaro* were both composed by

    (A) Modest Mussorgsky.
    (B) Giuseppi Verdi.
    (C) Wolfgang Amadeus Mozart.
    (D) Camille Saint-Saens.
    (E) Peter Ilych Tchaikovsky.

64. What time frame spanned the Classical period in music?

    (A) 1600–1750
    (B) 1750–1825
    (C) 1800–1900
    (D) 1850–1920
    (E) 1725–1850

65. *The Nutcracker* ballet is an annual Christmas event that was originally choreographed in 1882. Which of the following composers wrote the score?

    (A) Igor Stravinsky
    (B) Darius Milhaud
    (C) Peter Ilych Tchaikovsky
    (D) Aaron Copland
    (E) Johann Sebastian Bach

66. In which of the following works is the philosopher Gottfried Leibniz satirized as Dr. Pangloss?

    (A) *Light in August* by William Faulkner
    (B) *The Sufferings of Young Werther* by Johann von Goethe
    (C) *Thousand Cranes* by Yasunari Kawabata
    (D) *Interpreter of Maladies* by Jhumpa Lahiri
    (E) *Candide* by Voltaire

67. The music of the Middle Ages was almost always inspired by

    (A) weddings.
    (B) religion.
    (C) childbirth.
    (D) funerals.
    (E) good harvests.

68. A villanelle is a kind of
    (A) oil painting.
    (B) architectural nuance.
    (C) poem.
    (D) play.
    (E) orchestral movement.

69. Debussy, Ravel, and Monet were members of this school of art and music, which flourished in the late 1800s.
    (A) Romantic
    (B) Renaissance
    (C) Impressionist
    (D) Experimental
    (E) Neoclassical

70. The Romantic Age in music, art, and literature is associated with which attribute?
    (A) logic
    (B) delicacy
    (C) imagination
    (D) emotion
    (E) spectacular design

71. Of the following instruments, which one is least likely to be found in a classical orchestra?
    (A) flute
    (B) dulcimer
    (C) piccolo
    (D) viola
    (E) cymbals

Questions 72–74 are based on the following people.
    (A) Philip Glass, Johann Strauss, Stephen Sondheim
    (B) Jackson Pollack, Marc Chagall, Henri Matisse
    (C) Jane Austen, Marcel Proust, Tillie Olson
    (D) Martha Graham, George Balanchine, Jerome Robbins
    (E) T.S. Eliot, George Sand, Paul Auster

72. Which are composers?

73. Which are visual artists?

74. Which are choreographers?

75. Benjamin Britten, Felix Mendelsohn, Richard Wagner, and Karl Maria von Weber were all renowned as what type of artists?
    (A) opera singers
    (B) poets
    (C) composers
    (D) novelists
    (E) choreographers

76. The figures in Paul Gauguin's most famous paintings are for the most part
    (A) Tahitian.
    (B) Hawaiian.
    (C) Inuit.
    (D) Jamaican.
    (E) Alsatian.

GO ON TO THE NEXT PAGE

Questions 77–78 are based on the following choices.

(A) *La Sylphide, Giselle, Sleeping Beauty*
(B) *Don Giovanni, Tristan and Isolde, Carmen*
(C) *Don Quixote, Madame Bovary, Anna Karenina*
(D) *Sleeping Beauty, Snow White, Little Red Riding Hood*
(E) *La Traviata, The Marriage of Figaro, Faust*

77. Which is a group of ballets?

78. Which is a group of novels?

79. Describing a piece of music or a ballet as being "adagio" means that the work is

(A) jumpy.
(B) slow.
(C) a pas de deux.
(D) climatic.
(E) fast.

80. Jazz singers like Ella Fitzgerald gave life to a unique style of singing that ran up and down the scales instead of hitting certain notes. This type of singing is known as

(A) aria.
(B) recitative.
(C) Beat.
(D) scat.
(E) contained.

81. Futurism was an art movement that emphasized

(A) motion.
(B) line.
(C) primary colors.
(D) cool colors.
(E) juxtaposition of disparate objects.

82. In this film, an ordinary man realizes how much his life has affected others when an angel visits him on Christmas Eve.

(A) *It Happened One Night*
(B) *A Streetcar Named Desire*
(C) *Citizen Kane*
(D) *Gone with the Wind*
(E) *It's a Wonderful Life*

83. What does the poetic term "hyberbole" mean?

(A) the use of exaggeration for effect or emphasis
(B) the use of similar words that have different meanings
(C) the use of "like" or "as" to compare two different things
(D) the use of words to denote the sound objects or actions make
(E) the repetition of predominantly consonant sounds at the beginning of words or syllables

84. Which language is also known as the language of ballet?

(A) Russian
(B) English
(C) French
(D) Romanian
(E) Spanish

85. Which of the following plays has a tragic character lost in the illusion that "personality will win the day?"

(A) Tennessee Williams' *A Streetcar Named Desire*
(B) Arthur Miller's *After the Fall*
(C) William Saroyan's *The Time of Your Life*
(D) Arthur Miller's *Death of a Salesman*
(E) Tennessee Williams' *The Glass Menagerie*

86. Which of the following did T.S. Eliot NOT write?

    (A) "The Waste Land"
    (B) "Murder in the Cathedral"
    (C) "The Love Song of J. Alfred Prufrock"
    (D) "The Hollow Men"
    (E) "Goblin Market"

87. Which of the following was an ancient Greek poet?

    (A) Horace
    (B) Pericles
    (C) Sappho
    (D) Dante
    (E) Marcus Aurelius

88. William Shakespeare used the work of which of the following as sources for his plays?

    (A) Geoffrey Chaucer, Geoffrey of Monmouth, Plutarch
    (B) David Hume, Baruch Spinoza, Soren Kierkegaard
    (C) Edward Gibbon, Thomas Babington Macauley, Benjamin Disraeli
    (D) John Donne, Aphra Behn, John Dryden
    (E) Arthur Miller, Thornton Wilder, Lillian Hellman

89. Which of the following is NOT a device used in poetry?

    (A) synecdoche
    (B) metonymy
    (C) foreshortening
    (D) alliteration
    (E) assonance

90. Which of the following is an example of alliteration?

    (A) "this morning morning's minion"
    (B) "in the room the women come and go"
    (C) "Tell me, Ramon Fernandez, if you know"
    (D) "all seems yellow to the jaundiced eye"
    (E) "All my pretty ones? Did you say all?"

91. Kobo Abe, Yukio Mishima, and Yasunari Kawabata are all

    (A) Chinese artists.
    (B) Japanese novelists.
    (C) Korean poets.
    (D) sculptors.
    (E) installation artists.

Questions 92–94 refer to the following people.

    (A) William Wordsworth, Lord Byron, John Keats
    (B) Rabindranath Tagore, Rumi, Kahlil Gibran
    (C) Horace, Ovid, Virgil
    (D) James Welch, Leslie Marmon Silko, Joy Harjo
    (E) Marianne Moore, H.D., Edna St. Vincent Millay

92. Which group belongs in the Romantic period?

93. Which group is composed of Native Americans?

94. Which group would be considered Modernist poets?

95. Henry Moore was a sculptor from

    (A) England.
    (B) the United States.
    (C) Australia.
    (D) Iceland.
    (E) Canada.

Questions 96–98 refer to the following terms.

(A) installation art
(B) dance
(C) music
(D) poetry
(E) painting

96. Which of these activities would Niccolo Paganini be associated with?

97. Which of these activities would involve a choreographer?

98. Which of these activities first came into prominence in the second half of the twentieth century?

99. Which of the following types of art was brought into prominence in the Byzantine period?
(A) watercolor
(B) portrait painting
(C) landscape painting
(D) mosaic
(E) statuary

100. Spondee, anapest, and iamb all refer to what aspect of a poem?
(A) rhyme scheme
(B) theme
(C) trope
(D) meter
(E) stanza

Questions 101–103 refer to the following poem.

LXXXII.

I grant thou wert not married to my Muse
And therefore mayst without attaint o'erlook
The dedicated words which writers use
Of their fair subject, blessing every book
Thou art as fair in knowledge as in hue,
Finding thy worth a limit past my praise,
And therefore art enforced to seek anew
Some fresher stamp of the time-bettering days
And do so, love; yet when they have devised
What strained touches rhetoric can lend,
Thou truly fair wert truly sympathized
In true plain words by thy true-telling friend;
And their gross painting might be better used
Where cheeks need blood; in thee it is abused.

101. The text above was written by
(A) George Herbert
(B) William Shakespeare
(C) Wallace Stevens
(D) Coventry Patmore
(E) Gustave Apollinaire

102. What poetic form does the text above use?
(A) free verse
(B) prose
(C) sonnet
(D) metaphor
(E) simile

103. What is iambic pentameter?

    (A) a series of rhymed lines
    (B) a type of poem in which stressed and unstressed syllables alternate five times per line
    (C) an ironic work in which the author puts a lot of feeling into the text
    (D) a political rebuttal written in Britain during the Enlightenment
    (E) a rhyme scheme in which consonant sounds are repeated throughout each line

104. Gertrude Stein, William Carlos Williams, and Maria Rainer Rilke are all close contemporaries of which of the following?

    (A) I.M. Pei, Isamu Noguchi, Phillip Glass
    (B) Christopher Wren, Rembrandt, Johann Sebastian Bach
    (C) John Ruskin, Richard Wagner, Theodore Gericault
    (D) Frank Lloyd Wright, Paul Gaugain, Claude Debussy
    (E) Filippo Brunelleschi, Titian, Claudio Monteverdi

105. Which of the following figures of the twentieth century is INCORRECTLY matched to his/her art form?

    (A) Le Corbusier ... architect
    (B) Pablo Neruda ... conceptual artist
    (C) Moses Isegawa ... novelist
    (D) Jean Arp ... sculptor
    (E) Nelly Sachs ... poet

106. "Adonais" was an elegy for John Keats written by

    (A) William Wordsworth.
    (B) Percy Bysshe Shelley.
    (C) John Donne.
    (D) Dante Alighieri.
    (E) Heinrich Heine.

107. Which of the following musicians is a cellist?

    (A) Yo-Yo Ma
    (B) Jennifer Koh
    (C) Arthur Rubinstein
    (D) Vladmir Feltzman
    (E) Mischa Elman

108. Leopold and Molly Bloom are characters from a novel by which of the following authors?

    (A) Laurence Sterne
    (B) Moses Isegawa
    (C) Chinua Achebe
    (D) Kate Chopin
    (E) James Joyce

109. *Jane Eyre* is a novel written by whom?

    (A) Charlotte Bronte
    (B) Jane Austen
    (C) Aphra Behn
    (D) Anne Bronte
    (E) Emily Bronte

110. Which instruments form a string quartet?

    (A) two flutes, one piccolo, one trumpet
    (B) one clarinet, two French horns, one bass
    (C) one viola, two violins, one cello
    (D) two cellos, one saxophone, one double bass
    (E) one drum, one bass, one piano

GO ON TO THE NEXT PAGE

111. Thomas Hobbes' *Leviathan* argues for which kind of political system?

    (A) democracy
    (B) socialism
    (C) autocracy
    (D) communism
    (E) plutocracy

112. In the recent film as well as the novel by William Makepeace Thackeray, the protagonist, Becky Sharp

    (A) is born into a wealthy family.
    (B) is an Olympic swimmer.
    (C) schemes and connives her way into high society.
    (D) is a naive young woman in a wicked world.
    (E) doesn't care for material things.

113. What is the title of this novel by Thackeray?

    (A) *Vanity Fair*
    (B) *Look Back in Anger*
    (C) *Death Be Not Proud*
    (D) *The House of Mirth*
    (E) *The Age of Grief*

114. *The Human Comedy* was produced by

    (A) Georges Bizet.
    (B) Hector Berlioz.
    (C) Honore de Balzac.
    (D) Gustave Flaubert.
    (E) Arthur Rimbaud.

115. Photorealism is a movement in

    (A) photography.
    (B) installation art.
    (C) land art.
    (D) painting.
    (E) poetry.

116. In painting, chiaroscuro involves

    (A) light and shadow.
    (B) color.
    (C) theme.
    (D) the vanishing point.
    (E) figures.

117. You would most likely find a bas-relief

    (A) on a canvas.
    (B) in a video installation.
    (C) on the face of a building.
    (D) in an etching.
    (E) in a Post-Impressionist painting.

Courtesy of SuperStock, Inc.

118. Pointillism, developed by Georges Seurat, painter of *Bathers at Asniers* above, is a method involving

    (A) straight lines.
    (B) points of color.
    (C) pointed political commentary.
    (D) photorealism.
    (E) multiple vanishing points.

GO ON TO THE NEXT PAGE

Used by permission. See copyright page (iv) for information.

119. Who is the painter of this work?

    (A) Jacob Lawrence
    (B) Man Ray
    (C) Kenneth Noland
    (D) Andrew Wyeth
    (E) Mary Cassatt

120. Filippo Brunelleschi is most famous for his work on which of the following structures?

    (A) column
    (B) amphitheatre
    (C) statuary
    (D) dome
    (E) arch

121. Which of the following were both artists and poets?

    (A) Dante Gabriel Rossetti, William Blake, Michelangelo
    (B) Edith Wharton, Rene Descartes, Renzo Piano
    (C) Federico Garcia Lorca, Francisco de Zurburan, Gabriela Mistral
    (D) Gail Tsukiyama, Vikram Seth, Margaret Atwood
    (E) Robert Browning, Alfred Lord Tennyson, Charlotte Bronte

122. A novel concerning the moral and psychological development of the protagonist is called a

    (A) roman a clef.
    (B) bildungsroman.
    (C) young-adult literature.
    (D) fairy tale.
    (E) saga.

Questions 123–125 refer to the following artists.

    (A) Auguste Rodin, Michelangelo, Giovanni Bernini
    (B) Frank Gehry, I.M. Pei, Christopher Wren
    (C) Judy Chicago, Jenny Holzer, Barbara Kruger
    (D) Piet Mondrian, Vincent van Gogh, Jan Vermeer
    (E) Andy Warhol, Roy Lichtenstein, Richard Hamilton

123. Which is a group of Dutch-born painters?

124. Which is a group of Pop Artists?

125. Which is a group of sculptors?

126. Which of the following novels was NOT written by Ayn Rand?

    (A) *The Fountainhead*
    (B) *Atlas Shrugged*
    (C) *Anthem*
    (D) *We the Living*
    (E) *This Side of Paradise*

Question 127 refers to the following people.

(A) Charlotte Perkins Gilman
(B) Matthew Mauri
(C) Charles Dickens
(D) Charlotte Bronte
(E) Toni Morrison

127. Which is a twenty-first century author?

Questions 128–130 refer to the following people.

(A) Jacques Lipchitz
(B) George Eliot
(C) Federico Garcia Lorca
(D) I.M. Pei
(E) Fomich Nijinsky

128. Which is a sculptor?

129. Which is a woman?

130. Which is a poet?

131. The first three books of John Galsworthy's *The Forsythe Saga* revolve around the failed relationship of

(A) Tristan and Isolde.
(B) Novalis and Sophie.
(C) Hero and Leander.
(D) Soames and Irene.
(E) Clarissa and Peter.

132. "Naturalist" or "Realist" novels are works in which human beings

(A) triumph over nature.
(B) succumb to natural forces.
(C) come to understand the beauty of nature.
(D) retreat to idyllic, natural landscapes.
(E) tamper with nature through medical science.

133. Dadaism was a movement in which

(A) artists returned to classical techniques.
(B) artists subverted classical notions of art.
(C) drawing revolved around new sketching techniques.
(D) the human figure returned to oil painting.
(E) sculptors worked exclusively with marble.

Questions 134–136 refer to the following structure.

Photograph by Dean Fox. Courtesy of SuperStock, Inc.

134. The architect of this structure is

(A) Frank Lloyd Wright.
(B) Buckminster Fuller.
(C) Mies van der Rohe.
(D) Alexandre-Gustave Eiffel.
(E) Renzo Piano.

135. This piece is located in

   (A) Normandy.
   (B) Geneva.
   (C) Chicago.
   (D) Buenos Aires.
   (E) Paris.

136. It is primarily considered

   (A) a place of business.
   (B) a lighthouse.
   (C) a temporary edifice.
   (D) a storage facility.
   (E) a work of art.

137. The sonnets of Shakespeare and most of his plays are written in

   (A) iambic pentameter.
   (B) trochaic hexameter.
   (C) blank verse.
   (D) free verse.
   (E) spondaic tetrameter.

138. Assonance is the repetition of

   (A) vowel sounds.
   (B) interior consonant sounds.
   (C) initial consonant sounds.
   (D) verbs.
   (E) adjectives.

139. *The Laocoon Group* is a/an

   (A) Hellenic sculpture.
   (B) medieval sculpture.
   (C) Romanesque façade.
   (D) Egyptian sculpture.
   (E) Asian sculpture.

140. Lady Gregory and J.M. Synge were key figures in the dramatic Renaissance of which country?

   (A) England
   (B) Australia
   (C) Poland
   (D) the United States
   (E) Ireland

END OF TEST. STOP

THE ANSWER KEY APPEARS ON THE FOLLOWING PAGE.

ANSWER KEY

1. C	21. A	41. D	61. D	81. A	101. B	121. A
2. A	22. A	42. B	62. E	82. E	102. C	122. B
3. D	23. E	43. B	63. C	83. A	103. B	123. D
4. D	24. D	44. A	64. B	84. C	104. D	124. E
5. D	25. C	45. C	65. C	85. D	105. B	125. A
6. D	26. B	46. B	66. E	86. E	106. B	126. E
7. E	27. A	47. E	67. B	87. C	107. A	127. E
8. C	28. D	48. D	68. C	88. A	108. E	128. A
9. B	29. A	49. C	69. C	89. C	109. A	129. B
10. C	30. C	50. B	70. D	90. A	110. C	130. C
11. D	31. D	51. B	71. B	91. B	111. C	131. D
12. C	32. B	52. C	72. A	92. A	112. C	132. B
13. D	33. C	53. A	73. B	93. D	113. A	133. B
14. A	34. C	54. D	74. D	94. E	114. C	134. D
15. B	35. A	55. A	75. C	95. A	115. D	135. E
16. B	36. B	56. B	76. A	96. C	116. A	136. E
17. D	37. C	57. B	77. A	97. B	117. C	137. A
18. C	38. E	58. D	78. C	98. A	118. B	138. A
19. E	39. A	59. D	79. B	99. D	119. D	139. A
20. A	40. E	60. E	80. D	100. D	120. D	140. E

Answers and Explanations

1. (C)
O. Henry's short stories, published in the nineteenth century, are still renowned for the imaginative, surprise ending put in such stories as "The Gift of the Magi." While his stories do sometimes feature tragic or happy endings, this is not the reason for his beloved place in American literature.

2. (A)
Kafka and Ovid wrote these similarly titled works approximately two millennia apart. Edith Wharton wrote novels including *The Decoration of Houses*, and Virgil wrote *The Aeneid* (B). Alice Walker wrote *The Color Purple* and Geoffrey Chaucer wrote *The Canterbury Tales* (C). William Gaddis wrote *The Recognitions* and Robert Burns (D) wrote "The Twa Herds." Chinua Achebe wrote *Things Fall Apart* and Jhumpa Lahiri wrote *Interpreter of Maladies* (E).

3. (D)
The Baroqe era spans 1600–1750. Bach lived from 1735–1782 and Handel's life spanned 1685–1759, putting both solidly in the Baroque period. Richard Strauss (1864–1949) and Frederic Chopin (1810–1849) were Romantic composers (A). Ludwig van Beethoven lived from 1770–1827, while John Cage is a twentieth-century composer (B). Mozart lived during the eighteenth century in the Classical era (C). Mahler lived during the nineteenth century and Glenn Miller was a modern musician.

4. (D)
"I think therefore I am," is Descartes' statement of the only irrefutable fact of existence. "Cogito ergo sum" is Latin for "I think therefore I am."

5. (D)
In this great work, a middle-class French housewife's affair leads to her ruin and death. The other choices, while all famous novels, do not contain adulterous love affairs. Willa Cather's *Death Comes to the Archbishop* (C) is a tempting answer as "death" appears in the title, but it tells a very different story than *Anna Karenina*'s.

6. (D)
Victorio De Sica's *The Bicycle Thief (Ladri di biciclette)* deals with the real-life problems of a working man. De Sica used non-actors in the leading roles and shot on the streets rather than in a studio—all characteristic of the Italian Neorealism movement. The other movements are not depicted by *The Bicycle Thief*.

7. (E)
Socrates is considered to have set the standard for Western philosophy. Plato (D) was a student of Socrates, and an important philosopher who wrote down Socrates' ideas. Aristotle (A) lived in the fourth century, and was an important philosopher as well. Henry David Thoreau (B) was an American writer and philosopher who lived during the nineteenth century. Bertrand Russell (C) was a twentieth-century British philosopher and essayist.

8. (C)
All of these authors are African-American writers. Zora Neale Hurston died in 1960 and wrote during the Harlem Renaissance; her most notable work is *Their Eyes Were Watching God*. Toni Morrison is still alive and writing. Her first novel, *The Bluest Eye*, is taught in many classrooms, and is considered a modern classic. Rita Dove is a Pulitzer Prize-winning poet.

9. (B)
Aquinas' system was a belated reaction to St. Augustine's Platonic-based philosophy. Except for Marcus Aurelius, the other choices were born long after Aquinas.

10. (C)
Luis Buñuel lived from 1900–1983. The other individuals are known for their achievements in literature and the visual arts.

11. (D)
Even if you are unfamiliar with the plot of *Un chien andalou*, remember that Salvador Dali is a Surrealist and is connected with Surrealist work. Super-realism (A) occurred between 1965 and 1975 and exemplified true-to-form sculpture. Photorealism (B) occurred during the later 1960s and exhibited realistic paintings. Impressionism (C) occurred between the years 1860–1900 and was another form of painting. Classical cinema lasted through 1928 and

emphasized important narrative information. *Un chien andalou* was filmed during the Surrealist movement, which lasted from 1924 until the 1950s.

12. (C)

Paganini lived from 1782–1840, in the same era as Schubert. Answers (A), (B), and (D) are all twentieth-century composers. Verdi (E), a tempting answer, lived in the late 1800s.

13. (D)

Wittgenstein was the most prominent and influential philosopher of the twentieth century and was single-handedly responsible for philosophy's current preoccupation with language. While some of the other choices such as Rousseau (C) were philosophers, only Wittgenstein emphasized language's importance to philosophy.

14. (A)

Boccaccio's great bawdy look at Italian morality and culture was published in 1353. It was a collection of stories.

15. (B)

Eisenstein was, with American D.W. Griffith, one of the two pioneering geniuses of the modern cinema. The other filmmakers listed all made important contributions to Soviet cinema and the theory of montage.

16. (B)

"A change of key" is the definition of "modulation." While notes ascend and descend on a scale ((E) and (A)), they do not necessarily modulate. A diapason (C) is an outpouring of sound, utilizing the whole range of a person's voice or an instrument. A modulation is not built on a second scale step (D).

17. (D)

Buster Keaton's influence on comic filmmaking continues to this day. Chaplin (B) was a contemporary of Keaton's. Wilder (A), Hawks (C), and Capra (E) worked after Keaton in the sound era.

18. (C)

The twentieth-century dancer and choreographer George Balanchine's first ballet company was called Ballet Society. It later became New York City Ballet. The other choices are also ballet companies.

19. (E)

Examine the style of the selection for clues as to the author. F. Scott Fitzgerald is known for his lyrical prose, which is the style of the quote. He wrote *The Great Gatsby*, which features these lines.

20. (A)

These words from *The Great Gatsby* compare one thing or experience to another using *like* or *as*, the definition of "simile."

21. (A)

A book told in third person (B) removes the narrator's voice from the tale. Second person (C), which is rarely used, uses the pronoun "you."

22. (D)

Starry Night is a painting created by Vincent van Gogh. It is currently held in the Museum of Modern Art, in New York.

23. (E)

While these writers are not contemporaries of each other, all three of these novels poke fun at American culture and society. Instead of pleading for a return to small-town values (D), the novels suggest that these values have led to conformity and hypocrisy in American life. The novels did not all proclaim the rights of women (A), call for the end of government (B), or politicize world events (C).

24. (D)

"Conceit" (A) is a literary comparison, but the letter is not compared to any other item or person in the text. "Point of view" (C) refers to the method of narration used in the book, and "denouement" (E) refers to the end of a literary work. While *The Scarlet Letter* asks the reader to reconsider the morality of the time period, the scarlet letter itself serves as a *symbol* of this theme, not the theme itself (B).

25. (C)

Tom Jones is a novel written by Henry Fielding. The other novels were all written by Somerset Maugham.

26. (B)

All three of these writers are members of Native American tribes. Their books focus on daily life in modern Native American culture.

27. (A)

The film *Gigi* is based on Colette's short stories about life in Paris. While Simone de Beauvoir (E) is renowned as a feminist writer, she wrote in a later time period, as did Marguerite Duras (D).

28. (D)

Both novels concern themselves with a non-utopian society (A) where people and their surroundings are completely controlled by government forces. These are not democratic societies (C). "Pneumatic" (B) is not a type of society.

29. (A)

Steinbeck's landmark work is one of the most famous Depression-era novels, calling for compassion for those that suffered dire poverty. The other choices refer to different time periods.

30. (C)

The unfolding and often linked events within a traditional novel or play form the plot. Characterization (A) involves representing a character by presenting mannerisms and movement. Symbolism (B) involves attributing symbolic meaning to objects, events, and people. Denouement (D) is the winding down of the play, while the climax (E) is the culmination of a crisis or period of intensity.

31. (D)

E.M. Forster is renowned for such novels as *A Room with a View*. Robert Frost (A) wrote poetry, Yukio Mishima (C) wrote novels, and Marlowe (B) wrote Elizabethan-era plays. Machiavelli's fourteenth-century nonfiction book about leadership (E), *The Prince*, is still often read today.

32. (B)

A violin is the smallest string instrument in an orchestra. While viola (D) is a tempting answer, it resembles a large violin, not a smaller one. A cello (C) is a large instrument, sometimes requiring a musician to stand up while playing. Bass (A) and double bass (E) are the largest string instruments in an orchestra.

33. (C)

The novels are epistolary. Like many early novels, both of these texts are written in the form of letters to other characters. While other early writers concentrated on religious themes, neither *Pamela* nor *Lady Susan* is concerned with religious topics (E), nor were they written to formula (B).

34. (C)

This award-winning novel chronicles the famous epic poem of *Beowulf*, but it is written in the sympathetic point of view of the monster, Grendel. While "The Seafarer" (D) and "The Battle of Maldon" (E) are also early English works, they are incorrect choices.

35. (A)

A social satire, *Gulliver's Travels* pokes fun at the mores of author Jonathan Swift's contemporaries. To drive home the link between the brutish, human-like Yahoos and Englishmen, the protagonist Gulliver begins to confuse the two cultures within the novel. Answers (B), (C), and (D) all involve Americans, while choice (E) is a ridiculous answer meant to distract test-takers.

36. (B)

"Bard" is a Middle English word for "poet." The word "Bard" can also refer to playwrights who wrote in verse like Shakespeare, but never to the other choices listed.

37. (C)

Magical realism is a school of writing that introduces magical elements to ordinary lives, often without explanation. Epistolary (A) refers to a novel written in letters or missives, and an epic novel (E) often spans many generations of lives. Do not be led astray by the term creative nonfiction (B). While it may contain some fictional elements, creative nonfiction refers to actual events.

38. (E)

The opera *Eugene Onegin* is based on a work by Aleksandr Pushkin, a prose poem written in the heart of the Romantic era. The poem has the same title as the opera.

39. (A)
Li Po and So Shu are famous Chinese poets. Both are notable poets of the Tang Dynasty (618–907 C.E.). The other choices involve different nationalities and professions.

40. (E)
The harp is a string instrument, not a wind instrument. Wind instruments compress air to create sounds, or create sounds when the musician blows through their mouthpiece. Woodwinds are characterized by their tubular shape and typically have keys or holes allowing the musician to produce different notes. Oboe (A), flute (B), bassoon (C), and saxophone (D) are all woodwinds.

41. (D)
Virginia Woolf wrote *Mrs. Dalloway* at the turn of the century. Note that the other writers did not write at the turn of the century.

42. (B)
Hughes, Wright, Toomer, and Hurston were all part of the Harlem Renaissance in the twentieth century. None of the other answers are art movements like the Harlem Renaissance, which was a flowering of African-American literature and art in the 1920s.

43. (B)
The Romantic movement flourished from the late 1700s through the early 1800s in Britain, giving voice to novels like Mary Shelley's *Frankenstein*. The other choices include writers from the Renaissance and nineteenth-century England.

44. (A)
Sometimes rumored to be the true author of Shakespeare's plays—a theory often disputed—Marlowe was born the same year as Shakespeare (1564) and also wrote in the Elizabethan era. Dryden (B) wrote after Shakespeare's death in the Restoration era, as did Wycherley (C). Thornton Wilder (an American) (D) and Harold Pinter (E) are both modern writers.

45. (C)
Antonio Vivaldi (1678–1741) composed *The Four Seasons*. Each choice is a musical composer. Note that three of the options are Italian composers: Vivaldi, Corelli (D), and Casella (E). This suggests that one of them is the correct answer.

46. (B)
Farce refers to broad comedy, often involving mistaken identity. A farce is too lighthearted and nonsensical to be a tragedy (A), masterpiece (C), drama (D), or romance (E).

47. (E)
A Streetcar Named Desire (C) and *Sweet Bird of Youth* (B) are also by Tennessee Williams and may be tempting answers, since they are also about fading Southern women. Look for the hint of "isolated"; during *The Glass Menagerie*, Laura liked to be alone to stare at her glass animals. *Our Town* (A) and *After the Fall* (D) do not involve aging Southern belles.

48. (D)
Sometimes known as postmodern, experimental fiction pushes the boundaries of traditional writing. Test out each word in your mind: an experiment often results in "new" findings. None of the other terms work.

49. (C)
A male singer (A) has many different names depending on the tenor of his voice. A sequence of single tones (B) is called a progression. "Counterpoint" is two or more simultaneous melodies, not tones (D). Ascending notes (E) move up the musical scale and do not define counterpoint.

50. (B)
Only two of the plays mentioned feature supernatural elements. *The Tempest* (D) is a rational answer since it features magical elements, but Puck is the catalyst for the events in *A Midsummer Night's Dream*.

51. (B)

Modern dance is now popular in many countries, but it originated in the United States, spurred on by the great Isadora Duncan. Duncan is considered to be the founder of modern dance.

52. (C)

Webster and Johnson wrote during the Elizabethan era. This era spanned the many years of Queen Elizabeth's rule and spawned great playwrights, due to the queen's continuing interest and financial investment in the theater.

53. (A)

The three playwrights listed are concerned with the meaningless nature of life and are considered to be part of the philosophical movement of existentialism. If you have seen any plays by these writers, you probably would never consider them optimistic (B).

54. (D)

In a realistic play, the audience is contained by a "fourth wall" and should not be addressed. Shakespeare had his characters address the audience at times, and Bertolt Brecht's plays are particularly renowned for this effect.

55. (A)

The term *deus ex machina* literally means "god in the machine," referring to the practice in Greek plays of a god figure descending and solving all the problems of the play. While answer (E), a character arriving at the last minute, could occur at this time, answer (A), an implausible ending where everything is resolved, is the better choice. The term does not refer to a play ending in death of all the characters (B), a scene leading to another scene (C), or a particularly happy ending (D).

56. (B)

Aristotle wrote in his classic text, *Poetics*, that without character there is no plot to set in motion and vice versa. The two are always, according to his ideas, dramatically linked. The other terms are not linked to *Poetics*.

57. (B)

Look for key words like "English" and "nineteenth-century." Edith Wharton (E) was American, Victor Hugo (C) was a French writer, and Tolstoy (D) was Russian. Washington Irving (A), an American, wrote in the eighteenth century.

58. (D)

Kane famously intones the word "Rosebud" as he dies, which no one around him understands, but which was actually the name of his childhood sled. The word symbolizes Kane's lost innocence.

59. (D)

Wilder is the rare artist who conquered two mediums with utter success—he was a master playwright and novelist.

60. (E)

Beethoven died in 1827 and Lord Byron died in 1824. Remember that the nineteenth century refers to the 1800s.

61. (D)

George Gershwin's *Rhapsody in Blue*, often called the first jazz symphony, uses elements of jazz never before entwined with classical forms. Gershwin did not inspire ballet (A), piano (B), violin (C), or chamber (E) symphonic music.

62. (E)

As the characters in the plays listed meet their sad fate of death or, in the case of Oedipus, blindness, their downfalls are seen as great and unavoidable tragedies. None of the other choices are correct, especially choices (B) and (D). The tragic stories are far from being comedic, nor are they experimental (C) or quintessential romance (A).

63. (C)

Verdi (B) also wrote many famous operas, but Mozart's comic touch infuses the two operas listed. The other composers were not known for their operas.

64. (B)

The Baroque period spanned from 1600–1750 (A). The Classical period spanned from 1750–1825; the Romantic era was from 1825–1900.

65. (C)
Igor Stravinsky (A) composed many ballet scores; however, he was born in 1882 and lived until 1971, much later than the era of *The Nutcracker*. Aaron Copland (D) was also a twentieth-century composer. Clearly, Bach (E) lived long before *The Nutcracker* was written, and Milhaud (B) never composed for the ballet.

66. (E)
Gottfried Leibniz is satirized in *Candide*. The work ridicules Leibniz's optimistic outlook by having Pangloss repeatedly utter the philosopher's maxim, "This is the best of all possible worlds," in the face of atrocities and disasters.

67. (B)
The music of the Middle Ages, both intensely superstitious and religious, sprang from the church and monasteries. The other choices did not have as much of an influence on music of the Middle Ages.

68. (C)
A villanelle is an elaborately structured poem, a literary structure often employed by Edna St. Vincent Millay.

69. (C)
This new way of looking at art and the world often depicted a pastoral setting. Debussy's "Afternoon of a Faun" is one of the most famous pieces from this era.

70. (D)
Read the words carefully. "Romantic" refers not only to love, but to the sentimental as well. This period was associated with the emotions.

71. (B)
A dulcimer is a simple, three-stringed instrument used for centuries to accompany ballads. All the other instruments would be used in an orchestral piece, including cymbals, used at intervals.

72. (A)
Glass, Strauss, and Sondheim are all composers. Glass and Sondheim are modern composers, while Strauss worked during the late Romantic period.

73. (B)
Pollack, Chagall, and Matisse were all visual artists. The other choices contain artists, dancers and choreographers, composers, and authors.

74. (D)
Graham, Balanchine, and Robbins were all choreographers. Graham is known for her work in the modern dance movement, while Balanchine worked in classical ballet.

75. (C)
Be careful to read the entire list of names before deciding on an answer. All of the choices listed are composers.

76. (A)
Gauguin's greatest work was produced during his exile in Tahiti. Paul Gauguin lived from 1848–1903 and was a Post-Impressionist artist.

77. (A)
La Sylphide, *Giselle*, and *Sleeping Beauty* are all ballets. The other choices contain a mixture of operas, novels, and ballets. Note that while answer (D) contains "Sleeping Beauty," which is a famous ballet, the other works are operas.

78. (C)
Don Quixote, *Madame Bovary*, and *Anna Karenina* are all novels. *Madame Bovary* and *Anna Karenina* both end tragically.

79. (B)
Adagio is a slow movement in music as well as in ballet. The movement is not jumpy (A), a pas de deux (C), climatic (D), or fast (E).

80. (D)
While Beat (C) may look right, remember that the Beat era popularized writing styles, not singing styles. Ella Fitzgerald practiced the scat style of singing.

81. (A)

The Futurists were concerned with the dynamism of motion as it pertained to the technological advancements of the time. Each of the other options was emphasized by different movements.

82. (E)

This classic Jimmy Stewart movie has often been copied but never duplicated as it follows an ordinary life and the reverberations every man has on others. It airs frequently on television between Thanksgiving and Christmas.

83. (A)

Choice (B) is the definition for homonyms, choice (C) defines simile, choice (D) defines onomatopoeia, and choice (E) defines alliteration.

84. (C)

Since ballet originated in France, ballet terms such as pas de deux and bras (referring to the position of the arms) still exist in the French language today. While Russian (A) is a tempting answer since so many dancers are Russian, recalling balletic terms will help you to find the correct answer.

85. (D)

Often considered to have elements of Greek tragedy, Arthur Miller's *Death of a Salesman* features a protagonist who cannot accept the reality that he is no longer useful. While some of the other plays have tragic characters, none of them have the type of character that Willy Loman, the protagonist of *Death of a Salesman*, represents.

86. (E)

The noted and prolific poet T.S. Eliot composed many poems in his lifetime, including the other choices listed. "Goblin Market," however, is by Christina Rossetti.

87. (C)

Sappho's fragments compose one of the earliest bodies of verse known to us today. Pericles (B) was a famous Greek, but he was a statesman, not a poet. The remaining choices are Roman or Italian.

88. (A)

Only a select few of Shakespeare's plays have an original point of departure. It was important that the audience know the basic storyline of any play, so Shakespeare used preexisting tales by the three authors listed to formulate his own plays. The other answer choices feature authors who lived after Shakespeare.

89. (C)

Foreshortening is a technique used by painters. The other choices are all devices used in poetry.

90. (A)

This fragment from Gerard Manley Hopkins' poem "The Windhover" contains the repetition of initial consonant sounds that defines alliteration.

91. (B)

The trio are considered to be the greatest Japanese novelists of the twentieth century. Since the three writers are not from China or Korea and are not artists, the other answers cannot be correct.

92. (A)

Wordsworth, Byron, and Keats were English poets who wrote during the Romantic era. Poets in all of the other groups lived outside of the Romantic period.

93. (D)

Welch, Silko, and Harjo are all Native Americans. Each name under choice (D) is a poet of the latter half of the twentieth century. None of the other groups is composed of Native Americans.

94. (E)

Each woman in choice (E) wrote in the golden age of modern poetry. The Native American poets would be considered postmodern (or not attributable to any particular epoch). While the Romantics (as well as Tagore and Gibran) wrote in the modern era, they would not be considered Modernist, which is a distinct movement in the arts and philosophy.

95. (A)

Moore was England's most prominent sculptor (if not its most prominent artist) of the twentieth century. He lived from 1898–1986. The sculptor Henry Moore is not to be confused with the English painter of the same name, who lived from 1831–1895.

96. (C)

Paganini was a virtuoso violinist and composer during the Romantic period. The composer is not associated with installation art (A), dance (B), poetry (D), or painting (E).

97. (B)

A choreographer is primarily associated with dance. There may be some choreography involved in installation art (A), but the artist would not be considered a choreographer.

98. (A)

There may have been quasi-installation pieces from as early as the Byzantine period, but the art form didn't come into prominence until the past few decades. All of the other answer choices include art forms developed prior to the twentieth century.

99. (D)

Although not an exclusive mode for the Byzantine artist, mosaic became the popular medium of the Eastern portion of the Roman Empire. The other forms of art became prominent during different time periods.

100. (D)

Each term in the question refers to a system of stressed and unstressed syllables, which comprises a poem's meter. Although iamb can refer to a rhyme scheme (A), spondee, anapest, and iamb all refer to meter.

101. (B)

Note the focus on love, the iambic pentameter, and the fact that the poem is a sonnet. Shakespeare utilized all these devices/forms. George Herbert (A) was a seventeenth-century British poet who wrote about the metaphysical, which is not discussed in the poem above. Wallace Stevens (C) was a twentieth-century modern American poet, who would not use words such as "thou" in his work. Coventry Patmore (D) was a British poet of the Victorian era (nineteenth century), so his works would not contain the same language as Shakespeare's either. Gustave Apollinaire (E) lived in France during the nineteenth and twentieth centuries.

102. (C)

Shakespeare was famous for his sonnets—this piece of work is his eighty-second sonnet. Free verse (A) is poetry written without rhythm, form, meter, or rhyme, some of which the poem employs. Prose (B) is matter-of-fact and unmetered, which does not constitute the work in question. Metaphor (D) and simile (E) are literary devices, not forms.

103. (B)

Iambic pentameter is a poetic device in which stressed and unstressed syllables alternate five times ("penta" refers to "five"). Lines in iambic pentameter do not have to rhyme (A). Iambic pentameter has nothing to do with irony (C) and it is not a political rebuttal (D). Consonant sounds may be repeated throughout each line (E), but it has nothing to do with a rhyme scheme or the poetic device of iambic pentameter.

104. (D)

While Victorian critic Ruskin (C) died in 1900, he is of a different era than writers Gertrude Stein or Rilke and far distant from the prime of Williams. Wright, Gaugain, and Debussy are all close contemporaries of Stein, Williams, and Rilke.

105. (B)

Pablo Neruda was a great Chilean poet, known for his touching love poems among other work. He was not known as a conceptual artist. All of the other figures are correctly matched to their discipline and art form.

106. (B)

The poem was written by Shelley shortly after Keats' death. Two of the options are chronologically impossible—John Donne (C) and Dante Alighieri (D). Both lived well before John Keats.

107. (A)

Jennifer Koh (B) is a violinist, while Arthur Rubinstein (C) and Vladmir Feltzman (D) are pianists. Mischa Elman (E) is also a violinist.

108. (E)

Leopold and Molly Bloom are husband and wife, representing Ulysses and Penelope in Joyce's novel, *Ulysses*.

109. (A)

Charlotte Bronte's *Jane Eyre* bridges the Romantic and Victorian eras. Her sisters Anne (D) and Emily (E) were also writers, so those choices may confuse you. Anne wrote *The Tenant of Wildfell Hall*, while Emily composed *Wuthering Heights*.

110. (C)

While a trio or a piano quartet can include different instruments, a string quartet always consists of four instruments: two violins (first and second), a viola, and a cello. Drums, flutes, French horns, saxophones, and other instruments are not included in a string quartet.

111. (C)

Hobbes was suspicious of the masses (especially the undereducated, landless peasants) and felt that if they were given power, the state would decline into anarchy.

112. (C)

Becky Sharp is still a sympathetic character because Thackeray illustrates, through her, the difficulties and prejudices young women had to face in a male-dominated, materialistic society. Through scheming and conniving, Becky could make her way into high society.

113. (A)

Becky Sharp is a character in Thackeray's *Vanity Fair*. *The House of Mirth* (D), a tempting answer, is by Edith Wharton.

114. (C)

The Human Comedy refers to the group of novels in which Balzac, a French realist, attempts to depict life in Paris as accurately as possible.

115. (D)

Artists like Close and Estes have used painting techniques to render photographic images. Photography (A) may be a tempting answer, since the paintings of photorealism are supposed to look so much like actual photos, but that choice is incorrect.

116. (A)

While color (B) may be an element in chiaroscuro, by definition it refers to the manipulation of light and shadow. Theme (C), the vanishing point (D), and figures (E) are not central to chiaroscuro.

117. (C)

Bas-relief refers to a surface sculpture raised from a wall or door. None of the other choices could contain this feature.

118. (B)

Seurat's close study of the juxtaposition of colors enabled him to enhance certain colors, while producing novel effects of shadow and light. Pointillism is the use of points of color. The full effect of a Pointillist painting is often best when viewed from across a room.

119. (D)

The painting, *Christina's World*, is indicative of Wyeth's examination of perspective in American landscapes.

120. (D)

Brunelleschi's dome in Florence is a landmark in Renaissance art and architecture. While Brunelleschi worked with different architectural forms, he is most famous for his work on domes.

121. (A)

While some of the other people may have dabbled in one medium or the other, the only group that fits the question's criteria is answer choice (A). Michelangelo was a poet, but he was not famous for his poetry.

122. (B)

Hesse's *Siddhartha* is a perfect example of a bildungsroman type of novel. Siddhartha, the main character in the book, finds himself through a journey of internal and external reflection.

123. (D)

Though they painted in different styles, each artist in answer (D) was born in the Netherlands. The artists in the other choices were born in different places, including Italy, Austria, and America.

124. (E)

While there are elements of Pop Art in the feminist artists listed (C), they are not considered to be Pop Artists. Warhol is famous for his use of Campbell's soup cans and everyday cultural objects in his work.

125. (A)

While Judy Chicago (C) might be considered a sculptor, both Kruger and Holzer focus on installation art. Only group (A)—Rodin, Michelangelo, and Bernini—contains all sculptors.

126. (E)

This Side of Paradise was written by F. Scott Fitzgerald. All of the other choices were written by Ayn Rand.

127. (E)

Charlotte Perkins Gilman (A) wrote during the Victorian era, Matthew Mauri (B) is a made-up name, Charles Dickens (C) wrote in the 1800s in England, and Charlotte Bronte (D) also wrote during the 1800s. Toni Morrison, author of *Beloved* among other works, is the only twenty-first-century author.

128. (A)

Jacques Lipchitz was a sculptor. Lipchitz was a seminal figure in the modern art movement. None of the other choices are sculptors.

129. (B)

Born Mary Ann Evans, George Eliot took a man's name to gain credibility and went on to become the most prominent novelist of the Victorian period.

130. (C)

Federico Garcia Lorca was a prominent Spanish dramatist and poet mysteriously murdered by Franco's fascists early in the twentieth century. None of the other choices are poets.

131. (D)

Galsworthy uses the relationship of Soames and Irene to expose the overly materialistic transaction of marriage in the late Victorian period. Answers (A) and (C) refer to mythological or legendary figures, answer (B) refers to an actual relationship, and answer (E) refers to Virginia Woolf's novel, *Mrs. Dalloway*.

132. (B)

This turn-of-the-(twentieth)-century movement was inspired by Darwin and the new view of the natural world as hostile and indifferent.

133. (B)

There were no specific media or techniques attributable to Dadaism, rather it was a philosophical (or non-philosophical) examination of the deeply entrenched principles of art. The Dadaists named themselves based on the word "Dada," which has no meaning.

134. (D)

Alexandre-Gustave Eiffel constructed the Eiffel Tower. The French architect received the commission for this work amid much controversy.

135. (E)

After initial ambivalence from residents, the Eiffel Tower has come to symbolize the city of Paris. The Eiffel Tower is now a major tourist attraction for France, along with its wineries, metropolitan areas, and countryside villas.

136. (E)

The Eiffel Tower was erected for art's sake rather than from any utilitarian motivation. It was built in 1889 to commemorate the French Revolution.

137. (A)

While the sonnets occasionally and the plays often depart from this meter, it is the prominent mode in Shakespeare's work. There is some blank verse (C), though rarely any free verse (D), in his plays.

138. (A)

Assonance is a device used throughout lines of text to create a mood or atmosphere. No particular part of speech (such as verb, adjective, or noun) is preferred in the use of this literary device.

139. (A)
The sculpture depicts the torture of Laocoon and his sons for trying to warn the Trojans about the Trojan horse. The artist is unknown.

140. (E)
At the turn of the century, Ireland experienced a flourishing in the literary arts in general and the theater specifically, due in large part to the efforts of Lady Gregory and William Butler Yeats.

Chapter Fifteen: Practice Test 3

Time—90 minutes
140 Questions

Directions: For each of the following questions or incomplete statements, select the best answer or completion from the five options given.

1. John Ashberry, W.S. Merwin, Adrienne Rich, Louise Gluck, and Yousef Komunyaka were all poets of

    (A) the first half of the twentieth century.
    (B) the early Renaissance.
    (C) the second half of the twentieth century.
    (D) the late Victorian period.
    (E) the Imagist movement.

2. Which modern classical composer pioneered twelve-tone composition?

    (A) Gustav Mahler
    (B) Arnold Schoenberg
    (C) Frederic Chopin
    (D) Claude Debussy
    (E) Yo-Yo Ma

3. Which of the following would best describe the central concern of Wallace Stevens in his poetry?

    (A) the imagination
    (B) socialism
    (C) poverty
    (D) women's issues
    (E) science

4. The opening movement of an opera is called

    (A) a prelude.
    (B) an epilogue.
    (C) a prologue.
    (D) an overture.
    (E) an overtone.

5. Which of the following poets has a type of sonnet named after him/her?

    (A) Walt Whitman
    (B) Petrarch
    (C) Anna Swir
    (D) Cathy Song
    (E) Samuel Taylor Coleridge

GO ON TO THE NEXT PAGE

Questions 6–8 refer to the following authors and texts.

(A) James Joyce's *Ulysses*
(B) Virginia Woolf's *Orlando*
(C) Ezra Pound's *Cantos*
(D) Salman Rushdie's *The Satanic Verses*
(E) William Carlos Williams' *Paterson*

6. Which takes place in Dublin?

7. Which takes place in New Jersey?

8. Which is patterned after a work by Dante?

9. Which of the following matches the poet to his/her epoch?

   (A) Elizabeth Barrett Browning . . . Age of Reason
   (B) Johann Wolfgang von Goethe . . . Romantic
   (C) John Dryden . . . Hellenic
   (D) Imamu Baraka . . . medieval
   (E) Emily Dickinson . . . postmodern

Questions 10–12 refer to the following people.

(A) David Smith, Jean Arp, Louise Nevelson
(B) Praxiteles, Phidias, *The Laocoon Group* sculptor
(C) Michelangelo, Donatello, Lorenzo Ghiberti
(D) Auguste Rodin, Antonio Canova, Honore Daumier
(E) Gianlorenzo Bernini, Antoine Coysevox, Gregorio Fernandez

10. Which group is from the twentieth century?

11. Which group is from the fifteenth century?

12. Which group is from the nineteenth century?

Used by permission. See copyright page (iv) for information.

13. Who is the MOST likely painter of the above work?

    (A) Paul Cezanne
    (B) Agnes Martin
    (C) Jackson Pollock
    (D) Honore Daumier
    (E) Leonora Carrington

14. Which term describes the artist's method?

    (A) minimalism
    (B) action painting
    (C) happening
    (D) jugendstil
    (E) Cubism

GO ON TO THE NEXT PAGE

15. In which century was this work first shown?

    (A) seventeenth
    (B) eighteenth
    (C) nineteenth
    (D) twentieth
    (E) twenty-first

16. In this Dickens novel, Pip and Estella are manipulated by a jilted bride grown old.

    (A) *A Tale of Two Cities*
    (B) *Oliver Twist*
    (C) *Great Expectations*
    (D) *Our Mutual Friend*
    (E) *Hard Times*

17. Cassio, Iago, and Desdemona can all be associated with which Shakespearean protagonist?

    (A) Hamlet
    (B) King Lear
    (C) Troilus
    (D) Timon of Athens
    (E) Othello

Questions 18–19 refer to the following poets.

    (A) William Butler Yeats
    (B) Walt Whitman
    (C) Hart Crane
    (D) Sylvia Plath
    (E) Marianne Moore

18. Which of the above poets did not produce work in the twentieth century?

19. This poet examined small subjects such as strange animals, steeplejacks, and baseball fans. Rather than quoting Dante or Shakespeare, he/she used encyclopedia snippets and newspaper blurbs to compose poems.

20. "The Miller's Tale," "The Franklin's Tale," and "The Wife of Bath's Prologue" are all parts of which literary work?

    (A) *Moll Flanders*
    (B) *The Flowers of Evil*
    (C) *The Sorrows of Young Werther*
    (D) *One Hundred Years of Solitude*
    (E) *The Canterbury Tales*

21. Which of the following figures would you be LEAST likely to find in a painting by Edgar Degas?

    (A) a ballerina
    (B) a choreographer
    (C) a horse
    (D) a Greek god
    (E) a jockey

22. The Fugitive Poets like Allen Tate, John Crowe Ransom, and Robert Penn Warren were working in

    (A) the American South.
    (B) Wales.
    (C) Canada.
    (D) the Balkans.
    (E) New York.

23. Sophocles's *Oedipus Rex* presents a hero with

    (A) a tragic flaw.
    (B) humility.
    (C) good fortune.
    (D) brains, but no physical strength.
    (E) a comical sidekick.

24. "The Second Coming," "Sailing To Byzantium," "The Lake Isle of Innisfree," and "Under Ben Bulben" are all poems by

    (A) William Butler Yeats.
    (B) Walt Whitman.
    (C) Gwendolyn Brooks.
    (D) e.e. cummings.
    (E) Emily Dickinson.

25. Which of the following works is a Renaissance painting?

    (A) *The School of Athens*
    (B) *Las Meninas*
    (C) *Embarkation to the Island of Cythera*
    (D) *Guernica*
    (E) *The Fountainhead*

26. Which of the following is a group of Cubist painters?

    (A) Michelangelo, Leonardo da Vinci, Jan van Eyck
    (B) Pablo Picasso, Juan Gris, Georges Braque
    (C) Claude Monet, Camille Pissarro, Berthe Morisot
    (D) Jean Dubuffet, Alberto Giacometti, Francis Bacon
    (E) Ellsworth Kelly, Agnes Martin, Franz Kline

27. Which of the following authors wrote *One Hundred Years of Solitude*?

    (A) Isabel Allende
    (B) Gunter Grasse
    (C) Gabriel Garcia Marquez
    (D) Joyce Carol Oates
    (E) Charlotte Bronte

28. A full-length ballet consists of how many acts?

    (A) six acts
    (B) two acts
    (C) four, plus two intermissions
    (D) one, plus a finale
    (E) three acts

29. Which of the following were contemporaries of Jacques Louis David and Eugene Delacroix?

    (A) Napoleon, Goethe, Hegel
    (B) Margaret Thatcher, Gabriel Garcia Marquez, Jacques Derrida
    (C) Mohandas Gandhi, Gabriela Mistral, Simone de Beauvoir
    (D) Pericles, Sappho, Plato
    (E) Peter the Great, Alexander Pope, Gottfried Wilhelm Leibniz

30. *A Christmas Carol* by Charles Dickens has seen many film adaptations, including the comic movie, *Scrooged*. It was originally published as a

    (A) short novel.
    (B) narrative poem.
    (C) collection of essays.
    (D) short story.
    (E) chapter of a longer novel.

31. Which of the following is NOT a play written by Eugene O'Neill?

    (A) *Moon for the Misbegotten*
    (B) *The Ice Man Cometh*
    (C) *Mourning Becomes Electra*
    (D) *The Cherry Orchard*
    (E) *Long Day's Journey into Night*

32. How many acts would a full-length play most likely include?

    (A) five
    (B) eight
    (C) ten
    (D) twelve
    (E) one

33. Which of the following were the most prominent artists of the Surrealist movement?

    (A) Salvador Dali and Rene Magritte
    (B) Morris Louis and Yves Klein
    (C) Jan Vermeer and Hans Holbein
    (D) Titian and Tintoretto
    (E) Anthony van Dyck and Albrecht Durer

34. Which of the following terms refers to a stage actor?

    (A) cooper
    (B) thespian
    (C) aesthete
    (D) angler
    (E) chandler

35. Which of the following playwrights is matched with his/her own play?

    (A) Lillian Hellman ... *Accidental Death of an Anarchist*
    (B) August Strindberg ... *Twelfth Night*
    (C) Moliere ... *The Misanthrope*
    (D) Henrik Ibsen ... *The Infernal Machine*
    (E) Christopher Marlowe ... *Tiger at the Gates*

36. Which classical composer wrote the ballet music *Bolero*?

    (A) Vittorio Rieti
    (B) Maurice Ravel
    (C) Igor Stravinsky
    (D) Arnold Schoenberg
    (E) Werner Egk

Questions 37–38 refer to Marcel Duchamp's *Fountain*.

37. Duchamp's *Fountain* is a urinal placed on the floor of an art gallery. The piece is an example of

    (A) a found object.
    (B) rotogravure.
    (C) novice art.
    (D) Surrealism.
    (E) Neoclassicism.

38. Which of the following would best describe the piece's tone?

    (A) melodramatic
    (B) satirical
    (C) romantic
    (D) sober
    (E) celebratory

39. Who is R. Mutt?

    (A) Georgia O'Keefe
    (B) Fra Lippo Lippi
    (C) Robert Indiana
    (D) Marcel Duchamp
    (E) Hieronymus Bosch

40. Praxiteles and Phidias were close contemporaries of

    (A) Marcel Proust and Claude Debussy
    (B) Boccaccio and Petrarch
    (C) Jonathan Swift and Thomas Gainsborough
    (D) Euripides and Aeschylus
    (E) Horace and Ovid

41. Which of the following styles traces its roots to the Roman empire?

    (A) Romantic
    (B) Baroque
    (C) Romanesque
    (D) Rococo
    (E) postmodern

42. Which of the following artists is considered an "Abstract Expressionist"?

    (A) Paul Cezanne
    (B) Piet Mondrian
    (C) Odilon Redon
    (D) Pablo Picasso
    (E) Georges de la Tour

43. Bauhaus was an institution famous for producing

    (A) poets.
    (B) composers.
    (C) architects.
    (D) musicians.
    (E) literary critics.

44. Which of the following artists is NOT a famous portrait painter?

    (A) Thomas Gainsborough
    (B) Franz Hals
    (C) Chuck Close
    (D) Amedeo Modigliani
    (E) Wassily Kandinsky

45. Which of the following were close contemporaries of Georges Seurat and Henri Toulouse-Latrec?

    (A) Claude Debussy and Thomas Hardy
    (B) Ludwig van Beethoven and Lord Byron
    (C) Jonathan Swift and George Handel
    (D) Duke Ellington and Sylvia Plath
    (E) John Cage and Toni Morrison

Questions 46–48 refer to the following portion of a poem.

Hail to the virtues which that perilous life
Extracts from Nature's elemental strife;
And welcome glory won in battles fought
As bravely as the foe was keenly sought.
But to each gallant Captain and his crew
A less imperious sympathy is due,
Such as my verse now yields, while moonbeams play
On the mute sea in this unruffled bay;
Such as will promptly flow from every breast,
Where good men, disappointed in the quest
Of wealth and power and honours, long for rest;
Or, having known the splendours of success,
Sigh for the obscurities of happiness.

46. Who is the British poet who ushered in the Romantic era and wrote the poem above?

    (A) Sylvia Plath
    (B) Henry David Thoreau
    (C) William Wordsworth
    (D) Virginia Woolf
    (E) William Shakespeare

GO ON TO THE NEXT PAGE

47. What is a defining subject of Romantic poetry, found in this poem?

    (A) the evils of war
    (B) nature
    (C) relationships
    (D) taxation without representation
    (E) Britain's relationship with America during the nineteenth century.

48. Where did the poet write this poem?

    (A) in the middle of the woods
    (B) by the sea
    (C) beside a stream
    (D) in his house
    (E) in India

49. Tom Stoppard's *Rosencrantz and Guildenstern Are Dead* is based on a play by which playwright?

    (A) John Webster
    (B) Jean Racine
    (C) Antonin Artaud
    (D) Lady Gregory
    (E) William Shakespeare

50. Walt Whitman's *Leaves of Grass* can best be described as

    (A) an esoteric take on capitalism.
    (B) a return to classicism.
    (C) a concise, compact masterwork.
    (D) an overflowing celebration of humanity.
    (E) a dark, Kafkaesque appraisal of the new America.

51. Russian artist Kasimir Malevich was the progenitor of which of the following movements?

    (A) Impressionism
    (B) Vorticism
    (C) Fauvism
    (D) Suprematism
    (E) Pointillism

52. Akira Kurosawa's epic masterpiece *Ran*, in which an old Japanese warlord divides his land between his three children, is an adaptation of which play by Shakespeare?

    (A) *King Lear*
    (B) *Measure for Measure*
    (C) *Henry IV*
    (D) *Titus Andronicus*
    (E) *As You Like It*

53. Which of the following poets' work could be described as evocative nonsense?

    (A) Sir Philip Sidney
    (B) Thomas Hardy
    (C) Edith Sitwell
    (D) Lewis Carroll
    (E) Juana Ines de la Cruz

54. John Milton's *Paradise Lost* is written in

    (A) blank verse.
    (B) trochaic hexameter.
    (C) heroic couplets.
    (D) free verse.
    (E) spondaic tetrameter.

GO ON TO THE NEXT PAGE

Questions 55–56 refer to the following centuries.

(A) sixteenth
(B) seventeenth
(C) eighteenth
(D) nineteenth
(E) twentieth

55. Which century is known primarily as an era of science and logic?

56. Which century is the Victorian period predominantly situated in?

57. Which of the following women is renowned for her role in popularizing modern dance?

(A) Hilary Hahn
(B) Suzanne Farrell
(C) Billie Holiday
(D) Jane Austen
(E) Isadora Duncan

58. In which century did Rainer Maria Rilke publish *The Duino Elegies*?

(A) sixteenth
(B) seventeenth
(C) eighteenth
(D) nineteenth
(E) twentieth

59. Which of the following poets is matched with his/her own work?

(A) Robert Lowell . . . "The Quaker Graveyard in Nantucket"
(B) A.E. Housman . . . "The Marriage of Heaven and Hell"
(C) Pablo Neruda . . . *The White Goddess*
(D) Derek Walcott . . . "The Idea of Order at Key West"
(E) Amy Lowell . . . "The Drunken Boat"

60. This experimental filmmaker scripted, directed, edited, and performed in the central role of *Meshes of the Afternoon*.

(A) Stan Brakhage
(B) Kenneth Anger
(C) Godfrey Reggio
(D) Bruce Connor
(E) Maya Deran

61. Roy Lichtenstein's paintings resemble

(A) Rembrandt's portraits.
(B) John Constable's landscapes.
(C) comic strips.
(D) photographs.
(E) collages.

62. John Locke is responsible for which of the following philosophical theories?

(A) tabula rasa
(B) the categorical imperative
(C) communism
(D) language games
(E) idealism

Courtesy of SuperStock, Inc.

63. Which of the following is most closely associated with the artist of the painting above?

    (A) bas-relief
    (B) manipulation of light and shadow
    (C) etching
    (D) allegory
    (E) religious sentiment

64. Which of the following philosophers was a student of Socrates?

    (A) Xenophanes
    (B) Archimedes
    (C) Thales of Miletus
    (D) Plato
    (E) Hippocrates

65. Paul Cezanne painted which of the following objects over and over?

    (A) a cathedral
    (B) a mountain
    (C) a haystack
    (D) an ox
    (E) a boot sole

66. Which of the following are literary critics?

    (A) Helen Vendler, Jacques Derrida, Harold Bloom, Julia Kristeva
    (B) Joseph Haydn, Giacomo Puccini, Phillip Glass, Edvard Grieg
    (C) Charlotte Corday, Guy Fawkes, John Wilkes Booth, Aaron Burr
    (D) Anthony van Dyck, Hans Holbein, Frans Hals, Sir Joshua Reynolds
    (E) Auguste Rodin, Alberto Giacometti, Maya Lin, Jean Arp

67. John Constable, Frederic Church, and Claude Lorrain are all famous for painting

    (A) self-portraits.
    (B) the demise of historical figures.
    (C) with sand.
    (D) landscapes.
    (E) murals.

68. "Denouement" refers to which part of a novel?

    (A) the prologue
    (B) the opening paragraph
    (C) the climax
    (D) the middle
    (E) toward the end

GO ON TO THE NEXT PAGE

69. Jasper Johns is most famous for painting

    (A) nudes and landscapes.
    (B) portraits and battle scenes.
    (C) flags and targets.
    (D) political figures and ballet dancers.
    (E) dogs and birds.

70. The protagonist of Malcolm Lowry's *Under the Volcano* is

    (A) a bullfighter.
    (B) an alcoholic.
    (C) a princess.
    (D) a fireman.
    (E) a cancer patient.

71. A term often applied in the seventeenth century to ensemble music for voices and instruments is

    (A) "concerto."
    (B) "symphony."
    (C) "movement."
    (D) "chorus."
    (E) "harmony."

Questions 72–74 refer to the following choices.

    (A) idealism
    (B) Continental philosophy
    (C) empiricism
    (D) logical positivism
    (E) utilitarianism

72. This philosophy is concerned with constructive theories which are applicable to the functioning of daily life.

73. Bishop Berkeley is this philosophical school's most notable adherent.

74. This school is distinguished from Anglo-American philosophy.

75. A prose work consisting of around 120 pages would be considered

    (A) an epic.
    (B) a saga.
    (C) a novella.
    (D) a ballad.
    (E) a sestina.

76. An extended work for orchestra, usually in three or four movements, is called a

    (A) scherzo.
    (B) symphony.
    (C) trio.
    (D) concerto.
    (E) quartet.

77. In Toni Morrison's *Beloved*, the title refers to

    (A) an old woman.
    (B) a dead child.
    (C) a young boy.
    (D) a telepathic teenager.
    (E) an animal.

78. Which of the following is the highest voice in a polyphonic texture?

    (A) alto
    (B) tenor
    (C) bass
    (D) virtuoso
    (E) soprano

79. "Fallingwater" is a famous

    (A) painting.
    (B) opera.
    (C) ballet.
    (D) edifice.
    (E) tone poem.

80. In musical notation, how many lines are used to write music?

    (A) four
    (B) three
    (C) five
    (D) one
    (E) two

81. Which of the following works were published in 1922?

    (A) *Tristram Shandy* and "Essay on Man"
    (B) "The Waste Land" and *Ulysses*
    (C) *One Hundred Years of Solitude* and *Men of Maize*
    (D) *Hamlet* and *The Alchemist*
    (E) *My Last Duchess* and *In Memorium*

82. What is the name used to describe big-band jazz music from the 1930s and 1940s?

    (A) swing
    (B) tap
    (C) Dixieland
    (D) ballroom
    (E) bebop

83. Which of the following was NOT a Romantic composer?

    (A) Frederic Chopin
    (B) Niccolo Paganini
    (C) Felix Mendelssohn
    (D) Franz Liszt
    (E) George Frideric Handel

84. Gregg Toland, esteemed for his deep-focus cinematography on *Citizen Kane*, also shot this classic 1940 film directed by John Ford and adapted from a John Steinbeck novel.

    (A) *Stagecoach*
    (B) *The Long Voyage Home*
    (C) *Tobacco Road*
    (D) *The Grapes of Wrath*
    (E) *How Green Was My Valley*

85. Which of the words below is the definition of a composition, or compositional technique, in which a theme (or themes) is extended and developed mainly by imitative counterpoint?

    (A) chorus
    (B) fugue
    (C) stanza
    (D) madrigal
    (E) fandango

86. This major figure of the French New Wave made the films *The 400 Blows*, *Jules and Jim*, and *The Last Metro*.

    (A) Alain Resnais
    (B) Jean-Luc Godard
    (C) Claude Chabrol
    (D) François Truffaut
    (E) Louis Malle

87. Which of the following novels was written by Emile Zola?

    (A) *The Mill on the Floss*
    (B) *Germinal*
    (C) *Hard Times*
    (D) *Madame Bovary*
    (E) *La Bas*

GO ON TO THE NEXT PAGE

88. In which century was the sonata form of classical music invented?

    (A) eighteenth
    (B) nineteenth
    (C) twentieth
    (D) seventeenth
    (E) sixteenth

89. Film noir, a genre of American filmmaking so labeled by the French because of its cynicism, darkness, and despair, emerged during which period of American history?

    (A) the Depression
    (B) post-World War II
    (C) the McCarthy/blacklist era of the 1950s
    (D) the Vietnam War
    (E) the Watergate era

90. In Dostoyevsky's *Crime and Punishment*, where does Raskolnikov end up at the novel's conclusion?

    (A) Moscow
    (B) Paris
    (C) Siberia
    (D) Berlin
    (E) Australia

91. Who was considered by Dostoyevsky, Tolstoy, Turgenev, and others to be the "father" of Russian literature?

    (A) Mikhail Lermontov
    (B) Vladimir Nabokov
    (C) Victor Pelevin
    (D) Nikolai Gogol
    (E) Aleksandr Solzhenitsyn

Questions 92–94 refer to the following disciplines.

   (A) drama
   (B) poetry
   (C) ballet
   (D) architecture
   (E) philosophy

92. Which of these disciplines are Frank Gehry, Mies van der Rohe, and Le Corbusier associated with?

93. In which of these disciplines would the term "aside" be used?

94. In which of these disciplines would the terms "architrave" and "flying buttress" be used?

95. In Arthur Koestler's *Darkness at Noon*, the main character is awaiting

    (A) a thunderstorm.
    (B) an execution.
    (C) the birth of his first daughter.
    (D) the arrival of his beloved.
    (E) the coronation of his queen.

96. Oscar Wilde's *The Picture of Dorian Gray* tells the story of a man who

    (A) never looks any older.
    (B) is sent to prison for ten years of hard labor.
    (C) paints landscapes in the open air.
    (D) turns into a cockroach.
    (E) travels to the North Pole.

GO ON TO THE NEXT PAGE

97. Which of the following matches the artist to his/her country of birth?

    (A) Francis Bacon ... France
    (B) Berthe Morisot ... Holland
    (C) El Greco ... Spain
    (D) Titian ... Ireland
    (E) Edward Hopper ... the United States

98. All of the following are novels by Fyodor Dostoyevsky EXCEPT

    (A) *The Brothers Karamazov.*
    (B) *The Possessed.*
    (C) *The Idiot.*
    (D) *House of the Dead.*
    (E) *Doctor Zhivago.*

99. During the Baroque era, which composer worked as a church organist?

    (A) Johann Sebastian Bach
    (B) Franz Haydn
    (C) Wolfgang Amadeus Mozart
    (D) Richard Wagner
    (E) Johannes Brahms

100. Fauvism was a movement in which art form?

    (A) painting
    (B) music
    (C) ballet
    (D) drama
    (E) opera

101. Which of the following did Robert Frost describe as "playing tennis without the net"?

    (A) vorticism
    (B) free verse
    (C) writing plays
    (D) automatic writing
    (E) imagism

102. Of the following composers, which one is known as the *enfant terrible* of avant garde music?

    (A) Richard Wagner
    (B) Samuel Barber
    (C) Ralph Vaughn Williams
    (D) John Cage
    (E) Willem de Kooning

103. The author Dorothy Parker was renowned for her

    (A) wit.
    (B) epic novels.
    (C) prolific output.
    (D) dramatic depth.
    (E) kind-hearted protagonists.

104. Which of the following is a noted photographer?

    (A) Dorothea Lange
    (B) Andrea del Sarto
    (C) Buckminster Fuller
    (D) Isadora Duncan
    (E) Djuna Barnes

105. What does the musical term "lieder" mean?

    (A) a symphony
    (B) an operetta
    (C) a song
    (D) a violin solo
    (E) a cello solo

106. Which of the following was famous for his/her Civil War photographs?

    (A) Alfred Stieglitz
    (B) Ansel Adams
    (C) Matthew Brady
    (D) Edouard Vuillard
    (E) Edith Wharton

GO ON TO THE NEXT PAGE

107. The film *The Third Man* was based on a novel by which author?

(A) Lope de Vega
(B) Mark Twain
(C) Colette
(D) Graham Greene
(E) Laurence Sterne

Questions 108–110 refer to the following painting.

Courtesy of SuperStock, Inc.

108. Who is the man pictured?

(A) Paul Gauguin
(B) Fernand Leger
(C) Roberto Matta
(D) John Constable
(E) Vincent van Gogh

109. What type of painting is this?

(A) still life
(B) landscape
(C) fresco
(D) self-portrait
(E) portrait

110. What period is this painting associated with?

(A) Baroque
(B) postmodern
(C) Post-Impressionist
(D) Pre-Raphaelite
(E) Neoclassical

111. Which of the following Shakespearean characters does NOT serve as comic relief?

(A) Prospero
(B) Falstaff
(C) Feste
(D) Touchstone
(E) Puck

112. The main character in M. Scott Momaday's *House Made of Dawn* is

(A) a Native American.
(B) a gypsy.
(C) a fireman.
(D) an African-American.
(E) an Irish immigrant.

113. The Hellenistic sculptor's approach to the human form can be described as

(A) idealistic.
(B) understated.
(C) ambivalent.
(D) ironic.
(E) modest.

114. Many of the "Seven Wonders of the Ancient World" come from which period?

(A) Baroque
(B) Byzantine
(C) Medieval
(D) Romantic
(E) Hellenistic

GO ON TO THE NEXT PAGE

Questions 115–117 refer to the following choices.

(A) Charlotte Bronte's *Jane Eyre*
(B) Marcel Duchamp's *Nude Descending a Staircase*
(C) Georges Bizet's *Carmen*
(D) Carolyn Forche's "The Colonel"
(E) Ludwig van Beethoven's *Eroica*

115. Which is a symphony?

116. Which is a painting?

117. Which is a poem?

118. A libretto is a manuscript used in which genre?

(A) novel
(B) opera
(C) ballet
(D) epic ballad
(E) symphony

119. In which of the following novels does the main character die?

(A) George Eliot's *Middlemarch*
(B) Mark Twain's *The Adventures of Huckleberry Finn*
(C) Fyodor Dostoyevsky's *Crime and Punishment*
(D) Charles Dickens' *The Old Curiosity Shop*
(E) Edith Wharton's *Ethan Frome*

120. Ray Bradbury and Isaac Asimov are both authors associated with

(A) the Romantic movement.
(B) Naturalism.
(C) science fiction.
(D) Robert Browning.
(E) absurdist drama.

121. Which of the following would you most likely find in an Andy Warhol work?

(A) soup cans and Marilyn Monroe
(B) trees and peasants
(C) rocks and hawks
(D) horses and Napoleon
(E) sides of beef and Pope Urban II

Questions 122–124 refer to the following picture.

Used by permission. See copyright page (iv) for information.

122. What country is this scene taken from?

(A) Belgium
(B) France
(C) England
(D) the United States
(E) Mexico

123. The mood of this painting can best be described as

(A) tense.
(B) stark.
(C) light-hearted.
(D) violent.
(E) comical.

124. Who is the painter?

    (A) Jackson Pollock
    (B) Arthur Dove
    (C) Georgia O'Keefe
    (D) Edward Hopper
    (E) Andrew Wyeth

125. The novels of Joseph Conrad are chiefly concerned with

    (A) power, corruption, and evil.
    (B) the Black Death.
    (C) the passage of time.
    (D) love.
    (E) art and music.

126. Which of the following is another term for the main character of a novel?

    (A) deus ex machina
    (B) thespian
    (C) protagonist
    (D) comic relief
    (E) bridge

127. Which of the following artists wrote a famous autobiography?

    (A) Praxiteles
    (B) Vincent van Gogh
    (C) Benvenuto Cellini
    (D) Giotto
    (E) Lorenzo Lotto

128. Where would a J.M.W. Turner painting most likely be set?

    (A) the sea
    (B) the desert
    (C) a nursery
    (D) ancient Egypt
    (E) Sub-Saharan Africa

129. "Mrs. Dalloway would buy the flowers herself" is the first line of a novel by

    (A) James Joyce.
    (B) H.D.
    (C) Virginia Woolf.
    (D) L.F. Celine.
    (E) M.A. Marcom.

130. Gioacchio Rossini composed which opera?

    (A) *Don Giovanni*
    (B) *The Barber of Seville*
    (C) *Orfeo*
    (D) *Die Freischutz*
    (E) *Aida*

131. *A Bend in the River* and *Half a Life* are novels by

    (A) V.S. Naipaul.
    (B) Selma Lagerlof.
    (C) Thomas Hardy.
    (D) Kate Chopin.
    (E) Gail Tsukiyama.

132. The narrative structure of Faulkner's *The Sound and the Fury* can best be described as

 (A) third-person omniscient.
 (B) multiple first-person points of view.
 (C) second-person direct address.
 (D) first-person singular.
 (E) third-person limited.

Questions 133–135 refer to the following authors.

 (A) Michael Ondaatje
 (B) Oliver Goldsmith
 (C) Milan Kundera
 (D) Gore Vidal
 (E) Italo Calvino

133. Which of these authors was born in the United States?

134. Which of these authors did NOT publish a work in the twentieth century?

135. The film *The English Patient* was based on a novel by which of these authors?

136. The stories of James Thurber can best be described as

 (A) language based.
 (B) melodramatic.
 (C) mysterious.
 (D) dark.
 (E) comic.

137. Salman Rushdie's *The Satanic Verses* was controversial in its satire of which of the following religions?

 (A) Christianity
 (B) Islam
 (C) Buddhism
 (D) Hinduism
 (E) Zoroastrianism

Questions 138–139 refer to the following continents and countries.

 (A) Ireland
 (B) the United States
 (C) Australia
 (D) Africa
 (E) the Soviet Union

138. From which country/continent did Mark Rothko and Marc Chagall emigrate?

139. Where were William Butler Yeats and George Bernard Shaw born?

140. Where are J.M. Coetzee's *Disgrace*, Barbara Kingsolver's *The Poisonwood Bible*, Norman Rush's *Mating*, and Chinua Achebe's *Things Fall Apart* all set?

END OF TEST. STOP

ANSWER KEY

1. C	21. D	41. C	61. C	81. B	101. B	121. A
2. B	22. A	42. B	62. A	82. A	102. D	122. D
3. A	23. A	43. C	63. B	83. E	103. A	123. B
4. D	24. A	44. E	64. D	84. D	104. A	124. D
5. B	25. A	45. A	65. B	85. B	105. C	125. A
6. A	26. B	46. C	66. A	86. D	106. C	126. C
7. E	27. C	47. B	67. D	87. B	107. D	127. C
8. C	28. E	48. B	68. E	88. A	108. E	128. A
9. B	29. A	49. E	69. C	89. B	109. D	129. C
10. A	30. A	50. D	70. B	90. C	110. C	130. B
11. C	31. D	51. D	71. A	91. D	111. A	131. A
12. D	32. A	52. A	72. E	92. D	112. A	132. B
13. C	33. A	53. D	73. C	93. A	113. A	133. D
14. B	34. B	54. A	74. B	94. D	114. E	134. B
15. D	35. C	55. C	75. C	95. B	115. E	135. A
16. C	36. B	56. D	76. B	96. A	116. B	136. E
17. E	37. A	57. E	77. B	97. E	117. D	137. B
18. B	38. B	58. E	78. E	98. E	118. B	138. E
19. E	39. D	59. A	79. D	99. A	119. D	139. A
20. E	40. D	60. E	80. C	100. A	120. C	140. D

Answers and Explanations

1. (C)

All of these poets would probably be categorized as post-modernists. All the poets listed are from the second half of the twentieth century.

2. (B)

Schoenberg invented twelve-tone composition, an approach that rejected conventional tonality and harmony. Note the use of the word "modern," a hint toward the time period the composer lived in. Choices (A), (C), and (D) are earlier composers, while (E) is a cellist.

3. (A)

Stevens was never particularly concerned with society in general, only with ideas and the nexus of reality and the imagination. Issues of socialism (B), poverty (C), women's issues (D), and science (E) were not important to him. Stevens lived from 1879–1955, and produced such works as "Sea Surface Full of Clouds."

4. (D)

A prelude (A) is a musical introduction to a drama or composition, while an epilogue (B) is a concluding part of a literary work. A prologue (C) occurs at the beginning of a literary work, and an overtone (E) is a harmonic tone.

5. (B)

The Petrarchan (or Italian) sonnet is slightly different than a Shakespearean (or English) sonnet. An Italian sonnet contains fourteen lines and two stanzas. The first stanza is composed of eight lines and the second stanza is composed of six lines. None of the other poets listed are noted for writing sonnets.

6. (A)

In Joyce's *Ulysses*, the character Leopold Bloom wanders the streets of Dublin for an entire day before returning to his wife Molly. None of the other stories takes place in Dublin.

7. (E)

Paterson is a town in New Jersey by the Passaic Falls and is the name of a main character in the work. None of the other answer choices takes place in New Jersey.

8. (C)

Pound's *Cantos* is an homage to the Italian Bard (poet). It is patterned after a work by Dante, who lived in the thirteenth century.

9. (B)

Goethe was the quintessential Romantic poet. The rest are all far distant from their corresponding time periods.

10. (A)

Smith, Arp, and Nevelson are from the twentieth century. Praxiteles, Phidias, and the sculptor of *The Laocoon Group* are ancient Greek artists (B), while the group of Bernini, Coysevox, and Fernandez (E) worked in the seventeenth century. See explanations for questions 11 and 12 for the periods of other artists mentioned.

11. (C)

Michelangelo, Donatello, and Ghiberti (C) are from the fifteenth century. See explanations for questions 10 and 12 for the periods of other artists mentioned.

12. (D)

Rodin, Canova, and Daumier are from the nineteenth century. See explanations for questions 10 and 11 for the periods of other artists mentioned.

13. (C)

Jackson Pollock is most famous for his "drip" paintings. Pollock was the first "all-over" painter, forgoing the use of a palette and brushes, using his hands and movement to create works of art.

14. (B)

Pollock was revolutionary in his consideration of process, placing as much emphasis on "how" the work was produced as on the final product. The entire process of creating a work involved action on the part of Pollock, while pouring, dripping, and splashing paint over canvasses.

15. (D)

The "action painting" movement got underway in the 1950s. Never before had action painting been practiced and viewed as a form of acceptable art.

16. (C)

Miss Havisham, Pip, and Estella are three of the most notable characters in all of Dickens' work. The other novels do not contain a jilted bride grown old, nor do they contain characters with these names.

17. (E)

In *Othello*, Iago is the ultimate villain who entangles Cassio, Desdemona, and Othello in a purported love triangle which brings about the demise of all but Cassio. The other choices appear in *Hamlet* (A), *King Lear* (B), *Troilus and Cressida* (C), and *Timon of Athens* (D).

18. (B)

Walt Whitman lived from 1819–1892, prior to the twentieth century. Although Yeats (A) had a career that straddled two centuries, and he can be considered both a Victorian and a modern poet, the bulk of his most famous work was created after the turn of the century. Crane (C), Plath (D), and Moore (E) all created work during the twentieth century.

19. (E)

Like Williams' *Paterson* and Pound's *Cantos*, Whitman's *Leaves of Grass* (B) and Crane's *The Bridge* (C) are indicative of the epic or lofty ambitions of modern poets. In contrast, Moore (E) traces her lineage back to Emily Dickinson. While Plath's (D) poems are similarly thoughtful, they are self-reflexive.

20. (E)

The Canterbury Tales is a collection of medieval tales by author Geoffrey Chaucer. The *Tales* are written in Middle English verse. *Moll Flanders* (A) is a novel by Daniel Defoe, *The Flowers of Evil* (B) is a book of poems by Baudelaire, *The Sorrows of Young Werther* (C) is a novel by Johann Wolfgang Goethe, and *One Hundred Years of Solitude* is a novel by Gabriel Garcia Marquez.

21. (D)

Degas' chief preoccupations were horse racing and the ballet. You would be least likely to find a Greek god in one of Degas' paintings, since a choreographer (B) and a jockey (E) have to do with ballet and horse racing, respectively.

22. (A)

The "Fugitives" were in favor of a more colloquial, idyllic verse. They were poets of the American South.

23. (A)

Aristotle suggested that for a successful tragedy, the protagonist must have a tragic flaw that causes his downfall. For many centuries in the arts, the term "tragic flaw" has been applied to figures from Othello to Jay Gatsby. While some classic heroes may have humility (B), good fortune, (C) brains but no physical strength (D), or a comical sidekick (E), these qualities and instances are not found in *Oedipus Rex*.

24. (A)

The aforementioned are Yeats' most notable works and could not have been written by any of the other choices, except perhaps Whitman. Yeats lived from 1865–1939 and was an Irish dramatist and prose writer, as well as poet.

25. (A)

This painting by Raphael is representative of the Renaissance's fascination with classical Greek art, literature, and philosophy. *Las Meninas* (B) was painted by Diego Velazquez in 1656. *Embarkation to the Island of Cythera* (C) is a French Rococo painting, created in 1717 by Jean-Antoine Watteau. *Guernica* (D) is a modern antiwar statement, painted in 1937 by Pablo Picasso. *The Fountainhead* (E) is a novel by Ayn Rand.

26. (B)

Picasso, Gris, and Braque all worked to bring Cubism into prominence. Other artists listed who followed the Cubists may have been influenced by Cubist techniques, but would not be considered strictly Cubists.

Section Four: The CLEP Humanities Exam
Practice Test 3 Answers and Explanations

27. (C)
This book is one of the first novels to come under the rubric "magical realism." Marquez was Colombia's most famous writer, and was granted a Nobel Prize in Literature.

28. (E)
"Full length" always means an evening-long piece with at least one pause and one intermission. There are three acts in a full-length ballet.

29. (A)
David and Delacroix are seminal artistic figures in the Romantic period while the contemporaries listed are historical, literary, and philosophical figures. The other choices listed lived and worked during different time periods.

30. (A)
While Dickens did write many long novels and often published them as serial chapters in magazines, his lean masterpiece, "A Christmas Carol," is now considered a novella or short novel. The story is retold on stage every year at Christmas.

31. (D)
Though *The Cherry Orchard's* bleak outlook on life is characteristic of O'Neill, it is the most famous work of the Russian playwright, Anton Chekhov. All of the other choices are plays written by O'Neill. Eugene O'Neill was the winner of the 1936 Nobel Prize in Literature and lived from 1888–1953.

32. (A)
The standard full-length play usually contains five (though occasionally four or three) acts. If a play had only one act (E), by definition it would be considered a one-act play, rather than a full-length play.

33. (A)
Salvador Dali and Rene Magritte were the most prominent artists of the Surrealist movement. Louis and Klein (B) were predominantly Color Field painters and the rest were long dead by the advent of surrealism.

34. (B)
The title of "thespian" is usually reserved for serious stage actors, but is occasionally used for actors in general. A cooper (A) is a person who makes wooden barrels, an aesthete (C) is a person who highly admires beauty, an angler (D) is someone who is scheming or who fishes with a hook, and a chandler (E) is a person who sells or makes candles.

35. (C)
Only Moliere is matched with the correct play—he wrote *The Misanthrope*. Dario Fo is the author of *Accidental Death of an Anarchist* (A), Shakespeare created *Twelfth Night* (B), *The Infernal Machine* is by Jean Cocteau (D), and Jean Giaudoux wrote *Tiger at the Gates* (E).

36. (B)
The French composer Maurice Ravel (1875–1937) wrote *Bolero*. *Bolero* later became infamous when it was used as the theme music for the movie *10* in 1979.

37. (A)
Fountain is an example of a found object. Not to be confused with novice art (C) or mock-primitive art, the piece is an example of the artist's taking something found in everyday life and attributing artistic value to it. Rotogravure (B) is an Intaglio printing process, Surrealism (D) was a twentieth century artistic and literary movement, and Neoclassicism (E) is a revival of classical forms and aesthetics.

38. (B)
The piece is satirical. Duchamp was thumbing his nose at the art world and its rigid notions of what constituted "art."

39. (D)
R. Mutt was another name for Marcel Duchamp. Duchamp was the quintessential Dadaist. While a few of the other choices have playful elements in their work, none would likely present a toilet as "art."

40. (D)
Praxiteles and Phidias were ancient Greek sculptors while Euripides and Aeschylus were ancient Greek dramatists. None of the others were close contemporaries of Praxiteles and Phidias.

41. (C)

While Baroque style (B) has a peripheral relationship to classical art, Romanesque style is named for its Roman lineage. The Romantic era (A), Rococo (D), and postmodern (C) do not date back to the Roman empire.

42. (B)

Mondrian's work used simple colors and geometric shapes in a spare yet mesmerizing form. Georges de la Tour (E) predated Mondrian's work by several centuries, and while some of the other painters worked at roughly the same time as Mondrian, they all had greatly different styles.

43. (C)

Although there were many artists and artisans involved in programs at Bauhaus, the architectural school was the most famous. Poets (A), composers (B), musicians (D), and literary critics (E) came out of Bauhaus, but the school was predominantly known for architecture.

44. (E)

While he may have painted a portrait or two in his younger years, Kandinsky is known for his work in Abstract Expressionism. The first three options are almost exclusively portrait artists, while Modigliani's most famous pieces are his portraits with elongated faces.

45. (A)

Seurat and Toulouse-Latrec were working at the cusp of modernism. Debussy was perhaps the first great modern composer and Hardy had one career as a Victorian novelist and a second as a quasi-modern poet.

46. (C)

William Wordsworth was considered to have initiated English Romantic poetry, along with Samuel Coleridge. Sylvia Plath (A) was an American poet who lived during the twentieth century. Thoreau (B) was American as well, and although he lived during the Romantic era, he was a Transcendentalist. Virginia Woolf (D) was British but was a novelist who lived during the twentieth century. Shakespeare (E) was British also but lived during the sixteenth century.

47. (B)

Nature was at the center of Romantic poetry. Romantic poetry did not focus on war (A), taxation without representation (D), or Britain's relationship with America (E). Although relationships (C) can sometimes be found in Romantic poetry, nature is the main focus of Wordsworth's poetry, as shown at the beginning of the excerpt.

48. (B)

William Wordsworth wrote this poem in 1833 on an excursion to his son's house by the sea at Moresby. The poem is called "Composed by the Seashore" and can be found in Wordsworth's "Evening Voluntaries."

49. (E)

Rosencrantz and Guildenstern Are Dead is basically Shakespeare's *Hamlet* viewed from the perspective of Rosencrantz and Guildenstern (two minor characters who get caught up in the tragic twists of plot). The play is not as famous or acclaimed as *Hamlet*, as it was written in the twentieth century.

50. (D)

Whitman's work is neither esoteric (A) nor classical (B), nor compact (C). Whitman also does not express a dark, Kafkaesque appraisal of the new America in his poems (E).

51. (D)

Malevich was the progenitor of Suprematism. He employed single or dual colors to put forth simplistic paintings which tried to convey a sense of perfection and completion. Minimalists trace their roots to his work. Malevich was not part of any of the other artistic movements.

52. (A)

In Kurosawa's screenplay, Shakespeare's three daughters become three sons. Other characters such as the Fool also occupy central roles, aiding our understanding of the protagonist's descent into madness. "Ran" literally means "chaos."

53. (D)

The other answer choices are all particularly coherent poets.

54. (A)

Milton's *Paradise Lost* is written in blank verse: unrhymed iambic pentameter. While heroic couplets (C) are another form of iambic pentameter, they consist of sets of two rhyming lines. Alexander Pope frequently used this form. Free verse (D) has no rhyme or meter, while answers (B) and (E) represent different metrical patterns.

55. (C)

The eighteenth century was the age of Newton, the era of science and logic (also known as the Age of Reason). Traditional religious and aesthetic ideas were turned upside down, provoking a reaction in the nineteenth century. Galileo and Copernicus were key advocates of science in previous centuries, but they did not so thoroughly affect the ethos of their eras.

56. (D)

Queen Victoria ruled for over half a century, dying in 1901. There were some novelists (though few poets) still writing in the Victorian mode in the twentieth century, but the period is considered to last only as long as Victoria's reign.

57. (E)

Isadora Duncan virtually created the free-flowing movements that we know as modern dance. While Suzanne Farrell (B) is a tempting choice, she was a great ballerina, not a modern dancer.

58. (E)

Rilke was born in the nineteenth century but published the bulk of his work in the twentieth. *The Duino Elegies* strive to determine the meaning of humanity in the modern world.

59. (A)

Robert Lowell wrote "The Quaker Graveyard in Nantucket." (B), (C), (D), and (E) were respectively written by Blake, Bridges, Stevens, and Rimbaud.

60. (E)

Maya Deran performed every major production task on *Meshes of the Afternoon*. The film established the independent avant-garde film movement in the United States. All the other experimental filmmakers listed came after Deran.

61. (C)

Lichtenstein was a Pop Artist who tested the boundaries of artistic material by blowing up images from comic strips. The American artist lived from 1923–1997.

62. (A)

"Tabula Rasa" roughly translates as "blank tablet" and characterizes Locke's theory that the human mind begins in a pristine state and is the complete product of its environment. John Locke is not responsible for any of the other philosophical theories listed.

63. (B)

Vermeer's paintings are most concerned with the effects of shadow and light. The other options are not associated at all with this great artist.

64. (D)

There are no primary texts of Socrates. All of his work was passed on through his student, Plato. Archimedes was a student of Plato at the Academy in Greece.

65. (B)

Cezanne painted a local mountain from several different perspectives at different times of day. Monet had worked with haystacks (A) earlier on and worked with the Rouen Cathedral (A) in a similar way. Phillip Guston used the boot sole (E) as the central symbol of his work.

66. (A)

Vendler, Derrida, Bloom, and Kristeva are all literary critics. Answer (B) is a group of composers, answer (C) is a group of assassins, answer (D) includes portrait painters, and answer (E) comprises sculptors.

67. (D)

Each person was a prominent landscape painter in England, America, and France respectively. None of the other choices were facets of the painters' work.

68. (E)

Also known as "falling action," "denouement" refers to the post-crisis period in which the novel winds down. The denouement is not found in the prologue (A), which is at the beginning of a novel, the opening paragraph (B), the climax (C), or the middle (D).

69. (C)

Johns was one of many experimental American artists trying to present new perspectives on old symbols. Flags and targets had been subjects of art for a long time, but Johns tried to paint them differently. None of the other choices concerned Jasper Johns.

70. (B)

The protagonist of this novel is an alcoholic. The story revolves around the protagonist's drunken reveries and waking delusions, which eventually degrade into a desperate situation. The main character is not a bullfighter (A), a princess (C), a fireman (D), or a cancer patient (E).

71. (A)

Ensemble music for voices and instruments is called a concerto. While the other choices are musical terms, only "concerto" refers to ensemble music for both voices and musical instruments.

72. (E)

Expounded by John Stuart Mill and later picked up by John Dewey and William James, this philosophical approach wanted to do away with the fruitless questions philosophers had been asking for millennia and address practical questions about life. Utilitarianism involved asking questions that mattered to everyday functioning.

73. (C)

Berkeley was a prominent empiricist who believed that only perceptions are experienced, and experience is the source of most knowledge. His ideas are often compared to fellow empiricist John Locke.

74. (B)

Continental philosophy refers to European (especially German) philosophy's tendency toward involved, complex, and cerebral theories in contrast to those of Anglo-Americans' pragmatic, logical empiricism. This is a distinction of predominance rather than an absolute classification.

75. (C)

A novella is a relatively new distinction given to what used to be called a short novel or long short story. An epic (A) and a saga (B) are often much longer than 120 pages. A ballad and a sestina are poetic forms much shorter than 120 pages. A sestina contains six stanzas of six lines and one envoy of three lines.

76. (B)

An extended work for an orchestra is known as a symphony. Beethoven was considered to be the "Master of the Symphony."

77. (B)

In the novel, the dead child comes back as a ghost and torments the house's inhabitants. The child was the "beloved" person in the house, hence the name of the novel.

78. (E)

Soprano is the highest female voice and the highest voice in a polyphonic texture. Alto (A) is a lower female voice. Bass (C) is the lowest male voice, while tenor (B) is the highest male voice. A virtuoso (D) is a person highly skilled in the arts.

79. (D)

"Fallingwater" is the name of a home built by Frank Lloyd Wright. The building is masterfully integrated with its landscape. None of the other choices refer to "Fallingwater."

80. (C)

Five lines are used to write music on a staff. On the treble staff, the lines in ascending order correspond to the musical notes E, G, B, D, and F, with F being the highest.

81. (B)

1922 is considered by most critics to have been the advent of modernism in literature, which "The Waste Land" and *Ulysses* exemplify.

82. (A)

"Swing" is a name for big-band jazz music from the 1930s and 1940s. The name is derived from the "swinging" rhythms of the band.

83. (E)

George Frideric Handel lived from 1685–1759, in the Baroque period. All the other composers are from the Romantic era.

84. (D)

The Grapes of Wrath was published in 1939. The book and film concern a family of dispossessed farmers migrating to California across the Dust Bowl of the Southwest during the Depression. The other choices listed are other films directed by John Ford.

85. (B)

A fugue is a composition in which the theme is developed mainly by an imitative counterpoint. "Stanza" (C) is a poetic term. A madrigal (D) is a work for several voices featuring a poetic text. The form dates from the Middle Ages and Renaissance. Fandango (E) is music accompanying a Spanish-American triple-time dance.

86. (D)

Francois Truffaut made the films *The 400 Blows*, *Jules and Jim*, and *The Last Metro*. The other filmmakers listed were also important directors of the French New Wave.

87. (B)

Emile Zola wrote *Germinal*. The other novels were written by George Eliot (A), Charles Dickens (C), Gustave Flaubert (D), and J.K. Huysmans (E).

88. (A)

One of Johann Sebastian Bach's sons, Karl Philipp Emanuel Bach, helped create the piano sonata in 1744. Wolfgang Amadeus Mozart gave us the violin sonata as we know it today.

89. (B)

These films, characterized by a downbeat atmosphere and graphic violence, carried postwar American pessimism to the point of nihilism by assuming the absolute irredeemable corruption of society and everyone in it. Billy Wilder's corrosive *Double Indemnity* may be regarded as the prototypical film noir. The other time periods did not involve film noir.

90. (C)

Raskolnikov is sent to a prison camp in Siberia where he must begin to redeem himself. Dostoyevsky based the novel on his own experiences of serving time at a Russian prison camp.

91. (D)

Nikolai Gogol's *Dead Souls* was a landmark work and led the great Russian novelists of the nineteenth century to describe him as "the father of us all." Great Russian novelists at the time included Dostoyevsky, Tolstoy, Turgenev, etc.

92. (D)

All three were architects. Mies van der Rohe was closely associated with the minimalist Bauhaus school. Gehry and Le Corbusier were known for their highly original, stylistic structures.

93. (A)

An "aside" is a line spoken for the benefit of the audience, understood to be unheard by the other characters onstage. The term is not used in poetry (B), ballet (C), architecture (D), or philosophy (E).

94. (D)

Both terms are used in architecture. An "architrave" is the lowest division of an entablature and a "flying buttress" is a kind of support.

95. (B)

Koestler's narrative described the real-life terrors of Communism. In the book, the narrator is awaiting an execution, a common occurrence during Communist rule.

96. (A)

The "picture" or portrait of Dorian Gray ages and grows more and more grotesque with every sin he commits, while Dorian's youthful good looks remain untouched by time. None of the other choices apply. In "The Metamorphosis" by Franz Kafka, the main character turns into a cockroach (D).

97. (E)

Edward Hopper was born in the United States. Francis Bacon (A) was born in England, Berthe Morisot (B) was born in France, and El Greco (C) spent most of his career in Spain, but was born in Greece, hence the nickname "El Greco." Titian (D) was born in Italy.

98. (E)

Doctor Zhivago was written by the Russian poet, Boris Pasternak. All of the other novels were written by Fyodor Dostoyevsky.

99. (A)

Bach is the only one of the choices who lived and worked during the Baroque era. Haydn (B) and Mozart (C) are from the Classical era, while Wagner (D) and Brahms (E) are from the Romantic era. Bach is also the only one who worked as an organist.

100. (A)

Henri Matisse was the most notable member of the Fauvist movement, which advocated bright colors and (to the critic's eye) savage imagery. The impact of Fauvism on other disciplines was minimal.

101. (B)

While most subsequent poets have at least acknowledged the validity of free verse (poetry without fixed rhyme or meter), Frost saw it as an excuse for sloppiness. He preferred more structured forms of poetry.

102. (D)

John Cage was a twentieth-century composer who began the avant-garde music movement. Barber (B), Williams (C), and Wagner (A) were all composers, but did not participate in this movement. Willem de Kooning (E) was a twentieth-century painter.

103. (A)

Parker's stories are exercises in irony and sardonic humor. Dorothy Parker, an American poet and writer of short stories, was born in 1893 and died in 1967. Her poetic volumes include *Enough Rope* and *Sunset Gun.*

104. (A)

Dorothea made a name for himself in the Depression years by capturing the despair and resilience of Americans in their darkest age. Del Sarto (B) was an artist, Fuller (C) was an architect, Duncan (D) was a dancer, and Barnes (E) was an author.

105. (C)

"Lieder" literally means "song" in German. It was a popular form in the nineteenth century.

106. (C)

Matthew Brady's war-camp photographs compose the earliest body of work in what was then a new medium. Stieglitz (A) and Adams (B) were twentieth-century photographers. Edith Wharton (E) was a novelist and Edouard Vuillard (D) was a French Post-Impressionist/Nabi painter.

107. (D)

The film *The Third Man* was based on a novel by Graham Greene. Greene was a British author of the twentieth century whose novels involve mysterious plot twists and penetrate the psychological crises of the protagonist.

108. (E)

Gauguin (A) was a contemporary and for a short time a close friend of Vincent van Gogh, but he is not in the portrait. Van Gogh created many self-portraits over the course of his career.

109. (D)

This self-portrait is one of many Van Gogh painted over the course of his tortured life. A portrait (E) could be a painting of anyone and is not as specific as answer (D). A still life (A) is a painting of inanimate objects, such as fruit and a vase of flowers. A landscape (B) is a painting of the countryside, and a fresco (C) is a painting on plaster created with dissolved pigments.

110. (C)

Van Gogh was the foremost artist (retrospectively) in the move away from Impressionism toward more Expressionist art. He was a member of the Post-Impressionist movement, but not any of the other movements listed.

111. (A)

Prospero is the wizard banished to an island with his daughter Miranda in *The Tempest*. He is a more serious character, not a comic figure such as Puck (E) in *A Midsummer Night's Dream*.

112. (A)
Momaday's novel is one of the first award-winning novels written by a Native American. The main character does not represent any of the other choices.

113. (A)
The sculptures from this age all display the human form as athletic, muscular, and in perfect proportion. The sculptures of humans are idealistic, but not understated (B), ambivalent (C), ironic (D), or modest (E).

114. (E)
The key word in this question is "ancient." All the other periods occurred long after what is considered ancient.

115. (E)
Eroica was written in honor of Napoleon, but Beethoven removed Napoleon's name from the composition in disgust after Napoleon declared himself emperor.

116. (B)
Nude Descending a Staircase was the most notable painting displayed at the famous Armory show just prior to World War I.

117. (D)
"The Colonel" is a poem that relates an incident with a particularly brutal Colonel in El Salvador. Forche is a prominent late twentieth-century poet who, like many of her fellow postmodernists, is most concerned with sociopolitical realities.

118. (B)
A libretto is the script that goes along with the music in opera.

119. (D)
Little Nell's death at the conclusion of *The Old Curiosity Shop* is one of the most pathos-evoking scenes in all of literature. In the Dostoyevsky (C) and Wharton (E) novels, the main characters meet bad endings but survive.

120. (C)
Along with Kurt Vonnegut, these two authors are the most notable writers in the genre of science fiction. They are not associated with the Romantic movement (A) (which occured well before the twentieth century), the painting style of Naturalism (B), author Robert Browning (D), or absurdist drama (E).

121. (A)
Warhol's paintings of soup cans, movie stars, and political figures reproduced with slight modifications took the art world in a new direction in the middle of the twentieth century. Since Warhol did not focus on nature, you are not likely to find trees and peasants (B), or rocks and hawks (C), in his work. Warhol did not include horses and Napoleon (D), or sides of beef and Pope Urban II (E) in his work.

122. (D)
The painting is *Nighthawks* by Edward Hopper. Hopper's main concern was with a distinctly American loneliness. He painted scenes in desolate, depressed areas to show the futility and emptiness of the American Dream.

123. (B)
Hopper chose particularly barren, soulless scenes to portray the emptiness in the American Dream. His work was not tense (A), light-hearted (C), violent (D), or comical (E).

124. (D)
Among the work of American artists, Edward Hopper's paintings are perhaps the most easily identifiable due to the uniformity of his subject matter. Hopper chiefly uses American scenes of desolation in his work. In contrast, Georgia O'Keefe (C) primarily painted flowers.

125. (A)
Conrad's work delves into the machinations of colonial tyrants and corrupted natives. He studies the facets of power, corruption, and evil in novels such as *Heart of Darkness*. None of the other choices apply to Conrad's work.

126. (C)
"Main character" and "protagonist" are two terms that are generally interchangeable. "Deus ex machina" (A) refers to an unexpected character or plot device to solve a situation in a drama or fiction. A thespian (B) is a person who acts in plays, comic relief (D) presents a light-hearted moment, scene, or character for the audience of a play, and a bridge (E) is found in some string instruments as a thin, upright piece of wood.

127. (C)
Benvenuto Cellini's autobiography is read both as a great work in the genre as well as a means of examining the Renaissance through the eyes of one of its most prominent sculptors.

128. (A)
Turner's depictions of storms and sunsets at sea were a prelude to the Impressionist movement. Rarely will you find a Turner painting set elsewhere.

129. (C)
The line of text contains the name of the novel's title character, "Mrs. Dalloway." The novel was written by English writer Virginia Woolf in 1925 and covers the thoughts of several people during a single day.

130. (B)
The Barber of Seville (B) was written in 1816. *Don Giovanni* (A) was written by Wolfgang Amadeus Mozart, *Orfeo* (C) was composed by Claudio Monteverdi, *Die Freischutz* (D) was written by Carl Maria von Weber, and *Aida* (E) was written by Guiseppi Verdi.

131. (A)
V.S. Naipaul's books are mostly set in Africa and describe the relationship between natives and immigrants. Naipaul won the Nobel Prize in Literature in 2001, and he is considered the leading novelist of the Caribbean today.

132. (B)
Multiple first-person points of view are given in this novel. The story is told from one perspective and then retold from the point of view of other characters.

133. (D)
Gore Vidal is a noted novelist, critic, and historian and considered by many to be the foremost "man of letters" in the United States. None of the other authors was born in the United States.

134. (B)
Oliver Goldsmith was a British author of humorous novels in the eighteenth century. All the other authors published work in the twentieth century.

135. (A)
The film *The English Patient* (1996) was based on the novel by Michael Ondaatje. The Sri Lankan-born author's novel *The English Patient* magnifies the personal to coexist with the historical.

136. (E)
Thurber's modus operandi is satirizing certain kinds of people and social (or political) situations. His tone is lighthearted in works such as *My Life and Hard Times*. James Thurber is a twentieth-century author.

137. (B)
The Ayatollah Khomeini of Iran called for Rushdie's death in response to what he felt was the author's disrespectful treatment of the prophet Muhammad. *The Satanic Verses* was published in 1988.

138. (E)
Both Rothko and Chagall were persecuted by the Stalinist regime and exiled to the United States and France respectively. Rothko was an Abstract Expressionist, while Chagall was a stained-glass artist and painter.

139. (A)
While Yeats was widely traveled, he was always associated with the Irish landscape and political strife, whereas Shaw spent most of his life in England and is today considered to be an English satirist.

140. (D)
Rush and Coetzee are expatriates to Africa and Achebe is a native. Kingsolver has traveled to the continent, though she never actually visited the country in which her novel is set.

| SECTION FIVE |

The CLEP Social Sciences and History Exam

Chapter Sixteen: Practice Test 1: Diagnostic

Time—90 minutes
120 Questions

Directions: For each of the following questions or incomplete statements, select the best answer or completion from the five options given.

1. The part of the brain associated with balance, smooth movement, and posture is

   (A) the hypothalamus
   (B) the temporal lobe
   (C) the cerebral hemisphere
   (D) the cerebellum
   (E) more highly developed in older adults than in adolescents

2. Which of the following statements about the evolution of island species is true?

   (A) On islands, native species will die out due to the lack of genetic diversity.
   (B) Because of their isolation, islands will have relatively few endemic species.
   (C) Islands will have more endangered species due to a high rate of endemism.
   (D) Hawaii has fewer endangered species than any other state.
   (E) Native island species benefit from the introduction of foreign wildlife.

3. Which world leaders are most closely linked with bringing about the end of Soviet domination in Eastern Europe?

   (A) Ronald Reagan, Margaret Thatcher, Pope John Paul II
   (B) Jimmy Carter, Margaret Thatcher, Pope John Paul II
   (C) Ronald Reagan, Leonid Brezhnev, Pope John Paul II
   (D) Jimmy Carter, Anwar Sadat, Menachim Begin
   (E) George H. W. Bush, Margaret Thatcher, Tony Blair

4. The Egyptian president assassinated by radicals in his own country for making peace overtures toward Israel was

   (A) Menachim Begin
   (B) Hosni Muborak
   (C) Gamal Nasser
   (D) Hafez al Asad
   (E) Anwar Sadat

GO ON TO THE NEXT PAGE

5. Supply-side economics holds that lowering taxes

   (A) causes higher interest rates because of excess consumption
   (B) leads to recession because the government will have less money to spend
   (C) increases unemployment because of lowered demand for goods and services
   (D) causes the economy to expand because consumers have more money to spend
   (E) causes the Federal Reserve to lower the money supply

6. Which of these statements would the Luddites have agreed with?

   (A) Advances in technology are always good for society.
   (B) It is more important to preserve jobs than to produce lower-priced goods.
   (C) Taxation without representation is tyranny.
   (D) Trade with all other nations benefits all parties.
   (E) Mass-produced goods are preferable to individually created goods.

7. What is the deepest lake in the world?

   (A) Great Salt Lake
   (B) Lake Biwa
   (C) Lake Superior
   (D) Lake Victoria
   (E) Lake Baikal

8. The names "Johanson" and "Lucy" will forever be associated. What is their relationship?

   (A) Johanson discovered Lucy, the oldest known human ancestor.
   (B) Johanson cloned a sheep he nicknamed Lucy.
   (C) Lucy was Johanson's first wife and the author of Coming of Age in Samoa.
   (D) They were husband-wife paleontologists.
   (E) They were father-daughter archaeologists.

9. What are subduction zones?

   (A) areas where the temperature is lower than freezing for the majority of the year
   (B) regions with less than 10" of rain each year
   (C) areas where tectonic plates collide and slide under one another
   (D) areas where the ice caps are melting, causing the flooding of nearby lands
   (E) places where there is abnormal electromagnetic activity possibly due to sunspots

10. The term "Gilded Age" refers to what era of American history?

    (A) It comes from a Mark Twain novel and alludes to the outwardly showy but inwardly corrupt nature of American society in the late 1800s.
    (B) It was coined by F. Scott Fitzgerald to describe the decadent days of the "flappers" and "bootleggers."
    (C) It is an ironic term referring to the dark days after the stock market crash on Black Friday.
    (D) It was completely rejected by the "Beat Generation" as an inaccurate characterization of their intellectual movement.
    (E) It was Hemingway's term for the glamorous heyday of the expatriates in the early twentieth century.

11. Which of the following are methodologies used to study social groups?

    I. experiments
    II. surveys
    III. cross-cultural comparison

    (A) I only
    (B) II only
    (C) III only
    (D) I and II only
    (E) I, II, and III

12. In which of the following geographic features is a canal likely to be found?

    (A) archipelago
    (B) isthmus
    (C) cape
    (D) island
    (E) valley

13. Tornadoes occur when

    (A) there is lightening in the area
    (B) cool and warm air collide, forcing the warm air to rise rapidly
    (C) earthquakes on the ocean floor cause huge tidal waves
    (D) warm air blows debris over a wide area
    (E) barometric pressure rises from 900 to 1000 millibars

14. Which country is composed of the most islands?

    (A) Indonesia
    (B) Fiji
    (C) Japan
    (D) Malaysia
    (E) Philippines

15. The Great Wall of China was built

    (A) to repel potential invaders from the north
    (B) to prevent Chinese citizens from escaping
    (C) in the mistaken belief that it would keep out the plague
    (D) to prevent traders from bringing in goods without paying tariffs
    (E) to keep prisoners busy so they would not rebel

16. According to the map of Africa below, which of these countries is NOT labeled correctly?

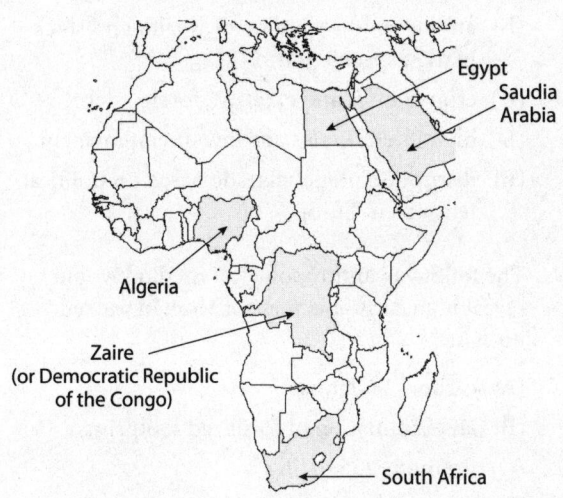

    (A) Zaire (or Democratic Republic of the Congo)
    (B) Egypt
    (C) Saudi Arabia
    (D) South Africa
    (E) Algeria

17. What was the name of Leningrad prior to 1924?

    (A) Moscow
    (B) Warsaw
    (C) St. Petersburg
    (D) Minsk
    (E) Kiev

18. What were the precipitating causes of the Great Depression?

    (A) World War II and a hard winter
    (B) an uneven distribution of wealth and stock market speculation
    (C) crop failures and excessive foreign debt
    (D) high interest rates and low unemployment
    (E) disruption of global trade based on political tensions in Europe

19. The following anthropological method would reveal if an early ape, man, or woman walked upright:

    (A) carbon-14 dating
    (B) an examination of fossilized footprints
    (C) uranium-235 dating
    (D) discovery of sticks near humanoid skeletons
    (E) process of elimination

20. In his Social Conflict theory, Karl Marx

    (A) proposed that the struggle between the "working class" and the "owner class" would result in a classless society
    (B) observed that class struggle inevitably leads to democracy
    (C) advocated suppression of the working class
    (D) anticipated the Solidarity movement
    (E) suggested that class struggle could be prevented

21. Chimpanzees are descended from an ancestor shared with the only hominid remaining today. What is the name of this contemporary hominid?

    (A) *Australopithecus robustus*
    (B) gorilla
    (C) *Homo sapiens sapiens*
    (D) orangutan
    (E) *Homo sapiens robustus*

22. Margaret Mead is best known for her work

    (A) focusing on adolescent boys in American Samoa
    (B) focusing on adolescent girls in British Samoa
    (C) with the elderly in New Guinea
    (D) on death and dying
    (E) focusing on adolescent girls in American Samoa

23. While aboard the *H.M.S. Beagle,* Charles Darwin developed his theory of

    (A) the origin of the cosmos
    (B) plate tectonics
    (C) evolution
    (D) natural rights
    (E) artificial selection

24. Which of the following statements about Ferdinand Magellan is true?

    (A) He discovered a land route to China.
    (B) He was commissioned by the Pope to prove that the earth was flat.
    (C) He sailed with the *Nina*, *Pinta*, and *Santa Maria*.
    (D) He sailed under the flag of England.
    (E) He was the first explorer to circumnavigate the globe.

25. Richard Milhouse Nixon was associated with what infamous organization that orchestrated the Watergate break-in?

    (A) The Quakers
    (B) The Labor Party
    (C) The Committee to Re-Elect the President
    (D) Whitewater
    (E) The Freemasons

GO ON TO THE NEXT PAGE

26. An earthquake would be least likely to occur in which geographic area?

    (A) the Sahara desert
    (B) California
    (C) France
    (D) Antarctica
    (E) Japan

27. What was the reason for the Twenty-sixth Amendment?

    (A) to abolish slavery
    (B) to limit the President to no more than two elected terms of office
    (C) to lower the voting age from twenty-one to eighteen
    (D) to repeal Prohibition
    (E) to prevent senators and representatives from voting for an immediate pay increase for themselves

28. Why do some economists prefer monetary policy over fiscal policy?

    (A) They believe monetary policy is less political and faster to implement.
    (B) They believe fiscal policy is less political.
    (C) They believe Congress is best suited to manage the economy.
    (D) Monetary policy is less likely to be overturned by the Supreme Court.
    (E) Monetary policy produces more concrete results.

29. Considered one of the "fathers of modern sociology," Emile Durkheim conceptualized

    (A) behaviorism
    (B) utilitarianism
    (C) the Oedipus complex
    (D) functionalism
    (E) survival of the fittest

30. Art, science, and philosophy flourished in Europe in the time following the Middle Ages. The name for this period, "Renaissance," is a French word that means

    (A) reason
    (B) related to the arts
    (C) relapse
    (D) reformation
    (E) rebirth

31. Which of the following statements is true about "socialization"?

    (A) Socialization is a static process.
    (B) Socialization begins at the close of enculturation.
    (C) Socialization is a lifelong process that begins at birth.
    (D) Those who are closest to us have the least effect on the socialization process.
    (E) Mass media is to blame for most alienation.

32. According to Max Weber,

    (A) division of labor is not necessary in a bureaucracy
    (B) society is characterized by status-quo maintenance
    (C) class struggle always leads to social harmony
    (D) social stratification is based solely on personal wealth
    (E) bureaucracies represent the ideal organization of large-scale modern societies

33. What is the difference between an archipelago and an atoll?

    (A) An archipelago is found in the Northern Hemisphere and an atoll in the Southern Hemisphere.
    (B) An archipelago is a chain of islands and an atoll is a ring of islands.
    (C) An archipelago is able to support only plant life, while an atoll can support plant and animal life.
    (D) An archipelago is natural and an atoll is man-made.
    (E) There is no difference.

34. Which of the following are symbolic components of culture?

    (A) values and norms
    (B) cultures and subcultures
    (C) folkways and mores
    (D) taboos and sanctions
    (E) language and gestures

35. Which of the following is true about deviance?

    (A) It always performs a negative function in society.
    (B) It sometimes performs a positive function in society.
    (C) It should never be encouraged or discouraged.
    (D) It is always a sign of societal dysfunction.
    (E) It operates independently of the wider society.

36. Which of the following explains the significance of Gresham's Law as it applied during the Great Depression?

    (A) During the Great Depression, people hoarded their money at home because they did not trust banks.
    (B) People were eager to trade their dollars for foreign currency because they thought it would hold its value better.
    (C) Congressman Gresham ordered the banks to remain open five days a week.
    (D) People held on to gold and spent paper money, causing the amount of gold in circulation to decline.
    (E) Simple bartering systems emerged to replace cash in day-to-day transactions.

37. The psychologist Erik Erikson is best known for his writings on

    (A) psychosocial development
    (B) class warfare
    (C) chaos theory
    (D) survival of the fittest
    (E) naval strategy

38. In her book, *On Death and Dying,*

    (A) Elizabeth Cady Stanton chronicles her husband's slow death from Alzheimer's
    (B) reincarnation and the afterlife are explored
    (C) Elizabeth Kubler-Ross introduces her theory about the stages of grief
    (D) Elizabeth Kubler-Ross debunks the stage theory of grief
    (E) Elizabeth Cady Stanton discusses the depression associated with dying

GO ON TO THE NEXT PAGE

39. Assuming that when we grow older we become less productive and examine our options for retired life, upon reaching this age

    (A) most people sink into irreversible depressions
    (B) our lives become increasingly less productive, therefore lacking in satisfaction
    (C) we long for social acceptance
    (D) we are able to develop integrity if we see ourselves as having led a successful life
    (E) despair and alienation are the most common experience

40. What was the significance of Richard Nixon's 1972 trip to China?

    (A) It was his first overseas trip.
    (B) He signed a peace treaty with Chairman Mao Tse-tung.
    (C) China agreed to withdraw from Hong Kong.
    (D) No American president had ever visited China before.
    (E) His cultural insensitivity increased tensions with China.

41. Whose victory at the Battle of Hastings in 1066 changed the culture of Great Britain?

    (A) Saladin
    (B) William of Normandy
    (C) Frederick the Great
    (D) Charlemagne
    (E) Attila the Hun

42. A country where all economic decisions are made by the government is best described as

    (A) socialist
    (B) capitalist
    (C) communist
    (D) fascist
    (E) totalitarian

43. The United States government is best described as a

    (A) monarchy
    (B) representative democracy
    (C) pure democracy
    (D) aristocracy
    (E) dictatorship

44. What was the argument against the creation of the Federal Reserve Bank?

    (A) It would give Congress too much power over monetary policy
    (B) It would be harder to open new banks
    (C) It would make it more difficult to implement fiscal policy
    (D) It would violate the system of checks and balances
    (E) It would concentrate power in the hands of Eastern bankers

45. The Federalist Papers are significant because

    (A) they contain the personal thoughts of George Washington, the nation's first president
    (B) they outline the manner in which our federal government should function
    (C) they outline basic rights and liberties reserved for the citizens of the United States
    (D) they provide the best insight into the framers' purposes in creating the Constitution
    (E) they lay out the civil liberties that members of a democracy enjoy

46. Which two adversaries did NOT sign a peace treaty at the end of World War II?

    (A) Japan and Italy
    (B) Japan and China
    (C) Russia and Japan
    (D) Germany and Italy
    (E) Canada and the United States

GO ON TO THE NEXT PAGE

47. Who created the American monetary system?

    (A) Aaron Burr
    (B) John Jay
    (C) James Madison
    (D) Alexander Hamilton
    (E) Thomas Jefferson

48. The purpose of the Electoral College is

    (A) to lengthen the election process, giving people longer to make up their minds
    (B) to involve additional parties in the electoral process, to prevent the likelihood of fraud
    (C) to give larger states more representation in the Electoral College
    (D) to give smaller states equal representation in the electoral process
    (E) to make sure every citizen's vote is counted

49. Which of the following is NOT a potential effect of global warming on worldwide food production?

    (A) Cold climates would be able to grow more food.
    (B) Hot climates would be able to grow less food.
    (C) Higher amounts of carbon dioxide in the atmosphere would have a fertilizing effect, aiding in agricultural production.
    (D) Weather prediction would be more difficult.
    (E) Demand for exotic ingredients would increase.

50. What did Andrew Carnegie, Cornelius Vanderbilt, and John D. Rockefeller have in common?

    (A) They opposed monopolies.
    (B) They married wealthy widows.
    (C) They were pro-Union.
    (D) They were known as "Robber Barons."
    (E) They were originally European royalty.

51. The Fall of Constantinople at the hands of the Turks resulted in

    (A) the defeat of Islam in the West
    (B) the rise of the Ottoman empire
    (C) the opening up of trade routes to the New World
    (D) the capture of Jerusalem
    (E) the conversion of millions of Muslims to Christianity

52. Lengthening the period of time a worker can collect unemployment benefits tends to

    (A) encourage job seekers to look harder for new jobs
    (B) make it harder for job seekers to find work
    (C) encourage illegal immigration
    (D) raise the unemployment rate
    (E) have no effect on the unemployment rate

53. Where in the United States Constitution does the phrase "separation of church and state" appear?

    (A) Article II, Section 1
    (B) The Bill of Rights
    (C) The Fifth Amendment
    (D) The First Amendment
    (E) These words do not appear in the Constitution

54. What is the "collective unconscious"?

    (A) Jung's name for knowledge passed automatically through generations
    (B) Freud's theory of human desires employed in dream analysis
    (C) A psychosocial memory that is encoded in DNA
    (D) An example of the negative effect of groupthink
    (E) An idea Freud introduced in opposition to Jung's theory of uniformity

GO ON TO THE NEXT PAGE

55. Which U.S. president said, "we have nothing to fear but fear itself" in response to enemy attacks on the United States?

    (A) Jimmy Carter
    (B) George W. Bush
    (C) Gerald Ford
    (D) Franklin D. Roosevelt
    (E) Ronald Reagan

56. The political party MOST likely to support lower taxes and less government spending is

    (A) the Democratic Party
    (B) the Green Party
    (C) the Republican Party
    (D) the Socialist Party
    (E) the Liberal Party

57. Presidents John F. Kennedy and Dwight D. Eisenhower are often held up as symbols of two radically different eras; which of the following is true?

    (A) Kennedy represents the prosperous, tranquil 1950s.
    (B) Kennedy himself was a product of the Eisenhower era and his policies are not necessarily as progressive as the Kennedy Myth maintains.
    (C) Eisenhower represents the turbulent, socially progressive 1950s.
    (D) Kennedy represents the socially and sexually repressive 1960s.
    (E) Eisenhower's policies are deceptively socialist in nature, advocating communal labor practices.

58. The Crusades were a series of wars

    (A) declared by Protestants on Catholics and Papal authority
    (B) initiated by Christians to win back their Holy Land from the Muslims
    (C) fought by the French and British for nearly one hundred years
    (D) fought between Jews and Palestinians over the Gaza Strip
    (E) initiated by Muslims to win back their Holy Land from the Christians

59. The term aboriginal typically applies to persons living in the

    (A) Gobi desert
    (B) south seas
    (C) western part of Africa
    (D) Australian outback
    (E) Amazon rainforest

60. Which country is the world's most populous democracy?

    (A) China
    (B) the United States
    (C) Russia
    (D) India
    (E) Japan

61. An example of a stateless people would be the

    (A) Kurds
    (B) Cambodians
    (C) Ethiopians
    (D) Panamanians
    (E) Irish

62. The Europeans were first interested in exploring Africa
    (A) because they wanted slaves to work in their colonies
    (B) because there were great sources of gold and diamonds
    (C) because Europe was becoming overpopulated and they needed new land to explore
    (D) to convert Africans to Christianity
    (E) because they were seeking a water route to India

63. In the stage of pre-contact,
    (A) societies are characterized by an openness to change
    (B) a primeval society has never encountered outsiders
    (C) an industrialized nation practices isolation
    (D) a primeval society aggressively pursues dominance
    (E) a society is not a part of the global technological revolution

64. What is the final stage of Freud's theory of psychosocial development?
    (A) anural stage
    (B) genital stage
    (C) Electra stage
    (D) oral stage
    (E) latency stage

65. Who is second in succession to the U.S. Presidency?
    (A) the secretary of state
    (B) the president pro tempore of the Senate
    (C) the vice president
    (D) the attorney general
    (E) the speaker of the House

66. The fertile crescent is known as
    (A) the cotton capital of the South
    (B) the breadbasket of Egypt
    (C) the cradle of civilization
    (D) the temple of the gods
    (E) the gateway to the east

67. World War I coincided with what other pivotal event in Russian history?
    (A) the breakup of the Balkan states
    (B) a return to feudalism and an agrarian lifestyle
    (C) the Russian potato famine
    (D) the Russian revolution, which ended the monarchy and brought Lenin to power
    (E) Stalin's rise to power and the beginning of a nascent democracy

68. Sir Isaac Newton's experiments and discoveries
    (A) led to a smallpox vaccination
    (B) allowed ships to sail around the world
    (C) led to today's scientists being able to design rockets
    (D) led to the discovery of microorganisms
    (E) allowed mapmakers to draw more accurate maps

69. Which skirmish was the final imperial struggle between the United States and Britain, leaving the Americans with undisputed control over their own destiny?
    (A) the Battle of Little Big Horn
    (B) the War of 1812
    (C) the Battle of Midway
    (D) the attack on Harper's Ferry
    (E) the Battle of Gettysburg

GO ON TO THE NEXT PAGE

70. Why do diamonds cost more than salt?

    (A) because there is more salt available on the earth than there are diamonds
    (B) because salt is necessary for human life, and diamonds are not
    (C) because salt is harder to mine than diamonds
    (D) because the price of salt is kept low by the government
    (E) because some countries export more diamonds than salt

71. The two variables represented by the Phillips curve are

    (A) interest rates and inflation
    (B) inflation and unemployment
    (C) aggregate supply and aggregate demand
    (D) price and quantity
    (E) money supply and money demand

72. What is the relationship between interest rates and inflation?

    (A) there is no relationship between interest rates and inflation
    (B) when interest rates fall, inflation rises
    (C) interest rates and inflation move in the same direction
    (D) when inflation falls, interest rates rise
    (E) there is not enough information given to answer

73. The Supreme Court decision *Brown v. Topeka Board of Education*

    (A) outlawed prayer in public schools
    (B) outlawed the practice of "separate but equal" education for minority children
    (C) forced public schools to stop saying the Pledge of Allegiance because of the words "under God"
    (D) forced public schools to offer equal athletics programs for girls
    (E) permitted the posting of the Ten Commandments in public schools

74. The social definition of a people based on cultural ties (such as language, dress, customs, and beliefs) is called

    (A) race
    (B) regionalism
    (C) social stratification
    (D) ethnicity
    (E) assimilation

75. Changing one's attitudes, beliefs, ways of thinking, or behavior in order to be more consistent with others is an example of

    (A) peer pressure
    (B) mimesis
    (C) disorientation
    (D) conditioning
    (E) conformity

76. Fiscal policy is implemented by

    (A) the Federal Reserve System
    (B) the Supreme Court
    (C) Congress
    (D) the Surgeon General
    (E) the FBI

77. The approach to researching societies known as cultural relativism

    (A) always involves an ethnocentric stance
    (B) is in stark contrast to ethnocentrism
    (C) views other cultures from the point of view of an individual's own values
    (D) never necessitates a suspension of judgment
    (E) involves family dynamics

GO ON TO THE NEXT PAGE

78. Which of the following is NOT a duty of the Federal Reserve System?

    (A) raising and lowering reserve requirements for member banks
    (B) examination and regulation of national banks
    (C) printing currency
    (D) setting the discount rate
    (E) keeping track of economic statistics

79. Which group of Americans was largely Republican in the years following the Civil War, but votes mostly Democratic today?

    (A) white men
    (B) women
    (C) African Americans
    (D) Hispanics
    (E) young adults

80. What was Winston Churchill referring to when he coined the phrase "the Iron Curtain"?

    (A) the rise of the communist party in China
    (B) ever-increasing government spending and the resulting budget deficit
    (C) the increasing industrialization of rural England
    (D) the military threat posed by a newly re-armed Germany
    (E) domination of Eastern Europe by the Soviet Union

81. Milton Friedman is the leading proponent of what school of economic thought?

    (A) supply-side economics
    (B) monetarism
    (C) Keynesism
    (D) socialism
    (E) fiscal policy

82. Which of the following statements is true in regards to the American construct of "Manifest Destiny"?

    (A) It was a phrase used by leaders and politicians to explain northward expansion
    (B) It expressed a sense of mission for many Americans to extend the boundaries of freedom and democracy
    (C) As the birth rate and immigration declined in the original thirteen colonies in the 1840s, continental expansion was not only desired but necessary
    (D) Frontier land was typically expensive but the overcrowding and disease of urban centers were bigger problems
    (E) Liberal racial policy offered uncommon opportunities for freed slaves

83. The suffrage movement resulted in

    (A) divorce rights for women
    (B) property rights for slaves
    (C) enfranchisement for women
    (D) voting rights for former slaves
    (E) the end of Prohibition

84. Which is true of crystallized intelligence?

    (A) It represents our acquired knowledge.
    (B) It is fluid in nature.
    (C) It refers to our ability to utilize acquired knowledge.
    (D) It is determined according to the Rorschach scale.
    (E) It represents our innate intelligence.

GO ON TO THE NEXT PAGE

85. Which is true of The New Deal?

    (A) It was Teddy Roosevelt's plan to put people back to work following the Great Depression.
    (B) It refers to the Pop Art movement popularized by Andy Warhol and Roy Lichtenstein.
    (C) It was a failed social program meant to force integration between whites and blacks in the rural South.
    (D) It opened up trade routes and reduced tariffs throughout North America in order to encourage free trade between Mexico, the United States, and Canada.
    (E) It included Franklin Delano Roosevelt's WPA projects, which put American artists to work on public arts projects.

86. Who was largely responsible for the Second Red Scare?

    (A) Joseph McCarthy
    (B) Vladimir Lenin
    (C) Benito Mussolini
    (D) Mikhail Gorbachev
    (E) Chairman Mao

87. The term "détente"

    (A) refers to the thawing out of international tension at the start of the Cold War
    (B) applies to the growing fear of nuclear holocaust after the Cold War
    (C) is a French term now typically used in reference to mounting Franco-American tension
    (D) refers to an accord established at the Geneva Convention
    (E) is usually associated with China, the Soviet Union, and the United States and refers to the relaxation of international tension

88. Which is true of *Uncle Tom's Cabin*?

    (A) It was heralded in the South and denounced in the North.
    (B) It was written by Catherine Beecher and advocated abolitionism.
    (C) It was a stop on the Underground Railroad.
    (D) It was not a cabin at all, but a mansion in Newport.
    (E) It was a bestselling book advocating emancipation.

89. The phenomenon in research where the subject's beliefs about the results of a study can significantly affect the outcome is known as

    (A) selection bias
    (B) the Moro reflex
    (C) the placebo effect
    (D) the Paracea effect
    (E) sample standard deviation

90. The Vikings were fierce warriors and skilled sailors who hailed from

    (A) Norway, Sweden, and Nova Scotia
    (B) Nova Scotia, the Ottoman empire, and Denmark
    (C) Norway, Sweden, and Denmark
    (D) Valhalla and Iceland
    (E) Greenland, Sweden, and Holland

91. The term "indentured servitude" refers to

    (A) a system of apprenticeship
    (B) written contracts between black immigrants and landholders
    (C) a common labor practice throughout the South today
    (D) an opportunity for refugees seeking political asylum
    (E) a system of importing servants to the New World

GO ON TO THE NEXT PAGE

92. One reason cartels can become unstable over time is that

    (A) countries will go to war over economic issues
    (B) buyers will stop buying if the prices are too high
    (C) when the goods are homogenous, the price will fall
    (D) people stop using drugs because they want to be healthier
    (E) a member will break with the cartel for individual gain

93. William Byrd was a gentleman planter who was educated in England and

    (A) whose sharp tongue landed him in jail after an argument with a colonial governor
    (B) whose detailed diaries are a valuable record of Southern colonial life
    (C) who founded a Utopian community in Virginia
    (D) who gained infamy after a scandalous affair with his slave Sally Hemings
    (E) who conducted tent-style revivals on his plantation

94. Which of these countries did Napoleon Bonaparte NOT attempt to conquer or control?

    (A) Italy
    (B) Russia
    (C) Germany
    (D) Switzerland
    (E) England

95. Nat Turner's Rebellion resulted in

    (A) the lynchings of more than twenty plantation owners in South Carolina
    (B) the "separate but equal" approach to segregation
    (C) the bloodiest insurrection by the Whigs against the Tories
    (D) the deaths of more than twenty white Virginians
    (E) the Fugitive Slave Act of 1866

96. The 1912 "discovery" of this inauthentic human ancestor was a hoax that set back the study of human evolution for at least 40 years. What was its name?

    (A) Java Man
    (B) Neanderthal Man
    (C) Cro-Magnon Man
    (D) Lucy
    (E) Piltdown Man

97. What was significant about the Missouri Compromise?

    (A) It marked the beginning of sectional reunification between the North and the South.
    (B) It allowed Missouri to enter the Union as a free state.
    (C) It permitted South Carolina to secede from the Union.
    (D) It granted fugitive slaves amnesty within the Missouri border.
    (E) It prohibited slavery above the 36°30' latitude line.

98. The Greek mathematician and inventor Archimedes is best known for

    (A) discovering that the earth revolves around the sun
    (B) proving that the earth is round
    (C) inventing calculus
    (D) discovering that mass can be measured by displaced water
    (E) inventing the telescope

99. Which statement does NOT explain why are some countries such as Japan, which lack nearly all natural resources, are still relatively wealthy?

    (A) They have a highly educated, industrious workforce
    (B) They have a high level of technology.
    (C) Their governments implement policies friendly to business and investment.
    (D) They have a financial system capable of supporting economic development.
    (E) They maintain colonial empires elsewhere in the world.

100. Which of these hypothetical individuals could not be elected President of the United States?

    (A) Bob, a 50-year-old man born in Ohio
    (B) Sally, a 36-year-old woman born in Florida
    (C) Howard, a 45-year-old man born in England
    (D) Ellen, a 60-year-old woman born in Montana
    (E) Antoine, a 40-year-old man born in Alaska

101. Considered the father of behavioral therapy, B. F. Skinner once stated that

    (A) with hard work and psychoanalysis a dysfunctional person may be reintegrated
    (B) personality is entirely genetically predetermined
    (C) our cognitions or thoughts control a large portion of our behavior
    (D) negative reinforcement and aversion therapy should never be used on children
    (E) with control of a child's environment, he could raise a child to become anything

102. The Spanish founded the first European colony in North America in 1565 and named it

    (A) St. Augustine
    (B) Plymouth
    (C) San Antonio
    (D) San Francisco
    (E) Acadia

103. In which way or ways was ancient Greek democracy, known as direct democracy, different from contemporary democracy?

    I. It did not presuppose equality of individuals.
    II. It limited democracy to natural-born citizens.
    III. It withheld political rights from women.

    (A) I only
    (B) II only
    (C) III only
    (D) I and III only
    (E) I, II, and III

104. The Magna Carta was the first attempt to

    (A) codify British common law
    (B) limit the power of a monarch
    (C) create a uniform tax code
    (D) impose taxation without representation
    (E) express individual civil liberties

105. The country once known as Ceylon is now called

    (A) Rhodesia
    (B) Indonesia
    (C) Ulan Bator
    (D) Sri Lanka
    (E) Myanmar

106. Abraham Lincoln was a member of which political party?

    (A) Republican
    (B) Federalist
    (C) Independent
    (D) Whig
    (E) Democratic-Republican

107. The origins of Rome are steeped in myth and legend. Many ancient Romans believed that

    (A) Zeus created Rome to house his oracle
    (B) Rome was built for the goddess Aphrodite
    (C) Rome was built in a day
    (D) the god Remus created the city
    (E) the city was founded by twin boys named Romulus and Remus

108. The three branches of the United States government are

    (A) the House of Representatives, the Senate, and the Congress
    (B) Legislative, Executive, and Judicial
    (C) the Federal Reserve, the Supreme Court, and the FBI
    (D) Democrats, Republicans, and Independents
    (E) the president, the vice president, and the speaker of the House

109. What war did the Treaty of Versailles end?

    (A) World War I
    (B) World War II
    (C) The Hundred Years' War
    (D) The French and Indian War
    (E) The French Revolution

110. Which is true of sensory memory?

    (A) It is very brief, lasting only a few seconds.
    (B) It differs depending upon the cognitive dissonance of the subject.
    (C) It takes over when our short-term memory expires.
    (D) It is possible only where displacement of old information occurs.
    (E) It is the opposite of semantic memory.

111. In 1940, four teenagers made what discovery in a cave at Lascaux, France?

    (A) paintings of bison and engravings of animals
    (B) evidence of the nomadic lifestyle of prehistoric humans
    (C) evidence of the gender-oriented division of labor in the Paleolithic Period
    (D) remains of the first tools
    (E) evidence of a mythological king

112. Why is Virginia Dare notable?

    (A) She was the first English child born in North America.
    (B) She was the last woman to be burned at the stake for practicing witchcraft in Salem, Massachusetts.
    (C) She was the designer of the first American flag.
    (D) She was the first settler to be held captive by Native American chief Powhatan.
    (E) She was the first woman to vote in America.

113. Why did Martin Luther nail his 95 Theses to the door of the Castle Church?

    (A) to protest against corruption in the Catholic Church, initiating the Reformation
    (B) in an effort to buy indulgences for his salvation from the Archbishop of Castlebury
    (C) as a written confession of his sins, ushering in the Reconstruction
    (D) to assert the authority of the Augustinian works over the Dominican self
    (E) in an effort to promote the Anglican movement in Germany

114. Aggressive behavior is an interpersonal style

    (A) where the long-term goals of an individual determine behavior
    (B) typically characteristic of passive personality types
    (C) where the needs of the self are considered rather than the needs of others
    (D) similar to assertive behavior, only with more anger involved
    (E) possessed by more CEOs than any other professionals

115. What is the strong bond that a child forms with his or her primary caregiver called?

    (A) pair-bonding
    (B) attachment
    (C) association
    (D) fraternal attachment
    (E) Oedipus complex

116. Reconstruction refers to the period

    (A) of community rebuilding after a natural disaster
    (B) after the American Civil War when the country attempted to reunite—physically, legally, and spiritually
    (C) after the Protestant Reformation when the Catholic church tried to reconstitute its power
    (D) of security and border reinforcement after the September 11, 2001 attacks
    (E) of economic prosperity as a result of the New Deal

117. What does a double-blind study mean?

    (A) random assignment will counteract the experimenter bias
    (B) only the subjects are blind to the purpose of the study
    (C) the researcher is blind to the purpose of the study but the subjects are not
    (D) both the experimenter and the subjects are unaware of the purpose of the study
    (E) the researcher and subject will never have a face-to-face meeting

GO ON TO THE NEXT PAGE

118. What occurred as a result of the Law of Primogeniture?

    (A) eldest sons joined the church
    (B) families tended to be smaller
    (C) younger sons tended to join the military or explore new frontiers
    (D) sons had more value than daughters
    (E) daughters tended to marry late in life

119. In 1630, what charismatic preacher led a Puritan migration of 900 colonists to Massachusetts Bay?

    (A) William Penn
    (B) Roger Williams
    (C) John Winthrop
    (D) Winthrop Fry
    (E) Brigham Young

120. What European explorer is credited with being the first to set foot on North America?

    (A) Ponce de Leon
    (B) Leif Ericson
    (C) Christopher Columbus
    (D) Amerigo Vespucci
    (E) Hernando Cortes

END OF TEST. STOP

THE ANSWER KEY APPEARS ON THE FOLLOWING PAGE.

ANSWER KEY

1. D	21. C	41. B	61. A	81. B	101. E
2. C	22. E	42. A	62. E	82. B	102. A
3. A	23. C	43. B	63. B	83. C	103. E
4. E	24. E	44. E	64. B	84. A	104. B
5. D	25. C	45. D	65. E	85. E	105. D
6. B	26. D	46. C	66. C	86. A	106. A
7. E	27. C	47. D	67. D	87. E	107. E
8. A	28. A	48. D	68. C	88. E	108. B
9. C	29. D	49. E	69. B	89. C	109. A
10. A	30. E	50. D	70. A	90. C	110. A
11. E	31. C	51. B	71. B	91. E	111. A
12. B	32. E	52. D	72. C	92. E	112. A
13. B	33. B	53. E	73. B	93. B	113. A
14. A	34. E	54. A	74. D	94. D	114. C
15. A	35. B	55. D	75. E	95. D	115. B
16. E	36. D	56. C	76. C	96. E	116. B
17. C	37. A	57. B	77. B	97. E	117. D
18. B	38. C	58. B	78. C	98. D	118. C
19. B	39. D	59. D	79. C	99. E	119. C
20. A	40. D	60. D	80. E	100. C	120. B

DIAGNOSTIC TEST QUICK REFERENCE TABLES

Use the following tables to determine which topics you need to review most.

Topic	Test Question
American History	10, 25, 40, 50, 55, 57, 69, 82, 83, 85, 86, 86, 91, 93, 95, 97, 112, 116, 119, 120
Western Civilization	6, 30, 41, 51, 62, 68, 80, 90, 94, 98, 102, 103, 104, 107, 109, 111, 113, 118
World History	4, 15, 4, 46, 58, 59, 60, 66, 67, 87
Political Science	3, 27, 42, 43, 45, 47, 48, 53, 56, 65, 73, 79, 100, 106, 108
Sociology	11, 20, 29, 31, 32, 34, 35, 38, 39, 74, 77
Economics	5, 18, 28, 36, 44, 52, 70, 71, 72, 76, 78, 81, 92, 99
Psychology	1, 37, 54, 64, 75, 84, 89, 101, 110, 114, 115, 117
Geography	2, 7, 9, 12, 13, 14, 16, 17, 26, 33, 49, 61, 105
Anthropology	8, 19, 21, 22, 23, 63, 96

Topic	Number of Questions on Test	Number Correct
American History	20	
Western Civilization	18	
World History	10	
Political Science	15	
Sociology	11	
Economics	14	
Psychology	12	
Geography	13	
Anthropology	7	

Answers and Explanations

1. (D)
The cerebellum is located at the bottom rear of the head directly above the brainstem and is important for a number of motor functions including skilled, voluntary, and precise movements. The temporal lobe plays a role in language, memory and emotion, so answer (B) is incorrect. Answer (E) is a distracter: an answer choice intended to draw attention away from the correct answer.

2. (C)
Because of their geographic isolation, islands are often home to a disproportionate number of endemic species. When the island habitat is threatened, affected species are often not present in any other location. Answer (D) is incorrect—Hawaii has *more* endangered species than any other U.S. state. Answer (E) is also incorrect—imported animals often destroy native species.

3. (A)
Common beliefs about the evils of repression and totalitarianism forged a bond between Reagan, Thatcher, and the Pope, emboldening countries in the Soviet bloc to break away and establish independent governments.

4. (E)
The Egyptian president Sadat and Israeli prime minister Begin (A) met at Camp David, pledging to work toward peace between the two nations. Muborak (B) followed Sadat as president of Egypt and Nasser (C) preceded Sadat as president, so both choices are incorrect.

5. (D)
Supply-side economics calls for lowering taxes to increase economic output because consumer spending accounts for two-thirds of economic activity. If consumers have additional disposable income they will spend it, causing business to increase output. This in turn will mean higher demand for the inputs involved in the production of goods, such as labor and raw materials.

6. (B)
The Luddites were radicals who roamed the English countryside smashing machinery, vandalizing factories, and even murdering the owners of factories that had begun to use emerging labor-saving technology. They believed that any innovation that resulted in jobs being lost was a threat, and resolved to stop such progress. Answer (E) directly contradicts the Luddite philosophy. In answer (A) the term "always" should indicate an incorrect answer choice; absolutes almost *always* appear *only* in wrong answers.

7. (E)
Lake Baikal, located in Siberia, in eastern Russia, is the world's deepest lake at 1620 meters, nearly one mile deep. It accounts for 20 percent of the Earth's fresh water.

8. (A)
In 1974, the anthropologist Johanson was in Ethiopia on a research expedition when he uncovered a dramatic discovery—the skeleton of a hominid he named "Lucy." The most amazing revelation came in the analysis of her leg bones, which indicated that she walked upright, making her the oldest known human ancestor at 3.2 million years old.

9. (C)
Subduction zones are areas of geological activity, where the Earth's tectonic plates collide with and slide under one another. The energy released can result in the formation of new volcanoes and undersea mountain ranges.

10. (A)
The term comes from a Twain novel of the same name and "Gilded Age" has come to represent American life in the late nineteenth century. This was a time when entrepreneurs with names like Carnegie and Vanderbilt celebrated their wealth with unprecedented lavish lifestyles.

11. (E)
This is a fairly straightforward sociology question about methods of study. Answer choices (A), (B), and (C) all refer to correct methodologies, but since there is only one answer to the question, (E) is the best answer. Pay careful attention to the word "only" when it appears in answer choices.

12. (B)

A canal is likely to be found crossing an isthmus—a narrow strip of land between bodies of water, as in Panama or Suez. A canal greatly benefits the inhabitants on either side by facilitating the transport of people and goods from one body of water to another. An archipelago (A) is a chain of islands already connected by water.

13. (B)

Tornadoes occur when atmospheric conditions force warm and cool air to collide. Since warm air rises, and cool air falls, a swirling motion results from this contact. Answer (D) describes one aspect of a tornado but is not the best answer.

14. (A)

Indonesia is made up of over 13,500 islands, of which about 6,000 are inhabited. In contrast, Japan has only around 2,000 islands while Fiji has a mere 332, 110 of which are inhabited; therefore (C) and (B) are also incorrect.

15. (A)

No one knows precisely when the building of the Great Wall began, but it is popularly believed that the Wall originated as a military fortification against invasions from Huns of the north.

16. (E)

The nation labeled as Algeria is actually Nigeria.

17. (C)

The city of St. Petersburg, once Russia's capital, has experienced a tumultuous history. The Soviet government renamed the city Leningrad in 1924 after the leader of the Bolshevik Revolution, V.I. Lenin. In 1991, with the collapse of the Soviet Union, the city of Leningrad regained its original name.

18. (B)

Two causes of the Great Depression were wild speculation in the stock market by investors using borrowed money and a trade war capped by the enactment by Congress of the Smoot–Hawley tariff act, which levied tariffs on imported goods. Other nations promptly enacted tariffs of their own, which reduced the sale of American-made goods abroad at a time when domestic demand was weak.

19. (B)

An analysis of ancient footprint impressions can reveal if primates walked upright in two-footed strides. Footprints also can help to establish weight transference and size. Carbon-14 (A) and uranium-235 (C) dating are used to determine the age of a fossil or artifact. Sticks (D) have been used as tools by apes regardless of their posture, so their presence does not indicate walking upright.

20. (A)

Marx was Communism's primary proponent but is not directly related to Poland's Solidarity movement; answer (D) can be eliminated. Answer (C) is in direct opposition to Marxist theory that champions the working class, and (E) is incorrect because Marx believed that class struggle was inevitable.

21. (C)

"Hominid" is a taxonomic term referring to humans and our ancestors. The hominids evolved and branched into at least twelve distinct species—humans (*Homo sapiens sapiens*) are the sole surviving hominids. *Australopithecus robustus* was actually a hominid but died out millions of years ago, so (A) is incorrect. Answer (E) is a scientific-sounding made-up name.

22. (E)

Margaret Mead published *Coming of Age in Samoa*; it became a bestseller and popularized cultural anthropology. This work advanced the idea that an individual's experience of developmental stages could be shaped by cultural expectations. Mead conducted her research with adolescent girls, not boys, so (A) is incorrect; she was studying in American Samoa, not British Samoa, so (B) is also incorrect.

23. (C)

In 1859 Darwin published his theory of evolution in the book *Origin of Species*, igniting a controversy that still rages today. Darwin formulated the idea of natural selection, not "artificial selection" (E). "Natural rights" (D) is a political term and does not relate to Darwin.

24. (E)

Magellan sailed under the flag of Spain and it took him fourteen months to find the southern opening to the Pacific Ocean. The unsuspecting navigator expected Asia to be only a few hundred miles past the coast of South America. Instead, the expedition traveled 12,600 miles before reaching the island of Guam. Only one of Magellan's five ships actually found its way back to Spain.

25. (C)

The Committee to Re-Elect the President—or CREEP as it was nicknamed—was an association working to help Nixon's second bid for the White House. The group was involved in the infamous Watergate cover-up scandal. President Nixon was a Quaker but Quakers are hardly an "infamous" group, so answer (A) is incorrect. Answer (D) uses the term "Whitewater," which refers to a different presidential scandal.

26. (D)

Earthquakes are least likely to occur in Antarctica as it is relatively free of the major fault lines that trigger this sudden movement of the Earth. Both California (B) and Japan (E) have well-known earthquakes in their history.

27. (C)

The Twenty-sixth Amendment lowered the voting age to eighteen. Because eighteen-year-olds were old enough to fight, and conceivably die, for their country, most Americans felt they had earned the right to vote for the elected officials who would make decisions on their behalf. Slavery was abolished with the Thirteenth Amendment, Prohibition was repealed by the Twenty-first Amendment, and presidential terms were limited with the Twenty-second Amendment.

28. (A)

Some economists advocate monetary policy over fiscal policy because they believe the Federal Reserve makes its decisions in a less political manner than Congress, and because of this it is able to act more quickly.

29. (D)

The starting point of functionalism is that all societies have certain basic needs or *functional* requirements that must be met if a society is to survive. The Oedipus complex (C) is a Freudian construct. The "survival of the fittest" concept (E) originated with Charles Darwin.

30. (E)

This question contains plenty of clues that point to the correct answer. Answers (A) and (B) are too narrow, and both answers (C) and (D) can be eliminated since neither "relapse" nor "reformation" make sense in the context of flourishing creativity.

31. (C)

Answer (A) expresses the opposite of (C). When there are two answer choices that are direct opposites, there is a good chance that one of them is the correct answer. Answers (D) and (E) are both nonsensical distracters.

32. (E)

German sociologist Max Weber was the first to observe and write about bureaucracies that developed in Germany during the nineteenth century. Weber saw bureaucracies as a big improvement over the haphazard style of government they replaced; he found bureaucracies to be rational, efficient, and honest.

33. (B)

Archipelagos and atolls are both island groups, differing only in shape. An archipelago is a chain of islands, while an atoll is a ring-shaped group of islands. This is a fairly straightforward geography question. Answer (D) is suspicious because there are few if any "manmade" islands.

34. (E)

The correct answer can be found by eliminating any choices that are not representative or "symbolic" in nature—only "language" and "gestures" fit this description. All words are really stand-ins for ideas; they represent or symbolize something else. Each of the other four answers refers to an "actual" cultural component.

35. (B)

Even if you know nothing about deviance, the answer choices contain information that can help you find the correct answer. Words like "never," "always," and "should" usually indicate potential wrong answers.

36. (D)

Gresham's Law states, "Bad money drives out good money." During the Great Depression, people believed that gold was safer than paper money, so they spent paper money and hoarded their gold money. This had the effect of reducing spending by consumers, making the Depression worse. In 1933, President Franklin D. Roosevelt made it illegal for Americans to own more than $100 in gold, other than in the form of jewelry and minor industrials.

37. (A)

The question lets you know that Erikson is a psychologist. Armed only with this knowledge, you can eliminate answer choices. "Class warfare" is a topic generally associated with sociology or political science, so (B) is wrong. Chaos theory (C) is a term from physics, so it must be incorrect. Similarly, (D) and (E) refer to evolution and the military, so they are also both incorrect.

38. (C)

Sociologist Elizabeth Kubler-Ross published *On Death and Dying* in 1969. She was a pioneer for the advancement of research into the psychosocial aspects of the dying process, particularly from the perspective of the dying individual.

39. (D)

When you encounter a question that asks you to assume a statement is true, treat it as fact. Don't let your personal opinion affect your answer. The key word "most" in (A) and (E) should also call attention to those selections as possible wrong answers.

40. (D)

President Nixon shook hands with the Chinese premier Chou En-Lai in what would become one of the most famous handshakes in diplomatic history. Nixon also met with Chairman Mao in what were the twilight days of China's Cultural Revolution. This trip was the first an American president had ever made to China and broke two decades of silence between the two nations.

41. (B)

William of Normandy brought the French language and French customs to Great Britain when he defeated the British at the Battle of Hastings and assumed the crown of England.

42. (A)

In a socialist country, the government makes all economic decisions. Communism is primarily a political description, not an economic one. In fact, answers (C), (D), and (E) are all terms used to describe political rather than economic systems.

43. (B)

The United States government is a representative democracy, in which all citizens have the right to vote for whomever they wish to represent them in the lawmaking process. In a dictatorship (E) or monarchy (A), the people have no voting rights and no control over how they are governed.

44. (E)

When Congress established the Federal Reserve System in 1912, politicians from the rest of the country feared that it would be a tool of the northeastern economic and business establishment.

45. (D)

The Federalist Papers, written by Alexander Hamilton, James Madison, and John Jay, were an attempt to convince citizens of the need to enact the proposed Constitution. Written under the pen name "Publius," they give insight into exactly what the framers of the Constitution were intending to accomplish and why they created the document as they did. Americans' civil liberties are laid out in the Bill of Rights, so (E) is incorrect.

46. (C)

More than a half-century after the close of World War II, Russia and Japan have yet to sign a peace treaty to formally end the war. To this day, the two nations are unable to resolve their dispute over four islands located to the north of Japan. Answers (D) and (E) can both be eliminated—in both cases the two countries named were allies.

47. (D)

Alexander Hamilton, the nation's first Secretary of the Treasury, was the principal designer of the American monetary system.

48. (D)

The Electoral College was formed to ensure that small states had a voice in national elections. Answer (C) is the opposite of answer (D). Whenever opposites appear in the answer choices, it is likely that one of these choices is correct.

49. (E)

The first four statements are all true, illustrating that global warming is a more complex issue than it might first appear to be. Option (E) is just there to confuse you—it is about globalization, not global warming.

50. (D)

These wealthy "Gilded Age" Americans garnered their fortunes as a result of monopolies, so answer (A) is incorrect. In addition, all three men were self-made, so (B) is also incorrect.

51. (B)

The Ottoman empire rose from the ashes of the old Byzantine empire, which collapsed at the hands of the Ottoman Turks in the mid-fifteenth century. The Turkish ruler, Mehmed II, made Constantinople his capital, renaming it Istanbul. Constantinople had been the Byzantine capital.

52. (D)

The unemployment rate tends to be higher in the presence of generous unemployment benefits, as the need to return to work is lessened. Logic alone can help solve this question. Answers (A) and (E) can be rejected—there is an obvious correlation between the amount of time individuals can collect benefits and the speed with which they will look for a new job. Unemployment benefits *may* very well contribute to illegal immigration but the question does not mention immigration trends; so (C) is also incorrect. Never read more into a question than the information provided.

53. (E)

Although the idea of keeping church and state separate appears in the First Amendment, which is in the Bill of Rights, the words "separation of church and state" do not appear anywhere in the Constitution.

54. (A)

Swiss psychologist Carl Jung was a longtime admirer of the eminent Dr. Freud, but though Freud saw Jung as his heir apparent, Jung had some different ideas. Jung, not Freud, applied the "collective unconscious" theory to dream analysis, so (B) is incorrect. Similarly, answer (E) can be eliminated. Freud or Jung appear in three of the five choices, indicating a high probability that they have to do with the correct answer.

55. (D)

Franklin Delano Roosevelt said this in response to the Japanese attack on Pearl Harbor in 1941. Answer choices (A) and (C) can quickly be eliminated, as neither the presidencies of Ford nor Carter were conducted in the context of fear.

56. (C)

The Republican Party has historically supported lower taxes and less government spending. Traditionally, the Democrats have endorsed higher taxes on the upper classes and increased entitlements for the poor, so (A) is incorrect.

57. (B)

This question is not as straightforward as some and requires more complex reasoning. Often this style of question is more easily managed by listing in two columns the various attributes of (in this case) Kennedy and Eisenhower and then comparing the two.

58. (B)

The desire to win back the Holy Land was an overriding concern among many European monarchs and nobles in the Middle Ages. Answer (D) can be ruled out because the Israeli-Palestinian clash is contemporary and the question is phrased in the past tense. Answer (E) can also be eliminated as most Christians have not inhabited their Holy Land in great numbers since well before the Crusades.

59. (D)

The native inhabitants of the Australian outback are typically referred to as "aborigines." Answer (B) is easy to rule out since it is highly unlikely that anyone lives *in* the vaguely defined "south seas."

60. (D)

It is tempting to assume that the United States is the biggest democracy because of its great land mass; however, India, with over one billion citizens, is the world's most populous democracy.

61. (A)

The Kurds are a stateless people: a recognizable, culturally homogenous group of people living within the borders of other nations because they have no nation of their own.

62. (E)

Interest in exploring Africa began as a means of finding a water route to India. Once Africa's riches came to the attention of the Europeans, mining, colonies, slaves and Christianity became reasons to exploit it, but all those reasons came after the desire to reach India by sea. Overpopulation in Europe would not necessarily have led to the desire to explore new lands; therefore, answer (D) can be eliminated.

63. (B)

This anthropology question can be solved by thinking logically, even if the term "pre-contact" is unfamiliar. By reading the answer choices, you can see that the term has something to do with "society" and "outsiders." An industrialized nation probably wouldn't be in a stage of "pre-contact" since technology relies upon the sharing of ideas between nations; so (C) is incorrect. Since (E) contains the clichéd and vague phrase "global technological revolution," it's pretty safe to eliminate this choice as well.

64. (B)

Freud postulated that individuals progress through a series of stages in a predetermined sequence that ultimately lead to a healthy/unhealthy personality, the last of which is the genital stage. Freud also theorized the Electra complex (C), but it is not one of the stages.

65. (E)

The speaker of the House is second in succession to the presidency, behind the vice president. Only elected officials may succeed to the presidency, so the secretary of state (A) and the attorney general (D)—both presidential appointees—are ineligible.

66. (C)

Located in what is currently Iraq, this rich area between the Tigris and Euphrates Rivers saw the birth of many great civilizations, including the Sumerians, the Assyrians, and the Babylonians.

67. (D)

At the same time as the Russians were fighting Germany in World War I, an internal political war raged at home: the Russian Revolution. The Great Potato Famine was an Irish, not a Russian, phenomenon, so (C) must be wrong. Feudalism is a medieval construct and since World War I took place in the twentieth century, answer (B) is also incorrect.

68. (C)

Sir Isaac Newton's Three Laws of Physics make up the foundation of modern rocket science.

69. (B)

From 1812 to 1815, the U.S. and Great Britain fought the War of 1812. The raid at Harper's Ferry, a slave rebellion, took place in 1834, so answer (D) is incorrect. Answer (C) is also wrong since the Battle of Midway was fought during World War II.

70. (A)

Diamonds are both rarer and harder to mine than salt—both factors that contribute to a commodity's overall value.

71. (B)

The Phillips curve graphically illustrates the relationship between inflation and unemployment. Typically, if one is low the other is high. For example, during a period of rapid economic expansion when businesses must hire additional workers, the rate of unemployment will decline. At the same time, however, production costs will rise as business is forced to utilize less efficient means of production to increase output. This leads to higher inflation.

72. (C)

Interest rates and inflation move in the same direction because inflation is a component of interest rates. The nominal, or stated interest rate is a function of inflation plus the perceived risk associated with the particular borrower. As the rate of inflation rises or falls, that component of the nominal interest rate will rise or fall as well.

73. (B)
In 1954, the Supreme Court ruled, in the case of *Brown v. Topeka Board of Education*, that the practice of "separate but equal" education for children of different races was unconstitutional. Supreme Court rulings sometimes have the power to force social change, as this one did.

74. (D)
This question addresses the reader's understanding of the often confused and confusing terms "race" and "ethnicity." *Race* is the social definition of people based on biological characteristics. *Ethnicity* is the social definition of people based on cultural characteristics (like style of dress, language, and norms).

75. (E)
The only other reasonable choice is answer (A). The term "peer pressure" is really a pop psychology term, and therefore is not correct.

76. (C)
Monetary policy refers to the manipulation of the money supply by the Federal Reserve System. *Fiscal* policy refers to Congressional spending of tax dollars. Clearly, the Surgeon General (D) and the FBI (E) are not involved with any economic policymaking.

77. (B)
The word "always" in answer (A) should indicate a potential wrong answer: ethnocentrism and cultural relativism are incompatible approaches. Similarly, answer (C) is incorrect since it is the *definition* of ethnocentrism.

78. (C)
The U.S. Mint—a division of the U.S. Treasury—prints all currency. Answers (A), (B), (D), and (E) fall under the umbrella of the Federal Reserve.

79. (C)
In the years following the Civil War, most of the newly freed slaves voted Republican, as the Democratic party was the favored party of the Southern states. Furthermore, President Abraham Lincoln, the individual most closely associated with the freeing of the slaves, was a Republican. Today most African Americans vote Democratic although the Republican Party regularly courts their vote.

80. (E)
In a 1946 speech, Winston Churchill said of Soviet domination of Eastern Europe that an "iron curtain has descended across the Continent." Some historians date the beginning of the Cold War to this pivotal speech by the former British prime minister.

81. (B)
Milton Friedman, who won the Nobel Prize for Economics in 1976, is one of the best-known economists of the monetarist school of thought. Answer (C) is incorrect: Keynesism is an economic school of thought but its primary proponent is more likely its founder John Maynard Keynes. Choice (E) is not even a school of thought.

82. (B)
Manifest Destiny is typically associated with a nineteenth-century ethos, a sense of duty to spread American ideals (as well as to expand settlement across the continent). The concept arose before the Civil War, so (E) is incorrect. Neither answer (D) nor answer (C) makes logical sense.

83. (C)
"Enfranchisement" and "suffrage" both refer to voting rights, but the suffrage movement focused on women, not former slaves, so (D) can be eliminated. Answer (E) may make you think of the Temperance movement, which was responsible for the enactment (not the end) of Prohibition.

84. (A)
Crystallized intelligence is the store of knowledge or information that a given society has accumulated over time. It is based on learning and experience, not innate intelligence (E). It remains relatively stable over time, so (B) is incorrect. Since it refers to acquired knowledge, not how we use it, (C) also is incorrect.

85. (E)
Answer (A) can be ruled out since, although Teddy was a Roosevelt, his presidency was before the Great Depression. Answers (B) and (C) are both distracters. Similarly, answer choice (D) describes the modern free-trade alliance, NAFTA.

86. (A)

McCarthy was a senator from Wisconsin in the 1950s. He was not above relying upon rumor, slander, or innuendo in his personal campaign to root out the communists who supposedly had infiltrated Congress.

87. (E)

Answer (A) is illogical; the very essence of the Cold War prevents a "thawing out." Similarly, the fear of "nuclear holocaust" was far greater during the Cold War than after, so answer (B) can also be eliminated.

88. (E)

Harriet Beecher Stowe's bestseller was published in 1852 and sold half a million copies in its first five years, breaking all records at the time. Catherine Beecher, Harriet's sister, was also a writer but this isn't her book, so answer (B) is wrong. The book was heralded in the North and denounced in the slaveholding South (A).

89. (C)

The placebo effect is the measurable, observable, or felt improvement in health not attributable to treatment (for example, among participants in medical studies). Many psychiatrists believe that the placebo effect is psychological, due to a belief in the treatment or to a subjective feeling of improvement.

90. (C)

The Vikings were a group of people indigenous to Norway, Sweden, and Denmark. Valhalla is the mythical home of the gods in Norse mythology, so answer (D) can be immediately ruled out. Nova Scotia, the Ottoman empire, and Denmark are too far removed geographically to have been the home of a common culture (B).

91. (E)

An indentured servant was a person who, in exchange for passage to the New World, agreed to work as a servant for a period of time to repay his or her debt. One-half to two-thirds of all immigrants to colonial America arrived as indentured servants. Even on the frontier, a small percentage of the population came under terms of indenture.

92. (E)

Cartels tend to be unstable over time because eventually one or more members will see an opportunity to undercut the prices charged by fellow members, increasing market share and profits at the other members' expense.

93. (B)

Answer choice (D) can be ruled out—Virginia planter Thomas Jefferson, not Byrd, had an affair with his slave, Sally Hemings. And though Byrd had a sharp tongue, as a plantation owner, he would not likely have found himself at the mercy of a colonial governor, therefore (A) is also incorrect.

94. (D)

Switzerland was one of the few European countries not coveted by the French general and emperor. Italy, Russia, England, and Germany were all targets of Napoleon.

95. (D)

Turner, who felt he was directed by God, led this 1831 rebellion; it is one of the most famous slave insurrections in American history.

96. (E)

The so-called "Piltdown Man" was an elaborate hoax. All of the remaining choices were legitimate anthropological finds.

97. (E)

In 1820, Missouri was admitted to the Union as a slave state and Maine was admitted as a free state, which maintained the balance of slave states and free states in the Union. Slavery opponents resisted allowing new slave states to join the Union, but agreed to accept Missouri with the stipulation that, except in Missouri, slavery would be banned north of the new state's southern boundary.

98. (D)

Archimedes' principle states that the weight of the water displaced by an object is equal to the weight of that object. This principle paved the way many hundreds of years later for the development of submarines. Archimedes lived in the third century B.C.E., in the city-state of Syracuse.

99. (E)
All of the other factors mentioned are reasons why a country such as Japan or Hong Kong is able to overcome significant obstacles to prosperity to become a major economic power.

100. (C)
Article II, Section 1 of the U.S. Constitution states that only native-born American citizens may be elected to the Presidency.

101. (E)
This question addresses the classic nature versus nurture question. Several of the answer choices contain key words indicating wrong answers. Absolute words like "entirely" in answer (B) and "never" in (D) are red flags.

102. (A)
St. Augustine, Florida was the first European colony in North America.

103. (E)
Although considered an enlightened society by ancient standards, the Greeks did not consider all individuals to be equal. In particular, slavery was the norm, women had no political rights, and only native-born Greek men were eligible to vote.

104. (B)
In 1215 the British noble class rose up and demanded that King John sign the Magna Carta, a document that limited the power of the monarch. The Magna Carta was an effort to express the rights of the nobility, but had little concern for average citizens.

105. (D)
The nation of Sri Lanka was known as Ceylon until 1972.

106. (A)
Abraham Lincoln was an early member of the Republican Party, formed in 1854 to oppose the expansion of slavery. The Republican Party evolved from the earlier Whig Party, so (D) is incorrect. In their time, the Whigs opposed the Federalists, another early American political party, so (B) is incorrect. The Democratic-Republican Party split in the 1820s into the Whig and Democratic Parties, so (E) is also incorrect.

107. (E)
Legend has it that twin brothers Romulus and Remus founded the city of Rome. Answers (A) and (B) can be eliminated since both Zeus and Aphrodite were Greek gods, not Roman gods.

108. (B)
In Articles I, II, and III of the U.S. Constitution, the government is divided into Legislative, Executive, and Judicial branches. Answer (D) can be immediately ruled out since it lists political parties, not branches of the government. The president, vice president, and speaker of the House are officeholders, not governmental branches (E).

109. (A)
The Treaty of Versailles, signed at Versailles on June 28, 1919, ended World War I, which had begun almost five years earlier.

110. (A)
Sensory memory only lasts a few seconds, when the senses send information immediately to the brain. This information is primarily unprocessed. Cognitive dissonance is an active way to process intellectual information (B). Sensory memory is even briefer than short-term memory (C). Options (D) and (E) are nonsensical and just there to confuse you.

111. (A)
Some boys were hiking in the woods when they discovered the amazing cave at Lascaux. It features paintings of people and animals on the walls, dating from c.15,000–13,000 B.C.E.

112. (A)
Virginia Dare was born in August 1587. A close reading of the answer choices reveals the word "first" in answers (A), (D), and (E), indicating that one of those is probably correct. Betsy Ross designed the American flag, so (C) is incorrect.

113. (A)
Martin Luther's act of protest started the Protestant Reformation in 1517. The "Archbishop of Castlebury" (B) is a made-up name designed to confuse you. Similarly, the term "Reconstruction" in choice (C) sounds a bit like "Reformation" and is a distracter.

114. (C)

In psychological terms, aggressive behavior is in opposition to passive (B) and assertive (D) behavioral styles.

115. (B)

The term "fraternal" refers to sibling relationships and since siblings are rarely primary caregivers, (D) can be eliminated. "Pair-bonding" refers to a life mate and is often romantic in nature, so (A) is also incorrect.

116. (B)

Reconstruction clearly refers to a "rebuilding" but natural disasters are not the best answer to this question (A). Answer (D) mentions "reinforcement" but that is not the same as reconstruction.

117. (D)

A "double-blind" study is a research method in which both the subjects and the experimenter are unaware or "blind" to the anticipated results. It is a mechanism to counteract bias, but not one based on randomness, so (A) is incorrect. Options (B) and (C) are also incorrect, since they both describe situations in which only one party to the experiment is "blind."

118. (C)

The Law of Primogeniture allowed eldest sons to inherit the family property and titles. Younger sons were left to strike out on their own in search of fortune. Many joined the military in search of new opportunities, or sought to explore new lands.

119. (C)

John Winthrop led the first mass emigration from England to the New World. They settled the Massachusetts Bay Colony in 1630. William Penn (A) founded Pennsylvania and Roger Williams (B) founded Rhode Island.

120. (B)

Leif Ericson is believed to have sailed from Iceland to establish a colony in Greenland around 980, some 500 years earlier than either Columbus or Vespucci in the late fifteenth century. Cortes and de Leon arrived in the early sixteenth century.

Section Five: The CLEP Social Sciences and History Exam | **385**

Chapter Seventeen: CLEP Social Sciences and History Review

- The Big Picture: CLEP Social Sciences and History
- Nuts and Bolts
- History
  - What You Need to Know
  - United States History
  - Western Civilization
  - World History
  - Master Timeline
  - History Resources
- The Social Sciences
  - What You Need to Know
  - Government/Political Science
  - Sociology
  - Economics
  - Psychology
  - Geography
  - Anthropology
- Final Thoughts

You have embarked on a quest to test your knowledge of the social sciences by taking the CLEP Social Sciences and History exam. Congratulations! Since the exam covers a wide range of subjects within the social sciences, you need to pick up concepts from several different subject areas in order to do well.

THE BIG PICTURE: CLEP SOCIAL SCIENCES AND HISTORY

The Social Sciences and History examination allows you 90 minutes to answer 120 questions. It covers a broad range of subjects from the social science and history fields. Emphasis is placed on Western cultural and intellectual history from ancient civilizations to the present; however, familiarity with world history also will help your score. Be particularly alert for questions that cross disciplines, movements, or periods. In addition it's especially important for you to have a clear understanding of the key terminology for each subject area covered.

NUTS AND BOLTS

The approximate subject area breakdown of the CLEP Social Sciences and History exam is as follows.

- 40% History
    - 17% United States History
    - 15% Western Civilization
    - 8% World History
- 13% Government/Political Science
- 10% Sociology
- 10% Economics
- 10% Psychology
- 10% Geography
- 6% Anthropology

Brace yourself: it is highly unlikely that you will achieve expert status in every section of the exam. The exam is designed so that you will *not* know the answer to every question. According to the test makers, the average college student completing a survey course in these subjects would get half the questions right. However, you can still rack up points within each subject area. While most students achieve a higher score in some sections than in others, it is a good strategy to keep in mind the percentage of the exam taken up by each topic. The higher the percentage for each topic, the more questions there will be in that subject area on the exam.

The goal of this review is to help you solidify what you already know and increase your familiarity with other important topics on the exam. With that in mind, you will find a brief summary of the scope of the questions for each field covered on the exam. The history review section includes a master timeline of important people and places from all periods. The social sciences section contains a list of important terms for each discipline; you'll find the timeline a useful tool for these portions of the test, as well. At the end of each subject review there are suggestions for further reading and study, as well as tips for better preparation in a shorter amount of time. Read on to begin compiling your knowledge database for the exam.

HISTORY

What You Need to Know

Since about 40 percent of the CLEP Social Sciences and History exam is devoted to history, it's essential that you brush up on different historical time periods and events. The history portion of the test will require a sound grasp of major chronological and geographical events in world history. You'll also need to understand the relationship between specific historical happenings and the development of ideas and major schools of thought—the big picture of human history. The questions will cover political, social, economic, intellectual and cultural material from a range of periods and geographical locales.

Economics, politics, social issues, the history of ideas, and scientific progress all influence the development of any society. Even more importantly, they are all interrelated. The sort of interconnectivity, or globalization, as we would call it today, of intellectual and cultural history has become more pronounced as technology and cultures have advanced. However, the seeds of globalization were planted a very long time ago. As international communications become more sophisticated, the various world economies and cultures have found themselves increasingly interrelated. As you study, keep up with current international events. Spend some time looking at an atlas or map. You can keep a notebook detailing current or past events, or make your own charts and timelines. Soon, the big picture of world history will start to make sense.

United States History

About 17 percent of the test questions will cover important events, people and movements in United States history—that translates to about 20 questions. The questions will cover the periods from the first European exploration of the New World at the close of the fifteenth century to the present. As you prepare yourself for this exam you will likely notice that many of the happenings on the American scene dovetail with events in Europe and across the globe. While you will not become an expert in the history of the United States just by reading this review, you will develop some useful test-taking skills and improve your approach to studying history.

Western Civilization

About 15 percent of the test questions will deal with major figures, occurrences, and intellectual movements of Western civilization from prehistory to modern times—approximately 18 questions. The questions will address ancient Western Asia, Greece, Rome, medieval and modern Europe, as well as European colonization of other regions around the world.

World History

About 8 percent of the test questions will cover important people, places, and events in the non-Western world from prehistory to the present. That means about 10 questions on the entire exam will be derived from world history. But the smaller percentage of questions does not mean you can gloss over world history. In fact, a sound grasp of this area of the test will probably result in a much better overall performance; the knowledge will overlap with both Western civilization and United States history. The questions often will be general and will address African, Asian, Australian, North American (non-U.S.) and South American history.

Master Timeline

The following timeline represents a chronological progression of major periods and events in United States history, Western civilization and world history. The timeline is intended to be a general overview and is by no means conclusive or absolute. It will give you a visual representation of the connections, or relationship, between the history of various regions of the world. Use it to direct and focus your studies. Make it your own: add images or graphs and charts, make a large version and post it on the wall . . . use whatever method works for you. The operating principle of the timeline is that once you get the big picture, the details will begin to stand out.

From a strategic standpoint, if you're familiar with time periods and their general characteristics, you'll be able to quickly rule out some of the multiple-choice answers on the test itself. Try to remember at least one important fact about each era. You could create a mnemonic device for each place or century. For example: "E" could stand for Enlightenment in England in the Eighteenth century. The more personal the mnemonic, the easier it will be for you to remember it.

Timeline Key

The different areas of history are denoted as follows:

United States History (roman type)

Western Civilization (bold type)

World History (italics)

Since the CLEP emphasizes United States history, you will notice more events from U.S. history than from Western civilization or world history in the timeline. Keep in mind that these dates are approximate and the terms are fluid with considerable overlap between periods and schools of thought.

Note: This exam uses the chronological designations B.C.E. (before common era) and C.E. (common era). These labels correspond to B.C. (before Christ) and A.D. (anno Domini), which are used in some other texts.

The Timeline

Ancient Civilization

The Fertile Crescent/Mesopotamia (pre-3500 B.C.E.–c. 500 C.E ending with *conquest by Persian empire***)**

    Ascent of the Sumerians (c. 3500 B.C.E.)

    Ascent of the Babylonians (c. 1800 B.C.E.)

    Ascent of the Assyrians (c. 1350 B.C.E.)

    Ancient Egypt (pre-3000 B.C.E–c.30 B.C.E. ending with **Roman invasion***)*

    Ancient Greece (pre-500 B.C.E.–500 C.E.)

The Golden Age of Greece (c. 460 B.C.E. beginning with *defeat of the Persians***–430 B.C.E.)**

The Peloponnesian War between Athens and Sparta (431 B.C.E.–404 B.C.E.)

Ancient Rome and the Roman Empire (c. 387 B.C.E. beginning with birth of Rome–c. 400 C.E.)

The Punic Wars (238 B.C.E.–204 B.C.E)

Africa and the Phoenicians

<ins>Other terms and names</ins>: *the Great Wall of China (at least 2000 years old), India and the Himalayas*

Medieval and Early Modern Civilization

The Middle Ages (c. 500–1500 B.C.E.)

The Crusades (the first c. 1095 B.C.E.)

The Renaissance (c. 1450 B.C.E.–c. 1700 B.C.E.)

<ins>Other terms and names</ins>: *The Huns, The Kurds,* **The Vikings,** *the Turks,* **Leonardo da Vinci, Michelangelo, Renaissance art**

The Seventeenth Century

Native American and Pre-Colonial Period (pre-1620)

Colonial Period (1620–c.1760s)

<ins>Other terms and names</ins>: **Spain, Italy and Age of Exploration, Martin Luther and the Protestant Reformation**

The Eighteenth Century

The Enlightenment (c.1700 B.C.E.)

Galileo, Newton and the Age of Discovery

The First Great Awakening (1730s–1740s)

Revolutionary Period (1775–1783 ending with the Peace of Paris)

Articles of Confederation Period and Constitutional Convention

Early Republic (pre-1763 to 1815)

Federalist Period (1789–1801)

<ins>Other terms and names</ins>: *Mexico and Central America,* **Spanish, French and Italian imperialism in the New World, Colonial Africa, and slavery**

The Nineteenth Century

Jeffersonian Era and War of 1812 (1801–1814)

The Second Great Awakening (c.1800–1861)

Reform Movements (1801–1861)

Nationalism and Sectionalism (1815–c.1865)

Jacksonian Era (1820–c.1845)

Expansion and Immigration

Antebellum America (1850–1861)

The Civil War (1861–1865)

Reconstruction (1865–1877)

The Frontier and Westward Expansion (1865–1900)

Early Industrial America (1865–1900)

Urban Culture (1865–1900)

> <u>Other terms and names</u>: *Australia and the aborigines*, massive immigration to U.S. from Western and Eastern European nations, **Triangular Trade**

The Twentieth Century

The Gilded Age (1890s–1914, ending with **World War I**)

The Progressive Era (1879–1920)

World War I (1914–1918)

The "Roaring '20s"

The Stock Market Crash and the Great Depression (1929–1941)

The New Deal (1932–1940s)

World War II (1941–1946)

The 1950s and the Cold War (1950s–1980s)

The Civil Rights Era (1950s–1960s)

The 1960s and the Protest Era

The Vietnam War (1960s–1970s)

Postmodern America (1990s–present)

> <u>Other terms and names</u>: **Russia and Communism; Hitler, Mussolini, and Fascism**; *Vietnam and Southeast Asia, Chinese Communism and the Cultural Revolution, conflict in the Middle East and international terrorism, American cultural imperialism, globalization and the Internet*

History Resources

To get yourself in an historical state of mind, watch the History Channel or *A & E Biographies*. Check out the Library of Congress and White House websites for American history reference. You also can find useful glossaries of terms in all sorts of subjects at ask.com and at about.com. In addition, mrdowling.com has excellent interactive Western civilization and world history information. The Public Broadcasting Service (pbs.org) is also a good resource for all sorts of fascinating information about historical happenings. If you can borrow history textbooks from your local library or school, they will help you prepare as well.

THE SOCIAL SCIENCES

What You Need to Know

Since about 60 percent of the CLEP Social Sciences and History exam is devoted to the social sciences, you'll need a plan of attack that can encompass a broad range of disciplines. The social sciences questions on the CLEP exam will cover the following fields: sociology, psychology, anthropology, geography, and government/political science. You will be expected to have a general, broad-based understanding of each of these fields. Many of the questions will cross periods, geographical areas, and disciplines—meaning they will address more than one subject at a time. So you must prepare yourself well and no one field can be entirely overlooked.

Just as with history, you should not expect to become an expert in each of the social sciences. The exam questions will give you the opportunity to demonstrate that you have a level of knowledge and general understanding expected of college students in an introductory survey course. Don't panic: this all may seem overwhelming at first, but as you begin preparing yourself for the exam by reviewing the individual subject areas, you will start to notice the connections between them. Many of the required skills, methodologies, and important terms are shared or similar.

As with history, paying close attention to connections between the areas of social science—the big picture—will help you score higher. Take note of these relationships in a journal or diary. Try out the methodologies of one field when you are studying another. Most importantly, make this knowledge your own; personalize it with mnemonics that work for you. Make your own color-coded flowcharts, tables, and graphs. If you have a friend who is taking the exam, you can do these things together. Tailor these study tools to your personal experiences, since the social sciences can be seen and experienced in everyday life. Train yourself to pay attention to how the social sciences are expressed around you on a daily basis. One way to start is by watching or reading the daily news.

Government/Political Science

About 13 percent of the exam will cover the fields of government and political science, which translates to approximately 16 questions. While we think of political science as pertaining only to government, it also has to do with power dynamics in all social arenas. In other words: who gets what, when, and how. You participate in politics in some fashion all of the time whether you know it or not—your goal now is to learn about the different aspects of politics.

The questions on this portion of the exam will require a familiarity with political science terminology, facts, methodologies, and general principles and theories. You will be asked to apply these abstractions to particulars. You will have to combine a working knowledge of the big picture of political science (and its relationship to the other social sciences) with an ability to apply its principles to specific data. Always remember to keep in mind the important connections between political science and the other disciplines on the exam, currently and throughout history. This is where your customized study aids can help.

Political Science Terms to Learn

Anarchy	Elites
Aristocracy	Equality of Opportunity and Equal Rights
Checks and Balances	Fascism
Communism, Marxism, and Socialism	Federalism
Conservatism	Immigration and Emigration
Democracy: Direct, Parliamentary, and Representative	Liberalism
	Natural Law
Despotism	Republicanism
Dictatorship	Tyranny
Electoral College	

Political Science Resources

The above list is just a sampling of the political science terms you should know for the exam. You can find their definitions easily by consulting political science textbooks or online resources. Check out the Thomson Nelson website, which contains hundreds of concise definitions of poli-sci terms, as do about.com and webref.org. A good source for American political information is thecapitol.net where you'll find a glossary of congressional terminology. You can also tune in to NPR (National Public Radio) for lively discussions of the contemporary political scene in this country and around the globe. If you're feeling especially ambitious, why not flip over to CSPAN to watch our democratic process in action?

Sociology

About 10 percent of the test questions will come from the field of sociology. That breaks down to about 12 questions. Sociology is the scientific study of human social behavior in collective or group situations. As with political science, you participate in sociological concerns all the time. A sociologist studies everything from group dynamics (in the workplace or in high school cliques) to the sort of kinship (or family) relationships you experience from day to day.

The test questions will require a familiarity with sociological terminology, major thinkers and their theories, general principles, and methodologies. You will be asked to apply these abstract concepts to particular situations. You will need an overall knowledge of the big picture of sociology, as well as the connections among the other social sciences currently and throughout history to do well on this portion of the exam. As you prepare for the exam, you will notice the cross-fertilization between sociology, political science, and anthropology. Remember to take note of the connections you observe in a journal or diary. Customizing your study aids to your personal experience is the best way to remember terms and concepts.

Sociology Terms to Learn

Behaviorism	Gender and Gender Theory
Cultural Determinism	Groups: Group Dynamics, Groupthink
Cultural Lag	Interaction and Interactionism
Cultural Relativism	Marxism
Demography	Samples: Random, Representative, etc.
Deviance	Social Conflict Theory
Ethnocentrism	Social Organization
Ethnography	Social Stratification
Family: Matriarchy, Patriarchy, etc.	

Sociology Resources

The above list gives examples of the sorts of terms and ideas that you'll likely encounter on the CLEP Social Sciences and History exam. For definitions of the terms, you can consult sociology textbooks; a good one is *Sociology—A Down-to-Earth Approach, Seventh Edition* by James M. Henslin (New York: Allyn & Bacon, 2004); or online reference sites. Check out glossarist.com for thousands of glossaries and topical dictionaries with terms and definitions (particularly strong in the Humanities and Social Science fields). You can also go to ask.com for a variety of resources. Visit your school or local library and read *The American Journal of Sociology*, which is also available online. Another good source for information on many of the Social Science topics is virtuallibrary.com.

Economics

About 10 percent of the social science test questions will come from the field of economics, which translates into approximately 12–13 questions. Economics can be loosely described as the study of how people allot scarce resources to produce needed commodities and how those commodities are distributed for consumption among the people in society. In other words: who makes, sells, and buys what; how commodities are produced, and at what cost. Some of the ways we participate in economics are obvious, but economics is at work in our lives all the time and in ways that you probably are not aware of. Today, economists are employed in almost every industry, from private corporations to the government and academia.

The questions on economics will require a knowledge of economics terms, methodologies, and principles. You will likely also be asked to interpret and analyze graphs or tables to test your ability to apply broad economic concepts to specific data. As you prepare for the exam, it will help if you start paying attention to how you participate in economics all of the time—from how you or your family manages the household economy to how your job allows you to participate in providing goods (i.e. commodities) and services. Keep in mind how the economy relates to the other social sciences, as well as to your personal life. You will begin to notice lots of connections with sociology and political science. Make sure to take note of these relationships, personalizing your study aids as you go along.

Economics Terms to Learn

Business Cycle
Capital and Capitalization
Commodities
Consumption
Depreciation and Appreciation
Distribution
Economies of Scale
Engel's Law
Free-Market Economy

Fiscalist and Monetarist View
Inflation and Deflation
Keynes Effect
Micro- and Macroeconomics
Obsolescence
Open and Closed Economies
Phillips Curve
Scarcity

Economics Resources

To learn more about these terms and others before the exam, here are some places to look: glossarist.com lists lots of economics reference sites; amosweb.com is an excellent source for definitions of terms as well as information about journals, international economics, and new research and data. You can also check out magazines like *The Economist* and read newspapers like *The Wall Street Journal*. When you're channel-surfing, why not stop at CNBC or one of the other financial channels, to further your knowledge of modern economics? For print resources, turn to your school or local library. A college-level economics textbook will be a help as well.

Psychology

About 10 percent of the test questions will come from the field of psychology. That breaks down to about 12 or 13 questions. We all use psychological principles every day without even thinking about it. Psychologists are interested in the study of human behavior, or how people behave in certain situations, how our brains grow and why we think the way we do, as well as how emotions develop and what impact they have on our interactions with others. In preparing for the CLEP Social Sciences and History exam, a heightened awareness of these functions in your own life will help you. For example: when you experience anxiety about taking this exam you are activating your autonomic nervous system. When you reward yourself with a treat for a job well done, you are also using a psychological principle.

The psychology questions on the exam will ask you about common terms, important figures, competing theories, and principles. The test will also ask you to apply certain research methodologies to specific data. As with all of the social sciences, psychology is intimately connected with the other disciplines—it is a good idea to keep a running tab of these connections. Pay attention to the behaviors of those around you. As you are learning a psychological theory, try to find an example of it in your daily life. Remember to personalize your study aids so that you remember terms more easily.

Psychology Terms to Learn

Aggression	Identity
Attachment	Intelligence
Behaviorism	Libido
Cognition	Lobes of the Human Brain
Collective Unconscious	Memory: Retrieval and Storage, Types of
Conformity	Perception
Conscious and Subconscious	Performance
Egocentrism	Personality
Extroversion and Introversion	Placebo Effect
Experimental Method	Reasoning: Deductive and Inductive
Gestalt Theory	Socialization
Group Process	Stage Theory
Id, Ego, and Superego	Variables

Psychology Resources

The list above represents a sampling of the types of terms you'll want to read about before the exam. You'll find a great web resource at allpsych.com—a virtual psychology classroom that has an extensive glossary of terms including all of those mentioned above. You can also check out glossarist.com as well as webref.org. Pick up a copy of *Psychology Today* magazine—it's available at most libraries and is an easy read. You can also look up *The Scientific American* at the library, or borrow an introductory psychology textbook. In addition, the Discovery Channel and the Learning Channel both often feature programs about topics like the human brain, dreaming, or childhood development.

Geography

About 10 percent of the CLEP Social Sciences and History test questions will be drawn from the field of geography—that means about 12 to13 questions. When most people think of geography they probably first think of maps, globes, or atlases. The practice of modern geography, however, involves much more than just memorizing the number of continents or the names of state capitals. Since World War II, the field has experienced an explosion of knowledge as a result of new technologies and the global communications revolution. Every time you get in a car or take a bus, train, or plane you are reaping the benefits of advances in geographical science.

The geography questions on the exam will require a familiarity with specific terms, tools, facts, and major principles. You will likely be asked to interpret data in the form of maps, charts, or tables. You will have to be able to apply a big-picture understanding of world geography to the particulars of a diagram or map. You can and do practice geographical methods all of the time—now you have to start paying attention to it. Look at a subway map with a fresh eye, and maybe check out the maps of your state capital or Washington D.C. Think about looking at the world from a bird's-eye view or from the top of a mountain.

Geography Terms to Learn

Acid Rain
Aerial Photography
Biological Diversity and Functional Diversity
Continental Drift
Demography
Distance
Ecology
Fault Zones
Location
Overpopulation and Underpopulation

Physiography and Topography
Plate Tectonics
Quantitative and Qualitative Analysis
Regional Geography
Remote Sensors
Space Accessibility
Spatial Interaction
Urban, Suburban, and Exurban
Weather and Climate

Geography Resources

The above list represents the kinds of terms and ideas you should investigate before you take the exam. You can learn these terms from a variety of sources: from textbooks to websites, journals, and magazines. Check out about.com for definitions of terms and mrdowling.com for excellent world geography and history information that is well illustrated, fun, and easy to navigate. Flip on the Weather Channel, the Discovery Channel, and the Learning Channel. These channels often feature programming that is weather related, particularly coverage of natural disasters. Remember to refer to traditional globes, maps, and atlases as well.

Anthropology

Only about 6 percent of the questions on the CLEP Social Sciences and History exam are drawn from anthropological subjects—that means approximately 7 questions. But that does not mean you can just skim over the subject. Nor will you want to once you start learning about this fascinating field. A general grasp of anthropology, the study of humankind in various regions of the world and over evolutionary time, will help you out in all of the other fields on the exam. You can hardly afford to overlook the study of human existence!

Anthropology Terms to Learn

Animism, Totemism, and Spiritualism
Archaeology
Artifact
Bipedalism
Biological Imperative
Brachiation
Chronometric Dating and Absolute Dating
Cultural, Physical, and Social Anthropology

Ethnography
Evolutionary Theory
Hominid
Linguistics
Matrilineal and Patrilineal Societies
Paleontology
Primate

Anthropology Resources

For definitions of the terms above you can go to the glossary of terms at the Leakey Foundation website: leakeyfoundation.org, where you can also learn about important figures and theories from the field. You should also check out the website for the American Anthropological Association at aaanet.org, where you'll get an excellent overview of the field and its many subfields. For a great interactive educational experience, visit the official website of the Cave at Lascaux: www.culture.fr/culture/arcnat/lascaux/en.; you'll feel like you're discovering prehistoric cave paintings for yourself. You also should look for anthropology textbooks and journals at your school or local library.

Final Thoughts

With all of these tools and resources, if you plan your study time well and follow through, you'll be well on your way to a great score on the CLEP Social Sciences and History exam.

Good luck!

Section Five: The CLEP Social Sciences and History Exam | 399

Chapter Eighteen: Practice Test 2

Time—90 minutes
120 Questions

Directions: For each of the following questions or incomplete statements, select the best answer or completion from the five options given.

1. Which of the following statements best characterizes social stratification?

    (A) The process serves as a cultural leveler
    (B) It is a hierarchical structure with a premise of the equal division of societies
    (C) The practice is a persistent characteristic of all societies throughout the world
    (D) It can be based on a broad range of factors including wealth, gender, and power
    (E) Social stratification is always fixed or static

2. With whom was Abraham Lincoln shaking hands when he famously remarked, "So this is the little lady who made this big war?"

    (A) Harriet Tubman
    (B) Rosa Parks
    (C) Harriet Beecher Stowe
    (D) Mary Todd
    (E) Harriet Jacobs

3. Which is true about the growth of the human brain?

    (A) It continues to grow into early childhood but at a slower rate than in infancy.
    (B) It begins to grow exponentially after the age of three.
    (C) It reaches 75 percent of adult size by age five.
    (D) It reaches 90 percent of adult size by age three.
    (E) It continues to grow throughout the lifespan of the average person.

4. What will be the likely impact of widespread Internet usage on closed/authoritarian societies?

    (A) Governments will outlaw the Internet.
    (B) It will become more difficult for governments to control information.
    (C) Citizens will be less informed about the world outside their own country.
    (D) Political and cultural change will be realized more slowly in closed societies.
    (E) People in these countries will be more content.

GO ON TO THE NEXT PAGE

KAPLAN

5. Which of the following is true about the role of the Catholic Church in early and medieval Europe?

   I. It was the largest and most powerful patron of the arts.
   II. It settled disputes between emerging nations.
   III. Popes annointed kings, conferring a sort of divine authority.

   (A) I only
   (B) III only
   (C) II and III only
   (D) I and II only
   (E) I, II, and III

6. Charles Horton Cooley concluded that human development is socially created—that our sense of self develops from looking at others. To describe this process, he coined the term

   (A) mirroring
   (B) mimesis
   (C) looking-glass self
   (D) social imprinting
   (E) imitation impulse

7. At the Battle at Bunker Hill, the American soldiers were ordered not to fire until they could see "the whites of their eyes" because

   (A) they had very little ammunition with which to attack the British soldiers
   (B) the Native Americans often used captured colonial soldiers as human shields
   (C) they knew the Native Americans were superstitious and would not fire back if they looked them directly in the eyes
   (D) many American revolutionaries had Loyalist relatives fighting on the side of the British Crown
   (E) French and British uniforms were easy to confuse from farther away

8. A colony is

   (A) located in a previously unexplored area of the world
   (B) often feared for its imperialistic tendencies
   (C) always expensive for the mother country to maintain
   (D) a settlement that is controlled by another country
   (E) usually a poor source of natural resources

9. Which of the following is NOT a component of the study of sociology?

   (A) demography
   (B) ethnography
   (C) culture
   (D) behaviorism
   (E) fascism

10. Abraham Lincoln eventually promoted which military man to general and commander of all Union forces?

    (A) Stonewall Jackson
    (B) Ulysses S. Grant
    (C) Jefferson Davis
    (D) Dwight D. Eisenhower
    (E) Donald Custer

11. Julius Caesar was assassinated because

    (A) his ambitious son was eager to ascend to the throne
    (B) he refused to return conquered lands to the Carthaginians
    (C) his political enemies believed he was planning to declare himself king
    (D) his wife was angry at his infidelities and lack of discretion
    (E) of his Christian belief system

GO ON TO THE NEXT PAGE

12. Conformity is common in the adolescent phase of an individual's life when one's sense of self is typically not entirely developed. Which of the following is NOT an example of conformity?

    (A) experimenting with fads like piercings or tattoos
    (B) adopting a popular hairstyle or fashion
    (C) abandoning interests or practices that are outside social norms
    (D) choosing pursuits based solely upon personal interest or affinity
    (E) the adoption of values that are out of step with one's core values

13. Henry Kissinger served in foreign policy positions under several presidents, but historians generally agree his greatest influence came under Nixon and Ford. Which of the following statements is true about Dr. Kissinger?

    (A) as Nixon's top security advisor, he guided Vietnam policy through the "Vietnamization" campaign
    (B) as President Ford's chief of staff he skillfully led the military invasions of Cambodia and Laos
    (C) under President Carter, he negotiated with South Vietnam leading to the 1976 cease-fire
    (D) he was the sole recipient of the Nobel Peace Prize in 1973
    (E) he advocated an aggressive policy of détente with China and the Soviet Union

14. Which of these is not a function of the United States government outlined in the preamble to the Constitution?

    (A) provision for the common defense
    (B) the establishment of a system of justice
    (C) the preservation of domestic tranquility
    (D) promotion of the general welfare of the body politic
    (E) the establishment of a uniform system of weights and measures

15. Who was the first Secretary of the Treasury in America?

    (A) Alexander Hamilton
    (B) Benjamin Franklin
    (C) John Jay
    (D) John Hancock
    (E) James Madison

16. When Jean Piaget studied children and IQ test results, he noted that young children consistently chose wrong answers while older children were able to give the expected answer. Piaget studied how children learn intellectually and how that ability matures, in other words, their

    (A) behavioral sociology
    (B) cognitive development
    (C) cognitive psychology
    (D) sensorimotor socialization
    (E) behavioral psychology

17. The impairment of the ability to communicate either through oral or written discourse as a result of brain damage is usually

    (A) due to genetic mutation
    (B) called amnesia
    (C) termed aphasia
    (D) totally reversible with therapy
    (E) called apoplexy

18. What is animism?

    (A) the attribution of human characteristics to animals
    (B) a belief that the world is inhabited by impersonal supernatural powers
    (C) a belief in spirit beings that are associated with nature or natural objects
    (D) the belief in several gods and/or goddesses
    (E) the belief in one god or goddess

19. Famous for his frugality, homespun witticisms, and inventions, this patriot quipped, "Early to bed, early to rise, makes a man healthy, wealthy, and wise."

    (A) Daniel Boone
    (B) Henry David Thoreau
    (C) James Fenimore Cooper
    (D) Davy Crockett
    (E) Benjamin Franklin

20. The "lost" city of Machu Picchu was built by the Incas in what is now

    (A) Argentina
    (B) Mexico
    (C) Columbia
    (D) Peru
    (E) Guatemala

21. One Frenchman was perhaps the most perceptive of all observers of American civilization; who is he?

    (A) Alexis de Tocqueville
    (B) William Dunlap
    (C) W.E.B. DuBois
    (D) Napoleon Bonaparte
    (E) Marquis de Sade

22. The African nations of Ethiopia and Eritrea have battled intermittently for many years over

    (A) illegal poaching of endangered species
    (B) the annexation of Eritrea by Ethiopia in 1962
    (C) trade arguments negotiated when Eritrea was an Italian territory
    (D) ownership of ancient artifacts with significance for both nations
    (E) rich mineral deposits along their shared border

23. Which of the following describes Easter Island?

    (A) It can be found off the coast of Chile
    (B) It is known for its unusually large rabbit population
    (C) It is named for its discoverer, the Earl of Easter
    (D) It is the site of the observations Charles Darwin wrote about in *The Origin of Species*
    (E) It resembles a cross in shape

24. Sigmund Freud's "Pleasure Principle" is his theory

    (A) regarding the eternal struggle between the id and the ego for gratification
    (B) that we remain in the oral stage of development in an effort to reenact the comfort we received from breast-feeding
    (C) of the id's desire to maximize pleasure and minimize pain in order to achieve immediate gratification
    (D) that all human pleasure is ultimately a result of parental approval
    (E) regarding the id's desire to minimize pleasure and maximize pain in order to achieve immediate gratification

25. What revivalist wrote the popular sermon "Sinners in the Hands of an Angry God" in the 1740s?

    (A) Lyman Beecher
    (B) Jonathan Edwards
    (C) William Bradford
    (D) Timothy Dwight
    (E) Benjamin Rush

26. Functionalism, structuralism, symbolic interactionism, and gender theory are all examples of theoretical approaches to what field of study?

    (A) sociology
    (B) literature
    (C) psychology
    (D) social anthropology
    (E) cultural anthropology

27. Rituals, often religious in nature, marking important stages in the lives of individuals such as marriage, birth, or death are known as

    (A) rites of intensification
    (B) the sacraments, or holy unctions
    (C) gender stratification rituals
    (D) either incorporation or reincorporation rituals
    (E) rites of passage

28. Sparta was known for its

    (A) industry and commerce
    (B) fierce warrior culture
    (C) intellectual freedom
    (D) scientific accomplishment
    (E) epic poetry

29. Which of the following is NOT an agent of socialization in the modern world?

    (A) the family unit
    (B) social class
    (C) sleep patterns
    (D) the mass media
    (E) religion

30. In 1802, Napoleon Bonaparte arranged for the sale of

    (A) St. Augustine, Florida, and its environs to the Seminole Indians for use as a reservation
    (B) the province of Louisiana to the Spanish Crown
    (C) exclusive trading rights to Lewis and Clark along the Mississippi River in exchange for an elimination of Creole tariffs
    (D) the Louisiana Territory to the United States
    (E) one thousand Haitian slaves aboard the *Amistad* in return for the Canadian province of Acadia

31. Psychology, like sociology, is often referred to as a social science or

    (A) absolute science
    (B) soft science
    (C) pseudoscience
    (D) life science
    (E) physical science

32. The Monroe Doctrine was significant because

    (A) President Monroe declared that presidents should not run for office more than twice
    (B) President Monroe was the first to receive a doctorate while in office
    (C) it stated the U.S. policy against European expansion in the western hemisphere
    (D) it officially declared the annexation of Texas by the United States
    (E) it proposed isolationism as official U.S. policy

GO ON TO THE NEXT PAGE

33. When conducting a study using a random sample, the experimenter obtains the subjects

    (A) by chance from the larger population being studied
    (B) using a specific set of demographic criteria
    (C) from a representative sample of the population
    (D) from groups that they have been observing over time
    (E) with no regard to personal bias

34. Which of these explorers was the first European to set foot in Florida?

    (A) Ferdinand Magellan
    (B) Robert de la Salle
    (C) John Cabot
    (D) Ponce de Leon
    (E) Christopher Columbus

35. A pattern in which a married couple may choose to live in the locality associated with either the husband's or the wife's relatives is known as

    (A) patrilocal residence
    (B) matrilocal residence
    (C) avunculocal residence
    (D) ambilocal residence
    (E) eneolocal residence

36. Heinrich Schliemann is significant because he

    (A) found and translated the first known version of Homer's *Iliad*
    (B) navigated the ship which charted the first trade route to China
    (C) was the archaeologist who found the ancient city of Troy
    (D) operated the first printing press famed for printing the Gutenberg Bible
    (E) discovered the tomb of King Tuthankamen and its archaeological treasures

37. The largest nonpolar desert in the world is the

    (A) Sahara
    (B) Gobi
    (C) Mohave
    (D) Kalahari
    (E) Arabian

38. The phenomenon that occurs when a collection of people are in total agreement and disinterested in entertaining any opposing viewpoint is known as

    (A) group polarization
    (B) social loafing
    (C) peer pressure
    (D) Stockholm syndrome
    (E) groupthink

39. As a result of mass immigration, by 1910, fully three-fourths of New York City's population

    (A) had been stricken with tropical viruses that traveled via steamer ships and locomotives
    (B) were either recent émigrés or first-generation Americans
    (C) were of Pacific Rim or Slavic ancestry
    (D) left the bustling city center for the relative calm of the outer boroughs
    (E) had displaced Native Americans, who were forced to move to the south or west

40. Formerly an American ally, what Panamanian dictator was overthrown by his countrymen and forced to seek refuge in the United States?

    (A) Daniel Ortega
    (B) Mario Vargas Llosa
    (C) Manuel Noriega
    (D) Juan Perón
    (E) Vicente Fox

GO ON TO THE NEXT PAGE

41. Emile Durkheim studied the social factors that underlie suicidal tendencies, concluding that

    (A) genetics is the sole determinant
    (B) suicidal fantasies are much more common among females than males
    (C) individual circumstance is a larger determinant of suicidal impulse than social factors
    (D) the degree to which people are tied to a social structure is as important as individual circumstance
    (E) individuals in urban environments are almost twice as likely to contemplate suicide as rural dwellers

42. Which of the following people was an escaped slave who became a well-known spokesman for abolitionism after the publication of his personal narrative?

    (A) Booker T. Washington
    (B) Washington Carver
    (C) Frederick Douglas
    (D) Frederick Jackson Turner
    (E) W.E.B. DuBois

43. Considered the upper house in the United States government, what power does the Senate possess that is not granted to the House of Representatives?

    (A) The power to levy and lower taxes
    (B) The ability to oversee and regulate the airline industry
    (C) The power to originate spending bills and propositions
    (D) The ability to override a Presidential veto
    (E) The power to ratify treaties with foreign nations

44. When alone, people tend to be more relaxed and less concerned with their outward behavior. When two or more people are together their behavior tends to change. What is the term for this phenomenon?

    (A) social facilitation
    (B) acquiescence
    (C) behavior modification
    (D) social morphism
    (E) antisocial behavior

45. Which of the following statements is FALSE about the Puritans, the original settlers of the American colonies?

    (A) They were devoted to doctrinal purity in their methods of worship.
    (B) They were dissatisfied with the influence of Roman Catholicism on their Anglican faith.
    (C) They were suspicious of the ritual, dogma, and political influence of the Catholic Church.
    (D) They were a mainstream group motivated by radical religious idealism that was popular in eighteenth-century England.
    (E) They were convinced that the Reformation had not gone far enough and that Queen Elizabeth I was too tolerant.

46. Which of the following monarchs was honored by Pope Leo X for an eloquent and vigorous defense of the Church against Martin Luther's attacks?

    (A) Henry VIII
    (B) Mary I
    (C) Frederick the Great
    (D) Richard I
    (E) Louis XVI

47. Which of the following is true of Transcendentalism?

    (A) It was practiced by Pennsylvania Quakers in an effort to communicate directly with the divine.
    (B) It was an intellectual, spiritual, and artistic movement that found its fullest expression at Brook Farm.
    (C) It represented the antithesis of the romantic ideals of Emerson and Thoreau.
    (D) It encouraged the practical and rational over the romantic and sublime.
    (E) It still thrives at Oneida, the utopian community in upstate New York.

48. The primary tools of fiscal policy are

    (A) restrictions on bank ownership
    (B) restrictions on interest rates
    (C) raising and lowering taxes and government spending
    (D) increasing and decreasing the money supply
    (E) raising and lowering the discount rate

49. This thinker coined the term "sociology" and suggested the use of positivism—applying the scientific method to the social world—though he never used the approach himself. Who was he?

    (A) Herbert Spencer
    (B) Max Weber
    (C) Wright Mills
    (D) Erik Erikson
    (E) Auguste Comte

50. The "shot heard round the world" refers to

    (A) the assassination of Archduke Ferdinand in Sarajevo, which signaled the beginning of World War II
    (B) the Japanese kamikaze-style attack at Pearl Harbor
    (C) the execution-style death of a Chinese student at Tiananmen Square
    (D) the unordered shot at Lexington that marked the beginning of the American Revolution
    (E) a misfired cannon that led to the Battle of Troy

51. Money, praise, intellectual stimulation—none of which are absolutely necessary for individual survival—are examples of

    (A) primary reinforcers
    (B) independent variables
    (C) secondary reinforcers
    (D) socially reinforced variables
    (E) situational attributes

52. The remains of the Ottoman empire, which collapsed following World War I, are known today as

    (A) Turkey
    (B) Mongolia
    (C) Russia
    (D) Iran
    (E) Morocco

GO ON TO THE NEXT PAGE

53. The Temperance movement of the ninteenth century

    (A) essentially pioneered the platform for the anger-management programs that are widely practiced in the workplace today
    (B) advocated the legalization and dispensation of birth control devices in overcrowded urban communities
    (C) was initially more successful at the state and local levels but eventually found universal acceptance
    (D) emphasized sexual abstinence until marriage with varying degrees of success
    (E) blamed the consumption of alcohol for a wide range of social ills, from poverty to insanity

54. Which of the following best explains the system of checks and balances?

    (A) The Federal Reserve System relies on people maintaining checking account balances in order to control the money supply.
    (B) The federal government checks into the background of individuals applying for sensitive government jobs.
    (C) Each of the three branches of the federal government has the ability to check the power of the other two.
    (D) The president and Congress work together to balance the federal budget.
    (E) Parties to a dispute can take their case all the way to the Supreme Court if they choose.

55. Polyandry is

    (A) the marriage custom of a woman having two or more husbands simultaneously
    (B) the marriage custom of a man having two or more wives simultaneously
    (C) a family consisting of related women, their offspring, and the women's brothers
    (D) a form of marriage in which a man or a woman marries a series of partners in succession
    (E) a family unit consisting of husband, wife, and more than one child

56. Which of the following groups did not invade Rome during the final days of the empire?

    (A) Huns
    (B) Visigoths
    (C) Vandals
    (D) Tartars
    (E) Ostrogoths

57. Which of the following describes ethnocentrism?

    (A) It is an attitude in the study of society that always takes cultural uniqueness into consideration.
    (B) It is more common in urban than in rural communities.
    (C) It is an approach which views other cultures and societies from the point of view of one's own values and beliefs.
    (D) It is a variation of cultural relativism.
    (E) It is a very progressive attitude toward the study of preliterate societies.

GO ON TO THE NEXT PAGE

58. Which of the following statements is FALSE when drawing a comparison between the Enlightenment in America and the same period in Europe?

    (A) In Europe, Enlightenment thinking tended to be a private affair of drawing rooms and personal correspondence
    (B) In America, where the king and the bishop were far away, the colonists were outspoken in their proclamation of new ideas.
    (C) Americans tended to be more abstract and less practical in the application of Enlightenment ideals than their European counterparts.
    (D) Europeans like Isaac Newton, Francis Bacon, and John Locke had done most of the technical thinking necessary for religious and political reform to flourish in America.
    (E) The abstract controversies of the European Enlightenment never made much of an impact on everyday life in America.

59. The story of human evolution has emerged slowly over the past two centuries. What was the effect of the discovery of the "Taung child" in 1925?

    (A) It failed to prove the evolutionary link between humans and chimps.
    (B) It was a true missing link between humans and chimps, the significance of which was overlooked for many years.
    (C) It was later proven to be a hoax that set back evolutionary studies for forty years.
    (D) It helped Franz Boaz prove that fossilized skulls were not always indicators of brain capacity.
    (E) It affirmed the link between the Piltdown Man and early hominids.

60. Who famously said, "Religion is the opiate of the masses?"

    (A) Adolph Hitler
    (B) Jerry Falwell
    (C) Vladimir Lenin
    (D) Sigmund Freud
    (E) Karl Marx

61. In 1848, Elizabeth Cady Stanton and Lucretia Mott held a convention in Seneca Falls, New York that helped launch

    (A) the women's rights movement
    (B) child labor legislation
    (C) the Temperance movement
    (D) women's colleges all over the Northeast, founding the Seven Sisters
    (E) groundbreaking divorce and women's property rights legislation

62. Cultural imperialism is the aggressive promotion of one's own (usually Western) culture, based on the assumption that its value system is superior to those of other cultures. Which of the following is NOT an example of cultural imperialism?

    (A) permitting students to wear their religious symbols to school even if they are not the same as those of the dominant culture
    (B) forcing capitalism on third-world countries before they are economically prepared for the change
    (C) Hollywood's exportation of American social mores in film, music videos, and television programming to the more conservative Middle East
    (D) McDonald's restaurants and Levi's stores opening in Red Square
    (E) the exportation of ideas like gender equality and democracy to non-Western nations

63. The term "bicameral legislature" means

    (A) legislators are elected every two years
    (B) two locations serve as the capital
    (C) the legislature meets every two years
    (D) both men and women may serve in the legislature
    (E) there are two houses in the legislature

GO ON TO THE NEXT PAGE

64. From the 1950s on, this team conducted a series of expeditions to Olduvai Gorge, producing several important discoveries of early primate fossils.

    (A) Louis and Mary Leakey
    (B) Donald and Lucy Livingstone
    (C) Louis and Lucy Leakey
    (D) Boaz and Benedict
    (E) Margaret and Mary Mead

65. Which of the following is NOT a means by which islands are formed?

    (A) Erosion between two land masses causes land to break away, leaving an unattached portion surrounded by water.
    (B) Skeletal remains of coral build up over millions of years.
    (C) Underwater volcanic eruptions create mountains of lava that eventually rise above the water.
    (D) A meteor crashes into the ocean.
    (E) Continental plates collide, creating undersea mountain ranges that break the surface of the water.

66. Peter the Great is credited with which of the following achievements?

    I. Opening new trade relationships between Russia and Western Europe
    II. Building the city of St. Petersburg
    III. Shaping Russia into a major European power

    (A) II only
    (B) I and II only
    (C) II and III only
    (D) III only
    (E) I, II, and III

67. Groups are the essence of life in society. Primary groups consist of

    (A) cooperative, intimate, face-to-face relationships
    (B) the extended family network
    (C) peer groups and superficial social networks
    (D) coworkers and authority figures
    (E) an individual's genus and species

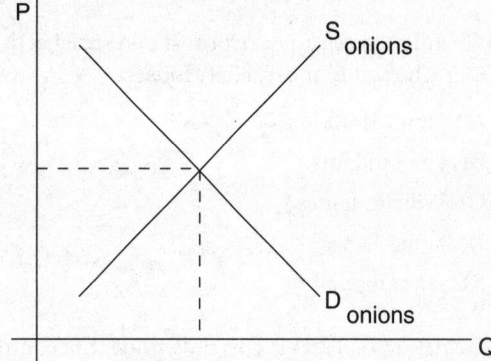

68. Assume that it is suddenly discovered that onions prevent hair loss and wrinkles. What will the impact be on the demand curve for onions?

    (A) The price elasticity of onions will rise.
    (B) The demand curve will shift to the right.
    (C) The demand curve will shift to the left.
    (D) There will be no change.
    (E) The price elasticity of onions will fall.

69. What was the Donation of Pepin?

    (A) a gift of land that sealed the alliance between the Frankish dynasty and the papacy
    (B) the return to the Huns of their rightful lands
    (C) a deed to the Catholic Church of tax-free land for cathedrals
    (D) a bribe that helped Charlemagne ascend the throne
    (E) a grant to the Spanish of the right to explore freely throughout the New World

GO ON TO THE NEXT PAGE

70. What is the significance of *Marbury v. Madison*?

    (A) It reiterated the official policy of separation of church and state.
    (B) It finally granted women the right to vote.
    (C) It extended the right to bear arms in the American West.
    (D) It established the tradition of judicial review.
    (E) It banned smoking in all government facilities.

71. Which Progressive-era reformist and social activist from Chicago founded Hull House?

    (A) James Hoffa
    (B) Jane Addams
    (C) William James
    (D) James Dewey
    (E) Jane Goodall

72. The nation of Tibet is currently under the control of what country?

    (A) Sri Lanka
    (B) the United Nations
    (C) India
    (D) Pakistan
    (E) China

73. Which of the following scientific accomplishments is NOT the result of Louis Pasteur's research?

    (A) the practice of heating milk to kill bacteria
    (B) vaccinations for anthrax, rabies, and cholera
    (C) the insight that germs do not originate spontaneously
    (D) saving France's silk industry by identifying bacteria that attacked silkworms
    (E) the use of X-rays to view inside the body

74. George Herbert Mead is known for

    (A) first distinguishing between the "I" and the "me" in the development of the self
    (B) his work with primates and tool usage in Nairobi
    (C) his groundbreaking research on adolescent females in Samoa
    (D) his first wife, Margaret, a famous anthropologist
    (E) first distinguishing between the "ego" and the "superego"

75. Do rivers always flow from north to south?

    (A) Yes.
    (B) No, in the southern hemisphere they flow south to north.
    (C) No, they flow with gravity, from higher to lower elevations.
    (D) No, they flow toward the largest body of water.
    (E) No, some rivers do not flow at all.

76. Which famous wearer of a coonskin cap became a celebrity in his own time as tales of his exploits were told in popular books and produced for the stage?

    (A) John Quincy Adams
    (B) Benjamin Franklin
    (C) James Fenimore Cooper
    (D) Daniel Boone
    (E) Davy Crockett

GO ON TO THE NEXT PAGE

77. The term "'centration"
    (A) refers to the bond a child forms with his or her primary caregiver
    (B) describes a demographic shift toward urban or population centers
    (C) denotes the tendency of a young child to focus only on his or her own perspective
    (D) was conceptualized by Elizabeth Kubler-Ross as one of the stages of grief
    (E) describes the tendency of parents to focus inordinately on their firstborn child

78. After 395 C.E., the Roman empire was divided into the Eastern empire and the Western empire. What was the capital of the Eastern empire?
    (A) Cairo
    (B) Mesopotamia
    (C) Baghdad
    (D) Constantinople
    (E) Peking

79. Which statement is NOT true about Queen Elizabeth I of England?
    (A) Her reign was a time of peace and prosperity.
    (B) Arts and culture flourished while she was in power.
    (C) England enjoyed resounding military triumph under her stewardship.
    (D) She never married, and she left her throne to her nephew.
    (E) She restored the Catholic church as the official church of England.

80. Which U.S. President said, "The buck stops here," meaning that he took full responsibility for his decisions?
    (A) Ronald Reagan
    (B) Richard Nixon
    (C) Franklin Delano Roosevelt
    (D) Bill Clinton
    (E) Harry S. Truman

81. The precipitating causes of the French Revolution did not include
    (A) economic disarray brought on by bad weather and poor crop harvests
    (B) dissatisfaction with an unwieldy and inefficient bureaucracy
    (C) higher taxes to support an increasingly expensive government
    (D) the inability or lack of desire of the king to address the need for real reform
    (E) the desire of French women to be given the right to vote and hold office

82. What leader emerged in the chaotic aftermath of World War II France to restore that nation to a position of European power?
    (A) Charles de Gaulle
    (B) Jean Monet
    (C) Georges Pompidou
    (D) François Mitterand
    (E) Pierre Mendes-France

83. Which of the following is NOT a condition for nationhood?
    (A) a sustained native population
    (B) a transportation system for people and goods
    (C) boundaries defined by a river or other natural landmarks
    (D) external recognition by other countries
    (E) an official currency

84. Memories for facts, life events, and information
    (A) are a product of the somatic memory response system
    (B) are most often stored in short-term memory
    (C) are rapidly displaced when traumatic events occur
    (D) are stored in declarative memory
    (E) are stored in sensory memory

GO ON TO THE NEXT PAGE

85. Niccolo Machiavelli was

   (A) the first man to circumnavigate the globe commanding the Spanish Armada
   (B) a sixteenth-century Italian writer who originated the idea of political pragmatism
   (C) a foreign policy advisor to King Ferdinand and Queen Isabella of Spain
   (D) the first scientist to determine that the earth revolves around the sun
   (E) a Renaissance sculptor from Napoli

86. What drawback is common to all counter-cyclical economic policy?

   (A) There are time lags involved in implementing the policy.
   (B) It is subject to political interference.
   (C) It may be hindered by Congressional recess.
   (D) The Supreme Court may declare it to be unconstitutional.
   (E) the Federal Reserve may choose not to act at all.

87. When a society adds a new cultural element—an invention or discovery—it takes some time for the culture to adjust; an example of this is the introduction of the automobile. What did William Ogburn call this tendency?

   (A) technological lag
   (B) symbiosis
   (C) cultural lag
   (D) the placebo effect
   (E) a cultural anomaly

88. The Hindu religion as we know it today was first practiced in

   (A) Malaysia
   (B) India
   (C) Nepal
   (D) Indonesia
   (E) Its origins are unclear

89. In the thirteenth century, the teenaged Marco Polo traveled to China with his father and uncle, where they were guests at the court of

   (A) Confucius
   (B) Mao Tse-tung
   (C) Liu Pang
   (D) Chairman Mao
   (E) Kublai Khan

90. The "Roundheads" and the "Cavaliers" were nicknames given to opposing factions in which country's revolution?

   (A) France
   (B) the United States
   (C) Russia
   (D) England
   (E) Chile

91. The decision-making process in which ideas are processed from the general to the specific is called

   (A) deductive reasoning
   (B) inductive reasoning
   (C) circular logic
   (D) reductive reasoning
   (E) logical reductivism

92. Which of the following is not attributed to the Mesopotamians?

   (A) calculus
   (B) metal coinage
   (C) flood control and irrigation
   (D) use of the arch and dome
   (E) a system of weights and measures

GO ON TO THE NEXT PAGE

93. Which of the following is a reasonable possible reaction to a period of rising inflation?

    (A) The Federal Reserve could lower interest rates.
    (B) Congress could increase government spending.
    (C) The FDIC could close the banks for a period of time.
    (D) The Federal Reserve could decrease the money supply.
    (E) Congress could either raise or lower taxes.

94. Who are the "Reagan Democrats"?

    (A) Republicans who switched to the Democratic party because they disagreed with Ronald Reagan
    (B) individuals who had traditionally been Democrats, but who began to vote Republican with Reagan's first presidential election
    (C) individuals who, like Ronald Reagan, switched from the Democratic party to the Republican party
    (D) Democrats who abstained from voting because they disliked both Ronald Reagan and his Democratic opponents
    (E) Republicans who became Democrats after Reagan's presidency because they disliked his successor

95. Which of the following does NOT contribute to acid rain?

    (A) sulphur dioxide emissions from industrial plants
    (B) nitrogen oxide emissions from automobiles
    (C) volcanic eruptions
    (D) lightning strikes
    (E) an unusually warm current in the Pacific Ocean

96. Karl Marx is considered the father of what philosophy of government?

    (A) democracy
    (B) nazism
    (C) fascism
    (D) communism
    (E) oligarchy

97. Which of these oil-producing countries is NOT a member of OPEC?

    (A) Mexico
    (B) Venezuela
    (C) Kuwait
    (D) Indonesia
    (E) Iran

98. In his "Fourteen Points" speech before Congress in 1918, President Woodrow Wilson began explaining his strategy for peace following World War I. In his speech, he introduced his idea of a "peace without victory." Which of the following is NOT one of the main tenets of his plan?

    (A) the idea of an "open" world after the war
    (B) freedom to navigate the seas
    (C) an affirmation of imperialism
    (D) equal trading practices and elimination of protective tariffs
    (E) an association of nations to ensure political independence and territorial integrity

99. An example of a government that has a ceremonial monarchy and an elected governing body is

    (A) Korea
    (B) Great Britain
    (C) Saudi Arabia
    (D) South Africa
    (E) Mexico

100. What is the name of the fault along which most of the major earthquakes in the United States have occurred?

    (A) San Jacinto
    (B) Balcones
    (C) New Madrid
    (D) Denali
    (E) San Andreas

101. Keynes argued that the level of economic activity is primarily determined by the level of

    (A) aggregate supply
    (B) unemployment
    (C) interest rates
    (D) inflation
    (E) aggregate demand

102. What word best describes American policy toward the Soviet Union from 1947 until the early 1980s?

    (A) containment
    (B) glasnost
    (C) appeasement
    (D) alliance
    (E) détente

103. Cartography is

    (A) a means of transporting goods over long distances
    (B) the study of handwriting analysis
    (C) the history of the automobile industry
    (D) the science of mapmaking
    (E) the charting of ancient trade routes

104. In 1954 the Supreme Court unanimously agreed that segregation in public schools is unconstitutional. What is the name of this landmark decision?

    (A) *Plessy v. Ferguson*
    (B) *Brown v. the Board of Education of Topeka, Kansas*
    (C) *Loving v. Virginia*
    (D) *Brown v. Charlotte-Mecklenburg Board of Education*
    (E) *Plessy v. the Board of Education of Topeka, Kansas*

105. Which of the following statements about political lobbying is true?

    (A) The McCain-Feingold Campaign Reform Act makes it illegal.
    (B) The practice is limited to the national level.
    (C) The practice has far-reaching effects on all aspects of the political process.
    (D) Only certain government-sanctioned groups are permitted to have lobbyists.
    (E) The practice is most common at the local level.

106. Which is NOT a reason why some countries with tremendous natural wealth may remain relatively poor?

    (A) They lack technology to fully utilize their natural resources.
    (B) There is government corruption and personal greed.
    (C) The infrastructure—such as roads, electricity, and transportation—is inadequate.
    (D) The uneducated workforce is not trained to make full use of natural resources.
    (E) The dominant culture encourages asceticism.

GO ON TO THE NEXT PAGE

107. Hurricane season in the United States is

    (A) June to November
    (B) September to January
    (C) March to August
    (D) October to May
    (E) Hurricanes occur year-round in the United States

108. Say's Law holds that

    (A) as inflation rises, interest rates will go up as well
    (B) the income earned by people for producing goods allows them to purchase the goods produced by others
    (C) people prefer tangible assets to paper currency during times of economic uncertainty
    (D) people prefer to hold liquid assets during times of rapid interest rate fluctuation
    (E) lower interest rates stimulate economic growth

109. The compromise that settled the dispute over how to count slaves for the purpose of Congressional representation was called the

    (A) Albany Compromise
    (B) Great Compromise
    (C) Connecticut Compromise
    (D) Three-Fifths Compromise
    (E) Forty Acres Compromise

110. Which economist espoused the theory of "creative destruction"?

    (A) Ludwig von Mises
    (B) Joseph Schumpeter
    (C) John Maynard Keynes
    (D) Anna Schwartz
    (E) Alan Greenspan

111. The Bikini atoll gained significance becuase

    (A) it was the site of early nuclear research in the development of the atomic bomb
    (B) the naval battle fought there led to the surrender of the Japanese Navy
    (C) the Rosetta stone was uncovered there, allowing archaeologists to decipher early writing
    (D) it was the site of a massive volcanic eruption
    (E) Napoleon was exiled there in 1812 and lived there until his death

112. Which of the following methods of amending the Constitution has never been used?

    (A) An amendment is proposed by a two-thirds vote in Congress and ratified by three-fourths of the state legislatures.
    (B) An amendment is proposed by Congress and ratified by conventions called for that purpose by three-fourths of the states.
    (C) An amendment is proposed by a national convention and ratified by conventions in three-fourths of the states.
    (D) An amendment is proposed by a national convention called by Congress and ratified by three-fourths of the state legislatures.
    (E) All four methods have been used.

113. The Southern Cross is

    (A) the criss-cross pattern made by the stars on the Confederate flag
    (B) a pattern of crosswinds in the southern Pacific ocean
    (C) a constellation entirely visible in the southern hemisphere
    (D) the labyrinthine approach to Mt. Everest originating in the southern part of Nepal
    (E) a group of islands south of Australia where Franciscan monks trace their roots

114. In economics, the term *equilibrium* means that

    (A) demand for a good exceeds the supply
    (B) the government has enacted price controls
    (C) prices of all similar goods are equal
    (D) demand and supply are equal
    (E) the number of sellers of a particular good is fixed

115. Senator Joseph McCarthy first entered the public spotlight in 1950 by claiming

    (A) that communists had infiltrated the American military and the FBI
    (B) that communists had "infested" the state department
    (C) that the Jews were running Hollywood and controlling the media
    (D) a vast conspiracy existed between the Soviets and traitorous American politicians
    (E) that no one in the government could be trusted

116. Supreme Court justices serve

    (A) for as long as the President keeps them
    (B) for ten tears
    (C) for life
    (D) as long as the President's political party remains in power
    (E) until the President who appointed them leaves office

117. Which of the following statements about outsourcing is true?

    (A) It typically leads to rising standards of living in developing countries.
    (B) It can lower a company's operational costs.
    (C) It exports technology around the world.
    (D) It may temporarily displace workers in developed countries.
    (E) All of the above statements are true.

118. What are the climatic consequences of the Andes Mountains on the surrounding regions?

    (A) The range blocks the sunlight from reaching the western slope of the mountains.
    (B) The snow in the mountains melts and provides water for the lower elevations.
    (C) The mountains prevent much of the moisture carried by the Atlantic trade winds from passing to the western side of the range.
    (D) The Andes shift the direction of Atlantic trade winds to the south.
    (E) The Andes shift the direction of the Atlantic trade winds to the north.

119. Which of the following is not a component of Gross National Product?

    (A) consumer spending
    (B) business investment
    (C) government expenditures
    (D) interest rates
    (E) exports

120. What was the policy toward Hitler's Germany advocated by British prime minister Neville Chamberlain?

    (A) to immediately go to war before Hitler could gain more strength
    (B) to impose economic sanctions, forcing Germany to withdraw troops from occupied territory
    (C) to allow Hitler to continue to occupy the land he wanted, and hope he would be satisfied
    (D) to have the United Nations send in troops in hopes of forcing the Germans to leave Czechoslovakia
    (E) to ask the United States for military aid in the event of war

END OF TEST.

THE ANSWER KEY APPEARS ON THE FOLLOWING PAGE.

ANSWER KEY

1. D	21. A	41. D	61. A	81. E	101. E
2. C	22. B	42. C	62. A	82. A	102. A
3. A	23. A	43. E	63. E	83. C	103. D
4. B	24. C	44. A	64. A	84. D	104. B
5. E	25. B	45. D	65. D	85. B	105. C
6. C	26. A	46. A	66. E	86. A	106. E
7. A	27. E	47. B	67. A	87. C	107. A
8. D	28. B	48. C	68. B	88. B	108. B
9. E	29. C	49. E	69. A	89. E	109. D
10. B	30. D	50. D	70. D	90. D	110. B
11. C	31. B	51. C	71. B	91. A	111. A
12. D	32. C	52. A	72. E	92. A	112. D
13. A	33. A	53. E	73. E	93. D	113. C
14. E	34. D	54. C	74. A	94. B	114. D
15. A	35. D	55. A	75. C	95. E	115. B
16. B	36. C	56. D	76. E	96. D	116. C
17. C	37. A	57. C	77. C	97. A	117. E
18. C	38. E	58. C	78. D	98. C	118. C
19. E	39. B	59. B	79. E	99. B	119. D
20. D	40. C	60. E	80. E	100. E	120. C

Answers and Explanations

1. (D)
Though social stratification *is* a hierarchical structure, answer (B) is incorrect since stratification is not premised upon the *equal* division of societies but, rather, a broad range of factors. Stratification can be fixed, but is more often a fluid process so (E) is incorrect.

2. (C)
Harriet Beecher Stowe (1811–1896) was an abolitionist who wrote *Uncle Tom's Cabin* in 1852. This controversial antislavery novel focused public attention on the issue of slavery and the underground railroad. Stowe became a celebrity who spoke out against slavery in America and Europe.

3. (A)
In early childhood, the brain continues to grow but not as quickly as in infancy. By age three, the brain has reached 75 percent of adult size, 90 percent by age five.

4. (B)
As access to and use of the Internet increases around the world, closed societies will find it more difficult to limit the exposure of their citizens to the rest of the world. Communication across national boundaries will allow citizens of these nations to learn about the freedoms enjoyed by people elsewhere, and they may be less satisfied with the limits placed on them by their own government.

5. (E)
The Catholic Church was the single unifying influence in early and medieval Europe for all of the reasons stated.

6. (C)
According to the sociologist, this process of identification has three steps. First, we imagine how we appear to others; second, we interpret how others evaluate us; and, third, we develop a sense of self. A favorable reflection in the "social mirror" helps to engender a positive self-image.

Answers (A) and (D) are examples of distracters: incorrect answers designed to resemble the correct answer in some way.

7. (A)
This battle was the first major clash between the British and the American troops during the American Revolution. The Americans actually did run out of ammunition and were left with only bayonets and stones to defend themselves. Terms like "human shield" in answer (B) would not have been in common usage during the colonial period and should indicate an incorrect answer.

8. (D)
A colony is a settlement established and controlled by another nation. During the Age of Exploration, colonies were valued as a source of wealth for the controlling nation (C). Answer (B) is illogical since colonies are the *result* of the imperialistic tendencies of the mother country. In addition, colonies are not necessarily restricted to previously unexplored areas of the world (for example, India and Iraq were both British territories at one time). Therefore, answer (A) is also incorrect.

9. (E)
Fascism is a form of government and so is part of the study of political science. All the other options are aspects of the field of sociology.

10. (B)
After his appointment, Grant soon became well known for his aggressive drives through enemy territory. The general led the Union forces to defeat the Confederacy in 1864. Stonewall Jackson (A) and Jefferson Davis (C) were famous Confederate leaders.

11. (C)
As Caesar's power increased, his political enemies in the Roman senate feared that he was planning to declare himself king, therefore eliminating their own power and influence.

12. (D)
When a question asks for a negative ("NOT an example of"), remember that means that all of the other answer choices must be correct. There can only be one right

answer per question—read all of the answer choices thoroughly and pick the one that does not fit in.

13. (A)
Dr. Kissinger did serve under President Ford but was not his chief of staff (B). He was awarded the Nobel Peace Prize, but he shared the honor with Le Duc Tho (although the Vietnamese leader ultimately declined), so (D) is incorrect.

14. (E)
The preamble to the Constitution outlined general goals of the new government, such as providing for the common defense. Specific powers and functions, such as establishing a uniform system of weights and measures, are listed in Article I, Section 8 of the Constitution.

15. (A)
Alexander Hamilton's signature appears on all United States currency.

16. (B)
In this context, the term "cognitive" refers to the way the brains of children process information. Cognitive psychology and behavioral psychology are competing disciplines, so (C) and (E) are incorrect. Answer (A) is scientific-sounding but incorrect, as there is no such field.

17. (C)
Answer (B), amnesia, sounds like answer (C). In answer (D), the absolute term "totally" ought to suggest that the answer is incorrect.

18. (C)
Common among preliterate societies, this belief system attributes consciousness or a "soul" to nature or natural objects.

19. (E)
Franklin is the only option recognized both for patriotism and witticisms. While both Thoreau and Franklin are known for frugality, Thoreau is not famous for his patriotism. Boone (A) and Crockett (D) are both known more as frontiersmen than as wits.

20. (D)
Machu Picchu is located in Peru. The city was originally built by the Incas in the early 1400s, and was unknown to the outside world until 1911. The means by which the city was constructed remains a mystery.

21. (A)
Alexis de Tocqueville was an aristocratic Frenchman who toured America in 1831. He later wrote *Democracy in America*, a two-volume study of the American people and their institutions. Covering everything from the press, race relations, money, and the judicial system, de Tocqueville's observations about American life are still widely studied.

22. (B)
Eritrea gained independence from Italy in 1952. Ten years later, Ethiopia annexed the new nation. The countries have been in conflict ever since. Although it is a poor country with relatively few natural resources, Eritrea does offer access to the Red Sea.

23. (A)
Easter Island, known for its great stone statues, is located off the coast of Chile in the Pacific Ocean.

24. (C)
Answer (E) is the exact opposite of answer (C), suggesting that one of these is the correct answer. Though answer (A) is close and employs Freudian terms, answer (C) is the most specific and the best choice.

25. (B)
Jonathan Edwards was one of the most important preachers during the "Great Awakening" in 1740s America. Timothy Dwight was also a preacher but he was part of the "Second Great Awakening" of the nineteenth century (D).

26. (A)
Though gender theory and structuralism are theoretical approaches to literature and anthropology, only sociology employs all four methodologies.

27. (E)

Answers (A) and (C) are both ritualistic practices, but they do not answer the question asked. Answer (D) is also wrong. If you encounter a choice using the either/or format, it is likely to be wrong because most questions have only one correct answer.

28. (B)

The Spartans were so dedicated to perfecting the perfect warrior that they deliberately led lives of great harshness to make themselves better able to cope with the rigors of war. They had no time for or interest in music, art, literature (E), or science (D).

29. (C)

Answers to NOT questions should be deduced using the process of elimination. Socialization occurs throughout a person's lifetime; the family unit, social class, religion, and the mass media can all influence the way an individual learns to participate in modern society. Sleep patterns have nothing at all to do with the socialization process.

30. (D)

Louisiana was a territory, not a province, so (B) is incorrect. The other wrong answer choices use terms like "Creole" and "Haitian" that have some relationship to the French.

31. (B)

Soft sciences is another term for the social sciences—these disciplines are not intrinsically absolute or empirical, so (A) is incorrect. The hard sciences, like chemistry or physics, rely much more heavily on empirical methods of observation and experimentation.

32. (C)

The Monroe Doctrine was named for the sixth president of the United States, James Monroe. In 1823, Monroe asserted that the American hemisphere was no longer available to be colonized by European nations, and that attempts to do so or to meddle in the affairs of sovereign nations would be considered "dangerous to the peace and safety" of the United States.

33. (A)

A random sample is selected by chance from the group being studied. By contrast, when conducting a study using a representative sample (C), the experimenter draws the subjects from a sample or subgroup of the population that possesses the same characteristics as the population.

34. (D)

Ponce de Leon, a Spanish explorer who had sailed with Columbus, arrived in Florida in 1513. Legend has it that he was seeking the "Fountain of Youth."

35. (D)

Even if you aren't familiar with these terms, you can eliminate many incorrect answers by looking at the prefixes of the answer choices. "Patri "is Latin for "father" (reflected in terms such as "patriarchy") and "matri" is Latin for "mother," so both (A) and (B) can be ruled out. "Ambi," used in the term "ambidextrous" for a person who can write with the left or right hand, implies an either/or meaning.

36. (C)

Heinrich Schleimann was a nineteenth-century German businessman who had a lifelong dream of finding the lost city of Troy. He pioneered modern archaeological techniques, and in 1872 he unearthed significant remains in what is now Turkey.

37. (A)

The Sahara desert, located in northern Africa, is the largest desert in the world, at 3.5 million square miles. The second largest, the Gobi, in Asia, encompasses only 500,000 square miles, so answer (B) is incorrect.

38. (E)

Though similar in function, peer pressure (C) is typically imposed from without while groupthink is conceived from within.

39. (B)

The correct answer is the most logical conclusion to the statement given. Answers (A), (C), (D), and (E) cannot be assumed with the information given in the introductory portion of the statement. Never read anything more into a question than what is actually supplied.

40. (C)

In 1989, Manuel Noriega was deposed by his countrymen and forced to seek asylum in the United States.

41. (D)

In answer (A) the word "sole" should be a red flag: absolutes usually indicate wrong answers. Durkheim did not study the relationship between urban/country dwellers and suicide, so answer (E) is also incorrect.

42. (C)

Abolitionist and orator Frederick Douglas was born into slavery, but in 1838 he escaped to freedom in New York. Though both Booker T. Washington (A) and W.E.B. DuBois (E) were famous proponents of African-American rights, they were of a younger generation than Douglas and are typically associated with the late nineteenth and early twentieth centuries.

43. (E)

The Senate is given the power to ratify treaties in Article II, Section 2 of the U.S. Constitution.

44. (A)

Social facilitation is the phenomenon that people perform tasks better in groups or in front of people than they do alone. Though scientific-sounding, answers (B) and (D) are made-up terms. Answers (C) and (E) are actual psychology terms that do not refer to the concept in question.

45. (D)

This answer is written in a deliberately confusing manner, but when read carefully, its lack of logic is clear. It just doesn't make sense that a group could be "mainstream" and "radical" at the same time.

46. (A)

In 1521 Pope Leo X awarded King Henry VIII of England the title "Defender of the Faith." Ironically, in 1529, Henry too, would break away from the Church.

47. (B)

Transcendentalism was an important American movement in philosophy and literature that flourished during the early to middle years of the nineteenth century. To its practitioners, the soul of each individual was identical with the soul of the world and contained the world's essence. Emerson and Thoreau were two of the most well-known transcendental writers, so answer (C) is incorrect. This was a romantic movement, so (D) is also wrong.

48. (C)

The primary tools of fiscal policy are the raising and lowering of taxes and government spending. These decisions are made by Congress.

49. (E)

Auguste Comte (1798–1857) was a French philosopher and the originator of positivism. He sought to apply methods of observation and experimentation, which were beginning to be used in the hard sciences, to the field we now know as sociology.

50. (D)

The assassination of Archduke Franz Ferdinand ignited World War I, so answer (A) can't be correct. Answer (C) is also an unlikely choice since the Tiananmen Square events are too recent. Answer (E) doesn't make sense because the Trojan War occurred in antiquity, long before the invention of the cannon.

51. (C)

The key here is the phrase "none of which are absolutely necessary for individual survival." Answer (A) must be incorrect since it only stands to reason that "primary" reinforcers *are* necessary for survival. Though answers (D) and (E) are sociological terms, they do not match the introductory portion of the question.

52. (A)

The nation of Turkey makes up the core of the former Ottoman empire, which held sway as a global power from the fourteenth century until the end of World War I.

53. (E)

The terms "essentially" and "widely practiced" in answer (A) and the phrase "with varying degrees of success" in answer (D) should alert the test-taker: such vague terms often indicate incorrect answers.

54. (C)

The U.S. government is structured so that each branch of government can check or restrain the power of the other two. The framers of the Constitution wrote in a system of checks and balances so that no one branch of government could become too powerful and subvert the will of the people.

55. (A)

Even if the test-taker recognizes that the prefix "poly" usually means "many," the correct answer is not obvious. Polygamy is when a man has two or more wives (B). Since polyandry and polygamy are similar words, (A) would be a good guess.

56. (D)

The Tartars, an Asian tribe, never invaded Rome, preferring to conduct their pillaging and plundering closer to home. The other four answer choices list Germanic tribes who were based nearer to Rome.

57. (C)

Ethnocentrism is the *opposite* of cultural relativism, so (D) is incorrect. Answer (A) contains the word "always" and (E) uses the word "very"—both of which should suggest a probable wrong answer.

58. (C)

This question is not as difficult as it may appear. When looking for an answer that is false, you can usually learn quite a bit about the subject from reading the answer choices carefully. Four of the five choices are true, so the challenge is to find the answer that does not fit in.

59. (B)

The Piltdown Man was the hoax that set back evolutionary studies, so both answers (C) and (E) are incorrect. Answer (A) is the opposite of the correct answer.

60. (E)

This is perhaps the best-known quotation by Karl Marx, originator of communism. What is less well known is that Marx actually viewed religion as the primary solace of the oppressed proletarian classes.

61. (A)

This is a straightforward history question but a few answers can be eliminated using careful reasoning. The year 1848 is a little early for child labor legislation (B), which didn't become an issue until the Industrial Revolution. Similarly, (E) is unlikely since women didn't even have voting rights until 1920.

62. (A)

Allowing students to freely express their religion even if it is not in line with the dominant culture would be an example of tolerance of difference rather than an imposition of dominant values.

63. (E)

A bicameral legislature is one with an upper and a lower house. In the formation of the U.S. government this model served the purpose of allowing smaller states equal footing with larger states in the Senate, while giving the larger states greater representation based on their size in the House of Representatives.

64. (A)

The Leakeys were a husband and wife archaeologist-anthropologist team famous for their work in Africa, in particular at the Olduvai Gorge site.

65. (D)

There is no evidence that a meteor has ever crashed into the ocean and created an island. Common means of island origin are by erosion of a land bridge, by growth of coral islands, and by volcanic activity.

66. (E)

Peter the Great ruled Russia from 1682 until 1725, propelling his country from a slumbering giant to a major factor in European politics.

67. (A)

The key word in this sociology question is "primary." Answer (B) is wrong since it uses terms like "extended" and "network" which, by definition, cannot be primary in nature. Likewise, the word "superficial" in (C) should signal an incorrect answer.

68. (B)

This new use for onions will cause a shift to the right in the entire demand curve. More onions will be demanded at every price because of a change in perception about their value to consumers.

69. (A)

Pepin, king of the Franks, earned the gratitude of the pope in 751 when he restored lands that had been seized by the Lombards to papal control.

70. (D)

Marbury v. Madison, heard by the U.S. Supreme Court in 1803, established the tradition of judicial review. The Court curtailed its own power by declaring the Judicial Act of 1789 unconstitutional, but in doing so, positioned itself as interpreter of the Constitution.

71. (B)

Jane Addams was an activist in the late 1800s who played a pivotal role in the development and promotion of social work. She founded Hull House in Chicago—a settlement home to provide support for the immigrants who were flocking to the city at the end of the nineteenth century.

72. (E)

Tibet, a holy place to millions of Buddhists all over the world, is under the control of China. Answer (B) can be ruled out since the UN is not a country.

73. (E)

Pasteur is responsible for discoveries that formed the foundation of many scientific advancements, but the X-ray is the result of pioneering work done by the Polish scientist Marie Curie.

74. (A)

George Herbert Mead was a sociologist who believed that the mind developed through one's interactions with the social environment. He called this idea "social behaviorism." Answers (B), (C), and (D) are all distracters as they refer to anthropologist Margaret Mead, who has no relationship to the sociologist.

75. (C)

To be a river the body of water must flow (E), and since water is subject to the effect of gravity, rivers always flow from higher to lower elevations.

76. (E)

Davy Crockett was a frontiersman, congressman from Tennessee, and hero of the Alamo. The popular play *The Lion of the West* told his story. He died at the Alamo in 1836. Adams and Franklin were statesmen and Cooper was a writer, so options (A), (B), and (C) are incorrect.

77. (C)

If you don't recognize a word, it can be useful to read all of the answer choices for clues about the question category. Answers (A), (C), (D), and (E) all involve psychology so it is pretty safe to assume the term is a psychological one.

78. (D)

After the Western empire fell, the Eastern half survived for a thousand years as the Byzantine empire. Constantinople was its the most important city.

79. (E)

As head of the Church of England, Queen Elizabeth was Protestant. When looking for one answer choice that is not true, always remember that the other four choices must be true.

80. (E)

Harry S. Truman, the thirty-third President of the United States, was known for his plain-speaking ways and is perhaps one of the most quotable of the American presidents.

81. (E)

In the late eighteenth century, when the French Revolution took place, almost no one championed the cause of women's suffrage. The other four answer choices are all true. Economic hardship brought on by bad harvests, and dissatisfaction with the response by the king and royal bureaucracy brought down the throne in 1789.

82. (A)

Charles de Gaulle, who had served his country during World War II, was twice elected President of France.

83. (C)

Nations can draw their boundaries in whatever way they choose. They do not have to be defined by natural landmarks.

84. (D)

Answer (B) is easy to rule out as it doesn't make sense that memories for "life events" would be stored in short-term memory. Sensory memory (E) would logically involve one of the five senses.

85. (B)

Machiavelli was an Italian political theorist who outlined strategies for achieving and maintaining power. The quote, "The end justifies the means," is from Machiavelli's most famous work, *The Prince*.

86. (A)

Monetary policy is conducted by the Federal Reserve and has nothing to do with politics; therefore (B) and (C) are incorrect. Likewise, (D) is wrong since the Supreme Court has no role in any economic policy-making.

87. (C)

William F. Ogburn was the American sociologist who coined the term "cultural lag." Answer (A) is a made-up distracter. The "placebo effect" (D) and symbiosis (B) are completely unrelated constructs.

88. (B)

The roots of the Hindu faith can be traced back to the Indus Valley in northwest India.

89. (E)

The Mongol emperor Kublai Khan founded the Yuan dynasty of China when he conquered that country in 1279. He was the grandson of Genghis Khan.

90. (D)

The "Roundheads" and the "Cavaliers" were opposing factions in the English Civil War. The names referred to the appearance of the two groups. The "Roundheads" were Puritans who eschewed frivolity and wore their hair in the classic bowl cut. In contrast, the fashionable "Cavaliers" donned long-haired wigs and extravagant costumes.

91. (A)

Answer (B) is the opposite. All of the other choices are distracters that sound like the correct answer.

92. (A)

Calculus was developed by Sir Isaac Newton (1642–1727), a scientist of the British Enlightenment. (The German scientist Leibniz also developed calculus at this time.) This occurred three thousand years after the Mesopotamian civilizations ended.

93. (D)

During a period of rising inflation, a decrease in the money supply can slow economic growth and ease inflationary pressures. Answer (E) contains the terms either/or, which should signal a possible wrong choice.

94. (B)

In the 1980s, a shift in voting patterns occurred as voters who had formerly been reliable Democrats began to vote Republican, especially in the South. This trend was first noted in the 1980 presidential election.

95. (E)

Options (A), (B), (C), and (D) can all contribute to acid rain, demonstrating the complexity of the problem. Option (E) describes El Niño, which contributes to unusual weather but not acid rain.

96. (D)

Karl Marx (1818–1883) was a German social and political theorist who, after a failed career in journalism, wrote *The Communist Manifesto* in 1848 with Friedrich Engels. His radical theories advocating the overthrow of existing economic and political systems were the model used by Lenin and the Bolshevik Party in the Russian Revolution.

97. (A)

Mexico, the world's sixth-largest oil-producing country, is not a member of OPEC.

98. (C)
A careful read of all of the answer choices reveals the only choice that does not fit in with the theme of the question. The term "imperialism" is out of place among the other choices, which emphasize ideas like freedom, equality, and openness.

99. (B)
The British monarchy has no role in the governing process. Mexico has not had a monarchy for many years, so (E) is incorrect. Saudi Arabia has no "elected" governing body, so (C) is also incorrect.

100. (E)
The San Andreas Fault runs north and south along the western portion of the United States.

101. (E)
In 1936, John Maynard Keynes, a British economist, was the first to develop the theory that aggregate demand determines the level of economic activity.

102. (A)
Containment refers to a policy of checking the expansion or influence of a hostile power or ideology such as communism. Détente (E) describes a relaxation of tensions between rivals. Glasnost (B) is a Russian term meaning "openness" and applies to the period following the containment policy when tensions between the United States and the Soviet Union began to gradually decline.

103. (D)
Cartography, the science of mapmaking, dates back as far as 2500 B.C.E., when Babylonians made maps on clay tablets.

104. (B)
Plessy v. Ferguson held that "separate but equal" railway cars were not an unconstitutional infringement of civil liberties. *Brown v. the Board of Education* overturned this decision and the "separate but equal" construct.

105. (C)
Lobbying of elected officials takes place at all levels of local, state, and national government.

106. (E)
Nations such as Zimbabwe and Tanzania, which are rich in mineral wealth, remain poor for a variety of reasons including the first four listed.

107. (A)
According to the National Hurricane Center, most hurricane activity in the U.S. occurs between the months of June and November.

108. (B)
The eighteenth-century French economist Jean-Baptiste Say formed the theory that the level of aggregate in an economic supply will drive the level of overall economic activity. This theory was the foundation for supply-side economics theory almost two hundred years later.

109. (D)
The Three-Fifths Compromise, reached by Northern and Southern states at the 1787 Constitutional Convention, called for each slave to be counted as three-fifths of a person for purposes of determining legislative apportionment.

110. (B)
Joseph Schumpeter, a twentieth-century economist, believed that economic progress was achieved through a continual process of technological advancement, in which old industries are replaced by new ones.

111. (A)
The Bikini atoll in the southwest Pacific Ocean was the site of extensive atomic and hydrogen bomb testing from 1946–1958. Before testing began, the indigenous population was relocated to neighboring islands.

112. (D)
Answers (A) through (C) are each methods that have been used to amend the Constitution. This question is an example of the importance of reading each answer choice thoroughly—Congress does not call national conventions. You may encounter questions with an "all of the above" option among the answer choices. Be sure to read all answer options thoroughly.

113. (C)

The Southern Cross, a kite-shaped constellation, is the signature constellation of the southern hemisphere. It was first seen by European explorers in the early sixteenth century, and was the inspiration for the Australian flag.

114. (D)

When a market is at equilibrium sellers are able to sell their product at just the price buyers wish to pay. There is no pressure for prices to rise or fall, and no shortage or surplus of the product.

115. (B)

A special Senate committee investigated the charges and found them groundless. McCarthy was undaunted and continued to use his position to wage a relentless anti-communist crusade.

116. (C)

Article III, Section 1, states that Supreme Court Judges "shall hold their offices during good behavior," which has since its inception been interpreted to mean that they serve life terms.

117. (E)

Be sure to read all answer choices carefully before making your selection. Outsourcing is a means of lowering costs by shifting production to areas where labor costs are lower. This has been a boon to countries such as India, where a well-educated, English-speaking workforce has enjoyed new prosperity and the availability of technology that might otherwise have been unavailable in that nation. Workers in higher-wage countries may find themselves displaced by these changes until job markets adjust to the changes in labor demand.

118. (C)

The Andes have a significant effect on the climate of the region. As air moves up over the eastern slope of the Andes, it cools, causing moisture to freeze and fall to the ground as snow. Once across the mountains, the air warms up as it descends and is able to hold on to its moisture as it passes west of the Andes. This part of South America, the Atacama desert, is one of the driest places on earth.

119. (D)

The term "rate" is the key word here. Interest rates have no set dollar value—they are always calculated in percentage form—as such, there is no definite dollar figure that can be assigned. The remaining answer choices can be assigned stable dollar values and all contribute to the GNP.

120. (C)

In 1938, British prime minister Neville Chamberlain and other European leaders met with Adolf Hitler in Munich to plot a peaceful solution to a crisis brought on by Hitler's seizure of a portion of Czechoslovakia. Hitler promised that if he were allowed to keep it, he would be satisfied and not invade additional lands. Chamberlain was convinced that this appeasement of the German dictator had worked, and promised his country "peace in our time." Months later, Hitler seized the rest of Czechoslovakia.

Section Five: The CLEP Social Sciences and History Exam | 429

Chapter Nineteen: Practice Test 3

Time—90 minutes
120 Questions

Directions: For each of the following questions or incomplete statements, select the best answer or completion from the five options given.

1. Which of the following was NOT a shortcoming of the Articles of Confederation?

   (A) Measures approved by Congress had to be approved by nine of the thirteen states.
   (B) Congress could not collect taxes to pay its bills.
   (C) There was no authority to regulate foreign trade.
   (D) The Articles of Confederation were very difficult to amend when the need arose.
   (E) Congress had no power to declare war.

2. Which Louisiana governor became one of the most powerful political bosses in the country, even announcing his intention to run for the Presidency against fellow Democrat Franklin Delano Roosevelt in 1935? He was assassinated just one month after declaring his candidacy.

   (A) David Duke
   (B) Huey Long
   (C) Sam Tweed
   (D) George McGovern
   (E) James Hoffa

3. Which two ancient city-states fought the Peloponnesian Wars?

   (A) Athens and Babylonia
   (B) Rome and Carthage
   (C) Athens and Sparta
   (D) Rome and Syracuse
   (E) Sumeria and Sparta

4. "Socialization" and "enculturation" are both terms describing the process by which an individual adopts/learns the behavior patterns of the surrounding culture. Which of the following is NOT a component of either process?

   (A) values
   (B) norms
   (C) mores
   (D) genetics
   (E) conformity

KAPLAN

5. Bipedalism is the fundamental characteristic used to define hominids. To what does the term refer?

   (A) two-legged upright gait
   (B) the ability to operate cognitively using both lobes of the brain
   (C) a stooped-over gait typically accompanied by knuckle-dragging
   (D) the propensity to pair-bond and typically mate for life
   (E) the use of tools

6. Carl Jung—a younger colleague of Sigmund Freud—took his mentor's idea of the unconscious and expanded upon it. Jung drew on religion, mythology, philosophy, and mysticism to develop what he called the

   (A) symbolic unconscious
   (B) conscious unconscious
   (C) collective unconscious
   (D) unconscious dialectic
   (E) seismic unconscious

7. Which of these events caused a dramatic deterioration in Arab-Jewish relations?

   (A) the creation of the nation of Israel
   (B) the death of the shah of Iran
   (C) the founding of OPEC
   (D) the collapse of the Soviet Union
   (E) the attacks on the World Trade Center

8. General Custer, who titled his memoirs *My Life on the Plains*, commanded his infamous "last stand" at the Little Big Horn in June 1876. Toward whom was this surprise assault directed?

   (A) a Cree Indian reservation in Idaho
   (B) a coalition of renegade mountain men and fur traders
   (C) French-Canadian soldiers from Acadia
   (D) the British
   (E) a Sioux/Cheyenne encampment

9. Which continent is home to the most countries?

   (A) Asia
   (B) North America
   (C) Europe
   (D) Africa
   (E) South America

10. What role did Charles de Gaulle play in the liberation of France?

    (A) He served in the government set up by the Germans and tried to negotiate their withdrawal from France.
    (B) He escaped to England where he met with Churchill, then addressed the occupied French nation over the radio, urging the people to continue to fight.
    (C) He hid in Paris for the entire duration of the occupation, spying on the Nazis and secretly sending intelligence information to the Allies.
    (D) He helped smuggle weapons into France to be used when the time came to liberate the country.
    (E) He was imprisoned in Germany during the war and was not able to participate in the liberation of Paris.

11. The United States Constitution grants the House of Representatives, but NOT the Senate, the power to do which of the following?

    (A) regulate TV and radio broadcasting
    (B) originate spending bills
    (C) declare war
    (D) approve Supreme Court nominees
    (E) override a presidential veto

GO ON TO THE NEXT PAGE

12. Known to his men as "Old Hickory," which Major General did the citizens of the Crescent City turn to for protection from the British in late 1814?

    (A) Andrew Johnson
    (B) Lafayette
    (C) Andrew Jackson
    (D) Washington Lee
    (E) John Laffitte

13. If the price of input I rises, the price of finished good G will rise if

    (A) there are ample acceptable substitutes for input I
    (B) there is no other way to produce finished good G
    (C) input I makes up a minor portion of finished good G
    (D) consumers will purchase good G only when its price is low
    (E) good G is an inferior product that consumers prefer in hard times

14. William Graham Sumner coined the term "folkways" as a subset of "customs" to denote group habits that are common to a society or culture. Which of the following is not an example of "folkways"?

    (A) accent
    (B) clothing fashions
    (C) modes of recreation
    (D) traditional garb
    (E) ceremonial headwear

15. Which of the following was NOT an objection to the Constitution raised by the Anti-Federalists?

    (A) the lack of a bill of rights
    (B) the failure to provide women the right to vote
    (C) increased powers of the central government
    (D) the process by which it would be ratified
    (E) the absence of a mention of God

16. The psychological term for the stable set of individual characteristics that make an individual unique is

    (A) perception
    (B) sense of self
    (C) genetic makeup
    (D) personality
    (E) genotype

17. Which of the following individuals did not leave written accounts of history?

    (A) Tacitus
    (B) Herodotus
    (C) Attila the Hun
    (D) Julius Caesar
    (E) Suetonius

18. South Dakota senator George McGovern ran for President in 1972 on the Democratic ticket, promising to bring home the remaining American troops from Vietnam. To whom did he lose?

    (A) Jimmy Carter
    (B) Lyndon Baines Johnson
    (C) Robert F. Kennedy
    (D) Gerald Ford
    (E) Richard Nixon

19. Which was the last Russian dynasty?

    (A) Romanov
    (B) Tolstoy
    (C) Federov
    (D) Kruschev
    (E) Godunov

GO ON TO THE NEXT PAGE

20. Which of the following was not a contributing factor to the collapse of the Roman empire?

    (A) a papal edict freeing all slaves
    (B) invading tribes from north of the empire
    (C) a costly bureaucracy increasingly unable to manage imperial affairs
    (D) such a vast expanse of territory was difficult to control
    (E) a series of corrupt and inept emperors

21. The primary significance of El Niño is that it

    (A) causes an increase in electromagnetic activity, which can interfere with radio transmissions.
    (B) lowers average ocean surface water temperatures, which causes less plankton growth.
    (C) affects the gravitational force exerted by the moon on the tides.
    (D) increases average ocean surface water temperature, causing climatic change around the world.
    (E) changes seismic activity on the ocean floor that can cause underwater volcanic eruptions.

22. Potassium-argon and carbon-14 are chronometric methods that determine

    (A) the age of trees by dating the rings of trunk cross-sections
    (B) the age of a specimen in number of years
    (C) the lifespan of primates
    (D) the age of a specimen with an accuracy of about a thousand years
    (E) the rate at which the earth is warming or cooling

23. Oligopoly is a market structure characterized by

    (A) few or no barriers to entry
    (B) many sellers offering similar products
    (C) aggressive price competition by sellers
    (D) a single seller
    (E) a few sellers offering similar products

24. While Karl Marx stressed economic conflict as the guiding force in social evolution and Sigmund Freud emphasized psychosexual maturation, Emile Durkheim's vision was more peaceful and progressive. Durkheim was one of the creators of

    (A) positivism
    (B) neo-positivism
    (C) progressive evolution theory
    (D) optimism
    (E) causal positivism

25. Which U.S. president said, "Go ahead, make my day," as a warning to Congress not to submit a tax increase?

    (A) Bill Clinton
    (B) Ronald Reagan
    (C) Gerald Ford
    (D) George H. W. Bush
    (E) Harry S. Truman

26. According to psychiatrists, a compulsive act is typically done in an attempt to alleviate the discomfort caused by

    (A) a fixation
    (B) a manic episode
    (C) bipolar disorder
    (D) an obsession
    (E) a repressed memory

GO ON TO THE NEXT PAGE

27. What is meant by the phrase "dirty war" as it was carried out in Argentina?

    (A) the use of radioactive devices to terrorize the population
    (B) secret forays into neighboring countries to assassinate political rivals
    (C) a secret campaign by the government against political dissenters
    (D) the dispute with Great Britain over the Falkland Islands
    (E) deliberate pollution of a neighboring country's waterways

28. William Bradford came to New England aboard the *Mayflower* in 1621 and became leader of the Pilgrims, eventually serving as governor of which colony?

    (A) Massachusetts Bay Colony
    (B) Chesapeake Bay Colony
    (C) Commonwealth of Rhode Island
    (D) Virginia Bay Colony
    (E) Plymouth Colony

29. What is a tsunami?

    (A) a giant wave caused by seismic activity in the ocean
    (B) a rainforest in central Asia
    (C) a large fish native to the South Pacific
    (D) a tornado that forms over water
    (E) a hurricane occurring in the Pacific Ocean

30. The patricians were noble families of Rome who, in 509 B.C.E., expelled the Etruscan king and decreed that Rome would become a republic. The other citizens of Rome, including farmers, merchants, and artisans, were known as

    (A) serfs
    (B) plebeians
    (C) drones
    (D) proletariats
    (E) vassals

31. Which of the following did NOT contribute to the decline of feudalism in Europe?

    (A) greater social mobility as a result of a more diversified field economy
    (B) the Black Plague, which reduced the labor force and resulted in higher wages
    (C) a papal edict declaring the feudal system to be in violation of Church law
    (D) rising growth and influence of urban towns
    (E) the rise of humanistic philosophy with its emphasis on individual self-worth

32. The policy of executive privilege came into effect during the Nixon administration when members of the executive branch were being questioned by authorities. What does executive privilege provide for?

    (A) the right for the president to plead the Fifth Amendment
    (B) the residence of impeachment powers exclusively in the executive branch
    (C) the need for presidential approval before Congress can question any executive branch staff member
    (D) the right for the president to grant pardons without any recourse from the judicial branch
    (E) the right to choose cabinet members without congressional approval

33. One argument for using fiscal policy rather than monetary policy to influence the economy is that

    (A) it is easier to implement than monetary policy
    (B) it takes effect more rapidly than monetary policy
    (C) monetary policy is unfair to the middle class
    (D) monetary policy is too extreme a measure
    (E) fiscal policy has a more precise effect on the economy

34. Modern humans and apes share the same brachiating anatomy of the upper torso. The style of movement this enables

   (A) is only present in upright-walking primates with a hunter-gatherer social past
   (B) has evolved over the last 25,000 years
   (C) allows humans to swivel their hips
   (D) is known as "arm-swinging" since the arms pull the body along while walking, as apes use their arms when moving through trees
   (E) has influenced traditional displays of physical strength (for example, chest-pounding among apes and muscle-flexing in modern humans)

35. "Theory" can be defined as "a general statement about how some parts of the world fit together and how they work." Which of the following concepts is primarily a sociological theory?

   (A) Marxism
   (B) fascism
   (C) monarchy
   (D) monopoly
   (E) anarchy

36. What is meant by the term "federalism?"

   (A) the Federalist Party is in control of the government
   (B) the division of power between a strong central government and several regional governments
   (C) the use of monetary policy by the Federal Reserve System to manage the money supply
   (D) a political-economic system where the federal government controls all industry
   (E) a political system in which all federal officers are elected

37. Which of the following thinkers is NOT associated with childhood developmental stages?

   (A) Jean Piaget
   (B) Sigmund Freud
   (C) Eric Erikson
   (D) Margaret Mead
   (E) Elizabeth Kubler-Ross

38. Which of the following was NOT a reason for the United States' entry into World War I?

   (A) the sinking of the *Lusitania* by the Germans
   (B) the discovery of a plot by Germany to get Mexico to enter the war against the United States
   (C) the bombing of Pearl Harbor by the Japanese
   (D) the disruption of Atlantic shipping lanes by unrestricted German submarine warfare
   (E) Germany's attempts to lure Japan into the war

39. With what traveling show did sharpshooter "Wild Bill" Hickock and his girlfriend "Calamity Jane" tour?

   (A) The Greatest Show on Earth
   (B) The Ringling Brothers Circus
   (C) P.T. Barnum's Side Show and Oddities
   (D) Buffalo Bill Cody's Wild West Show
   (E) The Columbia World's Exposition

40. Its defeat in World War II changed Japan in which of the following ways?

   (A) The emperor lost his complete control of the government and became a purely ceremonial figure.
   (B) A new constitution was written, and women were given the right to vote.
   (C) Western-style democracy was abolished.
   (D) Japan no longer strove to emulate the United States' economic success.
   (E) Japan reverted to its earlier reclusive ways.

GO ON TO THE NEXT PAGE

41. According to Charles Horton Cooley (1864–1929), our sense of self develops from interaction with others. For Cooley, this process contains three steps. Which of the following choices lists them correctly?

    (A) We imagine how we look to others, we negatively compare ourselves to others, we develop a self-concept
    (B) We develop a self-concept, we positively compare ourselves to others, we negatively compare ourselves to others
    (C) We imagine how we look to others, we interpret how others react to us, we develop a self-concept
    (D) We interpret how others react to us, we develop a self-concept, we perfect our self-concept with constant adjustments
    (E) We negatively compare ourselves to others, we positively compare ourselves to others, we interpret how others react to us

42. The low-pressure area of light variable winds near the equator is known to sailors as the

    (A) doldrums
    (B) trade winds
    (C) Bermuda Triangle
    (D) Corolis effect
    (E) Southern Cross

43. On April 14, 1775, the colonial governor of Massachusetts, General Gage, was secretly ordered by the British to suppress rebellion by any means necessary. Four days later, Gage sent seven hunded British soldiers to destroy the colonists' weapons depot; what famous event happened later that night?

    (A) John Hancock placed his signature—the largest and the final— on the Declaration of Independence.
    (B) George Washington declared war against King George of England.
    (C) Paul Revere set out from Boston to Lexington to warn the colonial militiamen.
    (D) Plans for the Underground Railroad were finally put into action.
    (E) Vast stores of English tea were thrown into Boston Harbor.

44. What is the relationship between real and nominal interest rates?

    (A) Nominal interest rates take inflation into account, while real rates do not.
    (B) Real interest rates are paid to borrowers and nominal interest rates are paid to lenders.
    (C) Real interest rates are paid on government bonds and nominal interest rates are paid on bank deposits.
    (D) Real interest rates take inflation into account, while nominal interest rates do not.
    (E) Real and nominal rates are the same thing.

GO ON TO THE NEXT PAGE

45. Great Britain's defeat of the Spanish Armada in 1588 is often considered a turning point in world history. Which of the following was NOT a result of this landmark victory?

    (A) English replaced Spanish as the most commonly spoken language in Europe.
    (B) Great Britain replaced Spain as the dominant world power.
    (C) Spain's influence in the New World gradually declined.
    (D) English imperial interests widened as the British gained superiority over the seas.
    (E) Spanish influence across Europe began to subside.

46. What is the meaning of the term "gerrymandering"?

    (A) attempts by interest groups to influence politicians by contributing to their campaigns
    (B) drawing of electoral districts to limit the voting strength of a particular group
    (C) the levying of poll taxes to discourage voting by minority groups
    (D) the process of choosing a political party's slate of candidates
    (E) a method to delay a vote on a bill by talking for hours to keep the debate open

47. What controversy surrounds the Elgin Marbles?

    (A) The Nazis commandeered them prior to the outbreak of World War II.
    (B) They have been discovered to be forgeries.
    (C) The government of Greece wants them back.
    (D) Museum officials have done restoration work that has altered their historical value.
    (E) Money raised for the building of a new wing of their museum was misappropriated by employees.

48. In 1729, Benjamin Franklin began publishing *The Pennsylvania Gazette* and two years later founded the first American public library. While visiting the library, colonists could have read Franklin's annual almanac written under the pseudonym of

    (A) Little Richard
    (B) Little Peter
    (C) Poor Little Richard
    (D) Poor Richard
    (E) Peter Pilgrim

49. The "Forbidden City" is located in

    (A) Beijing
    (B) Riyadh
    (C) Machu Picchu
    (D) Moscow
    (E) Tokyo

50. Sociologists employ many research methods when they are studying a given population, including demography. Which of the following is NOT an example of a demographic study?

    (A) a study of divorce rates in the rural Midwest based on statistical analysis
    (B) a study of marital satisfaction of women who married later in life based on perceived quality of life
    (C) a statistical analysis of birth rates in urban populations compared to the same rates in rural populations
    (D) a study of infant mortality rates in the Pacific Northwest
    (E) a comparison of divorce rates in families with no children and families with at least one child

GO ON TO THE NEXT PAGE

51. Which of the following was NOT a consequence of the 1991 Mt. Pinatubo eruption?

    (A) The height of the volcano was reduced by 800 feet
    (B) Valleys were buried by as much as 650 feet of ash and pumice
    (C) The earth's temperature fell by one degree
    (D) Ash covered the earth's stratosphere within twelve months
    (E) An ancient city was preserved as it was the day of the eruption

52. In psychoanalytical theory, the part of our personality that contains our primitive impulses such as sex, anger, and hunger is called

    (A) the ego
    (B) the id
    (C) the superego
    (D) the uber-ego
    (E) the under-ego

53. In 1857, the United States Supreme Court made a benchmark ruling; what did the Dred Scott decision determine?

    I. Black people, free or not, could not be citizens.
    II. Slaves brought into free territory by their owners remained property.
    III. Any escaped slave who reached the North would be granted citizenship and all the rights that came accordingly.

    (A) I only
    (B) II only
    (C) III only
    (D) I and III only
    (E) I and II only

54. An increase in the money supply will generally cause the economy to

    (A) stagnate
    (B) expand
    (C) contract, then expand
    (D) contract
    (E) inflate

55. Thermoluminescence is

    (A) a technique for determining the age of burnt flint or ceramics found at archaeological sites
    (B) the amount of heat or energy remaining in a skeleton after decomposition begins
    (C) a technique for determining the sex of primate remains by measuring light refracted through gender-specific cells
    (D) a gradual heating and cooling of the earth as a result of seismic activity
    (E) a technique for determining the age of archaeological artifacts by using a gradual heating and cooling process

56. Which of the following statements is TRUE about the relationship between the North and the South in the antebellum period?

    (A) The North was chiefly an agricultural region threatened by the South's economic strength
    (B) The South was chiefly an agricultural region eager to expand into factory-based industries
    (C) The North was chiefly a manufacturing region seeking justification to appropriate the natural resources in the South.
    (D) A flood of immigrants to southern cities had Atlanta and Chattanooga vying with Boston and New York to be the seat of education and culture in the country.
    (E) As the United States became more established, the two regions found themselves increasingly at odds over differences in economic, social, and political beliefs.

GO ON TO THE NEXT PAGE

57. Which political party would agree with the statement, "The government that governs best governs least"?

    (A) Socialist
    (B) Green
    (C) Democratic
    (D) Libertarian
    (E) Communist

58. Kai Erikson is known for his work on the function of deviance in group situations. Which of the following statements would he most likely agree with?

    (A) Deviant behavior typically serves a disruptive function and should therefore be discouraged as counterproductive to the group's long-term survival.
    (B) Deviant behavior should be encouraged as a force for innovation
    (C) A group will accept and sustain deviant behavior rather than eliminating it because it maintains the boundaries of acceptable and unacceptable behavior.
    (D) Deviance is never functional—it decreases group solidarity and encourages nonconformist group behavior.
    (E) As a group becomes more established, its standards of behavior become more rigid and codified.

59. Which of the following is true of the Salic Law?

    (A) It said that only male descendants of the king could inherit the throne.
    (B) It spelled out how the royal court of France should function.
    (C) It regulated the French winemaking industry.
    (D) It governed the French monetary system.
    (E) It made Paris the capital of France.

60. Which faith stresses the importance of meditation and the Middle Way?

    (A) Judaism
    (B) Hinduism
    (C) Buddhism
    (D) Islam
    (E) Jainism

61. According to psychologists, which of the following is an example of "inappropriate affect"?

    (A) smiling when recounting a happy childhood memory
    (B) crying when remembering a lost loved one
    (C) laughing when talking about the death of a loved one
    (D) a racing pulse and sweaty palms in a panic situation
    (E) inability to determine appropriate personal space

62. What happened in 1870 in Italy and in 1871 in Germany?

    (A) Unified nations were formed when smaller kingdoms agreed to join together.
    (B) Women were granted the right to vote, well before they were given that right in the United States.
    (C) The Catholic Church was made the official state religion resulting in a consolidation of papal authority.
    (D) They both joined the League of Nations, a predecessor to today's United Nations.
    (E) Their monarchs were assassinated and the tide of communism could no longer be contained.

GO ON TO THE NEXT PAGE

63. Although she did not live long enough to see women at voting booths, Susan B. Anthony fought tirelessly for women's suffrage in her lifetime. In 1872, she led a group of women to the polls in Rochester, New York, demanding that

    (A) black women and men be given the same voting rights as whites
    (B) women be given the same civil and political rights that had already been extended to black males under the Fourteenth and Fifteenth Amendments
    (C) landholding women—black or white—be given the same voting and civil rights given to black males under the Fourteenth and Fifteenth Amendments
    (D) white women who held property should have some say over how their tax dollars were spent
    (E) the ability to read and write, rather than one's gender, should be the test for voting rights

64. Henry the Navigator played an important role in the Age of Exploration because he

    (A) was the first person to circumnavigate the globe
    (B) encouraged Europeans to explore the African continent
    (C) invented the sextant, which was vital to marine navigation and mapmaking
    (D) discovered through scientific calculation that the world was not flat
    (E) financed Columbus' voyage to the New World

65. One definition of "sociology" is "the study of social order." The term was coined by a Frenchman, August Comte, but didn't come into usage until after the French Revolution. Which of the following conditions had to be in place before the study of social order could become established?

    I. the old absolutist monarchies were overthrown
    II. new classes demanding citizens' rights appeared
    III. Enlightenment philosophy emphasized humanism and the individual in relation to society

    (A) I only
    (B) II only
    (C) III only
    (D) I and II only
    (E) I, II, and III

66. When there are many sellers and few buyers for a certain product, which of the following will NOT occur?

    (A) More buyers will enter the market.
    (B) Prices will tend to rise.
    (C) Sellers may attempt to differentiate their product from the other similar products.
    (D) Prices will tend to fall.
    (E) Prices will remain constant.

67. From June through September of 1692, nineteen men and women were hanged at Gallows Hill in Massachusetts—many more languished in jails for months without trial. For what offense were teenagers Ann Putnam and Mercy Lewis eventually put on trial?

   (A) treason—they were both Tories and loyal to the British crown
   (B) witchcraft—after they exhibited some unusual behavior, the local magistrates attributed their afflictions to the supernatural
   (C) vandalism—they were the first to be charged with this crime in the New World
   (D) suicide—the girls were unsuccessful and since taking one's life went against Puritan doctrine, they were sentenced to life in prison
   (E) unlawful pregnancies—they were unwed mothers who would not reveal the fathers of their children

68. What was the primary significance of the Strategic Defense Initiative?

   (A) This act of Congress founded the first U.S. space program, which eventually put a man on the moon.
   (B) This international agreement compelled non-oil producing nations to stockpile oil in the event of a war in the Middle East.
   (C) This post-World War II committee ceded Israeli settlements in the West Bank, causing additional violence between Jews and Palestinians.
   (D) This policy motivated the Soviet Union to compete with the American arms program, spending much more than it could afford.
   (E) American surveillance satellites were launched to provide constant tracking of enemy movements.

69. The systematic picking through the hair of one individual by another to remove foreign matter and parasites is called "grooming behavior." Why is this practice so important for primates?

   (A) The activity reduces the spread of disease within particular communities.
   (B) Grooming behavior helps create and maintain social bonds.
   (C) As a mating ritual, this practice has its own well-defined and gender-specific roles.
   (D) This behavior helps establish desirable traits of physical attractiveness.
   (E) The practice helps regulate primate body temperature and metabolism.

70. The American Puritans only extended church membership to those they called "True Believers," people who made public professions of their faith. New members soon wanted their children to be baptized, creating a dilemma for the church elders. They advocated doctrinal purity but also sought to keep as many people as possible under the sway of the church. What was their solution?

   (A) the "Halfway" covenant
   (B) the Inner Light
   (C) the "One-Drop" rule
   (D) adult baptism
   (E) the original sin construct

71. The ancient nation of Nubia is now contained within the borders of what two nations?

   (A) Algeria and Libya
   (B) Iran and Iraq
   (C) Egypt and Sudan
   (D) Columbia and Venezuela
   (E) Brazil and Peru

GO ON TO THE NEXT PAGE

72. Which of two following sociological perspectives are in direct opposition to one another?

    (A) Marxism and socialism
    (B) socialism and cultural relativism
    (C) behaviorism and ethnocentrism
    (D) cultural relativism and ethnocentrism
    (E) behaviorism and Marxism

73. Which of the following is not one of the four major islands of Japan?

    (A) Nagasaki
    (B) Hokkaido
    (C) Honshu
    (D) Kyushu
    (E) Shikoku

74. The essay "The Crisis," written in 1776, was a call to arms for Americans. The essay opens with the following sentence: "These are the times that try men's souls." Who was its author?

    (A) Thomas Jefferson
    (B) James Madison
    (C) Benjamin Franklin
    (D) John Adams
    (E) Thomas Paine

75. The tendency of an individual to focus energy inward resulting in decreased social interaction, as opposed to focusing energy outward toward others and group activity, is known as

    (A) introspection
    (B) internal orientation
    (C) an internal locus of control
    (D) introversion
    (E) intrinsic motivation

76. What archaeological breakthrough was made possible by the discovery of the Rosetta Stone?

    (A) the discovery of the lost city of Atlantis
    (B) the ability to decipher the meaning of hieroglyphics
    (C) uncovering the secret of how the ancient Babylonians made fire
    (D) understanding the meaning of the ring of giant stones at Stonehenge
    (E) knowledge of the method the ancient Egyptians used to mummify their dead

77. Throughout the colonial period in America, one of the greatest sources of irritation between England and the colonies

    (A) was the religious dogma of the British colonial governors
    (B) was the restrictions placed on religious freedoms in the colonies
    (C) was the Navigation Acts, which protected British shipping while garnishing a profit for the king
    (D) was the insistence by the throne that debtors and criminals be sent to the New World rather than to prison
    (E) was King George's rampant profiteering of the abundant natural resources available in America

78. What was the outcome of the Bretton Woods conference?

    (A) It signaled the end of World War II.
    (B) It established the Federal Reserve System.
    (C) It returned the U.S. to the gold standard.
    (D) It established a system of fixed exchange rates.
    (E) It returned lands seized by Hitler to the French.

GO ON TO THE NEXT PAGE

79. Social anthropology seeks to understand cultural diversity including relationships between culture and power. Social anthropologists identify specific social issues and compare them across societies. Which of the following subjects would NOT be addressed by the discipline?

    (A) intelligence and its measurement
    (B) kinship and colonialism
    (C) class and caste
    (D) politics and power
    (E) myth and ritual

80. Which of these factors is contributing to deforestation of the Amazon rainforest?

    I. the land is needed for farming and ranching
    II. the trees themselves are used for lumber
    III. city dwellers seek land in the country for recreational use

    (A) I only
    (B) II only
    (C) III only
    (D) I and II only
    (E) I, II, and III

81. The research method using random assignment of subjects and the manipulation of variables in order to determine cause and effect is known as

    (A) the experimental method
    (B) the variation method
    (C) deductive reasoning
    (D) causal analysis
    (E) longitudinal study

82. What led to the establishment of the United Nations?

    (A) The world lacked an international standard of weights and measures.
    (B) Famine in Africa demonstrated the need for a humanitarian relief agency.
    (C) The charter of the League of Nations had expired.
    (D) The nations of the world wanted to fight terrorism.
    (E) The League of Nations had failed to keep the world at peace.

83. In the period from about 1900 through the 1920s, African-American literature, art, music, dance, and social commentary flourished. This movement was named for the community that was at its center; what is this cultural movement now known as?

    (A) the Jazz Age
    (B) the Village Revival
    (C) the Harlem Renaissance
    (D) the Delta Diaspora
    (E) the New Nubian Movement

84. The *Book of the Dead* is a remnant of what country's ancient culture and rituals?

    (A) China
    (B) Mexico
    (C) Egypt
    (D) Babylonia
    (E) Greece

GO ON TO THE NEXT PAGE

85. Psychologists use the term "learned helplessness" to describe a condition that occurs

    (A) after a period of sustained negative consequences when individuals begin to believe they have no control over their environment
    (B) when individuals are prevented from taking any proactive measures to improve their circumstances and subsequently believe they are powerless
    (C) when a child is rendered helpless and ineffectual because of a domineering mother figure
    (D) when either member of a pair-bond begins to rely too heavily on the other for their primary reinforcers
    (E) when invalids subconsciously prevent themselves from regaining physical health because they have become conditioned to expect constant care

86. Who were the two anarchists arrested for robbery in 1920s New York, resulting in one of the most sensational trials of the early twentieth century?

    (A) Plessy and Ferguson
    (B) Sacco and Vanzetti
    (C) Capone and Capellini
    (D) Katzmann and Coletti
    (E) Julius and Ethel Rosenberg

87. Why is the Dead Sea given this name?

    (A) No aquatic life can survive there.
    (B) Many ferocious battles have been fought nearby.
    (C) It is slowly evaporating.
    (D) Many of the sailors who set sail from there never returned.
    (E) It has a large shark population.

88. Which economist first advocated the concept of counter-cyclical economic policy?

    (A) Adam Smith
    (B) Arthur Laffer
    (C) John Maynard Keynes
    (D) Joseph Schumpeter
    (E) Milton Friedman

89. Frictional unemployment occurs when

    (A) factories close, leaving workers without jobs
    (B) individuals leave their jobs to seek other opportunities
    (C) consumers stop buying certain products, causing entire industries to falter
    (D) technology causes some products to become obsolete
    (E) individuals leave the labor force

90. Known for her unorthodox style, this proto-feminist declared herself the first woman candidate for President of the United States in 1870—she lost by a large margin. Who was she?

    (A) Susan B. Anthony
    (B) Charlotte Perkins Gilman
    (C) Victoria Woodhull
    (D) Dorothy Parker
    (E) Gloria Steinem

91. Charlemagne's reign was significant because he

    (A) was the first king of France to be crowned by the Pope
    (B) led the first Crusade to the Holy Land
    (C) defeated the British at the Battle of Hastings
    (D) established a central government over western Europe
    (E) built the Cathedral of Notre Dame in Paris

92. The most recent amendment to the Constitution of the United States

    (A) limited the Presidency to two terms
    (B) abolished the poll tax
    (C) lowered the voting age to eighteen
    (D) provided for Presidential disability
    (E) prohibited immediate Congressional pay raises

93. Thorndike's "Law of Effect" states that

    (A) those responses that are followed by negative reinforcers will be repeated more often than those that are not
    (B) those responses that are followed by a positive consequence will be repeated more frequently than those that are not
    (C) there is no relationship between positive reinforcers and negative behavior
    (D) those responses that are followed by negative reinforcers are repeated more frequently in some destructive personality types
    (E) most individuals alter unacceptable responses when repeatedly subjected to negative consequences

94. The only crime specifically mentioned in the U.S. Constitution is

    (A) tax evasion
    (B) mail fraud
    (C) perjury
    (D) counterfeiting
    (E) treason

95. During World War II, John Steinbeck worked as a war correspondent in Italy and northern Africa for the *New York Herald Tribune*. In 1962, Steinbeck was awarded the Nobel Prize for Literature. Which of the following did he pen?

    (A) *The Red Badge of Courage* and *The Grapes of Wrath*
    (B) *The Grapes of Wrath* and *Of Mice and Men*
    (C) *Of Mice and Men* and *The Old Man and the Sea*
    (D) *The Old Man and the Sea* and *The Grapes of Wrath*
    (E) *The Old Man and the Sea* and *The Red Badge of Courage*

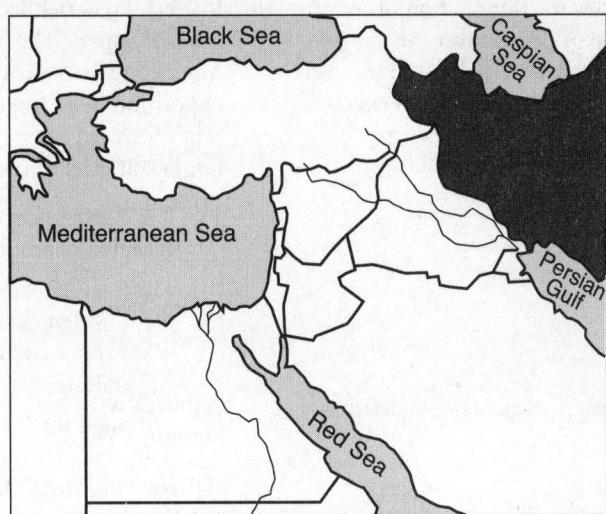

96. The darkly shaded country was once known as

    (A) Ceylon
    (B) Rhodesia
    (C) Persia
    (D) Burma
    (E) Siam

97. What does it mean to say that archaeological remains—such as fossilized animals—are found *in situ*?

    (A) They are located in an area previously beneath sea level.
    (B) They are not found in their original ecosystem.
    (C) They have been removed and relocated, perhaps by scavenging animals.
    (D) They are found in their natural position—buried in the place where they died.
    (E) They are found perfectly preserved.

98. What is the difference between a continental island and an oceanic island?

    (A) A continental island has the same plant and animal life as the nearest continent, and an oceanic island has its own plant and animal life.
    (B) A continental island lies off the coast of a continent, and an oceanic island is located in the ocean away from major land masses.
    (C) A continental island is a large island, and oceanic islands are small islands.
    (D) A continental island has fresh water and an oceanic island does not.
    (E) There is no difference.

99. Commonly used to describe the domination of one class, nation, or group of people over others, this notion was extended by Antonio Gramsci to denote dominance over people's political and cultural perceptions. Gramsci's idea was known as

    (A) hierarchy
    (B) imperialism
    (C) hegemony
    (D) cultural imperialism
    (E) cultural persuasion

100. What was Napoleon's primary motive in his desire to conquer Egypt?

    (A) to win glory for himself
    (B) to explore the tombs of the pharaohs
    (C) to crown himself king of Egypt
    (D) to cut off British access to India
    (E) to follow in the footsteps of his hero, Alexander the Great

101. A dream in which an individual is aware that he or she is dreaming and sometimes even able to manipulate the dream is called

    (A) R.E.M. state
    (B) an illusive dream
    (C) a waking dream
    (D) an out-of-body experience
    (E) a lucid dream

102. In 1893, Frederick Jackson Turner presented his seminal paper, "The Significance of the Frontier in American History" at the World's Columbia Exposition in Chicago. Turner introduced his concept of American "exceptionalism" in his presentation; what is its central premise?

    (A) It is a refutation of the previously widely accepted concept of "Manifest Destiny."
    (B) The frontier experience explains the development of democracy in the United States and is key to understanding a uniquely American cultural identity.
    (C) Although the literal American frontier essentially ended around 1865, the frontier experience imprinted itself on the American psyche.
    (D) The frontier ideal and the notion of "Manifest Destiny" were popular mythologies to justify unbridled westward expansion.
    (E) The American frontier took the place of the long-exploited European frontier in the imaginations of settlers.

103. The hypothesis, based on studies of modern human mitochondrial DNA, that all modern humans descended from one closely related population, or even one woman who lived in Africa approximately 100,000 to 200,000 years ago is

    (A) the Original Eden hypothesis
    (B) the Adam's Rib theory
    (C) the Hanging Gardens hypothesis
    (D) the African Eve hypothesis
    (E) the Hellenic Origins hypothesis

GO ON TO THE NEXT PAGE

104. Which of the following statements about Alexander the Great is NOT true?

    (A) The great Greek philosopher Aristotle was his tutor.
    (B) He ordered the construction of the Great Pyramid of Egypt.
    (C) His empire included Greece, Macedonia, Persia, Egypt, and parts of India.
    (D) His mother plotted to have his father assassinated.
    (E) His horse, Bucephalus, was said to be a horse no other man could ride.

105. What is meant by the expression, "There is no such thing as a free lunch"?

    (A) The government prohibits spoiled food from being given to charity.
    (B) There are costs associated with providing goods and services.
    (C) A restaurant will have to close if no one pays for the food.
    (D) In many cities it is illegal to serve meals to homeless people.
    (E) Regulation of the restaurant industry drives up the costs of doing business.

106. The exclusionary rule is derived from

    (A) Article I, Section 1 of the Constitution
    (B) English common law
    (C) the Fifth Amendment to the Constitution
    (D) Congressional mandate
    (E) the Fourth Amendment to the Constitution

107. Who were the Boers?

    (A) the ruling family of the Netherlands during World War II
    (B) a missionary order working to convert the Indians in South America
    (C) Dutch settlers in South Africa
    (D) a secret society of knights during the time of the Crusades
    (E) the family controlling most of the diamond trade in Africa

108. Edward Jenner was responsible for what life-saving scientific breakthrough?

    (A) the smallpox vaccination
    (B) the discovery of airborne germs
    (C) penicillin
    (D) using heat to sterilize surgical instruments
    (E) identifying the mosquito as a carrier of yellow fever

109. Who is considered to be the Father of the Constitution?

    (A) Thomas Jefferson
    (B) John Hancock
    (C) George Washington
    (D) John Adams
    (E) James Madison

110. A nation-state is one where the majority of citizens share a common culture, language, and ethnicity. Select the BEST example of a nation-state from the choices listed.

    (A) Switzerland
    (B) India
    (C) Australia
    (D) Iceland
    (E) the United States

111. As a result of the widespread bank failures that took place during the Great Depression, which of the following institutions was formed?

(A) the Federal Reserve System
(B) the Federal Deposit Insurance Corporation
(C) the Comptroller of the Currency
(D) the Federal Home Loan Bank Board
(E) the Office of Thrift Supervision

112. Lech Walesa was

(A) the first Pole to be elected to the papacy
(B) the discoverer of the element polonium
(C) the leader of the Solidarity trade union movement
(D) a leader in the Polish resistance to the Nazis
(E) the composer of the Polish national anthem

113. The Saffir-Simpson scale is used to measure

(A) the strength of hurricanes
(B) relative annual rainfall
(C) the strength of tornadoes
(D) the magnitude of earthquakes
(E) the level of particulate matter in the atmosphere

114. To which school of economic thought does the Laffer curve belong?

(A) monetarism
(B) supply-side economics
(C) capitalism
(D) Keynesianism
(E) socialism

115. Why did the Founding Fathers create the Bill of Rights?

(A) to ensure that the costs of the Revolutionary War would be repaid
(B) to reassure the small states that their right to participate in the decision-making process would remain safe
(C) because the citizens had been accustomed to similar protection under British rule
(D) to guarantee that individual liberties would be respected
(E) to prevent the states from enacting their own individual bills

116. The strength of a research study is only as good as its ability to be replicated. What does this mean?

(A) The scientific method requires duplicate studies before any results are accepted as fact.
(B) If a study has significant results but cannot be done again with the same results, it is difficult to assess whether the results were due to error.
(C) A good study is one that has predictable results.
(D) If a study has significant results and is well documented throughout, it is not necessary to replicate the study.
(E) if a study has insignificant results but it can be replicated, it is a good study.

GO ON TO THE NEXT PAGE

117. As the military and spiritual leader of the Sioux tribe, Sitting Bull

(A) advocated firm resistance to white encroachment and settlement

(B) encouraged assimilation, even intermarriage, between the Sioux and the American settlers

(C) never made peace with the U.S. Army and, as a result, the Sioux have no reservation today

(D) was educated abroad and therefore unused to the nomadic lifestyle of his fellow tribespeople

(E) sought conciliation with both the Cheyenne and Arapahoe tribes

118. Frederick Law Olmstead was an American landscape architect prominent for designing many well-known urban parks; which of the following is not one of his creations?

(A) Central Park

(B) Prospect Park

(C) Golden Gate Park

(D) Jackson Park at the World's Columbian Exposition

(E) Washington Park at the World's Columbian Exposition

119. What is the world's tallest waterfall?

(A) Victoria Falls

(B) Yellowstone Falls

(C) Niagara Falls

(D) Angel Falls

(E) Tugela Falls

120. The formation of OPEC led to

(A) lower domestic oil production

(B) falling oil prices worldwide

(C) a transfer of wealth from oil-consuming nations to oil-producing nations

(D) less concentration in the domestic oil industry

(E) government regulation of oil imports

END OF TEST. STOP

ANSWER KEY

1. E	21. D	41. C	61. C	81. A	101. E
2. B	22. B	42. A	62. A	82. E	102. B
3. C	23. E	43. C	63. B	83. C	103. D
4. D	24. A	44. D	64. B	84. C	104. B
5. A	25. B	45. A	65. E	85. A	105. B
6. C	26. D	46. B	66. B	86. B	106. E
7. A	27. C	47. C	67. B	87. A	107. C
8. E	28. E	48. D	68. D	88. C	108. A
9. D	29. A	49. A	69. B	89. B	109. E
10. B	30. B	50. B	70. A	90. C	110. D
11. B	31. C	51. E	71. C	91. D	111. B
12. C	32. C	52. B	72. D	92. E	112. C
13. B	33. E	53. E	73. A	93. B	113. A
14. A	34. D	54. B	74. E	94. E	114. B
15. B	35. A	55. A	75. D	95. B	115. D
16. D	36. B	56. E	76. B	96. C	116. B
17. C	37. E	57. D	77. C	97. D	117. A
18. E	38. C	58. C	78. D	98. A	118. C
19. A	39. D	59. A	79. A	99. C	119. D
20. A	40. B	60. C	80. E	100. D	120. C

Answers and Explanations

1. (E)

The Articles of Confederation were an attempt to craft an agreement by which the newly independent nation could function. There were many things the new federal government could not do, but it could declare war.

2. (B)

Huey Long ran the state of Louisiana like a virtual dictator and controlled every level of Louisiana state politics. David Duke (A) was also a notorious Louisiana politician, but he gained infamy from being a supporter of the Ku Klux Klan. Though James Hoffa (E) was famously murdered, he was a labor-union boss from Chicago.

3. (C)

Athens and Sparta fought the Peloponnesian Wars over the time period 431–404 B.C.E. Eventually, Sparta emerged victorious, but the extended conflict weakened both city-states grievously.

4. (D)

Both socialization and enculturation refer to lifelong processes by which cultural and social identity are learned or passed down to an individual: values, norms, mores, and conformity are all learned. Answer (D) is correct since genetic makeup is determined at birth and cannot be taught.

5. (A)

The key to this question is breaking down the term "bipedalism": "bi" means two, "ped" means foot. If you don't know this, you can see that two of the five choices have to do with gait, while four describe characteristics of modern humans. Answer (A) combines these ideas.

6. (C)

For Freud, the goal of psychotherapy was to make the unconscious conscious, so answer (B) is not Jung's idea. All of the other answer choices are sound-alike distracters.

7. (A)

Though answer (E) may have contributed to poor relations today, the best answer is (A). When the nation of Israel was created in 1948, already strained Arab-Jewish relations became dramatically worse.

8. (E)

The Battle of the Little Big Horn in 1876 was fought well after America had won its independence from Great Britain, so (D) is incorrect. Answer (B) is also wrong: mountain men and fur traders were typically loners or traveled in small apolitical groups.

9. (D)

Africa has the greatest number of countries. There are 53, of which 6 are islands. If you had listened to the advice in Chapter Three and bought a world map, you would probably know this.

10. (B)

Charles de Gaulle may have saved France when he addressed the nation from London in June 1940. He rallied his countrymen, assuring them they were not alone in their fight against the Nazis. De Gaulle formed the Free France movement, and fought with the French and the British to liberate France. He was later elected President of France.

11. (B)

Article I, Section 7 of the Constitution states that all bills for raising revenue must originate in the House of Representatives. Answer (A) is incorrect, since neither house has absolute authority over the media, and both houses must approve Supreme Court nominees (D).

12. (C)

The "Crescent City" in question refers to New Orleans, and the question is asking about Andrew Jackson's victory in the Battle of New Orleans. Answers (B) and (E) are French names meant to confuse you.

13. (B)

The effect of an increase in the price of I on the price of G will depend upon the dependence of G on I. If there is a significant amount of I involved in the production of G,

then the manufacturer will have to continue to use it, and pass the increase in price along to the customers. Options (A) and (C) describe scenarios where G does not depend on I, so G probably can be produced without the more expensive input.

14. (A)
The term "folkways" is used to describe the cultural output (often material) of a particular group, such as woven baskets or headdresses, as well as traditional customs in dance and song. Only answer (A) is incorrect; accent is not a result of custom but rather of geography, class, or linguistics.

15. (B)
Neither the Federalists nor the Anti-Federalists addressed the right of women to vote, as it was not an issue at the time and would not become one for a century.

16. (D)
This question is straightforward and may seem almost "too obvious," but there is no reason to read more into it than is already there.

17. (C)
Tacitus, Herodotus, Julius Caesar, and Suetonius were all avid writers who recorded ancient historical events. Attila could not read or write.

18. (E)
Lyndon Baines Johnson (B) was president during the Vietnam conflict, but he preceded Nixon. Robert F. Kennedy (C) was never president.

19. (A)
The Romanov dynasty ruled Russia from 1613 until 1917, when the royal family was executed by the Bolsheviks. Tolstoy (B) is the famous Russian author of *War and Peace*.

20. (A)
The Roman empire eventually collapsed under the weight of its own ineptitude and corruption; at the same time it was being battered from the outside by barbarian invasions. The papacy was not a factor.

21. (D)
El Niño is a regularly occurring climatic feature in which warm water moves back and forth across the Pacific ocean. The warmer water temperatures affect rainfall and temperature around the world.

22. (B)
The key to this answer lies in the term "chronometric." The Latin root "chronos" means "time" and "metric" has to do with "measuring." Three answer choices refer to measuring the age of something, so one of them probably is correct.

23. (E)
Oligopoly exists when there are only a few sellers in a market. It typically occurs in industries where there are significant barriers to entry (such as high start-up costs).

24. (A)
Answer (B) should suggest that either (A) or (B) is the correct answer. Test writers often simply add a prefix like "neo-" to the correct answer to create a distracter.

25. (B)
In 1985 Ronald Reagan quoted a Clint Eastwood movie when he spoke these words.

26. (D)
If you have heard of obsessive-compulsive disorder, the right answer will be clear. The incorrect answer choices employ other familiar-sounding terms from pop psychology.

27. (C)
From 1976–1983, thousands of political opponents of the Argentine government simply disappeared in the middle of the night. Many were tortured and eventually killed.

28. (E)
This is a difficult question because Plymouth was not one of the thirteen major colonies. Bradford was largely responsible for keeping the earlier Plymouth settlement independent of the Massachusetts Bay Colony for many years.

29. (A)
Tsunamis are huge waves caused by earthquakes on the ocean floor, sometimes powerful enough to cause damage hundreds of miles away. Since tornados never form over water, answer (D) can be eliminated.

30. (B)
Answers (A) and (E) both refer to feudalism, the medieval socioeconomic system. The proletariat is the working class in Marxist theory, so (D) is also wrong.

31. (C)
The Church did not take a position on feudalism. All of the other answer choices are logical contributing factors to the decline of feudalism.

32. (C)
Since every American can plead the Fifth Amendment in a court of law, answer (A) is incorrect. Impeachment powers (B) reside in Congress, not in the executive branch; in addition, the key word "exclusively" should indicate a potential wrong answer.

33. (E)
Those economists favoring fiscal policy (changes in taxation and government spending) over monetary policy (enacted by the Federal Reserve) believe that it can be more precisely targeted at those sectors of the economy in need of intervention.

34. (D)
Answer choice (A) contains the absolute word "only," and can probably be eliminated. Answer (E) is designed to confuse you—a "traditional display" has nothing to do with a "style of movement."

35. (A)
Marxism is a theory of social conflict, which is a subject for study by sociologists. Fascism (B), monarchy (C), and anarchy (E) are all political subjects. Monopoly (D) is an economic concern.

36. (B)
Federalism refers to the system of dividing power between a central government and regional governments. The division of powers is spelled out in a constitution or other document.

37. (E)
Elizabeth Kubler-Ross is a sociologist known for her pioneering work on death, dying, and the aging process. Margaret Mead is an anthropologist known for her research on adolescent girls (D), and Jean Piaget (A) is a famous developmental psychologist.

38. (C)
World War I lasted from 1914–1918. The Japanese did not bomb Pearl Harbor until 1941, and that attack led the United States to enter World War II.

39. (D)
Wild Bill Hickock represents one of the earliest commercial pop cultural icons in American history. Hickock starred as "Wild Bill" in the play *Scouts of the Prairies* and toured throughout America and Europe with Buffalo Bill Cody's Wild West Show in 1872–1873.

40. (B)
Japan was an imperial monarchy before World War II, but the emperor did not play a fundamental role in governing Japan. Choice (A) is close, but its extreme language makes it an unlikely correct answer. Before the war, women did not have the right to vote. When the United States defeated Japan, it became a role model for that country, as the Japanese sought to achieve a similar level of economic prosperity.

41. (C)
Cooley's three steps are as follows: 1) we imagine how we look to others; 2) we interpret other's reactions; and 3) we develop a self-concept. Comparison and constant adjustment are not steps in this process, so all the other choices can be eliminated.

42. (A)
The doldrums, also known as equatorial belts of calm, are areas slightly north and south of the equator characterized by warm moist air as well as various forms of severe weather. The doldrums are also known for calms, periods when the winds die down altogether, leaving ships stranded.

43. (C)
Answer (A) can be eliminated as it's unlikely that anyone signed the Declaration of Independence in the middle of the night. The Underground Railroad (D) was not in place until the following century.

44. (D)
Real interest rates take into account the effect of inflation on the rate of return the investor will receive. The word "real" used in economics always indicates that the effect of inflation has been considered.

45. (A)
Answers (B) through (E) are all accurate characterizations of the balance of imperial power in Europe after 1588. Spanish was never the most commonly spoken language on the continent.

46. (B)
Gerrymandering is the process of drawing legislative districts in such a way as to either minimize or maximize the voting strength of a particular group. It is done to benefit the political party that is drawing the districts. It gets its name from Eldridge Gerry, governor of Massachusetts from 1810–1812.

47. (C)
The Elgin Marbles, named for the Earl of Elgin who brought them from Greece to England in 1806, are a series of sculptures from the Parthenon in Athens. The Greek government contends that they were illegally sold to Lord Elgin, and wants them back.

48. (D)
From 1732–1757, Benjamin Franklin published *Poor Richard's Almanac*—an encyclopedic text containing weather predictions, proverbs, and epigrams, which sold nearly ten thousand copies per year.

49. (A)
The "Forbidden City" is in Beijing. It was built between the years of 1406–1420 during the Ming dynasty, and was the home of emperors of China until the end of the Qing dynasty in 1924.

50. (B)
A demographic is a statistic characterizing human populations, or segments of populations broken down by things like age, gender, or income. Demographic studies are quantitative—they can be measured in numbers. In answer (B), the phrase "perceived quality of life" indicates a study of qualitative rather than quantitative factors.

51. (E)
The eruption of Mt. Pinatubo in the Philippines in 1991 was one of the twentieth century's most devastating volcanic events. The environmental consequences of the Mt. Pinatubo eruption were far reaching and long lasting, but the city famously preserved by a volcanic eruption was Pompeii, which fell victim to the eruption of Mt. Vesuvius in 79 C.E.

52. (B)
Sigmund Freud created the concept of the id, the ego, and the superego as the driving structure of the personality, as well as ideas about ego defense mechanisms like denial and projection. Answers (D) and (E) are distracters that sound like Freudian terms.

53. (E)
The key to this question is the pre-Civil War date, 1857. The ruling probably did not go in favor of African Americans, so (C) can be immediately ruled out, as can (D).

54. (B)
An increase in the money supply typically causes lower interest rates, leading to additional investment by business, increased employment, and greater economic output.

55. (A)
Thermoluminescence is used on archaeological artifacts. The technique measures the amount of light emitted by electrons as heat forces them out of pockets in a crystal and converts that measurement into an age. The other answer choices all employ scientific-sounding language, but don't make sense upon closer reading.

56. (E)

This question is designed to test your understanding of the socioeconomic characteristics of the North and South. Often, drawing a chart can simplify this type of question: write "North" in one column and "South" in a second column and place the appropriate traits underneath. Options (A), (B), (C), and (D) are all false statements.

57. (D)

The Libertarian Party advocates the least possible amount of interference by government. Environmentalism is the primary platform of the Green Party (B). Both the Communist (E) and Socialist (A) Parties advocate a strong central government.

58. (C)

Watch out for terms like "should be" in answers (A) and (B) that express opinion instead of fact. In answers (D) and (E), words like "never" and "rigid" are warning signs of potential wrong answers. The more ambiguous and nuanced statement, answer (C), is the right choice.

59. (A)

The Salic Law required that only male descendants of the king inherit the throne. The desire for a male heir was one of many factors considered by the French monarchy when negotiating for a bride, or when discarding a wife who had failed to produce the desired heir.

60. (C)

Buddhists seek to find the Middle Way in life, avoiding extremism in all forms. One way they seek to do this is through meditation.

61. (C)

This psychology question can be deciphered even if you've never heard the term "inappropriate affect": expressing contradictory behavior when describing or experiencing an emotion. A careful reading of the answer choices reveals that answer (C) is out of place.

62. (A)

Prior to 1870, both Italy and Germany were made up of several smaller kingdoms sharing similar cultures. Both groups realized that to be taken seriously by the rest of Europe they would need to unite into larger nations.

63. (B)

Black men were granted the right to vote in 1868, well before women of any color, so (A) is incorrect.

64. (B)

Henry the Navigator, a prince of Portugal who lived from 1394–1460, was among the first to see the value of exploring beyond the known world. He founded a center for cartography and sponsored ocean expeditions.

65. (E)

This question draws on sociology, political science, and Western civilization, among other topics. The key to the answer lies in the Enlightenment idea of individualism and free will; because of this new emphasis on the individual's capacity for reason, new disciplines like sociology were born.

66. (B)

If there are many sellers and few buyers for a product, a seller cannot raise prices without losing market share.

67. (B)

The hysteria surrounding the Salem witch trials that had swept so rapidly through Puritan Massachusetts ended almost as suddenly as it had begun.

68. (D)

First proposed in the 1980s, the Strategic Defense Initiative was a plan to shoot incoming missiles out of the sky while they were too far away to damage the United States. It would have made Soviet missiles useless against the U.S. The plan forced the Soviet Union to spend huge amounts of money to find a way to neutralize the S.D.I. The aging Soviet economy could not support this expense, and the government was forced to cut subsidies to satellite nations. The communist governments in those nations were unable to hold on to power, and in 1991, the Soviet Union itself collapsed.

69. (B)

There is no evidence to suggest that disease is preventable as a result of grooming behaviors, so (A) is incorrect. Additionally, among primates this is not a gender-specific behavior, so answer (C) can also be eliminated.

70. (A)

The "One-Drop" construct (C) refers to a slavery-era idea, so (C) is incorrect. Similarly, the notion of "original sin" (E) predates the Puritans by centuries.

71. (C)

The kingdom of Nubia now lies within the borders of Egypt and Sudan. Modern inhabitants of southern Egypt and northern Sudan still speak the Nubian language.

72. (D)

Cultural relativism is a critical perspective that takes the uniqueness of a subject into consideration, whereas an ethnocentric approach looks at a subject through one's own cultural lens. Marxism and socialism are closely related so (A) can be immediately eliminated.

73. (A)

Japan is a nation of over two thousand islands. The four major islands are Hokkaido, Honshu, Kyushu, and Shikoku. Nagasaki is the Japanese city where the second atomic bomb was dropped by the United States in World War II.

74. (E)

Essayist and pamphleteer Thomas Paine (1737–1809) also wrote *Common Sense* in 1776—a strong defense of American independence from England.

75. (D)

This psychology question addresses the concepts of introversion and extroversion. These are familiar concepts to most test-takers—don't just choose an answer because it sounds more formal, as with (B), (C), and (E).

76. (B)

In 1799, a French soldier in Napoleon's army was working at a fort on the Rosetta branch of the Nile River. He discovered a stone slab with carved inscriptions that would unlock the mystery of hieroglyphics years later. French linguist Jean Champollion would use these inscriptions to translate the ancient writing.

77. (C)

Many colonists came to the New World for the expressed purpose of practicing their religion free from government interference. This makes it easy to rule out both answers (A) and (B).

78. (D)

In 1944, delegates from 45 nations met at Bretton Woods, New Hampshire, to discuss the postwar recovery in Europe, as well as other issues. Some of the outcomes were a system of fixed exchange rates and the establishment of the International Monetary Fund and the World Bank.

79. (A)

Answers (B) through (E) are all social anthropological concerns. Psychologists would be most likely to study intelligence and its measurement (A).

80. (E)

All of the factors listed contribute to the deforestation of the Amazon—the world's largest tropical rainforest, home to the greatest variety of plants and animals on Earth.

81. (A)

The experimental method uses observation and theory to prove or disprove a hypothesis.

82. (E)

The United Nations was established in 1945 to replace the League of Nations, which had been unable to maintain peace in the world. To do this, the United Nations is authorized to send troops into areas of instability. The League had no such authority.

83. (C)

The Jazz Age does encompass the Harlem Renaissance but refers to a much broader movement that crossed racial barriers, so (A) is incorrect.

84. (C)

The *Book of the Dead* is a collection of ancient Egyptian hieroglyphic texts, explaining funeral customs and the proper spells to send the dead on a successful journey to the afterlife. The earliest collection dates from approximately 1500 B.C.E.

85. (A)

To reach the correct answer here, eliminate the choices that don't make sense. Each incorrect choice contains deliberately confusing language. Answer (C) can be ruled out, as the phrase "domineering mother figure" is really a matter of opinion, not fact. Terms like "pair-bond" and "primary reinforcer" in answer (D) refer to psychological concepts but have nothing to do with "learned helplessness."

86. (B)

Nicola Sacco and Bartolomeo Vanzetti were two poor Italian immigrants (who happened to be anarchists). They were found guilty of attempted robbery and attempted murder with very little evidence of either crime.

87. (A)

The Dead Sea has its name because no plants or animals can live in it due to high concentrations of minerals.

88. (C)

John Maynard Keynes (1883–1946) is one of the most important figures in the history of economics. He revolutionized the field with his classic book *The General Theory of Employment, Interest and Money* in 1936. Prior to Keynes, it was considered best to let the business cycle run its course—the length and severity of the Great Depression led him to question whether governments ought to step in and attempt to restore a nation to prosperity.

89. (B)

In a free economy, individuals may choose to leave a job in search of other opportunities. This is called frictional unemployment, and may actually rise when the economy is prospering because job seekers perceive their chances of finding a better job than the one they have to be greater at that time.

90. (C)

Dorothy Parker (D) was an American writer of the 1920s, and Gloria Steinem (E) was part of the 1970s feminist movement.

91. (D)

Charlemagne established a central government over western Europe, restoring much of the unity of the old Roman empire and paving the way for the development of modern Europe.

92. (E)

In 1992, the Twenty-seventh Amendment to the Constitution was adopted. This law prohibits Congress from recklessly raising its own pay by requiring that no pay raises take effect until after the next election.

93. (B)

The phrases "destructive personality types" in answer (D) and "unacceptable responses" in (E) are both subjective terms, indicating that both choices probably are incorrect.

94. (E)

Article III, Section 3 of the Constitution defines treason as levying war against the United States, or adhering to or giving aid and comfort to the enemy.

95. (B)

Stephen Crane wrote *The Red Badge of Courage*; *The Old Man and the Sea* is by Ernest Hemingway.

96. (C)

Iran was known to Europeans as Persia until 1935, when the Persian ambassador to Nazi Germany suggested a name change to celebrate the country's Aryan heritage.

97. (D)

The Latin term *in situ* loosely means "on-site." It has nothing to do with "sea level" or "ecosystem."

98. (A)

It is likely that continental islands were once part of the continent with which they share plant and animal species.

99. (C)

Antonio Gramsci (1891–1937) was an Italian revolutionary, socialist, and political theorist. Gramsci developed the concept of hegemony in response to the rise of fascism in the late 1920s and 1930s and the failure of the socialist experiment—he was puzzled by the fact that the working class did not uniformly resist.

100. (D)

Although Napoleon was certainly motivated by dreams of personal glory, his primary goal was to cut off British access to their richest possession, India.

101. (E)

R.E.M. or Rapid Eye Movement is the sleeping state in which all dreams occur, so (A) is incorrect. Answer (B) is a distracter that sounds like the real answer.

102. (B)

Answer (A) can be ruled out since the concept of "Manifest Destiny" has not been refuted. The phrases "popular mythologies" and "unbridled westward expansion" are subjective statements of opinion, so (D) is incorrect. Similarly, the phrase "long-exploited" in answer (E) is the sort of value judgment that typically indicates a wrong answer.

103. (D)

Although they are Biblical references, Eden, Adam, and Eve all stand for ideas about human origins. The clues in this question are the location and the fact that the possibility of a common female ancestor is mentioned.

104. (B)

Alexander the Great (356–323 B.C.E.) led an extraordinary life, but the pyramids were built thousands of years before he was born.

105. (B)

This phrase was coined by the well-known economist Milton Friedman to make the point that there is a cost to providing all goods and services. If the consumer of those goods does not pay, then the cost will be borne by others.

106. (E)

The exclusionary rule, which states that illegally obtained evidence may not be used against an individual, is derived from the Fourth Amendment, which protects against unreasonable search and seizure.

107. (C)

The Boers were a group of Dutch settlers in South Africa. They arrived between the years 1652 and 1795 during the course of trade by the Dutch East India Company. These people were repeatedly driven further inland by British settlers and finally defeated in the Boer War of 1899–1902. "Boer" is the Dutch word for "farmer."

108. (A)

In 1796 Edward Jenner, a British doctor, injected a boy with material from a patient with a minor ailment called cowpox. Jenner believed that people who had cowpox introduced to their system were immune to smallpox. He then exposed the boy to smallpox, the most feared disease of the day. The boy did not become ill, and Jenner went on to inoculate thousands of people, saving them from the death and disfigurement that smallpox caused.

109. (E)

James Madison is considered to be the Father of the Constitution because he was the best-prepared delegate to the Constitutional Convention, took many notes on the proceedings, and wrote a number of the *Federalist Papers* in support of the Constitution.

110. (D)

The people of Iceland share an ethnicity and language. The United States and Australia are home to citizens of many different ethnicities, and in Switzerland and India, multiple languages are spoken.

111. (B)

The Federal Deposit Insurance Corporation was formed in 1933 to regulate the solvency of commercial banks and to insure the consumers' deposits in the event that the bank failed.

112. (C)
Lech Walesa was a Polish shipyard worker who led the trade union movement that eventually led to the end of totalitarianism in Poland, a former member of the Soviet bloc. He won the 1983 Nobel Peace Prize, and was elected president of Poland in 1980.

113. (A)
The Saffir-Simpson scale to measure hurricane strength was developed in 1969 by civil engineer Herbert Saffir and National Hurricane Center director Bob Simpson.

114. (B)
Economist Arthur Laffer theorized that at certain high levels of taxation actual output would fall short of potential output because of the disincentives created by excessive rates of taxation. He postulated that as tax rates were lowered, revenues to the government would actually rise, because there would be less incentive to avoid paying taxes. The name comes from the emphasis on the supply side of the economy.

115. (D)
The Bill of Rights was included to reassure citizens that their individual liberties would be protected from the abuses they had suffered under colonial rule. These assurances were essential before delegates agreed to approve the new Constitution.

116. (B)
Replication is critical in determining the strength or weakness of a hypothesis.

117. (A)
Sitting Bull (1831–1890) was vehemently opposed to assimilation and would never have tolerated intermarriage, so (B) is incorrect. However, the Sioux chief did make peace with the U.S. Army in 1868 in exchange for a sizable reservation free of white settlers. Therefore, answer (C) is incorrect.

118. (C)
Frederick Law Olmstead was fascinated with nature from the time of his youth and was known for his designs in the accidental, naturalistic style of the British landscape garden.

119. (D)
Angel Falls, in the Guayana highland region of Venezuela, plunges off the side of a flat-topped mountain, free-falling 2,421 feet. In total, Angel Falls is 2,937 feet high.

120. (C)
When OPEC was formed in 1973 (by Iran, Iraq, Kuwait, Saudi Arabia, and Venezuela) the days of low oil prices ended. Prior to 1973, oil was priced based on how much it cost to produce, which in OPEC countries was virtually nothing.

| SECTION SIX |

The CLEP Natural Sciences Exam

Chapter Twenty: Practice Test 1: Diagnostic

Time—90 minutes
120 Questions

Directions: Each question below has five lettered answer choices. For each question or phrase, choose the most closely related answer. For multiple questions that refer to the same group of lettered answer choices, each choice can be used more than once, once, or not at all.

Questions 1–3

(A) DNA
(B) Mitochondrion
(C) Vacuole
(D) Plasma membrane
(E) Cell wall

1. Not found in a prokaryotic cell

2. Not found in an animal cell

3. Storage organelle

Questions 4–6

(A) Apomorphy
(B) Homologous
(C) Analogous
(D) Homoplasy
(E) Adaptation

4. Similar features that share a common evolutionary origin such as the wings of a bat and the flippers of a whale

5. A novel feature that was derived over evolutionary time

6. A feature that provides a selective advantage to an organism

Questions 7–8

(A) Active transport
(B) Diffusion
(C) Facilitated diffusion
(D) Osmosis
(E) Concentration gradient

7. Term for chemical substances passing through a membrane with the expenditure of energy

8. A special term for the simple diffusion of water across a selectively permeable membrane

GO ON TO THE NEXT PAGE

Questions 9–10

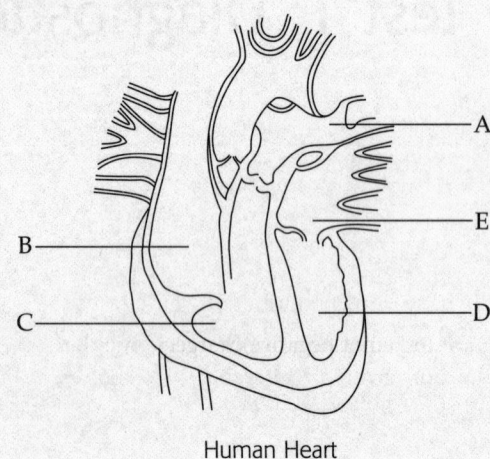

Human Heart

9. Left ventricle

10. Right atrium

Questions 11–13

(A) Phloem
(B) Xylem
(C) Roots
(D) Stomata
(E) Tracheids

11. Has its transport interrupted by cavitation

12. Transports food from sources to sinks

13. Regulate transpiration by opening or closing

Questions 14–16

(A) $H-C\equiv C-H$

(B) $\left[\begin{array}{c} H \\ | \\ H-N-H \\ | \\ H \end{array}\right]^+$

(C) $H-\overset{H}{\underset{|}{C}}=\overset{H}{\underset{|}{C}}-H$

(D) $H-\overset{H}{\underset{H}{\overset{|}{C}}}-H$

(E) CH_3-CH_2-OH

14. Ethanol

15. Methane

16. An ion

Directions: For each of the following questions or incomplete statements, select the best answer or completion from the five options given.

17. In natural selection, "fitness" is the ability of organisms to survive and reproduce successfully. At which of the following levels does natural selection act?

    (A) species
    (B) community
    (C) ecosystem
    (D) individual
    (E) population

18. A number of populations of different species in a given habitat represent a(n)

    (A) biosphere.
    (B) biome.
    (C) ecosystem.
    (D) community.
    (E) population.

19. Many species are capable of exponential (ever-increasing) population growth rates. In reality, which of the following organisms exhibit this pattern?

    (A) humans
    (B) rabbits
    (C) ants
    (D) algae
    (E) grasshoppers

20. The mass number of an atom is derived from which of the following?

    (A) the number of protons
    (B) the number of neutrons
    (C) the number of protons plus electrons
    (D) the number of neutrons plus electrons
    (E) the number of protons plus neutrons

21. Which of the following is TRUE of an atom having 12 protons and 12 electrons?

    (A) It has a net positive charge.
    (B) It has an atomic number of 12.
    (C) It has a neutral charge.
    (D) It has a mass number of 24.
    (E) It has a net negative charge.

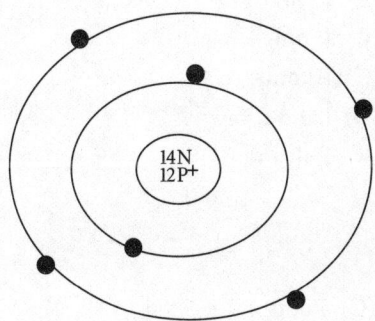

22. Based on the information from the periodic table entries, which of the following is true of the atom shown?

    (A) It represents boron.
    (B) Since it has two more neutrons than the carbon shown in the box it must be nitrogen N.
    (C) It cannot be carbon because the mass numbers are different.
    (D) It is carbon but must be synthesized in the lab.
    (E) It is a carbon isotope because the atomic numbers are identical.

GO ON TO THE NEXT PAGE

Questions 23–25 refer to the following diagram, which represents equal volumes of water being heated in two beakers of differing shape on a laboratory hot plate.

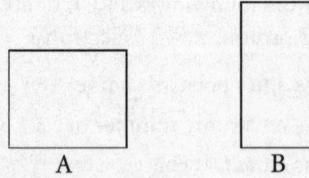

23. Which processes are involved in heating the water in these beakers?

    I. conduction
    II. convection
    III. radiation

    (A) I only
    (B) II only
    (C) III only
    (D) I and II only
    (E) I, II, and III

24. Between the contents of beakers A and B, which will increase in temperature faster and why?

    (A) A because there is less water to heat.
    (B) B because the container shape will make convection more efficient.
    (C) They will heat at the same rate.
    (D) A because there is a greater surface area for conduction.
    (E) There is no way to tell for sure with the information provided.

25. Which hypothesis could beakers A and B potentially test?

    (A) The shape of the container holding water has an effect on its heating rate.
    (B) Laboratory hot plates differ in heat efficiency.
    (C) Water heats at a faster rate than milk.
    (D) Heating rates of water are affected by the volume of water.
    (E) None of these could be tested.

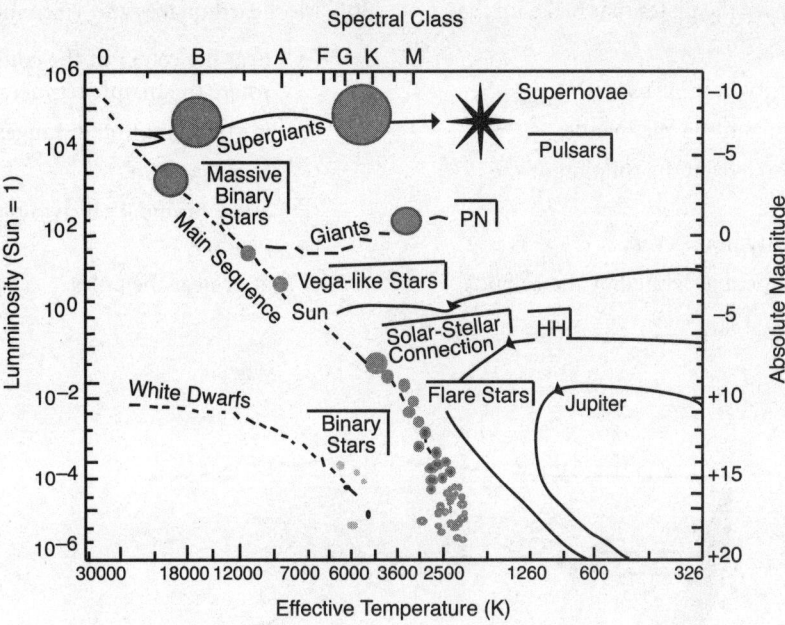

26. According to the above diagram, which of the following stars would have the highest surface temperature but lowest luminosity?

    (A) supergiants
    (B) pulsars
    (C) white dwarfs
    (D) giants
    (E) main sequence stars

27. Which of the following is NOT true of a black hole?

    (A) formed by the collapse of a very massive star
    (B) gravity can pull in light
    (C) requires a highly specialized form of telescope to view from earth
    (D) can warp space-time
    (E) cannot be viewed directly

28. What discovery did Edwin Hubble make that supports the Big Bang Theory?

    (A) background radiation from the big bang can still be detected
    (B) the existence of quasars
    (C) objects in the universe are moving away from each other
    (D) the existence of the asteroid belt
    (E) the existence of black holes

GO ON TO THE NEXT PAGE

29. The force that moves the plates that make up the Earth's crust arises from

    (A) volcanic activity in the crust.
    (B) convection currents in the mantle.
    (C) centripetal force from the rotation of the Earth.
    (D) tectonic activity in the crust.
    (E) the magnetic field generated by the rotating Earth.

30. Most earthquakes and volcanoes occur

    (A) near the center of the continental plates where the mantle temperatures are greater.
    (B) in young mountain ranges.
    (C) at the equator.
    (D) at the boundary of two moving continental plates.
    (E) at or near the poles.

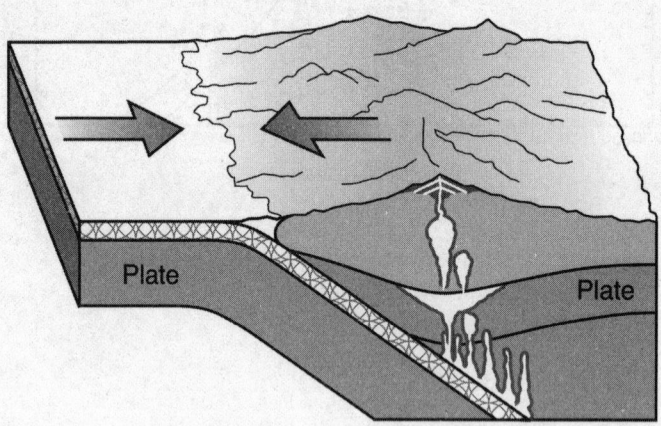

31. The boundary between two plates shown above would most likely result in

    (A) mountains.
    (B) earthquakes.
    (C) volcanoes.
    (D) none of the above.
    (E) all of the above.

GO ON TO THE NEXT PAGE

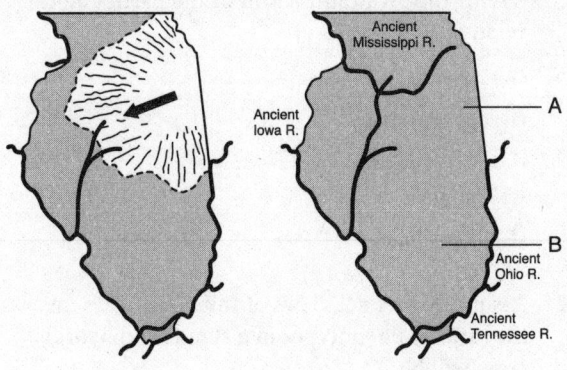

Illinois Glaciation: Before and After

32. The diagram shows the most recent glacial advance in Illinois. What is probably the main difference in soils between region A and region B today?

    (A) A is a much poorer soil.
    (B) B is a flat and poorly drained soil.
    (C) A has shallower topsoil.
    (D) A has a much younger and richer soil.
    (E) B has much older soil with more organic matter and nutrients.

33. Which of the following scientists provided the foundation for our current method of classification of organisms using binomial nomenclature?

    (A) Charles Lyell (1797–1875)
    (B) Charles Darwin (1809–1882)
    (C) Carolus Linnaeus (1707–1778)
    (D) Aristotle (384–322 B.C.E.)
    (E) Gregor Mendel (1822–1884)

34. All of the following contribute to variation in the genetic code EXCEPT

    (A) mutation.
    (B) cloning.
    (C) recombination.
    (D) crossover.
    (E) sexual reproduction.

35. Darwin used evidence from all of the following sources to construct his theory of evolution due to natural selection EXCEPT

    (A) embryology.
    (B) comparative anatomy.
    (C) genetics.
    (D) selective breeding.
    (E) population biology.

Questions 36–37 refer to the following figure of a theoretical cladogram.

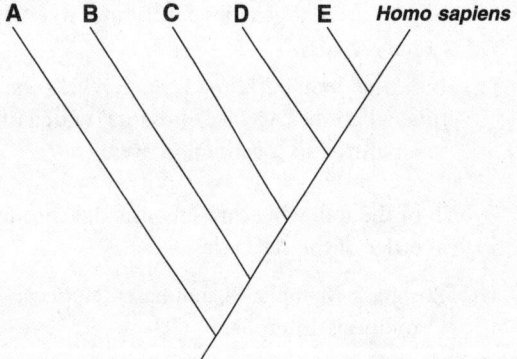

36. Which of the following statements can be correctly inferred from the cladogram?

    (A) Taxon A is an extinct animal.
    (B) Taxon C is a mammal.
    (C) Taxon D evolved from taxon C.
    (D) Together, taxon E and *Homo sapiens* form a monophyletic group.
    (E) *Homo sapiens* is the most advanced organism.

37. If taxon C is known to be a species of fish, which of the following statements must also be true?

    (A) Taxon D and taxon E must also be fish.
    (B) Taxon A and taxon B must also be fish.
    (C) Taxon B must be an amphibian.
    (D) Taxon D and taxon E must be vertebrates.
    (E) Taxon A and taxon B must be vertebrates.

GO ON TO THE NEXT PAGE

38. Which of the following statements describes the "Cambrian Explosion"?

    (A) It is the point in time when the universe came into being.
    (B) It is the period in evolutionary history when most of the major groups of animals appeared on Earth.
    (C) It is the period in evolutionary history when human impact caused the first great artificial extinction event.
    (D) It is the point in scientific history when the discovery of DNA led to the understanding of how molecular genetics contributes to evolutionary theory.
    (E) Indicated by the iridium layer, it marks the time when the "Age of Dinosaurs" ended due to a natural mass extinction event.

39. Which of the following correctly lists the chronological order of the cell cycle?

    (A) Prophase-Metaphase-Anaphase-Telophase-Cytokinesis-Interphase
    (B) Interphase-Anaphase-Prophase-Metaphase-Telophase-Cytokinesis
    (C) Prophase-Anaphase-Metaphase-Telophase-Interphase-Cytokinesis
    (D) Prophase-Interphase-Metaphase-Telophase-Anaphase-Cytokinesis
    (E) Interphase-Telophase-Metaphase-Anaphase-Cytokinesis-Prophase

40. What is the net energy yield from a molecule of glucose that is metabolized in the presence of oxygen?

    (A) 34 ATP
    (B) 2 ATP
    (C) 40 ATP
    (D) 4 ATP
    (E) 36 ATP

41. Which of the following groups of organisms represents the greatest fraction of the Earth's biodiversity?

    (A) Insecta
    (B) Mammalia
    (C) Annelida
    (D) Aves
    (E) Reptilia

42. Assuming Mendel's laws of inheritance are met, the ratio of phenotypes in a standard dihybrid cross will be

    (A) 3:1
    (B) 5:3:2:1
    (C) 1:1
    (D) 2:1
    (E) 9:3:3:1

43. The self-replicating molecules that were the possible precursors to life on Earth include

    (A) glucose polymers.
    (B) adenosine triphosphate.
    (C) amino acids.
    (D) nucleotides.
    (E) proteins.

44. The primary form of energy storage in plants is

    (A) simple sugars.
    (B) complex carbohydrates.
    (C) amino acids.
    (D) proteins.
    (E) triglycerides.

GO ON TO THE NEXT PAGE

45. Ribosomes are important cellular organelles involved in the production of

    (A) RNA.
    (B) DNA.
    (C) cellulose.
    (D) protein.
    (E) plasma membranes.

46. Which of the following contributes significantly to the compact tertiary structure of DNA?

    (A) histones
    (B) nuclear membrane
    (C) ribosomes
    (D) mRNA
    (E) tRNA

47. Gluconeogenesis describes the process of

    (A) synthesizing glycogen from glucose molecules.
    (B) metabolizing glycogen into glucose molecules.
    (C) synthesizing glucose from non-carbohydrate sources.
    (D) synthesizing lipids from glucose molecules.
    (E) metabolizing glucose to liberate energy for protein synthesis.

48. Meiosis is crucial for gametogenesis and sexual reproduction because it

    (A) produces very small gametes that are easily transported.
    (B) reduces the number of chromosomes from 2N to N.
    (C) creates the X and Y chromosomes that determine gender.
    (D) requires less energy than mitosis.
    (E) occurs in the early stages of development.

49. All of the following are parts of a flower EXCEPT

    (A) petal.
    (B) stamen.
    (C) sepal.
    (D) petiole.
    (E) anther.

50. The countercurrent exchange system is used to enhance the exchange of substrate between two oppositely directed flows of fluid. Which of the following systems employs a countercurrent exchange?

    (A) human circulation
    (B) bird gas exchange
    (C) amoeba food uptake
    (D) barnacle filtering
    (E) spider web-spinning

51. A sex-linked gene is one that has a locus

    (A) close to the promoter region of another gene.
    (B) on the same chromosome as another gene.
    (C) on the Y chromosome.
    (D) on the X chromosome.
    (E) on either the X or Y chromosome.

52. Which part of the human body produces insulin?

    (A) liver
    (B) spleen
    (C) pancreas
    (D) kidney
    (E) brain

GO ON TO THE NEXT PAGE

53. All of the following are true about protostome development EXCEPT

    (A) they have indeterminate cleavage.
    (B) they have holoblastic cleavage.
    (C) they have spiral cleavage.
    (D) they have holoblastic determinate cleavage.
    (E) the blastopore becomes the mouth.

54. Which of the following is a neurotransmitter eliciting a depolarization of skeletal muscle tissue, causing a contraction?

    (A) serotonin
    (B) dopamine
    (C) acetylcholine
    (D) calcium
    (E) histamine

55. A scientific hypothesis advances to the status of a theory after it

    (A) has been published in a scientific journal.
    (B) has been approved by a scientific committee.
    (C) has been among the scientific community for several years.
    (D) has been modified by a subsequent scientist.
    (E) has been supported by a significant amount of research.

56. All of the following are modes of pollination EXCEPT

    (A) wind.
    (B) water.
    (C) insects.
    (D) birds.
    (E) roots.

57. The main function of the small intestine is to absorb nutrients that are released during the digestion of ingested food. What is the main function of the large intestine?

    (A) storage of waste material
    (B) reclamation of water from the lumen
    (C) storage of water
    (D) concentration of urine
    (E) production of digestive enzymes

58. Which of the following is not one of the lobes of the human brain?

    (A) parietal
    (B) temporal
    (C) occipital
    (D) corpus callosum
    (E) frontal

59. Skeletal muscle provides the force for flexing and extending joints. How does smooth muscle function in animal bodies?

    (A) Smooth muscle provides regulatory functions such as peristalsis.
    (B) Smooth muscle has endurance for long-term flight.
    (C) Smooth muscle squeezes cells and aids in transport across cell membranes.
    (D) Smooth muscle keeps joints rigid during sleep.
    (E) Smooth muscle is located in jaw muscles for chewing tough fibers.

GO ON TO THE NEXT PAGE

60. Desert-dwelling animals have several adaptations that equip them for survival in arid environments. All of the following are some adaptations of desert plants and animals EXCEPT

    (A) waxy cuticle on leaves to prevent water loss.
    (B) structures with large surface area for dissipating heat.
    (C) moist, water-permeable skin to increase evaporative cooling.
    (D) extremely efficient kidneys relieving the need to drink water.
    (E) the ability to produce water internally through metabolism.

61. Which of the following diseases is inherited genetically from one or both of the parents?

    (A) Tay-Sachs
    (B) emphysema
    (C) AIDS
    (D) cirrhosis
    (E) hepatitis

62. Animals store calories in their bodies in the form of fat, but animals also will catabolize large amounts of glycogen during periods of low activity to make blood sugar available if needed in the future. Where is this glycogen stored?

    (A) brain
    (B) muscles and liver
    (C) blood
    (D) below the skin
    (E) bone marrow

63. Holometabolous insects undergo complete metamorphosis. This means that they

    (A) emerge directly from eggs as adults.
    (B) have no periods of hibernation as they develop
    (C) grow completely developed wings.
    (D) can reproduce asexually before reaching maturity.
    (E) have four different life stages: egg, larva, pupa, and adult.

64. Which of the mammals listed below has the longest gestation period?

    (A) mouse
    (B) bat
    (C) rhinoceros
    (D) elephant
    (E) wolf

65. The endocrine system involves which of the following structures and products?

    (A) digestive enzymes and the organs of digestion
    (B) aqueous gases and the lungs and airway
    (C) chemical messengers, the brain, and nerves
    (D) hormones and the glands that secrete hormones
    (E) antibodies and the lymph nodes

66. Every organism on Earth requires which of the following to be able to exchange gases with the external environment?

    (A) a steep diffusion gradient
    (B) moist membranes
    (C) gills
    (D) lungs
    (E) hemoglobin

GO ON TO THE NEXT PAGE

67. A scientist has a culture of flies that exhibit the dominant trait of red eye color, but does not know the eye-color genotypes of the flies in the culture. In order to determine the unknown genotype, she breeds them with flies that are homozygous recessive. This is an example of a

    (A) recombination experiment.
    (B) mutation experiment.
    (C) sex-linkage experiment.
    (D) genetic depression.
    (E) testcross.

68. In a seminal ecological paper, a sea star was removed from an intertidal zone and the population densities of other species changed drastically, upsetting the balance of the entire ecosystem. Which of the following statements is likely true about the intertidal zone?

    (A) The intertidal ecosystem was under pollution stress.
    (B) The sea star was a keystone predator species.
    (C) The intertidal ecosystem was being affected by global warming.
    (D) The sea star monopolized the ecosystem.
    (E) The sea star was a primary producer.

69. Which of the following terms best describes a large, continuous ecological system like a desert?

    (A) habitat
    (B) community
    (C) ecosystem
    (D) biome
    (E) niche

70. The logistic growth equation is a simple mathematical model to explain the growth of natural populations and is expressed as $\frac{\Delta N}{\Delta t} rN\left(\frac{K-N}{K}\right)$. Which term in the equation represents the carrying capacity of the environment?

    (A) $\frac{\Delta N}{\Delta t}$
    (B) r
    (C) K
    (D) N
    (E) $K - N$

71. A tree falls in the middle of a tropical rainforest, providing an open space for plants to colonize. This is an example of

    (A) exotic invasion.
    (B) primary succession.
    (C) secondary succession.
    (D) competition.
    (E) extinction.

72. All of the following factors will directly affect the number of individuals of a predatory species in a population EXCEPT

    (A) the predator's metabolic rate.
    (B) the predator's prey density.
    (C) the predator's home range.
    (D) the predator's reproductive rate.
    (E) the predator's natural enemies.

73. An r-selected species has which one of the following reproductive strategies?

    (A) producing one offspring when ecological conditions are most advantageous
    (B) a long gestation period and long-term adult care
    (C) producing a higher ratio of females to males
    (D) a short lifespan and the ability to produce a large number of offspring quickly
    (E) a reproductive rate responsive to environmental conditions

74. Species richness is an ecological measure of a habitat's

    (A) stage of succession.
    (B) conservation status.
    (C) nutrient availability.
    (D) age.
    (E) biodiversity.

75. Which organism below would be best suited for stage-dependent life table analysis?

    (A) human
    (B) housefly
    (C) freshwater sponge
    (D) bacterium
    (E) earthworm

76. Mistletoe utilizes the nutrients, structural support, and protection of other trees while providing no resources to the trees. The relationship between the mistletoe and a tree can be classified as

    (A) predation.
    (B) mutualism.
    (C) commensalism.
    (D) parasitism.
    (E) herbivory.

77. The half-life of the element thorium is twenty-five days whereupon it decays into protactinium. How much thorium will have decayed to protactinium in seventy-five days if there was 120 g of thorium to begin with?

    (A) 100 g
    (B) 40 g
    (C) 105 g
    (D) 15 g
    (E) 30 g

78. How many electrons does it take to fill the $3d$ subshell of an element with an atomic number over 30?

    (A) 2
    (B) 3
    (C) 6
    (D) 8
    (E) 10

79. Which of the following is the best possible definition of valence electrons?

    (A) the number of electrons an atom has in the outer shell
    (B) the number of electrons in surplus beyond the number of protons
    (C) the number of electrons an atom has in double bonds
    (D) the number of electrons an atom has in the $1s$ shell
    (E) the number of electrons an atom has in all of its shells

GO ON TO THE NEXT PAGE

80. What is the purpose of the cadmium rods in a nuclear reactor?

    (A) to dissipate heat so the reactor does not overheat
    (B) to absorb neutrons so the fission reaction occurs slowly
    (C) to donate neutrons to replenish the decaying uranium
    (D) to centralize electrons to harness electrochemical energy
    (E) to create a magnetic field to contain electrons

81. Which of the following subatomic particles is the smallest?

    (A) electron
    (B) proton
    (C) neutron
    (D) top quark
    (E) neutrino

82. How many electrons exist in the orbitals surrounding the nucleus of a neutral atom containing 10 protons?

    (A) 5
    (B) 6
    (C) 8
    (D) 10
    (E) 20

83. The atomic number of an element indicates

    (A) the molecular weight.
    (B) the order in which it was discovered.
    (C) the number of protons in the nucleus.
    (D) the number of elementary particles in the nucleus.
    (E) the energy state of the outer shell of electrons.

84. Heisenberg discovered that there was a certain level of uncertainty involved with electrons orbiting atomic nuclei. His uncertainty principle states that

    (A) it is impossible to know both the position and velocity of an electron.
    (B) it is impossible to know how many electron shells exist around the nucleus.
    (C) the probability of an atom ionizing in solution is not quantifiable.
    (D) charges of electron orbitals are unstable.
    (E) the speed of an electron varies disproportionately with the size of the nucleus.

85. How many neutrons are there in this isotope of uranium, $^{234}_{92}U$?

    (A) 92
    (B) 234
    (C) 117
    (D) 46
    (E) 142

86. Which of the following is the correct chemical formula for the compound silver chloride?

    (A) $FeCl_3$
    (B) $FeCl_2$
    (C) Ag_2Cl_3
    (D) $AgCl$
    (E) $CuCl_2$

87. Which of the following techniques involves quantifying the concentration of an unknown reagent by reacting the reagent until it is equivalent to a reagent with a known concentration?

    (A) titration
    (B) distillation
    (C) condensation
    (D) filtration
    (E) amalgamation

GO ON TO THE NEXT PAGE

88. Which of the following choices illustrates the balanced equation for the reaction NaOH + H_2SO_4 → Na_2SO_4 + H_2O ?

    (A) NaOH + $2H_2SO_4$ → $2Na_2SO_4$ + H_2O
    (B) 2NaOH + H_2SO_4 → Na_2SO_4 + $2H_2O$
    (C) NaOH + H_2SO_4 → Na_2SO_4 + H_2O
    (D) 2NaOH + $2H_2SO_4$ → Na_2SO_4 + H_2O
    (E) 4NaOH + H_2SO_4 → Na_2SO_4 + $3H_2O$

89. What is the percent by mass of carbon in the compound CO_2? (atomic weights: C=12.0 g/mole, O=16 g/mole)

    (A) 12.0 percent
    (B) 33.3 percent
    (C) 50 percent
    (D) 27.3 percent
    (E) 43.0 percent

90. Nonmetal elements adhere closely to the octet rule, which states that an atom

    (A) tends to lose or gain electrons so that there are eight electrons in the outer shell.
    (B) will form crystalline structures in a lattice of eight atoms.
    (C) releases energy to support the activation of eight electrons.
    (D) combines with another atom with eight valence electrons.
    (E) spins electrons eight revolutions before switching orbitals.

91. What volume of H_2O must be added to 100.0 ml of 10M HCl to obtain a 5M solution of HCl?

    (A) 100.0 ml of H_2O
    (B) 150.0 ml of H_2O
    (C) 250.0 ml of H_2O
    (D) 1000.0 ml of H_2O
    (E) 1500.0 ml of H_2O

92. A 70 kilogram man standing at rest on ice with a friction force of zero tries to push a resting mass of 70 kilograms forward by extending his arms. Which of the following is likely to occur?

    (A) The man pushes the mass away from him.
    (B) The man pushes himself away from the mass.
    (C) The man and the mass move away from each other at equal velocity.
    (D) Nothing moves because there is no friction.
    (E) An angular moment is created around the man's heels and he falls backward.

93. Water has physical properties that enable it to naturally exist in all three states of matter with only a limited amount of energy needed for it to transition between states and exist in liquid form at room temperature. What common metal exists in liquid form at room temperature?

    (A) mercury
    (B) gold
    (C) silver
    (D) potassium
    (E) magnesium

94. Air temperatures in areas near large bodies of water (coastline) are much more moderate than inland areas at the same latitude and altitude. What is the probable explanation for this phenomenon?

    (A) Large bodies of water retain heat and warm the soil at the soil/water interface.
    (B) The temperature difference between the ocean and coast is minimal so there is very little airflow (wind).
    (C) Water has a higher specific heat than soil so air temperatures above large bodies of water are more stable, while the air above land cools as the soil cools.
    (D) The air above large bodies of water is denser so it retains heat.
    (E) The ocean environment has greater primary productivity so creates more ambient heat from metabolic activity.

95. Which of the following examples would demonstrate the greatest increase in entropy?

    (A) A dead battery is recharged from AC current.
    (B) A child tows a sled up a snow-covered hill.
    (C) A puddle of water evaporates off hot pavement.
    (D) An avalanche drops fifty acres of snow down a mountainside.
    (E) A smoker strikes a match and lights a cigarette.

96. A 1 kilogram mass slides down a ramp so that it accelerates from a velocity of zero at the top of the ramp to a velocity of 50 m/s at the bottom of the ramp, where it reaches its top speed. What was the potential energy stored in the 1 kilogram mass at the top of the ramp?

    (A) 9.8 N
    (B) 1250 N
    (C) 2500 N
    (D) 5000 N
    (E) The mass had no potential energy while at rest.

97. A pressure cooker was a common kitchen appliance several decades ago, used less often today. What was the purpose of using a container with an airtight lid to cook on a stove?

    (A) The sealed container loses less water so the food does not dry out.
    (B) The pot loses less heat from heat dissipation into the air.
    (C) The lid creates a continuous connection of metal, spreading the heat more evenly.
    (D) The lid was a safety measure to protect the cook.
    (E) The boiling point of water increases with increased pressure so it allows cooking at a higher temperature.

98. Which of the following items does NOT pertain to the theory of relativity?

    (A) the Twin Paradox
    (B) A moving clock ticks slower than one at rest.
    (C) The speed of light in free space has the same value for all observers.
    (D) Planetary motion is elliptical in nature.
    (E) Moving objects are shorter than when they are at rest.

99. What happens to the angular acceleration of a particle as its radius of circular motion decreases?

    (A) It increases.
    (B) It decreases.
    (C) It stays the same.
    (D) Its tangential acceleration decreases.
    (E) Its tangential acceleration increases.

100. An object's weight is actually
    (A) the amount of matter it contains.
    (B) the force of gravity pulling it toward the Earth.
    (C) the resistance it exerts toward changes in motion.
    (D) the same quantity as its mass.
    (E) the weight of the volume of water displaced by the object.

101. The center of gravity of an object can be all of the following EXCEPT
    (A) the center of mass.
    (B) outside of the object.
    (C) the point where it can be suspended without rotating.
    (D) the average of the center of masses of the units that make up the object.
    (E) the point of minimum momentum of the moving object.

102. Which of the following substances requires the greatest amount of heat per kilogram for a given increase in temperature?
    (A) water
    (B) ice
    (C) steam
    (D) copper
    (E) aluminum

103. When a pistol fires it emits both a loud sound and a bright flash. An observer 100 m away is exposed to both effects of the firing of the gun. Which of the statements below is true?
    (A) The observer hears the shot and sees the flash at the same time.
    (B) The observer sees the flash before he hears the shot.
    (C) The observer hears the shot before he sees the flash.
    (D) The observer sees the flash, but does not hear the shot.
    (E) The observer hears the shot, but does not see the flash.

104. The magnitude of charge between two parallel plates of equal and opposite charge is
    (A) zero.
    (B) greater near the positive plate.
    (C) greater near the negative plate.
    (D) the same throughout.
    (E) twice the charge of either plate individually.

105. How many colors are there in the spectrum of light visible to most humans?
    (A) three
    (B) five
    (C) seven
    (D) eight
    (E) ten

106. What is the effect of a magnetic field on a charged particle?

    (A) It changes its charge.
    (B) It changes its direction.
    (C) It changes its mass.
    (D) It changes its energy.
    (E) It changes its velocity.

107. The main properties of a wave are defined by all of the following EXCEPT

    (A) duration.
    (B) wavelength.
    (C) amplitude.
    (D) frequency.
    (E) speed.

108. When a star explodes and releases an incredible amount of energy and light it is called a

    (A) supernova.
    (B) quasar.
    (C) pulsar.
    (D) black hole.
    (E) red giant.

109. The Doppler Effect is important to the science of astronomy because it allows scientists to measure

    (A) the size of celestial bodies.
    (B) the distance between celestial bodies.
    (C) the cosmological age of celestial bodies.
    (D) the gravitational pull between celestial bodies.
    (E) the speed celestial bodies move away from or toward the Earth.

110. Which celestial body possesses a body and a tail, orbits the sun, and is composed of frozen gas, ice, and rocky debris?

    (A) meteor
    (B) comet
    (C) asteroid
    (D) planet
    (E) moon

111. Which planet below has the longest year?

    (A) Mercury
    (B) Earth
    (C) Neptune
    (D) Mars
    (E) Venus

112. This scientist described three laws of planetary motion that mathematically predicted the shape of planets' orbits and their velocities.

    (A) Stephen Hawking (1942–)
    (B) Edmond Halley (1656–1742)
    (C) Nicolaus Copernicus (1473–1543)
    (D) Galileo Galilei (1564–1642)
    (E) Johannes Kepler (1571–1630)

113. A rainbow is a common atmospheric phenomenon created by the optical disturbance called

    (A) reflection.
    (B) illusion.
    (C) refraction.
    (D) flare.
    (E) diffusion.

GO ON TO THE NEXT PAGE

114. Which of the following describes the climatic condition that causes an arid area to form on the leeward side of a mountain range?

    (A) rain shadow
    (B) Santa Ana
    (C) El Niño
    (D) La Niña
    (E) zephyr

115. An earthquake with a magnitude of 4 on the Richter Scale is _____ time(s) greater in amplitude than an earthquake with a magnitude of 3.

    (A) 1
    (B) 1.5
    (C) 10
    (D) 31
    (E) 100

116. Which of the following answers describes a subduction zone?

    (A) Two tectonic plates collide, forcing an elevated ridge to form.
    (B) A thin area in the Earth's crust occurs, and volcanoes are more probable there.
    (C) Two tectonic plates collide and grind past each other at oblique angles.
    (D) Two tectonic plates collide and the older, denser plate bends under the younger, less dense plate.
    (E) An area has many quake faults.

117. Which of the following geologic periods is the oldest?

    (A) Cretaceous
    (B) Permian
    (C) Quaternary
    (D) Cambrian
    (E) Carboniferous

118. Which process from the following list is NOT part of the hydrologic cycle?

    (A) fixation
    (B) evaporation
    (C) condensation
    (D) transpiration
    (E) interception

119. By far, the most common gas in the Earth's atmosphere is

    (A) oxygen.
    (B) nitrogen.
    (C) carbon dioxide.
    (D) hydrogen.
    (E) water vapor.

120. The changing seasons on the Earth are best explained by

    (A) the tilt in its rotational axis.
    (B) its proximity to the sun.
    (C) the gravitational pull from the moon.
    (D) its ellipsoidal revolution around the sun.
    (E) the large amount of water on its surface.

END OF TEST. STOP

ANSWER KEY

1. B	19. A	37. D	55. E	73. D	91. A	109. E
2. E	20. E	38. B	56. E	74. E	92. C	110. B
3. C	21. C	39. A	57. B	75. B	93. A	111. C
4. B	22. E	40. E	58. D	76. D	94. C	112. E
5. A	23. D	41. A	59. A	77. C	95. D	113. C
6. E	24. D	42. E	60. C	78. E	96. B	114. A
7. A	25. A	43. D	61. A	79. A	97. E	115. C
8. D	26. C	44. B	62. B	80. B	98. D	116. D
9. D	27. C	45. D	63. E	81. E	99. A	117. D
10. B	28. C	46. A	64. C	82. D	100. B	118. A
11. B	29. B	47. C	65. D	83. C	101. E	119. B
12. A	30. D	48. B	66. B	84. A	102. A	120. A
13. D	31. E	49. D	67. E	85. E	103. B	
14. E	32. D	50. B	68. B	86. D	104. D	
15. D	33. C	51. E	69. D	87. A	105. C	
16. B	34. B	52. C	70. C	88. B	106. B	
17. E	35. C	53. A	71. C	89. D	107. A	
18. D	36. D	54. C	72. A	90. A	108. A	

GO ON TO THE NEXT PAGE →

DIAGNOSTIC TEST QUICK REFERENCE TABLES

Use the following tables to determine which topics you need to review most.

Topic	Test Question
Biological Sciences	
Evolution and Diversity	4, 5, 6, 33, 35, 36, 37, 38, 41
Cell Biology and Biochemistry	1, 2, 3, 7, 8, 39, 40, 43, 45, 46, 47, 48, 51
Organisms and Heredity	9, 10, 11, 12, 13, 34, 42, 44, 49, 50, 52, 53, 54, 56, 57, 58, 59, 60, 61, 62, 63, 64, 65, 66
Ecology and Population Biology	17, 18, 19, 55, 67, 68, 69, 70, 71, 72, 73, 74, 75, 76
Physical Sciences	
Atoms and Subatomic Structures	20, 21, 77, 78, 79, 80, 81, 82, 84
Elements, Molecules, and Compounds	14, 15, 16, 22, 83, 85, 86, 87, 88, 89, 90, 91
Energy, Matter, and Mechanics	23, 24, 25, 92, 93, 94, 95, 96, 97, 98, 99, 100, 101, 102
Electricity, Magnetism, and Waves	103, 104, 105, 106, 107
The Universe	26, 27, 28, 108, 109, 110, 111, 112
Earth Science	29, 30, 31, 32, 113, 114, 115, 116, 117, 118, 119, 120

Topic	Number of Questions on Test	Number Correct
Biological Sciences		
Evolution and Diversity	9	
Cell Biology and Biochemistry	13	
Organisms and Heredity	14	
Ecology and Population Biology	24	
Physical Sciences		
Atoms and Subatomic Structures	9	
Elements, Molecules, and Compounds	12	
Energy, Matter, and Mechanics	14	
Electricity, Magnetism, and Waves	5	
The Universe	8	
Earth Science	12	

Answers and Explanations

1. (B)
Prokaryotes do not have mitochondria or chloroplasts and it is surmised that these organelles in eukaryotic cells are descendants of prokaryotic organisms that took on a symbiotic relationship with eukaryotes.

2. (E)
Animal cells do not have cell walls. Cell walls are present in plant cells and some fungal and prokaryotic cells.

3. (C)
One sole purpose of a cell vacuole is for storage of substrate. Vacuoles may store products of cell synthesis, waste products, or water.

4. (B)
The wings of a bat and the flippers of a whale are homologous structures because they share all of the same bones and it is probable that these bones have a common origin. The contrary example would be the wings of a bat and the wings of a butterfly. Although both provide flight, the wings of a butterfly are formed from an exoskeleton and from completely different developmental tissues.

5. (A)
Apomorphy is defined as a derived or specialized characteristic. It is a novel trait that was not present in an organism's ancestor.

6. (E)
When an organism obtains an apomorphy, it may be advantageous or deleterious. Most derived traits are harmful to an already-successful organism, but some provide an advantage that makes the organism more successful and allows it to produce more offspring (higher fitness). Such a trait is adaptive and is naturally selected for within the population.

7. (A)
Active transport requires external energy. It involves the transport of a substance through the plasma membrane via a channel protein or membrane protein. Diffusion refers to movement of a substance across the membrane without the need for external energy.

8. (D)
Osmosis is the passive transport of water across a selectively permeable membrane.

Questions 9 (D)–10 (B)
Blood flow through the human heart is part of a continuous closed system, so a starting point is somewhat arbitrary (although conventionally we begin where the two vena cavae empty their blood into the right atrium). Blood returns to the heart through the vena cava and empties into the right atrium. The blood then passes to the right ventricle where it is pumped to the lungs through the pulmonary artery and oxygenated. Blood returning from the lungs enters the left atrium, the left ventricle, and is then pumped to the rest of the body through the aorta.

11. (B)
Cavitation is the suspension of a continuous flow of liquid. This prevents the proper functioning of the rising water column in the xylem.

12. (A)
Leaves produce sugar (source) and the sugar travels to other parts of the plant (sink) with lower sugar concentrations through a continuous chain of lower osmotic pressure. The transport occurs in the phloem.

13. (D)
Stomatal opening and closing controls the rate of gas exchange in the plant cells and controls the amount of water that is lost.

14. (E)
This question requires a certain amount of recall. Ethanol is the combination of the two-carbon molecule ethane and an alcohol unit. An alcohol is signified by the attachment of a hydroxyl group (-OH) to a carbon atom.

15. (D)

Methane is the simplest organic molecule, which combines one carbon atom with four hydrogens.

16. (B)

An ion is an atom that has donated or borrowed an electron or a proton so that it is no longer neutral. Ammonium (NH_4^+) has an extra proton so it has an unbalanced charge of +1.

17. (E)

It is the reproductive success in a given population that determines fitness. A population with a greater number of individuals better suited to their environment will have a greater number that survive and reproduce. Fitness can vary widely from population to population within a species as well as among individuals in a population.

18. (D)

A community exists when several species utilize the same geographic area and resources but generally do so in a sustainable way.

19. (A)

While many organisms could exhibit this pattern of population growth, limited resources, disease, predation or other factors generally prevent this. Humans, however, have developed extraordinary means of exploiting resources and have shown exponential population growth in modern times.

20. (E)

Since electrons have almost no mass the mass number is derived from the number of protons and neutrons in the nucleus of the atom

21. (C)

Protons are positively charged particles and electrons are negative. Since the atom described above has an equal number of positive and negative particles it is neutral.

22. (E)

Since the atomic numbers are identical, the element shown is in fact carbon but it is called carbon-14 because it has two additional neutrons. Carbon-14 is a radioactive isotope of the common carbon-12.

23. (D)

Conduction will pass heat directly from the hot plate through the glass and to the water. However as the temperature in the water rises, convection currents will form and the water will begin to circulate thus speeding up the heating process.

24. (D)

Although the two containers have the same volume of water, A has a greater surface area contact with the hot plate thus conduction will be greater.

25. (A)

Even though this experiment would be very simple it could provide a basic test of the effect of container shape on the rate of heating. Keep in mind that a true test of this would require a control situation and many replications of the experiment.

26. (C)

White dwarfs are small hot stars that have a very low luminosity.

27. (C)

Since light is not reflected but in fact pulled into a black hole it is not possible to view them with any standard telescope. Evidence for their existence is sought by looking for the effects they have on surrounding space.

28. (C)

As a bright object moves farther away the light energy it emits will gradually shift toward the red end of the spectrum (lower energy). This tendency is known as the Doppler Effect and it was the observation that the light emitted from stars and galaxies was shifting toward the low-energy end of the spectrum (Doppler Shift) that led Hubble to conclude the universe is expanding.

29. (B)

Because the mantle has molten areas, some of which are hotter than others, differential heating occurs and convection currents are formed which are capable of moving the continental plates.

30. (D)

When two tectonic plates meet pressure can build up because of opposing forces. Earthquakes and volcanoes are most common at these regions though they can occur with any type of fault or crack in a plate.

31. (E)

Earthquakes can occur at any tectonic boundary or fault. However when one of the earth's plates is pushed under another as shown, tremendous pressure causes subducted plate to turn to molten rock. The pressure from this molten layer will cause some to push upward which can cause uplift and form volcanic peaks. An example of this is the Cascade mountain range in the western United States.

32. (D)

Soils within the region impacted by glaciers are very young. In Illinois these soils are rich in organic matter and constitute some of the best agricultural lands in the world.

33. (C)

Linnaeus is the father of modern nomenclature and his hierarchy is still in use today. The binomen consists of the genus and species names such as *Homo sapiens* and is always portrayed in italics (or underlined), with the genus name capitalized.

34. (B)

A clone of an individual, by definition, is an exact duplicate. There cannot be any variation in a clone except through mutation.

35. (C)

Darwin stood on the shoulder of previous scientists, particularly geologists and Malthus who created important mathematical principles, and Darwin also collected data himself. Although Gregor Mendel was Darwin's historic contemporary, Mendel's work was not recognized and the appreciation for genetics was not realized until after Darwin's death.

36. (D)

Cladograms must be interpreted according to the relationships evident in the tree. The nodes of each branch can represent either extinct or extant taxa. The branching pattern can show relative ages of divergence, but not exact dates. Also, taxa more basal on the tree are not necessarily ancestral forms, but can be just as derived as the organisms at the tips of the top of the tree. A monophyletic group is one that is defined jointly by a derived characteristic (a synapomorphy) and is represented on the tree as sharing a branch.

37. (D)

If taxon C is a fish, then all of the taxa that are within the same monophyly must be part of an inclusive group that includes fish (i.e. fish, vertebrates, chordates, etc.), but are not necessarily fish. Taxa D and E do not have to be fish, but they must be vertebrates.

38. (B)

The Cambrian period occurred 500 million years ago and is noted for containing an incredible diversity of fauna. Up to this point in geological time the fauna was comparatively homogenous and static.

39. (A)

The cell cycle is composed of a long gap where cell growth and DNA replication takes place, called interphase, and mitosis. The order of mitosis is prophase, prometaphase, metaphase, anaphase, and telophase, followed by cell division or cytokinesis.

40. (E)

If metabolism occurs in the presence of oxygen the cells can use aerobic pathways in the mitochondria to obtain energy from pyruvate in addition to the ATP liberated during glycolysis.

41. (A)

The most diverse group of organisms by far is the arthropods, which make up over 80 percent of Earth's bio-diversity. The class Insecta is the largest and most diverse group within Arthropoda. There are over one million named species of insects and as many as ten million still undescribed.

42. (E)

The standard dihybrid cross is between parents that are both heterozygous for two different traits (TtWw). If the parent's gametes assort independently they will have offspring with the phenotype TtWw with a probability of 9 out of 16, offspring with the phenotype TTWw with a probability of 3 out of 16, offspring with the phenotype TtWW with the probability of 3 out of 16, and offspring with the phenotype of ttww with the probability of 1 out of 16.

43. (D)

The current prevailing hypothesis on the early origins of life is that nucleotides synthesized in an organic soup with lightning as a possible source of energy. Nucleotides then formed long chains that could act as a template to replicate themselves on a regular basis. These nucleotides went on to form the DNA of simple organisms like viruses and ultimately prokaryotes.

44. (B)

Unlike animals that store body fat, plants store energy in the form of long sugar polymers. Plants like the potato have been cultivated for their energy storage qualities and incorporated into the human diet.

45. (D)

Ribosomes are the organelles that translate mRNA from the nucleus into proteins. They read down the length of the mRNA molecule, adding amino acids brought by tRNA according to the DNA code.

46. (A)

During most of the life of a cell, the cell's DNA is stretched out and invisible, even under a microscope. During cell division the DNA condenses into thick chromosomes. The condensation is facilitated by specialized bodies called histones.

47. (C)

This process describes the synthesis of glucose rather than glycogen. The "neo-" prefix indicates that these are glucose rings that are formed from compounds other than from previous breakdown of sugar.

48. (B)

Gametes are not always small, especially in relation to the organism's body size. The key to carrying out sexual reproduction is that the gametes have to combine and result in a complete set of chromosomes. The chromosome number has to be halved first in meiosis, otherwise, the chromosome number would double after each generation.

49. (D)

Flowers are the reproductive part of a plant and are composed of structures that produce gametes and attract pollinators. Petiole is a descriptive term for a particular shape of a structure that is narrow at the base and widens toward the tip.

50. (B)

In a countercurrent exchange, a fluid with high osmolarity passes a fluid with low osmolarity, thus enhancing the exchange of substances across the cell membranes. These systems are used whenever extremely concentrated solutions are needed or when substrates need to be extracted from dilute solutions. Birds require hypoxic blood for both flight muscle and to dissipate heat.

51. (E)

Sex-linked genes are those on the sex chromosomes. They can occur either on the X or Y chromosome.

52. (C)

Insulin is produced by the pancreas. Insulin is released in response to elevated blood glucose and causes systemic response that is tissue specific.

53. (A)

Protostomes have determinate cleavage. Cells have a predetermined fate early in development, so that removal of a cell or region of cells causes abnormal development.

54. (C)

Skeletal muscle action potentials are enervated exclusively by acetylcholine. The signal for muscle contraction comes across the synapse of a motor neuron.

55. (E)
Despite common misconceptions, a theory is a well-supported hypothesis. Once a scientist proposes a hypothesis, she or he tests several sources of data to see if the hypothesis can be refuted. If the hypothesis stands up to these tests or is supported even more by the data, it eventually becomes a theory within the discipline.

56. (E)
Pollen must reach the female flower structures of a plant. Flowers are never located below the soil in roots, where pollen cannot gain access.

57. (B)
Waste is accumulated in the large intestine, but the body doesn't store waste material. The large intestine absorbs the majority of the remaining water from digested material or water that has been added to the lumen in digestive enzymes.

58. (D)
The medial portion of the brain is composed of a corpus callosum that joins the right and left sides of the brain. There is no medial lobe.

59. (A)
Smooth muscle tissue lines the walls of the arteries, digestive tract, and bladder. These muscles are controlled involuntarily through the parasympathetic nervous system.

60. (C)
Although evaporation would help in cooling an organism in a hot environment, moist tissues would allow too much water loss.

61. (A)
The only disease in the list that is not acquired from the environment is Tay-Sachs, which is caused by a lethal double recessive genetic inheritance. Although some children acquire HIV infections from their mothers, it is from contaminated blood rather than genes.

62. (B)
Although technically not storage, large concentrations of glycogen are accumulated in liver and muscle tissue during periods of high blood glucose concentrations and low activity.

63. (E)
Holometabolous insects have four stages of development. They begin life as an egg and hatch as a larva. The larva is the feeding stage of the insect until it grows to maximum size. The larva then pupates and emerges as an adult.

64. (C)
Elephants have the longest gestation period of any mammal, roughly 22 months.

65. (D)
The endocrine system release chemicals that affect bodily function. That is the purpose of the glands and their secretions.

66. (B)
Gases can only exchange across moist membranes, regardless of the possession of lungs or gills.

67. (E)
When an organism exhibits a dominant phenotype it could be because the individual is homozygous for the gene or because it is heterozygous dominant. The way to test this is to cross the individual with a recessive homozygote. This is called a testcross.

68. (B)
According to the hypothesis, a keystone predator species is so integral to the functioning of the ecosystem that it will collapse if the species is removed.

69. (D)
A biome is the largest division of the Earth's differential landscape. A biome is typically defined by climate, soil, and vegetation type.

70. (C)
The logistic growth curve has three parameters. The value r is the intrinsic growth rate of the population, which is mainly affected by rates of birth and death. The parameter N is the initial value of the population. The carrying capacity is designated by K.

71. (C)
Secondary succession explains the colonization of open space by organisms that are in nearby areas or that had been in that area before, perhaps represented by a seed bank. Primary succession takes place on soil that has never contained these organisms before, such as a new volcanic island.

72. (A)
Factors that affect the population density directly affect birth rate, death rate, and competition for resources with other populations in the same niche. Other factors more inherent to the individual that have less of an effect on community interaction will have less effect on population density.

73. (D)
A species that is r-selected is opportunistic. Exotic species and species that take advantage of a disturbance in the ecosystem are typical examples of r-selected species. By contrast, K-selected species take better care of their young by either providing them with nourishment or parental care.

74. (E)
Species richness is the count of the number of species in a continuous ecological unit. This is one of the ways ecologists measure biodiversity.

75. (B)
A stage-dependent life table analysis portrays the distribution of individuals in a population based on discrete developmental stages such as egg, larva, adult, etc. Organisms that have more ambiguous development or only one life stage are more appropriate for age-dependent analysis.

76. (D)
Since the mistletoe is taking away resources and not providing resources in this symbiotic relationship, this is an example of parasitism. Other examples of symbiosis have organisms sharing resources to enhance the survival of both organisms, i.e. food for protection, protection for structural support, etc.

77. (C)
In 75 days, thorium will go through three half-life decays and on average half of the thorium will have decayed. At day 25 the mass will have been reduced by half, to 60 g. By day 50 the mass will reduce to 30 g and by day 75 the mass will only be 15 g. If only 15 g is left then 105 g must have decayed.

78. (E)
All d subshells, no matter what their level, are full with 10 electrons.

79. (A)
Valence electrons are the electrons that are used by an atom to form electrochemical bonds with other atoms. These are the electrons in the outer shell, and only they can interact with the shells of other atoms.

80. (B)
The fission reaction in a nuclear reaction is only possible if the chain reaction is not allowed to take place too rapidly. Otherwise, the reactions would be like a nuclear bomb exploding. Rods of certain metals can act as neutron acceptors to limit the rate of the reaction.

81. (E)
It was once thought that atoms were the smallest particles, but even they are made up of parts. An atom has a nucleus composed of protons and neutrons (that contain mass) and electrons with no mass that circle the nucleus. Scientists have discovered that even these particles are made up of smaller units that have changing energy. A top quark is one of the most energetic quarks and a neutrino one of the less energetic.

82. (D)

A neutral atom has no charge. The charges are balanced because the number of positively charged protons equals the number of negatively charged electrons.

83. (C)

The atomic number does not indicate chronology or mass. Each atom in the periodic table is numbered based on the quantity of protons in its nucleus. The mass of atoms can change in different isotopes with different quantities of neutrons.

84. (A)

Since we measure and observe electrons according to the activity of those electrons, we cannot know both the position of an electron and the direction in which it is traveling.

85. (E)

When an isotope is signified as in the question, the bottom number indicates the number of protons (as well as the number of electrons in neutral elements). The top number indicates the number of particles in the nucleus (the protons and neutrons combined). By subtracting the two numbers, the number of neutrons can be determined.

86. (D)

Every atom combines with others so that the number of electrons in its outer shell is full. Silver has one s electron in the fifth subshell (the s subshell is full with two electrons) that can contribute to a bond and chloride has seven electrons ($3s^2\ 3p^5$) in its third subshell. These atoms combine one-to-one to make both of their outer shells filled.

87. (A)

Titration usually involves investigating a solution with an unknown concentration. Using some form of visible indicator such as a color change or precipitate, a solution with a reacting reagent and known concentration is added to the unknown until all of the reagent in the unknown has reacted. The concentration of the original can then be determined by quantifying the amount of known reagent used.

88. (B)

A balanced equation has the quantity of each type of atom equal on both sides of the arrow. The arrow is equivalent to an equal sign in a mathematical equation. Coefficients are placed in front of each compound formula by process of elimination until the counts of atoms are equal.

89. (D)

The entire mass of CO_2 is 12.0 g/mole + 2(16 g/mole) = 44 g/mole. The fraction of the mass contributed by carbon is 12.0 g/mole ÷ 44 g/mole = 27.3 percent.

90. (A)

The nonmetal elements try to fill their outer shell with eight electrons to attain the noble gas configuration of s^2p^6. Other elements either share their electrons or donate them to the outer shell to have a full outer shell of eight electrons.

91. (A)

Dilution equations can be solved with the equation $M_iV_i = M_fV_f$ where the subscripts i = initial and f = final. The initial volume of solution is 100 ml and the initial and final molarities are 10M and 5M respectively, so one simply needs to solve for the final volume of solution and find the difference. V_f = (10 M × 100.0 ml)/5 M = 200.0 ml; so the volume of water that was added was 100.0 ml.

92. (C)

Both bodies at rest have inertia that resists movement. The force exerted by the extended arms of the man must overcome either the inertia of the man's body or the inertia of the mass. Since the masses are equal and the ice is frictionless, both masses are equal; so if they move at all they will both move equally. Assuming the man can generate enough force to move the mass, both the man and the mass will move away from each other at the same velocity.

93. (A)

The element mercury is also called quicksilver because it is liquid metal. Mercury was used in thermometers because of its sensitivity to temperature and rate of expansion. Today, thermometers made of mercury have been replaced with electric and water thermometers due to mercury's toxicity.

94. (C)

Water has a higher specific heat than soil, so it retains heat better. Although air temperatures change rapidly, climates near large bodies of water are more moderate because the water temperature remains stable.

95. (D)

Entropy is a measure of discord and chaos. Systems that increase in entropy lose energy by going from states of order to disorder, such as the breaking of a glass. Systems that store energy lose entropy.

96. (B)

The potential energy at the beginning of the slide will equal the kinetic energy when the mass reaches its final velocity. Kinetic energy is equal to $1/2\ mv^2$, so the energy of the mass at final velocity is $1/2\ (1\ kg)(50\ m/s)^2 = 1250\ N$.

97. (E)

Water boils at a higher temperature when the pressure increases. Pressure cookers were used to increase the amount of heat that could be delivered to food to either decrease the cooking time or increase the temperature. The opposite occurs at altitudes where it takes much more heat to boil water.

98. (D)

Planetary motion only involves relativity in the sense that the moving bodies always move in relation to each other. The shape of the orbits is dictated by the combined gravitational pull of the objects with mass around the planets.

99. (A)

This can be observed in the spinning of an ice skater. The speed at which a skater spins is increased when the skater pulls his or her arms into his or her body. The skater's arms as they are pulled into the body decrease the radius of circular motion.

100. (B)

In physics, the object's weight is measured by how its mass is pulled by gravity. The larger the mass, the larger the force exerted, and the larger the weight.

101. (E)

The center of gravity is the point at which an object can be suspended and not rotate. It is the sum of the combined center of masses of all the atoms that make up the object. The center of gravity can be outside of the object such as in the hole of a doughnut. An object's center of gravity is the point at which all calculations of linear motion are made, since the center of gravity typifies the entire object. The momentum of the center of gravity is the object's momentum.

102. (A)

This question asks about the stability of temperature of the given substances. The substance that is most resistant to changes in temperature is water.

103. (B)

This question explores the wave speeds of sound and light. Sound travels at only about 330 m/s while light travels at almost 300,000,000 m/s. The light from the gun flash will reach the observer's eye long before the sound from the shot. The slow speed of sound is what causes the echo effect in large sports stadiums.

104. (D)

If two plates are arranged an equal distance from each other and have equal and opposite charge, the entire area between the plates will have a uniform charge. This is due to the electrons being able to leave from any place on the plate and pass to the other plate. The plates must be perfectly parallel in order for this to be true.

105. (C)

This question can be addressed by memorizing the mnemonic device ROYGBIV. The letters stand for red, orange, yellow, green, blue, indigo, and violet: the seven colors of the rainbow.

106. (B)

Since a magnetic field is a charged region with positive and negative poles, a charged particle will orient to these poles based on the charge of the particle. Electrons travel at right angles to the magnetic lines of an electromagnetic field so will usually change direction when entering the field.

107. (A)
A wave diagram shows the length, crests, frequency, and amplitude of a wave. The duration of a wave is dependent upon whether the source of the wave continues to emit the wave. The properties of the wave will be constant if the source of the wave does not change in frequency, amplitude, wavelength, etc.

108. (A)
Stars in the universe age and eventually collapse or explode. These explosions or supernovas are sometimes visible on Earth to astronomers using telescopes. Since the distance between Earth and these stars is so vast, explosions often take place millions of years before we can see them.

109. (E)
The Doppler Effect causes waves to be pushed together or spread apart directly in front of or behind a moving object that is emitting waves. This can be witnessed by listening to a car moving toward and away from you with its horn honking. The horn has a higher pitch when it is approaching and a lower pitch as it is moving away. Scientists can use this shift in the electromagnetic spectrum of objects transmitting light to measure their movement in relation to Earth.

110. (B)
Comets travel through the solar system in a large ellipse and begin to burn up as they approach the heat of the the sun. The gases released from the icy, rocky comet create a tail that can be many millions of miles long.

111. (C)
The planet that has the longest year is the planet that has the largest orbit. The planet with the largest orbit is the planet that is furthest away from the sun. This planet is Neptune.

112. (E)
Johannes Kepler was a mathematician who studied the motion of the planets. Kepler's laws are mathematical proofs that describe the conservation of periodicity of angular motion as the distance between a planet and the sun decreases.

113. (C)
When water or water vapor is present in the atmosphere the droplets act as little prisms that break up white light into the seven colors of the rainbow. This phenomenon is called refraction or bending of light. The rainbow is caused by different wavelengths of light bending at different angles through the prism.

114. (A)
When warm, wet air climbs up the face of a mountain, the air experiences drops in temperature and pressure. The water trapped in the air condenses and falls as rain or snow. As the air travels over the mountain and down the other side it warms up again, but has lost most of its moisture. This effect is called a rain shadow because very little rain occurs on the back side of the mountain range.

115. (C)
The Richter scale is measured logarithmically. A change in one unit on the Richter scale is equal to ten times the magnitude of the previous value. A magnitude 4 quake is ten times greater than a magnitude 3 quake and 100 times greater than a magnitude 2 quake.

116. (D)
When the Earth's tectonic plates move they run into each other at their borders. Some plates are more dense than others because of the varying consistency of the crust. The less dense plate floats above the more dense plate while the more dense plate bends downward. This kind of meeting between plates is a subduction.

117. (D)
There are no defined periods older than the Cambrian. Although pre-Cambrian time accounts for about 90 percent of Earth's history, there are few markers to distinguish divisions over that time period.

118. (A)
The hydrologic cycle describes the fate of water as it changes states of matter from liquid to gas during its use by organisms on earth and through evaporation and condensation. Fixation is a process that occurs in the nitrogen cycle.

119. (B)
Although living organisms rely mainly on the presence of CO_2 and O_2 gas, these are not the most common gases in the atmosphere. Nitrogen is the most common gas in the atmosphere, making up approximately 78 percent compared to the 21 percent made up by oxygen.

120. (A)
Earth's seasons occur over the duration of an annual cycle which takes the planet through an entire orbit around the sun. Although the Earth spins so that no one side is entirely away from the sun during the year, there is a tilt in the Earth's axis so that it doesn't spin perpendicular to the direction of the orbit. The portion of the Earth that faces away from the sun during the year is going through winter. The northern hemisphere faces away from the sun during the months of December through March.

Chapter Twenty-One: CLEP Natural Sciences Review

- The Big Picture: CLEP Natural Sciences
- Nuts and Bolts
- Biological Sciences
  - Evolution and Diversity of Life
  - Diversity of Life Chart
  - Cell Biology and Biochemistry
  - Organisms and Heredity
  - Ecology and Population Biology
- Physical Sciences
  - The Metric System
  - Atoms and Subatomic Structures
  - Elements, Molecules, and Compounds
  - Energy, Matter, and Mechanics
  - Electricity, Magnetism, and Waves
  - The Universe
  - Earth Science
- Natural Sciences Resources
- Final Thoughts

Congratulations on deciding to take the CLEP Natural Sciences exam! This review section and the accompanying practice tests will help ensure you test your best.

THE BIG PICTURE: CLEP NATURAL SCIENCES

The exam covers a wide range of science topics, so you will have to bring all of your knowledge of the sciences together. A full 50 percent of the test requires you to recall and apply knowledge of the biological sciences, while the remaining 50 percent of the exam requires you to tackle physical science topics. This may sound challenging perhaps, but it is not insurmountable. After all, the exam includes information that you would learn in introductory college-level science courses usually taken by non-science majors. It's time to borrow or purchase some introductory biology, physics, and chemistry textbooks and get cracking!

The problems on the exam test your knowledge of factual information (approximately 40 percent of the test), as well as the ability to apply concepts to problems (another 40 percent of the test). Most of the problems that require you to apply concepts are based on reasoning ability, but do include some math. The remaining 20 percent of the test involves the ability to understand and interpret information presented in paragraph form or as graphs, diagrams, tables, or equations.

NUTS AND BOLTS

The full CLEP Natural Sciences exam is composed of 120 multiple-choice questions, with 90 minutes to answer these questions. That means you need to answer more than one question per minute. The breakdown of topics on the exam is as follows:

Biological Sciences (50%)

Evolution and Diversity of Life	10%
Cell Biology and Biochemistry	10%
Organisms and Heredity	20%
Ecology and Population Biology	10%

Physical Sciences (50%)

Atoms and Subatomic Structures	7%
Elements, Molecules, and Compounds	10%
Energy, Matter, and Mechanics	12%
Electricity, Magnetism, and Waves	4%
The Universe	7%
Earth Science	10%

Keep in mind that some questions overlap biological and physical science topics, so they can fall into more than one category.

In the following review section, important terms to know for the exam appear in bold type. Be sure to look up any unfamiliar words or concepts in a college-level textbook.

BIOLOGICAL SCIENCES

Evolution and Diversity of Life

Although life on earth shows extreme diversity, it also shows incredible unity. All living things share certain characteristics. All have one or more of the basic functional units called cells. All require energy to carry out life functions and to maintain **homeostasis**, the maintenance of stable internal conditions. All living things carry genetic information in the form of **DNA** and **RNA** (deoxyribonucleic acid and ribonucleic acid), and all pass on that information in the process of reproduction.

The earliest fossil evidence indicates that the first living things on earth were single-celled, **prokaryotic** bacteria that appeared more than 3.5 billion years ago. Current theories on the origin of life focus on spontaneous formation of simple **amino acids** near thermal vents in the deep ocean or in subterranean caves, followed by incorporation of simple strands of nucleic acids, the building blocks of the genetic code. It is thought that all life on earth today represents changes in the genetic code of those earliest bacteria through the process of evolution due to natural selection, genetic drift, gene flow and mutation.

There are several kinds of evidence that support **evolutionary theory**. They include the fossil record, biogeographical evidence, **comparative anatomy** and physiology, and comparison of the genetic material itself. **Fossils** are the remains or traces of living things laid down in sediments that ultimately turned to rock. The fossil record is most complete for vertebrates—animals with backbones—and shows many transitional forms. **Biogeography** refers to the study of distribution of living things around the world. By comparing the structure and function of cells and organs, simple modifications can be seen in closely related organisms. Comparison of **genes** shared by many organisms is a powerful tool in understanding evolution.

Modern evolutionary theory originated when geologists began dating the age of rocks in which fossils were found. Charles **Lyell** wrote the *Principles of Geology* (1830) that suggested that the earth was much older than the few thousand years it was thought to be at the time. That, in conjunction with an essay on human populations written by Thomas **Malthus** in 1798, helped Charles Darwin develop his theory of evolution based on natural selection. Darwin calculated that two elephants could produce 19 million descendants in 750 years. Obviously, that was not happening, so it became clear that only some of the offspring survived. Darwin concluded that certain characteristics would favor survival for some individuals over others.

In 1809, Jean Baptiste **Lamarck** theorized that characteristics acquired by an organism during its lifetime could be passed on to its offspring. This theory was false, since organisms take tens of thousands of years to evolve and exhibit new traits that can be passed on to offspring. While Lamarck's theory was false, his acceptance of evolution as an explanation of biological diversity was important.

The theory of **natural selection** was written by Charles **Darwin** in his book *The Origin of Species* (1859). Darwin studied finches and tortoises on the Galapagos Islands, leading him to propose that organisms better adapted to their environment will survive (survival of the fittest) as opposed to their peers that are less well adapted. **Adaptations** that organisms acquire to best suit their environment are passed on to offspring through the process of natural selection.

Mutations. are rare changes in the DNA that can be passed on to succeeding generations. Many mutations make the organism less likely to survive and procreate, but a few mutations may help an organism adapt to the environment or cope with environmental changes. Over billions of years, favorable mutations have led to development of more complex and diverse organisms adapted to almost every environment on earth.

Mutation leads to **microevolution**—changes at the population level. **Macroevolution**—the formation of new species and mass extinction of existing ones. According to the Hardy-Weinberg theorem, the proportion of genes in a large, randomly breeding population will tend to stay the same over time. Changes in frequency of traits occur due to things like migration of a particular type of individual at a higher rate than other types of individuals or selection for favorable characteristics.

When organisms such as Darwin's finches produce many offspring, some tend to migrate and occupy new niches. New species are formed when populations of organisms adapted to specific conditions become reproductively isolated from other populations: unable to interbreed with them to produce fertile offspring.

To name and classify organisms, the system of taxonomy was developed. In taxonomy, organisms are categorized into increasingly closely related groups based on assumed evolutionary relationships and shared characteristics. Most systems currently recognize eight levels of classification according ot the revised Linear taxonomy: **Domain**, **Kingdom**, **Phylum** (**Division** for plants), **Class**, **Order**, **Family**, **Genus**, and **Species**.

There are three **Domains** of organisms. The **Archaea** are a small group of prokaryotes well adapted to extreme environments such as very hot or salty conditions. They are thought to be the most evolutionarily ancient group of organisms. The **Bacteria** include all other prokaryotic organisms. All prokaryotes lack a true cell nucleus and cellular organelles. Bacteria can be differentiated from Archaea by the presence of peptidoglycans in the cell walls. The third domain of organisms is comprised of all other living things, the **Eukaryota**. Eukaryotes have cells with a true cell nucleus and organelles. All plants and animals are members of the domain Eukaryota.

Most classification systems now recognize **six Kingdoms** of living things. They are: **Archaea**, **Bacteria**, **Protista**, **Fungi**, **Plantae**, and **Animalia**. Archaea and Bacteria are single-celled prokaryotes. Protists are unicellular eukaryotes. Protists can be heterotrophic, mixtotrophic, or photoautotrophic. Most are found in aquatic environments or as parasites. (**Photoautotrophs** such as green plants produce their own food while **heterotrophs** must obtain nutrition from outside sources.) Fungi are mostly multicellular, terrestrial, heterotrophic organisms with cell walls containing chitin. Plants are multicellular, terrestrial, autotrophic (photosynthetic) organisms with cell walls containing cellulose. Animals are multicellular aquatic and terrestrial heterotrophs and their cells lack a cell wall.

Viruses are agents that traditionally have not been considered to be living organisms. (Currently, scientists are debating this topic.) The defining characteristics of life include cellular structure and metabolic activity, and viruses lack both. Like living things, viruses are capable of reproduction and contain genetic information in the form of nucleic acids, but they cannot reproduce outside of a host cell.

The chart on the opposite page provides an overview of the origins of life and the classification system.

Diversity of Life

	Appeared (yrs before present)
Prokaryotes: The simplest and most ancient organisms	
Kingdom Archaea Kingdom Bacteria	3.5 billion
Eukaryotes	
Kingdom Protista: unicellular eukaryotes and algae	1.7 billion
Amoebas	
Flagellates	
Ciliates	
Sporozoans	
Algae (some are *multicellular)	*1 billion
Slime molds	
Complex Multicellular Eukaryotes	
Kingdom Fungi: filamentous hyphae, heterotrophic, chitin cell wall	500 million
Ascomycota—sac fungi, yeasts, truffles, morels	
Imperfect fungi—penicillium and aspergillis	
Basidiomycota—mushrooms, toadstools	
Zygomycota—black molds	
Kingdom Plantae: photosynthetic, terrestrial, cellulose cell wall	500 million
Nonvascular plants: bryophytes, liverworts, mosses	
Seedless vascular plants: ferns, horsetails, club mosses	400 million
Vascular seed plants	
Gymnosperms: seeds born "naked" on cones	300 million
Conifers	
Cycads	
Ginkgoes	
Gnetophytes	
Angiosperms: flowering plants	65 million
Monocots	
Dicots	
Kingdom Animalia: complex heterotrophs that lack cell walls	
Phylum Porifera: sponges	600 million
Phylum Cnidaria: jellyfish, anemones	
Phylum Platyhelminthes: flatworms	
Phylum Nematoda: roundworms	
Phylum Annelida: segmented worms	
Phylum Mollusca:	
gastropods—snails and slugs	
bivalves—clams and oysters	
cephalopods—squids and octopi	
Arthropoda Phylum:	450 million
crustaceans—crabs, barnacles	
arachnids—spiders and scorpions	
insects—the most abundant eukaryotes	
Phylum Echinodermata: sea stars, sand dollars	
Phylum Chordata: Tunicates, Lancelets, Vertebrates	
Vertebrates	
Fish	425 million
Amphibians	300 million
Reptiles	
Birds	150 million
Mammals	50 million
Humans	100 thousand

*The first organisms to inhabit land were plants and fungi, which appeared together 500 million years ago. The first animals to inhabit land were arthropods 450 million years ago.

Cell Biology and Biochemistry

All living things are composed of one or more cells. Cells are the functional unit of life and are composed of nucleic acids and other macromolecules surrounded by a **phospholipid plasma membrane**. Within the plasma membrane, all cells have ribosomes for protein synthesis in the **cytoplasm**. Cells move materials through the cell membrane by the processes of **active transport**, **osmosis**, and **diffusion**.

The DNA of prokaryotes (bacteria) is not separated from the rest of the cell in a membrane-bound nucleus but in a region called the nucleoid. Bacteria also lack membrane-bound structures called **organelles** and reproduce asexually through a process called **binary fission.**

Eukaryotic cells do have a membrane-bound nucleus and their genetic material is carried on by chromosomes in that nucleus. Eukaryotic organisms also have membrane-bound organelles that compartmentalize various cellular functions. The membrane-bound organelles of eukaryotic cells are as follows:

- **Chloroplasts (in plant cells)**—perform photosynthesis and contain chlorophyll; occur in leaves and stems of plants
- **Golgi apparatus**—lies adjacent to the nucleus of a cell; produces secretions within a cell
- **Lysosomes (in plant cells)**—contain hydrolytic enzymes; important in intracellular digestion
- **Mitochondria**—contain genetic material and enzymes necessary for converting food to usable energy; site of cellular respiration
- **Nucleus**—contains nucleoi (involved in ribosome formation) and chromatin (DNA).
- **Rough endoplasmic reticulum**—membrane network in the cytoplasm, covered with ribosomes; involved in the transport, synthesis, and modification of cellular materials
- **Smooth endoplasmic reticulum**—membrane network in the cytoplasm *not* covered with ribosomes; involved in the transport, synthesis, and modification of cellular materials
- **Vacuoles**—found in the cytoplasm of plants and fungi; pockets containing water, metabolic waste, or food

Cells and their organelles are composed of four basic kinds of complex **organic macromolecules**: **carbohydrates** (starches and sugars), **lipids** (fats), **proteins**, and **nucleic acids**. Carbohydrates and fats are primarily used as short- and long-term energy sources respectively. Proteins support cellular structure and carry out many important functions by acting as organic catalysts in the form of **enzymes**. Nucleic acids carry the genetic information as DNA and RNA.

Many organic macromolecules are **polymers** made up of simple units called **monomers**. The monomers of carbohydrates are called **monosaccharides**. **Glucose** is a common monosaccharide, and **sucrose** (table sugar) is a common **disaccharide**. Complex carbohydrates (**polysaccharides**) include **starch** and **cellulose**. The monomers of proteins are called **amino acids**. Amino acids form **polypeptide chains** that fold to form complex protein structures. Protein function is related to its structure. DNA and RNA are made up of nucleotide monomers, and the **nitrogenous base** of each monomer is what creates the genetic code.

All living things need to acquire energy. The usable form of energy for living things is in the high-energy bonds of a molecule called **ATP (adenosine triphosphate)**. ATP is often stored in the bonds of complex molecules such as glucose. Plants are **autotrophic**, meaning they can produce their own energy by using the sun's energy to fix carbon dioxide in the process of **photosynthesis**:

$$6\ CO_2 + 6\ H_2O + \text{light energy} \rightarrow 6\ O_2 + C_6H_{12}O_6$$

(translation: carbon dioxide + water + light energy → oxygen + glucose)

To release the energy in glucose and produce ATP, most organisms perform **cellular respiration**:

$$C_6H_{12}O_6 + 6\ O_2 \rightarrow 6\ CO_2 + 6\ H_2O + ATP$$

(translation: glucose + oxygen → carbon dioxide + water + ATP)

If no oxygen is present, organisms can produce energy via **fermentation**:

$$C_6H_{12}O_6 \rightarrow 2\ C_2H_5OH + 2\ CO_2 + ATP$$

(translation: glucose → ethyl alcohol + carbon dioxide + ATP)

Organisms that can produce ATP without oxygen by using fermentation are called **anaerobic** organisms. Yeast is an example of an organism that uses fermentation to produce ATP.

Chemical energy that was originally produced through photosynthesis is used by eukaryotic organisms in the form of sugars. Heterotrophic organisms (organisms that cannot perform photosynthesis) obtain their energy for cellular respiration by consuming other organisms.

Organisms build complex proteins from instructions carried on DNA molecules called **chromosomes**, and those proteins facilitate and control all other growth, development, and function. The genetic "blueprint" of organisms is stored in DNA in the form of long chains of nucleotides.

DNA is found in the nucleus of eukaryotic organisms and is expressed through the process of **transcription** and **translation**. The structure of DNA is composed of two complementary strands of nucleotides that wrap around each other to form a **double helix**. The two strands of nucleotides have a sugar-phosphate backbone. The bases are connected through hydrogen bonds. In each strand of DNA, **guanine** pairs with **cytosine** (G-C) and **adenine** pairs with **thymine** (A-T).

Sequences of DNA called **genes** code for the synthesis of a protein. Within each protein are amino acids that are coded by sequences of triplets of nucleotide bases. These triplets are called **codons** in mRNA. In the transcription of DNA to RNA for transport to the cytoplasm of the cell, DNA is copied to complementary RNA base pairs that would form the other side of the DNA double-helix, with the exception of the base **uracil (U)**. **Messenger RNA (mRNA)** contains uracil

(U) instead of thymine (T), and uracil matches with adenine (A) in DNA. Copying DNA to mRNA is called **transcription**. Once DNA has been copied to mRNA for transport to the cytoplasm for protein synthesis, the mRNA attaches to the ribosome, which contains **ribosomal RNA (rRNA)**. **Transfer RNA (tRNA)** strands contain codons that are complementary to codons on the strands of mRNA; these complementary codons are called **anticodons**. When an anticodon (of tRNA) binds to a codon (of mRNA), the tRNA knows to carry only a specific amino acid. The amino acid is packaged into a protein (series of amino acids) with the aid of a ribosome. The formation of the protein is called translation. Each amino acid that is formed is attached to the growing protein through a peptide bond.

In order for unicellular organisms to reproduce and for multicellular organisms to grow and develop, new cells must be produced. New cells can only arise from preexisting cells, so cells must divide to produce exact copies of themselves in order to transfer the genetic information necessary for protein synthesis.

The **cell cycle** is a repeating pattern of events during which cells grow, make copies of their DNA, and then divide to produce new cells. Most of the cell cycle alternates interphase, a period of growth and **DNA replication**, with **mitosis**, when the cell divides to form two new cells. There are several phases of the cell cycle:

> **Interphase**—DNA replication creates **sister chromatids** joined at a **centromere**
> **Prophase**—DNA condenses into distinct chromosomes
> **Prometaphase**—nuclear envelope disassembles.
> **Metaphase**—chromosomes line up along the **central metaphase plate**
> **Anaphase**—sister chromatids split and are pulled to opposite ends of the cell
> **Telophase**—nuclear envelopes begin to form, chromosomes uncoil and lengthen
> **Cytokinesis**—division of the cytoplasm and formation of two new cells

For organisms that reproduce sexually, meiosis reduces the number of **chromosomes** from the number found in somatic (body) cells to half the number of chromosomes, thereby forming **haploid gametes** (reproductive cells). **Diploid somatic cells** have twice the number of chromosomes as the haploid gametes. **Meiosis** involves one round of DNA replication followed by two rounds of cell division (meiosis I and meiosis II), which reduces the number of chromosomes by half.

During meiosis I, genetic variation can be introduced through the processes of **crossing over** and **independent assortment** of **homologous chromosomes**. Meiosis II is similar to mitosis. Four genetically unique haploid daughter cells are produced in meiosis, while two genetically identical daughter cells are produced by mitosis. The genetically unique haploid cells are called **gametes**. Gametes from male parents are called sperm and from females are called eggs. The gametes combine at fertilization to create a **zygote**. Since it has genetic information from both a mother and father, the zygote is **diploid**. **Genetic diversity** and **heredity** are two sides of the same diploid coin: different DNA combinations introduce new traits and create genetic diversity, while strong genetic characteristics that survive despite the introduction of new DNA are hereditary characteristics.

Organisms and Heredity

The study of the inheritance of traits can be termed **heredity**. Genes are the fundamental units of inheritance and are comprised of sequences of DNA that code for proteins that ultimately control the structure and function of living things, including appearance and other traits.

Much of what we know about heredity was first described by Gregor **Mendel** based on experiments he performed through breeding pea plants. Mendel's theories include the idea that inherited traits are carried on the factors we now call genes, that an individual inherits one copy of a gene from each parent (an **allele**), and the presence of one form of a gene (**dominant**) can mask the presence of the other (**recessive**). By looking at how multiple traits were passed from generation to generation, Mendel also determined that genes from each parent are passed to offspring independently of each other.

An allele is one of two or more alternative forms of a gene. In sexually reproducing organisms, each individual has two copies of a gene, one inherited from the mother and one from the father. If both inherited alleles are the same, the individual is **homozygous** for that gene. If the inherited alleles differ, the individual is **heterozygous**. A dominant allele is one that controls how the gene will be expressed; a recessive allele is one that is masked by expression of a dominant allele in a heterozygous individual. The **genotype** is the actual set of alleles at the gene locus on homologous chromosomes. The **phenotype** is the observable expression of the trait based on the two alleles.

Uppercase letters are used to represent dominant alleles. The same letter in lower case represents the recessive version of the allele. To represent the genotype of purple pea flowers (a dominant trait) and white pea flowers (a recessive trait) an uppercase letter is used to represent the dominant allele and the same lowercase letter is used to represent the recessive:

PP (homozygous dominant), Pp (heterozygous), and pp (homozygous recessive).

By using a simple diagram called a **Punnett square**, predictions about how traits will be passed to offspring can be made. Those predictions are based on the original observations Mendel made with traits in peas and were the basis for his theories. When a homozygous dominant individual is crossed with a homozygous recessive (the **P generation**), all of the offspring (the **F1 generation**) will be heterozygous and show the dominant phenotype. If members of the F1 generation are crossed (two heterozygotes) the ratio of offspring (the **F2 generation**) will be 1:2:1 homozygous dominant, heterozygous, and homozygous recessive respectively, such that 1 in 4 will show the recessive trait.

Humans have 23 pairs of chromosomes: 22 pairs of **somatic chromosomes** and one pair of **sex chromosomes**. Female humans have two X chromosomes and male humans have one X chromosome and one Y chromosome. Other species may have different chromosomes to determine gender.

Changes in the DNA sequence that can be inherited by offspring are termed **mutations**. Some mutations cause inheritable disease. Human diseases caused by detrimental genetic inheritance include sickle-cell anemia, hemophilia, Tay-Sachs disease, Huntington's disease, Parkinson's disease, and cystic fibrosis. If a condition is a recessive disorder, both parents must carry a copy of the defective allele to pass it on to offspring, and they will not show the trait unless they have homozygous alleles for the trait. If the allele for the condition is dominant, only one parent has to have the allele to pass it on, and that parent will be affected by the disorder. Other chromosomal disorders such as Down Syndrome (trisomy—3 copies of a chromosome instead of 2) are caused by changes in the number of chromosomes due to errors that occur during meiosis.

Some genetic conditions are **sex-linked**, most often carried on the X chromosome. Since males only have one X chromosome, they will be affected by a sex-linked recessive disorder, such as hemophilia. Since females have two X chromosomes, a dominant form of the allele will mask the disorder unless it is inherited from both parents, a relatively rare occurrence. Sometimes environmental factors affect the onset of a genetic disease. Other diseases may be characterized by late onset of symptoms. Huntington's disease, for example, typically isn't expressed until a person is at least in his or her thirties.

Organization of Systems

All living things are organized at varying levels of complexity. Organic macromolecules come together to form cells and their organelles. In multicellular organisms, similar cells make up **tissues**, and tissues make up **organs**. Organs are arranged in **organ systems** that work together to form a functioning organism.

The simplest unicellular organisms have only the cellular level of organization. Very simple fungi, plants, and animals may have only the cellular or tissue level of organization. The organs of plants include leaves (photosynthetic organs) and flowers (reproductive organs). Among animals, the simplest sponges and Cnidarians are the only groups that do not have organs and organ systems.

A **zygote** is a fertilized egg and starts out as a single cell containing all the genetic information for growth and development. As cell division occurs, more complex levels of organization are encoded to develop in multicellular organisms. A **morula** forms from the dividing zygote, a process called **cleavage**. By the time the morula has divided into about a hundred cells (a hollow ball of cells) it is called a **blastula**. **Gastrulation** is the process by which tissue differentiation begins. The outer layer of the gastrula called the **ectoderm** becomes epidermis (skin) and the nervous system. The middle layer or **mesoderm** becomes muscle, skeleton, and many internal organs. The inner layer, the **endoderm**, becomes the gut and associated organs. Very simple animals have no developmental germ layers or only two germ layers. Organisms with two germ layers can develop a tissue level of organization. Those with all three germ layers are more complex and form organs and organ systems.

Humans and other vertebrates have only four main types of tissue that make up all of their organs and organ systems. **Epithelial tissue** includes skin and linings of blood vessels and organs. **Connective tissue** includes bone and cartilage, ligaments and tendons, blood, and adipose (fat) tissues. Many organs contain structural connective tissue. **Muscle tissue** is contractile tissue and includes skeletal muscle, smooth muscle, and cardiac muscle. **Nervous tissue** is found in the brain, spinal cord, and peripheral nervous system.

Humans have many important organ systems that work together to maintain bodily function:

Cardiovascular System—the **heart**, blood vessels, and blood. The primary function of the cardiovascular system is transport of substances such as gases (oxygen and carbon dioxide). Through the transport of gases, organic nutrients like glucose and proteins are transported, as well as wastes. The heart is composed of cardiac muscle tissue and pumps blood throughout the body. Blood vessels include **arteries** and arterioles which carry blood away from the heart, and **veins** and venules that carry blood to the heart. **Capillaries** are beds of tiny blood vessels embedded in tissue and are the site of exchange for gases and nutrients. Arteries have thicker walls because they carry blood at high pressure. Conversely, veins have thinner walls because they carry blood at a lower blood pressure. Blood flow rate is slowest in capillary beds to allow for exchange of materials. The human heart has four chambers, two upper atria and two lower ventricles. There are two circuits of circulation in the cardiovascular system. The **pulmonary circuit** takes blood from the right ventricle to the lungs via the pulmonary arteries. Blood is returned to the left atrium of the heart through the pulmonary veins. In the **systemic circuit**, blood is pumped from the left ventricle to all of the tissues of the body via the **aorta**, the largest artery in the body. The right ventricle pumps blood to the lungs. Blood is composed of about 55 percent liquid plasma which contains proteins, nutrients, and waste products, and about 45 percent formed elements, the blood cells and platelets. Red blood cells (erythrocytes) contain the pigment hemoglobin, which carries oxygen. White blood cells (leukocytes) are associated with immunity and platelets help blood to clot.

Digestive System—the digestive tract (mouth, esophagus, stomach, small intestine, large intestine, anus) and accessory organs (liver, gall bladder, pancreas). The main functions are ingestion and absorption of energy and nutrients and removal of wastes. Food enters the body through the mouth and passes down the **esophagus** and into the **stomach**. The stomach begins digestion with a mixture of hydrochloric acid and pepsin. The food passes into the **small intestine** where bile and **pancreatic enzymes** continue digestion. Most nutrient absorption takes place in the small intestine. The large intestine includes the **colon**, which reabsorbs water and some minerals, and the rectum, which stores feces until they are expelled through the anus. The **liver** produces bile to emulsify fats and processes everything absorbed in the small intestine. The liver is important in detoxification of drugs and other substances. The **gall bladder** stores bile. The pancreas juices include **amylase** to digest carbohydrates, **lipase** to digest fats, and **trypsin** for digestion of proteins.

Endocrine System—a group of organs, **glands**, and tissues that secrete **hormones**. Hormones control many physiological processes by acting as chemical messengers. The pituitary gland secretes many hormones, some of which act directly and others that stimulate other endocrine organs. Some important hormones include the reproductive hormones (testosterone in males, estrogen and progesterone in females) and **pituitary** hormones such as growth hormone and thyroid stimulating hormone. Blood glucose levels are normally maintained by two hormones produced by the pancreas: insulin, which decreases glucose levels, and glucagon, which increases glucose levels. Adrenaline, the "fight or flight" hormone, is produced by the **adrenal gland**. Thyroid hormones affect normal tissue growth and increase metabolism.

Excretory System—kidneys, ureters, bladder, urethra. The **kidneys** filter blood to allow excretion of **nitrogenous wastes**, help maintain salt and water balance, and help regulate blood pH. The functional unit of the kidney is called the **nephron**, and each kidney has about a million nephrons. Blood under high pressure enters a dense bed of capillaries in each nephron called the glomerulus, where filtration occurs. The water portion of the blood and small molecules such as wastes, sugars, salts, and amino acids are pushed into tubules while blood cells and large molecules remain in circulation. In the tubules of the nephrons, selective reabsorption allows desirable molecules like glucose and amino acids to be reabsorbed and for salts to be retained or removed as needed, while wastes are passed on to collecting tubules and eventually to the ureters. **Ureters** take the wastes, now called urine, from the kidneys to be stored in the **bladder** until the urine is expelled from the body through the urethra.

Integumentary System—the skin and associated glands, hair, nails. Functions include protection from infection and dehydration, maintaining body temperature, allowing sensation, and synthesizing vitamin D.

Lymphatic/Immune System—lymph tissues, vessels, and lymphoid organs. The lymphatic system is responsible for recycling body fluids and combating disease. Lymphatic vessels throughout the body return tissue fluids to circulation. Lymphoid tissues such as the spleen and tonsils, help combat disease by trapping foreign matter, while structures such as the thymus and bone marrow produce white blood cells and cleansing pathogens from lymph tissue. Nonspecific defenses include the inflammatory reaction and involve production of white blood cells called phagocytes that ingest invading pathogens. Specific defenses involve white blood cells called lymphocytes and production of antibodies in response to a specific antigen—usually an invading pathogen. **Immunity** occurs when the body learns how to quickly produce an antibody to a specific condition because of previous exposure.

Musculoskeletal System—bones, cartilage, tendons and ligaments, skeletal muscle. The contraction of muscle anchored to bone allows complex movement when muscles contract. Bones come together at flexible joints, and are attached to one another by ligaments. Tendons bind muscle to bone. Muscles are made of proteins called **actin** and **myosin** which slide past one another when signals that are received from the nervous system cause muscles to contract.

Nervous System—brain and **spinal cord** (central nervous system), and **peripheral nerves** (peripheral nervous system). The nervous system is responsible for coordination and integration of sensory input and motor output. Nerve cells called **neurons** have branched dendrites that receive signals and long axons along which those signals are transmitted. The endings of Axons are called **synaptic terminals**; the connections between the terminals and target cells are called **synapses**. **Neurotransmitters** are chemicals released at **synaptic terminals** to transfer signals from one neuron to another. Important structures of the brain include the cerebrum (higher learning, language, rational thought), cerebellum (motor coordination), the thalamus (sensory processing), hypothalamus (basic drives like hunger, thirst, sex), and the brain stem (breathing and heartbeat). The brain and spinal cord are surrounded by membranes called meninges. The spinal cord connects the brain and the peripheral nervous system. Reflexes are unconscious responses of the nervous system that conveyed by the spinal cord and brain stem. **Sensory receptors** for touch, taste, smell, sound, and vision are part of the peripheral nervous system and are processed in the brain. Chemoreceptors in the tongue (taste buds) and nasal passages (olfactory receptors) react with chemical molecules that they come in contact with. Mechanoreceptors in the ear respond to physical movement in the form of sound waves or motion and allow us to hear and maintain our sense of balance. Photoreceptors in the eyes called cones and rods allow vision.

Reproductive Systems—Male: **testes**, seminiferous tubules, vas deferens, prostate gland, ejaculatory duct, penis. Female: **ovaries**, fallopian tubes, uterus, cervix, vagina, clitoris. Sperm is produced in the seminiferous tubules in males. Eggs are produced from oocytes in the female ovaries. Once each month, a mature egg is released from the ovaries, where it travels through the fallopian tubes to the uterus to be fertilized. If the egg is not fertilized, menstruation occurs, but if the egg is fertilized, a zygote implants in the endometrial lining of the uterus. Male sperm move from the scrotum through the vas deferens and the penis to fertilize an egg in the female uterus. When an egg is fertilized, becomes a zygote, and grows into an embryo, the embryo is provided nutrients and oxygen through the placenta. The embryo grows into a baby, which exits the uterus at the end of nine months via the cervix and vagina.

Respiratory System—the nasal passages, trachea, bronchi, and lungs. The primary function is to provide oxygen for cellular respiration and remove the carbon dioxide that is produced as a waste product by working in conjunction with the cardiovascular system to allow exchange of those gases in the lungs and body tissues. Oxygenated air enters the mouth or nose, and is passed into the **trachea** which branches into **bronchi** at the lungs. Each bronchus further branches into bronchioles, which terminate at capillary-rich **alveoli**, the site of gas exchange. Oxygen is absorbed and carbon dioxide is released by red blood cells in the capillary beds of the alveoli. Breathing involves muscular contraction of the diaphragm which increases the volume of the chest cavity, causing a reduction in pressure and inflow of air during inhalation. Exhalation follows when signals for contraction of the diaphragm are stopped, the volume of the chest cavity decreases, and elastic recoil of the connective tissue of the lungs forces air to be expelled.

Plant Tissues

Plants have many tissues and organs that differ from those of animals. Plants have actively dividing cells called **meristems** in the regions of growth. Growth at the tips of shoots (the aboveground portion) and roots (the underground portion) occurs at apical meristems. Increase in girth in woody plants occurs at lateral meristems in the vascular cambium.

Many plants have vascular tissue for transport of water and nutrients. **Xylem** is vascular tissue that allows transport of water and minerals up from the soil through the roots to the plant leaves. **Phloem** is vascular tissue that allows transport of sugars, the products of photosynthesis, throughout the plant and to the roots. Nonvascular plants lack specialized structures for transport of water and depend on moisture in the surrounding habitat. They are often low-growing and generally found in moist environments.

Leaves are specialized photosynthetic organs. Pores in the leaf surface called **stomata** allow carbon dioxide to enter the leaf and enter the cell chloroplasts, the organelles where photosynthesis occurs. Chloroplasts contain the pigment **chlorophyll**, which harvests the sun's energy by absorbing light. When leaf stomata are open, water evaporates from the leaves in a process called **transpiration**. Plants can regulate water loss by closing stomata.

Like many animals, plants produce hormones that regulate growth and development. In addition, special receptors in plants allow detection of light and shade, change in seasons, and other signals important to dormancy and reproductive cycles. Most plants grow flowers to enable them to reproduce. The male part of a flower is the **stamen**, which includes the **pollen**-producing **anther**. The pollen must find its way to the **pistil**, the female part of the flower, which contains the ovary and the egg cells. **Seeds** are created when the pollen and eggs meet.

Ecology and Population Biology

The study of the interaction between organisms and their environment is termed **ecology**. Most living things ultimately depend on the process of photosynthesis which harvests the sun's energy. Plants and other photosynthetic organisms are **primary producers** because they use the sun's energy to fix carbon dioxide into organic compounds. Plants also take up water and important nutrients like nitrogen from the soil. Plant bodies represent the first link in ecosystem **food chains** or **food webs**. All other organisms get their energy by being **consumers** of other organisms.

An **ecosystem** is a group of organisms and all of the nonliving (**abiotic**) environmental factors with which the organisms interact. The fish, algae, and snails in an aquarium, along with the water, food, and wastes of the organisms represent an ecosystem. The climate, soil, and organisms of a tropical rainforest represent an ecosystem as well.

Energy and matter are cycled through ecosystems via both **abiotic factors**, things like climate and water flow, and **biotic factors**, living organisms. The movement of matter and energy through ecosystems is called **biogeochemical cycling**. Several biogeochemical cycles are important to ecologists. The **water cycle** involves the movement of water via precipitation, evaporation, transpiration, movement as surface and ground water, and its use by organisms. The **carbon cycle** involves the uptake of atmospheric carbon dioxide via photosynthesis and its return to the atmosphere via cellular respiration and decomposition of carbon compounds by bacteria and fungi. Combustion of fossil fuels has become a very important element of the carbon cycle. **Nitrogen**, one of the primary components of proteins, is also cycled through ecosystems. Although most of the atmosphere is composed of nitrogen, only certain bacteria are able to fix it into a form usable by living things. Bacteria are also very important in breaking nitrogen back down into its gaseous form. Many important organic and inorganic molecules cycle through living things by way of complex food webs.

The **trophic level** of an organism is determined by the position of the organism on a food chain or within a complex food web. Autotrophic plants are the primary producers so they occupy the first trophic level. **Herbivores** occupy the second trophic level because they are animals that eat plants. **Carnivores** eat other animals and occupy the third trophic level, etc. Fungi and bacteria are important decomposers, breaking down plants and animals to return the organic elements they contain to the earth. Typically, the trophic structure of any ecosystem can be represented by a pyramid. The primary producers represent the greatest biomass, and the top carnivores the least biomass. This is because as energy and nutrients move up the food chain, some energy is used by each trophic level, making less energy available for the next higher level.

Organisms interact with each other in many ways. **Predator-prey** relationships exist when one organism consumes another, such as a cow eating grass or a wolf eating a cow. **Competition** exists when two organisms must use a limited resource such as food or water. Plants sometimes compete for sunlight. **Symbiotic relationships** occur when two organisms interact closely. In **mutualism**, both organisms benefit from the relationship. In **commensalism**, only one organism benefits from a relationship but no harm is done to the other. **Parasitism** involves benefit to one organism at the expense of the other.

Organisms live as members of **populations**, groups of individuals of the same species that live together. The availability of food, competition, predation, and other factors will influence the number of individuals within a population. Populations of different species within an area represent a **community**, and community dynamics will influence individual populations. Population growth without limits would be exponential and is called the population's **biotic potential**. Actual population growth is limited; some individuals die and others move in or out. The **carrying capacity** of a system is the number of individuals a system can actually support given environmental factors such as space, light, water, or nutrients.

Succession is the process by which ecological communities change over time. Many of the changes associated with succession are due to factors such as competition and symbiosis. Examples of succession include occupation of a cleared vacant lot by weeds, insects, and small animals over time, or the gradual filling of a small pond by sediment. When an existing community has been destroyed by some **disturbance event**, such as clearing a lot, it is called secondary succession. When organisms gradually inhabit an area previously barren, such as after a glacial retreat, it is called primary succession.

Biomes are areas characterized by patterns of climate and vegetation. Similar biomes can often be found at the same latitude around the world. In addition, biomes are related to altitude. Changes in biomes moving from low areas up to the top of mountains are similar to changes that occur as one moves north or south from the equator. The characteristics of various biomes determine what types of organisms will live there.

- **Tropical Rain Forest**—warm and wet most of the year, they contain at least half of the Earth's terrestrial plant and animal species. Rain forests are found near the equator. Because most nutrients are contained in the vegetation they have very poor soils.
- **Deciduous Forests**—distinct seasons with warm summers, cool winters, and plenty of moisture. Many species of birds and mammals, and hardwood trees such as oak and maple dominate these forests of North America and Eurasia.
- **Grasslands**—distinct wet and dry seasons, few dispersed trees, rich soil and low annual rainfall. They are found in temperate and tropical regions. Both the American prairie and African savannah are grassland biomes. Grasslands can support large populations of grazing mammals.
- **Taiga**—a coniferous forest that extends around the upper northern hemisphere with cold, dry winters and limited precipitation during a short summer. Moose, elk, and large carnivores such as bears and wolves live in a taiga. Marshes and lakes are common. Vegetation is dominated by cold-tolerant needle-bearing trees such as fir and spruce.
- **Tundra**—Arctic and alpine locations with permanently frozen soil layer (permafrost), low-growing plants and lichens, and many migratory species. The landscape is boggy (in the summer) and windy. Tundra regions are characterized by short growing seasons and long, cold winters. Tundra covers one-fifth of the Earth's land surface.
- **Deserts**—may be hot or cold, but are always very dry. Deserts tend to occur at around 30 degrees latitude north and south. Deserts are marked by low primary productivity and organisms adapted to conserve water.
- **Aquatic**—may be marine or freshwater. Freshwater has a low salt concentration and includes ponds, lakes, streams, rivers, and wetlands. Marine regions cover three-quarters

of the earth's surface and include oceans, coral reefs, and estuaries. Aquatic ecosystems are very diverse and are divided into **pelagic** (open water), **benthic** (deep water), **abyssal** (deepest ocean) and **intertidal** habitats. The pelagic zone is far from land but reaches the surface, where ocean-going mammals like whales and dolphins can breathe. The benthic zone is below the pelagic and may include the ocean floor. The intertidal zone is where the ocean meets land, and may feature rocky coasts and sandy beaches.

PHYSICAL SCIENCES

Many of the subjects in the physical sciences overlap and intertwine. For example, you need to have a basic understanding of chemistry in order to complete some physics and astronomy problems. The movement of planets in astronomy can be explained by physics. You can't have a basic understanding of one concept without considering how that subject interacts with and impacts other disciplines.

The Metric System

The metric system is used for measurement in everyday life, as well as in the biological and physical sciences. Units of measurement used in the metric system include:

Measurement	Units
length	meters
mass	grams
temperature	degrees Celsius
time	seconds
volume	liters

These units of measurement can be increased or decreased by powers of ten with the following prefixes:

Prefix	Amount Increased/Decreased by	Symbol
micro-	one millionth	μ^N
milli-	one thousandth	m^N
centi-	one hundredth	c^N
deci-	one tenth	d^N
kilo-	one thousand	k^N
mega-	one million	M^N

Atoms and Subatomic Structures

Matter has **mass** and occupies space. Air, rocks, water, and living organisms are all made of matter. **Elements** such as iron, carbon, and helium are matter. Elements are composed of **atoms**. Atoms are composed of three subatomic particles: protons, electrons, and neutrons. **Protons** and **neutrons** are found in the nucleus of each atom. **Electrons** occur in regions of probability called **orbitals**, centered around the nucleus. Each orbital contains **shells** designated by letters including s, p, d, and f.

An atom is composed primarily of empty space between the electrons and the nucleus, but the **nucleus** makes up over nearly all of the mass of the atom. The nucleus houses positively charged protons and electrically neutral neutrons. The number of protons in the nucleus, Z, determines the **atomic number** and what chemical element the atom is. The number of neutrons in the nucleus is denoted by N. The **atomic mass** of the nucleus, A, is equal to $Z + N$.

Elements, such as carbon (C), cannot be broken down into simpler compounds by chemical means. The chemical behavior of an element is determined by the number of electrons in its outer shell. An ionic form of an element occurs when an element either loses or gains an electron from its outer shell during ionic bonding. A neutral atom, with the same number of protons and electrons, is the form of an element that is placed in the **periodic table**. The elements of the periodic table are arranged according to increasing numbers of protons.

The electrons are placed in orbitals that are spherical shaped (s orbitals), or are more complex in shape (p, d, and f orbitals). The electron configuration of an element describes how the atoms are arranged in the element. The electron configuration notation of an element can be figured out by noting how many electrons are found in each orbital of an element. According to the **octet rule**, the outer orbital, or shell, of each element must be filled in order for an element to not react with other elements. In order to fill an outer shell that is not completely full, an element will share, donate, or obtain enough electrons to fill its outer shell (usually eight electrons, except in elements that only have one s shell).

An isotope of an element has the same atomic number but a different atomic mass—the number of neutrons differs. An element can have several isotopes. Among all of the known elements are approximately 270 stable isotopes, and more than 2000 unstable isotopes.

Radioactivity is the phenomenon whereby some unstable atomic nuclei spontaneously emit particles in a process called radioactive decay. Radioactive decay can lead to formation of isotopes or new elements. **Alpha particles** emitted by helium nuclei can be stopped by a piece of paper. **Beta particles**, electrons or positrons, are much smaller and have less effect on the mass of the atom emitting them. Beta particles convert neutrons into protons, increasing the atomic number of the element. The isotope 14C is unstable and emits a beta particle, becoming the stable isotope 14N. **Neutrinos** are associated with beta decay. **Gamma rays** are a type of electromagnetic radiation that results from a redistribution of electric charge within a nucleus. A gamma ray is a high-energy photon that is released when the neutrons and protons in the nucleus are rearranged. There is no change in mass or atomic number.

Half-life is the time required for half of the atoms in any given quantity of a radioactive isotope to decay. Each particular isotope has its own half-life. The half-life of 14C is 5730 years, so that is the time it takes for half of some mass of the isotope to disappear. Nuclear half-lives range from fractions of a second to many times the age of the universe.

If atomic nuclei come close enough together, they can interact with one another through strong nuclear force, and reactions between them can occur. Such nuclear reactions can either be exothermic and release energy or endothermic, requiring the input of energy to occur.

Fusion is a nuclear process in which two light nuclei combine to form a single heavier nucleus. The fusion reaction used in some nuclear weapons is the reaction between two different hydrogen isotopes to form an isotope of helium (thus the term "hydrogen bomb" or "H-Bomb"). The reaction releases a huge amount of energy— more than a million times greater than a typical chemical reaction. Fusion occurs when two light nuclei fuse such that the sum of the masses of fused nuclei is less than the sum of the masses of the initial nuclei. The mass that is lost in the reaction is converted into energy carried away by the fusion products. Fusion is the process that takes place in stars like our sun, providing all of the energy used by life on Earth.

Fission is a nuclear process in which a heavy nucleus, such as that in uranium, splits into two smaller nuclei. Fission reactions were used in the first atomic bombs and are still used in nuclear reactors and as triggers for fusion bombs. A great amount of energy is released in fission reactions because for heavy nuclei, the summed masses of the lighter product nuclei is less than the mass of the original heavy nucleus. Fission occurs because of the electrostatic repulsion created by the large number of positively charged protons contained in a heavy nucleus. The two smaller nuclei formed in the reaction have less internal electrostatic repulsion than one larger nucleus, allowing the larger nucleus to overcome the strong nuclear force that holds it together. Fission can be seen as a tug-of-war between the strong attractive nuclear force and the repulsive electrostatic force, which ultimately wins.

Elements, Molecules, and Compounds

The following types of elements can be found in the periodic table:

Type of Element	Features	Location in the Periodic Table
Metals	High densities, solid at room temperature, conduct electricity, shiny, malleable	Left side to center
Nonmetals	Many gaseous at room temperature, some react easily with other substances. Examples: carbon, nitrogen, oxygen, and hydrogen	Central-right, top to bottom
Halogens	Nonmetallic compounds that form gases (sometimes diatomic) at room temperature. Examples: fluorine, chlorine, bromine, and iodine	Second group (column #17) from far right
Noble Gases	Filled outer electron shells, do not react easily with other atoms. Examples: helium, argon, krypton, neon, xenon, and radon	Far right group (column #18)

Periodic Table of the Elements

Group	1	2	3	4	5	6	7	8	9	10	11	12	13	14	15	16	17	18
1	1 H 1.008																	2 He 4.003
2	3 Li 6.941	4 Be 9.012											5 B 10.81	6 C 12.01	7 N 14.01	8 O 16.00	9 F 19.00	10 Ne 20.18
3	11 Na 22.99	12 Mg 24.31											13 Al 26.98	14 Si 28.09	15 P 30.97	16 S 32.07	17 Cl 35.45	18 Ar 39.95
4	19 K 39.10	20 Ca 40.08	21 Sc 44.96	22 Ti 47.88	23 V 50.94	24 Cr 52.00	25 Mn 54.94	26 Fe 55.85	27 Co 58.93	28 Ni 58.69	29 Cu 63.55	30 Zn 65.39	31 Ga 69.72	32 Ge 72.61	33 As 74.92	34 Se 78.96	35 Br 79.90	36 Kr 83.80
5	37 Rb 85.47	38 Sr 87.62	39 Y 88.91	40 Zr 91.22	41 Nb 92.91	42 Mo 95.94	43 Tc (98)	44 Ru 101.1	45 Rh 102.9	46 Pd 106.4	47 Ag 107.9	48 Cd 112.4	49 In 114.8	50 Sn 118.7	51 Sb 121.8	52 Te 127.6	53 I 126.9	54 Xe 131.3
6	55 Cs 132.9	56 Ba 137.3	57–70	71 Lu 175.0	72 Hf 178.5	73 Ta 181.0	74 W 183.8	75 Re 186.2	76 Os 190.2	77 Ir 192.2	78 Pt 195.1	79 Au 197.0	80 Hg 200.6	81 Tl 204.4	82 Pb 207.2	83 Bi 209.0	84 Po (209)	85 At (210)	86 Rn (222)
7	87 Fr (223)	88 Ra 226.0	89–102	103 Lr (260)	104 Rf (261)	105 Db (262)	106 Sg (263)	107 Bh (262)	108 Hs (265)	109 Mt (268)	110 Uun (269)	111 Uuu (272)	112 Uub (277)	113 Uut	114 Uuq (289)	115 Uup	116 Uuh	117 Uus	118 Uuo

57 La 138.9	58 Ce 140.1	59 Pr 140.9	60 Nd 144.2	61 Pm (145)	62 Sm 150.4	63 Eu 152.0	64 Gd 157.3	65 Tb 158.9	66 Dy 162.5	67 Ho 164.9	68 Er 167.3	69 Tm 168.9	70 Yb 173.0
89 Ac 227.0	90 Th 232.0	91 Pa 231.0	92 U 238.0	93 Np 237.0	94 Pu (244)	95 Am (243)	96 Cm (247)	97 Bk (247)	98 Cf (251)	99 Es (252)	100 Fm (257)	101 Md (258)	102 No (259)

Atomic Number — 6
Symbol — C
Atomic Mass — 12.01

* Numbers in parentheses are the *mass numbers* of the most stable isotope of the element.

Molecules contain two or more atoms that are bonded together. **Compounds** are molecules composed of more than one element. Compounds are named by the types of bonds that hold them together. **Ionic compounds** are formed from the attraction between charged particles called ions. Ions are formed when one atom gives up an electron to another, so that both have filled outer orbitals. The atom giving up an electron gains a positive charge, while the atom receiving the electron gains a negative charge, causing an attraction that bonds the two elements. In **covalent compounds** electrons are shared between two atoms. **Hydrogen bonds** form between polar molecules such as water. Water molecules are **polar** because the electrons from hydrogen spend more time orbiting the more positively charged nucleus of the oxygen atom, creating unequal charges at opposite ends of the molecule.

A **solution** is a uniform mixture of different substances. Air is a solution of various gases, and sea water is a solution of various solids dissolved in water, a **solvent**. A solution differs from a compound in that a solution can be separated into elements or compounds it contains by boiling or freezing. A compound is not altered by a change in state and always has the same proportion of elements present.

Acids are substances that increase the concentration of hydrogen ions in water, decreasing the pH of the solution. They can be defined as proton donors (Bronsted-Lowry) or electron-pair acceptors (Lewis). Examples of acids include hydrochloric acid (HCl) and nitric acid (HNO_3). **Bases** are substances that produce hydroxide ions in water, increasing the pH of the solution. They can be defined as proton acceptors (Bronsted-Lowry) or electron-pair donors (Lewis). Examples of bases include sodium hydroxide (NaOH) and potassium hydroxide (KOH). The pH scale ranges from 1 to 14. It is a negative and logarithmic scale of the number of hydrogen ions, H^+, in a solution. A solution with more hydrogen ions is more acidic and will have a smaller pH number. A solution with a pH of 1 is ten times more acidic than a solution with a pH of 2 and a solution with a pH of 1 is 100 times more acidic than a solution with a pH of 3. A solution with a pH of 2 is 100 times more acidic than a solution with a pH of 4. A pH of 1 to 6 is acidic, a pH of 7 is neutral and pH from 8 to 14 is basic. A **buffer** absorbs moderate amounts of acids and/or bases with little change in pH.

Through **reactions**, compounds combine to form more complex products or break down into simpler components. Reactions occur when there is instability or when they can achieve a lower energy state by reacting. **Reactants** are the chemicals that combine or decompose to form **products**. Products are obtained from a chemical reaction. **Combustion** (burning) was the first extensively studied chemical reaction. Combustion always produces carbon dioxide and water. The mass relationships of reactants and products can be calculated for chemical reactions.

A **mole** of a substance is defined as its gram molecular or atomic weight, which always contains 6.022×10^{23} molecules **(Avogadro's number)** of that substance. The atomic mass of an atom has the same formula weight as one mole of the atom. For example, the mass of carbon is 12.0 grams per mole of carbon atoms. The **formula mass** of a substance is the sum of the atomic masses of the atomic elements it contains, each multiplied by the number of times it appears in the formula of the substance. A mole of carbon dioxide (CO_2) molecules has a mass of 44 grams: 12 grams of carbon and 32 (2×16) grams of oxygen.

When writing **chemical equations**, the atoms on each side of the reaction must balance. A chemical equation is used to express the changes that take place during a chemical reaction. The number of atoms of each element at the beginning of the reaction must be accounted for at the end of the reaction.

Chemical reactions such as combustion that release energy, often in the form of heat, are called **exothermic**, and the amount of energy released by the reaction can be predicted. Reactions that occur only when heat or other energy is added to the system are called **endothermic**. The law of conservation of energy shows that if a given reaction is exothermic, the reverse reaction will be endothermic and that the amount of heat absorbed or given off will be the same.

If a reaction is strongly endothermic it means that the reactants are relatively stable; it takes a lot of energy to break the bonds of those compounds. Reactants in exothermic reactions are unstable. **Chemical energy** is the **potential energy** of electrons—the potential for electrons to be transferred in chemical reactions.

Endothermic reactions always require an input of energy, but many exothermic reactions also do not occur spontaneously. **Activation energy** is the minimum amount of energy required to start some exothermic reactions by loosening or breaking some bonds of the reactants. That is why combustion of fossil fuels in your automobile cannot proceed without a spark plug. The rate of chemical reactions depends on the nature of the reacting substances, temperature, the amount of each reactant present, and the presence or absence of an appropriate catalyst. A **catalyst** is a substance that alters the rate of a reaction without being changed chemically by the reaction, often by lowering the activation energy.

Organic chemistry focuses on carbon compounds, especially as related to living things. Carbon tends to form strong covalent bonds, including double and triple bonds (multiple shared electrons). In addition to being important to living things (see Cell Biology and Biochemistry), organic compounds are also important as synthetic fibers and plastics in the form of polymers.

Energy, Matter, and Mechanics

Energy is the ability to do work. The basic unit of work is the **joule**. Energy takes several forms: **potential energy** is stored energy; a large rock on the edge of a steep hill has potential energy. **Kinetic energy** is the energy of motion; the rock rolling down the hill has kinetic energy, and the ability to damage objects in its path. **Mass energy** is the energy of **relativity** ($E = mc^2$). Einstein's equation shows that mass and energy are just two forms of the same thing and that each has the capability to become the other. In his famous equation, E represents energy, m stands for mass, and c^2 is the speed of light, squared. It demonstrates the equality of matter and energy relative to velocity.

Electrical energy is associated with the number and kinds of charges on the atoms of a substance and movement of electrons. **Chemical energy** is energy stored in chemical bonds. **Thermal energy** is the total internal kinetic and potential energy of an object due to the random motion of its atoms and molecules.

The first law of thermodynamics is the law of conservation of energy and states that energy cannot be created nor destroyed; it can only change form (potential →kinetic energy).

The second law of thermodynamics states that in every energy transformation, some energy is always lost as heat, increasing entropy.

Heat is the thermal energy of random molecular motion. The heat of an object depends on temperature, mass, and the physical properties of the object, such as density. The unit of heat is the joule. Heat is always transferred from areas of high energy (fast motion) to areas of low energy (slow motion). A **calorie** is the amount of heat energy necessary to raise the temperature of one gram of water one degree Celsius. The term "calorie" that we use on food labels actually represents a kilocalorie of energy. If a banana has 110 calories, then it has 110 kilocalories. A calorie, one unit of energy, is also a kilocalorie.

Temperature is a measure of the average energy of random motion of the particles of a substance. Absolute temperature is measured in degrees **Kelvin** with absolute zero representing no molecular motion. The **Celsius** scale is based on the freezing (0°C) and boiling (100°C) temperatures of water. Experimental evidence shows that absolute zero is −273.15°C, so the conversion formula is simply: °C = K − 273.15. **Fahrenheit** establishes 0°F as the stabilized temperature when equal amounts of ice, water, and salt are mixed and, rather arbitrarily, 96°F (originally) as the body temperature of a person in good health (the scale was recalibrated eventually, resulting in 98.6°F becoming the body temperature). The conversion formula is more complex: °F = (°C × 1.8) + 32

Matter exists in one of three states: **solid**, **liquid**, or **gas**. Solids have a fixed shape, with molecules held close together by strong bonds. Liquid molecules move around and trade places, while maintaining a strong attraction to each other. Gases have particles that are separated by large amounts of space and expand at high temperatures, due to rapidly moving and colliding molecules. A gas will fill the shape of a container enclosing it.

Most compounds can undergo **state changes** if temperatures are raised or lowered. It requires an input of heat energy to change the state of a substance from solid to liquid form (**melting**) or from liquid to gas form (**evaporation**). When gases are cooled they change to liquids (**condensation**) and then to solids (**crystallization**) and energy is released.

Everything in the universe is in constant motion, from the atoms in our bodies to the galaxies of the universe. Understanding **mechanics**, the effects of physical forces acting upon bodies, is one of the cornerstones of understanding the physical universe.

Speed (velocity) of a moving object, such as a molecule, is the constant rate at which it covers a distance ($v = d/t$, speed = distance/time elapsed). The rate of change of speed, or **acceleration**, can be calculated as the difference in the beginning (v_o) and ending speed (v_f) over some period of time ($a = (v - v_o)/t$). The acceleration due to **gravity** (g) is a constant 9.8 meters per second^2, a calculation established in 1901 based on Galileo's research during the early seventeenth century. Isaac Newton developed the Second Law of Motion based on Galileo's discovery of the constant acceleration of falling bodies due to gravity. The Second Law states that the force of attraction between two objects is a function of the masses of the objects and the distance

between them, described by the equation $F = g(m_1 m_2)/r^2$, where g is the gravitational constant, m_1 and m_2 are the masses of the two objects, and r is the distance between the two objects.

Classical mechanics is often referred to as "Newtonian mechanics" after Newton and his laws of motion. **Newton's first law of motion** states that an object will remain in its state of rest or its state of motion in a straight line at a constant speed if no net force acts upon it. A **force** is any influence that can change the speed or direction of motion of an object. An object will not begin to move by itself. A moving object in the vacuum of space continues to move at a constant speed. On earth or in our atmosphere, forces such as friction and resistance slow and eventually stop moving objects. **Inertia** is defined as the resistance of an object at rest or an object in motion to change its state of rest or motion. Inertia offers a way to measure the amount of matter in an object. Mass is a measure of the inertia of a body.

Newton's second law of motion states that force on an object is equal to the product of its mass and acceleration. The greater the force applied to an object, the greater the acceleration. The greater the mass of the object, the smaller the acceleration. This relationship can be expressed in the equation $F = ma$ (force = mass x acceleration). The unit of force is the Newton (N).

Newton's third law of motion states that when an object exerts force on another object, the second object exerts an equal force in the opposite direction. For instance, if you tried to push an object that has more mass than you do, you would find yourself being pushed backward. This occurs because while the force the object exerts on you is the same as the force you exert on it, your mass is smaller so your acceleration due to the force is greater. Newton's law restated says that for every action, there is an equal and opposite reaction. When a person walks, the action of walking causes the force of the earth's surface to push her or him forward.

Classical mechanics is subdivided into statics, which concerns objects at rest, kinematics, which concerns objects in motion, and dynamics, which concerns objects subjected to various forces. Classical mechanics does not apply for systems moving at high velocities near the speed of light, where quantum mechanics and relativity come into play. **Quantum mechanics** is used to describe motion in atoms, while **relativity** describes motion in the vastness of space.

Einstein's theory of general relativity concerns gravity and inertia of massive objects in space and is a modification of Newtonian gravitational theory based on special relativity. The **theory of special relativity** put forth by Einstein is based on two ideas. First, it assumes that the laws of physics are constant from any frame of reference. This means that the laws of physics observed by a hypothetical observer traveling with a particle near the speed of light must be the same as those observed by an observer who is stationary in an observatory. The second is that the speed of light is constant regardless of the speed of the observer. This idea is important when one considers planetary motion and the point from which one is making observations! The earth is moving relative to the objects being observed. Based on these two assumptions, Einstein showed that space and time are relative concepts rather than absolute concepts, that is, one is always a function of the other.

Electricity, Magnetism, and Waves

When you rub your stocking feet across the carpet in a dry heated house, you get a little shock when you touch an object. This is an electrical phenomenon that can't be explained by chemical equations or gravitational theory. In fact, all matter including our bodies has an electrical nature, because electrical forces are what keep electrons in orbit around the nuclei of all of our atoms. All of the properties of matter except mass are related to **electrical forces.**

All electric **charges** are either positive or negative. Like charges (two positives for example) repel each other and unlike charges (opposites) attract each other. Most objects normally contain equal amounts of positive and negative charges (protons and electrons). Sometimes, when two objects are rubbed together, such as your socks and the carpet, the frictional motion is enough to break some of the electrons away. Depending upon the materials rubbed together, one object will pick up the positive charges produced and the other the negative charges. While rubbing your feet, you've created a charge on your skin; when you touch an uncharged object, electrons fly to equalize the charge difference.

The unit of electrical charge is the **coulomb (C).** The smallest unit of charge is abbreviated (e) and based on the charge of single protons and electrons (+ or − $1.6 \leftrightarrow 10^{-19}$ C).

Coulomb's law of electric force states that the force between two electric charges is directly proportional to both charges and inversely proportional to the square of the distance between them. The force is termed repulsion if the charges are the same and attraction if the charges are different.

Conductors such as metals allow free movement of electrons. An **insulator** such as glass or plastic tends to inhibit the flow of electrons. **Semiconductors** are intermediate. The **ampere** is the unit that measures electrical flow or **current**. An ampere is equal to movement of 1 coulomb per second. The **volt** is the unit of potential difference between negatively and positively charged surfaces, such as the poles of a battery, and is expressed as joules per coulomb. **Current** is the term used to describe the actual movement of electrons and is described by **Ohm's law** (current = voltage / resistance, or I = v/r). The **resistance** is a function of the medium of flow; i.e. resistance is low for a good conductor like copper and high for a poor conductor (a good insulator) such as plastic. The amount of work that can be done by electricity is expressed as **watts** (W), and can be calculated as amperes x volts. This is derived from the idea that power = current $\leftrightarrow$ voltage.

Magnetism is the force that moving charges such as electric currents exert on each other. The magnetic force between charges is a function of both the charges and their relative motion. Magnetic forces always come in pairs, and they can occur without objects coming into physical contact. **Magnetic fields** are regions of space altered by an electric charge. Every electric current has a magnetic field around it. An electric motor uses magnetic fields to turn electrical energy into mechanical energy. A generator uses magnetic fields to turn mechanical energy into electrical energy. Electromagnetic waves are coupled electric and magnetic disturbances that originate from accelerated electrical charges. Examples of electromagnetic waves include gamma rays, x-rays, and light.

Some **waves**, such as those in water and sound waves, carry energy from one point to another via periodic motion of individual particles in a medium. There is no net transfer of matter in wave motion. In **transverse waves**, the particles of the medium move perpendicular to the wave, while in a **longitudinal wave**, they move parallel to the wave. **Sound waves** are longitudinal and are produced by vibration of an object, causing changes in the pressure and density of the surrounding medium, such as air or water.

Waves are described in terms of **frequency**, **wavelength**, and **amplitude**. The frequency of a wave describes how many wave peaks pass a given point per second. The wavelength describes the distance between crests. The amplitude is the vertical distance from trough to peak. Frequency and wavelength are related by the equation: $v =$ wavelength (λ) x frequency (f), where v is the wave speed. Amplitude is independent of frequency and wavelength.

Electromagnetic radiation with a very short wavelength, such as ultraviolet light, has high energy. Long-wavelength radiation, such as infrared radiation, is often associated with heat. Very long wave radiation, such as radio waves, has very low energy. Light has intermediate wavelengths and energy.

Light is a kind of electromagnetic radiation that exhibits properties of both waves and particles. Light generally travels in straight lines; just shine a flashlight into the nighttime sky. Light can also be reflected, refracted, and even transmitted through surfaces. Light is **reflected** when it bounces off a surface, such as a mirror. **Refraction** or bending of light occurs when light is bent when passing through different media, such as the transition from air to water. Each frequency or wavelength of light produces a visual image of a different color and the dispersion of light (as refracted through a prism), causes the appearance of a rainbow.

The Universe

The **big bang** theory is the most widely accepted theory among scientists about the origin of the universe. Based on recent calculations, scientists believe that the universe was created between 13 and 24 billion years ago. In 1930, Georges Lemaître was the first to visualize matter condensed into a "primeval atom" that exploded and created the universe. The idea gained support with astronomer Edwin Hubble's finding that distant galaxies in every direction are going away from us at speeds proportional to their distance. This phenomenon is known as the **red shift**, a displacement of the spectra of distant objects. It is due to the fact that light from an object moving away shifts toward the "red" region of the spectrum (red and infrared wavelengths).

Initially, a star is composed mostly of hydrogen and helium. The star continues to turn hydrogen to helium through the process of nuclear fusion. When hydrogen is exhausted, some stars burn into embers. If the star is large enough, it can suddenly expand and produce a huge explosion; this star is now called a **supernova**. Elements heavier than iron can be formed during the supernova phase, such as gold, lead, and silver.

The distance of planets from the sun, with a descending order of planet size, are as follows:

Planet	Diameter of planet (in approx. miles)	Distance from sun (miles $\times 10^4$)
Jupiter	88,700	48,300
Saturn	74,900	88,600
Uranus	31,800	178,300
Neptune	30,700	279,300
Earth	8,000	9,300
Venus	7,600	6,700
Mars	4,200	14,200
Mercury	3,000	3,600

Comets are aggregates of frozen matter that follow regular orbits in the solar system. They appear to viewers on Earth as patches of light accompanied by long tails when they near the sun. An **asteroid** is a solid body that orbits around the sun. Many asteroids form a belt between Mars and Jupiter. **Meteoroids** are very small pieces of solid matter moving through space; when they enter the Earth's atmosphere they produce flashes of light as **meteors**, and **meteorites** are the remains that reach the ground. It is thought that the mass extinction of dinosaurs 65 million years ago occurred when an asteroid or giant meteorite collided with the Earth, putting up a dense cloud of debris that disrupted the planetary climate. A thin layer of the element iridium, which is uncommon on earth but common in meteorites, can be found around the world in geologic strata of that era.

The origin of the Earth's moon is still a mystery, but the most widely accepted theory today is that an object struck the Earth some 4.5 billion years ago, sending large fragments of the object into space. Some of those fragments are thought to have been held by the Earth's gravitational field and aggregated into the orbiting moon. The moon has no atmosphere or water and has been bombarded by meteorites over long periods of time, forming lunar craters.

Lunar eclipses occur when the Earth passes between the sun and moon, casting a shadow on the moon. **Solar eclipses** occur when the moon passes between the Earth and sun, casting a shadow on the sun.

Our sun is a member of an immense swirling group of stars called the Milky Way galaxy. The Milky Way is one of an estimated hundreds of billions of **galaxies** in the universe. The universe is continually expanding. In addition to galaxies and clusters of stars, clouds of gas and dust called **nebulae** are scattered throughout the universe. A **black hole** is an old star that has contracted so much that its gravitational field prevents the escape of light.

Earth Science

The Earth and surrounding sky can be thought of as comprising several spheres. The **atmosphere** is an envelope of gases surrounding the Earth. The **lithosphere** is Earth's rocky shell. The **hydrosphere** is the water in and on the Earth, including what lies below the surface. The **biosphere** includes all the living things on Earth.

The air we breathe consists of mostly nitrogen (78 percent) and oxygen (21 percent) with traces of argon (0.9 percent) and carbon dioxide (0.03 percent). Water vapor is also present in various amounts (up to 4 percent) depending upon climate and weather. The lower atmosphere also contains particulate matter such as dust and pollen.

The atmosphere is divided into four layers. Near the Earth's surface, within the **troposphere**, atmospheric pressure and temperature both decrease with altitude. Between 7 and 17 km above the Earth's surface the atmosphere abruptly becomes less dense and colder, and most weather phenomena cease. This is the boundary of the **stratosphere**; it is slightly higher near the equator and lower at the poles. The stratosphere contains **ozone**, a form of oxygen that absorbs ultraviolet radiation and prevents it from damaging life on Earth. The layer lying between 50 and 80 km is called the **mesosphere**. At 80 km the atmosphere changes greatly. Ions become more abundant and temperatures increase up to 2000∞C, earning this outer layer the name **thermosphere**.

The hydrosphere includes all of the water on the surface of the Earth (such as oceans, rivers, and ponds), groundwater, water stored in soil, and water in the atmosphere. Water is important to living things and is an important erosive force that has shaped the earth. It is also important to climate and weather. The oceans and ocean currents serve as huge influences over climate, both by acting as temperature buffers and by transporting warm or cold waters.

The energy that powers climate and weather is **insolation**—incoming solar radiation balanced with radiation generated by the earth. The uneven heating of the Earth's surface by the sun along with atmospheric moisture create the climates and weather of the Earth. **Weather** is the day-to-day conditions of temperature, precipitation, and wind in a given area. **Climate** is the long-term pattern of weather in an area. **Clouds** form as atmospheric moisture rises and condenses when cooler temperatures are encountered at higher altitudes. Rain falls when air becomes saturated with water. Since warm air is less dense than cool air, winds are generated by temperature differences.

The **lithosphere** includes the Earth's **crust** and the outermost part of the **mantle**. The crust includes the surface to 40 km deep and is composed chiefly of **silicates** (compounds with silicon and oxygen), **carbonates** such as limestone, metals and metal ores, and coal, oil, and natural gas. The mantle (40–2900 km) is mostly silicates of magnesium and iron. The Earth's core is

composed mostly of iron and nickel.

Common silicate minerals include quartz, feldspar, mica, ferrous (iron) and magnesium silicates, clays, and calcites. Rocks are aggregates of minerals formed by various processes. **Igneous rocks** are cooled from a molten state and are often associated with volcanoes. **Sedimentary rocks** are formed by the deposition of materials following processes including compaction. **Metamorphic rocks** are existing rocks that have been changed by heat and pressure. **Soil is** a combination of rock fragments, clay particles, and decomposed organic matter.

The surface of the Earth represents millions of years of changes, some very slow and others very fast. **Erosion** is a term that refers to all of the processes by which rocks are worn down and debris carried away, changing the physical character of the Earth's surface. **Weathering** can be chemical or mechanical. Water does both. The Grand Canyon is an example of chemical and mechanical weathering of rock by water. Glaciers also erode the earth as do groundwater and wind.

The Earth's crust is actually a group of plates moving against one another. The forces exerted by the movement of these plates are called **tectonic forces** and are responsible for **continental drift**, **earthquakes**, **volcanoes**, and the formation of great mountain ranges and deep trenches or rifts. A **fault** is a fracture in the Earth's crust along which movement of the tectonic plates has occurred. Sudden jerking movements of such faults cause earthquakes.

Faults can also cause formation of cliffs such as those found in the Rocky Mountains. **Folding** takes place as slow, continuous tectonic movement, producing hills and depressions that erode into parallel ridges and valleys as in the Appalachians. Mountains form in several ways. They may represent accumulation of volcanic lava or be raised by faults. The largest and tallest mountain ranges in the world show sedimentation, faulting, folding, volcanic activity, **uplifts**, *and* erosion.

Movement of the Earth's crust is most dramatically demonstrated by continental drift and **sea floor spreading**. Looking at a modern map of the world, one can easily see that the land masses fit together like the pieces of a puzzle. At the edges of each continent, a **continental shelf** gradually slopes to a depth of around 130 m, where a dramatic drop occurs and the bottom slopes more steeply along the **continental slope** to the **abyssal plain**. When the margins of the land masses are extended to include their continental slopes, the fit of land masses is clearly evident. It is a near certainty based on geological and biogeographical evidence that the land masses were once a single land mass which has been named **Pangaea**. In addition, the sea floor is continuously producing new crust via volcanic activity in **mid-ocean ridges**, while other portions of crust are **subducted** back into the mantle in **deep ocean trenches**.

The Earth has been continuously changing since it was formed with the solar system some 4.5 billion years ago. The oldest surface rocks are around 3.8 billion years old, and are igneous rocks embedded with sedimentary and metamorphic rocks, suggesting that shaping of the Earth's surface had already begun. The splitting of Pangaea into two and then several land masses began less than 200 million years ago, long after life appeared on the planet. The geologic and biological history of the Earth is divided into **eras**, **periods**, and **epochs**, each associated with climate conditions, landforms, and with biota (living things) present.

The earliest era in the Earth's history is the **Precambrian Era**, which lasted from 4.5 billion to

around 570 million years ago. During the early Precambrian period, simple bacteria and marine algae were the dominant life forms. By the late Precambrian, marine invertebrates had evolved.

The **Paleozoic** era lasted from the Cambrian period 550 million years ago until the Permian period around 250 million years ago. The main geological event influencing this era was the repeated advance and retreat of shallow sea over the continents. During this era, the first marine vertebrates (fish) and land plants evolved. During the Carboniferous period of the Paleozoic, large forests of non-flowering plants lived and died, producing many of the fossil fuels we use today. By the end of the Paleozoic era 225 million years ago, the first reptiles had appeared and insects were abundant.

The **Mesozoic** era occurred between 245 and 65 million years ago and coincided with the splitting of Pangaea. In addition, the great impact thought to have led to extinction of the dinosaurs occurred during the late Mesozoic. During the Triassic period, dinosaurs and mammals appeared. During the Jurassic, dinosaurs dominated the land. By the end of the Mesozoic, during the Cretaceous, dinosaurs became extinct and the first flowering plants appeared.

The past 65 million years, the **Cenozoic** era, consist of the Tertiary and Quaternary periods. One characteristic of Cenozoic times has been significant volcanic and tectonic activity, forming the Alps and Himalayas. The first primates appeared during the Paleocene epoch around 65 million years ago, as did many large mammals over the next millions of years. Flowering plants have dominated the Earth's flora during the Cenozoic era. Modern man has only appeared in recent history, around 0.01 million years ago, although early hominids arose during the Pliocene epoch, over 2 million years ago. During the Pleistocene epoch the last ice age occurred, covering much of the northern hemisphere with glaciers. Although "ice age" is a term associated with the Pleistocene and is the major climatic change with which we are most familiar, many such climatic changes have occurred throughout the Earth's long history.

NATURAL SCIENCES RESOURCES

The CLEP Natural Sciences exam covers a broad range of topics. Many of these topics are discussed in the review you have just read. There is always room to study more about each subject, however. Keep in mind that the majority of the exam will require you to apply knowledge to problems or questions, so that you must be able to synthesize your knowledge of all natural sciences topics into a plausible answer to each question. Practice taking the sample tests in this book, and figure out what areas you need to work on.

Use textbooks, library materials, museum exhibits, television programs on Natural Sciences topics, and other sources to expand your knowledge of the natural sciences. While you most likely will not know the answer to every question, since students who have taken actual college courses in the natural sciences can typically only answer 50 percent of the questions correctly, you can increase your chances of getting a good score on the exam by broadening your base of natural sciences knowledge. Here are some books and websites you can look up when studying on your own.

Biology Resources

Cell & Molecular Biology Online (cellbio.com)

The Biology Project (biology.arizona.edu)

Ecology.com

Campbell, Neil A. and Jane B. Reece. Biology. 6 ed. Menlo Park, CA: Benjamin Cummings, 2001.

Chemistry Resources

WebElements Periodic Table (www.webelements.com)

Brown, Theodore L. et al. Chemistry: The Central Science. 9 ed. New York: Prentice Hall, 2002.

Houk, Clifford C. and Richard Post. Chemistry: Concepts and Problems. 2 ed. New York: Wiley, 1996).

Physics Resources

Goldstein, Herbert et al. Classical Mechanics. 3 ed. New York: Addison Wesley, 2002.

Griffiths, David J. Introduction to Electrodynamics. 3 ed. New York: Prentice Hall, 1998.

Shankar, R. Principles of Quantum Mechanics. Boston: Kluwer Academic, 1994.

Earth Science Resources

United States Geological Survey (geology.usgs.gov)

Bennett, Jeffrey. The Cosmic Perspective. 3 ed. New York, Addison Wesley, 2003.

Denecke Jr. Edward J. Let's Review Earth Science. 2 ed. New York, Barron's, 2001.

FINAL THOUGHTS

With the information and resources above, you're on your way to a great CLEP Natural Sciences score.

Good luck on the exam!

Chapter Twenty-Two: Practice Test 2

Time—90 minutes
120 Questions

Directions: Each question below has five lettered answer choices. For each question or phrase, choose the most closely related answer. For multiple questions that refer to the same group of lettered answer choices, each choice can be used more than once, once, or not at all.

Questions 1–3

(A) Lewis acid
(B) Lewis base
(C) Bronsted-Lowry acid
(D) Bronsted-Lowry base
(E) Buffer

1. A proton donor

2. Able to absorb small additions of either a strong acid or strong base with little change in pH

3. Electron pair donor during the formation of a coordinate covalent bond

Questions 4–6

(A) Competitive exclusion
(B) Niche breadth
(C) Food web
(D) Natural selection
(E) Ecosystem

4. Two species utilize the same limited resource, causing the elimination of one of the species from the community

5. A multidimensional hyperspace that contains all of the biotic and abiotic factors that affect a species

6. A homogenous ecological unit comprised of a community and the abiotic factors that affect the species in that community

Questions 7–9

    (A) Convection
    (B) Conduction
    (C) Radiation
    (D) Specific heat capacity
    (E) Triple point

7. The temperature and pressure at which a substance can be at equilibrium in all three states of matter

8. The transfer of heat from one place to another by the motion of a volume of hot fluid

9. The transfer of energy from one place to another in the form of electromagnetic waves

Questions 10–12

    (A) Proxima Centauri
    (B) Sun
    (C) Jupiter
    (D) Saturn
    (E) Mercury

10. The second-closest star to the Earth

11. The ringed planet

12. The planet with the most moons

Questions 13–16 refer to the following diagram of a cross-section of the Earth.

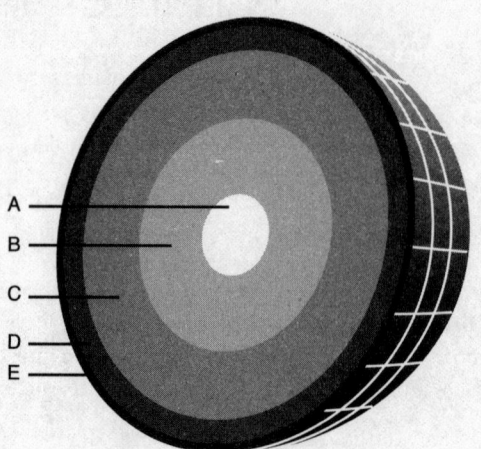

Cross-section of Earth

13. Mantle

14. Upper mantle

15. Crust

16. Outer core

GO ON TO THE NEXT PAGE

Directions: For each of the following questions or incomplete statements, select the best answer or completion from the five options given.

17. Had the Earth formed as a smaller planet with a lesser gravitational pull, what key event in the formation of life might not have been possible?

    (A) Living cells could not have evolved in a lower-gravity system.
    (B) The crust of the Earth might not have cooled enough for land masses and water to form.
    (C) The atmosphere would not have been able to produce enough oxygen for life.
    (D) The Earth could not have formed an atmosphere capable of retaining surface water.
    (E) The Earth might have become a moon of a larger planet.

18. A critical event in the development of living organisms was the formation of molecules that could

    (A) form complex cell organelles.
    (B) utilize oxygen.
    (C) self-replicate.
    (D) carry out photosynthesis.
    (E) carry out chemosynthesis.

19. The oldest fossils date to approximately 3.5 billion years ago and resemble what group of organisms found today?

    (A) algae
    (B) molds
    (C) primitive plants
    (D) protists
    (E) bacteria

20. As photosynthetic organisms increased the oxygen in the atmosphere, which adaptation then made the evolution of advanced life-forms possible?

    (A) anaerobic respiration
    (B) aerobic respiration
    (C) photosynthesis
    (D) transpiration
    (E) osmosis and diffusion

21. Which of the following adaptations is NOT found in mammals?

    (A) egg laying
    (B) four-chambered hearts
    (C) dry skin
    (D) mammary glands
    (E) cold-blooded

22. Which choice shows the five kingdom system of classification?

    (A) Monera, Protista, Plantae, Fungi, Animalia
    (B) Plantae, Fungi, Chordata, Amelida, Animalia
    (C) Monera, Fungi, Animalia, Chordata, Plantae
    (D) Animalia, Monera, Protista, Fungi, Bacteria

GO ON TO THE NEXT PAGE

23. Embryonic development can provide clues to evolutionary development by noting structure and form through the various stages of development. Which of the following structures is NOT found in human embryos?

    (A) gill slits
    (B) three-chambered heart
    (C) a tail
    (D) dorsal nerve cord
    (E) notochord

24. Which are in the correct order from general to specific?

    (A) kingdom, phylum, order, class, family, genus, species
    (B) kingdom, phylum, class, order, genus, family, species
    (C) kingdom, genus, family, order, class, phylum, species
    (D) kingdom, order, phylum, class, genus, family, species
    (E) kingdom, phylum, class, order, family, genus, species

25. Why has the status of viruses as living organisms been in doubt?

    (A) They can only reproduce inside of living cells.
    (B) They contain nucleic acids and can reproduce.
    (C) They lack major cell organelles.
    (D) They are found inside living organisms.
    (E) They cannot move independently.

26. What trait could be used to classify the following plants into two equal groups?

    Pine tree, maple tree, moss, fern, liverwort, carnation

    (A) Vascular vs. nonvascular
    (B) Seeds vs. spores
    (C) Land vs. aquatic
    (D) Photosynthetic vs. non-photosynthetic
    (E) Naked seeds vs. seeds contained in a fruit

27. You have found an unidentified species and need to place it into one of the five major kingdoms. Which characteristic below would prevent this organism from being placed into the animal kingdom?

    (A) multicellular
    (B) sessile (does not move freely)
    (C) no backbone
    (D) cell walls
    (E) lacks complex body organs

28. Which of the following is NOT a component of the process of natural selection?

    (A) Competition for limited resources occurs.
    (B) Surplus offspring are typically produced.
    (C) Traits acquired by parents are passed to offspring.
    (D) Some traits are more beneficial than others.
    (E) Traits must be genetic.

29. Which of the following components are required even in the most primitive cells?

   A. organelles   B. cell membrane
   C. cytoplasm   D. nucleus

   (A) A and B
   (B) B and C
   (C) A and C
   (D) B and D
   (E) C and D

30. Which of the following processes would NOT require energy to move substances across the cell membrane?

   I. active transport
   II. facilitated diffusion
   III. osmosis

   (A) I only
   (B) II only
   (C) III only
   (D) I and II only
   (E) II and III only

31. In a cell with 60 chromosomes, which of the following would be the sequence of chromosome numbers through the processes of mitosis and cell division?

   (A) 60-30-60
   (B) 30-60-120-60
   (C) 120-60
   (D) 60-120-60
   (E) 120-60-30

32. All of the following are a function of the plasma membrane of a cell except

   (A) cell-to-cell recognition.
   (B) regulation of movement into and out of the cell.
   (C) providing a rigid support structure.
   (D) signal reception.
   (E) containing cytoplasm.

33. Which organelle is responsible for energy production in the cytoplasm?

   (A) lysosomes
   (B) nucleus
   (C) ribosomes
   (D) mitochondria
   (E) endoplasmic reticulum

34. Which of the following is not a function of one of the forms of RNA in a eukaryotic cell?

   (A) duplicate the DNA molecule
   (B) carry transcripts of portions of DNA out of the nucleus
   (C) translate the code of DNA
   (D) protein manufacture
   (E) all are RNA functions

35. Which of the following do NOT represent human base-pairings?

   (A = Adenine, T = Thymine, C = Cytosine, G = Guanine, U = Uracil)

   I. A-T
   II. G-C
   III. A-U

   (A) I only
   (B) II only
   (C) III only
   (D) I, II, and III
   (E) None of the above

GO ON TO THE NEXT PAGE

36. In the process of DNA transcription and translation several forms of RNA are used: transfer RNA (tRNA), messenger RNA (mRNA), and ribosomal RNA (rRNA). Which of the following has these in the correct order of use from transcription through translation?

    (A) mRNA, rRNA, tRNA
    (B) rRNA, tRNA, mRNA
    (C) tRNA, rRNA, mRNA
    (D) rRNA, mRNA, tRNA
    (E) mRNA, tRNA, rRNA

37. During transcription, a specific code on the DNA molecule will signal the start and the end of transcription. The region of the DNA between these start and stop codes is called a

    (A) codon.
    (B) mRNA.
    (C) gene.
    (D) chromosome.
    (E) mutation.

38. In photosynthesis, how does the light energy actually interact with the plant pigments such as chlorophyll to start the process?

    (A) Chlorophyll uses light energy to produce carbohydrates like glucose.
    (B) The chlorophyll's temperature rises and drives the remaining processes.
    (C) Chlorophyll is split into smaller carbohydrates such as glucose and fructose.
    (D) ATP in the chlorophyll molecule is transported to the mitochondria in order to produce carbohydrates.
    (E) An electron in the pigments is boosted to a higher energy level and releases energy as it drops back to its original level.

39. In cellular respiration, it is the movement of electrons that makes the production of ATP molecules possible. What acts as the final acceptor of electrons in this process?

    (A) hydrogen
    (B) carbon
    (C) phosphorous
    (D) water
    (E) oxygen

40. Which of the following events during meiosis would result in a chromosome abnormality in the offpsring?

    (A) spermatogenesis
    (B) oogenesis
    (C) cytokinesis
    (D) crossing over
    (E) non-disjunction

41. The wings in bats and the wings in birds are said to be analogous structures because

    (A) they have a similar function but different structure.
    (B) they have a similar structure but different function.
    (C) they reveal a common ancestry.
    (D) they reveal a similar embryonic development pattern.
    (E) they have a similar function and structure.

GO ON TO THE NEXT PAGE

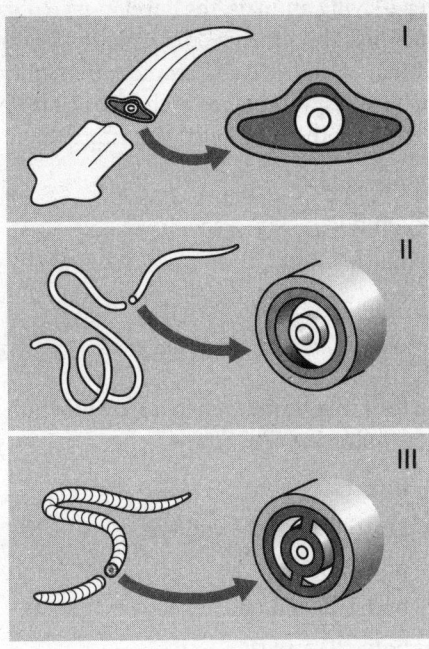

Acoelomate, Pseudocoelomate, Coelomate.

42. Which of the above cross-sections reveals an animal which would have the most complex body organs and systems?

    (A) I only
    (B) II only
    (C) III only
    (D) I and III only
    (E) I and II only

43. If a tree grows at 1.5 cm per year, how much higher would a nail hammered into the trunk of the tree be after 12 years?

    (A) 8 cm
    (B) 0 cm
    (C) 18 cm
    (D) 13.5 cm
    (E) 10.5 cm

44. What physiological feature helped early primitive plants move out of water onto land?

    (A) flowers
    (B) seeds
    (C) leaves
    (D) roots
    (E) cuticle

45. All animals but the sponges have some form of

    (A) dorsal nerve cord.
    (B) brain.
    (C) reproduction.
    (D) symmetry.
    (E) segmentation.

46. Which is actually considered a form of connective tissue in animals?

    (A) skin
    (B) blood
    (C) smooth muscle
    (D) neuron
    (E) skeletal muscle

47. When our body temperature approaches a certain point, the sweat glands are activated and we begin to perspire. This is an example of

    (A) a circulatory response.
    (B) an immune response.
    (C) a conditioned response.
    (D) positive feedback.
    (E) negative feedback.

48. Which of the following is/are NOT a part of the circulatory system?

    (A) arteries
    (B) veins
    (C) lungs
    (D) heart
    (E) capillaries

49. Organisms which exhibit the greatest diversity and the most adaptations generally utilize

    (A) sexual reproduction.
    (B) asexual reproduction.
    (C) binary fission.
    (D) budding.
    (E) regeneration.

50. A single cell resulting from fertilization of an egg by sperm is called a(n)

    (A) embryo.
    (B) fetus.
    (C) zygote.
    (D) trimester.
    (E) blastocyst.

51. In egg-laying animals, the developing embryo is nourished and protected by structures in the egg including a yolk sac and amnion. In mammals, the structure responsible for exchange of nutrients with the mother's bloodstream is/are the

    (A) placenta.
    (B) amnion.
    (C) uterine wall.
    (D) fallopian tubes.
    (E) ovaries.

52. The fruit in a flowering plant may function in any of the following EXCEPT

    (A) dispersal.
    (B) protection of the embryo.
    (C) pollination.
    (D) both (A) and (B)
    (E) both (B) and (C)

53. An insect changing from a larva to an adult or a tadpole developing into a frog does so in a process called

    (A) embryonic development.
    (B) binary fission.
    (C) oogenesis.
    (D) external fertilization.
    (E) metamorphosis.

GO ON TO THE NEXT PAGE

Questions 54–56 are based on the following pedigree.

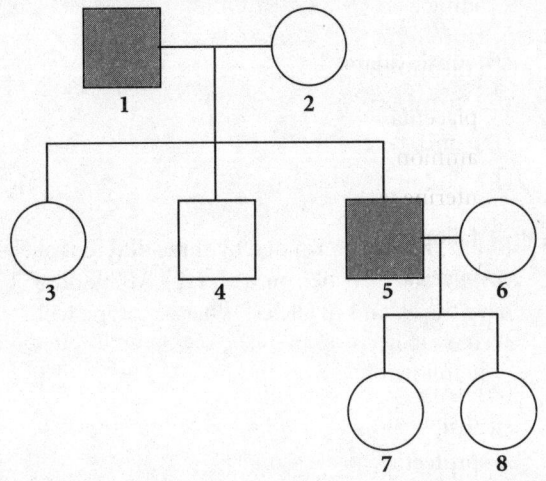

Pedigree

54. If the trait shown as shaded is an X-linked trait what chance is there that the mother (number 2) is a carrier?

    (A) 100 percent
    (B) 75 percent
    (C) 50 percent
    (D) 25 percent
    (E) 0 percent

55. Using the same pedigree for a recessive non sex-linked trait, what chance do the daughters (7 and 8) have of being carriers of this trait?

    (A) 100 percent
    (B) 75 percent
    (C) 50 percent
    (D) 25 percent
    (E) 0 percent

56. If the recessive allele of the trait in the pedigree is shown with a "t" and the dominant allele is shown with a "T," for which individual in the pedigree can a genotype not be determined?

    (A) 5
    (B) 6
    (C) 7
    (D) 8
    (E) all genotypes can be determined

Questions 57–59 are based on the following scenario.

In a certain plant red flowers (R) are dominant over white (r) and smooth seeds (S) are dominant over rough seeds (s). Two plants are crossed and produced the following offspring:

Red/Smooth:	26
Red/Rough:	24
White/Smooth:	30
White/Rough:	20

57. Given this information what must the parental genotypes have been?

    (A) RRSS × rrss
    (B) RrSs × RrSs
    (C) rrSs × rrSs
    (D) rrss × rrss
    (E) RrSs × rrss

58. Which of the following processes could result in a pattern of inheritance different than expected based on the principle of independent assortment and probability?

    (A) gene linkage
    (B) crossing over in meiosis
    (C) mutation
    (D) all of the above
    (E) none of the above

GO ON TO THE NEXT PAGE

59. In the example on the previous page, an Rr combination that produced a pink flower could be an example of

   (A) plietropy.
   (B) heterozygous traits.
   (C) codominance.
   (D) polygenic traits.
   (E) incomplete dominance.

60. Most genetic traits cannot be worked out with a Punnett square or pedigree because they are

   (A) not expressed.
   (B) monohybrid.
   (C) polygenic.
   (D) codominant.
   (E) too much affected by environment.

61. Inserting a gene into a bacterial strand of DNA to produce a specific compound would be an example of

   (A) DNA fingerprinting.
   (B) electrophoresis.
   (C) gene cloning.
   (D) karyotyping.
   (E) cross-breeding.

62. A mutagen that can affect a cell's DNA and cause cancer to form is called a

   (A) carcinogen.
   (B) antioxidant.
   (C) toxin.
   (D) oncogene.
   (E) codon.

63. Blood type is determined by three different alleles (iA, iB, and i). A person with type AB blood will have the iA and iB alleles. What genotype will account for type O blood?

   (A) iAi
   (B) iBi
   (C) ii
   (D) iiB
   (E) iiA

64. A gene that is more commonly expressed in one gender is said to be

   (A) sex-linked.
   (B) X-linked.
   (C) recessive.
   (D) sex-influenced.
   (E) dominant.

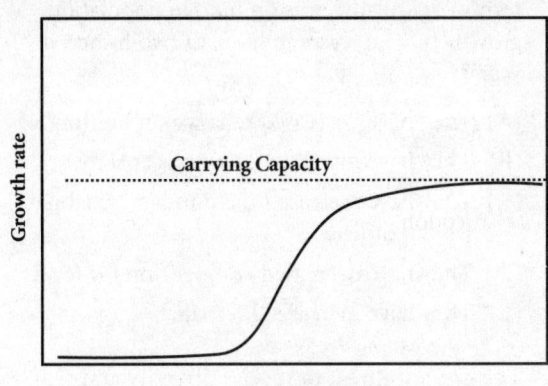

Time (Months)

65. The graph above shows the concept of habitat carrying capacity. As a population continues to increase some factor generally limits the rate of growth until it levels off or even declines. Which of the following is NOT a likely factor limiting the growth rate of a population?

(A) excessive food supply
(B) competition
(C) limited food supply
(D) predation
(E) limited space

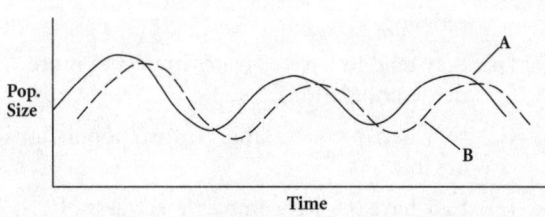

66. The graph above most likely shows which of the following interactions between species?

(A) competitive exclusion
(B) mutualism
(C) predator-prey
(D) overexploitation
(E) mimicry

67. Which of the following involves direct harm or exploitation of one organism by another?

(A) commensalism
(B) biological invasions
(C) competition
(D) mutualism
(E) parasitism

68. The effects of predation, carrying capacity, competition, disease, and parasitism are frequently density dependent, which means

    (A) their impact is greater when populations are growing.
    (B) they tend to have a greater impact in more dense populations.
    (C) they have a greater impact when populations are low.
    (D) they have the same impact regardless of density.
    (E) they have no impact at low densities.

69. Which of the following would most likely act as a density-independent factor?

    (A) predation
    (B) parasitism
    (C) seasonal food supply
    (D) weather
    (E) reproductive success

70. A scientist wanted to assess the reproductive success of a small mammal population and measured the following: population size, number of births, and number of deaths over three years. He found that the number of births in the population slightly exceeded the number of deaths but that population size had remained roughly the same.

    Which of the following estimates would help determine the reproductive success of this population?

    (A) immigration rate
    (B) emigration rate
    (C) survival rate
    (D) both (A) and (B)
    (E) all three of these estimates

71. What is the most direct effect of agricultural and technological advances on human population growth-rate increases in the past two hundred years?

    (A) They have decreased reliance on hunting.
    (B) They have increased carrying capacity.
    (C) They have increased the number of habitats we can utilize.
    (D) They have decreased competition for food.
    (E) They have increased lifespan.

72. The greatest threat to species diversity and survival today is

    (A) habitat loss.
    (B) predation.
    (C) disease.
    (D) exploitation/overhunting.
    (E) pollution.

73. The energy supplied by the sun is essential to life on Earth but is essentially unavailable to most living things. The organisms capable of converting this energy to a form usable by other organisms are called

    (A) herbivores.
    (B) primary consumers.
    (C) omnivores.
    (D) producers.
    (E) top consumers.

74. If carbon-14 has a half-life of 5730 years, how much of a 50-gram sample will remain after 17190 years?

    (A) 16.7 grams
    (B) 6.25 grams
    (C) 12.5 grams
    (D) 25 grams
    (E) 3.5 grams

Questions 75–76 are based on the following equation.

$$^{235}_{92}U + ? \rightarrow {}^{142}_{142}Ba + {}^{91}_{36}Kr + 3{}^{1}_{0}n$$

75. In the above fission reaction what is missing from the left side of the equation?

    (A) the element barium (Ba)
    (B) the element krypton (Kr)
    (C) a single neutron
    (D) both barium and krypton
    (E) three protons

76. A high amount of energy is released in a very short period of time from the above reaction. Which of the following contributes to the speed of this reaction?

    (A) the formation of barium and krypton, which contain high amounts of chemical energy
    (B) The three neutrons released will collide with other uranium atoms and start a chain reaction.
    (C) Over time much more krypton will be formed than barium, and krypton contains more kinetic energy.
    (D) Barium and krypton will combine with the released neutrons and will split again.
    (E) The by-products of fission reactions are radioactive and thus can be used as energy sources.

77. Given the ability of nuclear fission to accelerate so rapidly, what allows nuclear power plants to use these reactions to produce electricity?

    (A) They use other fuel sources such as plutonium.
    (B) The fission reaction is produced far underground.
    (C) Only trace amounts of radioactive materials are needed.
    (D) The reactions are controlled by using materials to slow down the flow of neutrons.
    (E) Fission by-products are encased in safe containers.

78. Each electron configuration represents the same hypothetical element. Based on these which of the following is NOT true?

    $$1s^2\ 2s^2\ 2p^8 \qquad 1s^2\ 2s^2\ 2p^6$$
    $$A B$$

    (A) The atom shown in A has eight electrons in its outermost energy level.
    (B) To be neutrally charged atom B will need to have eight protons in its nucleus.
    (C) Atom A is more likely to enter into a chemical bond.
    (D) Atom B could be an electron acceptor.
    (E) Atom A has a full outer electron shell.

79. The bond that forms sodium chloride (NaCl) is an ionic bond. Which of the following is true of this type of chemical bond?

    (A) can only be broken in water
    (B) based on the attraction of positively and negatively charged atoms
    (C) requires a minimal amount of energy to break
    (D) common in organic compounds such as glucose
    (E) involves the sharing of electrons between two atoms

GO ON TO THE NEXT PAGE

Questions 80–83 refer to the periodic table below.

Periodic Table of the Elements

1																	18
1 **H** 1.008	2											13	14	15	16	17	2 **He** 4.003
3 **Li** 6.941	4 **Be** 9.012											5 **B** 10.81	6 **C** 12.01	7 **N** 14.01	8 **O** 16.00	9 **F** 19.00	10 **Ne** 20.18
11 **Na** 22.99	12 **Mg** 24.31	3	4	5	6	7	8	9	10	11	12	13 **Al** 26.98	14 **Si** 28.09	15 **P** 30.97	16 **S** 32.07	17 **Cl** 35.45	18 **Ar** 39.95
19 **K** 39.10	20 **Ca** 40.08	21 **Sc** 44.96	22 **Ti** 47.88	23 **V** 50.94	24 **Cr** 52.00	25 **Mn** 54.94	26 **Fe** 55.85	27 **Co** 58.93	28 **Ni** 58.69	29 **Cu** 63.55	30 **Zn** 65.39	31 **Ga** 69.72	32 **Ge** 72.61	33 **As** 74.92	34 **Se** 78.96	35 **Br** 79.90	36 **Kr** 83.80
37 **Rb** 85.47	38 **Sr** 87.62	39 **Y** 88.91	40 **Zr** 91.22	41 **Nb** 92.91	42 **Mo** 95.94	43 **Tc** (98)	44 **Ru** 101.1	45 **Rh** 102.9	46 **Pd** 106.4	47 **Ag** 107.9	48 **Cd** 112.4	49 **In** 114.8	50 **Sn** 118.7	51 **Sb** 121.8	52 **Te** 127.6	53 **I** 126.9	54 **Xe** 131.3
55 **Cs** 132.9	56 **Ba** 137.3	57–70	71 **Lu** 175.0	72 **Hf** 178.5	73 **Ta** 181.0	74 **W** 183.8	75 **Re** 186.2	76 **Os** 190.2	77 **Ir** 192.2	78 **Pt** 195.1	79 **Au** 197.0	80 **Hg** 200.6	81 **Tl** 204.4	82 **Pb** 207.2	83 **Bi** 209.0	84 **Po** (209)	85 **At** (210)	86 **Rn** (222)
87 **Fr** (223)	88 **Ra** 226.0	89–102	103 **Lr** (260)	104 **Rf** (261)	105 **Db** (262)	106 **Sg** (263)	107 **Bh** (262)	108 **Hs** (265)	109 **Mt** (268)	110 **Uun** (269)	111 **Uuu** (272)	112 **Uub** (277)	113 **Uut**	114 **Uuq** (289)	115 **Uup**	116 **Uuh**	117 **Uus**	118 **Uuo**

Atomic Number ——— 6
Symbol ——— C
Atomic Mass ——— 12.01

* Numbers in parentheses are the *mass numbers* of the most stable isotope of the element.

57 **La** 138.9	58 **Ce** 140.1	59 **Or** 140.9	60 **Nd** 144.2	61 **Pm** (145)	62 **Sm** 150.4	63 **Eu** 152.0	64 **Gd** 157.3	65 **Tb** 158.9	66 **Dy** 162.5	67 **Ho** 164.9	68 **Er** 167.3	69 **Tm** 168.9	70 **Yb** 173.0
89 **Ac** 227.0	90 **Th** 232.0	91 **Pa** 231.0	92 **U** 238.0	93 **Np** 237.0	94 **Pu** (244)	95 **Am** (243)	96 **Cm** (247)	97 **Bk** (247)	98 **Cf** (251)	99 **Es** (252)	100 **Fm** (257)	101 **Md** (258)	102 **No** (259)

80. The majority of elements seen on the periodic table are classified as

(A) gases.
(B) metals.
(C) semi-metals.
(D) radioactive.
(E) synthetic.

81. The last column on the periodic table has the group number 8 and represents the "noble gases" which are largely non-reactive with other elements. What does the group number refer to?

    (A) The number of electrons in the outer shell of elements in a group.
    (B) The number of electron orbits or shells in elements from each group.
    (C) The average mass number of elements in that group.
    (D) The number of protons in the nucleus.
    (E) The average atomic number of elements in a group.

82. Which of the following is NOT true about elements when moving from the top to the bottom of the periodic table?

    (A) The number of electron orbitals or "shells" increases.
    (B) Elements generally become more metallic.
    (C) Elements become more stable and less reactive.
    (D) Mass numbers increase.
    (E) Atomic numbers increase.

83. The horizontal rows on the table are called "periods." Moving from left to right within one of these rows, which of the following is true?

    (A) The number of electron shells increases.
    (B) The number of protons increases.
    (C) The mass number remains roughly the same but the atomic number changes.
    (D) Elements become increasingly metallic.
    (E) An increasing number of synthetic elements occur.

84. Which of the following does NOT represent a compound?

    (A) H_2
    (B) H_2O
    (C) H_2O_2
    (D) CO
    (E) NaCl

85. A solution is a(n) _____ mixture in which one or more compounds are dissolved in a solute.

    (A) homogeneous
    (B) heterogeneous
    (C) suspension
    (D) colloidal
    (E) acidic

86. Metal alloys are examples of

    (A) pure forms of a given metal.
    (B) metals which are liquid at room temperature.
    (C) metals which can act as conductors.
    (D) homogeneous mixtures of two or more metals.
    (E) heterogeneous mixtures of two or more metals.

87. Two atoms which fill their outer electron energy levels by sharing electrons are forming

    (A) an ionic bond.
    (B) a mixture.
    (C) an alloy.
    (D) a covalent bond.
    (E) an electronic bond.

GO ON TO THE NEXT PAGE

88. Which is not a property of an acid solution?

    (A) can conduct electricity
    (B) corrosive to other materials
    (C) has an excess of H^+ ions
    (D) has an excess of OH^- ions
    (E) many are essential to living things

89. The pH scale is based upon of which of the following?

    (A) the electrical conductivity of an acid
    (B) the corrosive strength of an acid
    (C) the concentration of hydroxide (OH^-) ions
    (D) the ability of a base to neutralize acid
    (E) the concentration of hydrogen ions

Questions 90–91 refer to the following equation.

$$CH_4 + O_2 \rightarrow CO_2 + 2H_2O$$

90. Which of the following changes is needed to balance the equation above?

    (A) CH_4 should be $1CH_4$
    (B) Add H_2O to the left side of the equation
    (C) CO_2 should be $2CO_2$
    (D) $2H_2O$ should be $4H_2O$
    (E) O_2 should be $2O_2$

91. Which "Law" makes it important to balance chemical equations?

    (A) Law of Conservation of Matter
    (B) Law of Conservation of Energy
    (C) Law of Gravity
    (D) Law of Mechanics
    (E) Law of Thermodynamics

92. Energy is defined as the ability to do work. Which formula below defines the physical concept of work?

    (A) force ↔ distance
    (B) mass ↔ acceleration
    (C) distance/time
    (D) $E = mc^2$
    (E) energy/time

93. Which of the following is NOT a form of kinetic energy?

    (A) a moving car
    (B) a car battery
    (C) electrical current
    (D) molecules moving in a heated liquid
    (E) a falling rock

94. A thermometer (alcohol, mercury, or metallic spring) works because matter

    (A) contracts when cooled.
    (B) expands when heated.
    (C) contracts when heated.
    (D) both (A) and (B)
    (E) both (B) and (C)

95. Specific heat of a substance is the amount of energy required to raise the temperature of 1 gram of that substance 1° C. The formula is shown below.

$$S = \frac{\text{Energy Transferred (Joules)}}{\text{Mass (g)} * \text{Temperature Change}}$$

The resulting units for S are J/g °C

Given 100 g of the following substances which would require the most energy to increase in temperature by 1 degree Celsius?

(A) hydrogen (S = 14.3)
(B) mercury (S = .13)
(C) oxygen (S = .92)
(D) lead (S = .13)
(E) water (S = 4.2)

96. Two drills put the same amount of work into drilling a hole into a metal sheet. One drill is unable to make a hole as deep as the other even though the input of work energy was the same. Based on this which of the following is most likely true of the less efficient drill?

(A) It will generate less heat during the drilling process.
(B) It has a smaller drill bit.
(C) Both drills generate the same amount of heat because they put in the same amount of work.
(D) The more efficient drill actually worked harder because it drilled a deeper hole.
(E) It will generate more heat during the drilling process.

97. Which of the following would decrease the entropy in a body of water?

(A) heating
(B) freezing
(C) letting it stand
(D) adding an acid or a base
(E) stirring

98. When a piston is used to compress gas at constant temperature in a cylinder, which of the following will occur?

(A) pressure will decrease
(B) mass will decrease
(C) volume will increase
(D) temperature will increase
(E) pressure will increase

99. In rolling a ball down a ramp, which of the following measurements would have to be known to calculate velocity?

(A) slope and distance
(B) distance and mass
(C) distance and time
(D) slope and time
(E) force and mass

100. An astronaut on the moon once dropped a brick and a feather from the same height. Since the moon has no air resistance and only a fraction of the Earth's gravity which hit the surface first?

(A) the brick
(B) the feather
(C) they hit simultaneously
(D) neither hit because of low gravity
(E) none of the above

GO ON TO THE NEXT PAGE

101. The moon has one-sixth the gravitational pull of the Earth. An object which had a mass of 120 kg on Earth then would have a mass of _____ kg on the moon.

    (A) 100
    (B) 40
    (C) 60
    (D) 120
    (E) 20

102. A train car is moved along a track until it couples with another identical car which is not moving. Both cars move away together at half the original speed. What has happened to the momentum of the original car?

    (A) It has decreased by 50 percent.
    (B) It has doubled because of the weight of the two cars together.
    (C) It has decreased by 75 percent because the first car was moving.
    (D) It will increase by 50 percent.
    (E) It is the same as before because mass has increased.

103. A ball on the end of a string is twirled in a circle. What type of force is the string exerting on the ball?

    (A) centripetal
    (B) centrifugal
    (C) acceleration
    (D) frictional
    (E) gravitational

104. Which would NOT be true of a spaceship traveling very near light speed?

    (A) It would begin to lose mass and convert mass to energy.
    (B) The size and shape of the object would change.
    (C) Time would move more slowly for those on the spaceship.
    (D) The mass of the ship would approach infinity.
    (E) All of the above are true.

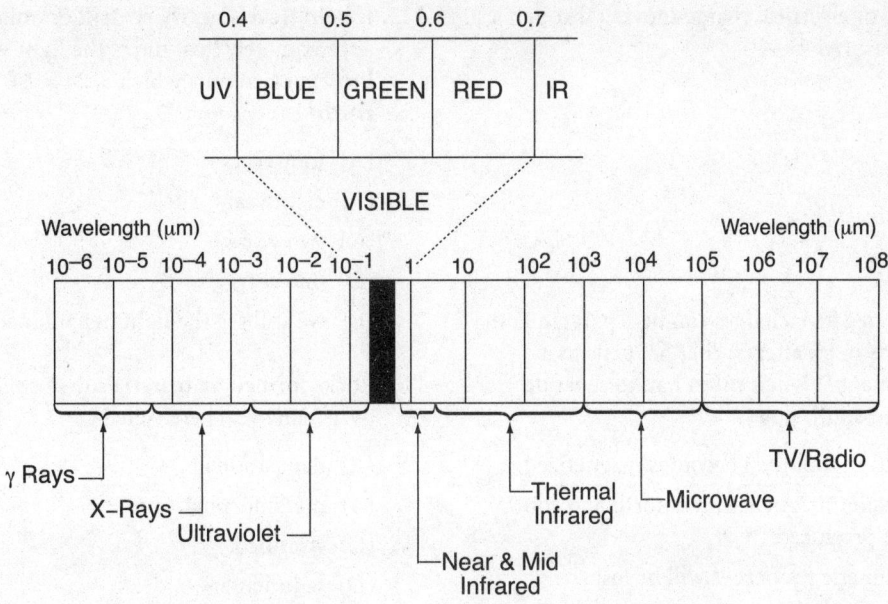

Electromagnetic spectrum showing wavelengths

Questions 105–106 are based on the above diagram.

105. Which region of the spectrum shown indicates the most high-energy form of radiation?

   (A) visible
   (B) ultraviolet
   (C) infrared
   (D) gamma rays
   (E) x-rays

106. In the electromagnetic spectrum, higher energy is indicated by having a higher

   (A) reflection.
   (B) refraction.
   (C) frequency.
   (D) amplitude.
   (E) wavelength.

107. Voltage is a measure of what type of energy?

   (A) magnetic
   (B) potential
   (C) atomic
   (D) kinetic
   (E) chemical

108. Resistors are placed into electrical circuits to

   (A) increase current.
   (B) decrease current.
   (C) divert current.
   (D) increase voltage.
   (E) decrease voltage.

109. The amount of electrical charge moving through a circuit is measured in

    (A) volts.
    (B) amperes.
    (C) ohms.
    (D) resistance.
    (E) joules.

110. Positive and negative charges can be separated and stored such as in a battery. What happens to a permanent magnet when cut in half to separate the north and south poles?

    (A) The cutting tool then becomes magnetized.
    (B) Two smaller magnets with a north and south pole are produced.
    (C) The magnetic properties will be lost.
    (D) The north pole will dominate.
    (E) The south pole will dominate.

111. The four inner planets in our solar system are known as

    (A) planetoids.
    (B) terrestrial.
    (C) gaseous.
    (D) Jovian.
    (E) solar.

112. What discovery by Galileo contradicted the idea that objects in space revolved around the Earth?

    (A) moons orbiting Jupiter
    (B) elliptical planet orbits
    (C) Halley's Comet
    (D) Saturn's rings
    (E) the existence of the asteroid belt

113. If light travels nearly six trillion miles in a year approximately how old is the light we see from Proxima Centauri which is 24×10^9 miles from Earth?

    (A) four years
    (B) eight years
    (C) two years
    (D) one year
    (E) we still see the light instantaneously

114. Rocks formed by materials deposited by water over many years are called

    (A) depositional.
    (B) metamorphic.
    (C) stratified.
    (D) sedimentary.
    (E) igneous.

115. What percentage of the Earth's atmosphere is comprised of oxygen?

    (A) 79
    (B) 21
    (C) 53
    (D) 14
    (E) 85

116. What percentage of water on Earth is NOT found in the oceans?

    (A) 10
    (B) 5
    (C) 3
    (D) 20
    (E) 50

117. The two most dominant processes in the water cycle are

    (A) evaporation and precipitation.
    (B) evaporation and transpiration.
    (C) transpiration and precipitation.
    (D) evaporation and runoff.
    (E) photosynthesis and respiration.

118. The vast majority of geologic history occurred during the

    (A) Jurassic era.
    (B) Precambrian era.
    (C) Paleozoic era.
    (D) Cenozoic era.
    (E) Mesozoic era.

119. Which of the following would be most useful for accurately estimating the age of a previously unidentified fossil?

    (A) the body form of the animal or plant
    (B) radiometric dating
    (C) the position of the fossil in the rock strata
    (D) the composition of the rocks around the fossil
    (E) the geographic location of the fossil

120. The greenhouse effect stems from the fact that CO_2 and other gases

    (A) block ultraviolet radiation thus causing the atmosphere to warm.
    (B) slow down evaporation and transpiration and thus alter precipitation patterns.
    (C) block infrared wavelengths that would have re-radiated back to space.
    (D) transmit infrared wavelengths but trap ultraviolet wavelengths thus decreasing ozone.
    (E) interfere with ozone creation thus increasing the effect of ultraviolet rays.

ANSWER KEY

1. C	19. E	37. C	55. A	73. D	91. A	109. B
2. E	20. B	38. E	56. B	74. B	92. A	110. B
3. B	21. E	39. E	57. E	75. C	93. B	111. B
4. A	22. A	40. E	58. D	76. B	94. D	112. A
5. B	23. B	41. A	59. E	77. D	95. A	113. A
6. E	24. E	42. C	60. C	78. C	96. E	114. D
7. E	25. A	43. B	61. C	79. B	97. B	115. B
8. A	26. B	44. E	62. A	80. B	98. E	116. C
9. C	27. D	45. D	63. C	81. A	99. C	117. A
10. B	28. C	46. B	64. D	82. C	100. C	118. B
11. D	29. B	47. E	65. A	83. B	101. D	119. B
12. C	30. E	48. C	66. C	84. A	102. E	120. C
13. C	31. D	49. A	67. E	85. A	103. A	
14. D	32. C	50. C	68. B	86. D	104. A	
15. E	33. D	51. A	69. D	87. D	105. D	
16. B	34. A	52. C	70. E	88. D	106. C	
17. D	35. E	53. E	71. B	89. E	107. B	
18. C	36. A	54. A	72. A	90. E	108. E	

Answers and Explanations

1. (C)

The Bronsted-Lowry system of acids and bases describes an acid as an element that can donate a proton to another atom in solution, namely a hydrogen atom. This system is more exclusionary than the Lewis system that only requires the liberation of electrons, which can be performed by any atom.

2. (E)

A buffer solution, such as human blood, has a mixture of both acid and base so that the addition of small quantities of other acids or bases does not greatly affect the pH. Buffers are necessary in biological systems because most reactions require or are at least maximized at specific pHs.

3. (B)

This is the definition of a Lewis acid. More kinds of atoms can be electron donors than proton donors.

4. (A)

Since these two species are utilizing the same resource, they are in competition. The competition causes the elimination (exclusion) of one of the species.

5. (B)

Niche breadth explains all the factors that contribute to the survival of a species and the fitness of the species. It is almost inconceivable to attempt to list all of the factors that make up one species niche.

6. (E)

A community is the collection of species that interact in a particular habitat. An ecosystem is the combination of the community and the environmental factors that affect the habitat.

7. (E)

The thermodynamic equilibrium of a substance occurs at a certain temperature and pressure that allows all three states of matter to exist simultaneously. The temperature and pressure for the triple point of water are 273.01 K and 611.73 pascals.

8. (A)

Heat can move in different ways. Convection is the movement of heat by the movement of heated liquids. Air is a less dense liquid than water, but air movements would be considered movement of liquid and considered convection.

9. (C)

Radio frequencies, heat from the sun, and x-rays are all different forms of electromagnetic radiation. These are forms of energy that transfer from one place to another with wave-like properties.

10. (B)

The star nearest the Earth itself is of course the sun. The closest star to the Earth's solar system is Proxima Centauri, which is 4.2 light years away. It isn't the brightest star, which is Sirius (the dog star), but it is closer to Earth than Sirius.

11. (D)

All of the giant planets have rings, but only the rings of Saturn are significant enough to be almost visible from Earth with binoculars. Neptune's rings are curiously oriented at a right angle to the direction of its orbit.

12. (C)

The planet with the most moons is Jupiter with an estimated sixty moons. The next largest number of moons occurs with the planet Saturn, with thirty-one moons, and Uranus, with twenty-seven.

13. (C)

The Earth is a dynamic object that is not solid all the way through. It has a solid crust around the outside surface, but most of the interior is composed of liquid, molten rock. The interior is made up of the mantle and the core, which are subdivided further based on distance from the center and temperature.

14. (D)
See explanation to question 13.

15. (E)
See explanation to question 13.

16. (B)
See explanation to question 13.

17. (D)
Had the Earth been smaller it is possible that gravity would not have been sufficient for an atmosphere to form that could have retained surface water and supported life.

18 (C)
All of these functions are critical to life but the formation of compounds that could actually replicate themselves (along with the development of plasma membranes) was a critical first step toward forming living cells.

19. (E)
These early cells were prokaryotic and resembled the bacteria found in today's mud flats, bogs, and pond mud where oxygen is largely absent.

20. (B)
Aerobic respiration is more efficient than anaerobic (without oxygen) respiration. Thus organisms capable of using the increasing oxygen in the atmosphere had an evolutionary advantage over those that could not and were capable of developing more complex structures.

21. (E)
While mammals actually do share some characteristics with groups like reptiles and amphibians, only birds and mammals have a constant and internally regulated body temperature. The duck-billed platypus is a mammal that lays eggs (A).

22. (A)
The five kingdom system (now outdated) consisted of Monera, Protista, Plantae, Fungi, and Animalia.

23. (B)
Like all other members of the phylum Chordata, humans possess at one time gill slits, a tail, a dorsal nerve cord, and a notochord.

24. (E)
These categories begin with all organisms in a group such as Animals and end with an individual species which is given a scientific name based on its genus and species. An example with the common housecat would be; Animalia, Chordata, Mammalia, Carnivora, Felidae, *Felis domesticus.*

25. (A)
Viruses can carry out many of the processes of living organisms but must reproduce using the cell organelles of other organisms and cannot reproduce themselves.

26. (B)
The mosses, ferns, and liverworts are all seedless plants and instead use spores and must remain near water to reproduce.

27. (D)
The animal kingdom is highly diverse and all of the above characteristics can be found except for cells containing cell walls.

28. (C)
Acquired traits cannot be passed from parent to offspring and only those traits that are hereditary can play a role in natural selection.

29. (B)
The cell membrane and cytoplasm are essential and found in all cells whereas the nucleus and organelles are only found in eukaryotic cells.

30. (E)
Diffusion and osmosis will move materials from higher to lower concentrations and require no external energy. Active transport can move materials against the concentration gradient when necessary and requires an input of energy.

31. (D)
Mitosis is the copying, duplication, and division of the nucleus. Cell division follows mitosis and chromosome numbers through this process will double and then divide.

32. (C)
Unlike a cell wall, the cell membrane is not a rigid structure but a lipid bilayer that regulates movement of materials into and out of the cell.

33. (D)
The mitochondria are the organelles where ATP is formed during the Krebs cycle and used to operate the activities within the cell.

34. (A)
Duplication of DNA takes place in the nucleus but is controlled by enzymes and does not require a specialized form of RNA.

35. (E)
The base pairings in DNA are identical for all organisms. Adenine will bond with thymine and guanine with cytosine. In the RNA molecule, uracil replaces thymine.

36. (A)
mRNA copies the code from the DNA molecule in the nucleus and carries it to rRNA which then attaches and allows the tRNA molecule containing the appropriate amino acid molecule to place that amino acid on the chain.

37. (C)
The regions of the DNA molecule between the stop and start codes will have information necessary to build a specific protein molecule in the cytoplasm. These units are known as genes.

38. (E)
It is the energy released by this initial electron movement that starts the electron transport chain that eventually drives the production of ATP.

39. (E)
Oxygen acting as an electron acceptor essentially pulls the electrons through the transport chain and makes aerobic respiration possible.

40. (E)
Non-disjunction involves two chromosomes that do not separate in meiosis I and hence an extra chromosome is sent through meiosis II. An example of this is Down syndrome; an affected individual has an extra twenty-first chromosome.

41. (A)
Both structures are used for flying hence they are analogous. However, the structure of the two wings is markedly different. Analogous structures can develop when two organisms occupy a similar habitat (such as whales and fish) or when a similar function is needed.

42. (C)
The presence of a lined body cavity means that more complex organs can develop and are better protected as organisms become larger.

43. (B)
Trees, like other plants, grow from the tips of the roots and shoots and thus the only growth on the trunk of a tree will be outward as its diameter increases.

44. (E)
Early land plants had to develop a means of avoiding water loss, and the waxy outer cuticle is found in all land plants.

45. (D)
Only the sponges lack any sort of regular body plan. Most animals we are familiar with have a bilateral symmetry with a distinct front, back, right, and left side.

46. (B)
There are really four general tissue types in most animals: connective, epithelial, muscle, and nervous. Blood in general is considered a fluid connective tissue.

47. (E)

Many of the body's mechanisms for maintaining homeostasis rely on negative feedbacks which will seek to return some condition such as temperature to a previous state. Other examples could be insulin responding to blood sugar levels, or water loss resulting from high salt intake.

48. (C)

Though the lungs work very closely with the circulatory system to deliver oxygen to cells and remove carbon dioxide, they are in the respiratory system.

49. (A)

Sexual reproduction results in greater genetic variety and hence is more advantageous in variable environments.

50. (C)

The first stage in development after fertilization is termed a zygote, which is a single 2n cell formed from the fertilization of the egg by the sperm.

51. (A)

The placenta is specialized tissue through which nutrients from the mother's bloodstream can pass and be carried through the umbilical cord to the developing fetus.

52. (C)

Fruits have a variety of functions but are formed after pollination and fertilization.

53. (E)

The cellular and physiological changes in changing from a larva to an adult can be dramatic and are termed metamorphosis.

54. (A)

Since X-linked traits are carried on the twenty-third X chromosome, there is no way the son (number 5) could have inherited this trait from his father. The trait had to be carried on one of his mother's X chromosomes.

55. (A)

Since the trait in this case is recessive, the father (number 5) must have both recessive genes and would have to pass at least one of them to all of his offspring regardless of gender.

56. (B)

Until at least one child actually shows up with both recessive alleles, there is no way to know for sure based on a pedigree whether the mother (number 6) is TT or Tt. Since only one allele will be sent with each fertilized egg, the dominant allele could appear in every child even if the mother is a carrier.

57. (E)

The important thing to note here is the relative proportion of each trait in the offspring. The proportions are approximately equal for each trait. However, since there are completely recessive individuals in the offspring, answer (A) is eliminated and since most had at least one dominant trait answer (D) is eliminated. Of the remaining combinations the only one that would produce an approximately equal number of each trait would be answer (E). If you look at the possible gametes from each parent you will see that the first parent has four possible combination (RS, Rs, rS, rs) and that the second has only rs. This combination predicts an equal proportion of each trait in the offspring.

58. (D)

Punnett squares show the probability of a particular combination of genes, but factors such as mutation or gene linkage (genes carried on the same chromosome) as well as crossing over (exchanging pieces of chromosome during meiosis) can all result in patterns somewhat different than expected.

59. (E)

When two traits appear to blend, then neither is completely dominant over the other. This is called incomplete dominance. In codominance, both traits are expressed equally and the offspring will express both traits. In the example in question this could be a flower with a mix of red and white petals or a plant with red and white flowers.

60. (C)
Most genetic traits are the result of two or more genes and are called polygenic. Eye color is an example of a polygenic trait with many factors affecting the actual eye color.

61. (C)
Since the new gene is now a part of the bacterial cell's DNA, it will be replicated and read each time the bacterial cell replicates and translates its own DNA. Hence the gene has been spliced and cloned.

62. (A)
Carcinogens are a specialized form of mutagens that are known to cause cancerous growth.

63. (C)
O is a recessive genotype where both the A and B factors are absent. A and B are codominant which is why a person can have type AB blood.

64. (D)
A sex-influenced trait is not one that is carried on the twenty-third X chromosome, rather it is one in which gender plays a role in expression and it will be found more in either males or females.

65. (A)
An excessive food supply will usually raise carrying capacity whereas the other factors can act (alone or in combination) to hold a population near carrying capacity.

66. (C)
Since species B increases after A but then decreases again when A declines this most likely represents a predator-prey cycle which can persist over time. An example is the apparent cycles between the lynx and snowshoe hare which seem to have a period of about ten years.

67. (E)
Although competition and invasive species can affect other species dramatically, parasites directly exploit their hosts in some way that can be harmful or in rare cases fatal to the host.

68. (B)
Though these factors can act at any population level, their impacts are frequently dependent on the density of individuals within a population (not population size). Highly dense populations can be more susceptible to predators, spread disease and parasites more easily, and place a great deal of stress on natural resources, which increases competition and can even exacerbate the effects of the other factors.

69. (D)
Factors like weather and climate generally act independent of population density. A severe flood can have devastating affects even in a healthy, stable population.

70. (E)
Since all of these factors can influence the size of a population, it is the combination of these plus the birth and death rates that would give a much more complete picture.

71. (B)
While these have had a number of impacts, they have greatly increased the number of people the planet can support because they have increased the overall food supply.

72. (A)
While any one of these factors does affect species survival, it is the loss of habitat that has occurred as human populations have grown which is the most significant threat.

73. (D)
By converting the input of solar energy to carbohydrates, and by taking in carbon dioxide and releasing oxygen in the process, producers such as plants are critical to life on Earth.

74. (B)
A half-life is the time during which 50 percent of the mass of sample is lost. The term of 17190 years is three "half-lives," which means that 6.25 grams will remain.

75. (C)

It is the bombarding of uranium with a neutron that causes the uranium atom to split, thus a single neutron should be shown as $_0^1 n$ in the equation.

76. (B)

This reaction is started from the addition of one neutron in order to split uranium; however, three neutrons are released which can then strike other uranium atoms that will release even more neutrons. This allows the reaction to accelerate very rapidly.

77. (D)

By using water or other materials the actual flow of neutrons is moderated or slowed so that the rapid acceleration and uncontrolled release of energy is prevented.

78. (C)

Because atom B has only six electrons in its outer shell but can hold up to eight, it will seek to fill that shell and would be more likely than A to form a chemical bond in order to gain two electrons.

79. (B)

To form sodium chloride, the Na$^+$ cation which is positively charged will bond with the Cl$^-$ anion, which is negative. These bonds are relatively strong, which is why most ionic compounds (such as sodium chloride, table salt) exist as solids at room temperature and pressure.

80. (B)

The molecules in the right quarter of the table are mostly gases but the majority of the elements are classified as metallic.

81. (A)

The group number is based on the number of electrons found in the outermost electron shell for an element. The noble gases each have eight electrons in their outer shell and thus do not need to fill this shell and are not commonly found reacting with other elements.

82. (C)

In general the elements in the lower portion of the table have more metallic properties than those at the top. There are exceptions to this (groups 7 and 8 are non-metals) but it is useful when trying to interpret the overall patterns in the table.

83. (B)

Within each period or row, elements are arranged by the atomic number which is the number of protons in the nucleus which increases from left to right. In addition, as one moves from left to right within a period the atomic radii decrease due to increasing nuclear charge.

84. (A)

A compound is a substance whose molecules consist of more than one element. Even though H_2 is a molecule with two atoms, it is still only one element and thus not a compound.

85. (A)

A solution is a mixture of compounds in which molecules cannot easily be separated and thus the mixture appears homogeneous throughout. Solutions can be solid, liquid, or gaseous.

86. (D)

Alloys are examples of solutions that are solids. Examples include bronze (copper and tin), and brass (copper and zinc).

87. (D)

The outer-shell electrons are called the "valence" electrons, thus "co-valent" refers to the sharing of these electrons.

88. (D)

For most acid solutions, the solvent is water. In a neutral water solution there are equal concentrations of each of these ions. When placed into water an acid will release H$^+$ ions and an acid solution will have a greater concentration of H$^+$ than OH$^-$. Bases on the other hand will have more OH$^-$.

89. (E)

The pH scale is based upon the negative logarithm of the hydrogen ion concentration. Hence the lower the value, the greater the concentration of hydrogen ions.

90. (E)

There are four oxygen atoms on the right side of the equation so to balance this there need to be four in the reactants on the left side as well.

91. (A)

The law of conservation of matter states that matter cannot be created or destroyed. A balanced equation is one which accounts for all present throughout the reaction.

92. (A)

If we push an object such as a car and make that object move, we have done work by applying a force to move an object. Work is calculated by multiplying the force we apply times the distance over which we apply it.

93. (B)

A car battery is a means of storing potential electrical energy. Until this energy is moving however it remains potential.

94. (D)

As the liquid such as mercury absorbs or loses heat energy it will expand or contract accordingly. Different measurement scales (Celsius, Fahrenheit) are used to note points along the scale where water will freeze or boil.

95. (A)

To determine the amount of energy required you need to rearrange the equation to get the following:

$$\text{Energy} = S \leftrightarrow \text{Mass} \leftrightarrow \text{Temperature Change}.$$

The mass in each case is 100 g and the temperature change in each case is 1°C, thus the sample with the largest specific heat is hydrogen and it will require 1430 joules of energy to raise the sample 1 degree. Hydrogen is much less dense than any of the other substances and thus energy conduction in a 100 g sample is much less efficient and more energy is required to heat the sample.

96. (E)

Since energy cannot be created or destroyed the input of work into both drills has to be accounted for as either mechanical work or as heat. Because the same energy was put into both machines, the one that drilled a deeper hole made more efficient use of the work energy. The less efficient drill will convert more of its energy to heat due to friction than the more efficient drill.

97. (B)

Since entropy is a measure of the disorder or randomness in a system, freezing water slows down the molecules in motion thus increasing the structure and order and decreasing entropy.

98. (E)

As a gas is compressed and the rate of collisions between molecules increases, pressure will increase. Unless controlled in some way (as in this scenario), temperature will generally increase as well.

99. (C)

Velocity is the distance divided by the time so no matter what other measures are made these must be available.

100. (C)

Because the pull of gravity is proportional to mass, acceleration due to gravity is constant for all objects regardless of mass. Without air resistance to slow the feather, the brick and feather fell at the same rate.

101. (D)

Mass remains constant no matter what the gravitational pull. Weight is a measure of the force of gravity on an object and the greater the mass the greater the weight.

102. (E)

Momentum is proportional to mass and velocity and since the mass has doubled, the velocity will change but the momentum is conserved.

103. (A)

The force which pulls an object into a circular motion is called centripetal. In this case the ball's momentum wants to travel in a straight line, but the string pulls inward and the path is circular.

104. (A)

Because energy and mass are equivalent but the speed of light is constant, $E = mc^2$ means that as more energy is put into making an object accelerate, mass must go up. This is true even of objects moving at everyday speeds here on earth. However when the speed of the object begins to approach that of light speed mass increases more and more rapidly and eventually the energy required to move the object would become infinite. As the object became more massive it would become harder to accelerate and some of the energy used to move it would not be converted to kinetic energy but instead would be converted to matter thus increasing the mass.

The increase in mass from moving objects in our everyday life is negligible but near light speed the increase is much greater. Physicists have proven this by accelerating particles to 99 percent light speed.

105. (D)

The gamma rays are very high-energy waves which are used in medicine but can be dangerous to humans because of the impacts their energy has on living tissue.

106. (C)

All of the waves have the same amplitude and as energy increases, wavelength decreases thus frequency must increase in higher-energy waves.

107. (B)

Voltage is the measure of the potential energy from the positive to the negative side of a circuit. This is essentially a measure of the amount of work possible with the amount of energy contained at one point of a circuit such as a battery.

108. (E)

Any component of a circuit has some level of resistance to electron flow, but resistors are used to specifically reduce the voltage by a predetermined level.

109. (B)

Amperes measure the unit of charge moving per second. This is a velocity measurement but is also similar to the amount of water coming out of a hose in a given time.

110. (B)

The result will be two smaller magnets each with a distinct north and south pole.

111. (B)

Unlike the gas giants Jupiter, Saturn, Uranus, and Neptune, the inner planets all have a solid surface and are called terrestrial planets. Pluto appears to be mostly ice.

112. (A)

Using a telescope of his own construction Galileo was able to see that Jupiter had moons that were in orbit around it casting doubt on the Earth-centered view of the universe.

113. (A)

At that speed it will take light four years to reach the Earth. Thus the closest star to our planet (apart from the sun) will appear to us as it existed four years ago.

114. (D)

Sediments dissolved in the water or other medium that are deposited over thousands of years form sedimentary rocks. Sandstone, limestone, and shale are common examples.

115. (B)

Around 78 percent of our atmosphere is nitrogen with only about 21 percent being oxygen. The nitrogen in the atmosphere is largely inert and species needing oxygen have adapted to the 21 percent present.

116. (C)

Humans depend on fresh water and it is a very limited resource on our planet. Ninety-seven percent of the Earth's water is found in the oceans.

117. (A)

The vast majority of the water cycle is driven by the processes of precipitation and evaporation. Water from the oceans and other bodies of water will evaporate, cool, and fall back to earth as precipitation. Some of this precipitation will find its way to the underground aquifers or be taken up by plants while some will end up in ponds, rivers, lakes, or the ocean to be evaporated again.

118. (B)

The Precambrian era lasted approximately four billion years and comprises over 88 percent of the time of Earth's history.

119. (B)

A variety of methods exist for placing a fossil in "relative time" where the general sequence of events can be determined and age may even be estimated. However, to estimate an accurate age of a fossil more precise measures such as radioactive dating are needed.

120. (C)

A greenhouse works on the principle that the sun's rays can pass through the glass but much of the infrared radiation radiated back from the ground does not and hence is trapped by the greenhouse, which raises the temperature. This is the same reason that a car heats up on a hot day. Higher-energy radiation can pass through the glass and heat the surfaces of the car but the heat energy in the form of infrared radiation cannot pass back through the glass windows and is trapped.

Chapter Twenty-Three: Practice Test 3

Time—90 minutes
120 Questions

Directions: Each question below has five lettered answer choices. For each question or phrase, choose the most closely related answer. For multiple questions that refer to the same group of lettered answer choices, each choice can be used more than once, once, or not at all.

Questions 1–2

(A) Chordata
(B) Cnidaria
(C) Porifera
(D) Platyhelminthes
(E) Echinodermata

1. The animal phylum that includes jellyfish and anemones

2. Simple multicellular organisms lacking tissues and organs

Questions 3–5

(A) NAD
(B) ATP
(C) RNA
(D) DNA
(E) AUG

3. A codon for amino acid production

4. The energy currency of the cell

5. The nucleic acid associated with translation

Questions 6–7

(A) Sex-linked
(B) Genotype
(C) Dominant
(D) Phenotype
(E) Heterozygous

6. The set of alleles at a gene locus of homologous chromosomes

7. A gene carried on the X or Y chromosome

Questions 8–10

(A) Nephron
(B) Neuron
(C) Myosin
(D) Cellulose
(E) Glucagon

8. A protein found in muscle

9. The functional unit of the kidney

10. A pancreatic hormone

GO ON TO THE NEXT PAGE

Questions 11–13

    (A) Cystic fibrosis
    (B) Hemophilia
    (C) Sickle-cell anemia
    (D) Huntington's disease
    (E) Down syndrome

11. A sex-linked recessive disorder

12. A defect affecting production of normal hemoglobin

13. A condition caused by non-disjunction of chromosomes during meiosis

Questions 14–15

    (A) Producers
    (B) Herbivores
    (C) Top consumers
    (D) Omnivores
    (E) Decomposers

14. Autotrophic organisms

15. Fungi and bacteria

Questions 16–18

    (A) Tundra
    (B) Taiga
    (C) Savannah
    (D) Desert
    (E) Tropical rain forest

16. A biome characterized by grasslands and large grazers

17. Alpine ecosystems

18. The biome with the greatest biodiversity

Directions: For each of the following questions or incomplete statements, select the best answer or completion from the five options given.

19. Which of the following is NOT a kind of evidence that supports evolutionary theory?

    (A) distribution of organisms on earth
    (B) fossils
    (C) homologous structures
    (D) DNA comparison
    (E) inheritance of acquired traits

Questions 20–21 are based on the following passage.

Microevolution occurs when changes in allele frequency for a particular trait lead to changes within populations. Macroevolution occurs when separate populations of a species become reproductively isolated from one another.

20. Which of the following is an example of microevolution?

    (A) industrial melanism in moths
    (B) sterile hybrids like mules
    (C) geographic isolation
    (D) formation of a new species
    (E) species extinction

21. Which of the following is an example of behavioral reproductive isolation?

    (A) reptiles unable to tolerate disparate environmental conditions
    (B) arthropods with incompatible reproductive structures
    (C) birds with different mating rituals
    (D) trees separated by a mountain range
    (E) incompatible gametes prevent zygote formation

22. While walking in the forest you come across a plant that has frond-like leaves and bears seeds naked on a reproductive structure called a strobilus. What type of plant is it?

    (A) a moss
    (B) a fern
    (C) a palm tree
    (D) a gymnosperm
    (E) an angiosperm

23. What is the most abundant group of terrestrial eukaryotes?

    (A) bacteria
    (B) protozoans
    (C) humans
    (D) birds
    (E) insects

24. Which of the following characteristics is NOT shared by all living things?

    (A) plasma membrane
    (B) cell wall
    (C) DNA
    (D) reproduction
    (E) metabolism

25. Which characteristic is common to all viruses?

    (A) plasma membrane
    (B) cell wall
    (C) DNA
    (D) reproduction
    (E) metabolism

GO ON TO THE NEXT PAGE

Questions 26–28 are based on the following passage.

   Reptiles and land plants such as conifers evolved during the Paleozoic era over 225 million years ago. During the Mesozoic era between 225 and 65 million years ago the phenomenon of continental drift began and progressed. Near the end of the Mesozoic, mass extinction of the dinosaurs and many coniferous plants was followed by the rise of mammals and flowering plants.

26. Based on the above, what might you infer to be true?

    (A) mammals should be similar all over the world
    (B) flowering plants should be similar all over the world
    (C) conifers should be similar all over the world
    (D) the rise of mammals likely led to dinosaur extinction
    (E) the rise of flowering plants likely led to extinction of many conifers

27. What type of evidence best supports the idea that a large asteroid impacted the earth and led to extinction of dinosaurs and many coniferous plants?

    (A) a layer of iridium in the geologic strata of the era
    (B) the distribution of conifers in the world today
    (C) the distribution of dinosaur fossils
    (D) the distribution of mammals in the world today
    (E) the absence of mammals and flowering plants during the Paleozoic

28. Why might an asteroid impact have been more devastating to conifers than flowering plants?

    (A) flowering plants have tougher leaves
    (B) herbivorous dinosaurs fed more on conifers
    (C) conifers have more resistant seeds
    (D) flowering plants reproduce more quickly
    (E) mammals feed more on angiosperm seeds

29. Which of the following organelles contains the cell's genetic information?

    (A) mitochondria
    (B) chloroplasts
    (C) the nucleus
    (D) the endoplasmic reticulum
    (E) the ribosomes

Questions 30–31 are based on the following passage.

   During interphase of the somatic cell cycle of an organism with a diploid chromosome number of 26, DNA replication produces sister chromatids that will divide during anaphase of mitosis. A germ cell from the same organism will undergo meiosis to produce haploid gametes via one round of DNA replication and two rounds of cell division.

30. What will mitosis of one of the organism's somatic cells produce?

    (A) two identical daughter cells with 26 chromosomes each
    (B) two unique daughter cells with 13 chromosomes each
    (C) four identical daughter cells with 26 chromosomes each
    (D) four unique daughter cells with 13 chromosomes each
    (E) four identical daughter cells with 13 chromosomes each

GO ON TO THE NEXT PAGE

31. During the first round of meiosis in the germ cell, genetic material is exchanged between homologous chromosomes. This phenomenon is called

    (A) non-disjunction.
    (B) crossing over.
    (C) independent assortment.
    (D) point mutation.
    (E) frame-shift mutation.

32. A template strand of DNA that codes for production of a series of amino acids has the following sequence of nucleotides: 3'-TACACAGAAGGA-5'. What would the complementary strand of mRNA produced be?

    (A) 5'-UACACAGAAGGA-3'
    (B) 3-AGGAAGACACAT-5'
    (C) 3'-AUGCUGUCUUCC-5'
    (D) 5'-ATGTGTCTTCCT-3'
    (E) 5'-AUGUGUCUUCCU-3'

33. Which is NOT a way materials enter cells?

    (A) osmosis
    (B) facilitated diffusion
    (C) endocytosis
    (D) exocytosis
    (E) active transport

Questions 34–36 are based on the following passage.

A laboratory experiment is set up to study the processes of photosynthesis and respiration. Four test tubes are filled with a pH indicator called phenol red. Under neutral conditions, the indicator is orange, under alkaline conditions it turns red, and under acid conditions it turns yellow. Addition of carbon dioxide to the solution will produce carbonic acid, while removal of carbon dioxide will make the solution more alkaline. The following experimental design is applied:

Tube 1–*Elodea* plants are added and placed in light.
Tube 2–Brine shrimp are added and placed in light.
Tube 3–*Elodea* plants are added and placed in the dark.
Tube 4–Brine shrimp are added and placed in the dark.

34. Which tube(s) would you expect to turn red over time?

    (A) Tube 1 only
    (B) Tubes 1 and 3
    (C) Tube 2 only
    (D) Tubes 2, 3, and 4
    (E) Tubes 2 and 4

35. Which of the tubes would you expect to turn yellow?

    (A) Tube 1 only
    (B) Tubes 1 and 3
    (C) Tube 2 only
    (D) Tubes 2, 3, and 4
    (E) Tubes 2 and 4

36. In which tubes is cellular respiration occurring?

    (A) Tubes 2 and 4
    (B) Tubes 1 and 3
    (C) Tube 2 only
    (D) Tubes 2, 3, and 4
    (E) All tubes

37. Which of the following is NOT an organic compound?

    (A) glucose
    (B) water
    (C) amino acid
    (D) lipid
    (E) nucleic acid

38. What is the primary function of the endocrine system?

    (A) transport of gases and nutrients
    (B) excretion of metabolic wastes
    (C) production of hormones
    (D) immunity and fluid balance
    (E) production of enzymes for digestion

39. What phase of embryonic development is associated with development of three distinct germ layers?

    (A) zygote
    (B) cleavage
    (C) morula
    (D) blastula
    (E) gastrula

40. Plant growth occurs in specific regions called

    (A) collenchyma.
    (B) phloem.
    (C) meristems.
    (D) tracheids.
    (E) stomata.

Questions 41–43 are based on the following passage.

In an experiment studying heredity, a P generation of true-breeding pea plants that produced purple flowers (a dominant characteristic) were cross-pollinated with those that produced white flowers (a recessive characteristic) and 500 offspring were produced in the F1 generation. A member of the F1 generation was allowed to self-pollinate and 400 F2 offspring were produced.

41. Which of the following represents the parental cross?

    (A) $Pp \times Pp$
    (B) $PP \times WW$
    (C) $Pw \times Pw$
    (D) $PP \times pp$
    (E) $PP \times ww$

42. How many white-flowered offspring would you expect in the F1 and F2 generations, respectively?

    (A) 0 and 100
    (B) 250 and 200
    (C) 125 and 300
    (D) 0 and 0
    (E) 250 and 0

43. What percentage of the F2 generation would you expect to be heterozygous for the trait?

    (A) 100 percent
    (B) 75 percent
    (C) 50 percent
    (D) 25 percent
    (E) 0 percent

44. Which of the following occurs in the sacs of the alveoli?

    (A) filtration of metabolic wastes
    (B) exchange of gases
    (C) absorption of nutrients
    (D) production of antibodies
    (E) filtration of lymph

45. What accessory organ is responsible for detoxifying materials in the blood that have been absorbed through the intestines before they enter general circulation?

    (A) the pancreas
    (B) the kidney
    (C) the spleen
    (D) the gall bladder
    (E) the liver

46. A person with type O blood

    (A) has both the A and B antigens on the surface of red blood cells.
    (B) can safely receive transfusions of any blood type.
    (C) does not have any naturally occurring blood type antibodies.
    (D) has both anti-A and anti-B antibodies.
    (E) has only anti-O antibodies.

47. Tay-Sachs disease is a recessive genetic disorder that affects production of an enzyme necessary for fat metabolism in the brain and usually causes death by age 5 for those homozygous for the mutation. Which of the following statements must be true?

    (A) the allele should disappear from the gene pool quickly
    (B) both parents must pass the defective allele to the affected offspring
    (C) at least one parent must show symptoms of the disorder
    (D) the mutated gene codes for many different proteins
    (E) mutation must involve a frame shift to be so serious

Questions 48–49 are based on the following figure.

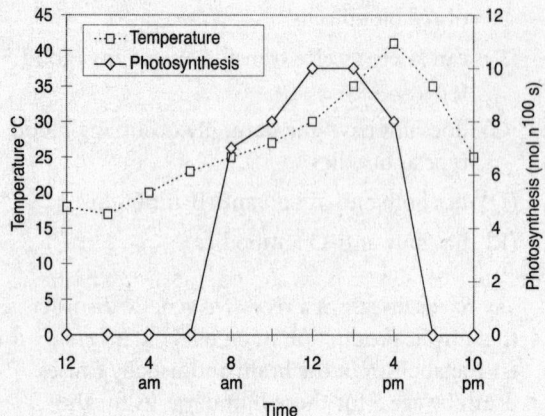

The figure above shows air temperature and the rate of net photosynthesis in plants during the course of single day. For the day shown, the sun rose at 6 am and set at 6 pm.

48. Which of the following statements is FALSE?

    (A) Photosynthesis was inhibited before sunrise and after sunset.
    (B) Temperature was highest at 4 pm.
    (C) Photosynthesis rate was highest between noon and 2 pm.
    (D) Photosynthesis rate increased consistently with temperature.
    (E) Both temperature and photosynthesis rate decreased after 4 pm.

49. Which of the following is NOT a possible explanation for the decreased rate of net photosynthesis from 2 pm until sunset?

    (A) less sunlight to provide energy for photosynthesis
    (B) inhibition of photosynthesis by low temperatures
    (C) increase in photorespiration due to high temperature
    (D) stomatal closure due to water stress
    (E) reduction in RUBISCO activity due to high temperature

50. Which of the following characteristics is NOT associated with a human embryonic development?

    (A) pharyngeal slits
    (B) post-anal tail
    (C) cartilaginous skeleton
    (D) notochord
    (E) oviparity

51. Which of the following is NOT a type of connective tissue?

    (A) blood
    (B) bone
    (C) nerves
    (D) tendons
    (E) adipose (fat)

52. How are nerve impulses transmitted along axons?

    (A) release of neurotransmitters at nodes of Ranvier on the myelin sheath
    (B) interaction between glial cells and dendrites
    (C) electrical signals transmitted at synapses
    (D) depolarization of the axon cell membrane
    (E) interaction of Schwann cells on sensory neurons

53. Peas can be either yellow or green and have smooth or wrinkled surfaces. There is no relationship between the way pea color and pea surface are passed from one generation to the next. This is an example of which phenomenon?

    (A) independent assortment
    (B) codominant alleles
    (C) incomplete dominance
    (D) pleiotrophic effects
    (E) continuous variation

GO ON TO THE NEXT PAGE

54. Which is NOT part of the water cycle?

    (A) transpiration
    (B) evaporation
    (C) precipitation
    (D) condensation
    (E) denitrification

55. Which of the following is NOT an example of a predator-prey relationship?

    (A) mycorrhizal fungi infecting plant roots
    (B) a cow grazing grass
    (C) a spider eating a fly
    (D) a caterpillar eating leaves
    (E) a bobcat eating a rabbit

56. If a population grows exponentially like the human population has done in the past 200 years, what will be the shape of the growth curve?

    (A) a straight diagonal line
    (B) a straight horizontal line
    (C) J-shaped
    (D) S-shaped
    (E) a bell-shaped curve

57. As energy flows from one trophic level to the next higher trophic level in an ecosystem, the amount of available energy

    (A) stays the same.
    (B) increases due to concentration of organic elements.
    (C) increases due to accumulation of biomass.
    (D) decreases due to loss as heat.
    (E) varies depending on the trophic structure of the community.

58. The gradual repopulation of an area by a sequence of plant and animal communities after a disturbance event such as a fire is called

    (A) primary succession.
    (B) secondary succession.
    (C) spontaneous generation.
    (D) restoration ecology.
    (E) primary productivity.

Questions 59–60 are based on the following figure.

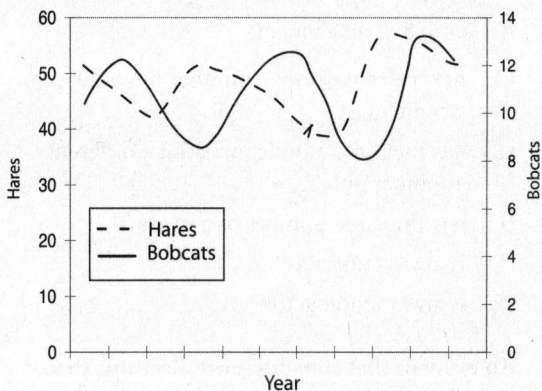

The figure above shows the number of hares and bobcats populating an area from 1970–1980.

59. Which of the following is probably NOT occurring in these populations?

    (A) the number of bobcats depends on the number of hares available as prey
    (B) competition between the hares and bobcats for limited food resources
    (C) the number of hares depends on the number of bobcat predators
    (D) competition between bobcats for limited food resources.
    (E) resource limitation for hares at high population density

GO ON TO THE NEXT PAGE

60. What might you expect to happen if wolves, which also preyed upon hares, were introduced to the system?

    (A) the number of bobcats would increase
    (B) the number of hares would increase
    (C) no change would be expected
    (D) both hare and bobcat numbers would decrease
    (E) the amount of food available at all trophic levels would decrease

61. An isotope of an element

    (A) has the same atomic number but a different atomic mass.
    (B) has the same atomic mass but a different atomic number.
    (C) has the same number of neutrons.
    (D) is always unstable.
    (E) is always radioactive.

62. An element that contains more electrons than protons is

    (A) neutral
    (B) a cation
    (C) an anion
    (D) positively charged
    (E) an isotope

63. Which of the following are examples of electrons and positrons?

    (A) photon strings
    (B) omega waves
    (C) alpha particles
    (D) beta particles
    (E) gamma rays

64. Splitting a heavy atomic nucleus into two smaller nuclei results in

    (A) a fusion reacton.
    (B) a fission reaction.
    (C) alpha particles.
    (D) beta particles.
    (E) gamma rays.

65. Which of the following are high-energy photons?

    (A) photon strings
    (B) omega waves
    (C) alpha particles
    (D) beta particles
    (E) gamma rays

66. If the half-life of radioactive carbon-14 is 5730 years, that means that

    (A) it takes 5730 years for it to be half as radioactive.
    (B) in 11460 years a sample will completely disappear.
    (C) the mass of C-14 present will be reduced by half in 5730 years.
    (D) the radioactivity of C-14 will double in 5730 years.
    (E) the rate of decay will decrease by half in 5730 years.

67. The electron configuration notation $1s^2\ 2s^2\ 2p^6\ 3s^2\ 3p^4$ indicates

    (A) there is one s electron in the first energy shell.
    (B) there are two p electrons in the second energy shell.
    (C) the element has six valence electrons.
    (D) the element has eleven total electrons.
    (E) there are three s electrons in the third energy shell.

GO ON TO THE NEXT PAGE

68. Indicate the number of each type of subatomic particle in a neutral atom of the radioactive isotope $^{60}_{27}$Co and its atomic mass.

	Protons	Neutrons	Electrons	Mass
(A)	33	27	33	60
(B)	27	60	27	87
(C)	27	27	60	54
(D)	60	27	60	87
(E)	27	33	27	60

69. Which of the following form diatomic gases at room temperature?

   (A) halogens
   (B) metals
   (C) nonmetals
   (D) noble gases
   (E) heavy metals

70. Which of the following are very non-reactive elements?

   (A) halogens
   (B) metals
   (C) nonmetals
   (D) noble gases
   (E) heavy metals

71. Which of the following are solid, malleable, and conductive at room temperature?

   (A) halogens
   (B) metals
   (C) nonmetals
   (D) noble gases
   (E) heavy metals

Questions 72–73 are based on the following equation.

$$C_3H_8 + 5O_2 \rightarrow 3CO_2 + ?\ H_2O + heat$$

72. How many molecules of H_2O will be produced by the reaction shown?

   (A) 1
   (B) 2
   (C) 4
   (D) 6
   (E) 8

73. Which of the following statements about the reaction is FALSE?

   (A) it requires activation energy
   (B) it is endothermic
   (C) carbon dioxide is one of the products
   (D) oxygen is one of the reactants
   (E) it is a combustion reaction

74. If you added a strong base such as KOH to a solution, what change would you expect in the solution?

   (A) the pH would increase
   (B) the hydrogen ion concentration would increase
   (C) the solution would become more acidic
   (D) the pH would not be affected
   (E) the KOH would act as a buffer, reducing pH

75. Which type of compound is most likely to dissociate in water?

   (A) a phospholipid
   (B) a protein
   (C) a covalent compound
   (D) an organic compound
   (E) an ionic compound

GO ON TO THE NEXT PAGE

76. If the atomic mass of carbon is 12.0 grams per mole, hydrogen is 1.0 grams per mole, and oxygen is 16, what percentage by mass of glucose ($C_6H_{12}O_6$) is carbon?

    (A) 10 percent
    (B) 20 percent
    (C) 30 percent
    (D) 40 percent
    (E) 50 percent

77. How do catalysts work?

    (A) by giving up electrons to reactants
    (B) by participating in oxidation reactions
    (C) by participating in reduction reactions
    (D) by being used up to form products
    (E) by lowering activation energy of reactions

78. Which of the molecules below is most abundant in the atmosphere?

    (A) N≡N
    (B) O=O
    (C) Cl–Cl
    (D) O=C=O
    (E) H–O–H

79. Which of the molecules shown is polar?

    (A) N≡N
    (B) O=O
    (C) Cl–Cl
    (D) O=C=O
    (E) H–O–H

80. The energy stored in the bonds of molecules is known as

    (A) kinetic energy.
    (B) chemical energy.
    (C) heat.
    (D) mass energy.
    (E) electrical energy.

81. Which is the energy of relativity?

    (A) kinetic energy
    (B) chemical energy
    (C) heat
    (D) mass energy
    (E) electrical energy

82. The energy of random molecular motion is called

    (A) kinetic energy.
    (B) chemical energy.
    (C) heat.
    (D) mass energy.
    (E) electrical energy.

Questions 83–85 are based on the following figure.

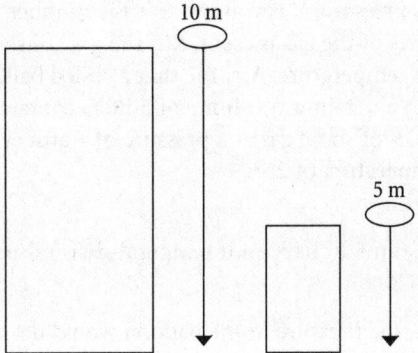

The figure above represents two watermelons of equal mass (1 kg) being dropped from rest (not thrown up or down) from the tops of two buildings. The distance to the ground is 10 meters from the top of the building on the left and 5 meters from the top of the building on the right. The acceleration of gravity is 9.8 m/s². The velocity of each watermelon when it reaches the ground can be calculated as $v = v_0 + at$ where v is the final velocity, v_0 is the initial velocity, a is acceleration, and t is time.

83. If the final velocity of the watermelon on the left was 50 m/s, how long did it take to reach the ground (to the nearest second)?

    (A) 1 second
    (B) 3 seconds
    (C) 5 seconds
    (D) 10 seconds
    (E) 15 seconds

84. Assume that the watermelon dropped from the building on the right took 3 seconds to reach the ground. What was its approximate final velocity?

    (A) 30 meters per second
    (B) 20 meters per second
    (C) 10 meters per second
    (D) 5 meters per second
    (E) 1 meter per second

85. How would these calculations be affected if the mass of the watermelons were doubled?

    (A) The final velocities of both would double.
    (B) The final velocities of both would be reduced by half.
    (C) The time to reach the ground would change but the final velocity would remain constant.
    (D) Both time to reach the ground and final velocity would be affected depending on height of building.
    (E) Changing the mass of the watermelons would not change the calculations.

86. The second law of thermodynamics states that in every energy transformation, some usable energy is lost as heat. Because of this

    (A) the amount of energy in the universe is steadily decreasing.
    (B) the disorder and entropy of the universe is steadily increasing.
    (C) heat is generated in every chemical reaction.
    (D) the amount of heat in the universe is steadily decreasing.
    (E) the entropy of the universe is the only constant.

Questions 87–88 are based on the following passage.

A glass of liquid water left outside freezes during a cold night. The following morning, a film of moisture can be seen on the outside of the glass. By late afternoon, some of the water from the glass has evaporated.

87. What process caused the film of moisture on the outside of the glass?

    (A) condensation
    (B) melting
    (C) sublimation
    (D) evaporation
    (E) crystallization

88. Which of the following shows the correct order of energy transformations that have occurred?

    (A) energy released → energy absorbed → energy released
    (B) energy absorbed → energy absorbed → energy released
    (C) energy released → energy released → energy released
    (D) energy released → energy released → energy absorbed
    (E) energy absorbed → energy absorbed → energy absorbed

89. What does Newton's first law of motion state?

    (A) The greater the force applied to an object, the greater the acceleration.
    (B) The greater the mass of the object, the smaller the acceleration.
    (C) An object will remain in its state of rest if no net force acts upon it.
    (D) The force on an object is equal to the product of its mass and acceleration.
    (E) For every force exerted there is an equal and opposite force at work.

Questions 90–91 are based on the following passage.

The universal gas law is written $PV = nRT$ where P is pressure, V is volume, n is the number of moles of the gas present, R is the gas constant, and T is temperature. Assume that a sealed balloon with a maximum volume of 5 liters contains 0.25 moles of some gas at a pressure of 1 atm at a temperature of 25°C.

90. What might happen if temperature is raised to 30°C?

    (A) the pressure in the balloon would decrease
    (B) the volume of the balloon would increase
    (C) the number of moles of gas in the balloon would increase
    (D) the pressure and volume of the balloon would decrease
    (E) the pressure would increase and the volume decrease

91. Assuming that volume and temperature were held constant, what effect would adding another 0.25 moles of gas to the balloon have?

    (A) it would double the pressure
    (B) it would reduce the pressure by half
    (C) it would increase the pressure by 25 percent
    (D) it would decrease the pressure by 25 percent
    (D) it would quadruple the pressure

92. The resistance of a moving object to change in its state of motion is called

    (A) entropy.
    (B) inertia.
    (C) force.
    (D) mechanics.
    (E) gravity.

GO ON TO THE NEXT PAGE

93. If the gravity of Mars is 0.4 times the gravity of Earth, what would be the mass of an object on Mars that has a mass of 1000 kg on Earth?

    (A) 4000 kg
    (B) 400 kg
    (C) 2500 kg
    (D) 250 kg
    (E) 1000 kg

94. What scientist first put forth the idea that all objects fall to earth with the same acceleration?

    (A) Aristotle
    (B) Newton
    (C) Galileo
    (D) Einstein
    (E) Copernicus

95. What is the unit of electrical charge?

    (A) coulomb
    (B) ohm
    (C) volt
    (D) ampere
    (E) watt

96. The electromagnetic radiation with the longest wavelength is

    (A) ultraviolet.
    (B) radio waves.
    (C) microwaves.
    (D) infrared.
    (E) visible light.

97. The electromagnetic radiation with the highest energy is

    (A) ultraviolet.
    (B) radio waves.
    (C) microwaves.
    (D) infrared.
    (E) visible light.

98. How does sound travel?

    (A) as transverse waves
    (B) as magnetic fields
    (C) as longitudinal waves
    (D) as particles
    (E) as gamma rays

99. When light bends as when passed through water or a prism it is termed

    (A) reflection.
    (B) transmission.
    (C) absorption.
    (D) refraction.
    (E) magnetism.

100. Evidence supporting the big bang theory includes

    (A) the asteroid belt.
    (B) supernovas.
    (C) red dwarfs.
    (D) the red shift.
    (E) black holes.

101. An old very massive star contracted on itself is called

    (A) the asteroid belt.
    (B) a supernova.
    (C) a red dwarf.
    (D) a white dwarf.
    (E) a black hole.

GO ON TO THE NEXT PAGE

Questions 102–104 are based on the following figure.

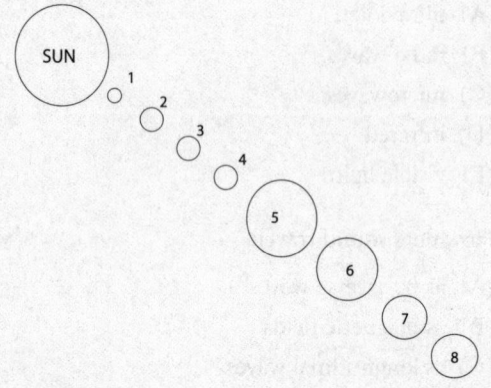

102. Which of the planets labeled above represents the earth?

    (A) 1
    (B) 3
    (C) 4
    (D) 5
    (E) 6

103. Which planet has a highly visible ring?

    (A) 1
    (B) 3
    (C) 4
    (D) 5
    (E) 6

104. Between which two planets does the asteroid belt occur?

    (A) 1 and 2
    (B) 3 and 4
    (C) 4 and 5
    (D) 5 and 6
    (E) 6 and 7

105. Aggregates of frozen material in regular elliptical solar orbits that appear as patches of light with long tails are known as

    (A) asteroids.
    (B) comets.
    (C) sun showers.
    (D) meteorites.
    (E) meteors.

106. The remains of objects from space that have passed through the earth's atmosphere and hit the ground are called

    (A) asteroids.
    (B) comets.
    (C) sun showers.
    (D) meteorites.
    (E) meteors.

107. What is a nebula?

    (A) a diffuse mass of interstellar gas and dust
    (B) a large group of distant galaxies
    (C) an old star contracted upon itself
    (D) the last remnants of the big bang
    (E) the remains of an ancient galaxy

108. What is the main composition of the planet Jupiter?

    (A) lead and zinc
    (B) hydrogen and helium
    (C) liquid iron
    (D) ice
    (E) frozen methane

109. Which is the atmospheric layer rich in ozone?

    (A) thermosphere
    (B) troposphere
    (C) lithosphere
    (D) stratosphere
    (E) hydrosphere

110. Which is the earth's crust and outermost mantle?

    (A) thermosphere
    (B) troposphere
    (C) lithosphere
    (D) stratosphere
    (E) hydrosphere

111. Which is the atmospheric layer closest to the ground?

    (A) thermosphere
    (B) troposphere
    (C) biosphere
    (D) stratosphere
    (E) hydrosphere

112. In general, as altitude increases, temperature and pressure decrease. As temperature decreases, air can hold less water. When water condenses, energy is released and the surrounding air is slightly warmed. On hot, humid days, warm, moist air masses tend to rise into the atmosphere. What happens when a warm, moist air mass rises in the atmosphere?

    (A) clouds form when water condenses at higher altitudes
    (B) the relative humidity of the air decreases as it rises
    (C) the temperature of the air mass increases as it rises
    (D) high pressure builds in the rising air mass
    (E) there is no change in the air mass as it rises

113. What causes rain?

    (A) sudden warming of a cloud causes ice crystals to melt
    (B) rapid vaporization of water from clouds
    (C) sudden cooling of clouds causes rapid condensation
    (D) sudden pressure changes in a cloud literally squeeze water out
    (E) rapid loss of condensation nuclei due to pressure changes

114. Movement of magma from the interior of the earth is known as

    (A) subduction.
    (B) folding.
    (C) tectonics.
    (D) vulcanism.
    (E) a fault.

115. A fracture of the earth's crust that displaces rock is called

    (A) subduction.
    (B) folding.
    (C) tectonics.
    (D) vulcanism.
    (E) a fault.

116. Descent of the edge of one crustal plate under the edge of an adjoining plate is known as

    (A) subduction.
    (B) folding.
    (C) tectonics.
    (D) vulcanism.
    (E) a fault.

117. Global warming is caused by

    (A) loss of long-wave radiation to the atmosphere due to increased albedo.
    (B) increased ultraviolet radiation due to loss of the ozone layer.
    (C) increased cloud cover due to the greenhouse effect.
    (D) retention of infrared radiation by gases such as methane.
    (E) decreased atmospheric moisture due to the greenhouse effect.

118. What is the depositional feature laid down from a stream issuing from a mountain canyon?

    (A) karst
    (B) alluvial fan
    (C) bluff
    (D) cirque
    (E) delta

119. Which is a relatively steep slope at the outer edge of a flood plain?

    (A) karst
    (B) alluvial fan
    (C) bluff
    (D) cirque
    (E) delta

120. Slowing of a stream's velocity leads to deposition of materials at the mouth of a river in a formation bearing what name?

    (A) karst
    (B) alluvial fan
    (C) bluff
    (D) cirque
    (E) delta

END OF TEST. STOP

THE ANSWER KEY APPEARS ON THE FOLLOWING PAGE.

ANSWER KEY

1. B	19. E	37. B	55. A	73. B	91. A	109. D
2. C	20. A	38. C	56. C	74. A	92. B	110. C
3. E	21. C	39. E	57. D	75. E	93. E	111. B
4. B	22. D	40. C	58. B	76. D	94. C	112. A
5. C	23. E	41. D	59. B	77. E	95. A	113. C
6. B	24. B	42. A	60. D	78. A	96. B	114. D
7. A	25. D	43. C	61. A	79. E	97. A	115. E
8. C	26. C	44. B	62. C	80. B	98. C	116. A
9. A	27. A	45. E	63. D	81. D	99. D	117. D
10. E	28. D	46. D	64. B	82. C	100. D	118. B
11. B	29. C	47. B	65. E	83. C	101. E	119. C
12. C	30. A	48. D	66. C	84. A	102. B	120. E
13. E	31. B	49. B	67. C	85. E	103. E	
14. A	32. E	50. E	68. E	86. B	104. C	
15. E	33. D	51. C	69. A	87. A	105. B	
16. C	34. B	52. D	70. D	88. D	106. D	
17. A	35. E	53. A	71. B	89. C	107. A	
18. E	36. E	54. E	72. C	90. B	108. B	

Answers and Explanations

1. (B)
The animal phylum Cnidaria includes jellyfish and anemones. Cnidarians have radial symmetry with tentacles arranged around a simple gut opening. They are almost all aquatic animals and represent one of the earliest phyla of animals, with only two cell layers making up the body wall. Their tentacles contain stinging cells called nematocysts.

2. (C)
The sponges are the simplest animals; they are multicellular but lack more complex organization into specialized tissues or organs.

3. (E)
AUG is a three-base sequence of RNA that codes to initiate protein production with the amino acid methionine.

4. (B)
The high-energy bonds of adenosine triphosphate (ATP) provide the usable form of energy for all living things.

5. (C)
Translation is the production of proteins at the ribosomes using the code transcribed by mRNA from DNA in the nucleus and the amino acids shuttled by tRNA to the ribosomes. DNA only actively participates in the transcription process . . . translation is carried out by RNA.

6. (B)
Although the set of alleles at a locus might be heterozygous, they might also be homozygous, so (E) is not the best answer.

7. (A)
Sex-linked characteristics are carried on the sex chromosomes, X and Y. Most sex-linked characteristics are carried on the X chromosome, which is much larger than the Y.

8. (C)
Myo- is a word root always associated with muscle.

9. (A)
Nephr- is a word root always associated with the kidney and its functional filtering unit, the nephron.

10. (E)
The pancreas produces two hormones that regulate blood glucose levels, insulin and glucagon. Insulin lowers blood glucose levels by getting the body's cells to take glucose out of the blood; glucagon raises blood glucose levels by stimulating the liver to convert glycogen to glucose and release it to the blood.

11. (B)
Hemophilia is a recessive disorder linked to the X chromosome.

12. (C)
Sickle-cell anemia is a recessive hereditary disorder associated with a point mutation on the gene that codes for production of hemoglobin, the protein that carries oxygen in red blood cells.

13. (E)
Non-disjunction leads to aneuploidy, an abnormal number of chromosomes. Down syndrome, a developmental disability, is caused by triploidy (3 copies) of chromosome 21.

14. (A)
Autotrophic organisms are capable of producing their own food energy, usually via the process of photosynthesis. They are the first link in ecosystem food chains, the producers. All of the other kinds of organisms listed are heterotrophic and must get their energy from other organisms.

15. (E)
The fungi and bacteria are the decomposers of the biosphere, converting complex organic molecules down into simpler inorganic compounds, often in the form of gases.

16. (C)

The savannah in Africa and prairie of North America are both grassland biomes that support large grazing animals such as zebras and bison.

17. (A)

Biomes at high altitudes are similar to those at high latitudes, and there is a progression as one moves down a mountain similar to that seen as one moves more toward the equator. The tops of mountains, like the polar regions of earth, are marked by the long, cold winters and small vegetation that characterize the tundra biome.

18. (E)

Because of consistently warm temperatures and heavy precipitation, tropical rain forests are home to more kinds of organisms than any other biome.

19. (E)

Evidence to support evolutionary theory includes biogeographical evidence, the fossil record, and comparative anatomy, physiology, and genetics of organisms. Inheritance of acquired traits was an idea put forth by Lamarck, later proven to be false.

20. (A)

The phenomenon of industrial melanism, an increase in the number of dark moths in areas with trees darkened by pollution, is an example of changes in allele frequency in a population due to adaptive advantages conferred by the trait. Answers (B) and (C) are examples of reproductive isolation, and answers (D) and (E) are examples of macroevolution.

21. (C)

Answer (A) represents adaptive isolation, answer (B) morphological isolation, and answer (D) geographic isolation. Non-viable zygotes (E) represent a form of reproductive isolation unassociated with behavior. The mating rituals are a form of behavioral reproductive isolation.

22. (D)

Mosses and ferns do not produce seeds, and palms are angiosperms, plants that produce seeds enclosed in a vessel. Gymnosperms are naked seeded plants.

23. (E)

Although bacteria outnumber insects, they are prokaryotic organisms. Most protozoans are aquatic, and insects far outnumber both birds and humans.

24. (B)

All living things are cellular and are bounded by a cell membrane, all contain DNA or RNA, all are capable of reproduction, and all use energy via metabolism. Not all living things have cell walls; animals do not, for example.

25. (D)

Often not considered living things, viruses do not have cells or cellular structures or carry out metabolism. Some viruses have DNA, while others have only RNA. All viruses are capable of reproduction (replication) within a host cell.

26. (C)

Given that conifers evolved before the land mass of Pangaea split, one would expect for examples around the world to share characteristics with a relatively recent common ancestor. Since the flowering plants and mammals arose after the split of the continents, they would be less likely to show similarities around the world. Although competition is one possible hypothesis for why dinosaurs became extinct and conifers reduced in number, it is not well supported and in no way can it be inferred from the limited information given.

27. (A)

Only answer (A) can be related to an asteroid as the cause of the mass extinctions during the late Mesozoic. Answers (B) and (C) might provide evidence for other events that occurred during or after the extinction, but they do not point to its cause. Answer (E) provides evidence for when mammals and flowering plants arose.

28. (D)

Answer (A) is incorrect because conifers tend to have tougher, needle-like leaves. (The fact that they are permanent and not deciduous would be a long-term disadvantage under stressful conditions.) All of the other choices except (D) would tend to favor conifers over angiosperms. It is thought that because angiosperms have tough seeds and reach reproductive maturity quickly, they were able to better withstand the stressful environment post impact and then multiply quickly when conditions became more favorable.

29. (C)

The nucleus contains the cell's genetic code in the form of DNA. The chloroplast is associated with photosynthesis in autotrophic organisms, the endoplasmic reticulum produces complex macromolecules, and the ribosomes are the site of protein synthesis. Mitochondria metabolize glucose to produce energy in the form of ATP via cellular respiration.

30. (A)

Mitosis is the process whereby a single cell divides to produce two genetically identical daughter cells with the same number of chromosomes as the parent cell. The somatic cells contain the diploid number of chromosomes, 26 in this example.

31. (B)

Crossing over occurs during synapsis, an event during prophase I during which homologous chromosomes intertwine and sometimes exchange genetic material. Non-disjunction is an error in cell division in which chromosomes don't separate properly, and independent assortment is movement of homologous chromosomes to opposite sides of the metaphase plate. Mutations are changes in the DNA sequences on chromosomes that result in formation of abnormal genes.

32. (E)

When mRNA transcribes the code from a template strand of DNA, it is transcribing the "antisense" strand (3'>-5'). The complementary bases are laid down such that uracil corresponds to adenine and cytosine to guanine.

33. (D)

All of the other choices listed describe movement of materials across the cell membrane; however, exocytosis by definition is movement of materials out of the cell.

34. (B)

Photosynthesis will reduce the amount of carbon dioxide in solution, turning the indicator red. The Calvin cycle, carried out by plants independent of light, also uses carbon dioxide, so tube 3 will turn red as well.

35. (E)

In every tube except tubes 1 and 3, cellular respiration would lead to production of carbon dioxide, which would acidify the solution and turn the indicator yellow. Cellular respiration is also occurring in tube 1, but photosynthesis is using more carbon dioxide than is being produced, making the solution more alkaline. In tube 3 the Calvin "dark" cycle also uses carbon dioxide in cellular respiration.

36. (E)

All of the organisms are respiring.

37. (B)

Organic compounds are those that contain carbon bound to hydrogen and other elements such as oxygen and nitrogen. Water does not contain carbon.

38. (C)

Answer (A) describes the function of the cardiovascular system, answer (B) refers to the urinary system, answer (D) is the function of the lymphatic system, and answer (E) is a sub-function of the digestive system.

39. (E)

Gastrulation is the point at which differentiation of the germ layers occurs. A zygote is a fertilized egg, which undergoes cleavage to form a solid ball of cells called the morula. A blastula is a hollow ball of cells, which will indent, ultimately developing into a gastrula.

40. (C)

Collenchyma is a type of thickened plant tissue that supports the plants, while phloem is vascular tissue used for

transport of sugars. Tracheids are xylem cells and stomata are pores formed by guard cells on leaves. Apical and lateral meristems are the areas of active growth in a plant body.

41. (D)
Dominant alleles for a trait are represented by an uppercase letter; the recessive form is indicated by a lowercase version of the same letter. True-breeding parental generation individuals are homozygous for their trait, dominant or recessive.

42. (A)
In a cross of true-breeding dominant and recessive individuals, all of the F1 offspring would be expected to be heterozygous for the trait and show the dominant phenotype. In the F2 generation, about 1 in 4 would be expected to be homozygous recessive and show the recessive phenotype.

43. (C)
The F2 generation is expected to show a ratio of 1:2:1 homozygous dominant, heterozygous, and homozygous recessive. Although 75 percent of the F2 generation shows the dominant trait, only half are heterozygotes.

44. (B)
The alveoli are the sites of exchanges for oxygen and carbon dioxide in the lungs.

45. (E)
Materials absorbed into the bloodstream from the intestine are shunted to the liver via the hepatic portal vein. One of the primary functions of the liver is detoxification.

46. (D)
ABO blood type is a function of antigenic glycoproteins on the surface of the erythrocytes. People with type A have the A antigen and type B the B antigen. Type ABs have both and type Os have neither. Naturally occurring antibodies to the blood type antigens we lack are the cause of blood transfusion reactions. Type O individuals have anti-A and anti-B and can only safely receive type O blood. There is no anti-O.

47. (B)
Allele frequency would not necessarily change if only homozygotes do not reach reproductive age, particularly if mating is non-random. Both parents must be heterozygous to produce a homozygous recessive offspring, and a homozygous recessive individual is not expected to live to reproductive maturity. Neither parent would show symptoms if the enzyme is produced sufficiently in heterozygotes. Tay-Sachs does in fact involve a point mutation, affecting production of a single amino acid, proving answers (D) and (E) to be false.

48. (D)
Although both photosynthesis and temperature increased for most of the day, after 2 pm temperature continued to rise while photosynthesis rate decreased.

49. (B)
Although photosynthesis can be inhibited by low temperature, clearly that is not the case in this data figure, since temperature is at its highest during the period in question. All of the other explanations are feasible. Reductions in radiant energy might be due to a setting sun or cloud cover, both of which induce stomatal closure. At high temperatures, photorespiration can increase, reducing *net* photosynthesis; in addition, the activity of RUBISCO, an important photosynthetic enzyme, is reduced at temperatures over 40°C. Loss of water during a hot afternoon might also lead to stomatal closure and reduced photosynthesis.

50. (E)
All of the characteristics listed in answers (A)–(D) are associated with human embryos. Oviparity occurs in some fish, amphibians, birds, and a few mammals and involves laying eggs outside the mother's body for complete development.

51. (C)
There are four types of human tissue: epithelial, connective, muscle, and nervous. Since nerves are composed of nervous tissue, one can easily rule it out as a type of connective tissue, which all of the other choices are.

Section Six: The CLEP Natural Sciences Exam
Practice Test 3 Answers and Explanations

52. (D)
Nerve impulses are transmitted along axons when excitation causes sodium channels to open allowing rapid depolarization of the membrane as sodium floods into the cell. Adjacent channels are stimulated to open, sending the impulse down the long axon in a wave.

53. (A)
Mendel found in his work with peas that many genes are passed independently of each other; one has no effect on the other. This is because of independent assortment of homologous chromosomes during the first meiotic division of genes on different chromosomes. Each of the other choices describes interaction of alleles or genes to affect expression of some trait.

54. (E)
Water enters the atmosphere through transpiration and evaporation and comes to earth via precipitation and condensation. Denitrification is part of the nitrogen cycle.

55. (A)
Mycorrhizae are plant-symbiotic mutualists that benefit the plant by helping it get water and nutrients from the soil. Each of the other relationships described involves one organism consuming another, the defining characteristic of a predator-prey relationship.

56. (C)
Until resources become limiting, exponential population growth shows a J shaped curve. Once carrying capacity is reached, death rate increases and an S curve develops.

57. (D)
According to the laws of thermodynamics, all energy transformations increase entropy, a decrease in the amount of usable energy due to loss as heat. Since every link in a food chain represents an energy transformation, there is always a loss of available energy at higher trophic levels.

58. (B)
Succession is the population of an area by various communities of organisms over time; primary succession occurs where no organisms previously existed, such as on a new island or after glacial retreat. Secondary succession is associated with disturbance events and repopulation.

59. (B)
Hare are herbivores and bobcats carnivores, so they would not compete for food resources. All of the other choices might directly or indirectly influence the population of the primary consumers (the hares) and their predators (the bobcats).

60. (D)
Increased predation on hares would be expected to reduce the hare population and increased competition for prey would be expected to reduce the bobcat population. The amount of vegetation available as a food source might actually increase due to reduced consumption by hares.

61. (A)
An isotope of an element has a different number of neutrons but the same number of protons; this affects the mass but not the atomic number of the element. An isotope may be radioactive, but this is not always the case.

62. (C)
An element with more electrons than protons is a negatively charged ion called an anion. A cation is a positively charged ion and an isotope is an alternative form of an element with a different number of neutral particles in the nucleus, which does not affect charge.

63. (D)
Beta particles are tiny radioactive particles that have little effect on the mass of the atom emitting them.

64. (B)
Fission splits heavy nuclei into smaller ones; fusion is the creation of a heavy nucleus from smaller ones, as occurs in stars like the sun. Both processes release energy.

65. (E)
Gamma rays are a form of electromagnetic radiation that results from the redistribution of electric charge within the nucleus of an atom.

66. (C)
Half-life refers to the amount of time it takes for half of the mass of a radioactive isotope to decay.

67. (C)

The configuration shows two s electrons in the first shell ($1s^2$), two s electrons and six p electrons in the second shell ($2s^2$, $2p^6$), and two s electrons and four p electrons in the third shell ($3s^2$ and $3p^4$) for a total of sixteen electrons, six of them valence electrons as they exist in the outermost shell.

68. (E)

The bottom number in front of the abbreviation for the element represents the number of protons in the nucleus (the atomic number). In a neutral atom the number of protons is equal to the number of electrons. The mass number is 60 and protons and neutrons each have a mass of 1 amu. Therefore this isotope has 33 neutrons.

69. (A)

Halogens have seven valence electrons so two atoms often share one electron to fill their outer shells, such as fluorine F_2 and chlorine Cl_2.

70. (D)

The noble or inert gases have full outer electron shells so tend not to react with other elements.

71. (B)

The metals tend to be dense and solid at ambient temperatures and are good conductors.

72. (C)

To balance the equation, eight atoms of hydrogen and ten of oxygen are needed on the right side of the equation. Four water molecules will satisfy both.

73. (B)

The reaction shown is combustion of propane in the presence of oxygen, an exothermic reaction that produces three molecules of carbon dioxide and four molecules of water for every molecule of propane combusted. The reaction requires activation energy; often a spark.

74. (A)

Potassium hydroxide (KOH) is a strong base and in solution will decrease the concentration of free hydrogen ions, thus raising pH, making it more alkaline.

75. (E)

Ionic bonds are loose bonds and ions tend to go into solution in water. The other types of compounds listed have stronger bonds that do not dissociate easily.

76. (D)

The total molecular mass of a mole of glucose is 180 grams ((6×12) + (12×1) + (6×16)). The contribution to the total by carbon is 72 grams (6×12), which is 40 percent of the total.

77. (E)

Catalysts alter the rate of chemical reactions without being changed by the reaction, all of which would occur in choices (A)–(D). Most often, catalysts lower the activation energy for chemical reactions.

78. (A)

Nitrogen makes up about 78 percent of the Earth's atmosphere, oxygen (B) around 21 percent. Carbon dioxide (D) and water (E) are also present in much smaller quantities. Chlorine (C) is rare.

79. (E)

Because of the disproportionate charges in the nuclei of the hydrogen and oxygen atoms in water, the shared electrons spend most of their time orbiting the oxygen atom, producing a more negative charge on that side of the molecule.

80. (B)

Chemical energy is the kind of energy released by exergonic reactions such as combustion reactions or respiration when the bonds of organic molecules such as fossil fuels (or glucose) are broken.

81. (D)

Einstein's theory of special relativity describes the equality of mass and energy at velocities greater than the speed of light ($E = mc^2$).

82. (C)

Heat is the thermal energy associated with molecular motion; the greater the rate of motion, the more heat energy an object has.

83. (C)
To solve this equation, use t from the equation above as the unknown. Since $v_0 = 0$ (the watermelons have zero initial velocity, they are at rest), the equation simply becomes $t = v/a$. Since final velocity $v = 50$ m/s and $a = 9.8$ m/s^2, solving for t becomes 50 m/sec ÷ 9.8 m/sec^2 = 5.1 seconds.

84. (A)
This time one simply multiplies t (3 seconds) × a (9.8 m/s^2) since v_0 is still 0 to get a final v of 29.4 m/s.

85. (E)
Mass is not part of the equation so it would not affect the calculated results. In practice, increased resistance due to more surface area of the watermelons might affect the outcome, but the mass could also effectively be increased without increasing resistance.

86. (B)
Entropy is a measure of the amount of disorder in a system, and with each energy transformation, when energy is "lost," entropy increases. Answer (A) is incorrect because energy is not destroyed, it is merely changing form to heat energy, which is a less available form of energy. Answer (C) is incorrect because some chemical reactions require input of energy. Answers (D) and (E) are both incorrect; the amount of heat in the universe is thought to be increasing along with entropy.

87. (A)
Condensation is a state change from gas to liquid. Water will condense on a surface when that surface is sufficiently cooled to saturate the air; warm air can hold more water than can cool air, so when air is rapidly cooled, water often condenses from it.

88. (D)
When the water's state changed from liquid to solid, molecular motion slowed and energy was released. When atmospheric moisture condensed on the glass, another energy-releasing transformation took place. Evaporation required the input of energy (heat from the sun) to make the state change from liquid to gas.

89. (C)
Answers (A) and (B) are restatements of Newton's second law of motion, given in choice (D). Answer (E) is Newton's third law. Answer (C) puts forth half of Newton's first law, which also states that an object in motion will remain in motion unless some force acts upon it.

90. (B)
All one needs to know here is that if the right side of the equation gets bigger, so must the left side, so as T goes up, so must P and/or V, ruling out answers (A) and (D). Answer (C) is false because more moles of gas cannot spontaneously appear in the sealed balloon. Answer (E) is incorrect because a gas will always occupy as much volume as possible at the lowest pressure possible for a given temperature.

91. (A)
If both volume (V) and temperature (T) are held constant, since R is always constant then doubling the number of moles of gas (n), as is the case in this example, will also double pressure (P).

92. (B)
By definition, inertia is the resistance of an object at rest or in motion to change in its state of rest or motion unless some force acts upon it, as described by Newton's first law of motion.

93. (E)
The mass of an object is not influenced by gravity, only its weight is. Mass is an inherent characteristic. Weight is the mass of an object times the acceleration of gravity, so the weight of the object would be reduced on Mars.

94. (C)
Galileo's ideas contradicted those of Aristotle, which were based on the idea of objects moving toward their natural places. Galileo conducted experiments with balls rolling down inclined planes. Ideas about gravity and motion put forth by Newton and Einstein came much later. Copernicus mainly concerned himself with planetary motion and the relative position of the earth, planets, and stars.

95. (A)
An ohm is a measure of resistance, a volt is the potential difference between oppositely charged poles, an ampere is a measure of electrical current, and a watt is a measure of work that can be done (amperes × volts). The coulomb is based on the charge of a single proton or electron.

96. (B)
Radio waves have the longest wavelength.

97. (A)
The order of short wavelength (high energy) → long wavelength (low energy) for the types of electromagnetic radiation shown is: ultraviolet → visible light → infrared → microwaves → radio waves.

98. (C)
As sound travels, particles in the medium that sound is traveling through vibrate parallel to the direction of energy, thereby producing longitudinal waves.

99. (D)
Refraction is the term for the bending of light waves.

100. (D)
The idea of the big bang gained support when astronomers found that distant galaxies in every direction are going away from us at speeds proportional to their distance, a phenomenon known as the red shift, a displacement of the spectra of distant objects.

101. (E)
When a star ages and contracts, its gravitation field becomes so great that even light cannot escape, creating a so-called "black hole" in space.

102. (B)
Earth is the third planet from the sun.

103. (E)
While other planets have rings, Saturn's are the most visible. It is the sixth planet from the sun.

104. (C)
The asteroid belt consists of thousands of small objects less than 1000 km in diameter that follow separate orbits around the sun in the region between Mars and Jupiter, the fourth and fifth planets from the sun.

105. (B)
The appearance of a comet is due to the fact that as it nears the sun, heating of the frozen material produces a trail of gas and dust. The solar wind pushes the debris away and forms the comet's tail.

106. (D)
A meteoroid is an object moving through space; when it enters the earth's atmosphere and produces a flash, it is termed a meteor, and what's left after it hits the ground is a meteorite.

107. (A)
The word "nebula" in Latin means "cloud." Nebulae come in different forms: planetary nebulae, supernova remnants, and diffuse nebulae. When stars form, they form as a result of a nebula condensing.

108. (B)
Jupiter, the largest of the gas giants, is similar in composition to the sun and is comprised mainly of hydrogen and helium.

109. (D)
The stratosphere is the atmospheric layer immediately above the troposphere and contains ozone, which is responsible for absorbing ultraviolet radiation, protecting life on earth from its damaging effects.

110. (C)
The lithosphere is part of the geosphere (the Earth itself) and not part of the atmosphere.

111. (B)
The lowest layer of the atmosphere is the troposphere.

112. (A)

In the lower atmosphere, as air rises it cools about 1°C for each 100 m increase in altitude. The amount of water it can hold is reduced as it cools. When dew point temperature is reached, water condenses, forming clouds. As the mass rises and is cooled, relative humidity increases (B). Since there is no volume limitation on an air mass in the atmosphere, warm air expands freely, decreasing pressure (D) and lowering temperature (C).

113. (C)

Answer (D) could be a correct alternative, although an apparatus or entity large enough to grasp and firmly squeeze a cloud would have to be found.

114. (D)

Vulcanism is most often associated with volcanoes but by definition refers to any movement of magma near the earth's surface.

115. (E)

Faults form when fractures in the earth forcefully move the crust either horizontally or vertically. Folding (B) is the bending for crustal rocks by compression and uplift.

116. (A)

The plates of the earth's crust are in constant slow motion. When two plates come together, one will be forced down and presumably melt into the earth's magma.

117. (D)

Global warming is an effect of the greenhouse effect. The greenhouse effect occurs when heat energy, mostly long-wave infrared radiation, is trapped by gases such as methane and carbon dioxide in the earth's atmosphere.

118. (B)

Alluvium is any stream-deposited sedimentary material. When such material is deposited from mountain canyons, a characteristic fan shape occurs.

119. (C)

The outer edge of a river's flood plain is usually marked by a clear change in slope that marks the outer limit of erosion and undercutting. There is an abrupt rise to the flat terrain above, forming a ring of bluffs.

120. (E)

Deltas are formed when a relatively fast-moving stream is suddenly slowed, usually when it moves into a lake or ocean. Most of the stream load is dumped in a characteristic deltoid (triangular) pattern.

| SECTION SEVEN |

Computing Your Practice Test Score

Chapter Twenty-Four: Scoring Your Test

Now for the exciting part of the exam—computing your score! The score you obtain on each sample test in this book is an approximate score of what you would get on the actual test. The questions on the actual test are not the exact same questions offered in this book, but they are as close as possible.

Let's recap some of the scoring information from Chapter One. The number of questions you get correct (designated by one point each) is called your *raw score*. Each *correct* multiple-choice answer receives one point, while each *wrong* or *skipped* answer does not receive any points. There are no points subtracted for wrong or skipped answers.

The raw score is adjusted according to a formula specified by the College Board, and the result is your scaled score. Total *scaled scores* on the CLEP exams can range from a 20 to an 80. The American Council on Education's minimum recommended score for CLEP credit is 50.

The College Board has not released the exact scoring guidelines for each test, but you can estimate whether or not you have achieved a passing grade on the sample tests in this book. This does not determine what you will get on the actual test, but it is a good approximation.

To obtain your score for each test, add up the number of questions you got right and place that number over the total number of questions on each test. Complete the following formula to obtain your approximate score:

$$\frac{\text{\# of questions right}}{\text{Total \# of questions on test}} = \text{decimal} \times 100 = \text{percent of the exam you got correct}$$

The percent of the exam that you got correct should be over 70 percent (a grade of C) for you to expect to get a passing grade on the CLEP exam. Again, this is approximate. Remember that practice test conditions are not the same as real test conditions, so don't take your score too literally. But your score should give you a ballpark estimate of how comfortable you are with the material and how well-prepared you are for the exam.

Good luck!

| SECTION EIGHT |

CLEP Resources

A Special Note for International Students

If you are an international student considering attending an American university, you are not alone. Over 600,000 international students pursued academic degrees at the undergraduate, graduate, or professional school level at U.S. universities during the 2004–2005 academic year, according to the Institute of International Education's Open Doors report. Almost 50 percent of these students were studying for a bachelor's or first university degree. This number of international students pursuing higher education in the United States is expected to continue to grow. Business, management, engineering, and the physical and life sciences are particularly popular majors for students coming to the United States from other countries.

If you are not a U.S. citizen and you are interested in attending college or university in the United States, here is what you'll need to get started.

- If English is not your first language, you'll probably need to take the TOEFL® (Test of English as a Foreign Language) or provide some other evidence that you are proficient in English. Colleges and universities in the United States will differ on what they consider to be an acceptable TOEFL score. Because American undergraduate programs require all students to take a certain number of general education courses, all students—even math and computer science students—need to be able to communicate well in spoken and written English.

- You may also need to take the SAT® or the ACT®. Many undergraduate institutions in the United States require both the SAT and TOEFL for international students.

- There are over 3,400 accredited colleges and universities in the United States, so selecting the correct undergraduate school can be a confusing task for anyone. You will need to get help from a good advisor or at least a good college guide that gives you detailed information on the different schools available. Since admission to many undergraduate programs is quite competitive, you may want to select three or four colleges and complete applications for each school.

- You should begin the application process at least a year in advance. An increasing number of schools accept applications year round. In any case, find out the application deadlines and plan accordingly. Although September (the fall semester) is the traditional time to begin university study in the United States, you can begin your studies at many schools in January (the spring semester).

- In addition, you will need to obtain an I-20 Certificate of Eligibility from the school you plan to attend if you intend to apply for an F-1 Student Visa to study in the United States.

KAPLAN ENGLISH PROGRAMS*

If you need more help navigating the complex process of university admissions, preparing for the SAT, ACT, or TOEFL, or building your English language skills in general, you may be interested in Kaplan's programs for international students.

Kaplan English Programs were designed to help students and professionals from outside the United States meet their educational and career goals. At locations throughout the United States, international students take advantage of Kaplan's programs to help them improve their academic and conversational English skills, raise their scores on the TOEFL, SAT, ACT, and other standardized exams, and gain admission to the schools of their choice. Our staff and instructors give international students the individualized attention they need to succeed. Here is a brief description of some of Kaplan's programs for international students:

General Intensive English

Kaplan's General Intensive English classes are designed to help you improve your skills in all areas of English and to increase your fluency in spoken and written English. Classes are available for beginning to advanced students, and the average class size is 12 students.

TOEFL and Academic English

This course provides you with the skills you need to improve your TOEFL score and succeed in an American university or graduate program. It includes advanced reading, writing, listening, grammar, and conversational English. You will also receive training for the TOEFL using Kaplan's exclusive computer-based practice materials.

OTHER KAPLAN PROGRAMS

Since 1938, more than 3 million students have come to Kaplan to advance their studies, prepare for entry to American universities, and further their careers. In addition to the above programs, Kaplan offers courses to prepare for the ACT®, GMAT®, GRE®, MCAT®, DAT®, USMLE®, NCLEX-RN®, and other standardized exams at locations throughout the United States.

Applying to Kaplan English Programs

To get more information, or to apply for admission to any of Kaplan's programs for international students and professionals, contact us at:

Kaplan English Programs
700 South Flower, Suite 2900
Los Angeles, CA 90017, USA
Phone (if calling from within the United States): 800-818-9128
Phone (if calling from outside the United States): 213-452-5800
Fax: 213-892-1360
Website: www.kaplanenglish.com

*Kaplan is authorized under federal law to enroll nonimmigrant alien students. Kaplan is accredited by ACCET (Accrediting Council for Continuing Education and Training).

Word Roots

Knowing roots of words can help you in two ways. First, instead of learning one word at a time, you can learn a whole group of words that contain a certain root. They'll be related in meaning, so if you remember one, it will be easier for you to remember others. Second, roots can often help you decode an unknown word. If you recognize a familiar root, you can get a good enough idea of the word to answer the question.

A, AN—not, without
amoral, atrophy, asymmetrical, anarchy, anesthetic

AB, A—from, away, apart
abnormal, abdicate, ablution, abnegate, absolve, abstemious, abstruse, annul, avert

AC, ACR—sharp, sour
acid, acerbic, exacerbate, acute, acrimony

AD, A—to, toward
adhere, adjacent, adjunct, admonish, adroit, adumbrate, accretion, accertion, alleviate, aspire, assail, assonance, attest

ALI, ALTR—another
alias, alienate, inalienable, altruism

AM, AMI—love
amorous, amicable, amiable, amity

AMBI, AMPHI—both
ambiguous, ambivalent, ambidextrous, amphibious

AMBL, AMBUL—walk
amble, ambulatory, perambulator, somnambulist

ANIM—mind, spirit, breath
animal, animosity, unanimous, magnanimous

ANN, ENN—year
annual, annuity, biennial, perennial

ANTE, ANT—before
antecedent, antediluvian, antiquated, anticipate

ANTHROP—human
anthropology, philanthropy

ANTI, ANT—against, opposite
antidote, antithesis, antacid, antagonist, antonym

AUD—hear
audio, audience, audition

AUTO—self
autobiography, autocrat, autonomous

BELLI, BELL—war
belligerent, bellicose, antebellum, rebellion

BENE, BEN—good
benevolent, benefactor, beneficent, benign

BI—two
bicycle, bisect, bilateral, bilingual, biped

BIBLIO—book
Bible, bibliography, bibliophile

BIO—life
biography, biology, amphibious, symbiotic, macrobiotics

BURS—money, purse
reimburse, disburse, bursar

CAD, CAS, CID—happen, fall
accident, cadence, cascade, deciduous

CAP, CIP—head
captain, decapitate, precipitate, recapitulate

CARN—flesh
carnal, carnage, incarnate

CAP, CAPT, CEPT, CIP—take, hold, seize
capable, capacious, captivate, deception, intercept, inception, anticipate, emancipation

CED, CESS—yield, go
cease, cessation, incessant, cede, precede, accede

CHROM—color
chrome, chromatic, monochrome

CHRON—time
chronology, chronic, anachronism

CIDE—murder
suicide, homicide, regicide, patricide

CIRCUM—around
circumference, circumlocution, circumspect, circumvent

CLIN, CLIV—slope
incline, declivity, proclivity

CLUD, CLUS, CLAUS, CLOIS—shut, close
conclude, reclusive, claustrophobia, cloister, preclude, occlude

CO, COM, CON—with, together
coeducation, coagulate, coalesce, coerce, collateral, commodious, complaint, concord, congenial, congenital

COGN, GNO—know
recognize, cognition, diagnosis, agnostic, prognosis

CONTRA—against
controversy, incontrovertible, contravene

CORP—body
corpse, corporeal, corpulence

COSMO, COSM—world
cosmopolitan, cosmos, microcosm, macrocosm

CRAC, CRAT—rule, power
democracy, bureaucracy, autocrat, aristocrat

CRED—trust, believe
incredible, credulous, credence

CRESC, CRET—grow
crescent, crescendo, accretion

CULP—blame, fault
culprit, culpable, inculpate, exculpate

CURR, CURS—run
current, concur, cursory, precursor, incursion

DE—down, out, apart
depart, debase, debilitate, defamatory, demur

DEC—ten, tenth
decade, decimal, decathlon, decimate

DEMO, DEM—people
democrat, demographics, demagogue, epidemic

DI, DIURN—day
diary, quotidian, diurnal

DIA—across
diagonal, diatribe, diaphanous

DIC, DICT—speak
abdicate, diction, indict, verdict

DIS, DIF, DI—not, apart, away
disaffected, disband, disbar, distend, differentiate, diffidence, diffuse, digress, divert

DOC, DOCT—teach
docile, doctrine, doctrinaire

DOL—pain
condolence, doleful, dolorous, indolent

DUC, DUCT—lead
seduce, induce, conduct, viaduct, induct

EGO—self
ego, egoist, egocentric

EN, EM—in, into
enter, entice, encumber, embroil, empathy

ERR—wander
erratic, aberration, errant

EU—well, good
eulogy, euphemism, eurythmics, euthanasia

EX, E—out, out of
exit, exacerbate, excerpt, excommunicate, elicit, egress, egregious

FAC, FIC, FECT, FY, FEA—make, do
factory, facility, benefactor, malefactor, fiction, fictive, rectify, vilify, feasible

FAL, FALS—deceive
infallible, fallacious, false

FERV—boil
fervent, fervid, effervescent

FID—faith, trust
confident, diffidence, perfidious, fidelity

FLU, FLUX—flow
fluent, affluent, superfluous, flux

FORE—before
forecast, foreboding, forestall

FRAG, FRAC—break
fragment, fracture, refract

FUS—pour
profuse, infusion, effusive, diffuse

GEN—birth, class, kin
generation, congenital, homogeneous, ingenious, engender

GRAD, GRESS—step
graduate, gradual, retrograde, ingress, egress

GRAPH, GRAM—writing
biography, bibliography, epigram

GRAT—pleasing
grateful, gratitude, gratuitous, gratuity

GRAV, GRIEV—heavy
grave, gravity, aggrieve, grievous

GREG—crowd, flock
segregate, gregarious, aggregate

HABIT, HIBIT—have, hold
habit, cohabit, habitat, inhibit

HAP—by chance
happen, haphazard, hapless, mishap

HELIO, HELI—sun
heliocentric, heliotrope, aphelion, perihelion, helium

HETERO—other
heterosexual, heterogeneous, heterodox

HOL—whole
holocaust, catholic, holistic

HOMO—same
homosexual, homogenize, homogeneous, homonym

HOMO—man
homo sapiens, homicide, bonhomie

HYDR—water
hydrant, hydrate, dehydration

HYPER—too much, excess
hyperactive, hyperbole, hyperventilate

HYPO—too little, under
hypodermic, hypothermia, hypochondria

IN, IG, IL, IM, IR—not
incorrigible, insomnia, interminable, incessant, ignorant, ignominious, ignoble, illicit, illimitable, immaculate, immutable, impertinent, improvident, irregular

IN, IL, IM, IR—in, on, into
invade, inaugurate, incandescent, illustrate, imbue, immerse, implicate, irrigate, irritate

INTER—between, among
intercede, intercept, interdiction, interject

INTRA, INTR—within
intrastate, intravenous, intramural, intrinsic

IT, ITER—between, among
transit, itinerant, transitory, reiterate

JECT, JET—throw
eject, interject, abject, trajectory, jettison

JOUR—day
journal, adjourn, sojourn

JUD—judge
judge, judicious, prejudice, adjudicate

JUNCT, JUG—join
junction, adjunct, injunction

JUR—swear, law
jury, abjure, perjure, jurisprudence

LAT—side
lateral, collateral, unilateral

LAV, LAU, LU—wash
lavatory, laundry, ablution, antediluvian

LEG, LEC, LEX—read, speak
legible, lecture, lexicon

LEV—light
elevate, levitate, levity, alleviate

LIBER—free
liberty, liberal, libertarian, libertine

LIG, LECT—choose, gather
eligible, elect, select

LIG, LI, LY—bind
ligament, oblige, religion, liable, liaison, lien, ally

LING, LANG—tongue
lingo, language, linguistics, bilingual

LITER—letter
literate, alliteration, literal

LITH—stone
monolith, lithograph, megalith

LOQU, LOC, LOG—speech, thought
eloquent, loqucaious, colloquial, circumlocution, monologue, dialogue

LUC, LUM—light
lucid, elucidate, pellucid, translucent, illuminate

LUD, LUS—play
ludicrous, allude, delusion

MACRO—great
macrocosm, macrobiotics

MAG, MAJ, MAS, MAX—great
magnify, magnanimous, magnate, magnitude, majesty, master, maximum

MAL—bad
malady, maladroit, malevolent, malodorous

MAN—hand
manual, manuscript, manifest

MAR—sea
submarine, marine, maritime

MATER, MATR—mother
maternal, matron, matrilineal

MEDI—middle
intermediary, medieval, mediate

MEGA—great
megaphone, megalomania, megaton, megalith

MEM, MEN—remember
memory, memento, memorabilia, reminisce

METER, METR, MENS—measure
meter, thermometer, commensurate

MICRO—small
microscope, microorganism, microcosm, microbe

MIS—wrong, bad, hate
misunderstand, misapprehension, misconstrue, mishap

MIT, MISS—send
transmit, emit, missive

MOLL—soft
mollify, emollient, mollusk

MON, MONIT—warn
admonish, monitor, premonition

MONO—one
monologue, monotonous, monogamy

MOR—custom, manner
moral, mores, morose

MOR, MORT—dead
morbid, moribund, mortal, amortize

MORPH—shape
amorphous, anthropomorphic, morphology

MOV, MOT, MOB, MOM—move
remove, motion, mobile, momentum, momentous

MUT—change
mutate, mutability, immutable, commute

NAT, NASC—born
native, nativity, cognate, nascent, renascent, renaissance

NAU, NAV—ship, sailor
nautical, nauseous, navy, circumnavigate

NEG—not, deny
negative, abnegate, renege

NEO—new
neoclassical, neophyte, neologism, neonate

NIHIL—none, nothing
annihilation, nihilism

NOM, NYM—name
nominate, nomenclature, nominal, synonym, anonymity

NOX, NIC, NEC, NOC—harm
obnoxious, internecine, innocuous

NOV—new
novelty, innovation, novitiate

NUMER—number
numeral, numerous, innumerable, enumerate

OB—against
obstruct, obdurate, obsequious, obtrusive

OMNI—all
omnipresent, omnipotent, omniscient, omnivorous

ONER—burden
onerous, exonerate

OPER—work
operate, cooperate, inoperable

PAC—peace
pacify, pacifist, pacific

PALP—feel
palpable, palpitation

PAN—all
panorama, panacea, pandemic, panoply

PATER, PATR—father
paternal, paternity, patriot, compatriot, expatriate

PATH, PASS—feel, suffer
sympathy, antipathy, pathos, impassioned

PEC—money
pecuniary, impecunious, peculation

PED, POD—foot
pedestrian, pediment, quadruped, tripod

PEL, PULS—drive
compel, compelling, expel, propel, compulsion

PEN—almost
peninsula, penultimate, penumbra

PEND, PENS—hang
pendant, pendulous, suspense, propensity

PER—through, by, for, throughout
perambulator, percipient, perfunctory, pertinacious

PER—against, destruction
perfidious, pernicious, perjure

PERI—around
perimeter, periphery, perihelion, peripatetic

PET—seek, go toward
petition, impetus, impetuous, petulant, centripetal

PHIL—love
philosopher, philanderer, philanthropy, philology

PHOB—fear
phobia, claustrophobia, xenophobia

PHON—sound
phonograph, megaphone, phonics

PLAC—calm, please
placate, implacable, placid, complacent

PON, POS—put, place
postpone, proponent, juxtaposition, depose

PORT—carry
portable, deportment, rapport

POT—drink
potion, potable

POT—power
potential, potent, impotent, potentate, omnipotence

PRE—before
precede, precipitate, premonition, preposition

PRIM, PRI—first
prime, primary, primordial, pristine

PRO—ahead, forth
proceed, proclivity, protestation, provoke

PROTO—first
prototype, protagonist, protocol

PROX, PROP—near
approximate, propinquity, proximity

PSEUDO—false
pseudoscientific, pseudonym

PYR—fire
pyre, pyrotechnics, pyromania

QUAD, QUAR, QUAT—four
quadrilateral, quadrant, quarter, quarantine

QUES, QUER, QUIS, QUIR—question
quest, inquest, query, querulous, inquisitive, inquiry

QUIE—quiet
disquiet, acquiesce, quiescent, requiem

QUINT, QUIN—five
quintuplets, quintessence

RADI, RAMI—branch
radiate, radiant, eradicate, ramification

RECT, REG—straight, rule
rectangle, rectitude, rectify, regular

REG—king, rule
regal, regent, interregnum

RETRO—backward
retrospective, retroactive, retrograde

RID, RIS—laugh
ridiculous, deride, derision

ROG—ask
interrogate, derogatory, arrogant

RUD—rough, crude
rude, erudite, rudimentary

RUPT—break
disrupt, interrupt, rupture

SACR, SANCT—holy
sacred, sacrilege, sanction, sacrosanct

SCRIB, SCRIPT, SCRIV—write
scribe, ascribe, script, manuscript, scrivener

SE—apart, away
separate, segregate, secede, sedition

SEC, SECT, SEG—cut
sector, dissect, bisect, intersect, segment, secant

SED, SID—sit
sedate, sedentary, supersede, reside, residence

SEM—seed, sow
seminar, seminal, disseminate

SEN—old
senior, senile, senescent

SENT, SENS—feel, think
sentiment, nonsense, consensus, sensual

SEQU, SECU—follow
sequence, sequel, subsequent, consecutive

SIM, SEM—similar, same
similar, verisimilitude, semblance, dissemble

SIGN—mark, sign
signal, designation, assignation

SIN—curve
sine curve, sinuous, insinuate

SOL—sun
solar, parasol, solarium, solstice

SOL—alone
solo, solitude, soliloquy, solipsism

SOMN—sleep
insomnia, somnolent, somnambulist

SON—sound
sonic, consonance, sonorous, resonate

SOPH—wisdom
philosopher, sophistry, sophisticated, sophomoric

SPEC, SPIC—see, look
spectator, retrospective, perspective, perspicacious

SPER—hope
prosper, prosperous, despair, desperate

SPERS, SPAR—scatter
disperse, sparse, aspersion, disparate

SPIR—breathe
respire, inspire, spiritual, aspire, transpire

STRICT, STRING—bind
stricture, constrict, stringent, astringent

STRUCT, STRU—build
structure, obstruct, construe

SUB—under
subconscious, subjugate, subliminal, subpoena

SUMM—highest
summit, summary, consummate

SUPER, SUR—above
supervise, supercilious, superfluous, insurmountable, surfeit

SURGE, SURRECT—rise
surge, resurgent, insurgent, insurrection

SYN, SYM—together
synthesis, sympathy, symposium, symbiosis

TACIT, TIC—silent
tacit, taciturn, reticent

TACT, TAG, TANG—touch
tact, tactile, contagious, tangent, tangential, tangible

TEN, TIN, TAIN—hold, twist
detention, tenable, pertinacious, retinue, retain

TEND, TENS, TENT—stretch
intend, distend, tension, tensile, ostensible, contentious

TERM—end
terminal, terminus, terminate, interminable

TERR—earth, land
terrain, terrestrial, extraterrestrial, subterranean

TEST—witness
testify, attest, testimonial, protestation

THE—god
atheist, theology, apotheosis, theocracy

THERM—heat
thermometer, thermal, thermonuclear, hypothermia

TIM—fear, frightened
timid, intimidate, timorous

TOP—place
topic, topography, utopia

TORT—twist
distort, extort, tortuous

TORP—stiff, numb
torpedo, torpid, torpor

TOX—poison
toxic, toxin, intoxication

TRACT—draw
tractor, intractable, protract

TRANS—across, over, through, beyond
transport, transgress, transient, transitory, translucent

TREM, TREP—shake
tremble, tremor, trepidation, intrepid

TURB—shake
disturb, turbulent, perturbation

UMBR—shadow
umbrella, umbrage, adumbrate, penumbra

UNI, UN—one
unify, unilateral, unanimous

URB—city
urban, suburban, urbane

VAC—empty
vacant, evacuate, vacuous

VAL, VAIL—value, strength
valid, valor, ambivalent, convalescence, avail

VEN, VENT—come
convene, intervene, venue, convention, adventitious

VER—true
verify, verity, verisimilitude, verdict

VERB—word
verbal, verbose, verbiage, verbatim

VERT, VERS—turn
avert, convert, revert, incontrovertible, divert, aversion

VICT, VINC—conquer
victory, conviction, evict, evince, invincible

VID, VIS—see
evident, vision, visage, supervise

VIL—base, mean
vile, vilify, revile

VIV, VIT—life
vivid, vital, convivial, vivacious

VOC, VOK, VOW—call, voice
vocal, equivocate, invoke, avow

VOL—wish
voluntary, malevolent, benevolent, volition

VOLV, VOLUT—turn, roll
revolve, evolve, convoluted

VOR—eat
devour, carnivore, omnivorous, voracious

Vocabulary Word List

In general, the very best way to improve your vocabulary is to read. Choose challenging, college-level material. If you encounter an unknown word, put it on a flashcard or in your vocabulary notebook. Memorizing the words on the following list can help. Here are some techniques for memorizing words.

1. Learn words in groups. You can group words by a common root they contain (see the Root List for some examples), or you can group words together if they are related in meaning (i.e. word families). Memorizing words this way may help you to remember them.
2. Use flashcards. Write down new words or word groups and run through them when you have a few minutes to spare. Put one new word or word group on one side of a 3 × 5 card and put a short definition or definitions on the back.
3. Make a vocabulary notebook. List words in one column and their definitions in another. Test yourself. Cover up the meanings, and see which words you can define from memory. Make a sample sentence using each word in context.
4. Think of hooks that lodge a new word in your mind—create visual images of words.
5. Use rhymes, pictures, songs, and any other devices that help you remember words.

To get the most out of your remaining study time, use the techniques that work for you, and stick with them.

ABANDON

noun (uh baan duhn)

total lack of inhibition

The flamenco dancer performed with complete *abandon.*

ABATE

verb (uh bayt)

to decrease, to reduce

My hunger *abated* when I saw how filthy the chef's hands were.

ABET

verb (uh beht)

to aid; to act as an accomplice

While Derwin robbed the bank, Marvin *abetted* his friend by pulling up the getaway car.

ABJURE

verb (aab joor)

to renounce under oath; to abandon forever; to abstain from

After having been devout for most of his life, he suddenly *abjured* his beliefs, much to his family's disappointment.

ABNEGATE

verb (aab nih gayt)

to give up; to deny to oneself

After his retirement, the former police commissioner found it difficult to *abnegate* authority.

ABORTIVE

adj (uh bohr tihv)

ending without results

Her *abortive* attempt to swim the full five miles left her frustrated.

ABROGATE

verb (aab ruh gayt)

to annul; to abolish by authoritative action

The president's job is to *abrogate* any law that fosters inequality among citizens.

ABSCOND

verb (aab skahnd)

to leave quickly in secret

The criminal *absconded* during the night with all of his mother's money.

ABSTEMIOUS

adj (aab stee mee uhs)

done sparingly; consuming in moderation

The spa served no sugar or wheat, but the clients found the retreat so calm that they didn't mind the *abstemious* rules.

ACCEDE

verb (aak seed)

to express approval, to agree to

Once the mayor heard the reasonable request, she happily *acceded* to the proposal.

ACCLIVITY

noun (uh klihv ih tee)

an incline or upward slope, the ascending side of a hill

We were so tired from hiking that by the time we reached the *acclivity*, it looked more like a mountain than a hill.

ACCRETION

noun (uh kree shuhn)

a growth in size, an increase in amount

The committee's strong fund-raising efforts resulted in an *accretion* in scholarship money.

ACME

noun (aak mee)

the highest level or degree attainable

Just when he reached the *acme* of his power, the dictator was overthrown.

ACTUATE

verb (aak choo ayt)

to put into motion, to activate; to motivate or influence to activity

The leaders rousing speech *actuated* the crowd into a peaceful protest.

ACUITY

noun (uh kyoo ih tee)

sharp vision or perception characterized by the ability to resolve fine detail

With unusual *acuity*, she was able to determine that the masterpiece was a fake.

ACUMEN

noun (aak yuh muhn) (uh kyoo muhn)

sharpness of insight, mind, and understanding; shrewd judgment

The investor's financial *acumen* helped him to select high-yield stocks.

ADAMANT
adj (<u>aad</u> uh muhnt) (<u>aad</u> uh mihnt)

stubbornly unyielding

She was *adamant* about leaving the restaurant after the waiter was rude.

ADEPT
adj (uh <u>dehpt</u>)

extremely skilled

She is *adept* at computing math problems in her head.

ADJUDICATE
verb (uh <u>jood</u> ih kayt)

to hear and settle a matter; to act as a judge

The principal *adjudicated* the disagreement between two students.

ADJURE
verb (uh <u>joor</u>)

to appeal to

The criminal *adjured* to the court for mercy.

ADMONISH
verb (aad <u>mahn</u> ihsh)

to caution or warn gently in order to correct something

My mother *admonished* me about my poor grades.

ADROIT
adj (uh <u>droyt</u>)

skillful; accomplished; highly competent

The *adroit* athlete completed even the most difficult obstacle course with ease.

ADULATION
noun (<u>aaj</u> juh lay shuhn)

excessive flattery or admiration

The *adulation* she showed her professor seemed insincere; I suspected she really wanted a better grade.

ADUMBRATE
verb (<u>aad</u> uhm brayt) (uh <u>duhm</u> brayt)

to give a hint or indication of something to come

Her constant complaining about the job *adumbrated* her intent to leave.

AERIE
noun (ayr ee) (eer ee)
a nest built high in the air; an elevated, often secluded, dwelling
Perched high among the trees, the eagle's *aerie* was filled with eggs.

AFFECTED
adj (uh fehk tihd)
phony, artificial
The *affected* hairdresser spouted French phrases, though she had never been to France.

AGGREGATE
noun (aa grih giht)
a collective mass, the sum total
An *aggregate* of panic-stricken customers mobbed the bank, demanding their life savings.

ALGORITHM
noun (aal guh rith uhm)
an established procedure for solving a problem or equation
The accountant uses a series of *algorithms* to determine the appropriate tax bracket.

ALIMENTARY
adj (aal uh mehn tuh ree) (aal uh mehn tree)
pertaining to food, nutrition, or digestion
After a particularly good meal, Sherlock turned to his companion and exclaimed, "I feel quite good, very well fed. It was *alimentary* my dear Watson."

ALLAY
verb (uh lay)
to lessen, ease, reduce in intensity
Trying to *allay* their fears, the nurse sat with them all night.

AMITY
noun (aa mih tee)
friendship, good will
Correspondence over the years contributed to a lasting *amity* between the women.

AMORPHOUS
adj (ay mohr fuhs)
having no definite form
The Blob featured an *amorphous* creature that was constantly changing shape.

ANIMUS

noun (<u>aan</u> uh muhs)

a feeling of animosity or ill will

Though her teacher had failed her, she displayed no *animus* toward him.

ANODYNE

noun (<u>aan</u> uh dyen)

a source of comfort; a medicine that relieves pain

The sound of classical music is usually just the *anodyne* I need after a tough day at work.

ANOMALY

noun (uh <u>nahm</u> uh lee)

a deviation from the common rule, something that is difficult to classify

Among the top-ten albums of the year was one *anomaly*—a compilation of polka classics.

ANTHROPOMORPHIC

adj (aan thruh poh <u>mohr</u> fihk)

suggesting human characteristics for animals and inanimate things

Many children's stories feature *anthropomorphic* animals such as talking wolves and pigs.

ANTIQUATED

adj (<u>aan</u> tih kway tihd)

too old to be fashionable or useful

Next to her coworker's brand-new model, Marisa's computer looked *antiquated*.

APHORISM

noun (<u>aa</u> fuhr ihz uhm)

a short statement of a principle

The country doctor was given to such *aphorisms* as "Still waters run deep."

APLOMB

noun (uh <u>plahm</u>) (uh <u>pluhm</u>)

self-confident assurance; poise

For such a young dancer, she had great *aplomb*, making her perfect to play the young princess.

APOSTATE

noun (uh <u>pahs</u> tayt)

one who renounces a religious faith

So that he could divorce his wife, the king scoffed at the church doctrines and declared himself an *apostate*.

APPOSITE

adj (aap puh ziht)

strikingly appropriate or well adapted

The lawyer presented an *apposite* argument upon cross-examining the star witness.

APPRISE

verb (uh priez)

to give notice to, inform

"Thanks for *apprising* me that the test time has been changed," said Emanuel.

APPROPRIATE

verb (uh proh pree ayt)

to assign to a particular purpose, allocate

The fund's manager *appropriated* funds for the clean-up effort.

ARABLE

adj (aa ruh buhl)

suitable for cultivation

The overpopulated country desperately needed more *arable* land.

ARCANE

adj (ahr kayn)

secret, obscure; known only to a few

The *arcane* rituals of the sect were passed down through many generations.

ARCHIPELAGO

noun (ahr kuh pehl uh goh)

a large group of islands

Between villages in the Stockholm *archipelago*, boat taxis are the only form of transportation.

ARREARS

noun (uh reerz)

unpaid, overdue debts or bills; neglected obligations

After the expensive lawsuit, Dominic's accounts were in *arrears*.

ARROGATE

verb (aa ruh gayt)

to claim without justification; to claim for oneself without right

Lynn watched in astonishment as her boss *arrogated* the credit for her brilliant work on the project.

ASKANCE

adv (uh skaans)

with disapproval; with a skeptical sideways glance

She looked *askance* at her son's failing report card as he mumbled that he had done all the schoolwork.

ASSENT

verb (uh sehnt)

to agree, as to a proposal

After careful deliberation, the CEO *assented* to the proposed merger.

ATAVISTIC

adj (aat uh vihs tik)

characteristic of a former era, ancient

After spending three weeks on a desert island, Roger became a survivalist with *atavistic* skills that helped him endure.

AUTOCRAT

noun (aw toh kraat)

a dictator

Mussolini has been described as an *autocrat* who tolerated no opposition.

AVER

verb (uh vuhr)

to declare to be true, to affirm

"Yes, he was wearing a mask," the witness *averred*.

AVUNCULAR

adj (ah vuhng kyuh luhr)

like an uncle in behavior, especially in kindness and warmth

The coach's *avuncular* style made him well-liked.

AWRY

adv (uh rie)

crooked, askew, amiss

Something must have gone *awry* in the computer system because some of my files are missing.

BALK

verb (bawk)

to stop short and refuse to go on

When the horse *balked* at jumping over the high fence, the rider was thrown off.

BALLAST

noun (baal uhst)

a structure that helps to stabilize or steady

Communication and honesty are the true *ballasts* of a good relationship.

BEATIFIC

adj (bee uh tihf ihk)

displaying calmness and joy, relating to a state of celestial happiness

After spending three months in India, she had a *beatific* peace about her.

BECALM

verb (bih kahm)

to stop the progress of, to soothe

The warm air *becalmed* the choppy waves.

BECLOUD

verb (bih klowd)

to make less visible, to obscure, or blur

Her ambivalence about the long commute *beclouded* her enthusiasm about the job.

BEDRAGGLE

adj (bih draag uhl)

soiled, wet and limp; dilapidated

The child's *bedraggled* blanket needed a good cleaning.

BEGET

verb (bih geht)

to produce, especially as an effect or outgrowth; to bring about

The mayor believed that finding petty offenders would help reduce serious crime because, he argued, small crimes *beget* big crimes.

BEHEMOTH

noun (buh hee muhth)

something of monstrous size or power; huge creature

The budget became such a *behemoth* that observers believed the film would never make a profit.

BENEFICENT

adj (buh nehf ih sent)

pertaining to an act of kindness

The *beneficent* man donated the money anonymously.

BERATE
verb (bih rayt)

to scold harshly

When my manager found out I had handled the situation so insensitively, he *berated* me.

BILIOUS
adj (bihl yuhs)

ill-tempered, sickly, ailing

The party ended early when the *bilious* 5-year-old tried to run off with the birthday girl's presents.

BLASPHEMOUS
adj (blaas fuh muhs)

cursing, profane; extremely irreverent

The politician's offhanded comments seemed *blasphemous*, given the context of the orderly meeting.

BLATANT
adj (blay tnt)

completely obvious and conspicuous, especially in an offensive, crass manner

Such *blatant* advertising within the bounds of the school drew protest from parents.

BLITHELY
adv (blieth lee)

merrily, lightheartedly cheerful; without appropriate thought

Wanting to redecorate the office, she *blithely* assumed her co-workers wouldn't mind and moved the furniture in the space.

BOMBASTIC
adj (bahm baast ihk)

high-sounding but meaningless; ostentatiously lofty in style

The lawyer's speeches were mostly *bombastic*; his outrageous claims had no basis in fact.

BOVINE
adj (boh vien)

relating to cows; having qualities characteristic of a cow, such as sluggishness or dullness

His *bovine* demeanor did nothing to engage me.

BRAGGART
noun (braag uhrt)

a person who brags or boasts in a loud and empty manner

Usually the biggest *braggart* at the company party, Susan's boss was unusually quiet at this year's event.

BROACH

verb (brohch)

to mention or suggest for the first time

Sandy wanted to go to college away from home, but he didn't know how to *broach* the topic with his parents.

BUCOLIC

adj (byoo <u>kah</u> lihk)

pastoral, rural

My aunt likes the hustle and bustle of the city, but my uncle prefers a more *bucolic* setting.

BURNISH

verb (<u>buhr</u> nihsh)

to polish; to make smooth and bright

Mr. Frumpkin loved to stand in the sun and *burnish* his luxury car.

BURSAR

noun (<u>buhr</u> suhr) (<u>buhr</u> sahr)

a treasurer or keeper of funds

The *bursar* of the school was in charge of allocating all scholarship funds.

CACHE

noun (caash)

a hiding place; stockpile

It's good to have a *cache* where you can stash your cash.

CACOPHONY

noun (kuh <u>kah</u> fuh nee)

a jarring, unpleasant noise

As I walked into the open-air market after my nap, a *cacophony* of sounds surrounded me.

CALUMNY

noun (<u>kaa</u> luhm nee)

a false and malicious accusation; misrepresentation

The unscrupulous politician used *calumny* to bring down his opponent in the senatorial race.

CANTANKEROUS

adj (kaan taang kuhr uhs)

having a difficult, uncooperative, or stubborn disposition

The most outwardly *cantankerous* man in the nursing home was surprisingly sweet and loving with his grandchildren.

CAPTIOUS

adj (kaap shuhs)

marked by the tendency to point out trivial faults; intended to confuse in an argument

I resent the way he asked that *captious* question.

CATACLYSMIC

adj (kaat uh klihz mihk)

severely destructive

By all appearances, the storm seemed *cataclysmic*, though it lasted only a short while.

CATALYST

noun (kaat uhl ihst)

something that provokes or speeds up significant change, especially without being affected by the consequences

Technology has been a *catalyst* for the expansion of alternative education, such as home schooling and online courses.

CAUCUS

noun (kaw kuhs)

a closed committee within a political party; a private committee meeting

The president met with the delegated *caucus* to discuss the national crisis.

CAUSTIC

adj (kah stihk)

biting, sarcastic

Writer Dorothy Parker gained her reputation for *caustic* wit, and her tombstone is inscribed with a fittingly clever "Excuse my dust."

CEDE

verb (seed)

to surrender possession of something

Argentina *ceded* the Falkland Islands to Britain after a brief war.

CELERITY

noun (seh leh rih tee)

speed, haste

The celebrity ran past his fans with great *celerity*.

CENSORIOUS

adj (sehn sohr ee uhs)

critical; tending to blame and condemn

Closed-minded people tend to be *censorious* of others.

CERTITUDE

noun (suhr tih tood)

assurance, freedom from doubt

The witness' *certitude* about the night in question had a big impact on the jury.

CESSATION

noun (seh say shuhn)

a temporary or complete halt

The cessation of hostilities ensured that soldiers were able to spend the holidays with their families.

CHARY

adj (chahr ee)

watchful, cautious; extremely shy

Mindful of the fate of the Titanic, the captain was *chary* of navigating the iceberg-filled sea.

CHIMERICAL

adj (kie mehr ih kuhl) (kie meer ih kuhl)

fanciful; imaginary, impossible

The inventor's plans seemed *chimerical* to the conservative businessman from whom he was asking for financial support.

CIRCUITOUS

adj (suhr kyoo ih tuhs)

indirect, roundabout

The venue was only a short walk from the train station, but a roadblock meant I had to take a *circuitous* route.

CIRCUMVENT

verb (suhr kuhm vehnt)

to go around; avoid

Laura was able to *circumvent* the hospital's regulations, slipping into her mother's room long after visiting hours were over.

CLOYING

adj (kloy ing)

sickly sweet; excessive

When Dave and Liz were together their *cloying* affection toward one another often made their friends ill.

COAGULATE

verb (koh aag yuh layt)

to clot; to cause to thicken

Hemophiliacs can bleed to death from a minor cut because their blood does not *coagulate*.

COGENT

adj (koh juhnt)

logically forceful; compelling, convincing

Swayed by the *cogent* argument of the defense, the jury had no choice but to acquit the defendant.

COLLOQUIAL

adj (kuh loh kwee uhl)

characteristic of informal speech

The book was written in a *colloquial* style so it would be more user-friendly.

COMMUTE

verb (kuh myoot)

to change a penalty to a less severe one

In exchange for cooperating with detectives on another case, the criminal had his charges *commuted*.

COMPLACENT

adj (kuhm play sihnt)

self-satisfied, smug

Alfred always shows a *complacent* smile whenever he wins the spelling bee.

COMPLIANT

adj (kuhm plie uhnt)

submissive, yielding

The boss was unused to an assistant who spoke her mind, but he grew to respect the fact that she wasn't *compliant*.

CONCOMITANT

adj (kuh kahm ih tuhnt)

existing concurrently

A double-major was going to be difficult to pull off, especially since Lucy would have to juggle two papers and two exams *concomitantly*.

CONCORD

noun (kahn kohrd)

agreement

The sisters are now in *concord* about the car they had to share.

CONDOLE

verb (kuhn dohl)

to grieve; to express sympathy

My hamster died when I was in third grade, and my friends *condoled* with me and helped bury him in the yard.

CONFLAGRATION

noun (kahn fluh gray shuhn)

big, destructive fire

After the *conflagration* had finally died down, the city center was nothing but a mass of blackened embers.

CONFLUENCE

noun (kahn floo uhns)

the act of two things flowing together; the junction or meeting place where two things meet

At the political meeting, while planning a demonstration, there was a moving *confluence* of ideas between members.

CONSANGUINEOUS

adj (kahn saang gwihn ee uhs)

having the same lineage or ancestry; related by blood

After having a strange feeling about our relationship for years, I found out that my best friend and I are *consanguineous*.

CONSTERNATION

noun (kahn stuhr nay shuhn)

an intense state of fear or dismay

One would never think that a seasoned hunter would display such *consternation* when a grizzly bear lumbered too close to camp.

CONSTITUENT

noun (kuhn stih choo uhnt)

component, part; citizen, voter

A machine will not function properly if one of its *constituents* is defective.

CONSTRAINT

noun (kuhn straynt)

something that restricts or confines within prescribed bounds

Given the *constraints* of the budget, it was impossible to accomplish my goals.

CONTEMPTUOUS

adj (kuhn tehmp choo uhs)

scornful; expressing contempt

The diners were intimidated by the waiter's *contemptuous* manner.

CONTENTIOUS

adj (kuhn tehn shuhs)

quarrelsome, disagreeable, belligerent

The *contentious* gentleman ridiculed anything anyone said.

CONTIGUOUS

adj (kuhn tihg yoo uhs)

sharing a boundary; neighboring

The two houses had *contiguous* yards so the families shared the landscaping expenses.

CONTINENCE

noun (kahn tih nihns)

self-control, self-restraint

Lucy exhibited impressive *continence* in steering clear of fattening foods.

CONVALESCE

verb (kahn vuhl ehs)

to recover gradually from an illness

After her bout with malaria, Tatiana needed to *convalesce* for a whole month.

CONVERGENCE

noun (kuhn vehr juhns)

the state of separate elements joining or coming together

A *convergence* of factors led to the tragic unfolding of World War I.

COQUETTE

noun (koh keht)

a flirtatious woman

The normally serious librarian could turn into a *coquette* just by letting her hair down.

COTERIE

noun (koh tuh ree)

an intimate group of persons with a similar purpose

Judith invited a *coterie* of fellow stamp enthusiasts to a stamp-trading party.

COUNTERVAIL

verb (kown tuhr vayl)

to act or react with equal force

In order to *countervail* the financial loss the school suffered after the embezzlement, the treasurer raised the price of room and board.

COVERT

adj (koh vuhrt)

secretive, not openly shown

The *covert* military operation wasn't disclosed until after it was determined to be a success.

CULL

verb (kuhl)

to select, weed out

You should *cull* the words you need to study from all the flash cards.

CUMULATIVE

adj (kyoom yuh luh tihv)

increasing, collective

The new employee didn't mind her job at first, but the daily, petty indignities had a *cumulative* demoralizing effect.

CURT
adj (kuhrt)

abrupt, short with words

The grouchy shop assistant was *curt* with one of her customers, which resulted in a reprimand from her manager.

DEARTH
noun (duhrth)

a lack, scarcity, insufficiency

The *dearth* of supplies in our city made it difficult to survive the blizzard.

DEBACLE
noun (dih baa kuhl)

a sudden, disastrous collapse or defeat; a total, ridiculous failure

It was hard for her to show her face in the office after the *debacle* of spilling coffee on her supervisor—three times.

DECLAIM
verb (dih klaym)

to speak loudly and vehemently

At Thanksgiving dinner, our grandfather always *declaims* his right, as the eldest, to sit at the head of the table.

DEFAMATORY
adj (dih faam uh tohr ee)

injurious to the reputation

The tabloid was sued for making *defamatory* statements about the celebrity.

DEMAGOGUE
noun (deh muh gahg) (deh muh gawg)

a leader, rabble-rouser, usually appealing to emotion or prejudice

The dictator began his political career as a *demagogue*, giving fiery speeches in town halls.

DENIZEN
noun (dehn ih zihn)

an inhabitant, a resident

The *denizens* of the state understandably wanted to select their own leaders.

DERIDE

verb (dih ried)

to laugh at contemptuously, to make fun of

As soon as Jorge heard the others *deriding* Anthony, he came to his defense.

DIFFUSE

verb (dih fyooz)

to spread out widely, to scatter freely, to disseminate

They turned on the fan, but all that did was *diffuse* the cigarette smoke throughout the room.

DIGRESS

verb (die grehs)

to turn aside, especially from the main point; to stray from the subject

The professor repeatedly *digressed* from the topic, boring his students.

DILAPIDATED

adj (dih laap ih dayt ihd)

in disrepair, run down

Rather than get discouraged, the architect saw great potential in the *dilapidated* house.

DILUVIAL

adj (dih loo vee uhl)

pertaining to a flood

After she left the water running in the house all day, it looked simply *diluvial*.

DISCOMFIT

verb (dihs kuhm fiht)

to disconcert, to make one lose one's composure

The class clown enjoyed *discomfiting* her classmates whenever possible.

DISCRETE

adj (dih skreet)

individually distinct, separate

What's nice about the CD is that each song functions as a *discrete* work and also as part of the whole compilation.

DISINGENUOUS

adj (dihs ihn jehn yoo uhs)

giving a false appearance of simple frankness; misleading

It was *disingenuous* of him to suggest that he had no idea of the requests made by his campaign contributors.

DISINTERESTED

adj (dihs ihn trih stihd) (dihs ihn tuh reh stihd)

fair-minded, unbiased

A fair trial is made possible by the selection of *disinterested* jurors.

DISPASSIONATE

adj (dihs paash ih niht)

unaffected by bias or strong emotions; not personally or emotionally involved in something

Ideally, photographers should be *dispassionate* observers of what goes on in the world.

DISSIDENT

adj (dihs ih duhnt)

disagreeing with an established religious or political system

The *dissident* had been living abroad and writing his criticism of the government from an undisclosed location.

DOCTRINAIRE

adj (dahk truh nayr)

rigidly devoted to theories without regard for practicality; dogmatic

The professor's manner of teaching was considered *doctrinaire* for such a liberal school.

DOGGED

adj (daw guhd)

stubbornly persevering

The police inspector's *dogged* determination helped him catch the thief.

DOLEFUL

adj (dohl fuhl)

sad, mournful

Looking into the *doleful* eyes of the lonely pony, the girl yearned to take him home.

DOUR

adj (doo uhr) (dow uhr)

sullen and gloomy; stern and severe

The *dour* hotel concierge demanded payment for the room in advance.

EFFLUVIA

noun (ih floo vee uh)

waste; odorous fumes given off by waste

He took out the garbage at 3 A.M. because the *effluvia* had begun wafting into the bedroom.

ELEGY

noun (eh luh jee)

a mournful poem, usually about the dead

A memorable *elegy* was read aloud for the spiritual leader.

ELUDE

verb (ee lood)

to avoid cleverly, to escape the perception of

Somehow, the runaway *eluded* detection for weeks.

EMOLLIENT

adj (ih mohl yuhnt)

soothing, especially to the skin

After being out in the sun for so long, the *emollient* cream was a welcome relief on my skin.

EMULATE

verb (ehm yuh layt)

to strive to equal or excel, to imitate

Children often *emulate* their parents.

ENCUMBER

verb (ehn kuhm buhr)

to weigh down, to burden

The distractions of the city *encumbered* her attempts at writing.

ENJOIN

verb (ehn joyn)

to direct or impose with urgent appeal, to order with emphasis; to forbid

Patel is *enjoined* by his culture from eating beef.

EPOCHAL

adj (ehp uh kuhl) (ehp ahk uhl)

momentous, highly significant

The Supreme Court's *epochal* decision will no doubt affect generations to come.

EPONYMOUS

adj (ih pahn uh muhs)

giving one's name to a place, book, restaurant

Macbeth was the *eponymous* protagonist of Shakespeare's play.

EQUIVOCATE

verb (ih kwihv uh kayt)

to avoid committing oneself in what one says, to be deliberately unclear

Not wanting to implicate himself in the crime, the suspect *equivocated* for hours.

ERSATZ

adj (uhr sahtz)

being an artificial and inferior substitute or imitation

The *ersatz* strawberry shortcake tasted more like plastic than like real cake.

ESCHEW

verb (ehs choo)

to shun; to avoid (as something wrong or distasteful)

The filmmaker *eschewed* artifical light for her actors, resulting in a stark movie style.

ESPOUSE

verb (ih spowz)

to take up and support as a cause; to marry

Because of his beliefs, he could not *espouse* the use of capital punishment.

ESPY

verb (ehs peye)

to catch sight of, glimpse

Amidst a crowd in black clothing, she *espied* the colorful dress that her friend was wearing.

EUPHEMISM

noun (yoo fuh mihz uhm)

an inoffensive and agreeable expression that is substituted for one that is considered offensive

The funeral director preferred to use the *euphemism* "passed away" instead of the word "dead."

EUTHANASIA

noun (yoo thun nay zhuh)

the practice of ending the life of terminally ill individuals; assisted suicide

Euthanasia has always been the topic of much moral debate.

EXCORIATE

verb (ehk skohr ee ayt)

to censure scathingly; to express strong disapproval of

The three-page letter to the editor *excoriated* the publication for printing the rumor without verifying the source.

EXPONENT

noun (<u>ehk</u> spoh nuhnt)

one who champions or advocates

The vice president was an enthusiastic *exponent* of computer technology.

EXPOUND

verb (ihk <u>spownd</u>)

to explain or describe in detail

The teacher *expounded* on the theory of relativity for hours.

EXPUNGE

verb (ihk <u>spuhnj</u>)

to erase, eliminate completely

The parents' association *expunged* the questionable texts from the children's reading list.

EXTIRPATE

verb (<u>ehk</u> stuhr payt)

to root out, eradicate, literally or figuratively; to destroy wholly

The criminals were *extirpated* after many years of investigation.

EXTRAPOLATION

noun (ihk <u>strap</u> uh lay shuhn)

using known data and information to determine what will happen in the future, prediction

Through the process of *extrapolation*, we were able to determine which mutual funds to invest in.

EXTRINSIC

adj (ihk <u>strihn</u> sihk) (ihk <u>strihn</u> zihk)

external, unessential; originating from the outside

"Though they are interesting to note," the meeting manager claimed, "those facts are *extrinsic* to the matter under discussion."

EXTRUDE

verb (ihk <u>strood</u>)

to form or shape something by pushing it out, to force out, especially through a small opening

We watched in awe as the volcano *extruded* molten lava.

FACETIOUS

adj (fuh <u>see</u> shuhs)

witty, humorous

Her *facetious* remarks made the uninteresting meeting more lively.

FACILE

adj (faa suhl)

easily accomplished; seeming to lack sincerity or depth; arrived at without due effort

Given the complexity of the problem, it seemed a rather *facile* solution.

FALLACIOUS

adj (fuh lay shuhs)

tending to deceive or mislead; based on a fallacy

The *fallacious* statement "the Earth is flat" misled people for many years.

FEBRILE

adj (fehb ruhl) (fee bruhl)

feverish, marked by intense emotion or activity

Awaiting the mysterious announcement, there was a *febrile* excitement in the crowd.

FECKLESS

adj (fehk lihs)

ineffective, worthless

Anja took on the responsibility of caring for her aged mother, realizing that her *feckless* sister was not up to the task.

FEIGN

verb (fayn)

to pretend, to give a false appearance of

Though she had discovered they were planning a party, she *feigned* surprise so as not to spoil the festivities.

FERAL

adj (fehr uhl)

suggestive of a wild beast, not domesticated

Though the animal-rights activists did not want to see the *feral* dogs harmed, they offered no solution to the problem.

FICTIVE

adj (fihk tihv)

fictional, relating to imaginative creation

She found she was more productive when writing *fictive* stories rather than autobiographical stories.

FILIBUSTER

verb (fihl ih buhs tuhr)

to use obstructionist tactics, especially prolonged speech making, in order to delay something

The congressman read names from the phonebook in an attempt to *filibuster* a pending bill.

FITFUL

adj (fiht fuhl)

intermittent, lacking steadiness; characterized by irregular bursts of activity

Her *fitful* breathing became cause for concern, and eventually, she phoned the doctor.

FLIPPANT

adj (flihp uhnt)

marked by disrespectful lightheartedness or casualness

Her *flippant* response was unacceptable and she was asked again to explain herself.

FLOUT

verb (flowt)

to scorn, to disregard with contempt

The protestors *flouted* the committee's decision and hoped to sway public opinion.

FODDER

noun (fohd uhr)

raw material, as for artistic creation, readily abundant ideas or images

The governor's hilarious blunder was good *fodder* for the comedian.

FOREGO

verb (fohr goh)

to precede, to go ahead of

Because of the risks of the expedition, the team leader made sure to *forego* the climbers.

FORGO

verb (fohr goh)

to do without, to abstain from

As much as I wanted to *forgo* statistics, I knew it would serve me well in my field of study.

FORMIDABLE

adj (fohr mih duh buhl) (fohr mih duh buhl)

fearsome, daunting; tending to inspire awe or wonder

The wrestler was not very big, but his skill and speed made him a *formidable* opponent.

FORTITUDE
noun (fohr tih tood)
strength of mind that allows one to encounter adversity with courage
Months in the trenches exacted great *fortitude* of the soldiers.

FORTUITOUS
adj (fohr too ih tuhs)
by chance, especially by favorable chance
After a *fortuitous* run-in with an agent, Roxy won a recording contract.

FRENETIC
adj (freh neht ihk)
frantic, frenzied
The employee's *frenetic* schedule left him little time to socialize.

FULSOME
adj (fool suhm)
abundant; flattering in an insincere way
The king's servant showered him with *fulsome* compliments in hopes of currying favor.

FURLOUGH
noun (fuhr loh)
a leave of absence, especially granted to soldier or a prisoner
After seeing months of combat, the soldier received a much-deserved *furlough*.

FURTIVE
adj (fuhr tihv)
sly, with hidden motives
The *furtive* glances they exchanged made me suspect they were up to something.

GALVANIZE
verb (gaal vuh niez)
to shock; to arouse awareness
The closing down of another homeless shelter *galvanized* the activist group into taking political action.

GAMELY
adj (gaym lee)
spiritedly, bravely
The park ranger *gamely* navigated the trail up the steepest face of the mountain.

GAUCHE

adv (gohsh)

lacking social refinement

Snapping one's fingers to get a waiter's attention is considered *gauche*.

GRANDILOQUENCE

noun (graan dihl uh kwuhns)

pompous talk; fancy but meaningless language

The headmistress was notorious for her *grandiloquence* at the lectern and her ostentatious clothes.

GREGARIOUS

adj (greh gaar ee uhs)

outgoing, sociable

Unlike her introverted friends, Susan was very *gregarious*.

GROTTO

noun (grah toh)

a small cave

Alone on the island, Philoctetes sought shelter in a *grotto*.

HARANGUE

verb (huh raang)

to give a long speech

Maria's parents *harangued* her when she told them she'd spent her money on magic beans.

HEDONIST

noun (hee duhn ihst)

one who pursues pleasure as a goal

Michelle, an admitted *hedonist*, lays on the couch eating cookies every Saturday.

HEGEMONY

noun (hih jeh muh nee)

the domination of one state or group over its allies

When Germany claimed *hegemony* over Russia, Stalin was outraged.

HERETICAL

adj (huh reh tih kuhl)

departing from accepted beliefs or standards, oppositional

Considering the conservative audience, her comments seemed *heretical*.

HIATUS
noun (hie ay tuhs)
a gap or interruption in space, time, or continuity
After a long *hiatus* in Greece, the philosophy professor returned to the university.

HISTRIONICS
noun (hihs tree ahn ihks)
deliberate display of emotion for effect; exaggerated behavior calculated for effect
With such *histrionics*, she should really consider becoming an actress.

HUBRIS
noun (hyoo brihs)
excessive pride or self-confidence
Nathan's *hubris* spurred him to do things that many considered insensitive.

HUSBAND
verb (huhz buhnd)
to manage economically; to use sparingly
The cyclist paced herself at the start of the race, knowing that if she *husbanded* her resources she'd have the strength to break out of the pack later on.

HYPOCRITE
noun (hih puh kriht)
one who puts on a false appearance of virtue; one who criticizes a flaw he in fact possesses
What a *hypocrite*: He criticizes those who wear fur, but then he buys a leather shearling coat.

IGNOBLE
adj (ihg noh buhl)
having low moral standards, not noble in character; mean
The photographer was paid a princely sum for the picture of the self-proclaimed ethicist in the *ignoble* act of pick-pocketing.

ILLUSORY
adj (ih loo suhr ee) (ih loos ree)
producing illusion, deceptive
The desert explorer was devastated to discover that the lake he thought he had seen was in fact *illusory*.

IMBIBE

verb (ihm bieb)

to receive into the mind and take in, absorb

If I always attend class, I can *imbibe* as much knowledge as possible.

IMPASSIVE

adj (ihm pahs sihv)

absent of any external sign of emotion, expressionless

Given his *impassive* expression, it was hard to tell whether he approved of my plan.

IMPERIOUS

adj (ihm pihr ee uhs)

commanding, domineering; urgent

Though the king had been a kind leader, his daughter was *imperious* and demanding during her rule.

IMPERTURBABLE

adj (ihm puhr tuhr buh buhl)

unshakably calm and steady

No matter how disruptive the children became, the babysitter remained *imperturbable*.

IMPLACABLE

adj (ihm play kuh buhl) (ihm plaa kuh buhl)

inflexible; not capable of being changed or pacified

The *implacable* teasing was hard for the child to take.

IMPORTUNATE

adj (ihm pohr chuh niht)

troublesomely urgent; extremely persistent in request or demand

Her *importunate* appeal for a job caused me to grant her an interview.

IMPRECATION

noun (ihm prih kay shuhn)

a curse

Spouting violent *imprecations*, Hank searched for the person who had vandalized his truck.

IMPUDENT

adj (ihm pyuh duhnt)

marked by cocky boldness or disregard for others

Considering the judge had been lenient in her sentence, it was *impudent* of the defendant to refer to her by her first name.

IMPUGN

verb (ihm pyoon)

to call into question; to attack verbally

"How dare you *impugn* my motives?" protested the lawyer, on being accused of ambulance chasing.

IMPUTE

verb (ihm pyoot)

to lay the responsibility or blame for, often unjustly

It seemed unfair to *impute* the accident on me, especially since they were the ones who ran the red light.

INCANDESCENT

adj (ihn kahn dehs uhnt)

shining brightly

The *incandescent* glow of the moon made it a night I'll never forget.

INCARNADINE

adj (ihn kaar nuh dien) (ihn kaar nuh dihn)

red, especially blood red

The *incarnadine* lipstick she wore made her look much older than she was.

INCHOATE

adj (ihn koh iht)

being only partly in existence; imperfectly formed

For every page of the crisp writing that made it into the final book, Jessie has 10 pages of *inchoate* rambling that made up the first draft.

INCIPIENT

adj (ihn sihp ee uhnt)

beginning to exist or appear; in an initial stage

The *incipient* idea seemed brilliant, but they knew it needed much more development.

INCORRIGIBLE

adj (ihn kohr ih juh buhl)

incapable of being corrected or amended; difficult to control or manage

"You're *incorrigible*," yelled the frustrated mother to her son, in the middle of his third tantrum of the day.

INCREDULOUS
adj (ihn krehj uh luhs)

unwilling to accept what is true, skeptical

The Lasky children were *incredulous* when their parents told them they were moving to Alaska.

INDOMITABLE
adj (ihn dahm ih tuuh buhl)

incapable of being conquered

Climbing Mount Everest would seem an *indomitable* task, but it has been done many times.

INGRATIATE
verb (ihn gray shee ayt)

to gain favor with another by deliberate effort, to seek to please somebody so as to gain an advantage

The new intern tried to *ingratiate* herself with the managers so that they might consider her for a future job.

INHERENT
adj (ihn hehr ehnt)

involving the essential character of something, built-in, inborn

The class was dazzled by the experiment and as a result more likely to remember the *inherent* scientific principle.

INQUEST
noun (ihn kwehst)

an investigation, an inquiry

The police chief ordered an *inquest* to determine what went wrong.

INSENSATE
adj (ihn sehn sayt) (ihn sehn siht)

lacking sensibility and understanding, foolish

The shock of the accident left him *insensate*, but after some time, the numbness subsided and he was able to tell the officer what had happened.

INSOLENT
adj (ihn suh luhnt)

insultingly arrogant, overbearing

After having spoken with three *insolent* customer service representatives, Shelly was relieved when the fourth one sympathized with her complaint.

INSULAR

adj (ihn suh luhr) (ihn syuh luhr)

characteristic of an isolated people, especially having a narrow viewpoint

It was a shock for Kendra to go from her small high school, with her *insular* group of friends, to a huge college with students from all over the country.

INSUPERABLE

adj (ihn soo puhr uh buhl)

incapable of being surmounted or overcome

Insuperable as our problems may seem, I'll come out ahead.

INTER

verb (ihn tuhr)

to bury

After giving the masses one last chance to pay their respects, the leader's body was *interred*.

INTERLOCUTOR

noun (ihn tuhr lahk yuh tuhr)

ones who takes part in conversation

Though always the *interlocutor*, the professor actually preferred that his students guide the class discussion.

INTERNECINE

adj (ihn tuhr nehs een)

mutually destructive; equally devastating to both sides

Though it looked as though there was a victor, the *internecine* battle benefited no one.

INTERREGNUM

noun (ihn tuhr rehg nuhm)

a temporary halting of the usual operations of government or control

The new king began his reign by restoring order that the lawless *interregnum* had destroyed.

INTIMATION

noun (ihn tuh may shuhn)

a subtle and indirect hint

Abby chose to ignore Babu's *intimation* that she wasn't as good a swimmer as she claimed.

INTRACTABLE

adj (ihn traak tuh buhl)

not easily managed or manipulated

Intractable for hours, the wild horse eventually allowed the rider to mount.

INTRANSIGENT
adj (ihn traan suh juhnt) (ihn traan zuh juhnt)
uncompromising, refusing to abandon an extreme position
His *intransigent* positions on social issues cost him the election.

INTREPID
adj (ihn trehp ihd)
fearless, resolutely courageous
Despite freezing winds, the *intrepid* hiker completed his ascent.

INUNDATE
verb (ihn uhn dayt)
to cover with a flood; to overwhelm as if with a flood
The box office was *inundated* with requests for tickets to the award-winning play.

INVETERATE
adj (ihn veht uhr iht)
firmly established, especially with respect to a habit or attitude
An *inveterate* risk-taker, Lori tried her luck at bungee-jumping.

IRASCIBLE
adj (ih raas uh buhl)
easily angered, hot-tempered
One of the most *irascible* warriors of all time, Attila the Hun ravaged much of Europe during his time.

IRONIC
adj (ie rahn ihk)
poignantly contrary or incongruous to what was expected
It was *ironic* to learn that shy Wendy from high school grew up to be the host of a talk show.

IRREVERENT
adj (ih rehv uhr uhnt)
disrespectful in a gentle or humorous way
Kevin's *irreverent* attitude toward the principal annoyed the teacher but amused the other children.

ITINERANT
adj (ie tihn uhr uhnt)
wandering from place to place; unsettled
The *itinerant* tomcat came back to the Johansson homestead every two months.

JETTISON
verb (jeht ih zuhn) (jeht ih suhn)

to discard, to get rid of as unnecessary or encumbering

The sinking ship *jettisoned* its cargo in a desperate attempt to reduce its weight.

JOCULAR
adj (jahk yuh luhr)

playful, humorous

The *jocular* old man entertained his grandchildren for hours.

JUNTA
noun (hoon tuh) (juhn tuh)

a small governing body, especially after a revolutionary seizure of power

Only one member of the *junta* was satisfactory enough to be elected once the new government was established.

KISMET
noun (kihz meht) (kihz miht)

destiny, fate

When Eve found out that Garret also played the harmonica, she knew their meeting was *kismet*.

LAMPOON
verb (laam poon)

to ridicule with satire

The mayor hated being *lampooned* by the press for his efforts to improve people's politeness.

LARGESS
noun (laar jehs)

generous giving (as of money) to others who may seem inferior

She'd always relied on her parent's *largess*, but after graduation, she had to get a job.

LAUDABLE
adj (law duh buhl)

deserving of praise

Kristin's dedication is *laudable*, but she doesn't have the necessary skills to be a good paralegal.

LAX
adj (laaks)

not rigid, loose; negligent

Because our delivery boy is *lax*, the newspaper often arrives sopping wet.

LEVITY

noun (leh vih tee)

an inappropriate lack of seriousness, overly casual

The joke added needed *levity* to the otherwise serious meeting.

LEXICON

noun (lehk sih kahn)

a dictionary; a stock of terms pertaining to a particular subject or vocabulary

The author coined the term Gen-X, which has since entered the *lexicon*.

LIBERTARIAN

noun (lih buhr tehr ee uhn)

one who advocates individual rights and free will

The *libertarian* was always at odds with the conservatives.

LIBERTINE

noun (lihb uhr teen)

a free thinker, usually used disparagingly; one without moral restraint

The *libertine* took pleasure in gambling away his family's money.

LICENTIOUS

adj (lih sehn shuhs)

immoral; unrestrained by society

Conservative citizens were outraged by the *licentious* exploits of the free-spirited artists living in town.

LILLIPUTIAN

adj (lihl ee pyoo shun)

very small

Next to her Amazonian roommate, the girl seemed *lilliputian*.

LIMBER

adj (lihm buhr)

flexible, capable of being shaped

After years of doing yoga, the elderly man was remarkably *limber*.

LITHE

adj (lieth)

moving and bending with ease; marked by effortless grace

The dancer's *lithe* movements proved her to be a rising star in the ballet corps.

LOQUACIOUS

adj (loh <u>kway</u> shuhs)

talkative

She was naturally *loquacious*, which was always a challenge when she was in a library or movie theater.

MACABRE

adj (muh <u>kaa</u> bruh) (muh <u>kaa</u> buhr)

having death as a subject; dwelling on the gruesome

Martin enjoyed *macabre* tales about werewolves and vampires.

MACROCOSM

noun (<u>maak</u> roh cahz uhm)

the whole universe; a large-scale reflection of a part of the greater world

Some scientists focus on a particular aspect of space, while others study the entire *macrocosm* and how its parts relate to one another.

MALAISE

noun (maa <u>layz</u>)

a feeling of unease or depression

During his presidency, Jimmy Carter spoke of a "national *malaise*" and was subsequently criticized for being too negative.

MALAPROPISM

noun (<u>maal</u> uh prahp ihz uhm)

the accidental, often comical, use of a word which resembles the one intended, but has a different, often contradictory meaning

Everybody laughed at the *malapropism* when instead of saying "public broadcasting" the announcer said "public boredcasting."

MALEDICTION

noun (maal ih <u>dihk</u> shun)

a curse, a wish of evil upon another

The frog prince looked for a princess to kiss him and put an end to the witch's *malediction*.

MALEVOLENT

adj (muh <u>lehv</u> uh luhnt)

exhibiting ill will; wishing harm to others

The *malevolent* gossiper spread false rumors with frequency.

MALFEASANCE

noun (maal fee zuhns)

wrongdoing or misconduct, especially by a public official

Not only was the deputy's *malfeasance* humiliating, it also spelled the end of his career.

MALLEABLE

adj (maal ee uh buhl)

easily influenced or shaped, capable of being altered by outside forces

The welder heated the metal before shaping it because the heat made it *malleable*.

MANNERED

adj (maan uhrd)

artificial or stilted in character

The portrait is an example of the *mannered* style that was favored in that era.

MAVERICK

noun (maav rihk) (maav uh rihk)

an independent individual who does not go along with a group

The senator was a *maverick* who was willing to vote against his own party's position.

MAWKISH

adj (maw kihsh)

sickeningly sentimental

The poet hoped to charm his girlfriend with his flowery poem, but its *mawkish* tone sickened her instead.

MEGALOMANIA

noun (mehg uh loh may nee uh)

obsession with great or grandiose performance

Many of the Roman emperors suffered from severe *megalomania*.

MELLIFLUOUS

adj (muh lihf loo uhs)

having a smooth, rich flow

She was so talented that her *mellifluous* flute playing transported me to another world.

MICROCOSM

noun (mie kruh kahz uhm)

a small scale representation of a larger system

This department is in fact a *microcosm* of the entire corporation.

MILIEU

noun (mihl yoo)

the physical or social setting in which something occurs or develops, environment

The *milieu* at the club wasn't one I was comfortable with, so I left right away.

MISANTHROPE

noun (mihs ahn throhp)

a person who hates or distrusts mankind

Scrooge was such a *misanthrope* that even the sight of children singing made him angry.

MISNOMER

noun (mihs noh muhr)

an error in naming a person or place

Iceland is a *misnomer* since it isn't really icy; the name means "island."

MISSIVE

noun (mihs ihv)

a written note or letter

Priscilla spent hours composing a romantic *missive* for Elvis.

MITIGATE

verb (miht ih gayt)

to make less severe, make milder

A judge may *mitigate* a sentence if it's decided that the crime was committed out of necessity.

MODICUM

noun (mahd ih kuhm)

a small portion, limited quantity

I expect at least a *modicum* of assistance from you on the day of the party.

MOLLIFY

verb (mahl uh fie)

to soothe in temper or disposition

A small raise and increased break time *mollified* the unhappy staff, at least for the moment.

MORDANT

adj (mohr dnt)

biting and caustic in manner and style

Roald Dahl's stories are *mordant* alternatives to bland stories intended for kids.

MORES

noun (mawr ayz)

fixed customs or manners; moral attitudes

In keeping with the *mores* of ancient Roman society, Nero held a celebration every weekend.

MOROSE

adj (muh rohs) (maw rohs)

gloomy, sullen

After hearing that the internship had been given to someone else, Lenny was *morose* for days.

MOTE

noun (moht)

a small particle, speck

Monica's eye watered, irritated by a *mote* of dust.

MUTABILITY

noun (myoo tuh bihl uh tee)

the quality of being capable of change, in form or character; susceptibility of change

The actress lacked the *mutability* needed to perform in the improvisational play.

MYOPIC

adj (mie ahp ihk) (mie oh pihk)

lacking foresight, having a narrow view or long-range perspective

Not wanting to spend a lot of money up front, the *myopic* business owner would likely suffer the consequences later.

NEBULOUS

adj (neh byoo luhs)

vague, undefined

The candidate's *nebulous* plans to fight crime made many voters skeptical.

NECROMANCY

noun (nehk ruh maan see)

the practice of communicating with the dead in order to predict the future

The practice of *necromancy* supposes belief in survival of the soul after death.

NEFARIOUS

adj (nih fahr ee uhs)

intensely wicked or vicous

Nefarious deeds are never far from an evil-doer's mind.

NEONATE

noun (<u>nee</u> uh nayt)

a newborn child

The *neonate* was born prematurely so she's still in the hospital.

NIHILISM

noun (<u>nie</u> hihl iz uhm)

the belief that traditional values and beliefs are unfounded and that existence is useless; the belief that conditions in the social organization are so bad as to make destruction desirable

Robert's *nihilism* expressed itself in his lack of concern with the norms of moral society.

NOMENCLATURE

noun (<u>noh</u> muhn klay chuhr)

a system of scientific names

In botany class, we learned the *nomenclature* used to identify different species of roses.

NON SEQUITUR

noun (nahn <u>sehk</u> wih tuhr)

a statement that does not follow logically from anything previously said

After the heated political debate, her comment about cake was a real *non sequitur*.

NOVEL

adj (<u>nah</u> vuhl)

new and not resembling anything formerly known

Piercing any part of the body other than the earlobes was *novel* in the 1950s, but now it is quite common.

OBDURATE

adj (<u>ahb</u> duhr uht)

stubbornly persistent, resistant to persuasion

The president was *obdurate* on the matter, and no amount of public protest could change his mind.

OBFUSCATE

verb (<u>ahb</u> fyoo skayt)

to confuse, make obscure

Benny always *obfuscates* the discussion by bringing in irrelevant facts.

OBSTINATE

adj (<u>ahb</u> stih nuht)

unreasonably persistent

The *obstinate* journalist would not reveal his source, and thus, was jailed for 30 days.

OLFACTORY

adj (ohl faak tuh ree)

relating to the sense of smell

Whenever she entered a candle store, her *olfactory* sense was awakened.

OLIGARCHY

noun (oh lih gaar kee)

a government in which a small group exercises supreme control

In an *oligarchy*, the few who rule are generally wealthier and have more status than the others.

ONUS

noun (oh nuhs)

a burden, an obligation

Antonia was beginning to feel the *onus* of having to feed her friend's cat for the month.

OPINE

verb (oh pien)

to express an opinion

At the "Let's Chat Talk Show," the audience member *opined* that the guest was in the wrong.

OPPORTUNIST

noun (aap ore too nist)

one who takes advantage of any opportunity to achieve an end, with little regard for principles

The *opportunist* wasted no time in stealing the idea and presenting it as his own.

OPPROBRIOUS

adj (uh proh bree uhs)

disgraceful, shameful

She wrote an *opprobrious* editorial in the newspaper about the critic who tore her new play to shreds.

ORNERY

adj (ohr nuh ree)

having an irritable disposition, cantankerous

My first impression of the taxi driver was that he was *ornery*, but then he explained that he'd just had a bad day.

OSCILLATE

verb (<u>ah</u> sihl ayt)

to swing back and forth like a pendulum; to vary between opposing beliefs or feelings

The move meant a new house in a lovely neighborhood, but she missed her friends, so she *oscillated* between joy and sadness.

OSSIFY

verb (<u>ah</u> sih fie)

to change into bone; to become hardened or set in a rigidly conventional pattern

The forensics expert ascertained the body's age based on the degree to which the facial structure had *ossified*.

OSTRACIZE

verb (<u>ahs</u> truh size)

to exclude from a group by common consent

Despite the fact that Tabatha had done nothing wrong, her friends *ostracized* her.

OUST

verb (owst)

to remove from position by force; eject

After President Nixon so offensively lied to the country during Watergate, he was *ousted* from office.

PAEAN

noun (<u>pee</u> uhn)

a tribute, a song or expression of praise

He considered his newest painting a *paean* to his late wife.

PALATIAL

adj (puh <u>lay</u> shuhl)

relating to a palace; magnificent

After living in a cramped studio apartment for years, Alicia thought the modest one bedroom looked downright *palatial*.

PALIMPSEST

noun (<u>pahl</u> ihmp sehst)

an object or place having diverse layers or aspects beneath the surface

Years ago, paper was very expensive, so the practice was to write over previous words, creating a *palimpsest* of writing.

PALPABLE

adj (pahlp uh buhl)

capable of being touched or felt; easily perceived

The tension was *palpable* as I walked into the room.

PALTRY

adj (pawl tree)

pitifully small or worthless

Bernardo paid the ragged boy the *paltry* sum of 25 cents to carry his luggage all the way to the hotel.

PANACHE

noun (puh nahsh)

flamboyance or dash in style and action

Leah has such *panache* when planning parties, even when they're last-minute affairs.

PANDEMIC

adj (paan deh mihk)

occurring over a wide geographic area and affecting a large portion of the population

Pandemic alarm spread throughout Colombia after the devastating earthquake.

PANEGYRIC

noun (paan uh geer ihk)

elaborate praise; formal hymn of praise

The director's *panegyric* for the donor who kept his charity going was heart-warming.

PARADIGM

noun (paar uh diem)

an outstandingly clear or typical example

The new restaurant owner used the fast-food giant as a *paradigm* for expansion into new locales.

PARAGON

noun (paar uh gon)

a model of excellence or perfection

She's the *paragon* of what a judge should be: honest, intelligent, and just.

PARAMOUNT

adj (paar uh mownt)

supreme, of chief importance

It's of *paramount* importance that we make it back to camp before the storm hits.

PARE

verb (payr)

to trim off excess, reduce

The cook's hands were sore after she *pared* hundreds of potatoes for the banquet.

PARIAH

noun (puh rie ah)

an outcast

Once he betrayed those in his community, he was banished and lived the life of a *pariah*.

PATENT

adj (paa tehnt)

obvious, evident

Moe could no longer stand Frank's *patent* fawning over the boss and so confronted him.

PATHOGENIC

adj (paa thoh jehn ihk)

causing disease

Bina's research on the origins of *pathogenic* microorganisms should help stop the spread of disease.

PATRICIAN

adj (puh trih shuhn)

aristocratic

Though he really couldn't afford an expensive lifestyle, Claudius had *patrician* tastes.

PATRONIZE

verb (pay troh niez)

to act as patron of, to adopt an air of condescension toward; to buy from

LuAnn *patronized* the students, treating them like simpletons, which they deeply resented.

PECULATE

verb (pehk yuh layt)

to embezzle

These days in the news, we read more and more about workers *peculating* the system.

PECUNIARY

adj (pih kyoon nee ehr ee)

relating to money

Michelle's official title was office manager, but she ended up taking on a lot of *pecuniary* responsibilities such as payroll duties.

PELLUCID
adj (peh loo sihd)

transparently clear in style or meaning, easy to understand

Though she thought she could hide her ulterior motives, they were *pellucid* to everyone else.

PENCHANT
noun (pehn chehnt)

an inclination, a definite liking

After Daniel visited the Grand Canyon, he developed a *penchant* for travel.

PENITENT
adj (peh nih tehnt)

expressing sorrow for sins or offenses, repentant

Claiming the criminal did not feel *penitent*, the victim's family felt his pardon should be denied.

PENURY
noun (pehn yuh ree)

an oppressive lack of resources (as money), severe poverty

Once a famous actor, he eventually died in *penury* and anonymity.

PEREGRINATE
verb (pehr ih gruh nayt)

to travel on foot

It has always been a dream of mine to *peregrinate* from one side of Europe to the other with nothing but a backpack.

PHALANX
noun (fay laanks)

a compact or close-knit body of people, animals, or things

A *phalanx* of guards stood outside the prime minister's home day and night.

PHILISTINE
noun (fihl uh steen)

a person who is guided by materialism and is disdainful of intellectual or artistic values

The *philistine* never even glanced at the rare violin in his collection but instead kept an eye on its value and sold it at a profit.

PHILOLOGY
noun (fih lahl uh jee)

the study of ancient texts and languages

Philology was the predecessor to modern-day linguistics.

PHLEGMATIC

adj (flehg maa tihk)

having a sluggish, unemotional temperament

His writing was energetic but his *phlegmatic* personality wasn't suited for television, so he turned down the interview.

PIQUE

verb (peek)

to arouse anger or resentment in; provoke

His continual insensitivity *piqued* my anger.

PLAINTIVE

adj (playn tihv)

expressive of suffering or woe, melancholy

The *plaintive* cries from the girl trapped in the tree were heard by all.

PLATITUDE

noun (plaa tuh tood)

overused and trite remark

Instead of the usual *platitudes*, the comedian gave a memorable and inspiring speech to the graduating class.

PLEBEIAN

adj (plee bee uhn)

crude or coarse; characteristic of commoners

After five weeks of rigorous studying, the graduate settled in for a weekend of *plebeian* socializing and television watching.

PLUCKY

adj (pluh kee)

courageous; spunky

The *plucky* young nurse dove into the foxhole, determined to help the wounded soldier.

POLITIC

adj (pah luh tihk)

shrewd and crafty in managing or dealing with things

She was wise to curb her tongue and was able to explain her problem to the judge in a respectful and *politic* manner.

POLYGLOT

noun (pah lee glaht)

a speaker of many languages

Ling's extensive travels have helped her to become a true *polyglot*.

PORE

verb (pohr)

to read studiously or attentively

I've *pored* over this text, yet I still can't understand it.

PORTENTOUS

adj (pohr tehn tuhs)

foreshadowing, ominous; eliciting amazement and wonder

Everyone thought the rays of light were *portentous* until they realized a nine-year-old was playing a joke on them.

POSIT

verb (pohz iht)

to assume as real or conceded; propose as an explanation

Before proving the math formula, we needed to *posit* that *x* and *y* were real numbers.

POTABLE

adj (poh tuh buhl)

suitable for drinking

Though the water was *potable*, it tasted terrible.

POTENTATE

noun (poh tehn tayt)

a ruler; one who wields great power

Alex was much kinder before he assumed the role of *potentate*.

PRECARIOUS

adj (prih caa ree uhs)

lacking in security or stability; dependent on chance or uncertain conditions

Given the *precarious* circumstances, I chose to opt out of the deal completely.

PRECIPITOUS

adj (pree sih puh tuhs)

steep

The *precipitous* cave was daunting for the first-time climber.

PRESAGE

noun (preh sihj)

something that foreshadows; a feeling of what will happen in the future

The demolition of the Berlin Wall was a *presage* to the fall of the Soviet Union.

PRESTIDIGITATION

noun (prehs tih dihj ih tay shuhn)

a cleverly executed trick or deception; sleight of hand

My hunch was that he won the contest not so much as a result of real talent, but rather through *prestidigitation*.

PRETERNATURAL

adj (pree tuhr naach uhr uhl)

existing outside of nature; extraordinary; supernatural

We were all amazed at her *preternatural* ability to recall smells from her early childhood.

PRIMEVAL

adj (priem ee vuhl)

ancient, primitive

The archaeologist claimed that the skeleton was of *primeval* origin, though in fact it was the remains of a modern-day monkey.

PRODIGAL

adj (prah dih guhl)

recklessly extravagant, wasteful

The *prodigal* expenditures on the military budget during a time of peace created a stir in the cabinet.

PROFFER

verb (prahf uhr)

to offer for acceptance

The deal *proffered* by the committee satisfied all those at the meeting, ending a month-long discussion.

PROGENITOR

noun (proh jehn uh tuhr)

an ancestor in the direct line, forefather; founder

Though he had been born here, his *progenitors* were from India.

PROLIFERATE

verb (proh lih fuhr ayt)

to grow by rapid production of new parts; increase in number

The bacteria *proliferated* so quickly that even the doctor was surprised.

PROMULGATE

verb (prah muhl gayt)

to make known by open declaration, proclaim

The publicist *promulgated* the idea that the celebrity had indeed gotten married.

PROPENSITY

noun (proh pehn suh tee)

a natural inclination or preference

She has a *propensity* for lashing out at others when stressed, so we leave her alone when she's had a rough day.

PROSAIC

adj (proh say ihk)

relating to prose (as opposed to poetry); dull, ordinary

Simon's *prosaic* style bored his writing teacher to tears, though he thought he had an artistic flair.

PROSCRIBE

verb (proh skribe)

to condemn or forbid as harmful or unlawful

Consumption of alcohol was *proscribed* in the country's constitution, but the ban was eventually lifted.

PROSTRATE

adj (prah strayt)

lying face downward in adoration or submission

My friends teased me for lying *prostrate* when I met my favorite musician.

PROVINCIAL

adj (pruh vihn shuhl)

limited in outlook, narrow, unsophisticated

Having grown up in the city, Anita sneered at the *provincial* attitudes of her country cousins.

PROXY

noun (prahk see)

a person authorized to act for someone else

In the event the shareholder can't attend the meeting, he'll send a *proxy*.

PSEUDONYM
noun (soo duh nihm)

a fictitious name, used particularly by writers to conceal identity

Though George Eliot sounds as though it's a male name, it was the *pseudonym* that Marian Evans used when she published her classic novel *Middlemarch*.

PUGILISM
noun (pyoo juhl ih suhm)

boxing

Pugilism has been defended as a positive outlet for aggressive impulses.

PUISSANT
adj (pwih sihnt) (pyoo sihnt)

powerful

His memoir was full of descriptions of *puissant* military heroics, but most were exaggerations or outright lies.

PUNCTILIOUS
adj (puhngk tihl ee uhs)

concerned with precise details about codes or conventions

The *punctilious* student never made spelling errors on her essays.

PUNDIT
noun (puhn diht)

one who gives opinions in an authoritative manner

The *pundits* on television are often more entertaining than the sitcoms.

PURLOIN
verb (puhr loyn)

to steal

His goal was to *purloin* the documents he felt belonged to him.

PURPORT
verb (puhr pohrt)

to profess, suppose, claim

Brad *purported* to be an opera lover, but he fell asleep at every performance he attended.

RANCOR
noun (raan kuhr)

bitter hatred

Having been teased mercilessly for years, Herb became filled with *rancor* toward those who had humiliated him.

RANKLE

verb (raang kuhl)

to cause anger and irritation

At first the kid's singing was adorable, but after 40 minutes it began to *rankle*.

RAPACIOUS

adj (ruh pay shuhs)

taking by force; driven by greed

Sea otters are so *rapacious* that they consumer 10 times their body weight in food every day.

RAPT

adj (raapt)

deeply absorbed

The story was so well performed that the usually rowdy children were *rapt* until the final word.

RAREFY

verb (rayr uh fie)

to make rare, thin, or less dense

The atmosphere *rarefies* as altitude increases, so the air atop a mountain is too thin to breathe.

RAZE

verb (rayz)

to tear down, demolish

The house had been *razed*; where it once stood, there was nothing but splinters and bricks.

REACTIONARY

adj (ree aak shuhn ayr ee)

marked by extreme conservatism, especially in politics

Her *reactionary* beliefs were misunderstood by her friends.

RECAPITULATE

verb (ree kuh pihch yoo layt)

to review by a brief summary

After the long-winded president had finished his speech, his assistant *recapitulated* for the press the points he had made.

RECIDIVISM

noun (rih sihd uh vih zihm)

a tendency to relapse into a previous behavior, especially criminal behavior

According to statistics, the *recidivism* rate for criminals is quite high.

REFRACT

verb (rih fraakt)

to deflect sound or light

The crystal *refracted* the rays of sunlight so they formed a beautiful pattern on the wall.

REFUTE

verb (rih fyoot)

to contradict, discredit

She made such a persuasive argument that nobody could *refute* it.

RELEGATE

verb (reh luh gayt)

to send into exile, banish; assign

Because he hadn't scored any goals during the season, Abe was *relegated* to the bench for the championship game.

REMISSION

noun (rih mih shuhn)

a lessening of intensity or degree

The doctor told me that the disease had gone into *remission*.

REMUNERATION

noun (rih myoo nuh ray shuhn)

payment for goods or services or to recompense for losses

You can't expect people to do this kind of boring work without some form of *remuneration*.

REPLETE

adj (rih pleet)

abundantly supplied, complete

The gigantic supermarket was *replete* with consumer products of every kind.

REPOSE

noun (rih pohz)

relaxation, leisure

After working hard every day in the busy city, Mike finds his *repose* on weekends playing golf with friends.

REPREHENSIBLE

adj (rehp ree hehn suh buhl)

blameworthy, disreputable

Lowell was thrown out of the restaurant because of his *reprehensible* behavior toward the other patrons.

REPROVE

verb (rih proov)

to criticize or correct, usually in a gentle manner

Mrs. Hernandez *reproved* her daughter for staying out late and not calling.

REQUITE

verb (rih kwiet)

to return or repay

Thanks for offering to lend me $1,000, but I know I'll never be able to *requite* your generosity.

RESCIND

verb (rih sihnd)

to repeal, cancel

After the celebrity was involved in a scandal, the car company *rescinded* its offer of an endorsement contract.

RESILIENT

adj (rih sihl yuhnt)

able to recover quickly after illness or bad luck; able to bounce back to shape

Psychologists say that being *resilient* in life is one of the keys to success and happiness.

RESOLUTE

adj (reh suh loot)

marked by firm determination

Louise was *resolute*: She would get into medical school no matter what.

RESPLENDENT

adj (rih splehn dihnt)

splendid, brilliant

The bride looked *resplendent* in her gown and sparkling tiara.

REVILE

verb (rih veye uhl)

to criticize with harsh language, verbally abuse

The artist's new installation was *reviled* by critics who weren't used to the departure from his usual work.

RHETORIC
noun (reh tuhr ihk)
the art of speaking or writing effectively; skill in the effective use of speech
Lincoln's talent for *rhetoric* was evident in his beautifully expressed Gettysburg Address.

RIFE
adj (rief)
abundant prevalent especially to an increasing degree; filled with
The essay was so *rife* with grammatical errors that it had to be rewritten.

ROSTRUM
noun (rahs truhm)
an elevated platform for public speaking
Though she was terrified, the new member of the debate club approached the *rostrum* with poise.

SACCHARINE
adj (saa kuh ruhn)
excessively sweet or sentimental
Geoffrey's *saccharine* poems nauseated Lucy, and she wished he'd stop sending them.

SACRILEGIOUS
adj (saak rih lihj uhs)
impious, irreverent toward what is held to be sacred or holy
It's considered *sacrilegious* for one to enter a mosque wearing shoes.

SALIENT
adj (say lee uhnt)
prominent, of notable significance
His most *salient* characteristic is his tendency to dominate every conversation.

SANCTIMONIOUS
adj (saangk tih moh nee uhs)
hypocritically devout; acting morally superior to another
The *sanctimonious* columnist turned out to have been hiding a gambling problem that cost his family everything.

SATIATE
verb (say shee ayt)
to satisfy (as a need or desire) fully or to excess
After years of journeying around the world with nothing but backpacks, the friends had finally *satiated* their desire to travel.

SATURNINE

adj (<u>saat</u> uhr nien)

cold and steady in mood, gloomy; slow to act

Her *saturnine* expression made her hard to be around.

SAVANT

noun (suh <u>vahnt</u>)

a person of learning; especially one with knowledge in a special field

The *savant* so impressed us with his knowledge that we asked him to come speak at our school.

SCRUPULOUS

adj (<u>skroop</u> yuh luhs)

acting in strict regard for what is considered proper; punctiliously exact

After the storm had destroyed their antique lamp, the Millers worked to repair it with *scrupulous* care.

SEAMY

adj (<u>see</u> mee)

morally degraded, unpleasant

The tour guide avoided the *seamy* parts of town.

SECULAR

adj (<u>seh</u> kyoo luhr)

not specifically pertaining to religion, relating to the world

Although his favorite books were religious, Ben also read *secular* works such as mysteries.

SEDITION

noun (seh <u>dih</u> shuhn)

behavior that promotes rebellion or civil disorder against the state

Li was arrested for *sedition* after he gave a fiery speech in the main square.

SEMINAL

adj (<u>seh</u> muhn uhl)

influential in an original way, providing a basis for further development; creative

The scientist's discovery proved to be *seminal* in the area of quantum physics.

SEQUESTER

verb (suh <u>kweh</u> stuhr)

to set apart, seclude

When juries are *sequestered*, it can take days, even weeks, to come up with a verdict.

SERAPHIC
adj (seh rah fihk)

angelic, sweet

Selena's *seraphic* appearance belied her nasty, bitter personality.

SIMIAN
adj (sih mee uhn)

apelike; relating to apes

Early man was more *simian* in appearance than is modern man.

SINECURE
noun (sien ih kyoor)

a well-paying job or office that requires little or no work

The corrupt mayor made sure to set up all his relatives in *sinecures* within the administration.

SOBRIQUET
noun (soh brih kay) (soh brih keht)

a nickname

One of former president Ronald Reagan's *sobriquets* was "The Gipper."

SOJOURN
noun (soh juhrn)

a temporary stay, visit

After graduating from college, Iliani embarked on a *sojourn* to China.

SOLICITOUS
adj (suh lih sih tuhs)

anxious, concerned; full of desire, eager

Overjoyed to see the pop idol in her presence, the *solicitous* store owner stood ready to serve.

SOPHOMORIC
adj (sahf mohr ihk)

exhibiting great immaturity and lack of judgment

After Sean's *sophomoric* behavior, he was grounded for weeks.

SPARTAN
adj (spahr tihn)

highly self-disciplined; frugal, austere

When he was in training, the athlete preferred to live in a *spartan* room so he could shut out all distractions.

SPECIOUS

adj (spee shuhs)

having the ring of truth but actually being untrue; deceptively attractive

After I followed up with some research on the matter, I realized that the charismatic politician's argument had been *specious*.

SPORTIVE

adj (spohr tihv)

frolicsome, playful

The lakeside vacation meant more *sportive* opportunities for the kids than the culinary tour through France.

SQUALID

adj (skwa lihd)

filthy and degraded as the result of neglect or poverty

The *squalid* living conditions in the building outraged the new tenants.

STALWART

adj (stahl wuhrt)

marked by outstanding strength and vigor of body, mind, or spirit

The 85-year old went to the market every day, impressing her neighbors with her *stalwart* routine.

STASIS

noun (stay sihs)

a state of static balance or equilibrium; stagnation

The rusty, ivy-covered World War II tank had obviously been in *stasis* for years.

STINT

verb (stihnt)

to be sparing or frugal; to restrict with respect to a share or allowance

Don't *stint* on the mayonnaise, because I don't like my sandwich too dry.

STIPULATE

verb (stihp yuh layt)

to specify as a condition or requirement of an agreement or offer

The contract *stipulated* that if the movie was never filmed, the actress got paid anyway.

STRATIFY

verb (straa tuh fie)

to arrange or divide into layers

Schliemann *stratified* the numerous layers of Troy, an archeological dig that remains legendary.

STRIDENT

adj (strie dehnt)

loud, harsh, unpleasantly noisy

The traveler's *strident* manner annoyed the flight attendant, but she managed to keep her cool.

STRINGENT

adj (strihn guhnt)

imposing severe, rigorous standards

Many employees found it difficult to live up to the *stringent* standards imposed by the company.

STYMIE

verb (stie mee)

to block or thwart

The police effort to capture the bank robber was *stymied* when he escaped through a rear window.

SUBTERRANEAN

adj (suhb tuh ray nee uhn)

hidden, secret; underground

Subterranean tracks were created for the trains after it was decided they had run out of room above ground.

SULLY

verb (suh lee)

to tarnish, taint

His outrageous gaffe *sullied* his public image.

SUPERFLUOUS

adj (soo puhr floo uhs)

extra, more than necessary

The extra recommendations Jake included in his application were *superfluous*, as only one was required.

SUPERSEDE

verb (soo puhr seed)

to cause to be set aside; to force out of use as inferior, replace

Her computer was still running version 2.0 of the software, which had been *superseded* by at least three more versions.

SUPPLANT

verb (suh plaant)

to replace (another) by force, to take the place of

The overthrow of the government meant a new leader would *supplant* the former one.

SURMOUNT

verb (suhr mownt)

to conquer, overcome

The blind woman *surmounted* great obstacles to become a well-known trial lawyer.

SYBARITE

noun (sih buh riet)

a person devoted to pleasure and luxury

A confirmed *sybarite*, the nobleman fainted at the thought of having to leave his palace and live in a small cottage.

TACTILE

adj (taak tihl)

producing a sensation of touch

The Museum of Natural History displays objects for people to touch so that they have a *tactile* understanding of how different peoples and animals lived.

TANTAMOUNT

adj (taan tuh mownt)

equal in value or effect

If she didn't get concert tickets to see her favorite band, it would be *tantamount* to a tragedy.

TAUTOLOGICAL

adj (tawt uh lah jih kuhl)

having to do with needless repetition, redundancy

I know he was only trying to clarify things, but his *tautological* statements confused me even more.

TAWDRY

adj (taw dree)

gaudy, cheap, showy

The performer changed into her *tawdry* costume and stepped onto the stage.

TEMERITY

noun (teh mehr ih tee)

unreasonable or foolhardy disregard for danger, recklessness

I offered her a ride since it was late at night, but she had the *temerity* to say she'd rather walk.

TEMPESTUOUS

adj (tehm pehs choo uhs)

stormy, turbulent

Our camping trip was cut short when the mild shower we were expecting turned into a *tempestuous* downpour.

TEMPORAL

adj (tehmp ore uhl)

having to do with time

The story lacked a *temporal* sense, so we couldn't figure out if the events took place in one evening or over the course of a year.

TENACIOUS

adj (teh nay shuhs)

tending to persist or cling; persistent in adhering to something valued or habitual

Securing women's right to vote required a *tenacious* fight.

TENET

noun (teh niht)

a principle, belief, or doctrine accepted by members of a group

One of the *tenets* of the school is that it is not acceptable to cheat.

TENUOUS

adj (tehn yoo uhs)

having little substance or strength; flimsy, weak

Francine's already *tenuous* connection to her cousins was broken when they moved away and left no forwarding address.

TERSE

adj (tuhrs)

concise, brief, free of extra words

Her *terse* style of writing was widely praised by the editors, who had been used to seeing long-winded material.

THWART

verb (thwahrt)

to block or prevent from happening; frustrate, defeat the hopes or aspirations of

The heavy lock *thwarted* his attempt to enter the building.

TITULAR
adj (<u>tihch</u> yoo luhr)

existing in title only; having a title without the functions or responsibilities

Carla was thrilled to be voted Homecoming Queen until somebody explained that the *titular* honor didn't mean she could boss anybody around.

TOADY
noun (<u>toh</u> dee)

one who flatters in the hope of gaining favors

The king was surrounded by *toadies* who rushed to agree with whatever outrageous thing he said.

TORTUOUS
adj (<u>tohr</u> choo uhs)

having many twists and turns; highly complex

To reach the remote inn, the travelers had to negotiate a *tortuous* path.

TOUT
verb (towt)

to praise or publicize loudly or extravagantly

She *touted* her skills as superior to ours, though in fact, we were all at the same level.

TRAJECTORY
noun (truh <u>jehk</u> tuh ree)

the path followed by a moving object, whether through space or otherwise; flight

The *trajectory* of the pitched ball was interrupted by an unexpected bird.

TRANSIENT
adj (<u>traan</u> see uhnt)

passing with time, temporary, short-lived

The reporter lived a *transient* life, staying in one place only long enough to cover the current story.

TRANSITORY
adj (<u>traan</u> sih <u>tohr</u> ee)

short-lived, existing only briefly

The actress' popularity proved *transitory* when her play folded within the month.

TREMULOUS
adj (<u>treh</u> myoo luhs)

trembling, timid; easily shaken

The *tremulous* kitten had been separated from her mother.

TROUNCE

verb (trowns)

to beat severely, defeat

The inexperienced young boxer was *trounced* in a matter of minutes.

TRUCULENT

adj (truhk yuh lehnt)

disposed to fight, belligerent

The bully was initially *truculent,* but eventually stopped picking fights at the least provocation.

TURGID

adj (tuhr jihd)

swollen as from a fluid, bloated

In the process of osmosis, water passes through the walls of *turgid* cells, ensuring that they never contain too much water.

TUTELAGE

noun (toot uh lihj)

guardianship, guidance

Under the *tutelage* of her older sister, the young orphan was able to persevere.

UNCANNY

adj (uhn kaa nee)

so keen and perceptive as to seem supernatural, peculiarly unsettling

Though they weren't related, their resemblance was *uncanny*.

UNCONSCIONABLE

adj (uhn kahn shuhn uh buhl)

unscrupulous; shockingly unfair or unjust

After she promised me the project, the fact that she gave it to someone else is *unconscionable*.

UNTOWARD

adj (uhn tō rd)

difficult to handle or work with

Charli's negative comments at work were a bit untoward.

USURY

noun (yoo zuh ree)

the practice of lending money at exorbitant rates

The moneylender was convicted of *usury* when it was discovered that he charged 50 percent interest on all his loans.

VARIEGATED

adj (vaar ee uh gayt ehd)

varied; marked with different colors

The *variegated* foliage of the jungle allows it to support thousands of animal species.

VEHEMENTLY

adv (vee ih mehnt lee)

marked by extreme intensity of emotions or convictions

She *vehemently* opposed the closing of the neighborhood garden, and was even arrested for protesting when the bulldozers came.

VERACITY

noun (vuhr aa sih tee)

accuracy, truth

She had a reputation for *veracity*, so everyone believed her version of the story.

VERBOSE

adj (vuhr bohs)

wordy

The DNA analyst's answer was so *verbose* that the jury had trouble grasping his point.

VERITABLE

adj (vehr iht uh buhl)

being without question, often used figuratively

My neighbor was a *veritable* goldmine of information when I was writing my term paper on the Civil Rights era because she had been a student organizer and protester.

VERNACULAR

noun (vuhr naa kyoo luhr)

everyday language used by ordinary people; specialized language of a profession

Preeti could not understand the *vernacular* of the South, where she had recently moved.

VERNAL

adj (vuhr nuhl)

related to spring; fresh

Bea basked in the balmy *vernal* breezes, happy that winter was coming to an end.

VICARIOUSLY

adv (vie kaar ee uhs lee)

felt or undergone as if one were taking part in the experience or feelings of another

She lived *vicariously* through the characters in the adventure books she was always reading.

VILIFY

verb (vih lih fie)

to slander, defame

As gossip columnists often *vilify* celebrities, they're usually held in low regard.

VIM

noun (vihm)

vitality and energy

The *vim* with which she worked so early in the day explained why she was so productive.

VINDICATE

verb (vihn dih kayt)

to clear of blame; support a claim

Tess was *vindicated* when her prediction about the impending tornado came true.

VIRULENT

adj (veer yuh luhnt)

extremely poisonous; malignant; hateful

Alarmed at the *virulent* press he was receiving, the militant activist decided to go underground.

VISCERAL

adj (vihs uhr uhl)

instinctive, not intellectual; deep, emotional

When my twin was wounded many miles away, I had a *visceral* reaction.

VITUPERATE

verb (vih too puhr ayt)

to abuse verbally, berate

Vituperating someone is never a constructive way to effect change.

VOCIFEROUS

adj (voh sih fuhr uhs)

loud, noisy

Amid the *vociferous* protests of the members of parliament, the prime minister continued his speech.

VOLLEY

noun (vah lee)

a flight of missiles; round of gunshots

The troops fired a *volley* of bullets at the enemy, but they couldn't be sure how many hit their target.

VOLUBLE

adj (vahl yuh buhl)

talkative, speaking easily, glib

The *voluble* man and his reserved wife proved the old saying that opposites attract.

WAN

adj (wahn)

sickly pale

The sick child had a *wan* face, in contrast to her rosy-cheeked sister.

WANTON

adj (wahn tuhn)

undisciplined, unrestrained; reckless

The townspeople were outraged by the *wanton* display of disrespect when they discovered the statue of the town founder covered in graffiti.

WAX

verb (waaks)

to increase gradually; to begin to be

The moon was *waxing*, and would soon be full.

WIELD

verb (weeld)

to exercise authority or influence effectively

For such a young congressman, he *wielded* a lot of power.

WILY

adj (<u>wie</u> lee)

clever; deceptive

Yet again, the *wily* coyote managed to elude the ranchers who wanted it dead.

WINSOME

adj (<u>wihn</u> suhm)

charming, happily engaging

Dawn gave the clerk a *winsome* smile, and he apologized for making her wait.

WORST

verb (wuhrst)

to gain the advantage over; to defeat

The North *worsted* the South in America's Civil War.

WRY

adj (rie)

bent or twisted in shape or condition; dryly humorous

Every time she teased him, she shot her friends a *wry* smile.

YEN

noun (yehn)

a strong desire, craving

Pregnant women commonly have a *yen* for pickles.

ZENITH

noun (<u>zee</u> nihth)

the point of culmination; peak

The diva considered her appearance at the Metropolitan Opera to be the *zenith* of her career.

ZEPHYR

noun (<u>zeh</u> fuhr)

a gentle breeze; something airy or unsubstantial

The *zephyr* from the ocean made the intense heat on the beach bearable for the sunbathers

Section Eight: CLEP Resources | **673**

Math in a Nutshell

This list covers basic math topics including arithmetic, algebra, geometry, and probability. Be sure to brush up on sets, logic, imaginary numbers, and other Odd topics on your own.

Use this list to remind yourself of the key areas you'll need to know. Do four concepts a day, and you'll be ready within a month. If a concept continually causes you trouble, circle it and refer back to it as you try to do the questions.

You've probably been taught most of these concepts in school already, so this list is a great way to refresh your memory.

NUMBER PROPERTIES

1. Number Categories

Integers are **whole numbers;** they include negative whole numbers and zero.

A **rational number** is a number that can be expressed as a **ratio of two integers. Irrational numbers** are real numbers—they have locations on the number line—but they **can't be expressed precisely as a fraction or decimal.** For the purposes of the SAT, the most important **irrational numbers** are $\sqrt{2}$, $\sqrt{3}$, and π.

2. Adding/Subtracting Signed Numbers

To **add a positive and a negative,** first ignore the signs and find the positive difference between the number parts. Then attach the sign of the original number with the larger number part. For example, to add 23 and −34, first ignore the minus sign and find the positive difference between 23 and 34—that's 11. Then attach the sign of the number with the larger number part—in this case it's the minus sign from the −34. So, 23 + (−34) = −11.

Make **subtraction** situations simpler by turning them into addition. For example, you can think of −17 − (−21) as −17 + (+21).

To **add or subtract a string of positives and negatives,** first turn everything into addition. Then combine the positives and negatives so that the string is reduced to the sum of a single positive number and a single negative number.

3. Multiplying/Dividing Signed Numbers

To multiply and/or divide positives and negatives, treat the number parts as usual and **attach a minus sign if there were originally an odd number of negatives.** For example, to multiply −2, −3, and −5, first multiply the number parts: 2 × 3 × 5 = 30. Then go back and note that there were *three*—an *odd* number—negatives, so the product is negative: (−2) × (−3) × (−5) = −30.

4. PEMDAS

When performing multiple operations, remember to perform them in the right order: **PEMDAS,** which means **Parentheses** first, then **Exponents,** then **Multiplication** and **Division** (left to right), and lastly **Addition** and **Subtraction** (left to right). In the expression $9 - 2 \times (5 - 3)^2 + 6 \prod 3$, begin with the parentheses: $(5 - 3) = 2$. Then do the exponent: $2^2 = 4$. Now the expression is: $9 - 2 \times 4 + 6 \prod 3$. Next do the multiplication and division to get: $9 - 8 + 2$, which equals 3. If you have difficulty remembering PEMDAS, use this sentence to recall it: **P**lease **E**xcuse **M**y **D**ear **A**unt **S**ally.

5. Counting Consecutive Integers

To count consecutive integers, **subtract the smallest from the largest and add 1.** To count the integers from 13 through 31, subtract: 31 − 13 = 18. Then add 1: 18 + 1 = 19.

NUMBER OPERATIONS AND CONCEPTS

6. Exponential Growth

If r is the ratio between consecutive terms, a_1 is the first term, a_n is the nth term, and S_n is the sum of the first n terms, then $a_n = a_1 r^{n-1}$ and $S_n = \dfrac{a_1 - a_1 r^n}{1 - r}$.

7. Union and Intersection of Sets

The things in a set are called elements or members. The union of Set A and Set B, sometimes expressed as $A \cup B$, is the set of elements that are in either or both of Set A and Set B. If Set $A = \{1, 2\}$ and Set $B = \{3, 4\}$, then $A \cup B = \{1, 2, 3, 4\}$. The intersection of Set A and Set B, sometimes expressed as $A \cap B$, is the set of elements common to both Set A and Set B. If Set $A = \{1, 2, 3\}$ and Set $B = \{3, 4, 5\}$, then $A \cap B = \{3\}$.

DIVISIBILITY

8. Factor/Multiple

The **factors** of integer *n* are the positive integers that divide into *n* with no remainder. The **multiples** of *n* are the integers that *n* divides into with no remainder. For example, 6 is a factor of 12, and 24 is a multiple of 12. 12 is both a factor and a multiple of itself, since $12 \times 1 = 12$ and $12 \prod 1 = 12$.

9. Prime Factorization

To find the prime factorization of an integer, just keep breaking it up into factors until **all the factors are prime.** To find the prime factorization of 36, for example, you could begin by breaking it into 4×9: $36 = 4 \times 9 = 2 \times 2 \times 3 \times 3$.

10. Relative Primes

Relative primes are integers that have no common factor other than 1. To determine whether two integers are relative primes, break them both down to their prime factorizations. For example: $35 = 5 \times 7$, and $54 = 2 \times 3 \times 3 \times 3$. They have **no prime factors in common,** so 35 and 54 are relative primes.

11. Common Multiple

A common multiple is a number that is a multiple of two or more integers. You can always get a common multiple of two integers by **multiplying** them, but, unless the two numbers are relative primes, the product will not be the *least* common multiple. For example, to find a common multiple for 12 and 15, you could just multiply: $12 \times 15 = 180$.

To find the **least common multiple**, check out the **multiples of the larger integer** until you find one that's **also a multiple of the smaller.** To find the LCM of 12 and 15, begin by taking the multiples of 15: 15 is not divisible by 12; 30 is not; nor is 45. But the next multiple of 15, 60, *is* divisible by 12, so it's the LCM.

12. Greatest Common Factor (GCF)

To find the greatest common factor, break down both integers into their prime factorizations and multiply **all the prime factors they have in common.** $36 = 2 \times 2 \times 3 \times 3$, and $48 = 2 \times 2 \times 2 \times 2 \times 3$. What they have in common is two 2s and one 3, so the GCF is $2 \times 2 \times 3 = 12$.

13. Even/Odd

To predict whether a sum, difference, or product will be even or odd, just **take simple numbers like 1 and 2 and see what happens.** There are rules—"odd times even is even," for example—but there's no need to memorize them. What happens with one set of numbers generally happens with all similar sets.

14. Multiples of 2 and 4

An integer is divisible by 2 (even) if the **last digit is even.** An integer is divisible by 4 if the **last two digits form a multiple of 4.** The last digit of 562 is 2, which is even, so 562 is a multiple of 2. The last two digits form 62, which is *not* divisible by 4, so 562 is not a multiple of 4. The integer 512, however is divisible by four because the last two digits form 12, which is a multiple of 4.

15. Multiples of 3 and 9

An integer is divisible by 3 if the **sum of its digits is divisible by 3.** An integer is divisible by 9 if the **sum of its digits is divisible by 9.** The sum of the digits in 957 is 21, which is divisible by 3 but not by 9, so 957 is divisible by 3 but not by 9.

16. Multiples of 5 and 10

An integer is divisible by 5 if the **last digit is 5 or 0.** An integer is divisible by 10 if the **last digit is 0.** The last digit of 665 is 5, so 665 is a multiple of 5 but *not* a multiple of 10.

17. Remainders

The remainder is the **whole number left over after division.** 487 is 2 more than 485, which is a multiple of 5, so when 487 is divided by 5, the remainder will be 2.

FRACTIONS AND DECIMALS

18. Reducing Fractions

To reduce a fraction to lowest terms, **factor out and cancel** all factors the numerator and denominator have in common.

$$\frac{28}{36} = \frac{4 \times 7}{4 \times 9} = \frac{7}{9}$$

19. Adding/Subtracting Fractions

To add or subtract fractions, first find a **common denominator,** then add or subtract the numerators.

$$\frac{2}{15} + \frac{3}{10} = \frac{4}{30} + \frac{9}{30} = \frac{4+9}{30} = \frac{13}{30}$$

20. Multiplying Fractions

To multiply fractions, **multiply** the numerators and **multiply** the denominators.

$$\frac{5}{7} \times \frac{3}{4} = \frac{5 \times 3}{7 \times 4} = \frac{15}{28}$$

21. Dividing Fractions

To divide fractions, **invert** the second one and **multiply.**

$$\frac{1}{2} \div \frac{3}{5} = \frac{1}{2} \times \frac{5}{3} = \frac{1 \times 5}{2 \times 3} = \frac{5}{6}$$

22. Mixed Numbers and Improper Fractions

To convert a mixed number to an improper fraction, **multiply** the whole number part by the denominator, then **add** the numerator. The result is the new numerator (over the same denominator). To convert $7\frac{1}{3}$, first multiply 7 by 3, then add 1, to get the new numerator of 22. Put that over the same denominator, 3, to get $\frac{22}{3}$.

To convert an improper fraction to a mixed number, divide the denominator into the numerator to get a **whole number quotient with a remainder.** The quotient becomes the whole number part of the mixed number, and the remainder becomes the new numerator—with the same denominator. For example, to convert $\frac{108}{5}$, first divide 5 into 108, which yields 21 with a remainder of 3. Therefore, $\frac{108}{5} = 21\frac{3}{5}$.

23. Reciprocal

To find the reciprocal of a fraction, **switch the numerator and the denominator.** The reciprocal of $\frac{3}{7}$ is $\frac{7}{3}$. The reciprocal of 5 is $\frac{1}{5}$. The product of reciprocals is 1.

24. Comparing Fractions

One way to compare fractions is to **re-express them with a common denominator.** $\frac{3}{4} = \frac{21}{28}$ and $\frac{5}{7} = \frac{20}{28}$. $\frac{21}{28}$ is greater than $\frac{20}{28}$, so $\frac{3}{4}$ is greater than $\frac{5}{7}$. Another method is to **convert them both to decimals.** $\frac{3}{4}$ converts to .75, and $\frac{5}{7}$ converts to approximately .714.

25. Converting Fractions and Decimals

To convert a fraction to a decimal, **divide the bottom into the top.** To convert $\frac{5}{8}$, divide 8 into 5, yielding .625.

To convert a decimal to a fraction, set the decimal over 1 and **multiply the numerator and denominator by 10** raised to the number of digits to the right of the decimal point.

To convert .625 to a fraction, you would multiply $\frac{.625}{1}$ by $\frac{10^3}{10^3}$ or $\frac{1000}{1000}$. Then simplify: $\frac{625}{1000} = \frac{5 \times 125}{8 \times 125} = \frac{5}{8}$.

26. Repeating Decimal

To find a particular digit in a repeating decimal, note the **number of digits in the cluster that repeats.** If there are 2 digits in that cluster, then every second digit is the same. If there are 3 digits in that cluster, then every third digit is the same. And so on. For example, the decimal equivalent of $\frac{1}{27}$ is .037037037..., which is best written $.\overline{037}$. There are 3 digits in the repeating cluster, so every third digit is the same: 7. To find the 50th digit, look for the multiple of 3 just less than 50—that's 48. The 48th digit is 7, and with the 49th digit the pattern repeats with 0. The 50th digit is 3.

27. Identifying the Parts and the Whole

The key to solving most fractions and percents story problems is to identify the part and the whole. Usually you'll find the **part** associated with the verb *is/are* and the **whole** associated with the word *of.* In the sentence, "Half of the boys are blonds," the whole is the boys ("*of* the boys"), and the part is the blonds ("*are* blonds").

PERCENTS

28. Percent Formula

Whether you need to find the part, the whole, or the percent, use the same formula:

Part = Percent × Whole

Example: What is 12 percent of 25?
Setup: Part = .12 × 25

Example: 15 is 3 percent of what number?
Setup: 15 = .03 × Whole

Example: 45 is what percent of 9?
Setup: 45 = Percent × 9

29. Percent Increase and Decrease

To increase a number by a percent, **add the percent to 100 percent,** convert to a decimal, and multiply. To increase 40 by 25 percent, add 25 percent to 100 percent, convert 125 percent to 1.25, and multiply by 40. 1.25 × 40 = 50.

30. Finding the Original Whole

To find the **original whole before a percent increase or decrease,** set up an equation. Think of the result of a 15 percent increase over *x* as 1.15*x*.

Example: After a 5 percent increase, the population was 59,346. What was the population before the increase?
Setup: 1.05*x* = 59,346

31. Combined Percent Increase and Decrease

To determine the combined effect of multiple percent increases and/or decreases, **start with 100 and see what happens.**

Example: A price went up 10 percent one year, and the new price went up 20 percent the next year. What was the combined percent increase?
Setup: First year: 100 + (10 percent of 100) = 110. Second year: 110 + (20 percent of 110) = 132. That's a combined 32 percent increase.

RATIOS, PROPORTIONS, AND RATES

32. Setting up a Ratio

To find a ratio, put the number associated with the word *of* **on top** and the quantity associated with the word *to* **on the bottom** and reduce. The ratio of 20 oranges to 12 apples is $\frac{20}{12}$, which reduces to $\frac{5}{3}$.

33. Part-to-Part Ratios and Part-to-Whole Ratios

If the parts add up to the whole, a part-to-part ratio can be turned into two part-to-whole ratios by putting **each number in the original ratio over the sum of the numbers.** If the ratio of males to females is 1 to 2, then the males-to-people ratio is $\frac{1}{1+2} = \frac{1}{3}$ and the females-to-people ratio is $\frac{2}{1+2} = \frac{2}{3}$. In other words, $\frac{2}{3}$ of all the people are female.

34. Solving a Proportion

To solve a proportion, **cross multiply:**

$$\frac{x}{5} = \frac{3}{4}$$
$$4x = 3 \times 5$$
$$x = \frac{15}{4} = 3.75$$

35. Rate

To solve a rates problem, **use the units** to keep things straight.

Example: If snow is falling at the rate of one foot every four hours, how many inches of snow will fall in seven hours?

Setup:
$$\frac{1 \text{ foot}}{4 \text{ hours}} = \frac{x \text{ inches}}{7 \text{ hours}}$$
$$\frac{12 \text{ inches}}{4 \text{ hours}} = \frac{x \text{ inches}}{7 \text{ hours}}$$
$$4x = 12 \times 7$$
$$x = 21$$

36. Average Rate

Average rate is *not* simply the average of the rates.

$$\text{Average } A \text{ per } B = \frac{\text{Total } A}{\text{Total } B}$$

$$\text{Average Speed} = \frac{\text{Total distance}}{\text{Total time}}$$

To find the average speed for 120 miles at 40 mph and 120 miles at 60 mph, **don't just average the two speeds.** First, figure out the total distance and the total time. The total distance is $120 + 120 = 240$ miles. The times are two hours for the first leg and three hours for the second leg, or five hours total. The average speed, then, is $\frac{240}{5} = 48$ miles per hour.

AVERAGES

37. Average Formula

To find the average of a set of numbers, **add them up and divide by the number of numbers.**

$$\text{Average} = \frac{\text{Sum of the terms}}{\text{Number of terms}}$$

To find the average of the 5 numbers 12, 15, 23, 40, and 40, first add them: $12 + 15 + 23 + 40 + 40 = 130$. Then, divide the sum by 5: $130 \div 5 = 26$.

38. Average of Evenly Spaced Numbers

To find the average of evenly spaced numbers, just **average the smallest and the largest.** The average of all the integers from 13 through 77 is the same as the average of 13 and 77:

$$\frac{13 + 77}{2} = \frac{90}{2} = 45$$

39. Using the Average to Find the Sum

$$\text{Sum} = (\text{Average}) \times (\text{Number of terms})$$

If the average of 10 numbers is 50, then they add up to 10×50, or 500.

40. Finding the Missing Number

To find a missing number when you're given the average, **use the sum.** If the average of 4 numbers is 7, then the sum of those 4 numbers is 4×7, or 28. Suppose that 3 of the numbers are 3, 5, and 8. These 3 numbers add up to 16 of that 28, which leaves 12 for the fourth number.

41. Median and Mode

The median of a set of numbers is the **value that falls in the middle of the set.** If you have 5 test scores, and they are 88, 86, 57, 94, and 73, you must first list the scores in increasing or decreasing order: 57, 73, 86, 88, 94.

The median is the middle number, or 86. If there is an even number of values in a set (6 test scores, for instance), simply take the average of the 2 middle numbers.

The mode of a set of numbers is the **value that appears most often.** If your test scores were 88, 57, 68, 85, 99, 93, 93, 84, and 81, the mode of the scores would be 93 because it appears more often than any other score. If there is a tie for the most common value in a set, the set has more than one mode.

POSSIBILITIES AND PROBABILITY

42. Counting the Possibilities

The fundamental counting principle: If there are *m* **ways** one event can happen and *n* **ways** a second event can happen, then there are *m* × *n* **ways** for the 2 events to happen. For example, with 5 shirts and 7 pairs of pants to choose from, you can have $5 \times 7 = 35$ different outfits.

43. Probability

$$\text{Probability} = \frac{\text{Favorable Outcomes}}{\text{Total Possible Outcomes}}$$

For example, if you have 12 shirts in a drawer and 9 of them are white, the probability of picking a white shirt at random is $\frac{9}{12} = \frac{3}{4}$. This probability can also be expressed as .75 or 75%.

POWERS AND ROOTS

44. Multiplying and Dividing Powers

To multiply powers with the same base, **add the exponents and keep the same base**:

$$x^3 \times x^4 = x^{3+4} = x^7$$

To divide powers with the same base, **subtract the exponents and keep the same base**:

$$y^{13} \div y^8 = y^{13-8} = y^5$$

45. Raising Powers to Powers

To raise a power to a power, **multiply the exponents**:

$$(x^3)^4 = x^{3 \times 4} = x^{12}$$

46. Simplifying Square Roots

To simplify a square root, **factor out the perfect squares** under the radical, unsquare them, and put the result in front.

$$\sqrt{12} = \sqrt{4 \times 3} = \sqrt{4} \times \sqrt{3} = 2\sqrt{3}$$

47. Adding and Subtracting Roots

You can add or subtract radical expressions **when the part under the radicals is the same**:

$$2\sqrt{3} + 3\sqrt{3} = 5\sqrt{3}$$

Don't try to add or subtract when the radical parts are different. There's not much you can do with an expression like:

$$3\sqrt{5} + 3\sqrt{7}$$

48. Multiplying and Dividing Roots

The product of square roots is equal to the **square root of the product**:

$$\sqrt{3} \times \sqrt{5} = \sqrt{3 \times 5} = \sqrt{15}$$

The quotient of square roots is equal to the **square root of the quotient**:

$$\frac{\sqrt{6}}{\sqrt{3}} = \sqrt{\frac{6}{3}} = \sqrt{2}$$

49. Negative Exponent and Rational Exponent

To find the value of a number raised to a negative exponent, simply rewrite the number, without the negative sign, as the bottom of a fraction with 1 as the numerator of the fraction: $3^{-2} = \frac{1}{3^2} = \frac{1}{9}$. If x is a positive number and a is a nonzero number, then $x^{\frac{1}{a}} = \sqrt[a]{x}$. So $4^{\frac{1}{2}} = \sqrt[2]{4} = 2$. If p and q are integers, then $x^{\frac{p}{q}} = \sqrt[q]{x^p}$. So $4^{\frac{3}{2}} = \sqrt[2]{4^3} = \sqrt{64} = 8$.

ABSOLUTE VALUE

50. Determining Absolute Value

The absolute value of a number is the distance of the number from zero on the number line. Because absolute value is a distance, it is always positive. The absolute value of 7 is 7; this is expressed $|7| = 7$. Similarly, the absolute value of −7 is 7: $|-7| = 7$. Every positive number is the absolute value of 2 numbers: itself and its negative.

ALGEBRAIC EXPRESSIONS

51. Evaluating an Expression

To evaluate an algebraic expression, **plug in** the given values for the unknowns and calculate according to **PEMDAS**. To find the value of $x^2 + 5x - 6$ when $x = -2$, plug in −2 for x: $(-2)^2 + 5(-2) - 6 = -12$.

52. Adding and Subtracting Monomials

To combine like terms, **keep the variable part unchanged while adding or subtracting the coefficients:**

$$2a + 3a = (2 + 3)a = 5a$$

53. Adding and Subtracting Polynomials

To add or subtract polynomials, **combine like terms.**

$$(3x^2 + 5x - 7) - (x^2 + 12) =$$
$$(3x^2 - x^2) + 5x + (-7 - 12) =$$
$$2x^2 + 5x - 19 =$$

54. Multiplying Monomials

To multiply monomials, **multiply the coefficients and the variables separately:**

$$2a \times 3a = (2 \times 3)(a \times a) = 6a^2$$

55. Multiplying Binomials—FOIL

To multiply binomials, use **FOIL.** To multiply $(x + 3)$ by $(x + 4)$, first multiply the **F**irst terms: $x \times x = x^2$. Next the **O**uter terms: $x \times 4 = 4x$. Then the **I**nner terms: $3 \times x = 3x$. And finally the **L**ast terms: $3 \times 4 = 12$. Then add and combine like terms:

$$x^2 + 4x + 3x + 12 = x^2 + 7x + 12$$

56. Multiplying Other Polynomials

FOIL works only when you want to multiply two binomials. If you want to multiply polynomials with more than two terms, make sure you **multiply each term in the first polynomial by each term in the second.**

$$(x^2 + 3x + 4)(x + 5) =$$
$$x^2(x + 5) + 3x(x + 5) + 4(x + 5) =$$
$$x^3 + 5x^2 + 3x^2 + 15x + 4x + 20 =$$
$$x^3 + 8x^2 + 19x + 20$$

After multiplying two polynomials together, the number of terms in your expression before simplifying should equal the number of terms in one polynomial multiplied by the number of terms in the second. In the example, you should have $3 \times 2 = 6$ terms in the product before you simplify like terms.

FACTORING ALGEBRAIC EXPRESSIONS

57. Factoring out a Common Divisor

A factor common to all terms of a polynomial can be **factored out.** All three terms in the polynomial $3x^3 + 12x^2 - 6x$ contain a factor of $3x$. Pulling out the common factor yields $3x(x^2 + 4x - 2)$.

58. Factoring the Difference of Squares

One of the test maker's favorite factorables is the **difference of squares.**

$$a^2 - b^2 = (a - b)(a + b)$$

$x^2 - 9$, for example, factors to $(x - 3)(x + 3)$.

59. Factoring the Square of a Binomial

Recognize polynomials that are squares of binomials:

$$a^2 + 2ab + b^2 = (a + b)^2$$
$$a^2 - 2ab + b^2 = (a - b)^2$$

For example, $4x^2 + 12x + 9$ factors to $(2x + 3)^2$, and $n^2 - 10n + 25$ factors to $(n - 5)^2$.

60. Factoring Other Polynomials—FOIL in Reverse

To factor a quadratic expression, **think about what binomials you could use FOIL on to get that quadratic expression.** To factor $x^2 - 5x + 6$, think about what **F**irst terms will produce x^2, what **L**ast terms will produce $+6$, and what **O**uter and **I**nner terms will produce $-5x$. Some common sense—and a little trial and error—lead you to $(x - 2)(x - 3)$.

61. Simplifying an Algebraic Fraction

Simplifying an algebraic fraction is a lot like simplifying a numerical fraction. The general idea is to **find factors common to the numerator and denominator and cancel them.** Thus, simplifying an algebraic fraction begins with factoring.

For example, to simplify $\frac{x^2 - x - 12}{x^2 - 9}$, first factor the numerator and denominator:

$$\frac{x^2 - x - 12}{x^2 - 9} = \frac{(x-4)(x+3)}{(x-3)(x+3)}$$

Canceling $x + 3$ from the numerator and denominator leaves you with $\frac{x-4}{x-3}$.

SOLVING EQUATIONS

62. Solving a Linear Equation

To solve an equation, do whatever is necessary to both sides to **isolate the variable.** To solve the equation $5x - 12 = -2x + 9$, first get all the x's on one side by adding $2x$ to both sides: $7x - 12 = 9$. Then add 12 to both sides: $7x = 21$. Then divide both sides by 7: $x = 3$.

63. Solving "In Terms Of"

To solve an equation for one variable **in terms of** another means to **isolate the one variable on one side of the equation,** leaving an expression containing the other variable on the other side of the equation. To solve the equation $3x - 10y = -5x + 6y$ for x in terms of y, isolate x:

$$3x - 10y = -5x + 6y$$
$$3x + 5x = 6y + 10y$$
$$8x = 16y$$
$$x = 2y$$

64. Translating from English into Algebra

To translate from English into algebra, look for the key words and systematically turn phrases into algebraic expressions and sentences into equations. Be careful about order, especially when subtraction is called for.

Example: The charge for a phone call is r cents for the first 3 minutes and s cents for each minute thereafter. What is the cost, in cents, of a phone call lasting exactly t minutes? ($t > 3$)

Setup: The charge begins with r, and then something more is added, depending on the length of the call. The amount added is s times the number of minutes past 3 minutes. If the total number of minutes is t, then the number of minutes past 3 is $t - 3$. So the charge is $r + s(t - 3)$.

65. Solving a Quadratic Equation

To solve a quadratic equation, put it in the "$ax^2 + bx + c = 0$" form, **factor** the left side (if you can), and set each factor equal to 0 separately to get the two solutions. To solve $x^2 + 12 = 7x$, first rewrite it as $x^2 - 7x + 12 = 0$. Then factor the left side:

$$(x-3)(x-4) = 0$$
$$x - 3 = 0 \text{ or } x - 4 = 0$$
$$x = 3 \text{ or } 4$$

66. Solving a System of Equations

You can solve for 2 variables only if you have 2 distinct equations. 2 forms of the same equation will not be adequate. **Combine the equations** in such a way that **one of the variables cancels out.** To solve the 2 equations $4x + 3y = 8$ and $x + y = 3$, multiply both sides of the second equation by -3 to get: $-3x - 3y = -9$. Now add the 2 equations; the $3y$ and the $-3y$ cancel out, leaving: $x = -1$. Plug that back into either one of the original equations and you'll find that $y = 4$.

67. Solving an Inequality

To solve an inequality, do whatever is necessary to both sides to **isolate the variable.** Just remember that when you **multiply or divide both sides by a negative number**, you must **reverse the sign.** To solve $-5x + 7 < -3$, subtract 7 from both sides to get: $-5x < -10$. Now divide both sides by -5, remembering to reverse the sign: $x > 2$.

68. Radical Equations

A radical equation contains at least one radical expression. Solve radical equations by using standard rules of algebra. If $5\sqrt{x} - 2 = 13$, then $5\sqrt{x} = 15$ and $\sqrt{x} = 3$, so $x = 9$.

FUNCTIONS

69. Function Notation and Evaluation

Standard function notation is written $f(x)$ and read "f of 4." To evaluate the function $f(x) = 2x + 3$ for $f(4)$, replace x with 4 and simplify: $f(4) = 2(4) + 3 = 11$.

70. Direct and Inverse Variation

In direct variation, $y = kx$, where k is a nonzero constant. In direct variation, the variable y changes directly as x does. If a unit of Currency A is worth 2 units of Currency B, then $A = 2B$. If the number of units of B were to double, the number of units of A would double, and so on for halving, tripling, etc. In inverse variation, $xy = k$, where x and y are variables and k is a constant. A famous inverse relationship is $rate \times time = distance$, where distance is constant. Imagine having to cover a distance of 24 miles. If you were to travel at 12 miles per hour, you'd need 2 hours. But if you were to halve your rate, you would have to double your time. This is just another way of saying that rate and time vary inversely.

71. Domain and Range of a Function

The domain of a function is the set of values for which the function is defined. For example, the domain of $f(x) = \frac{1}{1-x^2}$ is all values of x except 1 and -1, because for those values the denominator has a value of 0 and is therefore undefined. The range of a function is the set of outputs or results of the function. For example, the range of $f(x) = x^2$ is all numbers greater than all or equal to zero, because x^2 cannot be negative.

COORDINATE GEOMETRY

72. Finding the Distance Between Two Points

To find the distance between points, **use the Pythagorean theorem** or **special right triangles.** The difference between the x's is one leg and the difference between the y's is the other.

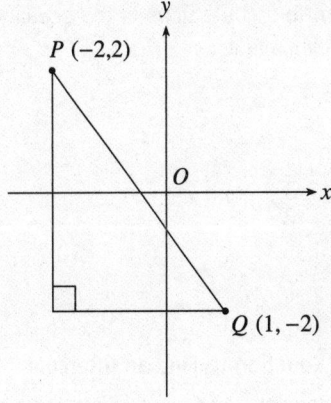

In the figure above, PQ is the hypotenuse of a 3-4-5 triangle, so $PQ = 5$.

You can also use the **distance formula:**

$$d = \sqrt{(x_1 - x_2)^2 + (y_1 - y_2)^2}$$

To find the distance between $R(3, 6)$ and $S(5, -2)$:

$$d = \sqrt{(3 - 5)^2 + [6 - (-2)^2]}$$
$$= \sqrt{(-2)^2 + (8)^2}$$
$$= \sqrt{68} = 2\sqrt{17}$$

73. Using Two Points to Find the Slope

$$\text{Slope} = \frac{\text{Change in } y}{\text{Change in } x} = \frac{\text{Rise}}{\text{Run}}$$

The slope of the line that contains the points $A(2, 3)$ and $B(0, -1)$ is:

$$\frac{y_A - y_B}{x_A - x_B} = \frac{3 - (-1)}{2 - 0} = \frac{4}{2} = 2$$

74. Using an Equation to Find the Slope

To find the slope of a line from an equation, put the equation into the **slope-intercept** form:

$$y = mx + b$$

The **slope is** m. To find the slope of the equation $3x + 2y = 4$, rearrange it:

$$3x + 2y = 4$$
$$2y = -3x + 4$$
$$y = -\frac{3}{2}x + 2$$

The slope is $-\frac{3}{2}$.

75. Using an Equation to Find an Intercept

To find the y-intercept, you can either put the equation into $y = mx + b$ **(slope-intercept)** form—in which case b **is the y-intercept**—or you can just **plug $x = 0$** into the equation and **solve for y**. To find the x-intercept, **plug $y = 0$** into the equation and **solve for x**.

76. Finding the Midpoint

The midpoint of two points on a line segment is the average of the x-coordinates of the endpoints and the average of the y-coordinates of the endpoints. If the endpoints are (x_1, y_1) and (x_2, y_2), the midpoint is $\left(\frac{x_1 + x_2}{2}, \frac{y_1 + y_2}{2}\right)$. The midpoint of $(3, 5)$ and $(9, 1)$ is $\left(\frac{3 + 9}{2}, \frac{5 + 1}{2}\right)$.

LINES AND ANGLES

77. Intersecting Lines

When two lines intersect, **adjacent angles are supplementary and vertical angles are equal.**

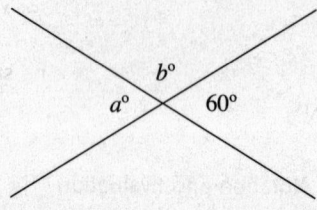

In the figure above, the angles marked $a°$ and $b°$ are adjacent and supplementary, so $a + b = 180$. Furthermore, the angles marked $a°$ and $60°$ are vertical and equal, so $a = 60$.

78. Parallel Lines and Transversals

A transversal across parallel lines forms **four equal acute angles and four equal obtuse angles.**

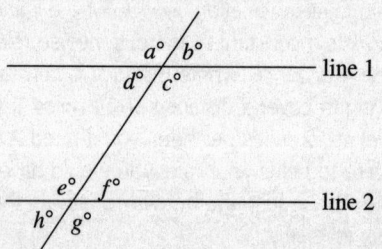

In the figure above, line 1 is parallel to line 2. Angles a, c, e, and g are obtuse, so they are all equal. Angles b, d, f, and h are acute, so they are all equal.

Furthermore, **any of the acute angles is supplementary to any of the obtuse angles.** Angles a and h are supplementary, as are b and e, c and f, and so on.

TRIANGLES—GENERAL

79. Interior and Exterior Angles of a Triangle

The 3 angles of any triangle **add up to 180 degrees**.

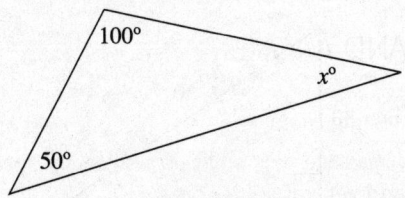

In the figure above, $x + 50 + 100 = 180$, so $x = 30$.

An exterior angle of a triangle is equal to the **sum of the remote interior angles**.

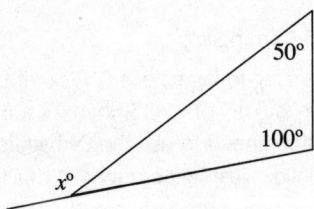

In the figure above, the exterior angle labeled $x°$ is equal to the sum of the remote angles: $x = 50 + 100 = 150$.

The 3 exterior angles of a triangle add up to 360 degrees.

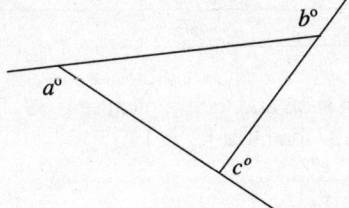

In the figure above, $a + b + c = 360$.

80. Similar Triangles

Similar triangles have the same shape: **corresponding angles are equal and corresponding sides are proportional**.

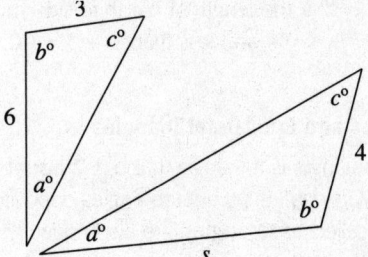

The triangles above are similar because they have the same angles. The 3 corresponds to the 4 and the 6 corresponds to the s.

$$\frac{3}{4} = \frac{6}{s}$$

$$3s = 24$$

$$s = 8$$

81. Area of a Triangle

$$\text{Area of Triangle} = \frac{1}{2}(\text{base})(\text{height})$$

The height is the perpendicular distance between the side that's chosen as the base and the opposite vertex.

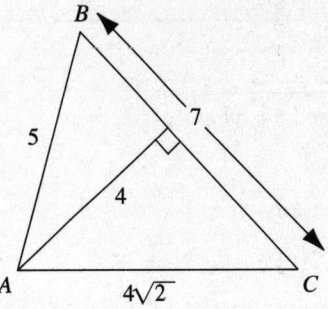

In the triangle above, 4 is the height when the 7 is chosen as the base.

$$\text{Area} = \frac{1}{2}bh = \frac{1}{2}(7)(4) = 14$$

82. Triangle Inequality Theorem

The length of one side of a triangle must be **greater than the difference and less than the sum** of the lengths of the other two sides. For example, if it is given that the length of one side is 3 and the length of another side is 7, then you know that the length of the third side must be greater than $7 - 3 = 4$ and less than $7 + 3 = 10$.

83. Isosceles and Equilateral Triangles

An isosceles triangle is a triangle that has **2 equal sides.** Not only are 2 sides equal, but the angles opposite the equal sides, called **base angles**, are also equal.

Equilateral triangles are triangles in which **all 3 sides are equal.** Since all the sides are equal, all the angles are also equal. All 3 angles in an equilateral triangle measure 60 degrees, regardless of the lengths of sides.

RIGHT TRIANGLES

84. Pythagorean Theorem

For all right triangles:

$$(\text{leg}_1)^2 + (\text{leg}_2)^2 = (\text{hypotenuse})^2$$

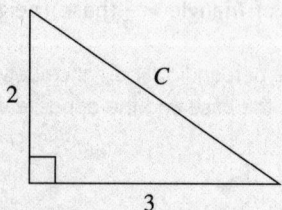

If one leg is 2 and the other leg is 3, then:

$$2^2 + 3^2 = c^2$$
$$c^2 = 4 + 9$$
$$c = \sqrt{13}$$

85. The 3-4-5 Triangle

If a right triangle's leg-to-leg ratio is 3:4, or if the leg-to-hypotenuse ratio is 3:5 or 4:5, it's a 3-4-5 triangle and you don't need to use the Pythagorean theorem to find the third side. Just figure out what multiple of 3-4-5 it is.

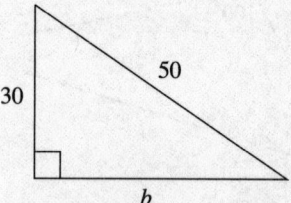

In the right triangle shown, one leg is 30 and the hypotenuse is 50. This is 10 times 3-4-5. The other leg is 40.

86. The 5-12-13 Triangle

If a right triangle's leg-to-leg ratio is 5:12, or if the leg-to-hypotenuse ratio is 5:13 or 12:13, then it's a 5-12-13 triangle and you don't need to use the Pythagorean theorem to find the third side. Just figure out what multiple of 5-12-13 it is.

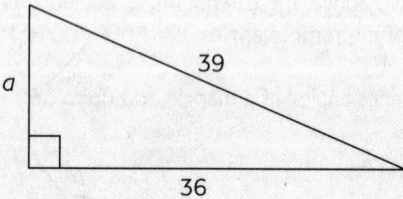

Here one leg is 36 and the hypotenuse is 39. This is 3 times 5-12-13. The other leg is 15.

87. The 30-60-90 Triangle

The sides of a 30-60-90 triangle are in a ratio of $x : x\sqrt{3} : 2x$. You don't need the Pythagorean theorem.

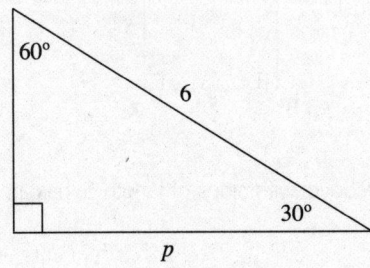

If the hypotenuse is 6, then the shorter leg is half that, or 3; and then the longer leg is equal to the short leg times $\sqrt{3}$, or $3\sqrt{3}$.

88. The 45-45-90 Triangle

The sides of a 45-45-90 triangle are in a ratio of $x : x : x\sqrt{2}$.

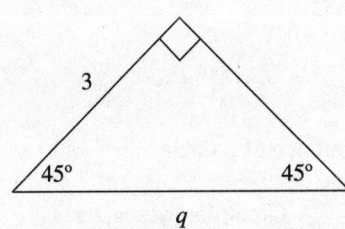

If one leg is 3, then the other leg is also 3, and the hypotenuse is equal to a leg times $\sqrt{2}$, or $3\sqrt{2}$.

OTHER POLYGONS

89. Characteristics of a Rectangle

A rectangle is a **four-sided figure with four right angles.** Opposite sides are equal. Diagonals are equal.

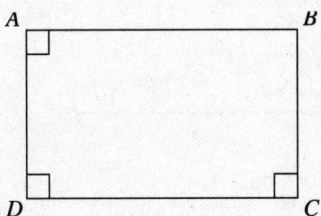

Quadrilateral *ABCD* above is shown to have three right angles. The fourth angle therefore also measures 90 degrees, and *ABCD* is a rectangle. The perimeter of a rectangle is equal to the sum of the lengths of the four sides, which is equivalent to 2(length + width).

Area of Rectangle = length × width

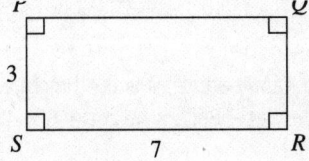

The area of a 7-by-3 rectangle is $7 \times 3 = 21$.

90. Characteristics of a Parallelogram

A parallelogram has **two pairs of parallel sides.** Opposite sides are equal. Opposite angles are equal. Consecutive angles add up to 180 degrees.

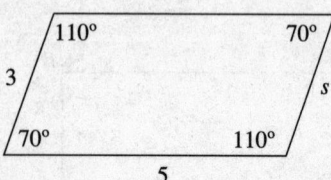

In the figure above, s is the length of the side opposite the 3, so s = 3.

Area of Parallelogram = base × height

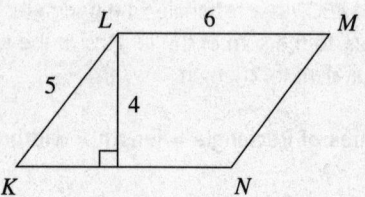

In parallelogram KLMN above, 4 is the height when LM or KN is used as the base. Base × height = 6 × 4 = 24.

91. Characteristics of a Square

A square is a **rectangle with four equal sides.**

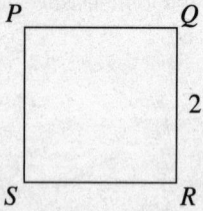

If PQRS is a square, all sides are the same length as QR. The perimeter of a square is equal to four times the length of one side.

Area of Square = (Side)^2

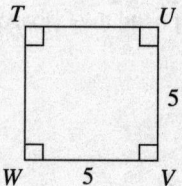

The square above, with sides of length 5, has an area of $5^2 = 25$.

92. Interior Angles of a Polygon

The **sum of the measures of the interior angles of a polygon** = $(n - 2) \times 180$, where n is the number of sides.

Sum of the Angles = $(n - 2) \times 180$

The eight angles of an octagon, for example, add up to $(8 - 2) \times 180 = 1{,}080$.

CIRCLES

93. Circumference of a Circle

Circumference = $2\pi r$

In the circle above, the radius is 3, and so the circumference is $2\pi(3) = 6\pi$.

94. Length of an Arc

An **arc** is a piece of the circumference. If n is the degree measure of the arc's central angle, then the formula is:

$$\text{Length of an Arc} = \left(\frac{n}{360}\right)(2\pi r)$$

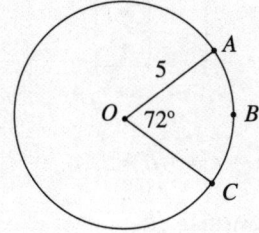

In the figure above, the radius is 5 and the measure of the central angle is 72 degrees. The arc length is $\frac{72}{360}$ or $\frac{1}{5}$ of the circumference:

$$\left(\frac{72}{360}\right)(2\pi)(5) = \left(\frac{1}{5}\right)(10\pi) = 2\pi$$

95. Area of a Circle

$$\text{Area of a Circle} = \pi r^2$$

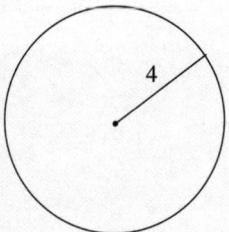

The area of the circle is $\pi(4)^2 = 16\pi$.

96. Area of a Sector

A **sector** is a piece of the area of a circle. If n is the degree measure of the sector's central angle, then the formula is:

$$\text{Area of a Sector} = \left(\frac{n}{360}\right)(\pi r^2)$$

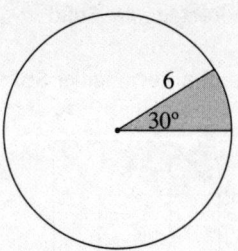

In the figure above, the radius is 6 and the measure of the sector's central angle is 30 degrees. The sector has $\frac{30}{360}$ or $\frac{1}{12}$ of the area of the circle:

$$\left(\frac{30}{360}\right)(\pi)(6^2) = \left(\frac{1}{12}\right)(36\pi) = 3\pi$$

97. Tangency

When a line is tangent to a circle, the radius of the circle is perpendicular to the line at the point of contact.

SOLIDS

98. Surface Area of a Rectangular Solid

The surface of a rectangular solid consists of three pairs of identical faces. To find the surface area, find the area of each face and add them up. If the length is l, the width is w, and the height is h, the formula is:

$$\text{Surface Area} = 2lw + 2wh + 2lh$$

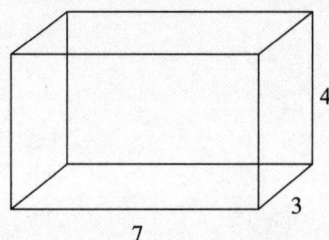

The surface area of the box above is:
$2 \times 7 \times 3 + 2 \times 3 \times 4 + 2 \times 7 \times 4 = 42 + 24 + 56 = 122$

99. Volume of a Rectangular Solid

Volume of a Rectangular Solid = *lwh*

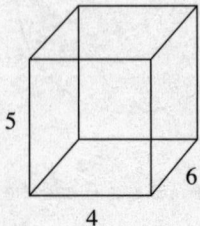

The volume of a 4-by-5-by-6 box is

$4 \times 5 \times 6 = 120$

A cube is a rectangular solid with length, width, and height all equal. If *e* is the length of an edge of a cube, the volume formula is:

Volume of a Cube = e^3

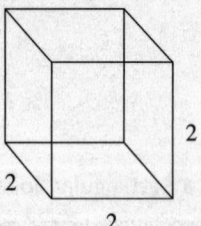

The volume of this cube is $2^3 = 8$.

100. Volume of a Cylinder

Volume of a Cylinder = $\pi r^2 h$

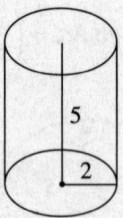

In the cylinder above, $r = 2$, $h = 5$, so:

Volume = $\pi(2^2)(5) = 20\pi$

Math Glossary

ABSOLUTE VALUE—the magnitude of a number, irrespective of its sign. Written as a number inside vertical lines: $|3|=3$ and $|-3|=3$.

ACUTE ANGLE—an angle measuring less than 90°. *A triangle with three acute angles is called an acute triangle.*

ADJACENT ANGLES—two angles having a common side and a common vertex.

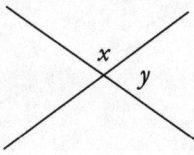

In the figure above, angles x and y are adjacent. (They are also supplementary.)

ALGEBRAIC EXPRESSION—one or more algebraic terms connected with plus and minus signs. *An algebraic expression is not an equation because it has no equal sign.*

ALTITUDE—a perpendicular segment whose length can be used in calculating the area of a triangle or other polygon.

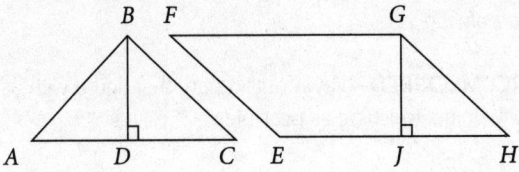

In the figure above, $\overline{BD}$ is an altitude of $\triangle ABC$, and $\overline{GJ}$ is an altitude of parallelogram EFGH.

ANGLE—two line segments coming together at a point called the vertex.

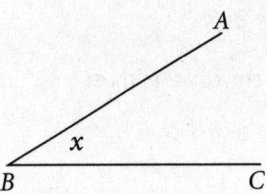

The angle above could be called $\angle ABC$, $\angle B$, or $\angle x$.

ARC—a portion of the circumference of a circle.

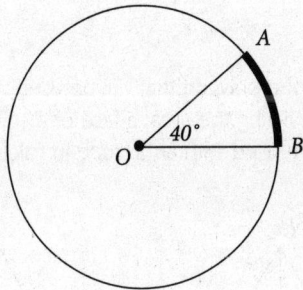

Because the central angle is $\frac{1}{9}$ of a full circle's 360°, the length of minor arc AB is $\frac{1}{9}$ the circumference.

AREA—a measure, in square units, of the size of a region in a plane. *Finding the area of a figure invariably involves multiplying two dimensions, such as length and width, or base and height.*

AVERAGE—the sum of a group of numbers divided by the number of numbers in the group. To find the average of 2, 7, and 15, divide the sum (2 + 7 + 15 = 24) by the number of numbers (3): 24 ÷ 3 = 8.

AVERAGE RATE—Average A per $B = \frac{\text{Total } A}{\text{Total } B}$. Average speed $= \frac{\text{Total distance}}{\text{Total time}}$. To get the average speed, don't just average the speeds.

AXES—the perpendicular "number lines" in the coordinate plane.

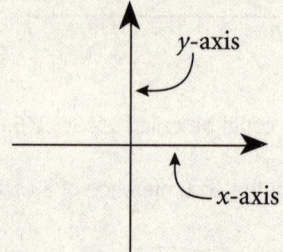

BASE—a side of a polygon that will be used with an altitude in calculating the area; a face of a solid, the area of which will be used with an altitude in calculating the volume.

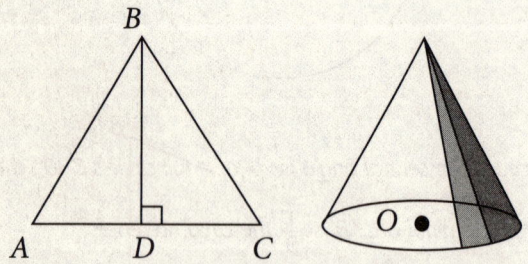

In the figure above, $\overline{AC}$ is the base of the triangle, and circle O is the base of the cone.

BINOMIAL—an algebraic expression with two terms. The FOIL method of multiplying works only for a pair of binomials.

BISECTOR—a line or line segment that divides an angle in half. The bisector of a 90° angle divides it into two 45° angles.

CENTRAL ANGLE—an angle formed by two radii of a circle.

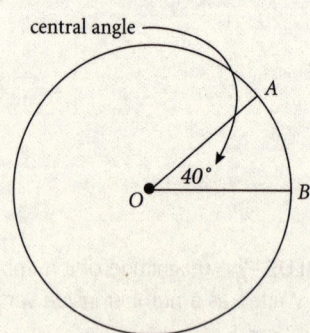

In the figure above, ∠AOB is a central angle.

CHORD—a line segment connecting two points on a circle.

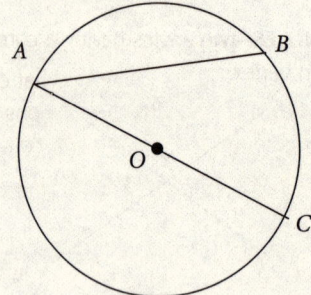

In the figure above, $\overline{AB}$ and $\overline{AC}$ are chords of circle O. Because it passes through the center, $\overline{AC}$ is also a diameter.

CIRCLE—the set of points in a plane at a particular distance from a central point. *A circle is not a polygon because it is not made up of straight sides.*

CIRCUMFERENCE—the distance around a circle. *The circumference of a circle is analogous to the perimeter of a polygon.*

CIRCUMSCRIBED—drawn outside another figure with as many points touching as possible.

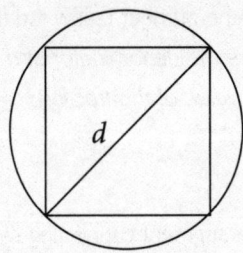

In the figure above, the circle is circumscribed about the square; d is both a diagonal of the square and a diameter of the circle.

COEFFICIENT—the numerical or "constant" part of an algebraic term. *In the monomial $-4x^2y$, the coefficient is -4. In the expression $ax^2 + bx + c$, a, b, and c are the coefficients.*

COMMON DENOMINATOR—a number that can be used as the denominator for two or more fractions so that they can be added or subtracted. *Before you can add the fractions $\frac{5}{6}$ and $\frac{5}{8}$, you first re-express them with a common denominator, such as 24: $\frac{5}{6} = \frac{20}{24}$ and $\frac{5}{8} = \frac{15}{24}$.*

COMMON FACTOR—a factor shared by two integers. *Any two integers will have at least 1 for a common factor.*

COMMON MULTIPLE—a multiple shared by two integers. *You can always get a common multiple for two integers by multiplying them, though that will not necessarily be the least common multiple.*

COMPLEMENTARY ANGLES—two angles whose measures add up to 90°. *A 30° angle and a 60° angle are complementary.*

CONE—a solid with a circle at one end and a single point at the other.

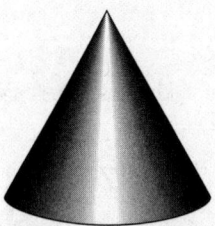

CONGRUENT—identical; of the same size and shape. *Congruent polygons have the same angles and side lengths.*

CONSECUTIVE—one after another, in order, without skipping any. *The numbers 6, 9, 12, 15, 18, and 21 are consecutive multiples of 3.*

COORDINATES—the pair of numbers, written inside parentheses, that specifies the location of a point in the coordinate plane. *The first number is the x-coordinate and the second number is the y-coordinate.*

COSECANT—the ratio of the hypotenuse to the opposite leg. *The cosecant of $\angle A$ in the figure below is $\frac{\text{hypotenuse}}{\text{opposite}} = \frac{13}{5}$.*

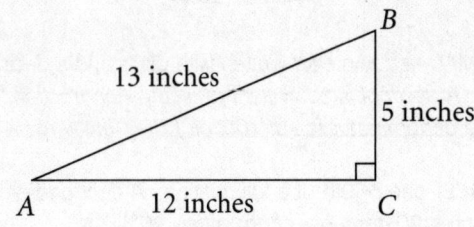

COSINE—the ratio of the adjacent leg to the hypotenuse. *The cosine of $\angle A$ in the figure above is $\frac{\text{adjacent}}{\text{hypotenuse}} = \frac{12}{13}$.*

COTANGENT—the ratio of the adjacent leg to the opposite leg. *The cotangent of ∠A in the figure above is $\frac{adjacent}{opposite} = \frac{12}{5}$.*

CUBE—a rectangular solid whose faces are all squares.

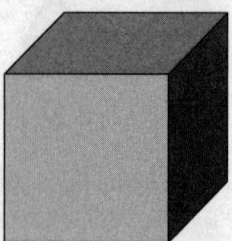

CUBE (of a number)—the third power. *The cube of a negative number is negative.*

CYLINDER—a solid with two circular ends connected by "straight" sides.

DECIMAL—a noninteger written with digits and a decimal point. *A decimal is equivalent to a common fraction whose denominator is 10, 100, or 1,000, etcetera.*

DEGREE—one 360th of a full rotation. *A right angle measures 90 degrees—often written 90°.*

DEGREE OF AN EQUATION—the greatest exponent in a single-variable equation. *The equation $x^3 - 9x = 0$ is a third-degree equation because the biggest exponent is 3.*

DENOMINATOR—the number below the fraction bar. *When you increase the denominator of a positive fraction, you decrease the value of the fraction: $\frac{7}{11}$ is less than $\frac{7}{10}$.*

DIAGONAL—a line segment connecting two nonadjacent vertices of a polygon. *A diagonal divides a rectangle into two right triangles.*

DIAMETER—(the length of) a line segment connecting two points on a circle and passing through the center. *A diameter is a chord of maximum length.*

DIFFERENCE—the result of subtraction. *The positive difference between 3 and 7 is 4.*

DIGIT—one of the numbers from 0 through 9. *In the 3-digit number 355, the hundreds' digit is 3, the tens' digit is 5, and the ones' digit is 5.*

DISTINCT—different, distinguishable. *The number 355 has 2 distinct digits: 3 and 5.*

EDGE—a line segment formed by the intersection of two faces.

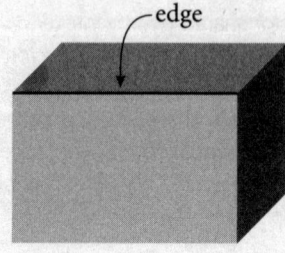

A rectangular solid has 12 edges.

ELLIPSE—a set of points in a plane for which the sum of the distances from two points (called *foci*) is constant.

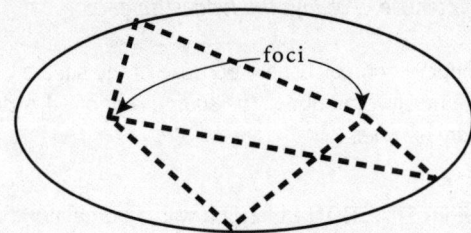

EQUATION—a statement of equality between two quantities. *It's an equation if it includes an equal sign.*

EQUATION OF A LINE—an equation that describes the relationship between the *x*- and *y*-coordinates of every point on the line in the coordinate plane. *The equation of the x-axis is y = 0, and the equation of the y-axis is x = 0.*

EQUILATERAL TRIANGLE—a triangle with three equal sides.

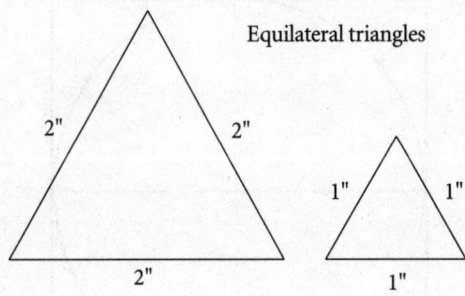

All equilateral triangles are similar—they all have three 60° angles.

EVEN NUMBER—a multiple of 2. *The set of even numbers includes not only 2, 4, 6, etcetera, but also 0, −2, −4, −6, etcetera.*

EXPONENT—the small, raised number written to the right of a variable or number, indicating the number of times that variable or number is to be used as a factor. *In the expression $-4x^3$, the exponent is 3, so $-4x^3 = -4 \cdot x \cdot x \cdot x$.*

EXTERIOR ANGLE—the angle created outside a polygon when one side is extended. *The exterior angles of any polygon add up to 360°.*

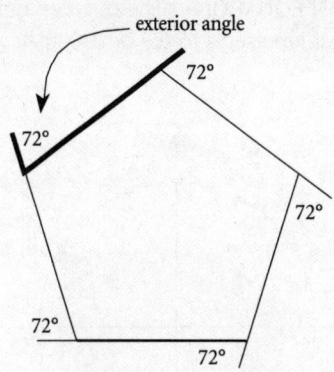

The exterior angles of a regular pentagon each measure 72°.

FACE—a polygon formed by edges of a solid.

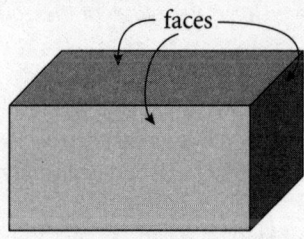

A rectangular solid has 6 faces.

FACTOR (of *n*)—a positive integer that divides into *n* with no remainder. *The complete list of factors of 18 is: 1, 2, 3, 6, 9, and 18.*

FACTORING (a polynomial)—re-expressing a polynomial as the product of simpler expressions. *The complete factorization of $2x^2 + 7x + 3$ is $(2x + 1)(x + 3)$.*

FRACTION—a number expressed as a ratio. *In everyday speech, the word fraction implies something less than 1, but to a mathematician, any number written in the form $\frac{A}{B}$ is a fraction.*

GRAPH OF AN EQUATION—a line or curve in the coordinate plane that represents all the ordered pair solutions of an equation.

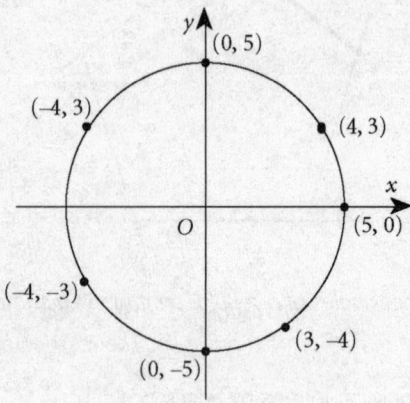

The figure above shows the graph of the equation $x^2 + y^2 = 25$.

GREATEST COMMON FACTOR—the greatest integer that is a factor of both numbers under consideration. *The greatest common factor (GCF) of relative primes is 1.*

HEXAGON—a six-sided polygon.

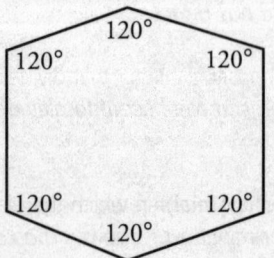

The six angles of a regular hexagon each measure 120°.

HYPOTENUSE—the side of a right triangle opposite the right angle.

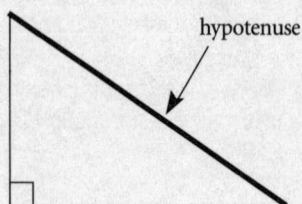

The hypotenuse is always the longest side.

IMAGINARY—not real, usually because of the square root of a negative number. *The square root of –4 is an imaginary number.*

IMPROPER FRACTION—a fraction with a numerator that's greater than the denominator. $\frac{35}{8}$ is an improper fraction and is therefore greater than 1.

INEQUALITY—a statement that compares the size of two quantities. *There are four inequality symbols: < ("less than"), ≤ "(less than or equal to"), > ("greater than"), and ≥ ("greater than or equal to").*

INSCRIBED—drawn inside another figure with as many points touching as possible.

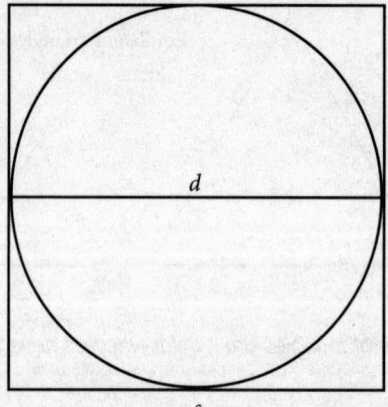

When a circle is inscribed within a square, the diameter d of the circle is the same as a length of a side s of the square.

INTEGER—a whole number; 325, 0, and –29 are integers.

INTERCEPT—the point where a given line crosses the x-axis or y-axis.

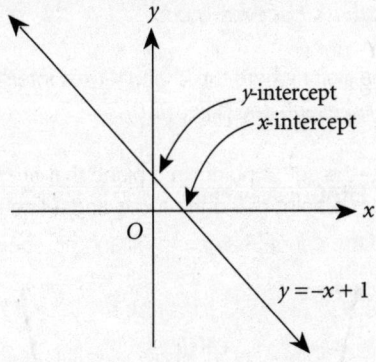

The y-intercept is the b in the slope-intercept form $y = mx + b$.

INTERIOR ANGLE—an angle inside a polygon formed by two adjacent sides. *Every polygon has the same number of interior angles as sides.*

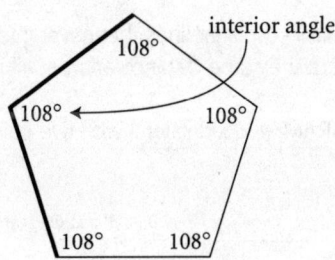

The interior angles of a regular pentagon each measure 108°.

IRRATIONAL—real, but not capable of being expressed as a ratio of integers. $\sqrt{2}$, $\sqrt{3}$, and π are irrational numbers.

ISOSCELES TRIANGLE—a triangle with two sides of equal length.

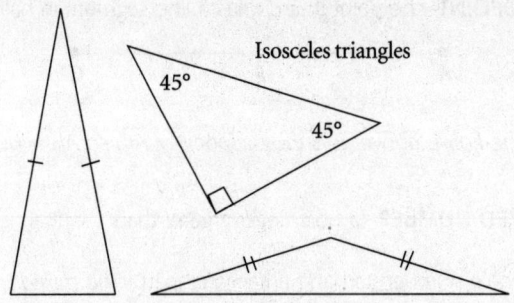

The angles opposite the equal sides of an isosceles triangle are also equal.

LEAST COMMON MULTIPLE—the smallest number that is a multiple of both given numbers. *The least common multiple of relative primes is their product.*

LEGS (of a right triangle)—the sides that make up the right angle.

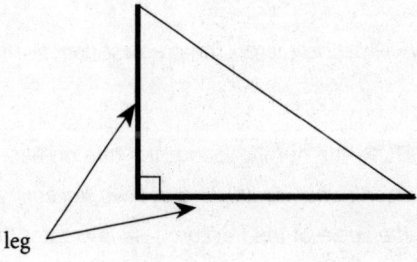

You can use the legs as the base and altitude to find the area of a right triangle.

LIKE TERMS—algebraic terms in which the elements other than the coefficients are alike. *$2ab$ and $3ab$ are like terms, and so they can be added: $2ab + 3ab = 5ab$.*

LINE—a straight row of points extending infinitely in both directions. *A line has only one dimension.*

LINE SEGMENT—a straight row of points connecting two endpoints. *Each side of a polygon is a line segment.*

LINEAR EQUATION—a single-variable equation with no exponent greater than 1. *A linear equation is also called a first-degree equation.*

MIDPOINT—the point that divides a line segment in half.

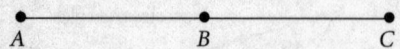

In the figure above, B is the midpoint of $\overline{AC}$, so AB = BC.

MIXED NUMBER—a noninteger greater than 1 written with a whole number part and a fractional part. *The mixed number $4\frac{2}{3}$ can also be expressed as the improper fraction $\frac{14}{3}$.*

MONOMIAL—an algebraic expression consisting of exactly one term.

MULTIPLE (of n)—a number that n will divide into with no remainder. *Some of the multiples of 18 are: 0, 18, and 90.*

NEGATIVE—less than zero. *The greatest negative integer is −1.*

NUMERATOR—the number above the fraction bar. *When you increase the numerator of a positive fraction, you increase the value of the fraction: $\frac{13}{17}$ is greater than $\frac{12}{17}$.*

OBTUSE ANGLE—an angle measuring more than 90° and less than 180°. *An obtuse triangle is one that has one obtuse angle.*

OCTAGON—an eight-sided polygon.

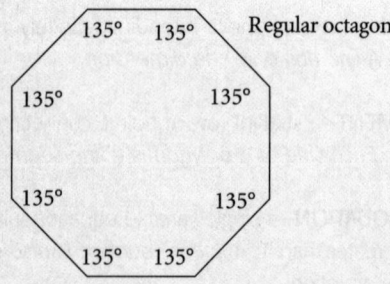

Each of the interior angles of a regular octagon measures 135°.

ODD NUMBER—an integer that is not a multiple of 2. *Any integer that's not even is odd.*

ORIGIN—the point where the *x*- and *y*-axes intersect. *The origin represents the point (0,0).*

PARABOLA—the set of points in a plane that are the same distance from a point called the *focus* and a line called the *directrix*.

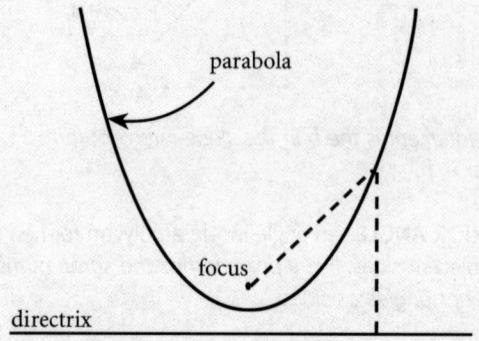

PARALLEL LINES—coplanar lines that never intersect. Parallel lines are the same distance apart at all points.

PARALLELOGRAM—a quadrilateral with two pairs of parallel sides.

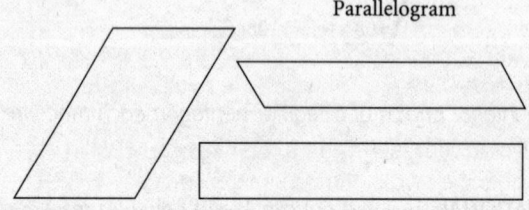

Opposite sides of a parallelogram are equal; opposite angles of a parallelogram are also equal.

PENTAGON—a five-sided polygon.

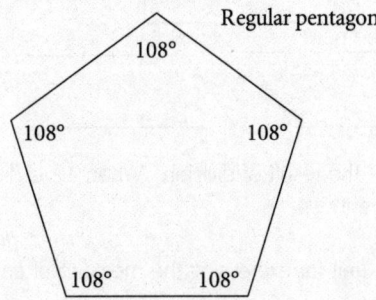

Regular pentagon

The interior angles of any pentagon add up to 540°. Each of the interior angles of a regular pentagon measures 108°.

PERCENT—one hundredth. 20% means 20 hundredths, or $\frac{20}{100} = \frac{1}{5}$.

PERCENT INCREASE/DECREASE—amount of increase or decrease expressed as a percent of the original amount. *A decrease from 100 to 83 is a 17% decrease.*

PERIMETER—the sum of the lengths of the sides of a polygon. *Two polygons with the same area do not necessarily have the same perimeter.*

PERPENDICULAR—intersecting at a right angle. *The altitude and base of a triangle are perpendicular.*

PI—an irrational number, approximately 3.14, which is equal to the ratio of the circumference of any circle to its diameter. The symbol for pi is π. *Pi appears in the formulas for the circumference and area of a circle, as well for the volumes of a sphere, a cylinder, and a cone.*

POINT—a precise position in space. *A point has no length, breadth, or thickness.*

POLYGON—a closed figure composed of any number of straight sides.

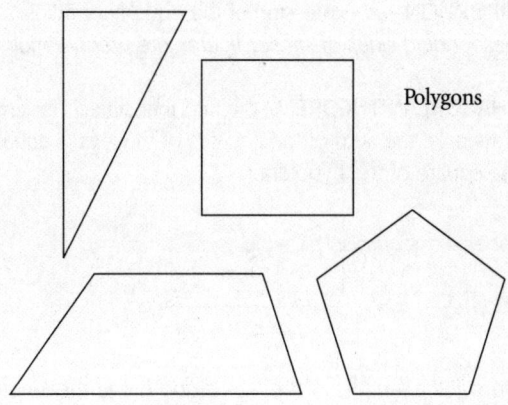

Polygons

Triangles, squares, trapezoids, and pentagons are all polygons, but circles and ellipses are not.

POLYNOMIAL—an algebraic expression that is the sum of two or more terms. *Binomials and trinomials are just two types of polynomials.*

POSITIVE—greater than zero. *Zero is not a positive number.*

POWER—a product obtained by multiplying a quantity by itself one or more times. *The fifth power of 2 is 32.*

PRIME FACTORIZATION—an integer expressed as the product of prime numbers. *The prime factorization of 60 is $2 \times 2 \times 3 \times 5$.*

PRIME NUMBER—an integer greater than 1 that has no factors other than 1 and itself. The first 10 prime numbers are: 2, 3, 5, 7, 11, 13, 17, 19, 23, and 29. Notice that 2 is the only even prime number.

PROBABILITY—the likelihood of a particular event, expressed as the ratio of the number of "favorable" occurrences to the total number of possible occurrences. *Probability is a part-to-whole ratio and can therefore never be greater than 1.*

PRODUCT—the result of multiplication. *The product of 3 and 4 is 12.*

PROPORTION—an expression of the equality of ratios. *Corresponding sides of similar figures are proportional.*

PYTHAGOREAN THEOREM—the rule that states, "for any right triangle, the sum of the squares of the legs is equal to the square of the hypotenuse."

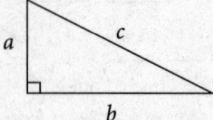

If you call the lengths of the legs a and b and the length of the hypotenuse c, you can write "$a^2 + b^2 = c^2$."

QUADRANT—one of the four regions into which the axes divide the coordinate plane.

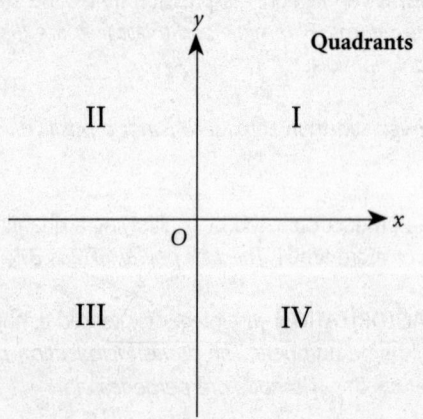

When you know the signs of the coordinates, you know which quadrant contains that point. For any point in Quadrant IV, for example, the x-coordinate is positive and the y-coordinate is negative.

QUADRATIC EQUATION—a second-degree equation. *Quadratic equations with one unknown often have two solutions.*

QUADRILATERAL—a four-sided polygon. *Squares, rectangles, parallelograms, and trapezoids are all quadrilaterals.*

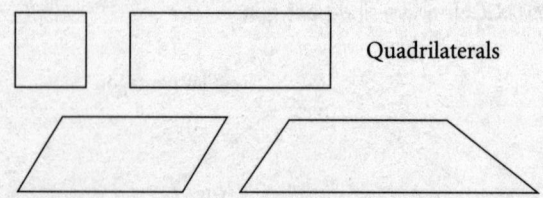

QUOTIENT—the result of division. *When 12 is divided by 3, the quotient is 4.*

RADIAN—a unit for expressing the measure of an angle.

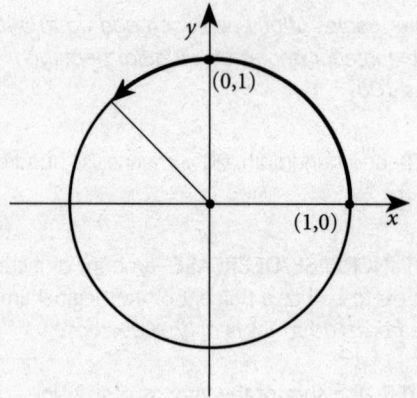

The angle shown in the figure above measures $\frac{3\pi}{4}$ radians, which is the same as 135°. It's no coincidence that $\frac{3\pi}{4}$ is also the length of the arc shown.

RADICAL—the symbol $\sqrt{}$, which by itself represents the positive square root, and with a little number written in—as in $\sqrt[3]{32}$—represents a higher root. *By convention, $\sqrt{}$ represents the positive square root only.*

RADIUS—(the length of) a line segment connecting the center and a point on a circle. *The radius is half the diameter.*

RATE—a ratio of quantities measured in different units. *The most familiar rates have units of time after the word per, such as: meters per second, pages per hour, inches per year.*

RATIO—a fraction that expresses the relative sizes of two quantities. *A ratio is generally expressed with the words "of" and "to": as in "the ratio of girls to boys."*

RATIONAL—capable of being expressed as a ratio of integers. *The repeating decimal .074074074074 . . . is a rational number because it can be written as $\frac{2}{27}$.*

REAL—having a place on the number line. *π is a real number because it has a location—somewhere just to the right of 3.14—on the number line.*

RECIPROCALS—a pair of numbers whose product is 1. *To get the reciprocal of a fraction, switch the numerator and denominator: the reciprocal of $\frac{2}{7}$ is $\frac{7}{2}$.*

RECTANGLE—a quadrilateral with four right angles. *All rectangles are parallelograms, but not all parallelograms are rectangles.*

RECTANGULAR SOLID—a solid whose faces are all rectangles.

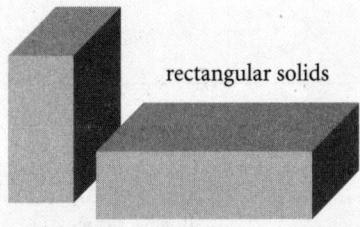
rectangular solids

REDUCING A FRACTION—expressing a fraction in lowest terms by factoring out and canceling common factors. $\frac{6}{8}$ reduces to $\frac{3}{4}$.

REGULAR POLYGON—a polygon with all equal sides and all equal angles. *Equilateral triangles and squares are regular polygons.*

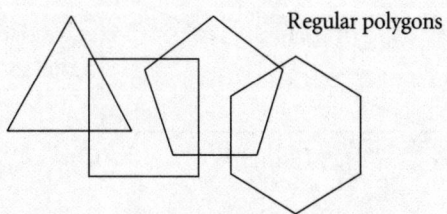
Regular polygons

RELATIVE PRIMES—positive integers that have no factors in common. *Thirty-five and 54 are relative primes because their prime factorizations (35 = 5 × 7, and 54 = 2 × 3 × 3 × 3) have nothing in common.*

REPEATING DECIMAL—a decimal with a digit or cluster of digits that repeats indefinitely. *The fraction $\frac{1}{7}$ is equivalent to the repeating decimal .142857142857142857. . . , which can be written as $.\overline{142857}$.*

RHOMBUS—a quadrilateral with four equal sides.

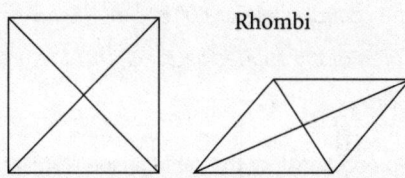
Rhombi

The diagonals of a rhombus are perpendicular.

RIGHT ANGLE—an angle measuring 90°. *A rectangle is a polygon with four right angles.*

RIGHT TRIANGLE—a triangle with a right angle. *Every right triangle has exactly two acute angles.*

ROOT—a number that multiplied by itself a certain number of times will yield the given quantity. *The third root of 8 is 2.*

SCALENE TRIANGLE—a triangle with sides of different lengths. *A 3-4-5 triangle is a scalene triangle.*

SECANT—the ratio of the hypotenuse to the adjacent leg. *The secant is the reciprocal of the cosine.*

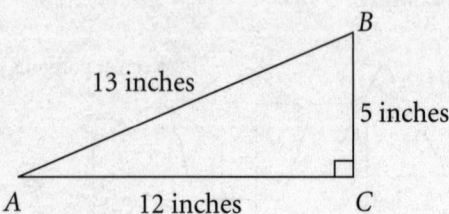

In the figure above, the secant of $\angle A$ is $\frac{13}{12}$.

SECTOR—a region bounded by two radii and an arc.

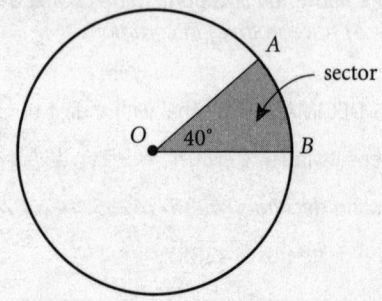

Because the central angle of 40° is $\frac{1}{9}$ of the full circle's 360°, the area of the shaded sector is $\frac{1}{9}$ of the area of the whole circle.

SIMILAR—proportional; of the same shape. Similar polygons have the same angles.

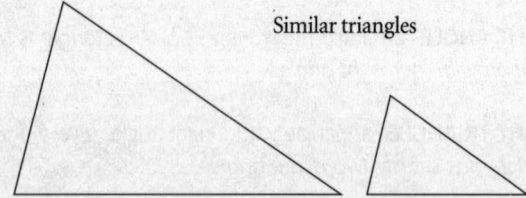
Similar triangles

SINE—the ratio of the opposite leg to the hypotenuse.

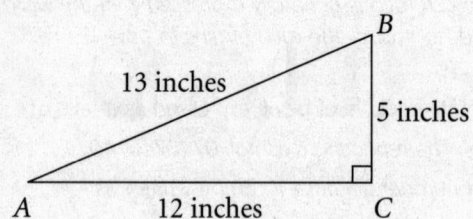

In the figure above, the sine of $\angle A$ is $\frac{5}{13}$.

SLOPE—a description of the "steepness" of a line in the coordinate plane, defined as $\frac{\text{Change in } y}{\text{Change in } x}$. Lines that go "uphill" (left to right) have positive slopes, and lines that go "downhill" have negative slopes. A horizontal line—that is, a line parallel to the x-axis—is "flat" and has a slope of 0.

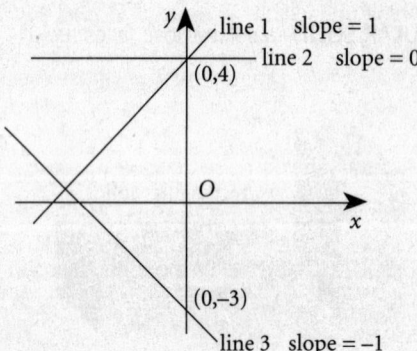

SLOPE-INTERCEPT FORM—an equation in the form $y = mx + b$. In this form, m is the slope and b is the y-intercept. Line 1 in the figure above has a slope of 1 and a y-intercept of 4, so its equation is $y = x + 4$. Line 2's equation is $y = 4$. Line 3's equation is $y = -x - 3$.

SOLID—a three-dimensional figure.

Cubes, cylinders, cones, and spheres are all solids.

SOLVING—isolating the given variable.

SPHERE—the set of all points in space a particular distance from a central point. *Visualize a sphere as a ball.*

SQUARE—a quadrilateral with four equal sides and four right angles. *A square can be thought of as a rectangular rhombus.*

SQUARE ROOT—a number that when squared yields the given quantity. *Positive numbers each have two square roots, but negative numbers have no real square roots.*

SUM—the result of addition. *The sum of 3 and 4 is 7.*

SUPPLEMENTARY ANGLES—two angles whose measures add up to 180°.

SURFACE AREA—the sum of the areas of the surfaces of a solid. *Surface area is measured in square units.*

SYSTEM OF EQUATIONS—two or more equations in which each variable represents the same quantity in one equation as in another.

TANGENT—the ratio of the opposite leg of a right triangle to the adjacent leg.

TANGENT (of a circle)—a line that intersects a circle at exactly one point. *Visualize a tangent as a line that just barely "touches" the circle.*

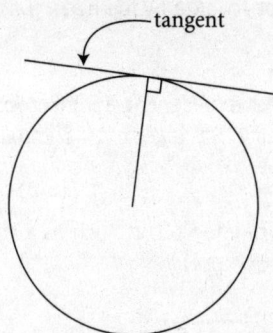

TERM—a part of an algebraic expression that either stands by itself or is connected to other terms with plus and minus signs. *A term has three parts: the coefficient, the variable(s), and the exponent(s).*

TRANSVERSAL—a line that intersects two parallel lines.

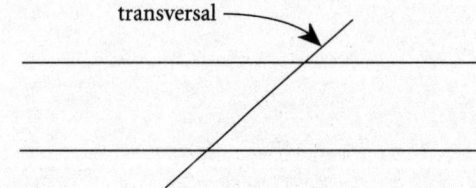

A transversal across parallel lines creates two sets of four equal angles.

TRAPEZOID—a quadrilateral with one pair of parallel sides.

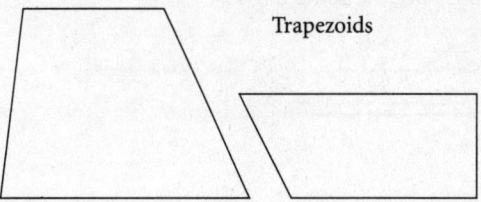

TRIANGLE—a three-sided polygon. *The three angles of a triangle add up to 180°.*

UNDEFINED—not covered by the rules. *Division by 0 is undefined.*

VARIABLE—a letter representing an unknown or unspecified quantity. *The letter most commonly used for a variable is x.*

VERTEX—a point of intersection, such as a corner of a rectangular solid or a polygon.

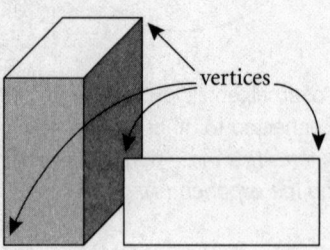

VERTICAL ANGLES—angles across the vertex of intersecting lines. *Vertical angles are equal.*

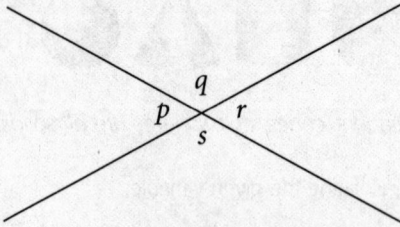

In the figure above, $\angle q$ *and* $\angle s$ *are vertical angles, as are* $\angle p$ *and* $\angle r$.

VOLUME—a measure of the amount of "space" contained within a solid. *Computing volume invariably involves multiplying three dimensions, such as length, width, and height.*

Notes

Notes